# The Anatomy of Prejudices

# The Anatomy of Prejudices

ELISABETH YOUNG-BRUEHL

Harvard University Press

Cambridge, Massachusetts

*On the twentieth anniversary of
her death, in grateful memory of my teacher*
HANNAH ARENDT
(1906–1975)

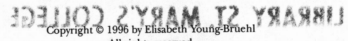

Copyright © 1996 by Elisabeth Young-Bruehl
All rights reserved
*Printed in the United States of America*
Second printing, 1998

First Harvard University Press paperback edition, 1998

Muriel Rukeyser, "Despisals," from *Breaking Open*
(1973), reprinted by permission of William L. Rukeyser.

Library of Congress Cataloging-in-Publication Data

Young-Bruehl, Elisabeth.
The anatomy of prejudices / Elisabeth Young-Bruehl.
p.   cm.
Includes bibliographical references and index.
ISBN 0-674-03190-3 (cloth)
ISBN 0-674-03191-1 (pbk.)
1. Prejudices.  I. Title.
BF575.P9Y686   1996
303.3´85—dc20          95-43754

# Contents

# Despisals

## MURIEL RUKEYSER

In the human cities, never again to
despise the backside of the city, the ghetto,
or build it again as we build the despised
backside of houses. Look at your own building.
You are the city.

Among our secrecies, not to despise our Jews
(that is, ourselves) or our darkness, our blacks,
or in our sexuality wherever it takes us
and we now know we are productive
too productive, too reproductive
for our present invention—never to despise
the homosexual who goes building another

with touch with touch (not to despise any touch)
each like himself, like herself each.
You are this.

    In the body's ghetto
never to go despising the asshole
nor the useful shit that is our clean clue
to what we need. Never to despise
the clitoris in her least speech.

Never to despise in myself what I have been taught
to despise. Nor to despise the other.
Nor to despise the *it*. To make this relation
with the it: to know that I am it.

# Prologue

*It is the not-me in thee that is to me most precious.*
—Quaker proverb

I have nearly four hundred undergraduates at Wesleyan University and Haverford College to thank for their patience with the visioning and revisioning, mapping and remapping lecture style that lies behind this book. Through five courses, rooms of students were gracious in their disbelief as the blackboards grew densely tangled and then were erased of abandoned ideas, as the new formulations were sketched, trimmed, contoured, synthesized. Invited to participate in a writer's thinking process, to come into the atelier, they learned to join a work in progress of theory building, and they did so with the kind of sharp—sometimes bemused—curiosity and feisty, critical intelligence that makes university teaching such a good education. And I certainly appreciated their company as we all felt the tension that always existed between my effort to explore various kinds of prejudices—chiefly, antisemitism, racism, sexism, and homophobia—and the constant reminder, in every morning's newspaper, that our topics unfortunately flourished in the world. We were constantly asking ourselves whether the approach being developed in the classroom could help us to understand these events in Bensonhurst or Crown Heights, those riots in Los Angeles, this wave of abortion clinic violence in Florida or Texas, the pronouncements about gays in the military, this horror—growing week by week—in Bosnia, those stories told by Rwandan refugees struggling over the border into Zaire, this bombing in Gaza, Belfast, Algiers.

While I worked my way through to this book, I kept remembering how perplexed I had been when I set out. I had wanted to teach a course on prejudices to explore the existing literature, a territory quite unknown to me. So I gathered a sample of books with titles like *The Nature of Prejudice, Towards the Elimination of Racism, Bigotry, Prejudice and Hatred, Children and Prejudice, Prejudice, Discrimination and Racism, The Social Psychology of Prejudice,* a dozen or so from each decade after World War II. But as I read along, I became more and more uneasy. These books seemed to arise from assumptions about prejudices that I thought were either banal or just wrong or not in any way adequate to the complexity of my experience or of the world. Turning to these books after reading my morning newspaper made me feel a deep sense of discrepancy.

The first part of this book, a kind of book-within-the-book, is an effort to say what is the matter with this literature—to describe that discrepancy between science and phenomena, theory and events, but also to ask why, on this topic of prejudices, so much has been written on such shaky foundations, with such a recycling of clichés and unfounded conclusions. I became convinced that the way we have learned to speak in postwar America about prejudices is a very large part of our prejudice problem, a part of which we are, daily, unaware. American discourse is also exported (while very little is imported from elsewhere), making American social science dominative in much of the world's academic and policy circles and weaving it into other peoples' prejudice problems. I realized that any book about prejudices that does not, first, address the mistaken, partial, or misleading American theories informing the current discussion will be just as misleading as the many educational programs, couched in the same hackneyed social science, that now exist for teaching tolerance in the schools. In this book I provide a tour of this territory because I think it is impossible to see what needs doing without a full sense of what has been done so obfuscatingly.

While I was trying to develop a critical path out of the social scientific morass, my students also brought close-to-hand case materials that kept us testing the evolving hypotheses and kept us arguing and searching for paths across the steep divides in our own experiences and expectations, too. A young man of ethnographic sensibility contributed a transcript of all the graffiti on ten selected men's room walls, so that we could make a survey of sexism and homophobia all around our town. Another analyzed for us the rugby team's astonishingly misogynistic victory anthem. On a trip home to Jamaica, a young woman interviewed in depth her cousin, the family bigot. The son of a Jewish mother and an African American father wrote about growing up in an extended family psychodrama of prejudices. We collected stories. In a trembling, enraged voice an Asian American described one day what had happened in the college locker room.

While the white varsity wrestlers were showering after a meet, their conversation focused on the observation that many of the younger wrestlers on the team were Asian American, a fact that seemed to make them apprehensive. The collective talk turned to reassuring remarks about how these Asian guys were not, however, going to be much of a threat in the competition for girls, because they have such small penises. Really, one entrepreneurial fellow suggested, condom manufacturers could make a killing if they designed a condom just for these small penises. And so they laughingly chatted on, not realizing that one of the young Asian American wrestlers was in the next aisle listening. When he reported the incident through the campus newspaper, an outcry from various minority groups brought the next chapter of the story. In late-night dorm discussions about what the reporter called "blatant racism," there was a clear divide between students who thought the incident was nothing to get excited about, just a bit of crude joking around—"dumb, but not racism"—and those for whom the incident recalled all their nightmares.

Like most publicized instances of prejudice, this one had two stages: one of word or deed, and one of interpretation. Prejudices manifested in slurs, acts of discrimination, attacks, are followed by prejudices—not necessarily the same ones—manifested in rationalizations, self-serving descriptions, denials, commentaries, often ones designed to discredit the victims' truthfulness or belittle their pain. Prejudices have histories, and the second stage commonly involves a reference to history or an argument about the applicability of history: this episode is like or unlike that one in kind or degree or intention. Theoretical or interpretive prejudices or spins, which can, of course, serve rawer forms of prejudice, come into play. There are wars, and there are culture wars.

For those of my students who identified themselves as "people of color," as well as for most of their white classmates—the sort to sign on for a class called "Studies in Prejudice"—the most painful part of this illustrative episode was the interpretive stage: it was bad enough that the wrestlers said what they said but worse that so many of their peers could not understand the prejudice or that the incident was an expression of prejudice. My students were discovering the larger problem that I discovered by reading the social science literature. Like the disinformation that protects codes, the interpretive vocabulary swirling around each and every publicized episode of prejudice promotes a kind of dis-education that prevents understanding. The students who dismissed this episode with their tacit definitions of prejudice were being emotionally insensitive and obtuse, but they were also operating out of the strong, although unknown to them as such, social scientific tradition. Intellectually and emotionally they had no sense at the elemental level of what prejudice is.

But students upset by the situation were also at a loss. They talked about the episode as an example of "blatant racism," while I argued that this was not racism of the varieties that whites typically display toward people of color, which involve accusing the victims of sexual power and primitiveness or mindlessness. Color was not the mark of difference. The prejudice was more like antisemitism, with the Asian Americans in the role of the Jews, people who are felt to be intellectually (and commercially) threatening and are therefore demeaned as sexually lesser. An Asian American, feared for his braininess and cunning, would be especially threatening if he were also a talented wrestler, a competitor in physical prowess, and so would have to be put down. The idea arises that maybe antisemitism and anti-Asianism of this sort are varieties of a single species of prejudice, while racism is another species.

To have this kind of discussion of the episode, you have to acknowledge that important differences exist between racism and antisemitism—they are not both "racism," and they are not just prejudice in the singular, an undifferentiated phenomenon, as implied in a title like *The Nature of Prejudice.* Our clichéd public discourse about prejudice virtually forbids such differentiation and nuance. Consequently, it virtually forbids inquiry into the different needs that different prejudices fulfill for different types of people in different social conditions.

My lectures—and this book—concentrate on these differences among the prejudices. This focus, of course, does not mean that the various prejudices have nothing in common. Psychologically, they all do involve some kind of projection of the victimizer's feelings onto the victimized; they all have an ingredient of "us versus them" identification and narcissism; they all operate as what I call social mechanisms of defense and are particularly acute in their adolescent onsets; they all require social learning or transmission. Sociologically, they all are aggravated by conditions of uncertainty, rapid change, migrations, and both downward and upward mobility; they all are fed by their own histories and accumulated stereotypes and cultural images. But, it seems to me, it is the differences among the types of prejudices that are particularly important, experientially and theoretically, and it is the differences that have been neglected. The differences are crucial to any educational work that attempts to alleviate prejudice with more than broadbrush "Just say no" pleading. Appreciating the differences allows the diagnoses—the differential diagnoses—without which there can be no cures.

My students have grown up in a period of acrimonious socio- and psychobabble, and they know it. They are skeptical—rightly—of anything intellectuals have to say about social and political problems. Theirs is a spirit of disillusionment, without direct experience of the illusions that have receded, which featured a certain 1960s hopefulness—the hopefulness of my own generation—that prejudices could be overcome. "We shall overcome!" is only a dream song to my students. But they do hope for agreement on what should be overcome. They want acknowledgment of the problem: "what those wrestlers said was not a joke," and what happened at their school in microcosm happens elsewhere writ larger and more horrific. Furthermore, they want their questions considered: what makes people say things like that? why should even the educated children of privilege need to make that kind of put-down? how is it that people cannot hear or will not change when they are told that they have been hurtful? what kind of education—if any—can address the prejudices?

This book is my diagnostic answer to my students' questions. After its extended reflection on how the way in which we talk about prejudices has become an obstacle, the book offers an alternative, a theory which is, at once, a claim that different prejudices are characteristic of different psychic or character types and a claim that different social conditions promote different character types and their corresponding prejudices. The theory is, on the one hand, psychoanalytic and, on the other hand, an appropriation of Max Weber's sociological theory, with its method of ideal type construction, and an adaptation of Hannah Arendt's method in *The Origins of Totalitarianism,* which contains a section on antisemitism that I consider the exemplary twentieth century historical analysis of a prejudice. The theory developed here is multilayered, antireductionistic (and thus sound bite proof), structurally very complex—complex, I hope, to the degree required by the vast web of phenomena it tries to explore. A book is not a blackboard, so the theory as you will read it here is necessarily not in creative motion, but it will become a work in progress again as it reaches its next audience—for your participation is invited.

In addition to my students, I thank the readers who participated in this book as a work in progress, M. T. Beecher, Jerome Kohn, Teresa Rittenhouse, and Ernest Sutton, and those who worked on it editorially, Angela von der Lippe, Elizabeth Hurwit, and Antonia Sunderland.

# Introduction: Studying Prejudices

As World War II drew to a close, the American Jewish Committee organized a group of American and émigré European scholars to produce a series of books. The six resulting volumes, collectively called Studies in Prejudice, attempted to answer in a careful, thorough social scientific manner the anguished, aching questions provoked by the events we now call (adopting a term proposed in the 1960s) the "Holocaust." How could this have happened? What kind of people perpetrated such hideous mass crimes? Why the Jews? What is antisemitism? Could the destruction of European Jewry have been predicted—and prevented? Will such events happen again? Under what conditions? What shall we tell children about it?

The six volumes were meant to advance America's discussion of prejudice "beyond mere commonsense approaches to problems of intergroup conflict," as Max Horkheimer, a director of the series, explained. "Prejudice," he went on, "is one of the problems of our times for which everyone has a theory, but no one an answer." Horkheimer and his colleagues wanted both theory and answers, and they thought they had both in the legacies they had received from Marx and from Freud. Behind all words and deeds of prejudice, their Marxist theory said sweepingly, there is a tangle of class conflict and socioeconomic inequalities. Revolutionize this context, drain this swamp, and prejudice will lose its breeding ground. In the hearts and minds of every prejudiced person, their Freudian theory said, just as sweepingly, a particular complex of personality traits can be found. A prejudiced personality is an "authoritarian personality," rigid, ideologically conservative, conventional, superficial, and disconnected from feelings. Reform the puritanical and punitive family contexts in which such people are raised, give children the kind of familial love from which they can learn to love, and prejudice will lose its psychic roots, its psychopathological roots.

These clear, powerful theoretical lines, which resonated so well with homegrown American progressive political traditions and efforts in child welfare and education, guided a decade of sequels to the Studies in Prejudice series. The Cold War encouraged just as much questioning as the immediate postwar moment had. Gordon Allport, one of the most brilliant and synthetic minds among the notable psychologists who gathered at Harvard in those years, surveyed the field in 1954 in a work called *The Nature of Prejudice*. His preface summarized both the sense of horror and the hope—the faith in science—shared by all the writers he considered:

> At the time when the world as a whole suffers from panic induced by the rival ideologies of east and west, each corner of the earth has its own special burdens of animosity. Moslems distrust non-Moslems. Jews who escaped extermination in Central Europe find themselves in the new State of Israel surrounded by antisemitism. Refugees roam in inhospitable lands. Many of the colored people of the world suffer indignities at the hands of whites who invent a fanciful racist doctrine to justify their condescension. The checkerboard of prejudice in the United States is perhaps the most intricate of all. While some of this endless antagonism seems based upon a realistic conflict of interests, most of it, we suspect, is a product of fears of the imagination. Yet imaginary fears can cause real suffering . . .
>
> [Recently there has appeared] the conviction that man can and should employ his intelligence to assist in his redemption. Men are saying, "Let us make an objective study of conflict in culture and industry, between people of different color and race; let us seek out the root of prejudice and find concrete means for implementing men's affiliative values." Since the end of the Second World War universities in many lands have given new prominence to this approach under various academic names: social science, human development, social psychology, human relations, social relations. Though not yet securely christened the infant science is thriving. It has found considerable welcome not only in universities, but likewise in public schools, in

churches, in progressive industries and government agencies, as well as in international bodies . . . Within the past decade or two there has been more solid and enlightening study in this area than in all previous centuries combined.[1]

Since Allport wrote his proud assessment of the young social sciences, they have grown into vast enterprises. In America, their practitioners continued to pore over the mysteries of antisemitism, although they gave more and more attention in the 1960s—following rather than leading the Civil Rights movement—to race prejudice directed against Negroes. The most comprehensive social scientific work that had ever been produced on that topic, Gunnar Myrdal's *The American Dilemma* (1944), was continually quoted, reviewed, and reassessed. Meanwhile the Negroes, who asserted themselves under the self-chosen names Blacks and then African Americans, repudiated a great deal of the white social scientific attention directed at them. Working mostly in non–social scientific genres and in history, they slowly revolutionized their subfield of Studies in Prejudice.[2]

One of the most striking changes that Negro theorists of prejudice insisted upon in the 1960s was simple in the extreme: they added the voices of the victims to the "data." Complex scales and questionnaires for assessing "social distance" and prejudice had already been developed, many of them outgrowths of social scientific work on antisemitism, but only in the 1960s did researchers argue that what Negroes thought about such topics as "the Negro family" ought to guide inquiries. Similarly, Black "self-esteem" had often been investigated, because it was assumed that loss of self-esteem is one of the marks of oppression, while what generations of Negro intellectuals had had to say on the topic of *white* self-esteem was not at all a part of the social scientific picture. These missing voices spoke when the Civil Rights movement and then the rise of Black Power made possible—for example—the publication of books with titles like *The Death of White Sociology*.[3] By the early 1970s, many African American intellectuals repudiated social science altogether and agreed with Albert Murray, author of *The Omni-Americans* (1970), that social science was not in any way the solution to the problem of racism—on the contrary, it was central to the perpetuation of the problem of racism. "The situation now is that the contemporary folklore of racism in the United States is derived from social science surveys in which white norms and black deviations are tantamount to white well-being and black pathology."[4]

Furthermore, as the Negro revolution in Studies in Prejudice unfolded during the 1960s, it gave impetus to another revolution, the Women's Liberation movement—so named in the late 1960s on the model of national and Black liberation movements. Feminists wrote Studies in Prejudice directed at the prejudice that came to be called "sexism," a neologism from the late 1960s modeled on the word "racism." As a vast library of studies in sexism appeared, theory became so important a part of women's liberation that a field and an activity called "feminist theory" grew up and became institutionalized in universities. This was a development for which there was no equivalent in Black Studies or African American Studies, where no one identified himself or herself as a theorist. The development was empowering because theory was, of course, the last thing in the world a woman should be capable of producing according to the prejudice that women set out to theorize about and eradicate—sexism. But the role of theory in feminism, and its entanglement with sexism, has become enormously complicated over three decades.

Theory also became a crucial mode of work in university social science more generally, and feminists both participated in this trend and helped shape it. A period of enormous self-consciousness and reflexivity began in the 1970s, and theory marked this venue. The term indicated that the kinds of social and psychological analyses that had been carried out under the banners of Marx and Freud could no longer be done. Such analyses had to be deconstructed, that is, exposed in all their internal contradictoriness, and shown as texts reflecting two universalizing, rationalistic "master narratives"—Marxism and Freudianism—whose truth claims were insupportable. Sexism was studied in a period, designated postmodern, in which all social phenomena and all social analyses were "read" as texts, and in which sexism could be construed—in the most general sense—as the way in which thought and language have been systematically structured to debase women. Linguistic change—starting with the now commonplace shift away from "he" as the generic pronoun—was understood as the paradigm for social change and the prelude to social change. Nonsexist language had to be created to speak of sexism; speaking of prejudice had to be a creative work, involving creative artists, not just a work of destruction. The emergence of feminist theory meant that for the first time in the history of Studies in Prejudice, the ideological character of a prejudice and the "totalizing" (to use a term of Michel Foucault's) of its discourse were really understood. The problem of eliminating sexism could be formulated clearly as an ultimately impossible Archimedean one: Give me a place to stand, and I will move the problem.

The migration of theoretical work on prejudice into the domain of sexism marked its exit from the domain of racism. Studies of the *effects* of racism still proliferated—indeed, they constitute by now a huge industry. But investigation of racism's motivations and contexts has nearly ceased. Little of the Marxism and even less of the Freudianism that had so informed the original Studies in Prejudice survived the waxing and then the waning of Black Power. Only recently has a new generation of African American intellectuals come forward—in a period when it is so obvious that racism is not part of our nation's past, an old aberration, but still our open wound, our founding injustice, our collective nemesis—to ask, again, "Why?"

This renewed "why," spurred by two decades of inquiry into sexism, is often posed now by African American women as part of feminist theory and in conjunction with Black feminist literary work, particularly in fiction. Studies of sexism were also extended and reworked by those concerned with "homophobia," a word coined in 1972 to indicate prejudice against homosexuals and to suggest that people who are homophobic both fear homosexuals and fear being homosexual. When homophobia became a topic in the 1970s, theorizing about the prejudice was built right into the designation of the prejudice: a revised Freudianism, Freudianism in a postmodern form, was announced with the word "homophobia."

Much of the theorizing about homophobia was done in the early 1970s by gay men, whose movement was called, on the model of Women's Liberation, the Gay Liberation movement. But the word "homophobia" was also applied by lesbians to prejudice against lesbians, even though the hostility to Freudianism in lesbian communities was—and to a large extent still is—so palpable. To this day "homophobia" implies that gay men and lesbians are the victims of the same prejudice, as does the newer term dating from the early 1980s, "heterosexism." Although these usages do capture the hatred aroused by life outside heterosexual norms, the analogizing also obscures the differences between prejudice directed at lesbians and prejudice directed at gay men, as well as differences along gender lines among those prejudiced against homosexuals.[5]

Gradually, over the course of the years since *The Nature of Prejudice,* the Studies in Prejudice conducted by victims of prejudice in non–social scientific media have parted company with those conducted by the university social science practitioners whose future achievements Allport had heralded. This is because, it is no exaggeration to say, most academic social psychologists and sociologists narrowed their object of study and their methods to a scandalous degree.

Among the social psychologists who studied antisemitism and racism, the clear, strong line of theoretical inquiry that came from Freudian psychoanalysis and was developed by the émigré group that produced *The Authoritarian Personality* (1951) grew fainter as psychoanalysis became both more and more woven into the fabric of American culture and more and more shallow, deradicalized, and mechanical. While every journalist could produce Freudian-sounding clichés about childhood sexuality, psychoanalytic clinicians by and large downplayed Freud's instinctual drive theory and kept it and themselves away from social theory. Social psychologists eventually studied prejudice in only the most literal sense: that is, they considered only the cognitive content of peoples' utterances, the record in their utterances or their prejudgments, their preconceived ideas, their stereotypes, their faulty generalizations. A prejudice, so the conventional academic understanding went for decades, is a distorting idea about a group, held without respect to individuals in the group or to actual experience with the group. Degree of prejudice is equivalent to the degree of rigidity or inflexibility or imperviousness to experience and education with which the faulty idea is held.

In Allport's day, extreme rigidity would have been explored as a matter of psychopathology, and Freudian categories would have been important to the exploration, as they were to Allport himself and to all of the Studies in Prejudice authors. But, as both psychoanalysis and the general idea that there is a distinction between rational and irrational thinking lost ground in social psychology, the cognitive approach came to be more focused on cognitive processes pure and simple, without regard to motivations and without concern for the unconscious. People thus acquire faulty generalizations because they are faultily educated— social learning is the culprit. We need not eliminate inequalities or question child-rearing practices and social habits.

Attributing prejudice to social learning or mislearning makes it seem a superficial matter, spread across all cultures in somewhat the same way that perceptual illusions and historical misinformation are. It normalizes prejudice. The obvious next step is to conclude that proper education can eliminate prejudice, that tolerance can be taught. Just say no to prejudice. Just say yes to the historically victimized. Or, as many social scientists said—"let them all learn social science!" This hope epitomizes the confident "just fix it!" attitude of many American educators since the 1950s. The attitude has been able to perpetuate itself because it has dictated the instruments for measuring prejudice—the statistically analyzable questionnaire and the opinion poll—and for judging the results of educational programs.

Since the 1950s, corrective educational programs and instruments for measuring their success have been developed and celebrated with little methodological sophistication. Academic social psychologists had no trouble assuming that a social psychologist could achieve unbiased, culturally neutral rationality or freedom from prejudice, and that such a pure state of mind and heart could provide a reliable or appropriate standard against which to measure others' prejudices. Few suspected that a questionnaire phrased entirely in negatives might suggest to respondents that they, too, should respond negatively—as it must have seemed to them that the questionnaire writers themselves already had. "Manual labor and menial jobs seem to fit the Negro mentality and ability better than more skilled or responsible work."[6] Agree or disagree? "It would be a mistake to have Negroes for foremen and leaders over whites." Agree or disagree? Similarly, educators and poll takers assumed that the people they questioned about their prejudices would be both willing and able to respond fully and truthfully. The Freudian idea that prejudices reflect unconscious fantasies and are themselves at least partly unconscious has no place in the brave new world of cognitive science. Meanwhile, the social pressure upon people to keep their prejudices to themselves has grown. Today, not many white participants in empirical studies are willing to tell a questioner or a pollster that, yes, in fact, they hate blacks—viscerally, violently.

As the social sciences became more scientific—or pseudoscientific— after the 1950s, that is, after they left far behind the kind of complexity and sense of depth that are evident in the postwar Studies in Prejudice, a divide opened between this kind of work and the rich, illuminating, nonacademic literary and historical traditions developed by American victims of prejudice. James Baldwin's *The Fire Next Time* (1963) and Milton Rokeach's *The Open and Closed Mind* (1960), for example, are books of the same period and place but from different planets of discourse. There are exceptions to this generalization—like the dialogue between James Baldwin and the anthropologist Margaret Mead published in 1972 under the title *Rap on Race*—and the study of sexism represents a departure from it, as I noted. But basically one can accurately say that nonacademic students of antisemitism and racism have learned from one another, not from the social scientists. And, as I implied before, this learning has been chronological; it constitutes a kind of genealogy of Studies of Prejudice.

Writers on racism in the 1960s drew eclectically on the Studies in Prejudice series, but they were much more strongly indebted to non–social scientific works like Jean-Paul Sartre's *Anti-Semite and Jew,* published in English in 1948. Feminists of the late 1960s drew heavily on Simone de Beauvoir's *The Second Sex* (1947), which shared a philosophy with Sartre's work of the same period, but their major debts were to the African American literary explorers of racism—Richard Wright, Ralph Ellison, James Baldwin, and Malcolm X. When white feminists were writing pieces with titles like "Woman as Nigger," they were not much concerned with the specific experiences of Negro women or of any other women who might, like Jewish women, know prejudice in more than one form. But since then that narrowness of focus—a theoretical prejudice—has been corrected somewhat. Urged on by works like Angela Davis's *Women, Race, and Class* (1981), a book in which the Marxist postwar theoretical line on prejudice got a full, complex refashioning, feminists of all backgrounds have begun to speak more inclusively of a hyphenated entity "gender-race-class," or sometimes "sexism-racism-classism."

In theorizing about homophobia, the touchstone literary *oeuvre* is Jean Genet's, but the debts to Black writers on racism and feminist writers on sexism are everywhere apparent. This theorizing, however, is also distinctive for doing much more than ignoring narrow academic social science; it has, by contrast, mounted a huge ground-clearing operation to show the theoretical prejudices in the whole history of psychological and sociological work on homosexuality, particularly insofar as this enterprise has classified homosexuality as a pathology. Black writers had complained bitterly that the Black victims of racism had been pathologized by white social science, and feminists noted again and again how being female was construed as a deviant condition. But homosexuality had the dubious distinction of being listed in psychiatric clinical manuals as an illness. Studies in Prejudice have become much more sophisticated theoretically as social scientific theory has become more deeply and completely understood as part of the problem of prejudice, not part of its solution.

Even though there has been some integration of the various kinds of Studies in Prejudice recently, no review or overview of the sort Allport attempted in *The Nature of Prejudice* has emerged. There is no written genealogy of Prejudice Studies. There is not even a work from within feminism that questions whether the currently in-vogue complex sexism-racism-classism contains constricting assumptions that do not allow any of its three parts to be illuminated. What we do have at the moment, however, is an exciting literature by people who are victims of multiple prejudices. There are, for example, anthologies like *This Bridge Called My Back: Writings by Radical Women of Color* (1981) with its poems and prose reflections by women who have known sexism and racism and homophobia. In this work can be found, at the least, a preliminary outlining of what kinds of inquiries would be needed to do not Studies in Prejudice but Studies in Prejudices—to give real acknowledgment to the plural.

To a certain extent, the absence on our current American intellectual scene of synthetic work on prejudices reflects three factors: that the social sciences are no longer the infants they were when Allport anticipated their futures; that the social sciences have been rigorously attacked by non–social science students of prejudice; and that the literature produced by literary and historical critics outside the social sciences has grown exponentially. No individual could read and review what has been written since 1954 on the subject of prejudices, or even what has been written since "sexism" was coined and added to the list of prejudices to be compassed. Moreover, new applications of the concept of prejudice are being generated all the time: we now speak, for example, of ageism and of prejudice against the disabled (or "differently abled" or "physically challenged"—terms intended, like Black and African American, to prevent prejudice from being displayed as it is being talked about).

## Obstacles to Synthesis

But more deters synthetic approaches to the study of prejudices than the size of the library existing for survey. Gordon Allport's way of thinking suited his time. He was able, without questioning himself, to build his entire book on the basis of a single assumption—one that I think is completely wrong. He went in search of "the nature of prejudice" and enjoined his fellow social scientists to "let us seek out the root of prejudice," an injunction that assumed prejudice is something singular with one nature and one root. Allport took for granted the singular nature of prejudice despite his cautious and careful stance on the question of causality: "It is a serious error to ascribe prejudice and discrimination to any single taproot, reaching into economic exploitation, social structure, the mores, fear, aggression, sex conflict, or any other favored soil. Prejudice and discrimination, as we shall see, draw nourishment from all these conditions, and many others." As his two contradictory root metaphors reveal, Allport could not bring himself to say that there are both many causes *and many prejudices*. He could explore the many causes, but he could not produce a phenomenology of prejudices (in the plural) because he was trapped by his assumption that prejudice is one.

Allport knew, of course, that prejudice comes in different forms, but he kept reducing these to variations of one thing:

> When we speak of prejudice we are likely to think of "race prejudice." This is an unfortunate association of ideas, for throughout history human prejudice has had little to do with race. The conception of race is recent, scarcely a century old. For the most part prejudice and persecution have rested on other grounds, often on religion. Until the recent past, Jews have been persecuted chiefly for their religion, not for their race. Negroes were enslaved primarily because they were economic assets, but the rationale took a racial form.

Much in that paragraph of Allport's preface is questionable, but I want to emphasize now only that prejudice was, for him, one thing that appears in different forms, under different conditions, and with different rationales, even though the one thing has plural causes. It is like a single disease arising under multiple causal conditions and displaying itself in different symptoms.

On the evidence of his book, it appears that Allport became dedicated to the idea that prejudice is one thing, with one nature, because of research done by himself and by his contemporaries that seemed to show definitively that a person who is prejudiced against, say, Negroes, will also be prejudiced against all kinds of other groups as well. He and his colleagues offered, again and again, social scientific versions of the famous cartoon from the *New Yorker* in which a barfly raises his glass and drunkenly announces, "I hate everybody—without regard to race, creed, or national origin!" Allport considered the equal opportunity sweep of hatred *a fact.* "One of the facts of which we are most certain is that people who reject one out-group will tend to reject other out-groups. If a person is anti-Jewish, he is likely to be anti-Catholic, anti-Negro, anti any out-group." When this stance of Allport's became dogma, the word "ethnocentrism" came into use for presenting the universal behind all variations of prejudice: they all involve not just prejudice against certain groups but a pervasive tendency to divide the world into in-groups and out-groups as well as a generally hostile frame of mind toward out-groups.[7] Prejudice is, in Allport's phrase, a "generalized attitude." And this single claim, this "certainty" about the generalized attitude of prejudice, both made possible Allport's synthetic endeavor and helped him doom all subsequent social scientific studies in prejudice to superficialities about the very different prejudices—like antisemitism, racism, and sexism.

Allport's broad idea, accepted throughout the academic halls of psychology and sociology, helped buttress two related ideas. One was that any differences of form a prejudice may assume over time or in different milieus are unimportant in comparison to prejudice's essence or nature. Antisemitism is one manifestation of prejudice in general, and not only is it essentially no different from white racism, but antisemitism in the time of Pontius Pilate is essentially no different from antisemitism in the time of Adolf Hitler. Similarly, we can distinguish no essential differences among modern antisemites who are children and antisemites who are adults, antisemites of one character type or another, antisemites who are upper class and antisemites who are lower class, and so forth. The second idea was that out-groups are virtually interchangeable. Ethnocentrism will focus on whichever one happens to live next door, or whichever out-group happens to be in direct economic competition, or whichever one has come into threatening prominence, or whichever one happens to be worse off and can thus be forced into the role of the oppressed (on the theory that prejudice runs downhill). Out-groups are, to put the matter another way, scapegoats onto which in-group members project feelings that must be put somewhere.

The idea that there are and always have been ethnocentric people and people who are (relatively) not ethnocentric gained ground throughout the 1950s, particularly because it accommodated the social psychological idea that prejudice is rigid and faulty generalization, a cognitive phenomenon. Behind many social policy and educational efforts to create the kinds of conditions (composites of many causal factors) in which (relatively) nonethnocentric, unprejudiced people would flourish lay the assumption that ethnocentric people can be cured of their wrong and harmful generalizations about out-groups if group barriers come down. Ethnocentrism has always existed because groups have eternally been divided, but this tragedy is not irreversible.

In the American context, hope for change took the form of turning up the temperature on the "melting pot," particularly in the schools. In practice such policies often meant using schools to make out-groups more acceptable to the in-groups controlling the schools—as minority groups quickly pointed out. But in theory the goal was less homogenizing or assimilatory. Significantly, American anti-ethnocentrism educational efforts in the 1950s went under the title "intracultural education," a term that implies bridge building among groups that have been out-groups to each other. This approach, of course, differs quite strikingly from the present "multicultural education" promoted by minority groups, which is an effort to maintain pluralism and give minority cultures recognition. Multiculturalism as an educational theory embodies the distrust of social science that has characterized victim-group studies of prejudice since the late 1960s. And thus it is no accident that most of the white middle-class intellectuals who currently oppose multiculturalism are blithely ignorant of the history that advocates of multiculturalism take for granted because it is their lives.

Since the 1950s, the assumption that prejudice or ethnocentrism is a single thing with many causes has governed social scientific work on prejudice, particularly in its narrow cognitive forms, even though revolutionizing challenges by victims of prejudice have sometimes temporarily disturbed it. Jews wrote the postwar Studies in Prejudice series as well as many other works on the topic, but few of them had challenged the ethnocentrism assumption because it fitted their hopes for assimilation. They wanted to be, as it were, victims no different than any others. Reform directed at a "generalized attitude" would benefit them as well as other immigrant groups and the Negroes, all of whom could work in coalitions to fight their common enemy. As Allport said, Jews were once persecuted for their religion, but more recently for their "race." Jew hatred and Negro hatred seemed to almost all theorists of the 1950s to be two forms of the same race prejudice problem (and they never even considered the problem of sexism).

But the Africans and African Americans who wrote after the war, and whose ideas gained ground in the 1960s, made no such assumption. They cited analogies between race prejudice and antisemitism, and they spoke of their fear that race prejudice could result in a genocide, another Holocaust, but Negro hatred seemed to them fundamentally unlike Jew hatred for the elementary reason that most Jews (particularly in America) are white. Jews are not hated for the color of their skin (and whatever skin color may represent), and many Blacks in the 1960s held it against their Jewish supporters in the early days of the Civil Rights movement that the specificities of prejudice against Blacks were not widely appreciated among the Jews. Similarly, feminists pointed out that sexism knows no religious or color boundaries; it is not a matter of distinguishing one native group from another native group. Sexism is both more universal and more intimate; it traverses groups, families, and social classes. Homophobia, too, knows no boundaries, but it— unlike sexism—involves alleging marks of difference. The male homophobe, for example, wants the male homosexual, who is invisible as such, to be a marked person so that his trespass—say, being a "woman" in a male body—will not be hidden and can be punished and also so that he, the male homophobe, being unmarked, will not be mistaken for a homosexual.[8] The Nazis made gays wear pink triangles.

To rescue the specificities of their experiences as victims from the great blurring of the "generalized attitude" approach, those who have written as witnesses, givers of testimony, have often accepted distorting ways of defining and typing prejudices. All of these distortions involve classifying prejudices according to their target groups. The extreme opposite of the claim that prejudice is one is the claim that each prejudice is uniquely received by a singular group or kind of group and that it is definable or analyzable in terms of the target group's experience. For people who begin with this particularizing approach, efforts to reach out and understand other peoples' experiences usually take the form of creating analogies.

But analogizing, in addition to being theoretically obfuscating, creates much more confusion than coalition when it serves as the basis for practical politics. For example, in the 1960s, when many Jews wanted to work with the Civil Rights movement to combat racism, they were willing to consider themselves a "race" like the Blacks (according to "race theory"). The Jews called prejudice against Jews "racism." This meant using the scientifically questionable word "race" for Blacks as well as failing to note that Jews are certainly not a "race" but a group defined by a religion or religiously based culture. It was European "race theory" that perpetrated the false conception of Jews as a race, "Semites." To take a second example: "People of color" is a phrase meant to indicate that African Americans, Native Americans, Hispanics, and Asian Americans—blacks, reds, browns, and yellows in the caricaturing color terms—are all victims of the same prejudice, racism, and all one kind of group. "People of color" is a phrase of great importance for coalition building and the practical politics of antiracism, and it has become the cornerstone concept of the struggling American political movement known as the Rainbow Coalition. But the umbrella "people of color" makes it difficult to see that many whites direct against Asian Americans, and particularly against those subgroups which are commercially successful, a type of prejudice that has much more in common with antisemitism than it does with racism against African Americans. And, from another angle, the prejudice now commonly directed by African Americans against commercially successful Asian American groups like the Koreans in Los Angeles or New York comes much closer to antisemitism than to either racism or what is known as "colorism" (prejudice by people of color against other people of color, usually *darker* color).

When victim groups and their representatives get caught up in the designation of prejudices according to their targets, they loose focus on the perpetrators and the circumstances, the social and political contexts, of the perpetration. They fail to perceive prejudices as fulfillments of needs or desires and to ask what needs or desires are being fulfilled. Classifying prejudices according to target groups obscures the fact that the same need or desire can be fulfilled by directing prejudice at a victim group defined by color or at one defined by sexual preference—or at people who can be hated for both color and sexual preference. The same need or desire can be fulfilled in one historical context by antisemitism and in another by anti-Communism and in another by "Japan bashing," each target group supplying a variation on the theme of "invidiously seeking international economic control."

The assumption that prejudice is a generalized attitude needs a critique, but not one that splinters prejudice into a series of pointers, named after the people pointed out. The literatures on prejudices written by members of victim groups have not explored the generalized-attitude idea theoretically. They have not questioned what purposes the idea served. As a result, the various victims of prejudice have not yet been able to make a clear survey of what the types of prejudice they have experienced have in common and do not have in common. They have not surveyed *the similarities and the differences.* Coalitions among victim groups will never be tied with strong theoretical ropes until both the similarities and the differences among the types of victimization are understood.

As the non–social scientific discourse on prejudice has grown (fortunately, finally) more multivocal, it has also (unfortunately) become more chaotic. Rather than coordinating their work, students of antisemitism, of white racism, of sexism, and of homophobia have either, on the one hand, stayed provincially within their distinct spheres or, on the other hand, created competing types of reductionism. Some theorists of the second sort hold that one type of prejudice—sexism, say—is the root of all others or of the two others in the trinity sexism-racism-classism. They view sexism as both the essence of prejudice and the proximate cause of all derivative forms. But no, say many Marxists, classism is the root. Others make the same argument for prejudice against people of color (which is no longer called racism among academic social scientists because the very notion that there are distinct races has been so thoroughly debunked and dispatched). Sometimes a plurality of causes for the basic form of prejudice is acknowledged, and sometimes a candidate for chief cause is nominated from Allport's list: "economic exploitation, social structure, mores, fear, aggression, sex conflict, and so forth." Recently, a third tendency has emerged: discourses about one kind of prejudice are used to talk indirectly about another—for example, discussions of gender construction and sex discrimination are used by some African American feminists to talk indirectly about racism when their discussion is with non–African American feminists, who cannot be expected to understand racism.

In schematic terms, some people say "X prejudice is all that I, a victim of it, am interested in"; others say "X prejudice is the root of all others or the key to their exploration"; and still others say "X prejudice can be used to show how Y prejudice operates when you must speak outside your own Y-victim group, because *they* don't get Y—because *they* are implicated." But, at the same time that these possibilities are being formulated, a strong movement has arisen against "essentialism" in any intellectual field. To avoid essentializing, one should speak of prejudices, not of prejudice, or, at least, one should give the various prejudices their due as distinct forms. Hence sexism-racism-classism. But usually advocates of this troika, rather than really framing questions about what the various prejudices do and do not have in common, either rule the topic of their interrelations out of theoretical bounds or judge the matter in advance (as I noted) by arguing reductively that one branch of the troika is fundamental.[9]

An additional theoretical complexity has also weighed against any synthetic approach. Allport, with his dedication to exploring a plurality of causes of prejudice, conscientiously tried to avoid favoring either psychological study of individuals or sociological study of groups or societies, even though his orientation was psychological and he appreciated psychoanalytic work. Many of the researchers whose contributions to the nascent field of "objective study of conflict" were reported by Allport assumed, as he did, that psychoanalytic psychology, empirical psychology, sociology, and political science were all complementary, overlapping. They anticipated that ways to explore the roots and manifestations of individuals' prejudices would mesh with social theories—Freudianism with Marxism. But this assumption, too, has unraveled, and not just because of specialization in the disciplines of social science, the ascent into prominence of cognitive models, and the impact of deconstructionist critiques of the master narratives. The synthetic hope has foundered primarily for two other reasons. First, the fortunes of Marxism as a practical politics have declined, which has given Marxist theory a very bad name. And second, any kind of social and political theorizing now being practiced lacks conceptual mediation between individual psyches and social processes.

As no coherent mediating notion of personality or character in which psychology and sociology could meet has ever appeared, discussions of the psychic causes of prejudice continue to compete with rather than mesh with social and economic theories. In the 1950s, the psychoanalytically oriented Marxists of the Frankfurt School, the ones who worked on the Studies in Prejudice series, attempted to be synthetic (even without a notion of character or personality), and they offered models that were later taken up by theorists of racism and sexism. But their goal has remained elusive. Other social scientific studies of the same vintage, like Gordon Allport's sequel, *Becoming: Basic Considerations for a Psychology of Personality* (1955), have exerted a wide influence in academic psychology but received little notice among the people of color and women who have since so effectively used anti-essentialist arguments to demolish the concept of personality (in the singular, and often the generic masculine).

I have been outlining a series of theoretical problems that have beset studies of prejudice. There is a split between work done by narrowly cognitive social scientists and work done by nonacademic victims of prejudices (who often focus on the prejudice of which they are the victims without linking their experiences to those of other victim groups). There is a "one and many" problem—an assumption that prejudice is one thing, a generalized attitude, even though it may have many causes, and the opposite assumption that prejudices can be defined by the group or kind of group they target. And there is a tendency to approach prejudice either psychologically or sociologically without consideration for the interplay of psychological and sociological factors. But this formidable array of obstacles is also embedded in yet another layer of complexity.

In the broader social and political context where both academic and nonacademic studies in prejudice have appeared, this additional layer of complexity has turned studying prejudice into a matter of competition for scarce resources of public attention and concern. Over the postwar decades in America, there have grown up, in political and cultural terms, three different public languages about prejudice, three different discourses. Those who learn one, or are acculturated to one, seldom learn the other two—or, at best, they tack on a second language, rarely a third, and never feel comfortable or fluent. In the diverse precincts of public policy, one or another language is spoken, but never more than one.

The first of these languages grew out of the immediate postwar discussion of antisemitism and of Nazism, which quickly became entangled with a discussion of Stalinism as the Cold War set in after 1948. Antisemitism, in this discussion, was an ideology (some said *the* ideology) of Nazism, and Nazism was one species of totalitarianism. Stalinism, the other totalitarianism, also involved antisemitism. Totalitarianism was the most hideous and perverted opposite to democracy that had ever appeared in history. This language, then, was a political language of war between democracy and totalitarianism, and its speakers felt that nothing in the world was more important, more crucial, than this planetary battle of democracy and totalitarianism, equated by some with a struggle between capitalism and socialism or Communism, and referenced by some to the old European political designations of right and left, conservative and progressive. Although many of the analytic categories that such speakers use resemble those developed by complex and subtle writers, like Hannah Arendt, the language itself has always been rigorously simple and Manichaean. The concern with antisemitism that was once so central to this language has atrophied, and, for similar reasons, so has concern with what was called, after World War I, "the minorities question," the question of how to achieve political equality for the many minority populations of Europe residing in majority-dominated nation-states. Anyone who has wanted to speak the democracy-versus-totalitarianism language intricately, and to keep it connected to its history and its original concern with antisemitism and minority problems, has had to strain against its unrelenting pull toward political ideology and superpower confrontational politics.

A second language grew out of the experiences of non-European colonial peoples with European colonialism and of African Americans with American racism. In colonial contexts, this was a language of national liberation from political and cultural oppression, while in the American context it was a language of liberation in which nationalism was problematic, in which Black nationalism was nationalism without a nation. (Politically, African Americans have periodically reworked the "Back to Africa" imperative so powerful in the 1920s, but more frequently they have advanced visions of cultural nationalism, which is now called Afrocentricity.) Many national liberationists considered socialism a goal, but always a socialism reconceived for non-European contexts—"Third Way" socialism, nonaligned socialism, and so forth—and removed to one degree or another from the democracy-versus-totalitarianism battle that was held to be a European, American, and Soviet affair. The basic dynamic—both psychological and sociopolitical—captured in this language was the rebellion of peoples once or even still labeled inferior and judged to be naturally fitted for servitude, against their oppressors and their oppressors' rationales.

Interestingly, in the last few years, as the Soviet satellites have broken away and the Soviet Union dissolved, American political circles have become more suffused with discussion of racism. There are domestic reasons for this shift, of course, and they have to do with the deteriorating economic position of a large portion of the African American and Hispanic populations and the erosion of hard-won civil rights gains. But it is also the case that while the discourse of totalitarianism versus democracy reigned supreme, hardly any discussion about national or cultural liberation could occur without immediate translation into the "them and us" superpower framework. In the 1950s the Civil Rights movement had to force its claims on the preoccupied federal government, and in the 1980s the Civil Rights movement had to try again to get through—less successfully. Whether the events in Eastern Europe and the former Soviet Union will, eventually, permit a greater American domestic appreciation of minority questions here and abroad remains to be seen, although the current wave of political conservatism and isolationism does not augur well. So, too, does it remain to be seen whether the plethora of different types of prejudice now flourishing in Eastern Europe and the former Soviet Union, released into new virulence by the political changes there, will be understood in all their differences or only in the simplifying categories like "ethnocentrism" or "ethnocentric nationalism" that now dominate the press.

The third language or type of discourse grew up in the course of the Women's Liberation movement and its fight for equality, which succeeded the prewar fight for suffrage. The terms of this language are built on a distinction between private spheres or forms of life and public ones. Feminist theorists, frequently to the incomprehension of people whose main modes of speaking and thinking are the two I have just noted, insisted that women had been largely confined to the private sphere, which was completely structured by the power relations of the public sphere. Men controlled social and political affairs, and men extended their power into the private sphere, where women were to be servants and mothers. "Patriarchy" is the concept that conveys the extension of male social and political power into domestic life, where it is wielded over women and children (as well as over slaves and servants, and also over those labeled in some way mentally or sexually deviant). Women's Liberation is liberation from patriarchy in all its manifestations: "the personal is political."

There is no nation of women, no customary social or political grouping by gender, so this language, and this liberation, have had to be invented. While nonsexist language has emerged as a goal, a needed invention, it has also been used to name a desired social order. Similarly, gay men and lesbians have had to establish an identity for themselves as a group—and to find a way to do that without simply adopting some

variation on the ways in which they have been castigated. Feminist and
gay forms of inventiveness have made reference to the politics of national liberation, so there have been, for example, a book called *Lesbian
Nation* and an agitprop group called Queer Nation. But this usage has
its obvious limits, and the feminist and gay movements have struck similar limits when they have invoked the democracy-versus-totalitarianism
discourse.[10]

Anyone who wants to discuss prejudice must start from a recognition
that people who speak these three languages and their variants do not
often understand one another. Furthermore, different theories of prejudice have been formulated against the background of these different
discourses, and thus they do not translate easily from one to another.
A synthetic approach will have to be polyglot.

## About This Book

In the vast library on prejudice and prejudices one finds little reflection
on how we theorize about prejudice, or on the conceptual and historical
frames in which we think about prejudice(s) and the causes of preju-
dice(s), although recently many short histories of theories of prejudice
have begun to appear.[11] Even the shift toward theory that came about
contemporaneously with the second wave of feminism has produced
theorizing not about prejudices but only about sexism and then sexism-
racism-classism. The obstacles to synthesis that I have sketched have
been too formidable.

Because there is so little reflection on how we theorize about prejudice, and because the histories of theory of prejudice that do exist are
in the nature of brief tour guides, not analyses, it is crucial to set the
discussion historically. As I have been noting, habits of thinking about
prejudice—and of *not* thinking theoretically or in terms of critical theory—have developed since the end of World War II, and these habits
have been reinforced as one type of prejudice after another has come
to center intellectual stage, particularly in America, where, as Allport
noted, "the checkerboard of prejudice is . . . perhaps the most intricate
of all." Broadly, as antisemitism has been succeeded by racism and racism by sexism and homophobia in the role of key focus of theorizing,
certain ways of thinking have become axiomatic and others have been
excluded. There are certainly many other types of prejudice that could
be considered, but these four—antisemitism, racism, sexism, and ho-

mophobia—are the four over which the determinative American discourse has arisen historically.

Although I proceed historically, this book is not simply a history of postwar theories of prejudice. It presents the genealogy of Studies of Prejudice that I consider a much-needed framework. But this historical approach is designed to reveal in detail the types of theoretical problems and obstacles that I have outlined quickly here, as well as to raise questions about what connections may exist between theoretical prejudices in the study of prejudice and prejudices themselves. Addressing the problems of theory and the obstacles to studying prejudices (in the plural) synthetically requires a typology of prejudices.

The first part of this book sets out the critical-theoretical agenda and treats work done within the social sciences, chiefly social psychology and sociology, and chiefly in America, as American work has dominated in Western social science. The second offers the new approach that this agenda calls for—it offers a typology. I focus on the needs and desires different prejudices fulfill. This approach is, initially, largely psychological, and it is rooted in psychoanalytic theory. But it broadens into a social theory. There are, I argue, characterologically based prejudice types and types of societies that reflect and promote, or refuse and demote, the different prejudices. Societies have, relatively speaking, prejudice inducements and prejudice immunities. Finally, in the third part of this book, I consider antisemitism, white racism, sexism, and homophobia as instances of the broad prejudice types and also as societal processes. This part is organized around issues that exemplify current forms of the various prejudices and engages literatures by the victims of the different prejudices, not the kind of social scientific studies that I criticize in the first part.

As a first step in the direction of a new typology, the notion that all prejudices are basically the same must be analyzed. I look at the history of the generalized—overgeneralized—notion "ethnocentrism" and incorporate the historical reconstruction to establish a more limited use for the term. Ethnocentrism, considered as a form of prejudice that protects group identity in economic, social, and political terms, is both universal—where groups are, ethnocentrism is—and ideologically or aspirationally limited. By contrast with ethnocentrism, there are prejudices that are not universal, which appear and grow in specific contexts, but that are, nevertheless, ideologically unlimited. Such prejudices have totalitarian sweep—they are prejudices promoting visions of world conquest, they are futuristic, supremacist, they make evolutionary claims. They are also prejudices aimed not at limited groups or *ethnoi*—a tribe, an ethnic group, a nation—but at *marks of difference,* aspects of human form, particular qualities that can be found in and across many groups. A person who hates what "black" signifies hates "blacks" wherever he finds or imagines them—in his own family or his own nation, as well as in groups he does not belong to and places he has never been. Sexists hate marks of the feminine, whether in women or in men. Antisemitism flourishes in Japan, in the absence of Jews. I call such prejudices ideologies of desire.

Ethnocentrisms take distinct historical forms. They vary with social circumstances and types of social and political organization, and they are influenced by technological developments. Thus the prejudice against out-groups that a nomadic tribe with simple technological resources can muster will be quite different from that expressed by the citizens of a walled polis with an imperial armada. But between ethnocentrisms and ideologies of desire we can trace distinctions of a fundamentally different sort. Ideologies of desire are prejudices that have consolidated—not originated, but consolidated—uniquely in the modern world. They presuppose specific modern conditions.

Looking at American history with this distinction in mind, we clearly see a profound shift in the forms and intensities of the ideological prejudices running through the 1870s and into the 1890s. In that two-decade span, antisemitism in its modern form appeared in America for the first time. That is, there appeared a prejudice against Jews distinguishable from earlier religiously based Jew hatred by its political and economic qualities. Describing a paradigmatic episode in his book *A Mask for Privilege: Antisemitism in America* (1948), the historian Cary McWilliams speculated about why a prominent Jewish banker and his family were refused accommodation in a Saratoga Springs resort hotel. They had set out on vacation in 1877, on the brink of "the second American Revolution," the revolution transforming American industry with astonishing quickness and bringing an entrepreneurial class, epitomized by a group of millionaire tycoons, to astonishing power. In this new and ferocious private business culture, successful Jewish bankers were envied and feared as operators of public business at the same time that the continuing waves of Jewish immigrants from Russia and Eastern Europe were feared as competitors in the middle-class clerical markets. The key sign of antisemitism—the charge that there is a powerful Jewish money conspiracy—appeared in its characteristic modern form: the government is being corrupted by this conspiracy. More generally, the period was also one in which, as Denis Tilden Lynch, author of *The Wild Seventies,* remarked, "class hatred was a new note in American life where all men were equal before the law." Strikes and violent antilabor actions broke out all over the country; 4 million people were unemployed in Northern cities. On the West Coast, Americans responded to immigration across the Pacific with anti-Chinese violence, and the federal government passed the Chinese Exclusion Act of 1882, a radical departure in policy and the first of a series of laws that culminated in the Immigration Act of 1924. This sweeping law barred not only Jews but Japanese, and it made first-generation Japanese Americans, like the Chinese earlier, ineligible for citizenship.

The *fin de siècle* also brought an end, as C. Vann Woodward argued in *The Strange Career of Jim Crow,* to Negro political progress after the Civil War ended, as segregation laws were promulgated—subtended by pseudoscientific evolutionary race theory—that for more than half a century relegated African Americans to a second American slavery. In addition, unwritten laws kept women in American households in their "separate sphere," reflecting a form of sexism laced with anxiety about the "new" women fighting for suffrage. A novel version of the ideology of female inferiority was hammered out with the same types of pseudoscientific tools that produced race theory. At the same time, physicians and sex researchers invented a new category with the name "homosexual." Homosexuals were, according to the sexological consensus, abnormal beings, perverts, deviants, whose acts were criminal—a judgment on the orientation that remained the official opinion until 1973, and a judgment on "sodomy" that still survives in many states. Antisemitism, racism, sexism, and homophobia were all "modernized" at the same moment.

Many social, economic, and political factors affected these fateful decades when prejudices solidified, grew encrusted with "science," became institutionalized, were made into law. The country had had its first modern war—the Civil War, fought with long-distance guns and cannons, involving massive civilian death as well as military losses—and was soaked in moral controversy as well as blood; a wrenching pace of social and economic change, industrialization and urbanization, had driven wedges between people, in many areas creating in an instant the class structures that had taken the centuries since feudalism to develop in

Europe; rank upon rank of immigrants had traveled over eastern, southern, and western boundaries and filled the country with their various
and often clashing customs and religious beliefs; there had been a complex cultural break with the democratic ethos that the prewar Tran-
scendentalists had extolled in the American character, the American
Creed. In Europe, where the modern prejudices also flourished, factors
comparable to these also existed, as did, in addition, a complex expor-
tation of racism to Africa, India, and China and a rebounding of it on
the colonializing countries. The French Revolution and the demand for
equality that came with it were crucial, for late-nineteenth-century prejudice production was in every sphere a backlash or counterrevolution,
a refusal to give up prerogatives, statuses, inherited or acquired securi-
ties.

     Ideologies of desire are, generally, backlashes against movements of
equality; they are regressive prejudices that reinstate inequalities and
distinctions when the force of movements for equality has been registered and (often unconsciously) rejected. As the psychoanalyst Ernst
Kris remarked: "Everywhere in Western civilization there exists some
sort of link between equalitarian beliefs and the growth of prejudicial
attitudes. Prejudice replaces social barriers of another kind."[12] Prejudices institutionalize at deeper and more inchoate individual and social
or political levels the differences between "us" and "them" that movements for equality address. In other words, ideologies of desire become
entangled with governments, with states proclaiming equality before the
law, either as they are used (like antisemitism) to destroy such states
and establish suprastate entities, or as they are institutionalized (like
racism) by such states, or as they extend (like sexism) state political
reach into nonpolitical arenas.

     I will try to show that the period between the last third of the nine-
teenth century and the last quarter of this century has an internal co-
herence as an epoch of prejudices. It is the period in which ideologies
of desire completely overshadowed ethnocentrisms and, often, mingled
with ethnocentrisms, making them peculiarly deadly—as the ethnic conflict in the former Yugoslavia has become genocidal by being mingled
with an anti-Muslimism that is horrifyingly similar to antisemitism. I certainly do not want to argue that wars between tribes, conflicts between
ethnic groups, battles under banners of nationalism, and religious controversies have not had enormous and dreadful play in this period. But
the era of state economies and world wars, of internationalism and what

is now known as globalism, which gives all local conflicts larger contexts of interference, has been an era in which "us versus them" has been both enacted and rationalized, converted into ideology, in quite distinctive ways. Moreover, since the end of World War II, as individuals and agencies of many sorts have tried to foster equality and eliminate prejudices, the specific qualities of the ideological prejudices have become clearer—unfortunately—because they have proven so peculiarly resistant, so recalcitrant, and even because they have proven so difficult to understand. As movements against the ideologies of desire have arisen, and victims have organized as resisters, these prejudices have often had to go under cover, in disguise, in code. Antiracism influences the forms of racism; feminism changes the expressions of sexism. Progress on legal fronts has changed the contexts of prejudices. But the needs these prejudices serve stay very much the same. Sometimes the needs simply find a new target when their familiar one becomes harder to hit because it is somewhat protected.

In the present moment, the expressions of the various types of ideologies of desire are enormously confused and confusing. The end of the Cold War as it existed from the late 1940s until 1989 has changed the way in which ideologies of world domination affect local situations and particular prejudices, especially those prejudices that feature visions of their target groups bent on world conquest. The great surge in immigration to Europe and America from the Third World in the wake of (often failed) colonial liberation movements and the slow but sure shifting of the world's population to the marginalization of "white" people have changed the context of racism. The emergence of women into workplaces, educational institutions, and professions in unprecedented numbers has changed the expressions of sexism, as the repercussions of the 1960s "sexual revolution," spreading around the globe, have changed the social and legal status of allegedly deviant sexual identities and the prejudices against them. The needs manifested in the various types of ideological prejudices are, as the end of the twentieth century approaches, being challenged not so much by antiprejudice efforts and campaigns for tolerance and human rights as by peoples once victims and now more powerful, each in a different mode—by gaining international standing, by gaining numerical strength, by appearing in public, and so forth.[13]

Antisemitism, racism, and sexism (with which, I will argue, homophobia is crucially linked) represent three different types of this kind of historically specific modern prejudice. They are all ideologies of desire. On a cognitive level, they have a great deal in common with one another and with ethnocentrism—all involve faulty generalizations, projection, and stereotyping. But beyond that the types of ideology of desire are quite distinct, first and foremost because they derive from three distinct types of psychic configurations or what I call "characters." I use this word to refer all at once to peoples' reigning desires, their instinctual drive organization, their developmental levels and psychic structures, their identifications, and their internalizations of their familial, social, cultural, and political surroundings. "Character" is both a psychological and a sociological designation, and it has a historical current—the modern historical conditions I have been sketching both produce and reflect modern forms of the character types that are particularly suited to sustain the various ideologies of desire.

But "character," it is important to note clearly at the outset, is not in this study a clinical designation, a diagnosis referring to disorders. Rather, it describes a series of predominating traits, in the manner that the Greek word *ethos* was used in the Greco-Roman characterological tradition. Many people have what clinicians term character disorders; when I use the word "character," however, I am not specifying a psychopathology but referring instead to a spectrum from normal to pathological that can be compassed with "narcissistic character," for example.

There is, in fact, no empirical evidence at all that people who are prejudiced are any more pathological than the general population, and also no evidence that particular pathologies subtend either prejudice as a "generalized attitude" or specific prejudices. On the contrary, many people have prejudices *instead of* the conventional forms of various pathologies, somewhat as people have perversions instead of neuroses if they act on their forbidden desires rather than repressing them. It has often been noted that many neurotics "recover" in terrible social circumstances—in war zones, for example—where the pain of the external world distracts them from the pain of their internal worlds. Participating in a supremacist movement can have a similar effect. It gives people "real" (to them) targets for hatreds they might otherwise expend on themselves. And it gives them a context in which their hatreds are "normal" (which may mean, of course, that the *society* is pathological). In 1961, when the political philosopher Hannah Arendt attended the trial of Adolf Eichmann in Jerusalem and pronounced him "terrifyingly normal,'' ''banal,'' she raised a storm of controversy, but I think she was quite correct in the sense that Eichmann functioned better in his bureaucracy than he would have without it.

I give the three broad character types that I discuss rather clinical sounding names—obsessional, hysterical, narcissistic—but I do so to utilize existing theory of character, not to point to pathologies. I also use these names to delineate the types as they have come to dominate subsocieties and even whole societies in particular historical circumstances and contexts. That is, I study character both psychologically and sociologically. I consider antisemitism, for example, an obsessional prejudice, the sort of prejudice that people of rigid, superego-dominated characters often display and the sort of prejudice that societies organized and functioning obsessionally are riddled with. In America, prejudices other than antisemitism have taken this form. As I implied before, anti-Communism of the McCarthyite sort did so in the 1950s, and Japan bashing (focused on Japanese commercialism) is currently a new contender for inclusion in the category, providing a terrible echo of the prejudice against Japanese Americans interned during the war (as the Germans had interned the Jews) to keep them from traitorous acts. Similarly, a contemporary obsessional form of homophobia features gay moguls ruling Hollywood and pushing ''the homosexual agenda'' by bankrolling political candidates. In fact, this plurality of obsessional modes constitutes one reason why antisemitism has never reached full lethal proportions in this country—new ''enemies,'' proliferating conspiracies, keep distracting the focus of obsessional movements.

Obsessional prejudices are the prejudices toward which people who are given to fixed ideas and ritualistic acts gravitate and through which they can behave sadistically without being conscious of their victims—as though in a trance, completely ''in cold blood.'' Obsessional characters are cut off from their own feelings and intentions; they know not what they say or do. So they are apt to sound like the elderly Long Islander of the late 1960s who responded to the invasion of his small town's commercial street by long-haired hippie entrepreneurs with characteristic obsessional lack of responsibility—''We should kill them, or else there will be violence.''

The obsessional prejudices feature conspiracies of demonic enemies everywhere, omnipresent pollutants, filthy people, which the obsessionally prejudiced feel compelled to eliminate—wash away, flush away, fumigate, demolish. The obsessionally prejudiced attribute to their victims a special capacity for commercial or economic conspiracy and diabolical behind-the-scenes cleverness, and they both envy this capacity and, acting imitatively, turn the fruits of this cleverness (particularly in the domain of technology) on their victims. They imagine the conspirators as having the capacity to penetrate them, get into their bowels and their privacies.

Racism, by contrast, exemplifies hysterical prejudice, by which I mean a prejudice that a person uses unconsciously to appoint a group to act out in the world forbidden sexual and sexually aggressive desires that the person has repressed. Racism is a prejudice that represents or symbolizes genital power or prowess and sexual desires by bodily features like skin color, thick hair, muscularity, or big breasts; it equates strength, size, and darkness with primitivity, archaic and unrestrained sexual activity forbidden in "civilization." The victims are, like victims of the most common forms of classism, another hysterical prejudice, "lower." Racism is a prejudice of desire for regression expressed as a charge that people who are "other" and sexually powerful—as parents or siblings are in the eyes of children—have never progressed, are intellectually inferior, are uncivilized. The "lower" men are imagined as brutal, the "lower" women as either (and sometimes both) sexually lascivious or maternally bountiful, milk giving and care giving.

Racists are people who, in the manner of hysterics, prevent themselves from regressing into infantile helplessness and incestuous love of their own family members by cordoning off their desires and by loving or forming partial, unconscious identifications with the victims of their prejudices. The "others," either as domestic servants or slaves or as a fantasized part of the prejudiced person's household, are love and hate objects in the loving and hating of whom no bans on incest or on rivalry are violated; they are the safe—for the prejudiced person—objects of childhood passions. Ideally, the victims do not get destroyed completely or flushed away as the obsessional's victims do; they are needed alive, so that they can be loved like mammies, prostituted or raped like whores, sexually mutilated, beaten, deprived of their power, crippled, emasculated—and in all instances, kept in their places.

Societies that are marked by hysterical trends like conversion of psychic conflicts into physical symptoms, that is, societies in which hysterical individuals are common and sexual repression or puritanism rife are societies split. They are committed to visions of equality and fairness, to courtly and carefully coded and elaborately theatrical ways of life, and they are, at the same time, sexually and aggressively explosive. Such societies would, as Gunnar Myrdal noted, embrace an American Creed of equality and justice for all and then fail miserably to put that creed into practice. Hypocrisy is normal—it is, as François La Rochefoucauld said, the homage that vice offers to virtue, or that one side of a split character offers to the other.

In historical periods and in particular social circumstances when racism is more muted, more disguised, its image systems are more subtle. The archetypical racist milieu, in which "superior" children grow up with "lower" (black or lower-class) domestics whom they can take as familial love and hate objects, is much more easily interpretable than a milieu in which the domestics are domestics in fantasies—as African Americans still are in the American national household fantasy, a fantasy in which whites are served and blacks serve. This is the fantasy, for example, that produced a remark by a white psychiatry student, son of a mother whom he felt was cold, as he explained why he was not racist: "I grew up in Wisconsin, so I hardly knew any Blacks, but I loved Aunt Jemima on the pancake box, because she seemed so warm and caring."[14]

Sexists, finally, are people (usually but certainly not always male) who cannot tolerate the idea that there exist people not like them, not—specifically—anatomically like them. Their prejudice has a narcissistic foundation, and it is, of the ideologies of desire, the most universal—as universal as narcissism is—even though it is most life defining and extreme in people whose narcissistic desires dominate their character. The narcissistic prejudices are prejudices of boundary establishment, of genital intactness asserted and mental integrity insisted upon. On the other side of the narcissists' boundaries there is not a "them," a "not-us," but blank, a lack—or at the most, a profound mystery.

Women challenge male gender identity and represent the possibility of castration. Control over women, and especially over women's sexuality and reproductive capacities, equals control over the marks of difference between males and females; it is the deepest counter to anxiety over gender identity and over castration. Sexism is expressed in many ways, but its essential meaning is control over female sexuality and reproduction, and its essential purpose is to keep men from recognizing women in their difference or from succumbing to their fear of becoming women. The most sexist societies are those in which narcissism is encouraged—and vice versa. But several major subtypes of narcissism exist, and the societies that sponsor these exhibit different sorts of (particularly) familial arrangements.

Many, but not all, homophobic acts and institutions also seek to preserve sameness. Men who play women's roles—that is, "passive" male homosexuals as homophobic people understand them—threaten men as much as women do; they, too, are castrati. Such male homosexuals must be repudiated as forcefully as any admixture of femininity in a "real" man must be. But women who act male—that is, "active" female homosexuals as homophobic people understand them—are more intricately, less directly threatening: they do what men do—they compete for women—while they demonstrate that the phallus is not necessary for doing what men do. They confuse the fact of anatomical difference, they upset the world of sexual identity concepts or boundaries. Neither "macho" male homosexuals nor "femme" female homosexuals disturb homophobic peoples' desires so profoundly, so they are less victimized, and the "presentation of self in everyday life" that they adopt is known by homosexuals to be safer, more invisible. The homophobia directed at the less threatening homosexual types bears much more envy and fear of imitation and similarity than that aimed at the more directly threatening types.

Homophobia is crucially linked to sexism. Many of the psychological and social elements that combine in sexism similarly merge in homophobia. But homosexuals are distinctive as a victim group by virtue of their abilities (as assigned to them by homophobes, of course) to fulfill the needs of all of the types of ideologies of desire. They share this distinction, in some historical contexts, with the group called "adolescents." Homosexuals (particularly males) can be filthy lucre for the obsessionally prejudiced, who maintain—to take the common example I alluded to before—that the Jews and the gays control Hollywood, or that all the Jews who control Hollywood are gay. The obsessionally prejudiced may insist that there are no gays in the American military—mendacious newspaper stories to the contrary notwithstanding—because the gays are much too interested in making money to bother with the military. And so forth. Homosexuals can also be "Negroes" (especially the ones who *are* Negroes) for the hysterically prejudiced: they are imagined as hypersexual or sexually monomaniac, they have huge phalluses or abnormal genitalia, they engage in all manner of exciting and forbidden perversities; they are "black" pornography, they are always ready for rape. Homosexuals can be, in short, all-purpose victims, and

gay people belonging to groups typically victimized for other purposes—African Americans, for instance—can either get a double dose
of one type of prejudice or different doses of different prejudices.

There are, as already indicated, social and political conditions in
which the various character types and their characteristic prejudices
flourish, in which they have political and social power and also ideological power, power to influence peoples' ideas. There are societies or
subsocieties in which obsessionality is normative—to use a stereotype,
"Prussian" societies. And there are societies in which conditions encourage hysterical splitting, even to the point where social forms and
laws for sanctioning double lives develop, providing the equivalent for
racists of what the coexistence of marriage and prostitution has been
for sexists. Splitting societies, for example, favor costumes and styles that
allow the hysterically prejudiced person to be both more visible and
more invisible, more distinctive and more indistinguishable, possibilities
well represented by either the Ku Klux Klan's white-on-white hooding
or the skinhead's dehooding. And there are societies that actually deserve the designation made fashionable (I think quite wrongly) in the
1970s with reference to America—"the culture of narcissism." These
societies encourage everyone (which usually means everyone male) to
take himself as the standard by which to judge everyone else and by
which to promote or hinder social ventures and technologies according
to whether they do or do not flatter the powers that be and would always
be. Such societies do not necessarily put the self first. That is, they do
not produce the kind of heedless self-promotion that earned the American middle and upper classes the title "narcissistic" in the 1970s. I will
suggest later why it seems to me that "Me first!" is more often the cry
of rivalrous, love-seeking hysterics. Narcissistic societies are, rather, ones
in which enormous innovative ambitions for power, great futureward
thrust, rest on profoundly conservative self-images—bodily or mental—
that ultimately will not allow innovation. The tragedies of such societies
are tragedies of ambition, in which women bear the marks of the conflicts on their bodies and minds.

In nations, different sorts of societies and subsocieties coexist and
overlap, people are influenced by—exposed to, educated by, ruled by—
any or all of the different types. And very seldom does a pure example
of any one type of society—or, for that matter, any one type of individual
character—exist. The prejudices overlap. People who are sexist can also
be racist, as people who are antisemitic can also be sexist, through all

the possible variations. But most people who are prejudiced usually have a fundamental prejudice, which, in turn, determines the way they acquire other prejudices or respond to other peoples' prejudices. A fundamental prejudice operates like a rigidly patterned way of falling in love or like a recurrent masturbation fantasy; it is an ideology of social love and hate.

The opposite idea—the Allportian one that prejudice is a generalized attitude—grew up from insufficient attention to the kind of information that no survey or questionnaire will ever turn up. One might think at first glance that a man who said, as one American paramilitary rightist of the 1960s did, "A nigger is nothing but a Jew turned inside out," was a classic example of an all-purpose bigot, a man who hated everybody.[15] But, if we analyze this remark as a condensed fantasy, we see a man who is basically an antisemite. He knows Jews to be filthy, fecal blackguards and has concluded that they really control the Blacks—inside and out, as it were. This man in his ideological obsession or fixation resembles a better known man, Adolf Hitler, who made many—obsessionally many—remarks like the following one from *Mein Kampf*:

> From time to time illustrated papers bring it to the attention of the German petit-bourgeoisie that some place or other a Negro has for the first time become a lawyer, teacher, even a pastor, in fact a heroic tenor, or something of the sort. While the idiotic bourgeoisie looks with amazement at such miracles of educational skill, the Jew shrewdly draws from it a new proof of his theory about the equality of men that he is trying to funnel into minds of nations. It doesn't dawn on this depraved bourgeois world that this is positively a sin against all reason: that it is criminal lunacy to keep on drilling a born half-ape until people think they have made a lawyer out of him, while millions of members of the highest culture-race must remain in entirely unworthy positions.[16]

Here the racism, the anti-Negro viciousness, simply serves the most fundamental charge—that the Jews are doing this criminal educating of Negroes, that the Jews are polluting the whole world with an idea of equality and thus depriving pure German working people of their rightful inheritance.

The moment that this study of prejudices—like any other—shifts register and presents not a theoretical discussion but actual examples of the phenomena, pieces of prejudice like the two just cited, it is obvious that typologies will always be outstripped by reality. No typology can capture individuals or societies in their full complexity or in their dynamism—or in their perversity. The value of a typology, however, provided that it is built up cautiously and flexibly, is that it can give a sense of the territory—even if this means only that it helps us raise new questions, that it operates in the manner of a many-faceted hypothesis. It is like a preliminary map. And we use a map only to benefit from others' efforts in our own exploration, to avoid beginning from scratch. Once we have been there, we can make our own map and discover all the ways in which the terrain as we experience it defies the map that gave us an orientation.

# I

## A Critique of Pure Overgeneralization

# 1

# Theories of Prejudice:
# A Preliminary Classification

If, as I have been suggesting, the only path to an understanding of prejudices (in the plural) is through the dark wood of existing theoretical prejudices, we must begin the journey at the basic unit of obstacle—the definition of prejudice. Since the end of the war, studies in prejudice of the most diverse sorts have typically shared an opening definitional focusing procedure. The writers' lenses are first trained on the word "prejudice," which receives an initial zoom-twist for historical background; *praejudicum,* we are told, is Latin for a judgment formed in advance of a trial. Various features of prejudgments are then noted: they are rigid, relatively impervious to concrete experiences that might challenge them; they are conveyed in completely conventionalized adjectives (Jews are filthy rich, Negroes are lazy, and so forth); and they are accompanied by ritualized affect. With the catalog of features comes a general definition in "prejudice is X" form to launch the inquiry: for example, "Prejudice is a negative attitude toward a socially defined group and toward any person perceived to be a member of that group."

Then, having set the terms for "prejudice," writers switch to fine focus for recognition that prejudgment involves many elements. We readers are reminded that prejudice has two valences, positive as well as the much more frequently studied and much more definitionally important negative. Prejudice is, we learn, most commonly understood to compass groups, but it can be trained on individuals, particularly when the experiences informing it are highly specific and traumatic. There are affective, conative, and cognitive components to prejudice. Most important, prejudice also is said to have measurable degrees. It can be as slight as a preference, as great as an aversion leading to segregation, and as intense and deadly as an attack or even a program for exterminating a group. These degrees relate to a rank of valuations commonly associated with prejudices: *preferences* seem more "normal" and tolerable; *aversions* seems less normal and more complex, especially when words like "justifiable" and "unjustifiable," "provoked" and "unprovoked" come into play; and *violence* crosses over a moral line (drawn at different places by different evaluators). Prejudiced people, too, are said to have different degrees. They can be considered "normal" people with particular deformations; they can be grouped by their prejudices, defined by them, as examples of the "prejudiced personality"; or they can be judged clinically psychotic, in which case it becomes reasonable to define paranoia as pathological prejudice. The differences of degree, furthermore, are assumed to be on a causal line: if a person ends up at the gravest or greatest degree, he or she got there by going through the lesser degrees. Progressing through the degrees may presume changing external conditions or deteriorating internal or intrapsychic conditions, or both.

## Definitions as Habits of Thought

As this quick review indicates, narrowly focused, qualifying discussions of prejudice rest on the assumption—Gordon Allport's assumption—that prejudice is one thing appearing in many forms. "Prejudice is X" and has different valences, different ranges, different degrees of intensity, and different degrees of pathology. Any typological statements about prejudice, then, are statements about the qualifying differences in a universal thing.

The sway of this "prejudice is one" assumption, this all-determining overgeneralization, has been, as I noted in the Introduction, almost complete within the social sciences. But there have been a few efforts to combat it. Most of these date from the late 1960s, when the dominance of a generation of theorists—Allport's generation—came to be challenged by a next generation, in a historical moment fraught with intellectual-political challenges in almost every domain. A brief period of iconoclasm ensued in the social sciences—a moment instructive for any effort to break out of the habits of thought social science has created.

At this time, and mostly in reaction to challenges by Black intellectuals issued either outside academia or through angry academic volumes like *Death of White Sociology* (1973), a few white social scientists began to reconsider the various kinds of universalizing theories of prejudice. They often started with specific questions about whether universalizing theories could take into account the particular qualities of prejudice against people of color, but these questions led to larger agendas. Caution and skepticism reverberate through the article entitled "Prejudice" in the 1968 *International Encyclopedia of Social Sciences,* for example. The author, Otto Klineberg, argues that using "prejudice" as a general category is tricky because "no typology of forms of prejudice is yet available, and since there will always be intervening and transitional varieties, perhaps no such typology will ever be fully acceptable."[1]

Klineberg emphasizes the point that Allport had made so clearly— that the causes or sources feeding into prejudice are multiple. But he also tries to draw the non-Allportian conclusion that this multiplicity implies that prejudices themselves are multiple, not just in degree but in kind as well. His formulation of that conclusion, however, does not do it justice: "Socially and psychologically attitudes differ depending on whether they are the result of deep-seated personality characteristics, sometimes of a pathological nature, or of a traumatic experience, or whether they simply present conformity to an established social norm."

It is interesting to note that even this critical approach to prejudice— to prejudices, in the plural—focuses only on attitudes, either psychologically or sociologically viewed. Klineberg still assumes the unitary nature of prejudice, though in an attenuated form. All prejudices are alike in being attitudes that can be considered independent of both their objects or victims and their specific content, what they allege about the victims. The methodological implication is that key interactive elements for constructing a typology are left out. We do not discover how the victims are constructed, what the victims' own story is, or what relations exist between the victims' story and what the prejudiced person says about it, how the prejudiced person interprets it, relates to it. The varieties of prejudice, in Klineberg's view, have to do with the varieties of racists' psychologies, histories of trauma, and social influences, but there is no indication of how these can be assessed. The varieties, in effect, once again turn out to be variations of degree—a scale of prejudice runs from the most psychologically rooted to the most sociologically rooted, with traumatic learning as a middle case (a case of social influence putting down a psychically deep root).

In Klineberg's cautious assessment can be found both an image of system and a refusal to attempt being systematic. He raised the possibility of something that had not been tried, a typology of forms of prejudice. But he immediately backed away because he assumed that the multiplicity of forms of prejudice—"there will always be intervening and transitional varieties"—would stand in the way of a typology rather than preventing such a typology from being too schematic. He thought that the varieties of prejudice would grow over the boundaries of any typology like plants over the edges of garden rows, and pruning would be, by definition, falsifying.

I find Klineberg's caution salutary, though it came to nothing because it was a caution without an alternative. He was—to use the current parlance—a deconstructor, not a reconstructor. And he did not analyze his own healthy theoretical skepticism. Specifically, he left in place his own theoretical prejudice about the centrality of differences *of degree* for distinguishing prejudices, while I think it is crucial, on the contrary, to make distinctions *of kind*. But as far as I can determine, only one scholar in this brief period of iconoclasm actually began to make a distinction of kind and base a typology on it. This was the South African sociologist Pierre van den Berghe, one of the very few writers on "race relations" who understood the value of a comparative approach. In his book *Race and Racism* (1967), he focused on the United States and South Africa, Mexico and Brazil, proceeding historically, comparing economic and social institutions.

Van den Berghe made his studies with the awareness that racism is different *in kind* from ethnocentrism, and that terms of degree like "preference" and "aversion" do not capture the difference. As he said summarily: "[Racism] unlike ethnocentrism is not a universal phenomenon. Members of all human societies have a fairly good opinion of themselves compared with members of other societies, but this good opinion is frequently based on claims to cultural superiority. Man's claims to excellence are usually narcissistically based on his own creations. Only a few human groups have deemed themselves superior because of the content of their gonads."[2] This basic distinction of kind served van den Berghe as a starting point for distinguishing two broad subtypes of racism, called paternalistic (typical of plantations) and competitive (typical of urban milieus), according to the use made in them, among other things, of biological pseudoscience. (He did not, however, compare racism with any other type of prejudice making use of pseudoscience, such as sexism.) He began to suggest that the first form lives on, psychically and socially, in the second form. The earlier is like a repressed desire or network of desires—an idea taken for granted by so many African American writers on the theme of unconscious memory, the theme concerning white racism of—for example—Ellison's *Invisible Man,* which starts as a study of paternalism in the South and ends as one of competitiveness in a Northern city.

Van den Berghe was not trapped by the unilluminating conception of prejudices as distinguishable by differences of degree, as Klineberg was, and he was also free of the notion, also apparent in Klineberg's approach, that there is a great divide between psychological theories of prejudice and sociological ones, with no way over the chasm—or no way across the hall from the Department of Psychology to the Department of Sociology. Van den Berghe, however, was not attuned to psychological phenomena, and his analysis stayed to the economic and sociological side, as he was aware. He did not share the "never the twain shall meet" theoretical prejudice about psychology and sociology, but neither did he analyze it. Just such an analysis, it seems to me, is the place to mount an attack on the whole "prejudice is one" overgeneralization with its single definition "prejudice is X (to different degrees)" corollary.

By the 1970s the overgeneralizing, definitionally rigid habit of thought in the social sciences was so set that studies in prejudice were just repetitions, recyclings. Not surprisingly, historical surveys of the social scientific work on prejudice that had been done since midcentury began to appear. Such surveys are typical of times when a younger generation is ready to supplant its elders but does not have a new vision. Searching for a new approach, the surveyors set up two conflicting general models of prejudice study, a psychological model and a sociological model, criticized both, and then, sometimes taking elements of both, went on to struggle for a third and higher ground. Currently, twenty years later, this struggle is still going on—the higher ground is still being invoked, and still proving elusive. Again and again, authors announce that psychological theories and sociological theories must yield to . . . to what? The higher ground has many names: "cognitive learning theories" is a common one when it is claimed by social psychologists; "social [or cultural] systems approaches" is preferred among sociologists. But it is simpler to define this higher ground by what is totally absent from it—any reference to psychoanalysis.

Interestingly enough, and also not surprisingly, the immediate postwar generation that produced the psychological and sociological theories judged so inadequate in the 1970s had also been a generation needing ways to go beyond its predecessors. In the early 1950s, while the theories now classified as psychological and sociological were being formulated, there was also a great effort afoot to establish a new and higher ground. Throughout the 1950s, Allport and his contemporaries had rejected the exclusively psychological and the exclusively sociological theories of their own predecessors, too.

What they had been looking for was not a neither/nor alternative but a synthesis, often called "culture and personality," which required a bridging notion. Many variations of the concept that David Riesman called "social character" or that Theodor Adorno and his associates called "a pattern of personality" had appeared as the meeting ground of psychology and sociology, a meeting ground typically located with the aid of psychoanalytic concepts—the very tools that were completely jettisoned by the 1970s.[3]

To get further oriented in the field of social science definitions and their analytical uses, we need a map of the recent surveys of the terrain of studies in prejudice and a guidebook to those earlier 1950s efforts at synthesis. We must take two steps back (in reverse chronological order) and bear with some critique of what has been done in order to go forward. The reason for this circuitousness is simple. During the 1950s, and again during the recent years when the psychological and sociological theories of the 1950s (now deemed inadequate) were being surveyed, all concerned assumed that these theories represented, and should represent, two approaches to the same thing—prejudice. No one noted that this conviction was so embedded in studies of prejudice that it defined the territory, making any pluralistic view of prejudices seem baroque, overcomplicated, strange. No one said—so it became nearly impossible to say—well, some kinds of prejudice are best initially approached sociologically, and some kinds psychologically; the two approaches ought to be complementary, the first predominating for some kinds of prejudice, the second for others.[4] The kind of prejudice van den Berghe had defined as ethnocentrism, for example, can be thoroughly approached with the tools of historically sophisticated sociology and then explored psychologically; but the prejudice he defined as racism must be considered through psychology before bringing in sociology.

## A Tour of Social Science Guides

I will set out on my tour of the key overgeneralization about prejudice from the place where many American college students of 1970s vintage made their first encounter with efforts to study prejudice—Barry E. Collins's textbook *Social Psychology* (1970). This representative work of its period shows clearly the critical survey technique as it was practiced by social psychologists. (How the survey technique was practiced by sociologists will be studied later.) I focus on the "authoritarian personality" as it came to center stage in social psychology and then was deposed— while leaving a legacy of overgeneralization that has never stopped being determinatively influential.

The chapter in Collins's text called "The Problem of Intergroup Prejudice" offers, first, a lengthy and typical discussion of how to define prejudice. As I noted earlier, a definition of prejudice is the *de rigueur* point of departure, and the result of this effort is the uninspiring sentence I cited before: "Prejudice is a negative attitude toward a socially defined group and toward any person perceived to be a member of that group." That definition established, problems of measurement arise in assessing both people's self-reports (their responses to questionnaires) and trained observers' observations. Then comes the survey of theories, classified by type of explanation: "societal-level explanations" and "individual-level explanations"—that is, sociological theories and psychological theories. Collins gives absolutely no indication that theories have psychosocial or historical contexts, that they arise in particular circumstances, and that they reflect those circumstances.

His survey lists two major types of sociological theories, one called "Exploitation" and the other "Realistic-group-conflict theory." The first is, basically, neo-Marxist. Prejudice, in such theories, is part and parcel of the exploitation ruling classes wreak upon ruled classes. It is used by exploiting classes to justify their exploitation—it singles out groups, insists that they are inferior, and then makes the charge of inferiority stick by keeping the groups down. Prejudice, such a theory assumes, is conscious and manipulative; it is the work of a group imagined as conspiratorial. The Collins survey does not mention the liberal, non-Marxist version of this approach, commonly used in the late 1960s, when liberals stressed the socioeconomic advantages to middle- and lower-middle-class whites in maintaining a stable black underclass and argued for policies designed to raise the underclass out of poverty.[5] Presidents Kennedy and Johnson took this approach in formulating their domestic agendas.

Realistic-group-conflict theory, by contrast, does not focus on a particular prejudiced class—the bourgeoisie—but considers types of relations that exist among groups of all sorts. Groups that have common goals and are "positively interdependent" do not hate and stigmatize each other, while groups that are vying for dominance or competing with each other develop derogatory attitudes that explain their animosity. This theory implies that dominant groups develop prejudices that function to keep their subordinates in place. Their prejudices increase when they feel threatened, when the subordinates seem to be engaging in either rebellion or increased competition. Allies or partners do not need prejudices: negative prejudices do not exist among equals.

The textbook's historical survey does not note the tradition of research out of which these societal-level theories grew, but I will set that historical marker for future reference. In America between World Wars I and II social scientists had focused on a phenomenon, usually labeled "ethnocentrism," sometimes "xenophobia," that they held to be normative or universal, a natural part of group relations of all sorts, and an especially prominent feature of the social landscape in societies—like our own—made up of wave upon wave of immigrant groups. All groups need to mark themselves off from others, protect their territories of identity, assert their distinctiveness. Much empirical attention was given to describing stereotypes and creating scales that could measure attitudes.

A sociologist named Emory Bogardus formulated the most widely used measuring device, which he called the "social distance" scale, and he produced longitudinal work with his scale between the 1920s and the 1950s. It was Bogardus who established a common "pattern of prejudice" among diverse American groups. Each light-skinned American group, Bogardus showed, put a great social distance between itself and any dark-skinned group, and the darker the group the greater the distance. The distances did not remain constant over thirty years. They were slow to change—but they did change. Bogardus was able to demonstrate empirically that social norms are not cast in bronze as earlier theorists of ethnocentrism, like William Graham Sumner, had urged with memorable formulations—"stateways cannot change folkways."[6] At the same time, Bogardus's scales reinforced the notion that all prejudices are the same—all involve distance—because distance is content-less; he gave no indication of why or how prejudices work or of whether different prejudices might involve different feelings of distance.

The most important thing to note about the survey of societal-level explanations in *Social Psychology* is not the lack of concern for earlier research like Bogardus's, but the selectivity in relation to contemporaries. Sociology had contributed many and much more interesting theories than the exploitation and realistic-group-conflict ones. Collins's text, completely typical in its ignorance of African American intellectual history, does not even mention the strong tradition of Black Marxism in this country and its important variants. Those variants go from the simplest idea (Eugene Debs's) that white racism is part of the ruling-class "divide and conquer" strategy for dominating the working class to the more influential idea, propounded during the 1930s within the American Communist Party, that African Americans constitute a Black Nation, oppressed both in its working-class status and as a nation. The Black Nation approach was elaborated and infused with more sophisticated notions of cultural nationalism in the prewar work of W. E. B. Du Bois, Richard Wright, and C. L. R. James and, after World War II, in Oliver Cox's *Caste, Class, and Race* (1948).[7]

Students learning social psychology in 1970 from Collins's text could have read in their daily newspapers about contemporaries who had appropriated this Black Marxist tradition—the Black Panther Party. But they would have had to search further for a second tradition Collins excluded. Theorists of mass society such as Karl Mannheim or C. Wright Mills or David Riesman had focused attention on how specific features of contemporary mass societies had changed the ways that prejudice is acquired and expressed. In its most extreme formulations, the theory of mass society implied that the interest groups into which a mass society is splintered have tremendous power over peoples' opinions and behavior in a given situation. People who are deracinated, disconnected from traditions, without affiliations, "massified" attach themselves to a group and then do as the group dictates and does. "Individual behavior is, for all practical purposes, made a fiction. Hence a distinctly personal attitude toward minority groups may be of little consequence in explaining an individual's behavior.''[8] A view like this, of course, makes social psychology as a discipline practically irrelevant.

In the neo-Marxist exploitation and realistic-group-conflict societal-level theories, as in the earlier social distance approach, prejudice serves a function. It furthers the aspirations of an exploiting group, or it aids the dominative and competitive purposes of a group rising to power or working to maintain power. It consolidates group identity. Similarly, in individual-level explanations, to which we turn now, prejudice is said to function for an individual. But at the individual level the question of whether prejudice is ubiquitous and normal or pathological and confined to pathological subgroups is not usually left aside (certainly not when a degree of intersocietal violence and destruction propels the theory). In most individual-level theories of prejudice prior to 1970, before the ascent of cognitive learning theory, pathology was assumed.

*Social Psychology* offers three types of individual-level explanations. All of them suppose that individuals have conflicts which their prejudices then help them to manage or to direct outward. Prejudices are, on this model, symptoms. As symptoms or outbreaks of conflict, they may, however, prevent a worse pathology, as a steam escape valve prevents an explosion. Or they may, by contrast, create an atmosphere in which aggression is aggravated. Each of the three individual-level explanations also involves some form of scapegoating. Prejudices as outlets for conflict require a target, a group onto which the individual's conflict can be displaced or projected.

In the first variant, it is aggression that is externalized in prejudice. For example, people may feel anger and frustration when a loved one disappoints them, or when an impersonal force like a set of rules or an economic crisis stops them from getting what they want, so they draw back and vent their anger and frustration on another party, the scapegoat. Generally, in this theory aggression results from prior frustration, and the greater the frustration the greater the aggression.

This frustration-aggression theory is a rather mechanical version of Freud's claim that experiences of internal or external frustration *(Versagung)* precipitate neuroses and psychoses.[9] Almost everyone in this train of work was indebted to John Dollard and his associates at Yale, who had produced several important studies of white racism in the American South and a general statement entitled *Frustration and Aggression* (1939). But the theory has also received a good deal of empirical investigation, much of it using various kinds of social distance scales developed on the basis of Bogardus's work in the 1920s. Such studies have shown, for example, that non-Jewish Americans who feel themselves victims of economic forces and are distrustful of politicians tend to be more antisemitic than those who do not feel victimized. Similarly, many different attitude measurements taken in the 1950s revealed that Jewish students who felt themselves victims of prejudice tended to be more anti-Negro than those who did not, while Catholic students feeling victimized ranked high on tests of both antisemitism and anti-Negro prejudice. More generally, there is some empirical evidence that children who live with frustrating authoritarian parents, and have a history of being punished harshly, are more prejudiced.

In its catalog of individual-level theories, Collins's *Social Psychology* makes a distinction between the frustration-aggression scapegoat theory of prejudice, operating by displacement, and a second type of symptom theory, one operating by projection—hence the "projection theory of prejudice." There seems to be an overlap in the two varieties of symptom theory, but the second type seems to imply more stress on the means people develop for resolving or at least silencing their internal conflicts. If they feel angry but also feel that they should not express anger, they project the anger onto someone else. If they feel afraid, they attribute the source of their fear to someone else, who becomes the "frightening one." Psychoanalytically based students of racism have suggested, for example, that whites project onto blacks the sexual desires that they feel guilty for having themselves, and then they find the blacks sexually powerful and uninhibited.

Similarly, students of antisemitism have suggested that people with aggressive, ambitious desires, which are in conflict with the demands of their own superegos, project those desires onto the Jews, whom they then find avaricious and ambitious. One of the volumes in the postwar Studies in Prejudice series, *Dynamics of Prejudice* (1952) by Bruno Bettelheim and Morris Janowitz, suggested that the 150 white veterans who made up the authors' research group projected onto blacks their unacceptable id impulses—making blacks sloppy, dirty, immoral people—and projected onto Jews their superego demands for goodness and honesty, making Jews into underhanded, corrupt businessmen.

*Social Psychology* does not offer much detail on the history of the projection theories of prejudice, nor does it even mention the Studies in

Prejudice series. Collins attributes this neglect, in part, to the scanty empirical (as opposed to clinical psychoanalytic) research history: "Unfortunately, there has not been much subsequent research on this model of projection-based prejudice, so it remains primarily an interesting possibility." The projection theory certainly did not lend itself to questionnaire research. (Other empirical techniques specifically designed to show projectivity, like Rorschach testing, have seldom been used by students of prejudice.) But the main reason why the projection theory remained underexplored was that it was not primarily a result of social psychological research—it came from other, usually more literary, historical, and psychoanalytic sources.

I will present some of this important work later, but here I want to note for future reference that social psychologists have made so little use of projection theory that they do not even recognize that it comes in two quite different psychoanalytic versions. One model stresses conflicts in prejudiced people between their superegos and their egos and postulates an anti-authoritarian rebellion against the demands of the superego. People rebelling against their internal superego demands project those demands onto another group, which they then portray as demanding, aggressive, shrewd, cunning, manipulative. By contrast, a second model emphasizes the pressures prejudiced people feel from their instinctual drives, their ids. This model presents id-ego conflicts and tracks projections that charge another group with being lecherous, sensuous, lazy at work, inferior—a fountain of instinctual drive. But, even though these two types of projections have been presented—sometimes separately, sometimes together as in the Bettelheim and Janowitz volume—they have not been used to distinguish different types of prejudice. Furthermore, if prejudice is assumed to be a generalized attitude, no sense can be made of a result like the one Bettelheim and Janowitz themselves reported on the basis of their interviews with the veterans—a result they could not interpret:

> In the majority of the cases . . . tolerance toward Jews was coexistent with stereotyped and even more marked intolerance of the Negro. As the degree of intolerance toward the Jew increased, it was generally accompanied by an even greater degree of intolerance toward the Negro. The reverse pattern—that is, tolerance toward the Negro accompanied by outspoken antisemitism—occurred in only one case. This case may be explained by the fact that this man's hostility toward Jews was limited to a special class of Jews, namely, alien Jews.[10]

The exceptional man last mentioned was neither antisemitic nor racist; he was—to use Pierre van den Berghe's term—ethnocentric: he opposed immigration. The most strenuous antisemites in the group also expressed racist attitudes. But the racists did not regularly express antisemitic attitudes. To my mind, this pattern suggests that antisemitism is a type of prejudice, crucially involving conflict with the superego, with a generalizing dynamic. Antisemites will tend to become, as it were, all-purpose bigots. But racism, more rooted in conflicts with the id, does not have this generalizing dynamic; it is more single-minded, single-focused. To make these sorts of distinctions, however, you have to assume both that projection is at work in prejudice and that not all prejudiced people project alike.

In addition to the aggression-frustration theory and the (unexplored) projection theory, *Social Psychology* notes a third individual-level approach. Research into the relations that exist between authoritarian upbringings and prejudice have been key since the late 1940s in the development of this theory, the most systematic and far-reaching individual-level scapegoating theory of prejudice. Known specifically by the title of its main report, *The Authoritarian Personality* (1951), the theory was the work of a team of German-Jewish émigré social theorists of the so-called Frankfurt School—Theodor Adorno, Max Horkheimer, and Else Frenkel-Brunswick (the chief child researcher)—and a group of American empirical social psychologists located at the University of California in Berkeley.

Researchers of the authoritarian personality assumed that prejudiced people displace aggression onto scapegoats—that is, they incorporated Dollard's frustration-aggression model into their work—but they did not assume that the scapegoats would be either a particular group or a single group. Like most projection theorists, they thought the displacement would be general, or limited only by some kind of distinctiveness in the selected group, perhaps a defenselessness and lack of ability to retaliate. Prejudiced people are prejudiced toward all kinds of different groups, so each sort of prejudice is a variation on a basic attitudinal syndrome. The syndrome, in turn, stems from a few basic personality traits laid down in early childhood, as a product of child-rearing methods and socialization. Authoritarian personalities are rigid, conventional, aggressive, stereotyping and superstitious, cynical, and have problematic—usually puritanical—attitudes toward sex. They are also drawn to conservative, fascistic, or protofascistic rightist ideologies. The authoritarian personality is the prejudiced personality, and the same empirical scales used to measure authoritarianness will measure prejudice—and vice versa.

Volumes of reflections—most of them methodological—have been issued in response to *The Authoritarian Personality*.[11] It is the major social psychology contribution of the 1950s, the one that absorbed the other two kinds of individual-level theories and made them part of a larger whole. Moreover, it was a huge monument (of a thousand pages) to the brief union—never revived again afterward—of modified Marxist social theory, psychoanalysis, and empirical research of the American sort. Even by 1970, when Collins wrote *Social Psychology*, the historical context of *The Authoritarian Personality* had disappeared from view. I am going to reconstruct it briefly in the following chapter in an effort to show where the book's ambitious sweep and its guiding assumptions—so influential—came from in intellectual-historical terms. My reconstruction will take off from two sentences in the book's introduction that reflect how deeply the events of World War II hung over the project and how clearly the authors, particularly the émigré authors, felt that the war had not ended, that the forces that had produced Nazism were still very much alive—in America, no less: "Observers have noted that the amount of outspoken antisemitism in pre-Hitler Germany was less than that in this country at the present time [1950]; one might hope that the potentiality is less in this country, but this can be known only through intensive investigation, through the detailed survey of what is on the surface and the thorough probing of what lies beneath it" (p. 4). "The present writers believe it is up to the people to decide whether or not this country goes fascist" (p. 10).

# 2

## What Happened to the "Prejudiced Personality"

Individual-level psychological theories of prejudice are generally quite static. They assume a human nature, a human functioning, that stays the same. If people are frustrated, they take out their frustrations on scapegoats; if people are conflicted, they relieve themselves by projecting some or all of the elements of their conflict onto others. But Theodor Adorno and Max Horkheimer, the guiding theoreticians of the Institute for Social Research in New York City, where the first stages of *The Authoritarian Personality* were conceived, were Marxists. They brought a societal-level assumption to their psychology: particular modern conditions produce particularly modern ways of life and thought, a particularly modern form of prejudice marked by its tendency to spread out over many victim groups.

*The Dialectic of Enlightenment,* which Adorno and Horkheimer wrote together over a number of years and published in 1944, is the book dedicated to this assumption, for which *The Authoritarian Personality* supplies the scientific proofs. Following the evolution of their work from the first book to the second reveals how this one great postwar effort at a synthetic Marxian-Freudian vision developed before becoming reduced to a shadow of its former self as it was assimilated into American social science. I also want to note for later rescue some of the Freudian ingredients that did not survive the translation of their vision across the Atlantic and into American social scientific research. When the modern

57

type whom Adorno and Horkheimer delineated and named the "fascist" became measurable with the "F-Scale," much was gained for the social scientific project of studying prejudice (in the singular), but much was lost for the study of prejudices (in the plural).

## Theoretical Antecedents of the F-Scale

Adorno and Horkheimer did not consider the class struggle between bourgeoisie and proletariat the driving force of history, so their Marxist "exploitation" explanation for prejudice was not based on class struggle. Rather, they had evolved from their strictly Marxist earliest work an interest in another more fundamental conflict between dominative human reason and nature. In *The Dialectic of Enlightenment,* they postulate their basic conflict theory and track the ascendancy in Europe since the ancient Greeks of the human dominative attitude. During the Enlightenment, they argue, human thinking that was once embedded in and attuned to nature finally became conventionalized and formulaic, mathematical or quantitative, and subjective in the sense that it located all value and life in the human subject and attributed none to the inferior, external natural world. The subject's value was not, however, as an individual, an embodied and expressive human being, but as dominative reason, as domination. Ways of being in the world, in nature, that were considered primitive, especially all modes involving imitation of nature, were ruled out of the bounds of Enlightenment "instrumental reason." Those holding power—the bourgeoisie in the modern world—tended to treat the classes below them in the same way as they treated the external world or nature, that is, as inferior and valueless. And they also tended to treat the Jews as relics of the past, as primitives, as people practicing "the mimetic impulse which can never be completely destroyed." The Jews thus represent all modes of life Western people have learned to repress. They speak, as it were, for nature, for the past, and for the id.

Much of *The Dialectic of Enlightenment* is an intricate philosophical analysis of the modes of instrumental reason and the evolution of reasoners who project their instrumental visions upon the world and see, then, nothing else, although they suffer from the repressed nature in themselves. But in the chapter "Elements of Antisemitism," Adorno and Horkheimer examine the content of the projections of the quintessential modern dominative type, whom they call, simply, "fascist."

The fascist is determined not by his class—fascists can be found in all classes—but by the forces that shape his reasoning, which is dominative and, moreover, destructive. The explanation offered for this destructiveness is Freudian, based on Freud's essay "Some Neurotic Mechanisms in Jealousy, Paranoia, and Homosexuality" (1922) and his case study of the paranoid Doctor Schreber (1911). In prose that is dense and didactic in both the original German and the English translation, Adorno and Horkheimer argue:

> The psychoanalytical theory of morbid projection views it as consisting of the transference of socially taboo impulses from the subject to the object. Under the pressure of the super-ego, the ego projects the aggressive wishes which originate from the id (and are so intense as to be dangerous even to the id), as evil intentions onto the outside world, and manages to work them out as abreaction onto the outside world; either in fantasy by identification with the supposed evil, or in reality by supposed self-defense. The forbidden action which is converted into aggression is generally homosexual in nature. Through fear of castration, obedience to the father is taken to the extreme in an anticipation of castration in conscious emotional approximation to the nature of a small girl, and actual hatred of the father is suppressed. In paranoia, this hatred leads to a castration wish as a generalized urge to destruction.[1]

These interpretive terms are quite vague: they focus on the paranoiac's projections and homosexual submission to a father figure but give no indication of why the Jews became the focus of a "generalized urge to destruction." The authors make no comparative inquiry about other groups construed as archaic or primitive—as Africans were to so many European whites; they conduct no questioning of whether there is a type of archaism specific to the Jews, and not attributed to others—a difference, for example, between dirty anal archaism and potent genital archaism. The terms are hardly suitable for an empirical study. But they do indicate the direction in which the empirical study, *The Authoritarian Personality*, was to evolve. They suggest that antisemitism is a symptom of a modern disease, a personality condition, characterized by this "generalized urge to destruction." *Any* group that could be construed as repressed nature could become the object of a fascist pogrom. The interpretive terms further suggest that the key to prejudice is submission to paternal authority, which in *The Authoritarian Personality* is construed not as homosexual submission but more generally as conformity.

For Adorno and Horkheimer, it followed, then, that fascists in political power would make antisemitism just one item on their agenda of destruction: "Antisemitism has virtually ceased to be an independent impulse and is now a plank in the platform. Anyone who gives a chance to Fascism, subscribes to the destruction of trade unions and the crusade against Bolshevism; he automatically subscribes too to the destruction of the Jews. The conviction of the antisemites—however artificial it may be—has been absorbed in the predetermined and subjectless reflexes of a political party." This claim is reflected in *The Authoritarian Personality* by a single statement, key to the idea that prejudice is a generalized attitude or that ethnocentrism encompasses all out-groups: "Fascistic social movements have shown consistent tendencies to oppose a variety of minority groups."[2]

As Horkheimer noted in his preface to *The Authoritarian Personality*, by using questionnaires, statistical surveys, in-depth interviews, and characterological assessments based on clinical categories, the research group assessed the personality they were studying as "a new anthropological type." They presented themselves as explorers in a new world. But they did not acknowledge (except in their bibliography) that *The Dialectic of Enlightenment* had preceded them. Rather, they referred occasionally to others' work on personality types—for example, to that of their former associate Erich Fromm.

Fromm's prewar work on authoritarianism and family structure had recently been reflected in a 1941 volume called *Escape from Freedom*, where he had characterized the "authoritarian personality" in modified (actually, quite desexualized) Freudian terms as essentially sadomasochistic. In authoritarian societies, Fromm had argued, masochism manifests itself in passive acceptance of a hypostatized fate, submission to duty, or to God's or a leader's will. Any or all of these hypostatized forces provide the masochist with a pleasurable release from anxiety as well as a feeling of power. The masochist is yearning to be free—of himself.

In earlier work, before he became a critic of Freud's libido theory, Fromm had noted as characteristic of the masochist a regression from genital or heterosexual sexuality to pregenital, especially anal pleasures, and he had postulated homosexual identification with leader figures among men who accepted as a matter of course their society's patriarchal elevation of men over women. But in *Escape from Freedom* he spoke much more generally about the isolation and loneliness of modern people and their desire to overcome their isolation. The key ingredient of a nonauthoritarian personality was, in Fromm's understanding, an ego strong and individualized enough to resist the allures of sadomasochistic authorities.

Fromm tended to find sadomasochistic authoritarians clustered in the lower middle class, an understanding that reflected an opinion held by almost every Marxist analyst of Nazism, including Wilhelm Reich, another Freudian whose work was important to Adorno and Horkheimer. In *The Mass Psychology of Fascism* (first edition, 1933), Reich, also using psychoanalytic categories, focused on the lower-middle-class family as the crucible of authoritarianism, and emphasized the inculcation of sexual inhibition and fear. But Reich was also convinced that the puritanism and repression of the middle-class "sex economy" influenced the working class whenever the working class emulated the middle class rather than rebelled against it. So authoritarians could be found, he argued, in every class—to the consternation of socialist theorists and to the defeat of Social Democratic party politics in Germany.

In Reich's view, the sex economy of the middle class prevented mature sexuality, which he equated with self-regulated heterosexual genitality. The middle class, he argued, produced sexually inhibited, passive men and women who were prepared to submit themselves to a patriarchal führer figure and to accept all the bogus race theory mysticism propounded by the führer. Fascistic men were, in effect, homosexually inclined men trapped in an "indissoluble sexual fixation" to their mothers and marked by their "incapacity to enter into other sexual relations." The fascist leadership could manipulate such males in much the same way that the antisexual Catholic Church had:

> The youth's sexual drive develops in a passive homosexual direction. In terms of the drive's energy, passive homosexuality is the most effective counterpart of natural masculine sexuality, for it replaces activity and aggression by passivity and masochistic attitudes, that is to say by precisely those attitudes that determine the mass basis for patriarchal authoritarian mysticism in the human structure. At the same time, however, this implies unquestioning loyalty, faith in authority, and ability to adapt to the institution of patriarchal compulsive marriage.[3]

Reich recommended that socialist political and sexual liberationists make it their goal to "pit natural genital demands against the secondary (homosexual) and mystical drives" inculcated in fascist youth.

It is interesting to note that the German Marxist appropriators of Freud for social theory again and again equated, to one degree or another, fascism with the homosexualization or effeminization of German youth in the confines of the German authoritarian family. The recurrent theme was submission to the führer, construed as passive homosexual submission to a dominating father figure. As I argue later, this homophobic theory misses the key psychodynamic of authoritarianism and of the obsessional prejudices because it mistakes pervasive *fear of homosexuality and passivity* for homosexuality and passivity; it mistakes pervasive *homophobia* for pervasive homosexualization.

But for the moment it is important to observe that this theory, though it never disappeared in the work of the Frankfurt School in America, was muted, softened, and Americanized in *The Authoritarian Personality*— and thus never received a proper debating in America. Not Fromm's early emphasis on immature, anal sexuality, nor Reich's discussion of the genital immaturity of German youth, nor *The Dialectic of Enlightenment* with its focus on homosexuality and paranoia are directly represented in *The Authoritarian Personality*'s list of authoritarian character traits. One of the key conditions for the generality of the "authoritarian personality" seems to have been the elimination from it of any of the ingredients of Freud's libidinally based theory of character formation and also of Freud's association of libidinal stages and certain types of pathology. These ingredients do not translate comfortably into questionnaire-based research—even assuming that researchers, particularly American researchers, might desire to investigate them. Ironically—one might even say tragically—the very depth of analysis that might have helped the Adorno group comprehend the bottomless horror of Nazi antisemitism and channel its attack on American fascism was exactly what it erased from its efforts over time. This erasure, I think, says more about antisemitism—about the type of prejudice it is and also about its effects *on those who study it*—than anything in *The Authoritarian Personality*. Few researchers wish to see the dynamics of antisemitism, which crucially involve anal sadism and deep anxiety about passivity—the home psychic territory of such obsessional defenses as intellectualization and splitting off of emotion from intellect.

The most quoted page of the one thousand pages that make up *The Authoritarian Personality*—the page reproduced in all of the brief surveys of theories of prejudice like Collins's—is the one on which the émigré authors and their American coauthors summarize the personality's traits. This summary, which would not have troubled the waters of American social science, includes of the Freudian psychoanalytic framework only a vague notion of submission or passivity as conformity, "projectivity" rather than paranoia, and instead of homosexuality (or fear of homosexuality) a completely contentless "interest in sexual goings-on." Thus, the authoritarian personality is characterized by:

Conventionalism. Rigid adherence to conventional middle-class values.

Authoritarian submission. Submissive uncritical attitude towards idealized moral authorities of the in-group.

Authoritarian aggression. Tendency to be on the lookout for, and to condemn, reject, and punish, people who violate conventional values.

Anti-intraception. Opposition to the subjective, the imaginative, the tender-minded.

Superstition and stereotypy. The belief in mystical determinants of the individual fate; the disposition to think in rigid categories.

Power and "toughness": Preoccupation with the dominance-submission, strong-weak, leader-follower dimension; identification with power figures; overemphasis upon the conventionalized attributes of the ego; exaggerated assertion of strength and toughness.

Destructiveness and cynicism. Generalized hostility, vilification of the human.

Projectivity. The disposition to believe that wild and dangerous things go on in the world; the projection outwards of unconscious emotional impulses.

Sex. Exaggerated concern with sexual "goings-on."[4]

The Adorno group's F-Scale, designed to reveal the presence or absence of these characteristics and to indicate whether subjects have high or low proclivity for affiliation with authoritarianism or fascism, was a composite scale made up of ingredients from more specific scales developed by the Berkeley group. It was the end point of the five-year development of the group's empirical work in the direction of a generalized concept of prejudice. Researchers had begun with the quite specific "Antisemitism Scale," moved to one measuring "Political-Economic Conservatism," and then subsumed both in an "Ethnocentrism Scale." Empirically, they felt they had proven that those scoring high for antisemitism tend to score high on conservatism, and they wanted to move on to a larger correlation. Their working hypothesis was that people who show prejudice toward Jews also show it toward Negroes, toward labor groups, indeed, toward any "out-group." They disregarded differences among these types of prejudice despite making admissions like the following: "It would be erroneous, then, to regard high scorers as 'all alike'; they have in common a general way of thinking about groups, *but there were wide individual differences in the imagery and attitudes regarding various groups*" (p. 146, italics added). No exploration whatsoever of these "wide individual differences" followed.

Antisemitism became, then, simply a facet of "ethnocentrism," a particular variation on prejudice in general. In the final step of their work, the researchers developed the F-Scale to "measure prejudice without appearing to have this aim and *without mentioning the name of any minority group*" (italics added). Methodologically, their intention was twofold: first, they wanted to circumvent their respondents' defenses against discussing difficult topics; second, they wanted to be able to include in the sample people from groups traditionally victimized by others' prejudice. But the rationale of the F-Scale also went deeper: "Might not such a scale yield a valid estimate of antidemocratic tendencies at the personality level? It was clear, at the time the new scale was being planned, that antisemitism and ethnocentrism were not merely matters of surface opinion, but general tendencies with sources, in part at least, deep within the structures of the person."

The F-Scale, in other words, was designed to show exactly what Adorno and Horkheimer had argued in *The Dialectic of Enlightenment:* a generalized prejudice stemming from a type of personality—the fascist, or the protofascist. But, significantly, research for *The Authoritarian Personality* showed no correlation between measures of authoritarianism and any form of character or psychopathology, including paranoia, although words clinically associated with obsessionality and narcissism—rigidity, inflexibility, intolerance of ambiguity, attraction to discipline as well as to disciplinarians—abound in the text. The authoritarian, so the argument went, was not a particular character type or a psychopath; he was a "new anthropological species."

## The Patriarchal Family: Nexus of Prejudice

As the scope of the generalization in the Adorno group's work grew—as antisemitism merged into ethnocentrism and ethnocentrism merged into the authoritarian personality—a theme latent in the group's prewar work came into prominence. If *The Authoritarian Personality* had been a product of the early 1970s instead of the early 1950s, this theme would have been given the conceptual title "patriarchy produces prejudice." When it was, in fact, taken up in the 1970s by feminist scholars adapting Marxism and psychoanalysis for their purposes, it did not have the Institute for Social Research label attached to it, but it was handed down, mediated, from them.[5]

In the 1930s, particularly in Erich Fromm's work, authoritarian personalities were said to be stamped out of a particular familial configuration: a strong patriarchal family, conventional and defensive about its conventions during rapidly changing times. In such families the father represented arbitrary domination and the mother played the role of the relatively warm and protective buffer between father and children. The identification of sons with their father in the bourgeois patriarchal family was, Fromm had argued, always ambivalent, and the sons typically did not resolve their oedipal ties to their mothers. As I noted, Fromm tended to lay a good deal of authoritarianism at the door of latent homosexuality in men, and psychodynamically this meant an undissolved mother bond. The authors of *The Dialectic of Enlightenment* agreed.

The authors of *The Authoritarian Personality,* however, were impressed by the empirical finding that men who scored low on the F-Scale—that is, relatively unprejudiced men—tended to have mothers who were both strong and loving. The liberal males were also less defensively macho and more willing both to treat women as equals and to admire feminine traits—including those in themselves. If these men remained tied to their mothers, tolerance was served, not disserved. So the authors postulated that the authoritarian personality in males is marked by a lack of qualities associated with maternal solicitude, such as pity, and that authoritarians are locked into rigidly defined gender roles. Finally, they argued that when the Nazis destroyed the German bourgeois family—no matter what their pro-family propaganda claimed—they destroyed with it the greatest fortress against harsh, authoritarian socialization.

These discrepancies between images of "the authoritarian producing family"—which really come down to a difference in assessment of males' maternal bonds, or a difference in assessment of proclivities for authoritarianism implied by homosexuality—point up how difficult, if not impossible, it is to isolate a single family configuration at the root of authoritarianism. The problem becomes obvious if we bring clinical material (rather than questionnaire and interview results) into consideration. In Nathan Ackerman and Marie Jahoda's contribution to the

Studies in Prejudice series, *Anti-Semitism, an Emotional Disorder* (1950), twenty-seven markedly antisemitic psychoanalytic patients are described as having in common families in which *both* parents were harshly authoritarian, very strict with their children, and, behind facades of respect, hostile toward each other. As children, these patients were afraid to be submissive to *either* parent, and *fear of passivity*—from which sexual identity confusion might stem—governed their later lives. They constantly struggled for active roles and for conventional acceptability rather than for any deeper group affiliation, which would have entailed submission. Ackerman and Jahoda describe a pattern in their antisemites that is nowhere to be found in *The Authoritarian Personality:*

> The child's fear of passive submission to either [authoritarian] parent impedes the process of identification. Often the child begins by making a partial identification with the weaker parent, who represents, if not the kinder, at least the less menacing of the two. In many instances, this is the father, the mother being the dominant partner. The identification with the weaker partner, however, reinforces the child's exposure to the destructive hate of the stronger parent, more frequently the mother. Because of this danger, and because of the great need for the protection of a strong parent, the child tends, defensively, to renounce identification with the weaker parent and to strive for an exaggerated identification with the more aggressive parent (identification with the enemy). Under such circumstances, of course, there can be at best only a partial, ambivalent identification with the stronger parent. As a result, the patient withdraws; the identification remains incomplete and distorted with both parents. This produces a lifelong indecisiveness and confusion as to sexual identity; the patient gives his wholehearted allegiance neither to father nor mother, and, correspondingly, neither to male nor female attributes . . . In the unconscious, Jewishness is sometimes equated with the image of an aggressive, domineering mother. In other cases, it may be symbolized in the father . . . One is tempted, on the basis of these observations, to speculate that conflict between male and female, between mother and father, becomes later symbolized as conflict between Jew and Gentile.[6]

In this conception, authoritarians produce authoritarians in the medium of failed identification processes. The family is not patriarchal in emotional terms. And submissiveness, rather than being the child's characteristic mode or desire, is the great, the determinative, fear. Such people join organizations to be defensively active, not to submit to a leader.

Results like these did not turn up in the Adorno group's work, probably because it was so focused on fathers and sons and because concern with what sorts of families produce authoritarians and what sorts do not overshadowed any concern with women. Adorno and his colleagues focused on male children, despite the predominance of women among their wartime university student research subjects, and they spoke of patriarchy without regard to what patriarchy meant for wives or daughters. Their only effort to consider prejudice against women, typically, fused into their larger agenda, ethnocentrism: "Although prejudice is usually thought of as directed against minorities—in the sense of small numbers, and as opposed to a vague majority—one may ask if prejudice is not sometimes directed against a group containing more than one half the population. The phenomenon of contempt for the masses and the subordination of women were considered examples of ethnocentrism of this type."[7] How much this approach confined the prejudice later known as sexism is obvious in their next query: "Can the attitude that 'women's place is in the home' be considered a prejudice? It would appear that it is, *to the extent that people with this attitude have others which are more obviously ethnocentric*" (italics added). The circular idea that a prejudice is identifiable as a prejudice by virtue of being part of a network of prejudices espoused by a prejudiced or ethnocentric personality is the logical outcome of the conviction that all prejudices are, in essence, one.

*The Authoritarian Personality* demonstrated vividly the allure of a monolithic idea. Its authors could not attend to prejudices that did not fit their model of in-group against out-group, since women are not an out-group to men the way one ethnic or "racial" group is to another. They could not see any family configuration that did not fit their model of the patriarchal family or any personality configuration that did not fit their model fascist. As the most encompassing product of midcentury social theory, *The Authoritarian Personality* stood in the way of any more nuanced inquiry into modes and contents (in the plural) of projection, differences among patriarchal families in psychological terms, and differences among prejudices in relation to differences among personalities. The book stood squarely in the grand European tradition of social theoretical inference from a key condition of life (the patriarchal family) to a novel form of character or personality (the authoritarian personality), and it spoke, as the great representatives of that tradition had, to a persistent desire for a sweeping view tying a single cause to a single characterological effect. Karl Marx had concentrated on how the changes in property relations and technological innovations produced by modern capitalism in turn produced the destructive alterations in workers' characters that are summarized in the term "alienation." Max Weber had charted the extension of bureaucracy through all domains of modern life and written about its concomitant depersonalizing, dehumanizing effects. Alexis de Tocqueville had singled out the historical effects of the principle of equality as it was elevated by the French and American Revolutions, generating in France, where it was only partially victorious, envy and resentment and pools of violence in the various classes and generating in America, where it was much more sweepingly victorious, the ambition and restlessness still so associated with American "national character." Gustave Le Bon had studied the breakdown of traditional religious and political orders as the precondition for mass hysteria and crowd behavior. Émile Durkheim had charged the characteristic modern depression and isolation up to social instability, dissolution of religious forms, and anomie. And Sigmund Freud had focused on the ways in which sexually repressive modern "civilized morality" produces specifically modern neuroses. But the claim of the Adorno group was even bolder—a "new anthropological species," the *omniprejudiced* fascist, had grown out of the modern authoritarian patriarchal family. The claim of novelty was the only one that seemed adequate to what the "new anthropological species" had wrought—the unprecedented phenomena of the Holocaust.

Certain types of theories of prejudice, because of the way they are framed, virtually forbid inquiry into sexism; they are self-blinding with respect to sexism. And in certain social atmospheres—crisis atmospheres, killing atmospheres—sexism, even if it is seen, seems less important than other prejudices. The Adorno group wrote in fear that America would go fascist, and that anxiety overshadowed everything. It even ruled out of consideration questions about whether antifascists or leftists could be authoritarians—a consideration that, in the beginning years of the Cold War, was on many American minds. *The Authoritarian Personality* focused on fascism as an anti-Bolshevist, antileftist, ideology. Was there left-wing or Communist authoritarianism? Authoritarianism for the gulag? Many of the Adorno group's most strident critics, who were not people of the Left themselves, thundered that Communism was as much of an internally coherent ideology as fascism and that Communism, too, should be equated with a prejudiced personality.[8]

But this partisan American domestic Cold War warfare obscured the related oversight by Adorno and his colleagues, who did not question whether the antisemitism they saw around them in America was connected to and reflected in a mode of American opposition to Nazism, and then opposition to Stalinism and Communism. That is, they failed to ask whether they were witnessing a complex *particular type* of prejudice adaptable to different enemies, as long as those enemies lent themselves to being conceptualized as an international conspiracy, a group aiming at world conquest—a group resembling the Jews as antisemites imagine them. The commonest rhetoric of the day might have suggested this line of inquiry. In 1945 speeches of the following sort were standard: "Evil doctrines of discrimination frequently imported from gangster nations plague certain areas of America. Racial and religious intolerance is being preached and practiced here by agents of our enemies as well as by innocent victims of their propaganda. With relentless determination, our deadly opponents will seek to apply the ancient doctrine of 'divide and rule' in their drive for world domination."[9] This statement attempted to explain why it was important for Americans to oppose religious and racial intolerance—because it is a foreign importation, urged by the country's enemies, the Nazis, that could weaken the country's united fighting front. The speaker, President Harry Truman, did not point out that the country had, independently of any foreign assistance, quite a history of such preaching and practice.

The American writer who did raise the possibility that Americans have periodically been dominated by a "paranoid style" in their politics—a style suitable to all sorts of enemies—was Richard Hofstader of Columbia University, whose work I will consider in detail later. For the moment note that Hofstader's description of a paranoid style in politics, written in 1964,[10] is quite consonant with the style of prejudice the Adorno group attributed to the authoritarian personality. But Hofstader's broader approach implied that the authoritarian personality can be prejudiced against Communists or prejudiced against Negroes and other minority groups insofar as these seem threatening in a stereotypically "Jewish" manner, that is, as power-seeking, commerce-controlling, conspiratorial. (Other types of personalities could, then, also be prejudiced against any of these groups, but in different ways, for purposes different than those driving the authoritarian personality.)

Similarly, the idea that there are different types or styles of prejudice makes possible the conclusion that the generalized attitude assumed by the Adorno group, as well as by Allport and most other social psychologists, may be a feature of only one type of prejudice, not of prejudice *tout court*. In other words, a prejudice that has at the center of its image system an international conspiracy would be very likely to tie all outgroups into that conspiracy. A paranoid style multiplies and links enemies; it has what I earlier called a generalizing dynamic. And the result looks like the following quote from a 1952 pamphlet issued by Germany's postwar fascistic Socialist Reich Party, which Allport cited as an example of prejudice as a generalized attitude: "The Jew, as dictator of democracy, Bolshevism, and the Vatican rule over all of you. Have you not realized that? Stand fast. Remain German. Do not vote but wait. We shall return."

## From the Prejudiced Personality to "Modern Racism"

I am suggesting that the authoritarian personality is one type of prejudiced personality, with one type of prejudice (that may take a number of groups as its object). And I will pursue this suggestion in detail later. For now I want to return to the way in which *The Authoritarian Personality* has come to exist as a historical creation in recent social psychology.

The various societal-level and individual-level theories surveyed in Collins's *Social Psychology* have reappeared, with just about the same titles, again and again in the social psychology literature. They appear, for example, with the same titles and in the same order in Phyllis A. Katz's important anthology *Towards the Elimination of Racism* (1976).[11] The theories will come up again and again in the pages following, too. But it is important to note how they have become, in the social science of recent years, pale versions of their 1950s selves.

Nearly twenty years separate Collins's *Social Psychology* from Frances Aboud's work *Children and Prejudice* (1988), which I will use as a representative example of how theories of prejudice are being surveyed currently. Her book makes a sustained argument for taking seriously a "social-cognitive developmental" approach to prejudice, and her review of the literature serves this goal. She finds that there are two alternatives for understanding prejudice, "social reflection theory" and "inner state theory." The range of variations surveyed in Collins's book—already very selective—has been reduced to a bare minimum. What remains is, *tout simple,* one sociological theory and one psychological theory.

The social reflection theory "claims that prejudice simply reflects the differential values attached to different groups in a stratified society." This claim means that "people are essentially a product of their social milieu; they adopt attitudes and stereotypes about groups that correspond to the relative power and status held by those groups." But, of course, that crude version of the theory cannot be correct—or else children would be like little social scientists, able to analyze the structures of the society around them, estimate influences, and stereotype accordingly. So most more sophisticated variants of the theory designate parents as the source of attitudes. Parents may not have prejudices that reflect the actual structure of the society, but they do simply convey ingroup and out-group likes and dislikes or the ethnocentrism presumed to be characteristic of all groups, regardless of their status. Children then adopt their parents' attitudes by imitation or in order to please their parents. But this notion of learning, as Aboud rightly remarks, presumes that children are blank slates passively receiving the impress of their surroundings. Such sociological behaviorism cannot account for the different forms that prejudice takes in children of different ages—that is, it is not a developmental theory.

In Aboud's survey, the "inner state" or psychological theory of prejudice is also a single item—the work of Adorno's group. Aboud describes this work by presenting what is actually not Adorno's thesis but Dollard's frustration-aggression hypothesis. She says that children experience frustration, feel hostility, are punished, feel anxiety, and develop prejudices as displacements when they are unable to overcome their anxiety. They are the products of child-rearing practices that interfere with conflict resolution. But, Aboud notes—as most commentators on the Adorno group's work have—a theory of this sort is unable to explain why one group rather than another becomes the object of a child's or an adult's prejudice. She also remarks that this theory, like the social reflection theory, makes no distinctions among different forms of prejudice typical of different age levels. It presumes a stable inner state of prejudice and has no developmental dimension.

Having set up two unsatisfactory extremes, each set out in a few sentences, Aboud follows the transcending or "third way" procedure so common in recent social science. She presents an alternative theory in which children start out (from age one to about three) egocentric and dominated by their emotions, building preferences on the basis of their anxieties about strangers. They then, in a second, less egocentric or more sociocentric stage, evolve preferences along with their more complex perceptions of differences in skin color, clothing, hair texture, and language and along with their sense that those who are different are unpredictable. Only when they have cognitive capacities for forming concepts and categories, for appreciating similarities as well as differences, do children understand people both in terms of their ethnicities, their groups, and in terms of the individual characteristics and qualities that they have enduringly (not as a matter of what they wear or how they appear at the moment or how their group is organized). Children eight to ten years of age, who have gained these conceptual and comparative abilities, who have done the three-step Piagetian development from centering on the self to focusing on group differences to understanding individuality, usually become less prejudiced.

What Aboud presents as the alternative explanation is a systematic, developmental version of a group of social learning theories gathered unsystematically together at the end of the survey in Collins's *Social Psychology*. These stress how prejudices are socially learned—how attitudes from parents, schools, peer groups, media, and other institutions are inculcated in children. They show, for example, that members of each subgroup in a society learn to rank their group first in their preferences—and how group norms are perpetuated. These explanations suggest that prejudice is learned as culture generally is learned, and as cultural stereotypes particularly are learned. If children see a group treated prejudicially, they conclude that the group members are as the prejudice directed against them says they are. Blacks are treated as inferiors, so they must be inferior. And, as racism persists in the form of institutional racism (*de facto* rather than *de jure*) throughout a culture, in everything from discrimination in education to legally supported employment and housing discrimination, it seems normal to children. It is normal to them because it is their norm. Such social learning notions give the content to the cognitive capacities Aboud studied.

In part, both Collins and Aboud prefer these cognition and learning alternatives, I think, because they can be studied in more or less controlled experiments. They are well suited to social psychological research projects. Groups of children in an elementary school or groups of college students can provide the data. The experimental subjects can answer questions, fill out questionnaires, rank their preferences for groups. But the understanding of prejudice that results, valuable as it is, particularly in its stress on developmental stages, is limited. A mob scene on a city street, a rash of anonymous propaganda, the formation of a hate group—events in the world—do not lend themselves to intra-mural academic study, and neither do people's unconscious needs and fantasies, which only show up in clinical interviews or (to some extent) projective tests. It is not difficult to take a life history from a research project volunteer, but it is very difficult—even in long-term therapy—to discover a need that has never been admitted, a conflict or a trauma that has been repressed, an unconscious desire, as it is very difficult to find out from a member of the Ku Klux Klan what moves him to wear a hooded white robe and commit murder.

Both Collins's learning theories and Aboud's specifically cognitive developmental approach are geared to prejudice as it frequently ex-ists—so these authors suggest—in modern advanced industrial societies like our own. As members of the most recent generations of social psy-chologists, those working in the 1970s and 1980s to lay down the third way of social psychological research, they are studying what some call "modern racism"[12] and others call "symbolic racism." This is racism when—at the level of public rhetoric, and to a certain extent at the level of public policy—it is not sanctioned. In many areas of American ge-ography and life, it is socially unacceptable or politically incorrect to be a racist or, in general, to be prejudiced. The language of prejudice, consequently, often becomes subtle, coded, indirect. In such contexts, many recent social psychologists suggest, modern racists accept stereo-types from their surroundings and then conform to them, behave in conformity to them, often without realizing or acknowledging what they are doing. Supposedly, they have no need to invent or adopt stereotypes on the basis of deep motives or personality structures of the sort the Adorno group was trying to discover.

The claim of a modern racism is meant to refute any psychoanalyti-cally oriented theorists, including the authors of *The Authoritarian Per-sonality,* who might think that unconscious motivations stimulate prej-udices or who might believe that uncoded prejudices do influence the modern racist's stereotyping by coexisting, repressed, along with the unconscious motivations. Conformity is the central category of analysis, but conformity is not thought to involve any unconscious motivation; it is more like adaptation. Modern racists, according to cognitively ori-

ented social learning theory, are divided and ambivalent. More seriously, they act to protect their nonprejudiced self-images—often in dis-
regard for the effects of their behavior on minority people, and often
by some form of "blaming the victim" maneuver that makes minority
people responsible for minority group sufferings. When whites who are
modern racists find themselves in conflict with African Americans, or
when modern racist Gentiles conflict with Jews, they understand their
behavior in the terms available from traditional public discourse about
immigration and ethnocentrism. They present themselves as protectors
of the interests of their group against another. So, if there is affirmative
action for "them," it must not be at "our" expense; we must not lose
jobs to them; our property must not be devalued if they move into the
neighborhood. It is all the same whether "they" are blacks or poor Irish,
refugees from Iran or Vietnam, Eastern Europeans or Soviet Jews.

I must emphasize that these complementary contemporary theories
of cognitive learning and modern racism represent a new way of claiming that all prejudices are alike. When theorists of modern racism speak
of racism, they mean both prejudice against people of color and antisemitism—they mean any prejudice against any group that was, in nine-
teenth- and early-twentieth-century pseudoscientific race theory, designated a "race." Even though they repudiate psychoanalysis and deny
any of the depth psychological dimensions that the Adorno group had
tried to consider, they come to *The Authoritarian Personality*'s conclusion:
all prejudices are ethnocentrism. All are instances of the attitudes and
practices members of in-groups—any in-groups—hold with respect to
their out-groups.

## Toward a Definition of Antisemitism

As this conclusion has permeated the entire field of Prejudice Studies
and as attention in America has shifted toward considering racism the
most pressing ethnocentrism to understand, antisemitism has been less
and less investigated. The submersion of antisemitism into the larger
category of ethnocentrism that the Adorno group accomplished has
meant that historical study of antisemitism has come only from historians, not from social theorists with historical-developmental visions like
the one in *The Dialectic of Enlightenment* and *The Authoritarian Personality*.

In the absence of new work, however, a number of studies have appeared that try to survey the vast existing literature on antisemitism and

bring order, clarity, even a certain definitiveness to it. But the heritage of *The Authoritarian Personality* and the ethnocentrism thesis it shared with Allport's *The Nature of Prejudice* has hobbled this effort. And this is so even in works of great theoretical self-consciousness like *Toward A Definition of Antisemitism* (1990) by the Scottish historian Gavin Langmuir, a collection of essays that shows great familiarity with the entire range of individual-level and societal-level postwar theorizing about antisemitism. A brief look at this fine book shows in one more dimension—the historiographical—how the midcentury work on the prejudiced personality and on the generality of prejudice has shaped current efforts.

Langmuir began by doing something rare in the history of writings about antisemitism: as his title indicates, he turned his attention directly to the problem of definition, and not just as the sort of semantic issue so commonly on display in social scientific efforts to define prejudice. He saw that any history of antisemitism required a thorough theoretical prolegomena, a clearing of obstacles and a mapping of territories. At the outset, for example, he felt unusually self-conscious about using a word, "antisemitism," which had been coined in the 1870s by a German antisemite: the word itself was and is part of the history of antisemitism, part of the problem of antisemitism, not part of its solution.[13]

Continuing in his outsider's mode, Langmuir allowed himself to be struck forcefully by something obvious: studies of antisemitism have motives, they represent different needs, serve different purposes. He was aware that all studies of prejudice contain theoretical prejudices. It was not, however, types or forms of theorizing that he viewed as prejudicial; he concentrated on specific motives and agendas. "I could not help noticing," he explained, "how diversely scholars dated the appearance of antisemitism and explained its causes. From religious motives, some depicted antisemitism as a millennial reaction to the unique values of Judaism. Others, concerned to assess the responsibility of Christianity for what Hitler had done, located its emergence in the first centuries of Christianity. Others, less concerned with religion or determined to absolve Christianity more completely, held that antisemitism was a secular phenomenon that only appeared in the nineteenth century." In works on postbiblical Jewish history published before the 1970s by both Jews and non-Jews, Langmuir found attitudes that he called "remarkably parochial or seriously biased."

For Langmuir, the crucial question that cried out for an answer was the very one that had moved the authors of *The Authoritarian Personality:* when and why had the kind of antisemitism that eventually led to Auschwitz come into being? He looked backward, over the history of antisemitism, using Auschwitz "as a touchstone." And, attempting to supply historians with a definition of that kind of antisemitism, he drew upon "Gordon Allport's magisterial work, *The Nature of Prejudice,*" for there he had discovered "ethnic prejudice" or ethnocentrism, a concept that did not depend on the theological premises employed by Jewish and Christian historians, and also one that accorded with his touchstone, Auschwitz, because it "emphasized the role of irrationality in prejudice." "My conception of antisemitism depended, not on the beliefs of any religion, but on the empirical studies of various examples of prejudice by sociologists and psychologists, and on the facts of the 'Final Solution.'"

Langmuir also centered his work on the idea that antisemitism was something different from the anti-Jewish hostility of the ancient Persians, Greeks, and Romans, which he called "ethnocentric hostility," that is, hostility occasioned by "a real Jewish characteristic, their insistence on maintaining their Judaic identity as a separate people." This ethnocentric hostility required no engagement with Judaic beliefs, no sense such as the early Christians had of Judaism as a source, an originary religion. But Langmuir also argued that antisemitism is something different from anti-Judaism, the attitude of early Christians who criticized Jews because their belief did not include the divinity of Jesus of Nazareth. Anti-Judaism certainly became, in the first centuries of the Christian era, the first "systematically elaborated rationalization that justified hostility to Jews," and it certainly was xenophobic, full of a sense of menace. But xenophobic anti-Judaism, a religious prejudice, did not have the irrationality that Langmuir had identified as the key characteristic of antisemitism.

As he pursued his historical investigation, Langmuir was drawn to what he saw as a change in the mentality of European Christians—a change that began to be apparent in the eleventh century, at about the same time as the first major massacre of Jews in Europe, 1096. Theological doubts of new sorts began to surface among the Christians, and this made Jewish disbelief in the divinity of Jesus more menacing. More materially, the Jews became increasingly threatening as they developed money-lending institutions. Christian ecclesiastical authorities forbade usury, and the Jewish practice of it made Christian debtors feel themselves subject to Jewish power, while it made those Christians who did sinfully act as creditors desire a stereotypical Jewish usurer onto whom their guilt could be displaced. Moreover, because the Jews had a distinctive legal status, and lived separately, they could easily be exploited in retaliation for their economic role and for their theological distinctiveness. Christians began to indulge a key form of self-protective exploitation by creating irrational fantasies: "that Jews ritually crucified young children, engaged in ritual cannibalism, tried to torture Christ by attacking the consecrated host of the Eucharist, and attempted to destroy Christendom by poisoning wells and causing the Black Death." Here, in these fantasies, Langmuir saw the emergence of the irrational antisemitism, the antisemitism of "chimerical character," which paved the way to Auschwitz.

But Langmuir's investigation, and his careful delineation of the "chimeria" at the center of antisemitism in the late Middle Ages, led him to turn away from his initial inspiration, Allport's *The Nature of Prejudice.* "What had started me on my quest was the concept of ethnic prejudice developed by psychologists and sociologists. It was an important advance in the study of intergroup conflict, but . . . [w]hen I examined the theories of prejudice more closely, I found that they did not enable me to distinguish clearly between an unusual kind of hostility to Jews and more normal forms of intergroup hostility." He noted that the Allportian definition of prejudice, although it had arisen from studies focused "primarily on the apparently unusual kind of hostility directed against African Americans, Jews, and some other groups . . . was so broad as to be applicable to almost any form of strong intergroup hostility." The broad-stroke Allportian approach also did not "answer the historical question of how those attitudes came into existence."

In the terms that I have been using, Langmuir felt the need for a distinction between an ethnocentrism and an ideology of desire. He met this need effectively by drawing a line with the concept "chimeria." Ethnocentrism is expressed in xenophobic assertions that have at least a tangential relation to the characteristics of real groups or subgroups, especially to those living separately, preserving their distinctiveness in and by isolation, while ideologies of desire are expressed in "chimerias", or fantasies that have irrational reference to real, observable, or verifiable characteristics of a group or marks of difference. To answer questions of historical origin by linking individual motivations—the "why?" of the fantasies—to ideational and socioeconomic contexts and specific historical conditions, Langmuir proposed a developmental scheme and a dynamic concept, "the self-fulfilling prophecy." "To deal with [the] historical characteristics of chimeria and to explain why only certain outgroups become objects of chimeria and scapegoats *par excellence* and why they came to be seen as inhuman or subhuman, we need to introduce the concept of the self-fulfilling prophecy."

When an in-group aims chimerical assertions at an out-group and exploits the out-group using the assertions for justification, he argued, the out-group is pushed into becoming what it has been charged with being. But this process takes different forms depending on the type of out-group targeted. First, in-group members can aim at a subgroup (especially a class, like agricultural or industrial workers) within their own group, which is then maintained in its exploitable condition by adopting *per force* ways of life that conform to the chimeria. But the self-fulfillment of the prophecy is not complete, for certain exceptional individuals can escape their class—upward mobility is possible. An in-group can, second, stigmatize a group that originated elsewhere and is culturally distinct, like the captured slaves of antiquity. But such slaves could eventually assimilate to their captor societies; their stigmatizing legal status might only retard their assimilation, not confine them permanently to legal limbo.

No exceptions to a self-fulfilling prophecy emerge from culturally distinct groups, originating elsewhere, that either cannot or will not overcome the consequences of the self-fulfilling prophecy dynamic. This third kind of out-group only becomes more exploited and more deeply branded as inferior. Eventually, the group is labeled subhuman. Such a group has characteristics that the in-group cannot dissociate from the charge of inferiority and that it will not detach from all kinds of institutionalized exclusions from its own political processes, professions, armies, schools. The key Jewish characteristic—from the medieval Christian point of view—was disbelief in Christ's divinity, which the Jews would not give up. The key characteristic for white racists is skin color, which cannot be given up. "In the case of blacks, the judgment that they are so fundamentally inferior in culture that they could be exploited as physical labor was inextricably associated with enduring physical characteristics that distinguished them—save for some of the offspring of sexual unions with members of the ingroup—from all other populations and all members of the ingroup."

Over time chimerias become embedded in the in-group's culture, they sustain its social fabric, and they are widely institutionalized or legalized. "However personal and individual in origin, chimerical assertions are now widely accepted and effect social policy." But they retain a personal dimension in the sense that they mean different things to different people. Some accept them as their original propagators intended them, some recite them but do not believe them, and some simply adopt and use them for their own purposes. And some, Langmuir notes, merge old chimerias, handed down, into their ethnocentrism, their xenophobia. Nonetheless, it is possible to learn to read the different forms that hostility takes. Langmuir summarizes two kinds of threats to Jews (of the sort that I have been attributing to ethnocentrisms and ideologies of desire):

> On the one hand, there are situations in which Jews, like any other major group, are confronted with realistic hostility, or with that well-nigh universal xenophobic hostility which uses the real conduct of some members of an outgroup to symbolize a social menace. On the other hand, there may still be situations in which Jewish existence is much more seriously endangered because real Jews have been irrationally converted in the minds of many into a symbol, "the Jews," a symbol whose meaning does not depend on the empirical characteristics of Jews yet justifies their total elimination from the earth.

Gavin Langmuir's work goes very far toward showing the ingredients a definition of antisemitism requires—farther than any historical work that has preceded it. But it does not supply those ingredients. Because the path from the eleventh century to Auschwitz, which Langmuir described theoretically in terms of a dynamic of self-fulfilling prophecy, was a long path and had many outbreaks of anti-Judaism, it is not clear in Langmuir's own terms *when* it had outbreaks of antisemitism. At the time the word "antisemitism" was coined, at the end of the nineteenth century, "the Jews" were once again becoming a symbol in the minds of many Europeans, but a political historian like Hannah Arendt would argue that this phenomenon was different. There was a new element—conflation of the Jews and the government, a joint turn against the state and against the Jews as the invisible manipulators of the state. And there were new conditions—prolonged economic crises and violence, including the devastating first world war, that could be charged to the account of Jewish-run states.

Langmuir could distinguish ethnocentrism from antisemitism, but he could not distinguish types or developmental courses of antisemitism because the concept of self-fulfilling prophecy is too monolithic. It implies that once a process starts, once chimerical antisemitism breaks off from ethnocentrism, there is a direct route to the worst outcome. Langmuir is, in his own way, of the opinion that Sartre voiced much more blatantly: "Antisemitism leads straight to National Socialism." But he also could not distinguish antisemitism from racism except in terms of the marker of difference—disbelief in the divinity of Jesus, skin color. Are there no differences between antisemitism and white racism other than those stemming from the unchanging Jewish or unchangeable black out-group characteristics? Both these "unusual hostilities" are, as Langmuir argued so cogently, different from ethnocentrism—but are they, in their chimerical assertiveness and their exploitation dynamic, so like each other?

Langmuir stood on the edge of an investigation that might be called comparative chimerias, but he did not go this way. He had not made the careful exploration of white racism and its history that he had made of antisemitism, and he simply extrapolated to white racism from antisemitism. In addition, despite his obvious respect for the psychoanalytic tradition he saw informing Allport's work and *The Authoritarian Personality*, he did not ask why, of all the chimerias that the eleventh-century Christians could have created to control their doubts and deny their complex materialism, they came to charges of ritual child crucifixion, cannibalism, Christ torture, and pollution (well poisoning and plague). As Gordon Allport and the Adorno group transmitted it to him, psychoanalysis supplied Langmuir with the concept of "projection" but not with means to explore *what* was projected. On this lack, the postwar social psychological tradition has foundered again and again.

# 3

# Sociology Surveys the
# American Dilemma

All of the brief historical surveys of theories of prejudice produced in the last twenty years by social psychologists have operated with the two classifications "societal-level" and "individual-level." The alternative, third ways proposed recently have focused on how individuals assimilate to the norms of groups, how they become social beings and learn the prejudices of their groups, especially the "modern" coded prejudices of their groups. In other words, these theories focus on prejudice learning, connecting this kind of learning with stages of cognitive development in general and with specific other kinds of learning, like learning moral reasoning. The key individual-level social psychological theory to be overcome has been the one attributed, often quite superficially, to *The Authoritarian Personality*.

The terrain of theories of prejudice looked different when it was surveyed historically by sociologists. Different formations stood out on the landscape. Sociologists were not looking for data that could be obtained in experimental settings—by administering questionnaires to college students, by interviewing nursery school children and then following up when the children reached age ten, and so forth. They also were not reacting as strongly as the social psychologists were to the intramural history of their own discipline and to a generational struggle for control of the field. They had an extramural concern, with questions about how their field was going to serve, or refuse to serve, the political purposes of the time.

81

## Antisemitism and Racism

There is, however, one crucial way in which the history of sociology was a disciplinary battleground: in the 1960's a vocal generation of African American sociologists challenged the history of sociology—as "white sociology"—for its ignorance of African American life and for its complicity in institutionalized racism. This dispute—although no one remarked on it at the time, and no social scientist that I know of has remarked on it since—pointed to a key difference between work on antisemitism done right after the war and work on racism done in the 1950s. Antisemitism was studied by Jews (and to a large extent still is). The Studies in Prejudice series was written by Jews and underwritten by the American Jewish Committee. Many intra-Jewish controversies arose about antisemitism and about what tactics of resistance were right for the Jewish communities, and these were particularly ferocious between Marxists and Zionists. But there was never a work called *The Death of Gentile Sociology* to compare with *The Death of White Sociology*. Studies of racism produced by social scientists in the 1950s, and on into the 1960s, were studies of white racism by—predominantly—liberal whites, mostly male, including many Jews, who tended to think of racism as similar to antisemitism and who tended to think of themselves as without prejudices.

This difference can be expressed another way by noting that the Studies in Prejudice series focused on antisemitism and on antisemites, whereas the only series of comparable extensiveness, commissioned by the Carnegie Foundation, focused not on racism and racists but on the American Negro. Gunnar Myrdal's *The American Dilemma* was the flagship volume in this series, but the others all show the emphasis in their titles: Melvin Herskovits's *The Myth of the Negro Past* (1941), Charles S. Johnson's *Patterns of Negro Segregation* (1943), Richard Sterner's *The Negro's Share* (1943), and Otto Klineberg's edited volume *Characteristics of the American Negro* (1944). In part, this attention to Negroes rectified a bias built into work from the 1930s in which American social scientists had struggled to free themselves from race theory. The Carnegie volumes answered a debate about whether slavery had been a benign institution, justified by the inferiority of the slaves, or a horrible institution, unjustifiable on any grounds. Among 1930s historians, supporters of old plantation mores and modern abolitionists had conducted a kind of historiographical civil war, and in the wake of this historiographical war the 1940s Carnegie writers assumed that the story in need of telling was the slaves' story, the Negro story. They assumed, as the historian Richard Hofstader put it, that "any history of slavery must be written in a large part from the standpoint of the slave."[1]

But this corrective seldom yielded any insight into white racism or white racists. A step was missing; a question went unposed. How, exactly, can the perpetrators' motivations be read from their behavior, their institutions, the damage they have wrecked upon their victims? All of the Carnegie work on the Negro, because it did not pose such questions and did not illuminate white racism, lent itself to the later sociological tendency to blame the Negroes for their oppression. It also fostered a distinct decline in interest in racism during the late 1940s and early 1950s, when studies of antisemitism dominated the American scene. Furthermore, while antisemitism was at the center of social scientific attention, the terms of its study dominated social scientific understanding of prejudice in general, or prejudice as a generalized attitude, just as its urgencies commanded funding. Gunnar Myrdal, looking back on *The American Dilemma* (1942) thirty years afterward, noted that "from the time of its appearance there set in a decisive decline of interest in the scientific study of race relations in America on the part of foundations as well as the academic community, lasting until after the Negro rebellion more than ten years later."[2]

This American postwar state of social scientific affairs widely diverged from discussions unfolding at the American headquarters of the newly established United Nations (UN). There, although Nazi antisemitism was the precipitating cause for the many discussions that wove protest over "race discrimination" into key UN declarations, antisemitism was not the focus of these discussions. "Race discrimination" referred to relations between white people and colored peoples, and it referred historically not to Europe and the lands Hitler had wanted to make part of the Thousand Year Reich but to the lands that white Europeans had, for four hundred years, plundered and colonialized. Since "race theory" was assumed to be the common denominator between Nazi antisemitism and European racism, the United Nations sponsored conferences like the one that eventually produced the "UNESCO Statement of 1950 on Race" and its 1951 sequel. These texts were designed to expose the pseudoscientific foundations of race theory, to offer strictly delimited, depoliticized definitions of "race" and to indicate areas needing scientific clarification.[3]

But theoretical critique was out of step with practice at the United Nations. At the very first UN meeting in New York, called while the Nuremberg Trials were in process, a resolution was introduced by Egypt. With the backing of all the African and Asian and most of the Latin American delegations, the resolution condemned racial and religious persecution and discrimination, but with phrasing that made it clear to all that many countries which had fought Hitler were implicated. The very nations that had sent delegates to draft the UNESCO statements on race were being accused of racism. Nonetheless, the resolution passed without opposition because it entailed no principles of enforcement or sanction. A more direct challenge was needed, and India promptly supplied it in June 1946. India's spokesperson, Vijaya Pandit (Nehru's sister)—like all her country people—presented herself as indebted to Gandhi's principles and then challenged the General Assembly to consider South Africa's treatment of people of color and specifically to sanction South Africa for its "Ghetto Act" directed at people of Indian origin. Her move brought the UN charter's restrictions on UN interference in the domestic affairs of member states into dispute. Jan Smuts of South Africa and those who agreed with him—including the United States—argued that no precedent for UN interference in the domestic affairs of member states should be countenanced. The resulting General Assembly resolution, while it went against South Africa by acknowledging the Indian complaint clearly, made no call for action.

In October 1947, inspired by India's example, and while the iron of discussion was still hot, the African American sociologist W. E. B. Du Bois and the National Association for the Advancement of Colored People (NAACP) submitted to the UN an appeal on behalf of the fourteen million African American citizens of the United States: "It is to induce the nations of the world to persuade this nation to be just to its own people that we have prepared and now present to you this document."[4] UN officials hesitated and then directed this explosive appeal to the newly formed UN Human Rights Commission, chaired by Eleanor Roosevelt, who quickly felt intense pressure from the U.S. State Department to avoid this exposure of the American race problem. In the context of the opening phase of the Cold War, United States diplomats were frightened by the prospect of such an inflammatory discussion in the UN, as they were horrified when Du Bois warmly welcomed the support given to his appeal by the Soviet Union and its Communist allies. The Du Bois petition never did receive a public airing, but its existence, the discussions it provoked, and the harsh light it cast on racism in the United States helped push American diplomats to cooperate in the great first achievements of the UN Human Rights Commission—the Universal Declaration of Human Rights and the Convention of the Prevention and Punishment of the Crime of Genocide (although the United States was not a signatory to the latter). Similarly, the discussions influenced President Truman's decision to desegregate the U.S. Armed Forces and to sponsor the civil rights cases that came before the Supreme Court in 1948.

In the postwar international context, the reluctance in America to focus on race relations, noted in Gunnar Myrdal's retrospective account, was part of a widespread desire to keep America's race problem out of view. It was complemented by State Department efforts to show that the Soviet Union, too, had a race problem—antisemitism—and thus had no pulpit of purity from which to preach against the United States. This kind of politicizing of prejudice did nothing to bring conceptual clarity to studies of antisemitism and racism, and it certainly had the effect of making it nearly impossible to draw comparisons between racism in America and racism in the colonialized world. American social scientific studies in racism were effectively cut off from those that emerged throughout the colonialized world in the period of the postwar national liberation movements. Texts like Frantz Fanon's *The Wretched of the Earth* (originally published in 1961), seized upon by many African American political activists as guidebooks to the effects of racism, looked to most white American social scientists like texts from another world, a world not relevant to the American race problem.

Even though the international context had a great impact on the way American studies in prejudice were—and were not—conducted, the main source of unclarity about the differences between antisemitism and racism was the habit, developed during the war and immediately afterward, of thinking in terms of prejudice in general and using antisemitism as the basis for generalizing analogies, a habit still central in the fine work I discussed in the last chapter, Langmuir's *Toward a Definition of Antisemitism.* Perhaps the high point—or the low point—of this whole tradition was a work called *Slavery: A Problem in American Institutional and Intellectual Life* (1959), in which the author, Stanley Elkins, compared Southern plantations to concentration camps and Negroes to Jewish prisoners, reduced to a childlike state of helplessness and dependence on their masters. The Negroes came to think of their masters as "somehow really 'good,' " while they evolved strategies and person-alities—such as "Sambo"—for winning their masters' approval. All prej-udices are alike, all victims share victim personalities and survival strat-egies.

Most commonly, the analogy between Jews and African Americans built upon the assumption that the social and political problems en-dured by African Americans as they migrated out of the South and into the cities of the North resembled problems that Jewish immigrants had faced. They were problems of acculturation—not of racism—and they simply required that the Negroes be cured or cure themselves of their unassimilatable preurbanized state.[5] When the worst phase of wartime and postwar antisemitism had faded, when many of the refugees from Hitler had safely entered the middle class, and the focus of American social science was shifting, crude comparisons emerged—why can't the Negroes be more like the Jews? or the Irish, or the Poles? Nowhere in the American social scientific literature was there any acknowledgment of the most elemental experience of racism, a lacuna that Frantz Fanon had forcefully denounced upon reading Sartre's *Anti-Semite and Jew*. Sar-tre had argued that antisemitism and racism are just two forms of scape-goating—all prejudiced people need scapegoats, and they turn to whichever group is to hand, inflicting on others their "idea" of them. And Fanon had said, so bitterly that he almost seemed unsympathetic to "the Jew, who is a white man": "They [the Jews] are hunted down, exterminated, cremated. But these are little family quarrels. The Jew is disliked from the moment he is tracked down. But in my case, every-thing takes on a new guise. I am given no chance. I am overdetermined from without. I am the slave not of the idea that others have of me but of my own appearance."[6]

White studies of white racism did not start off with statements about the difficulties of studying a prejudice endemic to the writers' own group—a little family deformation. Such admissions, still rare, only be-gan to seem important in the 1970s, when feminists conducted a sus-tained assault on the great ideal of scientific objectivity in social studies. This problem of prejudice in theorizing was, indeed, so little thought about by white social scientists, including the Jewish experts on preju-dice in general (meaning both racism against blacks and racism against Jews, or ethnocentrism directed at both out-groups), that they were usu-ally bewildered when African Americans shot off angry paragraphs like the following by Albert Murray, who never tired of indicating how self-serving was the white social scientific acceptance of the idea that an accommodating "Sambo" image was a staple of black life:

> On principle, white liberals and radicals give or "grant" sympathetic assistance to the civil rights movement, to be sure; but few Negroes are convinced that this indicates a comprehensive commitment to equality or even represents a truly intimate intellectual involvement with the fundamental issues of citizenship in an open, pluralistic society. Indeed, the most serious as well as the most universal Negro indictment against the so-called liberal and radical writers is that at bottom they are just as white-oriented as the mass media journalists. Even some U.S. Jewish intellectuals seem to regard WASPS as the chosen people. It is not at all unusual for second generation Jewish writers to refer to native-born multi-generation U.S. Negroes (most of whom, it so happens, are part-white) as a non-white, unassimilatable minority. Unassimilatable with whom? Is Norman Podhoretz [the editor of the Jewish then-liberal weekly *Commentary*] more assimilated than Count Basie?[7]

But sociology as a whole, even though it had produced shelves of studies to more than deserve this kind of accusation, which often brought the rejoinder "but that's antisemitism!" down on Murray, was more attuned to events in the world than psychology was. Sociologists also showed more concern with institutionalized prejudice—including that within the discipline of sociology itself. At the time that social psychologists were beginning to construct their image of past studies in prejudice as a range between societal-level and individual-level theories, sociologists were reading the so-called Moynihan Report—*The Negro Family: The Case for National Action* (1965)—and the educator James Coleman's *Equality of Educational Opportunity* (1966) and then the *Report of the National Advisory Committee on Civil Disorders* (1968). That is, a collection of texts had brought sociology very close to public policy. The collection focused not on antisemitism, or even ethnocentrism as a generalized characteristic, but specifically on white racism. As the Civil Rights movement gained momentum into the 1960s, and a decade—from 1954 to 1964—of antidiscriminatory legal achievements ensued, sociology became more and more oriented toward policy.

This difference between social psychology and sociology can be stated another way. Many social psychologists viewed the antidiscriminatory legal achievements, particularly the Supreme Court's 1954 decision against segregated schooling in *Brown v. Board of Education,* as signals that the era of American racism had ended, or all but ended—an interpretation in effect declared bankrupt twenty years later with the propagation of theories of modern racism and the persistence of racism. Sociologists, a generally more historically minded and cross-culturally aware group, realized that, if anything, the Supreme Court's decision signaled a change in the form of racism. Few would have subscribed to the view proudly set forth by the Columbia University social psychologist Otto Klineberg in 1955:

> Some years ago a psychologist suggested that the unprejudiced persons are the non-conformists, those who refuse to accept the current patterns of behavior. That theory does not sound quite so reasonable today. Prejudice is becoming less fashionable; racialism, at least of the overt variety, has almost gone underground. There are fewer voices raised to defend a hierarchy of races. It has become almost an insult to say to someone, "You are prejudiced." There is a growing awareness of the harm that prejudice does both to the minority and the majority, and an increasingly troubled conscience regarding what remains to be done. We are moving toward a society in which the prejudiced person will be the non-conformist.[8]

*The Authoritarian Personality,* the original version of the idea that prejudiced people are conformists, was conceived and written under the press of émigré Jewish despair; it was declared obsolete by homegrown American psychological optimism and repudiation of the weight of the past, which theorists of modern racism find embedded in cultural institutions but which can also be described as the workings of repressed wishes.

## Eliminating Racism: Social Experimentation

Most sociologists, unlike social psychologists, being accustomed to thinking in terms of societies, which are notoriously made up of more than one or two subgroups and ways of thought, would have found Klineberg's opinion blithe. In the late 1960s the majority of sociologists, white and African American, wanted to show that prejudice, and white racism in particular, could not be explained by any psychologically oriented theory. Racism, they argued, is not an individual aberration, not a matter of conformity or nonconformity, and in America it is neither concentrated in a particular group or class or region of the country nor associated with a particular ideology like the rightist conservatism presumed in the authoritarian personality model. Racism is embedded in the culture as a multifaceted whole—deeply and almost intractably embedded, some theorists said, while others said alterably embedded.[9]

Focusing on the culture as a whole also should not, many liberal and radical sociologists went on to say, imply that victims of racism live in a separate culture, what the Moynihan Report had called a "culture of poverty," which marks them off and defines their ways of life, perpetuates their victimhood by becoming a cause—or even the key cause—of their alleged failure to develop. Liberal sociologists attributed this idea that the victims of racism live in a separate culture to social psychology—and, especially awkwardly, to one African American social psychologist, Kenneth Clark.

In the late 1950s and early 1960s, while social psychologists were criticizing the work of Adorno and his group on the authoritarian personality but only beginning their search for an alternative cognitive learning theory path, they generated an important body of work on victims of prejudice. Most concerned Negroes, following in the footsteps first of the Carnegie series from the 1940s and then later of research conducted by Kenneth Clark, who had been a research assistant on Gunnar Myrdal's *The American Dilemma* project. Clark had then gone on to write influential, accessible books like *Prejudice and Your Child* (1955) and many detailed empirical studies like his pioneering examinations of desegregated schools. Much of his research was incorporated into *Dark Ghetto* (1965). Clark's studies, in turn, became the models for work on Indians (now called Native Americans), Mexican immigrants in the Southwest, West Indians and Puerto Ricans in the Northeast, and Asian immigrants in the West. The category "people of color" began to emerge as the experiences of Negroes were generalized (often quite falsely).

Social psychological studies of Negroes—particularly those by Clark and his wife, Mamie—had been key to *Brown v. Board of Education*, which featured a lengthy appendix, a novelty in Supreme Court proceedings, demonstrating the education the justices had received from social scientific sources. The Court's extensive use of social scientific research then set a precedent for similar policy uses throughout the government of works like Thomas Pettigrew's *A Profile of the American Negro* (1954). Two shifts in the ideas about prejudice that were shared among reform-minded Americans emerged from this intersection of Race Relations Studies and social policy.

The first shift arose as the conclusion Kenneth Clark drew from his empirical studies of desegregated schools filtered into social psychology and reversed the conventional wisdom in that field. The changes in people's behavior that will be necessary for school desegregation to work—so that conventional wisdom had declared—require and come from attitudinal changes. Clark simply countered that the opposite is true: changes in social arrangements can produce changes in attitudes. At a roundtable discussion in 1955, sponsored by the *American Journal of Orthopsychiatry*, Clark's challenge started to become a commonplace. A group of social workers and child guidance professionals noted: "The prevalent approach which is almost axiomatic in psychotherapy and casework is that attitudinal changes must precede behavioral changes . . . Our training and our theories in therapy and casework are predominantly in the direction of understanding attitudes of both youngsters and parents, of altering these attitudes and ideas, and through this route, altering behavior." But Clark's conclusions, they said, had persuaded them to the contrary view that "situationally determined behavioral changes generally precede any attitudinal changes."[10]

Again and again, Clark's conclusion appeared in the mid-1950s social psychological literature, signaling that those who would eliminate prejudices should start by adjusting institutions. Not personality theory but socialization theory would and should dominate studies in prejudice. In 1957, for example, Milton Kirkpatrick, director of a psychiatric hospital in Kansas City—a border state metropolis with a long history of segregation in schools and hospitals—described to another *Journal of Orthopsychiatry* roundtable the success of his hospital's integration program. He, too, referenced his experience to recent social science.

It has been said that "in different institutional settings the same individual with the same prejudices and personality will manifest entirely different behavior, and that group interests, standards and definition of the situation can outweigh the prejudices of individuals." Sociologists have pointed out that an institution may develop organizational systems and patterns of interpersonal relationships, independently of other institutions, and that many individuals can move from one institutional role to another with a minimum of confusion. They further suggest that "leaders who control the operating practices of an institution or social environment can establish intergroup practices for

that environment within a wide range of community customs . . . even
if they differ from generally accepted prior practices.''[11]

At the same roundtable, Leon Eisenberg, a child psychiatrist at the
Johns Hopkins Hospital, seconded Kirkpatrick's position: ''Everyday
clinical experience teaches us that changes of patterns of behavior
brought about by social redirection change attitudes and values. Do we
any longer argue that insight must precede improvement?'' Both psychiatrists realized that the position they were arguing against, that insight or attitudinal change brings about changes in behavior, had become the principal support for policies of gradualism or do-nothingism
advanced by those conservatives who feared or opposed desegregation.

But they did not acknowledge that the approach for which they felt
such enthusiasm implied that attitudes do not have unconscious roots.
In their enthusiasm, the clinicians were just as much behaviorists as the
social planners. Nor did they acknowledge that the new theory also implied that old attitudes of prejudice can and will reappear if the social
institutions revert to old prejudice-reinforcing forms. Attitude changes
are no more permanent than institutions, which are, of course, set in
larger contexts of social and historical change. Social revolutions, as the
émigrés from Hitler's Germany who had worked on *The Authoritarian
Personality* knew, can also have as their purpose the inculcation of prejudice, socialization for prejudice.

The second shift ushered in with the new close tie between the social
science establishment and social policy circles was related to the one
reflected in the discussion of attitudes and behavior. Victim groups, too,
have attitudes and behavior, and many wanted to argue that a history
of being victimized in social institutions leads to attitudes that perpetuate victimization. The very liberal social scientists who rushed to alter
attitudes of prejudice with behavior-shaping institutions were slow to
realize that applying the behavior-changes-attitudes formula to victim
groups was dangerous. It encouraged the argument that their victimhood has produced their attitudes. By the early 1970s, particularly because African Americans began to have some influence in the liberal
wings of sociology, there was widespread concern that psychological
studies of victims were providing policymakers and the general citizenry
with opportunities for ''blaming the victim'' (a phrase given currency
in William Ryan's 1971 book by that title). But this view was not welcomed in 1965, when the Moynihan Report, prepared as a policy paper

by Daniel Moynihan in his capacity as Assistant Secretary of Labor, generated a storm of controversy.

The Moynihan Report stressed the "deep-seated structural distortions in the life of the Negro-American" and set out to show how the institution of the Negro family was shaping Negro attitudes.[12] Moynihan judged the lower class Negro American family to be a "tangle of pathology" (the phrase was Kenneth Clark's) composed of absent and often derelict, emasculated fathers, mothers as heads of household, and sons with neither discipline nor male role models and thus potentially delinquent. The document tacitly held up the "American"—that is, white middle-class nuclear patriarchal—family as a model of normalcy and stability and used it to stigmatize the lower-class Negro American "matriarchy." It advanced an argument—in the manner of *The Authoritarian Personality*—for a particular family configuration as the cause of character deformation.

Stigmatization had not, as is clear in parts of the document, been Moynihan's intention. He had carefully acknowledged how three hundred years of slavery and then postslavery racism had effected Negro family life and thus Negro attitudes, although he showed no appreciation whatsoever for the strength and resilience in Negro families by speaking only of distortions. He blamed slavery and postslavery institutions. But he went on to make claims that the Negro family "pathology" had become self-perpetuating: "At this point, the present tangle of pathology is capable of perpetuating itself *without assistance from the white world.* The cycle can be broken only if these distortions are set right" (italics added). Throughout his report Moynihan spoke of racism as a virus, an analogy which implies that, once contracted, the racist viral infection has a course of its own. But the virus and pathology metaphors in his report made it clear that he thought the disease was lodged *in its victims.*

The theoretical argument underlying Moynihan's claim and his analogy was a reduction to the bare ungrammatical minimum of the approach used by the Adorno group: "The family is the basic social unit of American life; it is the basic socializing unit. By and large, adult conduct in society is learned as a child. A fundamental insight of psychoanalytic theory, for example, is that the child learns a way of looking at life in his early years through which all later experience is viewed and which profoundly shapes his adult conduct." This was all that was needed of psychoanalytic social psychology—and it was applied not to families in which racism is taught but to families victimized by racism and supposedly prone to socializing their children into deformation. The outline of a figure that might be called the "victim-of-prejudice personality" began to appear, a creature of the authoritarian personality and its successor, as the subject of study in the field of "race relations."[13]

For deploying his argument, Moynihan drew on Clark's work and a wealth of sociological studies of the "Negro family," but one book in particular was of great importance: *Beyond the Melting Pot* (1963), co-authored by Nathan Glazer and Daniel Moynihan himself. The authors had argued that family patterns were key to successful assimilation in America. So the Moynihan Report summarized:

> As with any other nation, Americans are producing a recognizable family system. But that process is not completed by any means. There are still, for example, important differences in family patterns surviving from the age of the great European migration to the United States, and these variations account for notable differences in the progress and assimilation of various ethnic and religious groups. A number of immigrant groups were characterized by unusually strong family bonds; these groups have characteristically progressed more rapidly than others . . . But there is one truly great discontinuity in family structure in the United States at the present time; that between the white world in general and that of the Negro American.

In its historical section, the Moynihan Report began to draw a distinction between the ethnocentrism that had greeted white immigrants to "the white world in general" in America and the racism that enwrapped the African slaves and their descendants. But as the historical sketch reached the late nineteenth century, after the failure of Reconstruction, when so many rural Southern Negroes emigrated to the North, the distinction collapsed. African American internal immigrants were simply treated as an especially unsuccessful group of immigrants. For example, Moynihan, himself a child of a broken Irish immigrant home, argued that *any* group which undergoes abrupt urbanization will be traumatized: "It was this abrupt transition that produced the wild Irish slums of the 19th Century Northeast. Drunkenness, crime, corruption, discrimination, family disorganization, juvenile delinquency were the routine of that era. In our time, the same transition has produced the Negro slum—*different from but hardly better than* its predecessors, and fundamentally the result of the same process" (italics added). In this passage, there is no peculiar legacy of racism distinguishing it and its victims from ethnocentrism (in-group to out-group prejudice) and its victims; there is only the big social cause—rapid urbanization.

The kind of biases informing the Moynihan Report became common fare. The Coleman Report, also tremendously influential in social policy circles, used the same tacit middle-class family norm to show that black children fail frequently in schools principally because their home and family environments are so inadequate. It makes no mention of racism in the schools, much less all around those home and family environments. Both of these reports, despite their authors' antiracist stances and intentions, ended up lending weight to arguments that the U.S. government under Lyndon Johnson was wasting money on programs for compensatory education, like Project Head Start, which had had the theoretical and practical result of disproving the idea that intelligence is based on heredity and linked to race. In 1969 the psychologist Arthur Jensen added another controversial stroke to the backlash against compensatory education by publishing an account of IQ heritability among white twins that included a leap of his imagination to differences in IQ score between black and white children.[14] Similar arguments about IQ heritability have appeared in every subsequent backlash against compensatory education or affirmative action (most recently in Richard Hernstein and Charles Murray's *Bell Curve,* 1994), and they always come tied to images of intellectually inferior blacks who are sexually or reproductively out of control, unfit for "normal" family life.

## When Racism Refused to Go Away: An Impasse

While many sociologists of the 1970s criticized the stigmatizing in these reports and research projects, they certainly did not counter them with any form of personality theory or make use of any psychoanalytic work done after the publication of *The Authoritarian Personality.* Personality theory in any form fell into disfavor. At the same time, sociologists could not agree on whether or not to distance themselves from materialist theories once crucial to their own discipline. Socialists came forth to explain racism as a product of capitalism—as Oliver Cox had for the previous generation in his *Caste, Class, and Race* (1959)—and to suggest that government domestic policy visions of "black capitalism" as a way to overcome the effects of white capitalist racism were visions infected with the very racism they were supposed to ameliorate. Marxism and neo-Marxism were both faulted for arguing that economic conditions determine the level and form of prejudice in a society.

But among the sociologists who rejected as simplistic the Marxist idea that racism is an epiphenomenon of economic forces many were eager to think about other ways of describing the interaction of socioeconomic forces and attitudes—particularly if adjustments in socioeconomic conditions could bring about changes in attitudes. They speculated about how various kinds of values (or ideologies), cultural norms, and notions of status (or group identity) interact with changing economic contexts and changing modes of competition. When Gordon Allport wrote a preface for a 1987 edition of *The Nature of Prejudice,* he stressed that over the course of some thirty-five years of research, social learning (or socialization) and conformity to cultural and group norms had emerged as the key concepts for indicating how much more important societywide factors are than individual personality factors. But it is also the case that these concepts were much more congenial to centrist and conservative American sociologists than any concepts derived from Marxism.

Sociologists in the late 1960s and early 1970s, in other words, tended to organize along national political lines, with leftists of both the liberal and the socialist sorts arrayed against conservatives of the liberal and rightist sorts. What this meant as far as sociological studies in prejudice were concerned was that almost all of the work was governed not by historically or motivationally oriented questions about the origin and development of prejudice but by practical questions like "how is prejudice institutionally sustained now?" and "who or what is to blame?" But two other factors also distinguished the work of this period from social psychological work in the older Allportian tradition.

First, sociologists had no need to emphasize the Allportian assumption that "prejudice is one thing with many causes." Most sociological researchers certainly did hold this view, but they did not debate or discuss it; they simply took it for granted, because white racism—or prejudice against people of color—was the only prejudice being considered. The very tacitness of the assumption gave it great—I think all-pervasive—influence. This influence took the form of a construction of white racism as a type of ethnocentrism. Moynihan operated with this equation but so, too, did his critics: African Americans are—or *should be*—an ethnic group like any other. The second feature distinguishing the sociological work from that in the Allportian tradition was its attitude toward causality. The sociological search *was* for a single, or a dominant, cause. Cruder forms of determinism were rejected; instead many forms flourished of what came to be called "particularism"—focus on a particular cause while acknowledging that other, less significant causes exist. Sociology became, in effect, a competition among particularisms, including a competition among various versions of socialization theory, and it has largely remained so.[15]

Among the broad spectrum of liberal theorists, one type of causal analysis commanded bipartisan support. Research projects came into favor that focused on residential separation or isolation of social groups and the ways in which lack of social interaction or social networking fuels prejudice.[16] So-called contact theory (particularly the work of Henri Tajfel) was a powerfully argued version of the idea that the institutions which shape behavior also shape attitudes. When whites and Negroes live apart, in largely separated racial areas, so that there is little contact among them of an equal character—that is, no contact as employees to employers, domestics to homeowners, service suppliers to service users—then prejudice grows and social mythology develops. Groups have few opportunities to learn about one another, and journalists in all the media contribute to the problem rather than helping to solve it if they do not present stories of minority life. The prejudice-reducing effects of desegregation in schools are counteracted by segregation in the rest of a child's life.

This kind of description assumes, in the terms I have been using, that racism is a type of ethnocentrism, a type of in-group prejudice toward an out-group like that which made assimilation complex for the Irish or the Italians. It contains no acknowledgment that the barriers separating white and black neighborhoods are not the same as those between upper- and lower-class white neighborhoods or between the neighborhoods of different white immigrant groups. It does not acknowledge that there may be prejudices that are organized from their starts by fantasies, not by the reality factors said to transform somehow into mythologies under conditions of segregation. A theory that holds, in effect, that unfamiliarity between groups breeds contempt—and posits that familiarity will breed respect—speaks to the problem of ethnocentrism but not to complexes of feelings and images of the "Other" that are unconscious, as resistant to familiarity as the unconscious is to reasoned arguments or progressive social visions.

Sociologists themselves, however, had assembled the data that pointed up the need for a distinction between ethnocentrism and racism, or between layers of feeling that can be described as ethnocentric and layers that are deeper. For example, as they tried to measure the impact of the 1954 Supreme Court desegregation decision, opinion researchers and pollsters revealed a significant change in America. Between 1942, when Myrdal's *The American Dilemma* was published, and 1956, there was a steady increase in approval of integration in the schools. In 1942, fewer than one third of the respondents in a national poll had favored integration; by 1956, over 50 percent did. Among white respondents in the South, the trajectory was from 2 percent in 1942 to 14 percent in 1956; among white respondents in the North, the shift was from 41 to 61 percent over the nearly fifteen-year period. Comparable statistics were assembled for opinions about integration in housing. But there was no change whatsoever on the question, "Do you approve or disapprove of marriage between white and colored people?" In 1958, only 4 percent approved, most of them college graduates.[17]

Miscegenation was, and remains to this day, the core where racism and its ideology can be seen most clearly—and where the empirical techniques that show racism most clearly make exploration the most difficult. But the ideological stratum of racism also showed up in the sociological research on another front. The National Opinion Research Corporation asked the Myrdalian question, "Do you think most Negroes in the United States are being treated fairly or unfairly?" The idea was to try to register the shortfall Myrdal had proposed between American commitment to social justice (the ideals of the American Creed) and the existence of racism. The answer "fairly" was given by 66 percent of the nation's white population in 1944 (77 percent in the South, 62 percent in the North). And it was given by 69 percent in 1956 (79 percent in the South, 63 percent in the North). That is, the percentage of those feeling that there was some discrepancy between creed and practice in race relations was about a third and remained about a third. An ideology may be defined as a belief system that protects itself against the possibility of revealing its internal contradictions. It is a belief system that virtually forbids its holder self-consciousness.[18]

Some acknowledgment that racism is more and different than ethnocentrism was finally made in another type of theorizing that became important in the 1970s. Sociology, because it had moved so far away from social psychology and individual-level theories, was without a way to inquire about its own data on issues like miscegenation or phenomena like prejudice blindness. But historians were not so self-constricted, and the period of the late 1960s sexual revolution—or, more generally, cultural revolution—was a brilliant one in social history. Neglected individual-level approaches, especially the psychoanalytic projection theory, had a new life in historical narratives. Historians of slavery, particularly, contributed significantly to this trend. Winthrop Jordan, for example, argued in *White over Black* (1968), a historical reconstruction of slavery before 1812, that Americans have a persistent blindness to what the history of racism teaches and has taught in different forms: "white men projected their own [sexual] conflicts onto Negroes in ways which are well known though not well acknowledged today."[19] Jordan was one of the most important scholarly voices representing the view reverberating everywhere in the books of African American male writers in the late 1960s that the sexual meaning of white racism had never been understood by whites despite being common knowledge among blacks. Eldridge Cleaver made the case in his explosive *Soul on Ice* (1968), while James Baldwin made it much more cogently in a series of books and essays. Calvin Hernton summarized it in his *Sex and Racism in America* (1965) with passage after passage like this one:

> Whether the white supremacist is virile or not, he *fears* he is inadequate, and he feels guilty about this fear—he therefore says Negroes are oversexed. The racist *fears* his sexuality is sinful, immoral. He therefore creates, out of the Negro female and Negro male, objects of degradation upon which he can act out his own feelings of iniquity and vulgarity. The racist *fears* the relationships between Negro men and women are healthier and freer than those between himself and white women. He also *fears* that black men can be better with white women than he is. He therefore transforms the white woman into a "lily lady," no longer a woman, but an idol, and he fills her with his paranoid fears of Negro men. And, finally, as he craves to maim the Negro, the racist acquires a false sense of superiority and justification for his actions by imagining the Negro is bent on deflowering the symbol of his guilt and inadequacy—"sacred white womanhood."

This type of analysis, very Freudian—and very much like Wilhelm Reich's *The Mass Psychology of Fascism* in its liberationist tone as well as in its social application of analytical categories—assumed that earlier forms of racism persist in later forms, that the past persists in modern racism and in all efforts to combat racism.

The late 1960s were also rich in social historical and cultural-theoretical elaborations of Myrdal's *The American Dilemma,* each attributing racism to some American ideology running against the grain of the American Creed. The historian C. Vann Woodward captured this approach in the title of one of his books—*American Counterpoint* (1971). Cultural theorists noted that many Americans subscribe to some form of the ideology of white supremacy, whether or not they belong to white supremacist organizations. Others in the majority population, while not accepting white supremacy, believe in some form of individualism dictating that each person should be responsible for his or her own advancement and none should be beholden to the state for his or her welfare—the kind of belief that translates into arguments against not just affirmative action but social welfare programs as well.

Leftist cultural theorists, often without any of the optimism about the American Creed that characterized Myrdal's work, studied these competing ideologies and sometimes argued that racism itself is an ideology that predates the American Creed and has always had equal weight with it in our history. Racism has been woven into American social and legal practices, they argued, and it has been key to the conceptions of national unity that have emerged as the nation has developed. From a psychohistorical perspective, Joel Kovel searched out in *White Racism* (1970) the roots of racism in American culture. This book is too sweeping in its claims, but it does include an effort to distinguish types of racism, and it arrives at two, "dominative" and "aversive," that resemble the "paternalistic" and "competitive" types sketched by Pierre van den Berghe in his *Race and Racism* (1967).[20] Van den Berghe had argued that in slaveholding contexts, racism is bound up with the sexual relations that exist between the master "race" and the slaves, and, on American plantations, with the child care given white infants by Negro women. The paternalistic racism of plantation life differs from the racism that develops with urbanization and the migration of freed Negroes into the cities, where they are kept down—economically and educationally—as a kind of class in the competitive world of capitalism. Still the habits, images, and expectations of paternalistic racism do not simply disappear in the cities, van den Berghe argued; they remain like a core, an undertow.

These Freudian (often without the name) investigations, which I will come back to later, were the most important and suggestive of the period. But they were overshadowed within sociology by a second cultural-theoretical (and neither very historical nor very Freudian) approach.

Indeed, on the evidence of textbooks of sociology written in the 1970s, as well as of then-current journals and books, it seems that neither the work of American historians nor that of African American writers was much read or registered in sociology departments, so this second approach had little competition. I will call it—since it has no name— autonomous norms.

Liberal sociologists, in the train of Myrdal, argued that American racism, even after the particular conditions that sustained it earlier in the country's history had lost much of their sway, had become a normative practice. Racism, they asserted, is part of life for most people because it is part of institutions, requiring no formal enforcement. People can be discriminatory as followers of institutional norms without being prejudiced, or at least without being bigoted—or so the sociologist Robert Merton had argued in a 1949 article that gained a new lease on life in the early 1970s.[21] Racism operates in the manner of a self-fulfilling prophecy (as Gavin Langmuir had argued in *Toward a Definition of Antisemitism*). Those who benefit from cultural norms learn to expect minority group members to behave as the cultural norms predict and participate in the fulfillment of the prophecy, just as—so later generations of feminists would argue—people who are not self-knowingly sexists nonetheless help girls and women conform to the expectations that delimit female achievement. This "institutionalized racism" and autonomous norms theory is the sociological version of the social psychological contribution that I discussed before, modern racism.

As to how ideologies or prejudices develop and are transmitted, the emphasis on autonomously operating cultural norms is apsychological, and the few psychologically minded critics working in sociology pointed this out. Like theories of social learning or socialization, theories emphasizing institutional influence and autonomous cultural norms have little to say about how, specifically, cultural norms are transmitted. But the main objection to the theory from within sociology came from those on the Left who did not believe in agentless social theory. Emphasis on autonomously functioning cultural norms was not acceptable to sociologists who leaned more toward Marxist "exploitation" analyses and even more offensive to those who wanted to understand American racism as a form of colonialism. The most widely read exponents of the latter approach were Stokley Carmichael and Charles Hamilton in their *Black Power* (1967). They, too, spoke of institutionalized racism, but they did so in portraying the Black ghettos of America as colonies that white

colonialists establish and rule for the economic good of the larger surrounding white society. White economic control means cultural control
as well, which results in systematic destruction of the indigenous culture.
White control deprives Blacks of any sense of their history in Africa or
in America and any sense of themselves, any racial self-esteem. As in
African national liberation theory—particularly Frantz Fanon's manifesto *The Wretched of the Earth,* available in English in 1963—political and
cultural revolution was presented as the only possible reply to exploitation by colonialists.

In part, this theory of African American communities as colonies reworked the earlier theory, mentioned above, of the Black Nation, which
had been constructed by African American Communists during the
1920s and 1930s. And in part it was inspired by the 1930s and 1940s
African and Afro-Caribbean "Black pride" cultural movement called
*négritude,* which had been a great influence on Fanon's early work. But
I think that the strongest single ingredient of it was the Vietnam War,
a war that many African American intellectuals viewed as an imperialist
American attempt to crush a Third World national liberation movement—an extraterritorial version of what was happening in American
cities, against Black people.

Astonishment at calls for Black national liberation, whether from
Black social theorists or from members of the Nation of Islam, who were
Black separatists, was as deep among white American social scientists as
it was among white Americans in general. And many African American
intellectuals felt that this astonishment existed because American social
science had, for decades but with special intensity in the 1960s, been
giving America the wrong message about the "Negro." The "Negro"
had been presented as a broken, emasculated, uneducated, child of
slavery. And this poor creature was then held to be trapped, living not
among actual racist white people with psyches, needs, and motivations,
but in a web of agentless norms, cultural habits, and faceless institutions.
"No wonder," Albert Murray said sarcastically in 1970, "white Americans continue to be so shocked and disoriented by the intensification
of the civil rights struggle." Why would a broken down people without
living, breathing oppressors to hold accountable be bothering to march
on Washington?

Instead of relying on what is now known about the nature of social
uprisings, white Americans keep allowing themselves to expect the

theoretical Sambo promised, as it were, by Stanley M. Elkins in *Slavery: A Problem in American Institutional and Intellectual Life,* implicitly confirmed by the pronouncements of Kenneth Clark in *Dark Ghetto,* and conceded by so much [Negro] self-deprecating rhetoric. But what these same white Americans keep running up against is such bewildering, outrageous and (to some of them) terrifying behavior as the intransigent determination of leaders like Charles Evers of Mississippi; the mockery and high camp of media types like H. Rap Brown on all networks; and people like those in Watts, Newark, and Detroit, who respond to the murderous hysteria of white police and national guardsmen with a defiance that is often as derisive as it is deepseated.[22]

But it also seems to me that if you had borne in mind the theories of modern racism, with their emphasis on how racism has become subtle and coded, as you read in your newspaper about the Los Angeles riots of May 1992 or watched the South Central section of that city—a raging epicenter of ethnocentric hostilities among African Americans, Koreans, and Hispanics—go up in flames on your television, you would have felt that you also bore in your mind a dreadful discrepancy, an ominous disjunction between theory and reality. Theoretically, this disjunction stems from an assumption key to the modern-racism conceptualization: that one form of racism can give way to another without residue, without carryover. It certainly is the case that many people in America now are modern racists—they would reject the label "racist" and opine that prejudice is morally wrong. But it does not follow that such people have no connection to uncensored, old-fashioned racism.

Albert Murray was pointing to the key problem with American sociological theories of racism, particularly those generated to compass modern racism with its (allegedly) autonomous norms. The past is missing from these theories; the idea that there is a connection between earlier and later forms of individual or societal racism is missing. Even victims of racism who get entangled in such social scientific ahistoricism cannot find their way out of it. Take, for example, an article written in 1968 by Dr. Herbert Walker, "Some Reflections on the Death of Dr. Martin Luther King—A Commentary on White Racism." This talk begins with the frank recognition that racism "appears to be culturally transmitted and forms a part of white character structure"—an approach of depth psychology that would have struck the Adorno group as correct. Racism, Walker asserts, is "a group of unconscious attitudes, the most basic of which is [a] hierarchical slave-owner to slave gradient."

But even while he claims that unconscious attitudes with historical sources operate in modern racism, Walker carefully distinguishes modern racism from the racism of bigots: "The black is perceived as a 'thing,' dehumanized and not responsive with human relatedness. Hence, he is inferior. This is not the blatant bigoted inferiority claimed by the militant white racist with emphasis upon the hypersexed, filthy, indolent savage, but rather the subtly dehumanized black as seen by the white moderate."[23] Walker's conclusion that moderate white racists have broken with blatant bigotry was endorsed by Dr. Hugh F. Butts of Columbia University, an African American psychoanalyst, who referred to Walker's article as he described the form that modern racism took in his professional life. Colleagues would refer white patients to him after warning the patients that Butts was black and assuring them that he was (nonetheless) well trained. When white patients did arrive, they brought their stereotypes with them: "I see in consultation and treatment a fair number of white women, many of whom upon initial contact, or soon thereafter, discuss their sexual fears with respect to me. They resort to the usual myths and stereotypes about black men regarding sexual potency, lasciviousness, drunkenness, and the like, and act toward me as if I were a reflection of those traits." Butts went on to say that he had found in Eldridge Cleaver's recently published *Soul on Ice* an exact description of the corollary attitude of white men toward the black man's phallus. The whites are saying, Cleaver wrote: "To prove my omnipotence I must cuckold you and fetter your balls . . . I will have access to the white woman and I will have access to the black woman . . . By subjecting your manhood to the control of my will, I shall control you." Reviewing his own experience and Cleaver's book, Butts conceded that moderate modern white racism is suffused with just the images of black hypersexuality that suffuse blatant bigotry, but he felt it important—at the same time—to distinguish moderate modern white racism from blatant bigotry.

Within sociology—and not just "white sociology"—any idea that the sexual, familial racism, the racism of "the slave-owner to slave gradient," can coexist in individuals and societies with the more impersonally expressed, coded, competitive modern racism has proven intolerable. This idea flies in the face of the very hope for progress that has motivated sociological research through the whole postwar era. When rioting erupts in our cities, whether in 1968 or 1992, it must not be the past speaking, the repressed returning.

# 4

## The Prejudice That Is Not One

Whether social psychologists or sociologists, American social scientists were unanimously impressed, particularly after the urban riots of the late 1960s, by the persistence of racism—modern racism—in America. Racism became *the* prejudice for study and extended to minority groups other than African Americans, specifically, to the newest wave of immigrants, largely "people of color."

### What "Prejudice" Has Become

In the 1970s the designation "people of color" referred primarily to Native Americans, Hispanics (which included Mexican Americans and immigrants from Central and South America, all Spanish speakers, but of very diverse cultures), and Puerto Ricans.[1] By the 1980s Asian Americans joined the category, though despite that they were sometimes understood as victims of a somewhat different kind of prejudice than that directed at people of color who could be more easily associated with Blacks.

Among people of color, social scientists made few distinctions about types of prejudice, but members of the Black, Native American, Hispanic, and Puerto Rican communities had no doubt that the prejudices they experienced were not all the same. Puerto Rican and Hispanic families where different "races" mingled encountered especially obvi-

104

ous differences as the fairer-skinned would be discriminated against because of their cultural (including language) difference while the darker-skinned, more "African," members would be treated as Blacks—the former were an ethnic minority, the latter a racial minority. Native American writers detailed the peculiar blend of ethnic disparagement and exoticizing that their communities endured. Considered "drunken Indians" even more than the Irish were "drunken Irish," they were called primitive in areas where Protestantism and Catholicism declared tribal religions to be primitive. As provincial on their reservations as Ozarkies in their hills, they were also termed noble savages, a defeated people, but one with special virtues of closeness to the earth, uncorrupted wisdom, untainted beauty. They were pitiable but also enviable, especially to New Age imitators and commercial exploiters of their cultures. In terms of policy, terrible abuse and neglect has mingled with compensatory guilt about the genocidal actions of the Old West settlers. In short, prejudice against Native Americans has mixed with patronization, an attitude pervasive since the creation of the Bureau of Indian Affairs and since citizenship was extended to them (and not to the Negroes).

Except for Asian Americans, the various people of color did, however, share a fate that in a sense justified considering them all as victims of racism (on the model of prejudice against Blacks). That is, they—as groups—were comparatively economically marginalized or stuck near the poverty level. Each group did produce a middle class, and from each arose individuals who made fortunes. But the position of the groups on average seemed a very strong argument for the shared status "victims of racism." The same general status was accorded to the children of these groups in school systems, where the confident expectation that altered social situations—particularly school integration—would eliminate prejudice had faded. In the 1970s, educators began to design curricula for teaching tolerance—something that had not been in educational fashion since the late 1940s, when the antisemitism felt so acutely by Adorno and other Jewish émigrés flourished. At the time there had been many efforts, in New York and New England particularly, to provide "intercultural education," which really meant education for overcoming ethnocentrism, for aiding assimilation while teaching respect for diverse cultural traditions. And those efforts had been successful.[2] But they were not translated—they were hardly even remembered—for the 1970s, a decade when nothing from the past seemed adequate to the violent and fragmented present.

When earnest educators sponsored programs for eliminating racism they inadvertently precipitated an educational response from African Americans and other minority groups called "multiculturalism," the term for representing minority cultures in classrooms and for protecting them from the encroachments of the majority culture and its racism, including the racism in its programs for eliminating racism. The multiculturalists particularly feared that those American schools which had become somewhat integrated were tracking children according to intelligence test results and producing segregation by this new means. In 1969, the American Association of Black Psychologists had taken the dramatic step of calling for a moratorium on all testing of Black people "until more equitable tests are available."[3] In general, social scientific assessment of the state of the schools became such a remarkably complicated, politically charged, and unsuccessful venture that one pair of reviewers, evaluating twenty years of research on education policy and race in 1976, sighed in frustration over it: "The technical sophistication of recent research on desegregation is such as to inspire more confidence than twenty years ago [when Kenneth Clark's work was done] that the results of any given study are valid. But these changes have led to more studies that disagree, to more qualified conclusions, more arguments, and more arcane reports and unintelligible results. If any given study is more valid, the inference to policy from the lot seems much more uncertain."[4]

As confidence waned in the notion that institutions, including schools, can change attitudes just by being integrated, there was a waxing of the idea that a particular attitude—self-esteem—could be changed programmatically. Both those who wanted to teach tolerance and those who wanted to preserve minority cultures became fixated on the same approach—improvement in self-esteem. Young people who feel good about themselves do not need to be intolerant of others, and young people who feel good about themselves do not submit to cultural robbery and cultural denigration. "Self-esteem" became an educational mantra among psychologists and sociologists, even though they disagreed about whether it implied a new type of integration—attitudinal integration, so to speak—or whether it would lead to a new kind of separation as empowered minorities stood up for themselves.

Extensions of the modern-racism approach flourished in the 1970s and reflected demographic shifts in America and in American schools. But the political situation of the period also sponsored a revival of the strand of social psychological work that grew out of *The Authoritarian Personality*, which had been thin during the 1960s, although it had been reflected in searches for personality types like Milton Rokeach's *The Open and the Closed Mind* (1960), James Martin's *The Tolerant Personality* (1964), and Richard Christie's *Studies in Machiavellianism* (1970). Not surprisingly, the authoritarian personality approach found fertile soil in a political period when various kinds of conservatism—which the Adorno group had cited as the political ideology of authoritarians— regained prominence in American and British politics and when neo-fascist groups began to flourish in these countries and in Germany, the Netherlands, and Austria. In 1973, G. Wilson published a collection of essays called *The Psychology of Conservativism,* and by 1992 momentum had gathered for a volume called *Strength and Weakness* and explicitly subtitled *Studies in the Authoritarian Personality Today.*[5]

But this revival also included a number of important efforts at correction. Robert Altemeyer, a Canadian social psychologist, whose research convinced him that the Adorno group was justified in associating authoritarianism with conservatism, developed a scale—the Right-Wing Authoritarianism Scale (RWA)—with which to elaborate and test the results achieved with the Adorno group's F-Scale. High scorers on the RWA shared a profile:

> High RWAs tend to support unjust acts by their governments, denial of the right to peaceful protest, and systematic police harassment . . . [They] are quite punitive toward "common criminals" when they are asked to recommend jail sentences . . . High RWAs tend to be prejudiced. In South Africa, high whites are quite hostile toward blacks. In the Soviet Union, Russian highs are prejudiced against many ethnic minorities in the country. In North America, research has shown that high RWAs dislike Jews, blacks, Hispanics, homosexuals, feminists, Native Americans, East Indians, Japanese, Chinese, Pakistani, Filipinos, Africans, Arabs and . . . French Canadians. You could say that right-wing authoritarians are "equal opportunity bigots," disliking all "different" people regardless of race, color or creed . . . Highs have little love for democracy . . .[Such] persons tend to be highly fearful. They have invested heavily in the established order, and from their point of view the waves of sin and rebellion constantly pound against their shrinking island of respectability.[6]

The RWA research did not, however, confirm the Adorno group's conclusions about family structure as the root of authoritarianism—high scorers *do not* resemble their parents in RWA—and Altemeyer did not find that authoritarianism was formed in childhood. Rather, it seemed to have an adolescent onset. These conclusions reflected Altemeyer's social learning perspective and his rejection of the psychodynamic or psychoanalytic ideas that had informed *The Authoritarian Personality*. And, like most social learning theorists, Altemeyer emphasized that what has been learned can be unlearned. High RWA is not an indelible condition: "Most highs never guess that the research with the RWA Scale applies to them; but if they discover it does, they typically show a very encouraging desire to change."

While the authoritarian personality strain of Studies in Prejudice gained this new lease on life, the Marxist exploitation theory of prejudice and, in general, any effort to link prejudice to a class—a dominating class—disappeared from the scene of American social science altogether as the country's political life moved toward the right and its left atrophied. But the theory appeared outside the social science disciplines in new forms. For example, Manning Marable, one of the founding members of the Democratic Socialists of America, published *How Capitalism Underdeveloped America* (1983), which painted a devastating picture of the social and economic odds against African Americans—the unemployment statistics for Black youth, the high school graduation rates for the inner city poor, the poverty levels for Black children, the arrest and prison and police violence numbers, the rate of death by homicide. The volume also implicated the "Black bourgeoisie" and "Black capitalism" in the process of pauperization and underdevelopment it describes.

For Cornel West, an exponent of the "prophetic Christianity" that has grown up in American Black churches, by contrast, the Black bourgeoisie is not part of the problem of racism but part of the solution, in that it is producing the intelligentsia to comprehend the history of those "European supremacist discourses" that have accompanied the rise of capitalism. West has expounded on the Judeo-Christian discourse emerging out of interpretations of the biblical story of Ham, whose progeny was cursed with blackness; the scientific discourse that produced race theory; and "the psychosexual racist logic," which he has described in these freewheeling terms:

> The psychosexual racist logic arises from the phallic obsessions, Oedipal projections, and anal-sadistic orientations in European cultures

which endow non-European (especially African) men and women with sexual prowess; view non-Europeans as either revengeful fathers, frivolous carefree children, or passive long-suffering mothers; and identify non-Europeans (especially black people) with dirt, odious smell, and feces. In short, non-Europeans are associated with acts of bodily defecation, violation and subordination.[7]

Passages like this one signal that the cultural-theoretical analyses and versions of the projection theory offered in the late 1960s by historians like Joel Kovel and Winthrop Jordan, which I mentioned before as not being much heeded by sociologists, have found their elaboration in a new African American sensibility, one not hostile to psychoanalysis or psychohistory, one in the line so brilliantly represented by Ralph Ellison's *Invisible Man*. Some of the frankness about what Calvin Hernton called "the sexualization of racism" has returned and engaged with analyses of sexism produced by feminists. Cornel West is the most widely known American currently continuing both this cultural-theoretical tradition and the cultural Black Marxist tradition that developed through the work of W. E. B. Du Bois, Richard Wright, and C. L. R. James.

Within these continuations of the individual-level and societal-level traditions of Studies in Prejudice another tendency can be noted. One finds a longing for synthesis, a deep frustration with the plethora of social scientific theories of prejudice, each growing more and more researched, investigated, written over—and trivialized. Nowhere is this longing for synthesis more obvious than in a work published in 1992 by a South African, John Duckitt's *The Social Psychology of Prejudice*, a bibliographic *tour de force*. It displays an extraordinary acquaintance with American and British social scientific studies of prejudice since the end of World War II, and it offers a thorough, if schematic, history of theories of prejudice—a history much more suggestive than any to be found in the early 1970s, when historical surveys like Collins's in his *Social Psychology* came into fashion.

By reviewing most of the major types of theories of prejudice that have been offered by social science and pointing up the limitations and weaknesses of each, Duckitt attempts to make an eclectic synthesis. To take the wheat and leave the chaff. Central to his enterprise is his conclusion that in the "bewildering variety of theories and approaches attempting to elucidate the causes of prejudice" four types recur: those focused on the psychological fundamentals of prejudice; those concerned with individual differences or personalities supporting prejudice; those searching for the mechanisms involved in the transmission of prejudice from group to individual; and, finally, those aimed at the social and intergroup dynamics of prejudice. There are, in other words, individual-level psychological and societal-level sociological theories—as has been noted repeatedly since the end of the war—and they all need to be taken into account.

Missing from this earnest effort is any critical thought about why the history of theories of prejudice runs so redundantly along two levels, individual and societal; why it is so relentlessly social scientific and closed to literary and philosophical voices, especially those representing victim groups (Duckitt himself ignores the literary and historical work of both South African and African American intellectuals entirely); why it is so monolithic—why, that is, it keeps being concerned with prejudice in the singular, not types of prejudice. On this last count, observe that *The Social Psychology of Prejudice* is not only tied to "Prejudice" in the singular but that the word "Prejudice" in this title refers *only* to race prejudice. Duckitt gives no indication that he considers any other kind of prejudice relevant to his inquiry or to his project of offering a theory of prejudice (race prejudice) that would synthesize the history of postwar theories of prejudice. Antisemitism, the prejudice over which social psychology had its immediate postwar flourishing, has disappeared from "*the* social psychology of prejudice." To find it, you must consult separate volumes, such as Walter Bergmann's *Error without Trial: Psychological Research on Anti-Semitism* (1988), which contains essays from the whole postwar period, each representing a different approach to antisemitism so that the volume is a veritable encyclopedia. The book resembles Duckitt's synthetic enterprise, but for antisemitism rather than racism.

While race prejudice has become Prejudice, sexism, like antisemitism, has had its own books. But sexism has its own books without ever having been, historically, included in the Studies in Prejudice traditions. As I noted in reviewing *The Authoritarian Personality*, it had occurred to the Adorno group in 1950 to raise the question, is prejudice against women prejudice? Should it be taken into account in the general rubric "ethnocentrism"? Can it be right to call an attitude toward an out-group that is not a minority a prejudice?[8] The book offered no answer, and the group made no effort to include prejudice against women in its research program. Gordon Allport was not so inhibited. Noting in *The Nature of Prejudice* that "the in-group of sex males makes an interesting study," he offered a short summary of then-current research:

A child of two normally makes no distinction in his companionships: a little girl or a little boy is all the same to him. Even in the first grade the awareness of sex groups is relatively slight. Asked whom they would choose to play with, first grade children on the average choose opposite-sex children at least a quarter of the time. By the time the fourth grade [age ten] is reached these cross-sexed choices virtually disappear: only two percent of the children want to play with someone of the opposite sex. When the eighth grade [age fourteen] is reached friendships between boys and girls begin to re-emerge, but even then only eight percent extend their choices across the sex boundary. For some people—misogynists among them—the sex-group remains important throughout their lives. Women are viewed as a wholly different species from men, usually an inferior species. Such primary and secondary sex differences as exist are greatly exaggerated and are inflated into imaginary distinctions that justify discrimination . . . But for many people [a] "war of the sexes" seems totally unreal. They do not find it a ground for prejudice.[9]

For Allport, men who consider "men" an in-group, consider women an out-group. The in-group and out-group dynamic can and should be discussed in the same terms as native born and immigrant, white and Negro, Gentile and Jew. The fact that all of those groups—native born people, immigrants, whites, Negroes, Gentiles, Jews—are about half female did not enter into his picture. And he made not the slightest glance at the complex question of *how* a male "sex group" is constructed by men, with what inclusions and exclusions on grounds other than sex—say, race. What happens in the fourth grade?

When social psychologists and sociologists did begin to take sexism into consideration, they assimilated it into their old patterns—deeming it an in-group and out-group matter, an ethnocentrism (in the Adorno group's sense) like any other. The simple facts that men are not generally given birth to by their ethnic and racial enemies, that they do not generally marry them and procreate with them (being unable to procreate without them), that they do not have them as daughters, and so forth, did not loom large in social science. Prejudice against women was too close, too intimate, too intrafamilial to be seen in its uniqueness— especially by the predominantly male community of social scientists, where the prejudice was far from absent.

Sexism helped rule sexism out of social scientific consideration, and this process received additional social scientific support during the

1970s. After E. O. Wilson published his *Sociobiology: The New Synthesis* (1975), many sociobiological and ethological studies were generated to show that both male dominance and female subservience (or confinement to reproductive responsibilities and relationships of dependence) are genetically based characteristics that further human evolution. Sociobiology also made in-group prejudice against out-groups, ethnocentrism, seem like a normal, universal human phenomenon based upon "kin altruism." This phrase, popularized by Pierre van den Berghe, who converted to sociobiology in the 1970s, abandoning the important steps he had taken toward distinguishing ethnocentrism and racism in *Race and Racism*, indicated that breeding populations develop genetic closeness and exclusivity sufficient to generate ferocious hostilities to all out-groups and sufficient to sustain preservative altruism within their own ever-expanding group. Sexism could be, with the help of these notions, conceived of as a natural human condition and part of natural ethnocentric intergroup relations.

If Duckitt had considered the sexism built into the whole history of theories of prejudice and looked out on recent developments like sociobiology, he would have realized that his project of using what is valuable in this history and leaving aside the rest was very problematic. Almost all the empirical results in that long history were reached without regard to gender issues. For example, I noted that the Adorno group abandoned much of the Freud-inspired work the Frankfurt School and its associates had done before their emigration. Specifically, the group deemphasized the idea that had informed *The Dialectic of Enlightenment*, Erich Fromm's work, and Wilhelm Reich's early theorizing: the idea that the submission of antisemites to their leaders, their führer in the Nazi case, should be construed as homosexual. This analysis presumed, of course, that the antisemites in question were male (as were their victims). And no distinct consideration of female antisemites (or female victims) appeared in any prewar psychoanalytic Marxist text. Social scientists seem to have just assumed that women, like homosexual males, passively submitted to the führer's will, without any indication that one group's submission is "unnatural" or "perverse" (by the social and psychiatric standards of the time and place) and the other's "natural." The Freudian strain of the Frankfurt School's work diminished as the research became Americanized, but submissiveness or conformity remained a key trait in the authoritarian personality. And this personality was construed in *The Authoritarian Personality* as male, as "he," even though the authors made it clear that the research populations available in Berkeley during the war were largely female. The text obscures the crucial theme of passivity and submissiveness. And certainly no one asked: Are there differences between antisemitisms or, generally, between ethnocentrisms directed at out-group men and at out-group women?

During the 1950s and 1960s, when American sociologists treated racism as their major concern, sex differences among racists had not been considered. When sociologists issued studies of racism, they seldom considered questions like, are women predisposed, or taught, or allowed, or encouraged to be racist in ways different from men? The archetypical racist was male. The vocabulary for discussing racism kept this bias in place—racism is a form of "paternalism," for example. But many historians and sociologists of race relations realized that gender distinctions among the victims of racism matter. Male and female slaves were often treated differently, historians noted. In the Negro family, the construction that was the subject of the Moynihan Report, the effects of racism travel along gender lines. The Negro women, strong matriarchs, are less damaged than the men, who were said to be (as racist stereotypes wishfully say them to be) emasculated and derelict. The "at risk" children in the Negro family are the young males, without fathers and male role models, while the young females are likely to bear children out of wedlock and remain enmeshed in the matriarchal pattern.[10] The extent to which this vision of disabling matriarchy was sexist was questioned only ten years later.

A curious situation exists now in social scientific research on race prejudice. After two decades of feminist influence on the disciplines of psychology and sociology, research populations are often divided into males and females. All the statistics come in two columns. But nothing much is made of the differences that show up. For example, in a British work that bears the title *Personality, Self-Esteem, and Prejudice* (1979)—in which "prejudice" means race prejudice and low self-esteem explains intolerance—the authors make gender distinctions but give indecipherable results, as the following display of the book's contemporary jargon and grammar shows:

> Being in a low stream [a low track in school], having a lower IQ and being a sociometric isolate all predict racialism to a significant extent for boys. Parents' social class is overall an insignificant predictor of

prejudice, but having a parent in a lower white-collar occupation emerged as the most powerful predictor of racialism in the total analysis. This unexpected finding is however in accord with the analysis of data from our national survey of prejudiced attitudes in adults, when it was found that the highest amount of prejudice was observed in . . . the lower white-collar category. One implication of this finding is that the feelings about status which presumably underlie the manifestation of prejudice in lower white-collar workers are transmitted to some extent to their sons . . .

. . . In boys lower white-collar class membership remains a significant predictor of prejudice, as does introversion and neuroticism, and friendship influence . . .

. . . In girls the self-esteem component B, lack of family concord, correlates significantly with the attitude component of racialism, suggesting that in contrast to boys, where school is a more important source of self-esteem, the family is an important source of poor self-esteem, and its concomitant reaction of racialist attitudes . . .

. . . It appears that in girls, self-esteem is a less consistent predictor of prejudice than in boys . . .

. . . Father's support was particularly related to self-esteem [among] adolescent boys . . . The same-sex parent acts as an important model for the child, both in the acquisition of values, and in the acquisition of self-esteem.[11]

There is such a tangle of ideas behind these sentences that they seem to produce more questions than they answer. School is the most important source of self-esteem for boys—but, then, the father's support is crucially important. Lack of family concord is a crucial factor undermining self-esteem in girls—but, then, *this* self-esteem is not as good a predictor of prejudice as is low self-esteem in boys. To make any sense of these currents would require an inquiry into the topic of sexual roles, and then of sexism. But this is a book about prejudice in the sense of race prejudice only.

In sum, the prejudice that emerged into great social prominence in the late 1960s and early 1970s, which was given the name "sexism" and analyzed in hundreds of feminist volumes, has yet to be included in books with titles like *The Social Psychology of Prejudice* or *Personality, Self-Esteem, and Prejudice*.[12] Correspondingly, the prejudice that emerged in the 1980s into great social prominence, homophobia, has also yet to be registered in the official texts of social science as a prejudice. The literature on homophobia is growing at an astonishing rate and a social psychological *Journal of Homosexuality* has existed since 1981, but my point is that these prejudices have not been drawn into the social scientific ambit of the word "prejudice" or into studies of what that word has been taken to refer to—that is, either prejudice in general as ethnocentrism or (more recently) prejudice in general as racism.

One of the key elements involved in these phenomena—the absence of sexism and homophobia from the category "prejudice," the failure to study differences in male and female prejudices, and the failure to study sexism and homophobia as they relate to other prejudices—is a function of the old assumption, which we have looked at now from many angles, that prejudice is a generalized attitude. If all prejudices are one, sexism has no specificity. If all prejudices are one, men and women will entertain them the same way. And if all prejudices are one, victims will be affected only by one thing. There is no tradition within the history of studies and theories of prejudice for looking at people as the victims of multiple prejudices. Nor is there much attention to the prejudices of victims of prejudice—to the sexism of black males, to the racism of white females, to the antisemitism of black females, and so forth—or to the ways in which intragroup prejudices relate to these cross-group prejudices: how the attitudes of white males toward Blacks, male and female, are related to their attitudes toward white women, for example.

Why are these permutations and variations not studied? In part, social science research methods lack the means for taking sexism into account; for all the years since the war, social science has been based on questionnaires (with interviews added when funding or time permit). Asking about prejudice against women immediately raises the question—whom shall we ask? just men? men and women? And if we asked women about their sexism, should we use the same terms used for asking men about theirs? Or should there be some designation like "colorism," which sets the color preferences and prejudices of people of color off from those of racists, meaning white racists? Shall we question people of different ethnic groups, racial groups, socioeconomic statuses? If we talk to black males, shall we ask about black females, or about females in general? Gender distinctions, that is, cut across all the other in-group and out-group distinctions.

Furthermore, if we admit sexism into consideration, all the neat simplicities stemming from the "prejudice is one" assumption will be ruined. It will no longer be possible to consider a black woman as just a black, or a white male as just a white. The same challenge to research methods and assumptions will come up if we take into account the homosexuality or heterosexuality of prejudiced people and victims of prejudice. And what would happen if attention were given to refinements like "manifest" and "latent" homosexuality, "closeted" and "open" homosexuality, bisexuality in fantasy or in practice, and so forth? How can research distinguish the facets of identities, determining which facet contributes to which experience of prejudice or victimization, when people cannot even make these distinctions in the privacy of their own self-understandings?

Theoretical prejudices about prejudice and complex methodological issues have certainly combined to keep sexism and homophobia out of the range of social scientific studies of prejudice. But, in principle, they should be as empirically explorable as any other prejudices, as should their roles in other prejudices. Impetus for inclusion of sexism and homophobia in social scientific studies has, of course, come from the victim groups, but the silence in social scientific studies has also been influenced by the ways studies of sexism and homophobia have been undertaken by feminists and gay liberationists. As so-called second-wave feminism gathered force in the early 1970s, feminist theorists had great difficulty situating their topic, sexism, in the terrain of prejudices, particularly with respect to racism, and this difficulty, in turn, stemmed from how they experienced sexism and interpreted their experience.

## How "Sexism" Came to Consciousness

Most striking in the early 1970s American feminist literature that set out to analyze and destroy "sexism" (the word that vied with and finally won over "male chauvinism" as the enemy ideology's name) is the emphasis on "consciousness raising." The first thing that the writers, most of them middle-class and educationally privileged, had to do was convince themselves and other women that they were, indeed, oppressed and oppressed *as women*. They had to legitimate their status as victims, something that no victim of "racism"—the word on which "sexism" was modeled—ever had to do. But they specifically had to alter their consciousnesses, their minds, their thoughts; they had to resist as thinkers. Eventually, the designation "theorist" was appropriated, and "feminist theory" was born. This focus on thinking, on theory, was the answer to the central modality in which the oppression of women was felt by that generation of educated, middle-class, and predominantly urban and white feminists. Women felt that they could not move forward until they had once and for all refuted the charge that women are mindless, that they are only bodies, sexual objects, reproductive machines. Victim groups must respond to their oppression first at the site where it most threatens their ability to respond—so a group attacked for its appearance responds with *négritude* or "Black is beautiful," and a group attacked for its mindlessness, which means body-onlyness, responds with consciousness raising.

For privileged women to say, clearly and unequivocally, "we are oppressed," or "we are the victims of sexism," required analysis of sexism as a complex and multifaceted form of mind control and body control. This analysis showed how vast claims in the shape of philosophical arguments, theologies, histories, and historiographies, reaching out to encompass all of time and space, all of human life, have denied women in one way or another: they derive her from man, they do not tell her story, they say she has no intellect, they reduce her to her unreasoning body and her reproductive functions. In the very language people speak, the denial is registered in thousands of variations on the theme of "he" as the generic pronoun for human beings. All of these huge intellectual constructions with their corollary institutions were of, by, and for men. They have made the cosmos, the divinity, the shape of history, the syntax of languages, masculine. In psychological terms, these constructions and institutions were obviously products of male narcissism, but for reasons that need examining, analysis of male narcissism only very slowly came to inform feminist analysis of sexism.

Even though so much of second-wave feminist analysis of sexism focused on—and took place in the medium of—linguistic constructions, it drew its power from the idea that women are oppressed as other groups are. They, like other groups, are scapegoats. In the American context, women became equated with African Americans. In the late 1960s and early 1970s, many white American feminists built their initial theories of sexism on their understandings of racism, recapitulating the turn-of-the-century intertwining of first-wave feminism's critique of paternalism and the Abolitionist movement's critique of slavery. There were many echoes of Elizabeth Cady Stanton's famous speech before the New York State Legislature of 1854, in which she tried to demonstrate the parallels between slavery and the social, economic, and political oppression of women. "The basic premise of women's liberation is that women are an exploited class, like black people" went a typical formulation in "Woman as Nigger," a 1969 article by Gayle Rubin, a student of anthropology who later became one of the key feminist theorists in the emerging field of Women's Studies.[13] But this very American analogizing of sexism and racism (with its inexact use of "class" as a synonym for "group") was also grafted onto a conceptual framework supplied by the European touchstone feminist text, Simone de Beauvoir's *The Second Sex*, which furnished this comparison:

> [There] are deep similarities between the situation of woman and that of the Negro. Both are being emancipated today from a like paternalism, and the former master class wishes to "keep them in their place"—that is, the place chosen for them. In both cases the former masters lavish more or less sincere eulogies, either on the virtues of "the good Negro" with his dormant, childish, merry soul—the submissive Negro—or on the merits of the woman who is "truly feminine"—that is, frivolous, infantile, irresponsible—the submissive woman. In both cases the dominant class bases its argument on a state of affairs that it has itself created.[14]

This same approach is echoed in *The Creation of Patriarchy* (1985), written nearly forty years later by the historian Gerda Lerner—a book with a scope and verve nearly equal to Beauvoir's. But Lerner incorporates the feminist effort of the intervening decades to establish the uniqueness of sexism:

> Sexism defines the ideology of male supremacy, of male superiority and of beliefs that support and sustain it. Sexism and patriarchy mutually reinforce one another . . . Sexism stands in the same relation to paternalism as racism does to slavery. Both ideologies enabled the dominant to convince themselves that they were extending paternalistic benevolence to creatures inferior and weaker than themselves. But there the parallel ends, for slaves were driven to group solidarity by racism, while women were separated from one another by sexism.[15]

Racism and sexism, though parallel, make different impacts on their victims. Slaves, who had their own culture, who had memories of a time before slavery and oral traditions for keeping those memories alive, who had experience of other forms of hierarchy—class hierarchy among whites, for example—had the elements necessary for group solidarity and resistance. They could see the slavery system in political terms. But women in households, experiencing domination in the paternalistic mode, "mitigated by mutual obligations and reciprocal rights," did not see themselves as a group and did not perceive themselves as potentially political, as resisters. (Slaves in more paternalistic contexts, Lerner notes, suffered the same isolating and depoliticizing effects.) Consciousness raising was the necessary step to resistance for women, who had to make themselves into a group and learn solidarity.

In *The Second Sex,* the analogy of sexism and racism flowed strongly against the basic premise about sexism that Beauvoir wanted to establish. "Otherness," she claimed in the book's introduction, "is a fundamental category of human thought. Thus it is that no group ever sets itself up as One without at once setting up the Other against itself." Women are the Other to men (or, as social scientists would say, women are the out-group to the male in-group). But this particular relationship of One and Other, Beauvoir argued, is unique. To state the matter in the form of a premise: like all who have been set up as others, a woman is bound to her master, but "the bond that unites her to her oppressors is not comparable to any other." This is so chiefly, Beauvoir contended, because the division of the sexes is a biological fact, not a historical event or process. Women are not a class or a collective unit like the proletariat; they are not a group once conquered in a war; they are not a minority "authentically assuming a subjective attitude," a "we," and struggling with a majority—indeed, they are an unorganized majority that has protested its condition with only "symbolic agitation."

There is, certainly, a history to this unique bond of One and Other, including a particularly complex recent history of Enlightenment emancipation followed by nineteenth-century counteremancipatory trends like those that oppressed races, classes, and castes in the imperialist expansion of European and American capitalism. Thus the analogy of sexism and racism. But Beauvoir wanted to concentrate on the uniqueness of the second sex's subservience. A *factum brutum,* biological difference, sex difference, has been turned into gender difference, a difference of social roles and possibilities. "A woman is not born but made," as she put the matter succinctly and famously. And what this statement meant to Beauvoir was that if gender (social) differences can be overcome, the sex (biological) difference will not matter—women will have escaped their biological condition.[16]

All the American feminist theorists who followed Beauvoir in analogizing sexism and racism hit upon the same complex task of redeeming sexism's uniqueness, a task that makes the introduction to *The Second*

*Sex* such a puzzle. Many, like Gerda Lerner, came upon the solution of emphasizing women's political and social isolation rather than, like Beauvoir, emphasizing their biological otherness and its social meaning. But, in general, it can be said of these theories of sexism that they were the only kind of theories of prejudice to have as a distinguishing trait that, no matter how much they subscribed to historical analogies, they also had to proceed *via negativa*. They insisted that sexism is not like any other kind of prejudice as though fearing the dissolving force of the very analogies with other prejudices, especially racism, that they also offered. Finally, the only way to protect the uniqueness of sexism seemed to be to make sexism the fundamental form of prejudice, the *Ur*-prejudice, the fountain of prejudice. This is how Kate Millett, introducing the title and the concept of her *Sexual Politics,* explained why sexism is more fundamental than racism, even though both are analogous in involving "the general control of one collectivity, defined by birth, over another collectivity, also defined by birth":

> [A] disinterested examination of our system of sexual relationship must point out that the situation between the sexes now, and throughout history, is a case of that phenomenon Max Weber defined as *herrschaft,* a relationship of dominance and subordination. What goes largely unexamined, often even unacknowledged (yet is institutionalized nonetheless) in our social order, is the birthright priority whereby males rule females. Through this system, a most ingenious form of "interior colonization" has been achieved. It is one which tends moreover to be sturdier than any form of segregation, and more rigorous than class stratification, more uniform, certainly more enduring. However muted its present appearance may be, sexual dominion obtains nevertheless as perhaps the most pervasive ideology of our culture and provides its most fundamental concept of power.[17]

Millett expected that the forward march of American history would reveal that "the priorities of maintaining male supremacy might outweigh even those of white supremacy; sexism may be more endemic in our society than racism." The male writers whose literary texts she made her chief objects of study confirmed her view. She did not hold this opinion because she had noted that women of color are oppressed by both white males and males of their own groups; rather, she held it because she believed that "the female of the non-white races does not figure in [white authors' texts] save as an exemplum of 'true' womanhood's servility, worthy of imitation by other less carefully instructed females." Millett's own perspective was white, and she attended only to specific white male fantasies and literary texts; she was not taking into account the experiential realities or analyses of sexism that women of color present in their texts.

For the first decade during which the word "sexism" flourished, almost all white users of the term took for granted its analogy with "racism." Black women objected time and again to such formulations as (to cite the well-known 1969 essay I noted before) "Woman as Nigger." Only white women, they noted, would come up with such a formulation, which really failed to acknowledge that half of the "niggers" are women and need not be analogized to themselves. And only white women would think, if they did think about black women at all, that black women would identify themselves first as women rather than first as blacks, or would see sexism, not racism, as their primary oppression. Hazel Carby, for example, noted that there were many theoretical problems with drawing parallels between race and gender, but she also stressed: "The fact that black women are subject to the *simultaneous* oppression of patriarchy, class and 'race,' is the prime reason for not employing parallels that render their position and experience not only marginal but invisible."[18] Finally, these objections were acknowledged. The poet Adrienne Rich was courageously frank in naming the problem "white solipsism." Such solipsism is not, she wrote, "the consciously held belief that one race is inherently superior to all others, but a tunnel-vision which simply does not see nonwhite experience or existence as precious or significant, unless in spasmodic, impotent guilt-reflexes, which have little or no long-term, continuing momentum or political usefulness."[19]

Another way of describing the problem, I think, is to note that the dynamic—the unacknowledged principle—animating feminist theory in the tradition of Beauvoir was that narcissism can only be fought with narcissism. The "white solipsism" in feminist theory derived from an effort to meet an ideology, sexism, viewed as spread out over all of human life, with one of equal compass, one embracing the particular and the universal, the individual and the social, the intimate and the cosmic, the practical and the theoretical. White feminists extrapolated from their own immediate experience, blew it up, as it were, to the macrocosm, to Everywoman. As a result, they did unto nonwhite women what had been done unto them in sexist ideologies—they denied nonwhite women their voices, their histories, their particularities (including the diversities within and among nonwhite communities). And the same problem existed in relation to other forms of particularity in ethnicity, religion, and culture (for example, in relation to Jewish women who have experienced both sexism and antisemitism) as well as sexual preference. There is a crucial lesson here, which needs—and has not yet received—a psychosocial theory: the narcissism of sexism compels from its victims a compensatory narcissism.

Situating sexism in relation to racism has been recognized as a problem—although not one afflicting the larger tendency of studies in prejudice to subscribe to the idea that all prejudices are essentially the same. There are, however, other complexities that arise from the impulse to fight narcissism with narcissism, to construct sexism transhistorically and universally. Feminist theory that presents sexism as all-pervasive is hard-pressed to provide an alternative. If sexism has been and is everywhere, at all times and in all places, how can there be an alternative to it— where would the alternative come from, how would it grow? If sexism's most notable feature has been its reach, its omnipresence, then how did it or might it permit an alternative? This problem pervades one of the most widely read and influential anthologies of feminist writings to appear on the American scene in the early 1970s, *Woman, Culture, and Society* (1971), edited by two Stanford University anthropologists, Michelle Rosaldo and Louise Lamphere.

The anthology came under the spell of the French theorist Claude Lévi-Strauss and his structuralism: "The current anthropological view draws on the observation that most and probably all contemporary societies, whatever their kinship organization or mode of subsistence, are characterized by some degree of male dominance." Most of the writers extended this observation to include societies throughout history—and thus they justified the presence of the three vast monoliths in the title, "Woman," "Culture," "Society." But this same anthology had to take into account a counterview—that patriarchal social organizations had grown up on the ruins of earlier matriarchies. The counterview implied that matriarchies, once existing, could be appropriated to provide images or ideals for the future—if there had once been an alternative to patriarchy, there could be one again.

This view itself had a long history, and it was—ironically enough—a male production. In the mid-nineteenth century, it had flourished under the influence of various kinds of evolutionary theories, especially Marxism as Engels presented it in *The Origin of the Family, Private Property, and the State*. The Marxist evolutionary implication of the matriarchist view was that sexism is a prejudice that will wither away with the social organization that produces and fosters it, patriarchy, and this transformation will come with socialism. The classless societies of socialism, then, would reverse what Engels called "the world defeat of women": the establishment of patriarchal systems, associated with the rise of far-flung and populous agricultural states organized along class lines. In such settled circumstances—so different from smaller, nomadic or semi-nomadic groupings—women first became wives, controlled by their husbands, domesticated, relegated to a private sphere, their sexuality and reproduction regulated. Male assertion of paternity, which, Engels stressed, required knowledge of how reproduction takes place, replaced the natural, obvious maternal filiation.

As soon as the matriarchal thesis appeared at the turn of the century—from the German Bachofen and the American Morgan, as well as from Engels—it was contested by anthropologists opposed to evolutionary theories and opposed to the idea that in the beginning of human life there had been any kind of organization that was not patriarchal and that did not reflect the (alleged) biological facts of male superiority in strength. During the second wave of feminism, the same position was reiterated despite efforts like Ashley Montagu's in *The Natural Superiority of Women* (1952) to debunk pseudoscientific claims about male strength (which always equated strength with adult physical size and muscle mass, not lower infant mortality rates, greater longevity, or better endurance). Masculine hunting parties, so Lionel Tiger argued in *Men in Groups* (1969), provided the foundations of human kinship orders. Or, in the less tendentious Lévi-Straussian formulation, which Simone de Beauvoir had echoed, asymmetry between the sexes has always and everywhere characterized human societies. In Beauvoir's words: "Society has always been male; political power has always been in the hands of men"; "the triumph of the patriarchate was nèither a matter of chance nor the result of a violent revolution. From humanity's beginnings, their biological advantage has enabled males to affirm their status as sole and sovereign subjects."[20]

But the evolutionary strain persisted, and in recent feminism it has been refined and made much more plausible than it was in Engels's version. Contemporary feminists realize that the idea that a matriarchy—a social form in which women rule in the political or governmental sense—preceded patriarchy is implausible and as yet without empirical or archaeological support.[21] But much evidence can be summoned for the more modest claim that when women became wives and their reproductive capacity was put at the service of husbands-fathers, they lost the relative equality of their earlier condition. Agricultural societies depend upon labor, and children are the labor of the future—so children have, for the men who cannot produce them, great value. Patriarchy, in this view, was initially the form of social organization that promoted high fertility rates and male control over children and labor. It kept women in a condition of pregnancy or child care for the better part of their mature lives. As the Danish scholar Marielouise Janssen-Jurriet put the matter summarily in her *Sexism: The Male Monopoly on History and Thought* (1976): "The quintessence of patriarchy is the male control of reproduction, which is oriented to maximize security for the individual paterfamilias, the oldest member of the clan, the chieftain or the men of the ruling social classes."[22]

Her version of Marxism takes reproduction resulting in surplus population, not production resulting in surplus value, as its central analytical category for criticizing capitalism. For feminist activists, the implication of such an analysis of sexism is that women must take control of their own reproductive capacities. What Janssen-Jurriet calls "birth strike" is the ultimate antisexism, and such political struggles as the one over freedom of choice in the matter of abortion are key. In general, this kind of theorizing suggests that women must understand independently what mothering is or can be and what it implies, and such a focus connects political theorists and activists with a turbulent stream of thought coming from a contested source—psychoanalysis.

## Psychoanalytic Interpretations of Sexism

During the 1960s and early 1970s—a period of rage in American feminist circles about Freud's supposedly sexist view of female development and psychology, as well as rage in homosexual circles about the way in which Freudian therapists were treating homosexuality as a psychopathology and working to "cure" homosexuals—few noticed that the very same feminists who were dynamiting Freud's views on women were using his views on men. Kate Millett, for example, who ferociously denounced Freud, was completely indebted to him for her understanding of sexism as a form of unacknowledged male bonding—unacknowledged male homoeroticism—purveyed most intimately "at the level of copulation." Her *Sexual Politics* had enormous shock-power as it presented a gallery of male characters in American novels who were entranced with violent anal intercourse, which Millett interpreted as intercourse they would, unconsciously, rather have had with males. In psychological terms, "sexual politics," the feminist claim that "the personal is political," meant that male psychology as interpreted by Freud is inflicted on women sexually. But it also meant that male psychologizing, indebted to Freud, circumscribes understandings of female psychology.

Two developments were necessary to make it possible for feminists to appropriate psychoanalytic theorizing about female psychology. The socialist theoretician Juliet Mitchell provided the first, thoroughly and forcefully, with publication of her *Psychoanalysis and Feminism* in 1974. Mitchell's intricate and courageous book suggested that Freud's view of female psychology—or, rather, views, as Mitchell understood that there was no single, finished view—could profitably be read as a portrait of female psychology under patriarchy. Freud did not present Woman without context; he presented his patients, middle-class Viennese women at the turn of the century, suffering from historically situated pathologies, and Freud himself was working in the same context, delimited by it. Freud both reflected turn-of-the-century patriarchy and *analyzed it* in the medium of his patient's illnesses. To interpret Freud richly, Mitchell argued, requires reading *him* sociopsychologically and understanding his work sociopsychologically. (One consequence of this approach—not, I think, intended by Mitchell—has been that psychopathology has been construed by many feminists as socially induced, rather than just socially shaped, so that Freud's nosology, or his typology of the neuroses and psychoses, which relied so heavily on notions of unconscious causation or "the return of the repressed," has been disregarded in feminism.)[23]

The second development that made psychoanalysis newly appropriable by feminists was also fostered by Mitchell's work. She noted that Freudian psychoanalysis is not the only kind of psychoanalysis, and she introduced her English and American readers to the controversial French theoretician Jacques Lacan. In the next several years, a literary critic, Dorothy Dinnerstein in *The Mermaid and the Minotaur,* and a sociologist, Nancy Chodorow in *The Reproduction of Mothering,* added to the expanding knowledge of psychoanalytic alternatives by introducing their readers to the largely English tradition generally called "object relations." This theory had gathered force in the 1940s spurred by the work of an émigré to England from Germany, Melanie Klein, and then developed through the work of analysts like Harry Guntrip, W. R. D. Fairbairn and, less directly, Donald Winnicott. Feminists combined these alternatives to the more strictly Freudian tradition of analysis, especially to the favored American development of that tradition, called "ego psychology," with a well-known earlier alternative, "cultural Freudianism," especially as expounded by Karen Horney and reflected in the "interpersonalist" work of Harry Stack Sullivan. Horney's theories had been used by Kate Millett and other late 1960s critics of Freud as well as by therapists like Jean Baker Miller in *Toward a New Psychology of Women* (1976) because Horney's seemed to them to be the one existing psychoanalytic critique of the most hated Freudian doctrine, "penis envy."[24] But cultural Freudianism did not have the ingredient that was key to the object relations alternative—focus in the domain of female psychology on the preoedipal period of development, the first two years of life. In the 1970s, the rise of the "preoedipal" into the forefront of psychoanalytic work was both fostered by and conducive to feminism's purposes. Viewing the preoedipal, posited as the determinative period of human development for males and females, as a period under female control, meant it was reformable by females.

The psychoanalytic alternatives were, because of their emphasis on developmental origins, the equivalents in depth psychology of the theories of origin developed by Marxist feminists. Psychoanalytic feminists looked to the era in individual development that was dominated by women, by mothers, as the social theorists had looked to matriarchy. The story of how baby girls become women and baby boys become men is the story of mothering, or of the internalization of mothering practices and mother images. In addition, feminists developing object relations and cultural psychoanalysis moved away from not just Freud's emphasis on the oedipal period but also his theory of instinctual drives. They did not subscribe to the notion that developmental phases are organized around oral, anal, and phallic erotogenic zones or that mature sexuality—heterosexuality—is genital dominance over all other libidinal urges and zones. It was just this theory—caricatured with the phrase "anatomy is destiny"—that had seemed to feminists to assign females, as nonphallic creatures, to sexual submission ("passivity") and eternal longing for the phallus. If psychoanalysis could be appropriated without giving up the key feminist achievement—distinguishing sex from gender, biological femaleness from socially constructed femininity—that is, if there could be a psychoanalysis that did not say "anatomy is destiny," then the anathema against psychoanalysis could be lifted.

The alternative psychoanalytic traditions, except for Lacanianism, begin with an elementary notation as their starting point: both females and males are born from a mother and begin their lives at her breast, in her care, psychically undifferentiated from her, in the womb of her feelings, her mothering. Both female and male children experience with a mother both their first pleasures and their first frustrations, they know hunger and satiation. She is, as her children grow and grow slowly separate from her—as they begin to individuate—an awesome figure to them. She has the power of pleasure and displeasure over them, she has the power to give and withhold narcissistic supplies. Individuating involves, necessarily, loss. For little girls and for little boys, however, the process takes very different forms. And these alternative psychoanalytic traditions emphasize the differences in female and male individuation processes as the key differences, in contradistinction to the emphasis placed in Freud's work on differentiation taking place over discovery of anatomical sexual dissimilarity. It is not the boy's horror (felt and then immediately denied) at the girl's "castrated" state or the girl's envy (felt immediately on viewing the phallus and then sustained) that mark the divergence in their psychic conditions. The ways in which the girl identifies with her mother and the boy disidentifies are what make them part company.

Along with the focus on mother-infant or "dyadic" interactions, the object relations school stresses the common tendency in people of both sexes to split their first object, their mother, into "good" and "bad"—supplying and frustrating—aspects. They banish the "bad" and very frighteningly powerful mother from later consciousness and retain the "good" in the form of later objects. Thus, men look for the "good" mother in women, which requires that their women be only nourishing, giving, comforting, warm, unthreatening, submissive. The wife they look for is the mother minus her power, which makes the husband the little boy minus all the littleness and powerlessness he felt in relation to his mother. The male's capacity to reverse the power equation with his mother in his relation with his wife means that he does not have to disparage his wife or devalue her—her qualities are very valuable, indeed, ideal. This is sexism of the "women are wonderful as long as they are wonderful to and for me" sort.

But sexism as active devaluation is, of course, also common, and within the Melanie Klein object relations tradition, it is charged primarily to envy. Klein, who defined envy generally as the angry feeling one person experiences when another person possesses and enjoys something desirable, which produces an impulse to steal or spoil that something, believed that the infant's first and paradigmatic envious feelings are directed at the mother's breast. Children want to incorporate the breast, to gain for themselves its milk, its awesome power. She felt that a girl's penis envy rests, ultimately, on this breast envy—that the penis is experienced as a source of power on the model of the breast. Formulations like Klein's, moreover, allowed analysts to bring into the sphere of their investigations a phenomenon in males that Freud had noted—particularly in his case study of five-year-old "Little Hans"—and that Karen Horney had explored but which had not been widely pursued: the envy that little boys display of breasts and also of wombs, of the woman's capacity to make babies. "Womb envy" became a staple concept. And analysts noted that the strongest defense men (and women) summon against envy is devaluation. Sexism, in this sense, is a defense against the desire to have the maternal breast, to be maternal or to regain the merger or symbiosis with the mother that is given up with growing up.

Both the sexism of idealizing women—which implies circumscribing them, allowing them only certain ideal qualities—and the sexism of devaluing them, then, can be tracked to the complexities of individuation, of separating from the all-powerful mother. In crude terms, the psychoanalytic ideas that came into feminism in the late 1970s are ideas that distinguish girls as members of their mother's domain and boys as exiles into the domain of the fathers, where they achieve their autonomy with respect to their early dependency on the mother. To males, the mother represents lack of autonomy, regression. Sexism, then, is the social manifestation of the psychic legacy in men of their separation, their disidentification, their rejection of the feminine in their mothers and also (as a product of early identification) in themselves. The right social therapy for sexism, it follows, will be one that repairs the separation of male and female spheres and the family configuration that results in what the analyst Grete Bibring had diagnosed (in 1953) as "too much of mother" and too little of father.[25] Generally, the therapy has been called "shared parenting," which means bringing the fathers into the domain of mothering, diminishing their not-mother status, their status as other and better because not tied to the dangerous aspects of the mother's power. If fathers were also nourishers, providers, objects of earliest identifications, children of both sexes would be more mixed in terms of their object relations—more fully relational.

As the feminist movement theoreticians used the various psychoanalytic theories focused on the mother-child dyad, making these common fare, some also found it possible to reuse some of the older, more Freudian theorizing as well. For example, there are feminists now who think that the therapy for the separation of male and female spheres and its attendant complexes is not shared parenting but positive reevaluation of the maternal sphere. To these feminists, the argument that sexism flows from the fact of mothering, the types of mothering, and the psychosocial complexities of children's individuation processes, looks like blaming women for sexism. Male dominance escapes focus. The problem of sexism, this argument goes, is located further along the developmental line of childhood. It stems from the ways in which preoedipal differences are sealed into place not by mothers but by the great weight of patriarchal marriage. Women are, as the sociologist Miriam Johnson puts it in her book title, *Strong Mothers, Weak Wives* (1988), and it is in their marriages that they are unable to protect their children from the sexist habits and arrangements of the family. The origin of sexism, in other words, is a predominantly oedipal matter; it has to do with how girls turn toward their fathers and learn from them how to be, forever, Daddy's little girl; and it has to do with how boys enter into their father's world and into male peer groups, especially adolescent peer groups, learning there the basics of male dominance.

The assumption behind this kind of argument is that people can be helped to appreciate the maternal qualities that have been devalued. They can come to see that what has been called "lack of autonomy" or lack of achieved disidentification with the mother in women is really lack of the cold, distant, abstractly logical, unrelational, or monadically differentiated male life-form that has been so destructive, for women, for men themselves, for the world. Women are uniquely able to mother, and also could be uniquely able to foster in their children antisexist attitudes if they could learn to value what they do, who they are—if their self-esteem could be improved. The goal of diminishing differences between the sexes, minimizing gender distinctions, then, looks like a loss for women, as it minimizes or undervalues their essential mothering capacity. From this point of view, the "reproduction of mothering" should give way not to the production of androgyny but to an appreciation of mothering. Feminists who took this "celebration of difference" position often noted that visions of androgyny can operate as covers for sexism in the way that visions of all group differences as ethnic differences can cover for racism. If one argues that all differences between men and women are socially constructed and can be socially reconstructed in the direction of androgyny, then the history of sexism as an ideology based on alleged biological differences may disappear from view or be underestimated. Androgyny then looks like an invitation to women to assimilate into masculinity as blacks have been urged to assimilate into white culture (and then been blamed when they failed to do so).[26]

## A Hidden Dynamic

Neither the feminist theories that emphasize the social construction of gender identity and look forward to a more androgynous future nor those that emphasize the essential female capacity, motherhood, and look forward to a future in which this capacity and femaleness in general are understood and appreciated really focus in on the psychosocial dynamics of male dominance or male supremacy. Neither disidentification with their mothers nor identification with their fathers explains how and why men become sexist. Psychoanalytic theories of sexism have shown that sexism has many modes: it can involve idealizing women, derogating them and emphasizing their "castrated" physical and mental inferiority, envying and fearing their bodies and reproductive capacities, viewing them as "other" than the fathers, excluding them from male peer groups, using them indirectly for homoerotic purposes. These different modes have diverse developmental origins—developmentally, they constitute many layers of sexism—and they command or suffuse diverse kinds of social organizations. But how these modes relate is not clear, and analyses of these modes have not revealed sexism's specificity as a prejudice.

Sexism, in contrast to antisemitism and racism, is a prejudice or an ideology of desire marked by its multiplicity or layering of manifestations and by its grandiosity as it embraces nature and social organization, as it permeates all cultures. Both the layering and the grandiosity reveal what I call the narcissism of sexism, which, it seems to me, is rooted in an elementary narcissistic experience, one portrayed by the anthropologist and psychoanalyst George Devereux in these terms:

> The fact that mankind is made up of males and females has never been accepted as an *irreducible* fact, which just happens to exist. It was experienced both as an intellectual challenge and as a source of anxiety as far back as human records—including myths—go . . .
>
> Now, it is self-evident that man seeks to "justify" ( = explain metaphysically) or to mythologize only those natural phenomena whose irreducible character he refuses to concede. Hence the fact that mankind has always mythologized—most recently in scientific jargon—the existence of the two sexes, is *prima facie* evidence that he refuses to accept this as an *irreducible* fact, whose understanding can only be impeded by the assumption that it is something to be "explained," i.e., to be justified metaphysically . . .
>
> In short, each human being was and is perplexed by the fact that another being, congruent in nearly every respect with his (or her) self-model, should, in one respect—sexuality—be so different. One's bewilderment and exasperation in the presence of the opposite sex is not unlike that experienced in the presence of the ape, who simply has no "right" to be at once so much like one's self-model and yet so different from it. Moreover, men and women are probably even more perplexed than dogs would be if they could think about it, that the opposite sex should also belong to their own species simply because sexual dimorphism is *more pronounced* in mankind—though not to the same extent in all races—than in most other mammals. Moreover, much of mankind's high degree of sexual dimorphism is due to the *women's* conspicuous femaleness; she is sexually always receptive and has permanent breasts. Man is not much more obviously male than the stallion; woman is more conspicuously female than the mare.[27]

Devereux here pinpoints an elemental experience that can take on diverse meanings in the different stages of children's lives and in the events of adults' lives, in diverse configurations of individuals' characters and in different social organizations and cultural traditions. There is an elemental anxiety, an inability to tolerate difference, a threat to narcissism—"She (or he) is not like me." And the anxiety that surrounds the experience is frequently silenced with an elemental denial—"Yes, she (or he) is really like me; or I am really like him (or her), or I will be in the future." But reality, the reality of difference, always challenges this kind of denial. Sexism keeps the denial in place, it keeps the hope of sameness alive. In its most elementary forms sexism keeps alive the male child's belief that his mother is like him, even to the point that she has a phallus like his. The female child's belief that her mother is like her is not challenged, although she may experience great anxiety about when and how she will have breasts, pubic hair; she and her mother can remain, as it were, a narcissistic "we" as she discovers male difference.

Why, Henry Higgins wanted to know in the archetypically sexist manner, can't a woman be more like a man? Why can't she be as the mother initially was—all-powerful, all-providing, part of him, not other or different? Why, women want to know, can't my oneness with my mother last forever, without interruption from him?

Feminist theory has taken Difference as its focus, its organizing theme. What do the anatomical and reproductive differences between the sexes mean—what have they meant historically, what do they mean, what can they mean? what should they mean? Or, to put the matter the other way around in terms of the distinction between sex and gender, how do socially constructed differences influence people's experiences of biological differences? how do familially and socially constructed differences become institutionalized—in our bodies and psyches, in our societies? The problem with all of these questions has been and remains finding a place to stand to pose them, finding a language to speak about experiences and institutions that have thoroughly shaped and determined language (and, some would say, even the "language" that is the unconscious). In historical terms and psychological terms, there has been a search for Before Difference—an originary state with which the psychic and social history of Difference could be compared, a state that, if reached, could be the place to stand for comprehending Difference. In recent feminism, Before Difference has meant the "preoedipal" or the matriarchal. Correlated with the various images of Before Difference have been visions of After Difference, a redemptive future in which differences either minimize and disappear or are reevaluated so that women do not loose out or come in second.

Nevertheless, although sexism has been generally understood, by theorists of otherwise diverse views, as the sum total of ways in which Difference has been claimed, evaluated, and instituted, its motivational dynamic has been neglected. Under or behind the vast scope and weight of the ways in which Difference has been claimed, evaluated, and instituted, that motivational dynamic has been obscured. Sexism is propelled not by desire for Difference but by nostalgic desire for Before Difference or denial of Difference, and feminist analyses of sexism often partake in this nostalgia and denial, creating as they do images of Before Difference female superiority, a kind of countersexism or female narcissistic idealizing of the mother-infant daughter bond or a matriarchal period. They reveal a longing to return to unchallenged narcissism, to which psychoanalysts give the name "primary narcissism," a deep regressive pull: "we are all alike here."

But sexism is also propelled by the defeat—the inevitable defeat—of that nostalgia, as all nostalgic people (male and female) who are not psychotically disconnected from reality must confront what Devereux called the "irreducible fact" again and again. Reactively, they may stress Difference, accentuating the irreducible fact in diverse ways, separating the spheres of male and female characteristics and activities, even to the point of pushing the different one, the Other, so far away as to make her (or him) virtually inhuman, monstrous, or nonexistent. Or they may construct a realm After Difference, a transcendent, angelic future, an androgynous utopia, or a vision of humankind, a oneness of people in comparison with which all differences are superficial, trivial, or nonexistent. They may say "different but equal," hoping that equality will minimize differences. Most basically, they may formulate ideas about the naturalness of simple heterosexual desire, that is, desire for members of the opposite sex conceived *only* as simply male/masculine or simply female/feminine, rather than as complexly layered sites of sex and gender images of diverse sorts. But these ideological formations all represent the failure of a nostalgic desire for what might be called the homo-sex world.

I am not just reconstructing and criticizing a theoretical history here but making a claim about sexism, about the deepest motivational layer of sexism, a layer of denial of difference hidden beneath upper layers where sexual difference is emphasized, even exaggerated. In succeeding chapters, I will return to this claim from many angles and try to support it, argue for it, show its social significance. But I advance it here to make one further observation about why sexism has not had a place in the all-prejudices-are-one and racism-is-the-prejudice social science traditions.

Contemporary feminism descends from Beauvoir's formulation that "otherness is a fundamental category of human thought" and that women are the Other to men. Sartre, in *Anti-Semite and Jew,* had used the same existentialist premises to argue that all antisemites need an

Other, a scapegoat, against whom to direct their passions. And social scientists, as I have noted again and again, put forth the version that all groups establish out-groups, all peoples are ethnocentric. But precisely these formulations block access to a prejudice that denies differences, that, fundamentally, under layers of difference marking, wants no others.

.There certainly are prejudices in which an Other is wanted and needed. The racist uses external marks of difference—skin color, hair texture, and so forth—to be able to say "that woman is completely other than my mother" (loving her is not incestuous), "that man is not like my father" (loving him is not incestuous, murderous feelings toward him are not parricidal), "those people are not my siblings" (rivalrous hatred toward them is not fratricidal). Antisemitism also establishes an Other. But there the similarity ends, for Other must be eliminated. The antisemite does not want to keep the Other in place; he or she wants to attack the Other (who is viewed as attacking and soiling) and cleanse the world of him or her. In quite distinct ways, then, the formulation that prejudices are directed at the Other will hold for racism and antisemitism, but not for sexism.

When white American feminists tried to draw analogies between racism and sexism, African Americans protested their insensitivity to the experiences of women of color, victims of both prejudices. Rightly, black feminists insisted on the troika race-gender-class. But this formulation has its limits, too, even though it effectively reminds everyone that racism, sexism, and classism (or, more simply, relegation to poverty) come together in and into black women's lives. What the formulation does not show is the specificities of the combination. The racism and classism of white men and women say to the black woman "you are the Other" (not a pure white woman, you are lower), and images of her as a loose woman, a whore, follow. But the sexism of males says to her "you are the same" (a man like us). This last denial of difference is not as well hidden as when it is expressed by an in-group, without the racism-classism combination: the black woman is said to be matriarchal, meaning that she wears the pants in the Black family, is the head of the house, is the man, but also meaning that she is the Mammy, the first (and phallic) mother who is like the man.

In saying that sexism has helped rule sexism out of social scientific consideration, I mean on one level that male-dominated scientists have not cared about or even seen women, women's issues, or issues that should be approached with sex or gender differences in mind. But I also want to suggest that there exists a dynamic in sexism itself—or in the narcissism that manifests itself in sexism—that keeps sexism from view even when it is being studied or considered.

As part of its functioning, each of the prejudices involves modes in which it defies understanding or refuses to come out into the open, ways in which it blocks access to its dynamics, even when being studied. Studies of racism keep returning to superficiality because the hard truths about racism's deep sexual roots, which have been spoken clearly—particularly in the late 1960s—by racism's victims, are intolerable. The victims' voices have been, I think, felt as voices exposing the hidden past, the sexual sins, the family secrets that bind "higher" and "lower" to each other intimately; their voices have been experienced as "the return of the repressed"—and they have been rerepressed by racists. Studies of racism get caught up in this dynamic of racism itself. And the characteristic psychology of racists fills those who approach it with anxiety, because it is so mobile, so chameleon-like, volatile, changeable, usually moody. The typical duplicity of racists—their tendency to live double lives, often one of respectability and one of scandal, one of genteel uprightness and one of violence, in turns—makes analysts distrust their perceptions. They feel the missing life, sense the repression, but are confused, particularly when the "good" side of racist psychology is showing.

Repression, the key defense of racists, is not, however, the mode that keeps antisemitism from view. Antisemites undo or make disappear the history of their thoughts and deeds. They specialize in the peculiar psychic business of making what has happened disappear—they split it off from their own consciousnesses, as they have split off any feelings they have for their victims, and they write what has happened out of history. They engage in a kind of obsessive magical thinking, for example, that subtends the most widespread current form in which antisemitism is perpetrated—denial of the Holocaust. Students of antisemitism suffer from incredulity when they encounter this splitting off and undoing in antisemitism and in antisemites. The psychology of the antisemite baffles them. It is so unfeeling, so dissociative, so cut off from affect or emotion, so rigid and self-perpetuating, so impervious to influence, that it seems completely foreign. In either a mode of charmed fascination or a mode of moral repulsion—or sometimes both—their incredulity paralyzes their investigations.

Studies of sexism, by contrast, have been circumscribed—although in their ambitions they have been as sweeping as the prejudice they have sought to compass. Many elements of the psychodynamics and sociodynamics of sexism have been isolated, described, and analyzed; but they have not, then, been framed developmentally, and, most important, the question of origins has not been put clearly. The narcissism that is sexism has been fought with the narcissism that is feminism, but the feminist fighters have been restricted by the punch and counterpunch. As a mode of nostalgia, narcissistic desire is aimed at a fantasized originary condition—but cannot understand *another's* way of fantasizing an originary condition. Visions of matriarchies or of empowering pre-oedipal mother-daughter dyadic relations are visions that are blind to the male nostalgic narcissistic vision of phallic mothers, also a blindness, which is the origin of sexism.

# 5

## The Homophobias

Each of the prejudices that have commanded attention in the growth era of American social science—antisemitism after the war, racism in the late 1950s and 1960s, sexism in the 1970s—has a dynamic history that renders it opaque to inquiry. Antisemitism, which is manifested in analsadistic chimeria that repel investigation, took a form in Nazi Germany that was too horrible to contemplate; racism involves a form of repression that makes it difficult (anxiety producing) to see its paternalistic, erotic past operating in its competitive present; sexism is "natural" (ego syntonic) for half the species and also takes a great diversity of forms stemming from different developmental moments and referenced to different social conditions that obscure it for the other half. These complexities mean, I have tried to show, that any approach to these prejudices must go through the cumulative history of studies in prejudice to chip away the crust of distortions the complexities have produced. The key distortion obscuring the origins and developmental histories of the prejudices themselves is the idea that prejudice is one. And this distortion has become, as the postwar decades have unfolded, more and more debilitating. It has helped set the study of sexism—a prejudice of vast multiplicity—theoretically and practically out of bounds of the social sciences. And the same problem has arisen over the latest focus of study, homophobia, which has met with a similar resistance but which is even more obscure in its multiplicity because all the types of prejudice can appear in homophobic forms.

137

In the sexism theories I have outlined, individual-level and societal-level approaches (psychology and sociology) are obviously much better integrated than in theories of antisemitism and racism. Both the types of societal-level theories I surveyed—the Marxist evolutionary ones and the Lévi-Straussian nonrevolutionary ones—imply that families and child-rearing practices contribute to sexism, and in this claim they meet up with the psychoanalytically informed individual-level theories. The patriarchal family is the mediating term, as it was in *The Authoritarian Personality*. This integration was made possible, however, because the psychoanalytically informed individual-level theories are almost free of such Freudian ingredients as the unconscious and unconscious fantasies, the instinctual drive theory, the whole Freudian psychopathology. In the Freudian view, these concepts helped explain the uniqueness of individuals, but in the feminist appropriation of psychoanalysis sees no individuals: there are girls and boys, females and males, mothers and fathers. Women are their feminine roles and men are their masculine roles.[1]

The integration—problematic as it is—of individual level and societal-level theories in feminist work on sexism is essential for studying prejudices. It will provide a point of departure for the study of prejudices offered later in this book. But first I conclude this critical historical tour of theoretical work on antisemitism, racism, and sexism with a discussion of how "homophobia" came into being and, like sexism, fell outside social scientific study of prejudice (as ethnocentrism or as race prejudice). This story also merges individual-level and societal-level theorizing, but the condition for the merger was not a mediating or bridging focus—the family's child-rearing practices—but rather the destruction (more technically, the deconstruction) of the concept of normality.

## Depathologizing

In 1973, under great pressure from homophile groups, the American Psychiatric Association revised its *Diagnostic and Statistical Manual* and removed "homosexuality" from its list of diseases. Homosexuality had been considered a disease for the better part of a century, while continuing to be a religious sin and, indeed, an abomination. This climatic change had begun when into the arsenal of homophile activists came a major statistical study of American men—Alfred Kinsey's *Sexual Behavior in the Human Male* (1948)—that indicated, to the astonishment of most

Americans, that 37 percent of the population surveyed would admit to homosexual activity of some degree. Kinsey's surprising work then inspired *Patterns of Sexual Behavior* (1951), by Clellan Ford and Frank Beach, which showed male homosexual activity of some sort to be normal and acceptable in forty-nine out of seventy-seven cultures studied through an anthropological data archive. As far as clinicians were concerned, the most influential item in the developing literature of the 1950s was Evelyn Hooker's research with a nonclinical homosexual population of thirty men, whose performances on projective tests like the Rorschach she compared to those of thirty heterosexuals of similar backgrounds and educational levels. The results, adjudicated and reviewed by a panel of clinicians, showed that in terms of pathology the homosexuals were no different from the heterosexuals—two-thirds of each group ranked as well adjusted as the average or better. Hooker's research also revealed a great diversity of personality types and patterns of sexual behavior within the homosexual population. She found no "homosexual personality." Drawing on Gordon Allport's *Nature of Prejudice*, Hooker, in addition, showed how the victimization and victim status of homosexuals produced disturbances in them, and this part of her research particularly informed the work she did later as head of the National Institute for Mental Health Task Force on Homosexuality, which produced a progressive report in 1972.[2]

In the 1960s, particularly after several psychiatrists came forth with strident works on homosexuality as a disease, the homophile movement focused its attention on the idea that homosexuality is a sickness and began using the growing sociological, anthropological, and clinical literature to articulate a forceful critique. The movement was aided in this effort to fight science with science by many within the psychotherapeutic community who saw no justification for the clinical assumption that homosexuals are pathological. These professionals did not cite Freud, as they might have. Indeed, mental health professionals, including most psychoanalysts, seemed quite unaware that Freud had explicitly condemned the psychiatric practice in his day of treating homosexuals as pathological. "Psychoanalytic research is most decidedly opposed to any attempt at separating off homosexuals from the rest of mankind as a group of special character," he had written in 1915.[3]

By studying sexual excitations other than those that are manifestly displayed, it has been found that all human beings are capable of making a homosexual object-choice and have in fact made one in their unconscious. Indeed, libidinal attachments to persons of the same sex play no less a part as factors in normal mental life, and a greater part as a motive force for illness, than do similar attachments to the op- posite sex. On the contrary, psychoanalysis considers that a choice of object independently of sex—freedom to range equally over male and female objects—as it is found in childhood, in primitive states of so- ciety and early periods of history, is the original basis on which, as a result of restriction in one direction or the other, both the normal and the inverted types develop. Thus from the point of view of psy- choanalysis, the exclusive sexual interest felt by men for women [or women for men] is also a problem that needs elucidating, and is not a self-evident fact based upon an attraction that is ultimately of a chem- ical nature.

Optimistically, Freud had predicted that the comparative studies then being produced by anthropologists, which had reached conclusions sim- ilar to those in Ford and Beach's *Patterns of Sexual Behavior,* would take discussions of homosexuality out of the domains of medical men: "The pathological approach to the study of inversion has been displaced by the anthropological," he had announced in 1905. Unaware of Freud's clearly stated views, or unable to find them behind half a century of distortion and misuse of his science, the homophile critics attacked the versions of psychoanalytic theory that presented heterosexuality as nar- rowly normative.

As with feminists, the attack on psychoanalysis generally focused on any formulation of a biological or an instinctual drive theory, and the alternative always emphasized the social construction of gender identity and sexual preference. At the same time, in the process of critique, the notion took shape that there is a specific kind of prejudice against ho- mosexuals, which has operated in society at large and in psychiatry's definition of normality. The general American public, and many ho- mosexuals, found the most important summary of the emergent critique of heterosexuality-as-normality in the book that popularized the word "homophobia" (coined in the late 1960s): George Weinberg's *Society and the Healthy Homosexual* (1972).[4]

Homophile organizations burgeoned in the 1960s and, learning from the Civil Rights movement, grew more assertive. By 1968, analogies be- tween racism and prejudice against homosexuals flourished, and the reply of the victims—"Gay is good"—explicitly followed "Black is beautiful." But it is important to note that no sustained theoretical elaborations of the analogy with racism were developed; homosexuality was not seen as a kind of slavery or as a form of paternalism. The analogy was, rather, a matter of practical politics as Gay pride was born and tested. In June of 1969 the emergent movement had its refusal to go to the back of the bus: customers of a gay bar in Greenwich Village, the Stonewall Inn, responded to a police action against the bar with a violent protest that spread out over the neighborhood and went on for days. The watershed protest was and still is celebrated annually at rallies and demonstrations.

But, unlike the Civil Rights movement, the Gay Liberation movement, although it had its large public marches and many of its organizations focused on legal challenges to combat workplace and housing discrimination, had a specific point of attack—the psychiatric establishment. Critical theory and practical politics combined when the most assertive and unrestrained of its demonstrations took place at the annual meetings of the American Psychiatric Association and other professional groups. Rightly, the leadership realized that until the stigma of being diseased was removed, homosexuals would never be able "to live in dignity" or to combat the older but still powerful form of prejudice against homosexuals prevalent in Jewish and Christian milieus—the charge that their sexual practice, being nonreproductive, was immoral. The psychiatric associations were understood, that is, to be the keepers of the definition of homosexuality and the official pathologizers of the homosexual. When psychiatry formally, officially relented, the churches were the next target.

## Capturing the Ground of Definition

The first thing that should be noted about the category "homosexual" is that it is not clear who should be registered in it. It is not a visibility category like "woman" or "person of color." In terms of visibility, "homosexual" has more of the indeterminacy of "Jew," which compelled Nazi antisemites to mark physically those whom they considered Jewish with a yellow Star of David, for example. But the Jews are a birth group; they have a genealogical history, and they extend their identity as a group from generation to generation, debating as they do which laws of inclusion and descent will keep them defined by themselves and not by antisemites. Homosexuals are given birth to if not always by heterosexuals at least by means of heterosexual intercourse (except in artificially aided conceptions). Like women, homosexuals pervade all "racial" and most if not all ethnic population groups; the chances that a homophobe will be hating someone who is kin are very great. Homosexuals are not a group unless they are made to be one or unless they respond to discrimination by organizing; they do not have a culture until they have been made into a subculture. Jean-Paul Sartre once remarked that if the Jews did not exist the antisemites would have invented them—a remark which is quite untrue of the antisemites and the Jews, but which covers the situation of the homophobes and the homosexuals very well. The homophobes *have* invented the homosexuals.

In societies where homosexual activity is not framed in identifying rituals, a homosexual is not visually identifiable unless he or she chooses to be by behaving, dressing, or talking in manners agreed to be homosexual, or by adopting homosexual insignia, or by joining homosexual organizations. A homosexual is not identifiable by the company he or she keeps, unless, again, a choice is made to be so identifiable. A homosexual is not even identifiable by the sex of his or her sexual partners, as many people who will, at some point, identify themselves as homosexuals have had sexual partners of the opposite sex, exclusively or most or some of the time. (In homophobic cultures, heterosexuals do not generally chose to have homosexual partners openly—but this does happen under conditions of deprivation, when partners of the opposite sex are unavailable, and the technical term for it is "contingent homosexuality.") The term "sexual preference" is ambiguous, as many people do not act on their preferences, so those preferences can be known only if the preferrers know them and make them known. (There are, that is, "psychological homosexuals"—those in whom homoerotic desires and fantasies preponderate—who are heterosexual in object choice and may not even be conscious of their homosexuality.) But as Kinsey so clearly emphasized, the homosexual is a kind of fiction, because homosexual behavior occurs along a continuum, ranging from entertaining homoerotic fantasies to having a single experience or period of experience to exclusive preference. And at least some people can move back and forth on the continuum during their lifetime—from a homosexual preference in adolescence, for example, to heterosexuality in adulthood, or vice versa. Such complexities have led many people to say, simply, a homosexual is a person who identifies himself or herself as a homosexual.

A homosexual's self-identification means, however, nothing to a homophobe. Homophobia is an assertion of control over the category "homosexual." Homophobes try to seize the power of definition. As all the cognitively inclined students of prejudice note, prejudice—and they would used the singular—involves faulty generalizations. Such generalizations take the form "All Jews [or most, if tokens and exceptions are needed] are filthy [or filthy rich] and always scheming for power"; or "Negroes are ignorant, lazy, and primitively sexual"; or "Women cannot reason—they're too emotional—and they were meant by nature to stay home and serve men [sexually]." Prejudices against homosexuals do not take such a form. People do, of course, speak of homosexuals as a general category (sometimes divided in two, gay men and lesbians), but no standard adjectives follow. Each generalizer's focusing fear or anxiety provides the predicate—if there is one, and there may be only a blank full of vague anger or discomfort, or a tautological spinning of the definitional wheels ("gays are . . . pansies [meaning female])." What is directed at homosexuals is not a standard, stereotyping adjective but the charge "he/she is a homosexual." The category itself—and whatever it means to the individual using it—is the main accusation: "Faggot!" "Dyke!"

Homophobia is mainly a category accusation because it is primarily directed at acts and what acts represent in fantasy, and only secondarily at the people who commit those acts, even though this century has given those people a distinct name. This is the one ideological prejudice that aims at *doing*, not *being*. Homophobic Christian fundamentalists, for example, currently rail against the "homosexual lifestyle," which they hold to be immoral and unnatural, and they are willing to tolerate homosexuals as long as the homosexuals do not declare themselves or engage in homosexual acts. The American military has currently adopted this view and tolerates homosexuals but not homosexual acts (or identifications). Homosexual acts—"sodomy"—are criminal. In other words, homophobes hate acts that they themselves can and usually do engage in, so, to repudiate these acts they must assign them clearly to another category of people. The category is all that stands between them and those acts. In Freudian terms, as they are repudiating their own pasts, their childhood and adolescent desires, they must be able to say "only *those* people do *that*," or "*this* is wrong only when done by *them*." When the differences between themselves and certain types of homosexuals are clear, homophobes are less strident about categories. They can go to Mardi Gras in New Orleans and enjoy being photographed with the drag queens. But when homosexuals are too close to home—when they hold hands or kiss in public like heterosexuals—the line of difference, the categorization, is threatened and homophobes are enraged.[5]

Because control of the definition of "homosexual" and control over who is to be registered in the category are central to homophobia, definitional questions are also central to—and tend to contaminate—efforts made by scientists, social scientists, and declared homosexuals to understand what homosexuality is, a question that logically precedes the question of who is homosexual. In current debates, there are those who say that homosexuality is a type of desire determined by some biological predisposition—some gene, some hormonal or neurohormonal configuration, some anatomical feature—and then manifest in behaviors that, in even the most varied cultural contexts, are rooted in those biological invariants. There is same-sex desire, that is, and it appears in different culturally influenced forms, so it is really not accurate to speak of "sexual preference," as homosexuality is not a matter of choice or "sexual orientation." Some subscribers to this view would go on to say that same-sex desire appears everywhere to some extent, in fact to the extent of the population cited in Kinsey's report as admitting to *being* homosexual—10 percent.

In the early days of the Gay Liberation movement, this essentialist, biologically oriented position was assumed by gay activists to be homophobic (as feminists assumed that "anatomy is destiny" is sexist). But since then it has exercised a great appeal among homosexuals for the simple reason that it implies they have no choice about their sexuality. If homosexuality is biologically determined, then, of course, no homosexual can help being homosexual. The shift toward accepting this position came about during a time when gay activists sought to counter charges of homosexual "promiscuity," either because they needed to assert that they could control disease (especially AIDS) transmission within their communities or because they needed to assert that homosexuals cannot influence the sexuality of children and should thus be legally free to parent. But many individual homosexuals also discovered that their parents could be much more accepting if absolved of their anxieties about having done something "wrong" by producing a homosexual child. Unlike biologically based theories of racial and sexual inferiority, the biologically based theories of homosexuality have seemed controllable to many of their victims: the victims hope that determinism can be shown to imply only difference, not inferiority. Such a hope (delusory, in my opinion) simply shows that power over definitions is the goal of both homophobes and (reactively, defensively) many homosexual activists.

The opponents of such essentialist theorists, who usually call themselves "constructionists," argue that sexual identity and sexual behaviors are not biologically preprogrammed but develop over time in social contexts, through interactions with other people. This argument owes a great deal to the array of feminist claims that gender identity is socially constructed, that anatomy is *not* destiny. But recently the nonessentialist position has also been linked with arguments about the historical construction of the category "homosexuality." Often influenced by Michel Foucault's *History of Sexuality,* constructionists locate in eighteenth- and nineteenth-century Western bourgeois societies the use of "heterosexuality" and "homosexuality" with reference to exclusive sexual object choices and discrete cultures or subcultures. "Compulsory heterosexuality"—to use Adrienne Rich's phrase—is relatively recent and culturally specific, and so is its corollary or offshoot, exclusive homosexuality.

Homosexuality as it was practiced among the ancient Greeks—traditionally the society held up as the one most inclined and favorable toward homosexuality in the European world—was behavior initiated by married men with young boys, initiates, who would later be married men and themselves initiators of homosexual relationships. This was not homosexuality in the modern sense, as it involved neither exclusivity nor subcultural segregation, and to distinguish it most constructionists call it "pederasty." And neither is this pederasty the same thing as the ritualized fellatio practiced by not yet married older youths on younger youths in certain tribes in Papua New Guinea, which is a kind of transmission of potency from one male to another in cultures where it is felt that young men need male nurture to become maturely masculine. Nor is Greek pederasty like the ritualized intercourse between a Native American *berdache,* a male who has from childhood been dressed as a female and assigned certain female functions, and the older male to whom the *berdache* has been married in a public ceremony.

Both essentialists and constructionists recognize that prejudice against homosexuals in any given time and place will be related to either the specific form that the constant same-sex desire takes (in the essentialist view) or the current form of the variable homosexuality (in the constructionist view). Most recent historians who have studied Greek homosexuality agree that it was quite acceptable, even celebrated, as long as it took the prescribed forms—as long as older men initiated young men, behaving actively toward them and being the ones who enjoyed the activity, and as long as the older men did not deplete the resources of their households on these pleasures. (Some historians would go further and add other restrictions—some, for example, make the claim that the pederastic sexual activity did not involve penetration of the young man's body.) Relations between two young men were not usually considered acceptable. It was also not acceptable for younger men to behave like women, and effeminacy was both scorned and felt to be a threat to the political and military well-being of the city-states. But this disapproval of types of behavior that departed from the norms, deviant behaviors, was not prejudice against homosexual persons or homosexuality in the modern sense.

Historians and anthropologists have also begun recently to notice that lesbianism, like male homosexuality, varies enormously with cultural contexts. This notice has been slow in coming because in many cultures—including the cultures of the researchers—lesbianism is much less apparent, more hidden and silent, than male homosexuality. In some cultures, however, female homosexuality does exist in ritualized forms integral to rites of passage. In such contexts—Sappho's community on Lesbos is an example—girls are homosexually initiated to sexual activity by older women, learning skill in love along with domestic skills and crafts to prepare them for marriage. Similarly, in some sexually egalitarian or relatively nonsexist cultures—among Native American tribes, for instance—women assume gender roles elsewhere considered masculine (roles like soldiering and hunting, which would be exclusively male in cultures with more rigidly dichotomous divisions of labor) and are permitted to take female sexual and marital partners. A kind of rule of thumb has emerged from this research that says the more sexist and stratified a culture is, the more female homosexuality will be confined to informal or clandestine activities in the second class and segregated realms allowed to women. Lesbian activity is, for example, part of life in harems or in the Muslim institution of purdah—and is harshly punished if it appears in public, in male domains. If conditions permit a separate world of all-female activity to develop—like women's colleges in turn-of-the-century America, or an educated, wealthy female class in the Near East—female homosexuality has a slightly more public arena.

By contrast, societies in which women are less constrained by their roles as wives and childbearers, and less submissive to males, are characterized by forms of female homosexuality that are more public. Among some African tribes, like the Azande, where men exert loose control over marriage institutions, a relationship between two women can be ceremonially acknowledged and also built up as a trading partnership.[6] The forms of lesbianism are tied, that is, to the forms of sexism.

But it is also important to note that some forms of woman-to-woman love can virtually disappear in homophobic milieus and periods. Throughout much of the nineteenth century in America, a form of female friendship sometimes known as a "Boston marriage" was common: two women, either living together as a couple or living apart, each in a marriage, would make a vow of fidelity, a declaration that each was for the other the center of her emotional world. Such relationships do not seem to have been sexual (meaning involving genital contact), but they were certainly passionate (as attests the surviving evidence, largely in the form of effusive, unrestrainedly passionate love letters). But, toward the end of the century, when "homosexual" came into scientific existence and won wide acceptance and held cultural sway, romantic female friendships virtually ceased, because women in such relationships could not escape the label. They could not be impassioned friends, they had to be "lesbians."[7]

Historical and cross-cultural research directed at male and female homosexual social forms is generally of the "social constructionist" sort. Accordingly, preponderantly societal-level or cultural theories have been generated to explain homophobia. They have linked the prejudice to the cultural contexts, and often to the specifically modern cultural contexts. But there is also a literature devoted to the psychological question, what motivates the homophobe? It contains an array of answers. As all the contributors note, the prejudice was originally explained psychologically; it was called a phobia on the assumption that fear of homosexuals, which ultimately meant fear of *being* homosexual, was the key condition. Partly because this definition existed, and mostly because the tendency within studies of prejudice of all sorts has been to collapse distinctions among types of prejudice and subscribe to the assumption that prejudice is one, there have seldom been any nuanced psychological studies of prejudice against homosexuals. In the late 1980s, however, a critique of homophobia caused a shift.

The critics noted that both the attacks on psychiatry generated within the late 1960s homophile movements and the discussions then within psychiatry had focused on male homosexuality and on male homophobia (and homophobia within psychiatry itself was largely male, as the profession was). Critics pointed to the assumption that prejudice against lesbians was part of the same phenomenon, not a separate topic. The little research devoted to female homosexuality attempted to analyze it by extrapolation from the much larger body of anthropological fieldwork and clinical theory and practice devoted to male homosexuality. Like male homosexuality, it was further assumed, female homosexuality must have a single root cause, whether ultimately biological or ultimately social. To this day, lesbianism receives far less attention from social scientists than male homosexuality does—and this discrepancy provides one of the important clues to the dynamics of antilesbian prejudice. Gender variables, in short, were as absent from discussions of homophobia as they were from all other sorts of studies of prejudices.

Those psychologists who have focused their attention on male prejudice against male homosexuals are almost unanimous in seeing this prejudice as a particular sort of sexism. They view it as a male's denigration of the femaleness and femininity in other men and in himself. The psychoanalyst Richard Isay has even argued that fear of homosexuality per se is secondary in homophobic men to their fear and hatred of what they perceive as feminine in other men and in themselves.[8] According to the most common social psychological explanation of this fear and hatred, men in contemporary cultures like ours have learned that they are supposed to be tough, dominant, and independent and that no real man should be feminine or homosexual. Homophobia helps men meet these requirements. They try not to appear feminine or to have intimate relations with other men, as they try to succeed with women. Beyond such an emphasis on learned roles lies the territory of developmental explanations. In many ways, developmental explanations resemble feminist appropriations of psychoanalytic theory—that is, they focus on the preoedipal period and children's separation and individuation from their mothers. Essentially, they hold that the complexities of separation and individuation in childhood can leave people vulnerable or ready to subscribe to the homophobia they encounter later in their surrounding cultures.

As far as males are concerned, developmental theorists assert that separation becomes linked to a boy's sense of his maleness or his gender identity (sometimes "core gender identity"). A boy's experience of his body and his genitals, the way in which his gender is ascribed to him by those who surround him, and the presence in him of the biological-hormonal factors that effect his size, weight, and general development combine to produce his sense that "I am male," which is usually in place by the time he reaches age three but is then deepened by his own interpretations and his culture's contributions as he matures. Many psychologists believe that a boy's gender identity is typically less secure than a girl's because it involves—as hers does not—disidentification with the mother. Female children, those who follow the "reproduction of mothering" model note, do not have to establish themselves as not-mother, as males do.[9] Antihomosexual bias in the culture and the presence (or image) of feminized male homosexuals, then, may stimulate in boys archaic fears of being merged with or not individuated from their mothers, fears of being female.

Those psychologists who do look at female prejudice against homosexuals note that social surveys generally indicate that women are less prejudiced against male homosexuals than males are—or, at least, they are less affectively prejudiced, although they may be doctrinally opposed as members of Jewish, Christian, or other groups. Very few episodes of violence against male homosexuals involve female perpetrators, most involve late adolescent or young adult males, often acting in groups. Psychologists also note that some predominantly heterosexual women are homophiles as far as gay men are concerned, preferring the company of gay men (as so-called fag hags) because these men are not threatening to them as men and because they make excellent confidants. Gay men are connoisseurs of males, after all, and understand more about males than many women, even if they identify themselves psychologically as feminine and are enjoyed by women for their gifts at "girl talk."

Women's prejudice against female homosexuals is generally understood as a function not of insecure gender identity but of their more complex development toward opposite sex object choice. Girls, so this argument goes, are relatively secure in their gender identities because they do not have to disidentify with their mothers, but this same circumstance complicates their turn toward opposite sex objects, through whom they leave the domain of the females, a domain they have grown accustomed to. The move to a heterosexual object has stages, and female homosexuals who represent loving the mother can stimulate anxieties for those who have not securely completed those stages—who are, to some degree, and in some way, homosexually tied themselves.

Psychologists have begun in recent years, in summary, to recognize that homophobia or antihomosexual prejudice is a composite of prejudices, differing (at the very least) according to the sex and gender identity of the prejudiced people and the sex and gender roles of their objects. The simplest of typological maps would have to include eight variations:

> males prejudiced against males perceived as feminine
> males prejudiced against males perceived as masculine
> males prejudiced against females perceived as masculine
> males prejudiced against females perceived as feminine
> females prejudiced against females perceived as masculine
> females prejudiced against females perceived as feminine
> females prejudiced against males perceived as feminine
> females prejudiced against males perceived as masculine

I do not know of a work on homophobia that takes all of these variations into account. But many writers recognize, for example, that men are contemptuous of feminine gay men and anxious about being approached or raped by masculine gay men—although both feelings may be registrations of the same anxiety about feminization. Similarly, many note that men are not generally prejudiced against lesbians for the same reasons that they are prejudiced against gay men. Many men view masculine lesbians more as competitors for women, and feminine lesbians as betrayers of femininity because they have chosen a female to do a male's love or sex work. Masculine lesbians attract more violence—men war against them as though they were men—and feminine lesbians attract ridicule and sometimes condescending indulgence (she would get over her delusion if a real man properly showed her what only a real man can show her, and so forth). Women can fear being approached or even raped by a "butch" or masculine lesbian while they react to a "femme" with what might be called an anxiety of similarity—"she is just like me, so I could be a lesbian like her."

Because homophobia is, as I noted, a prejudice of categorization, a good deal of it is directed by homophobic people *against heterosexuals.*

That is, a good deal of it is baiting. A group of boys keep one of their peers in terror by threatening to tell everybody he is a queer. A heterosexual woman is told by a man who wants to dominate her or punish her that he thinks she is a lesbian. Lesbian baiting is so common a method of control, particularly among wife beaters, that there are analysts of homophobia who take it to be completely describable as sexism—thus the title of a well-known work by Suzanne Pharr, *Homophobia: A Weapon of Sexism* (1988).

A simple—simplistic—map of variations does not take into account factors that run on different axes of meaning. For example, many people have very different feelings toward homosexuals, male and female, when they think of them as having relations with children than when they think of them engaging in acts with adults, and one ingredient of homophobia is the tendency to imagine that homosexuals seduce and molest children, despite the well-established fact that the vast majority of child abusers are heterosexual. (When child abuse is being investigated, anxieties about the same-sex nature of the abuse often color interpretations of what actually occurred without the interpreters being aware that they are operating with categories other than "adult" and "child.") Similarly, different sorts of sexual practices arouse different sorts of anxieties, and these have not been much explored in and of themselves or as the practices are held by prejudiced people to typify different homosexuals. For instance, the two male practices, fellatio and anal intercourse, have quite different meanings to those who are made anxious by them. For those who think or allow themselves to think that lesbians engage in sex, which is not everyone who is homophobic toward lesbians, practices such as cunnilingus and digital intercourse also have different meanings to those who are made anxious by them. Lesbians themselves express quite a range of opinion about whether some sexual practices—particularly sadomasochistic ones—should be considered lesbian or treated as homophobic invasions of lesbian communities. Heterosexual transvestites, homosexual cross-dressers, and transsexuals arouse different anxieties, with, again, differences along gender lines, but these have been little explored (and the differences among these categories are not widely understood by the general public). Finally, as I noted before, it is not at all uncommon for terrifically homophobic people to love transvestite entertainments, to enjoy drag queens at Mardi Gras, and to appreciate "screaming faggot" vaudevillians.

## Resetting the Problem: A Plea for More Complexity

To my mind, this vast array of permutations and complexities has been addressed with only sporadic forays of social science because no clear way has emerged to put the basic question, what purposes do the forms of homophobia serve? The form of homophobia that approximates sexism—a male supremacy dominating and denigrating the feminine in men and setting the terms for what is feminine in women—has, however, headed researchers in the direction of the basic question. Reasoning from their investigations of sexist homophobia (if I may use that designation as a shorthand), researchers have tried to make the general claim that homophobia is a form of defense for sexual identity or for shoring up core gender identity. The common denominator among the homophobic types is, then, that homosexual acts represent, and homosexuals embody, identity trespassing or transgressing. Homosexuals shake up the gender boundaries. They are, as the current slang goes, "gender benders."

Interestingly, this direction has brought about a return to—and was in part brought about by—the framework for research represented by *The Authoritarian Personality*. Researchers using questionnaires and interviews have developed a profile of the homophobic person. He or she is authoritarian, status conscious, intolerant of ambiguity, and both cognitively and sexually rigid. But the homophobes thus profiled are motivated less by conventional sexual morality than by a desire to preserve a double standard between the sexes, that is, to preserve traditional—traditionally sexist—masculine and feminine gender roles. They "condemn the homosexual to reduce sex-role confusion" induced by considering feminized men and masculinized women. At the opposite pole, those who are least homophobic support equality between the sexes. In short, the new strand of authoritarian personality research suggests that the homophobe is a sexist and the nonhomophobe is an antisexist.[10]

This kind of empirical work, though interesting, perpetuates the bias in the study of homophobia toward concentrating on the sexism variety and ignoring all the many other functions that homophobias may fill. It makes homophobias into one thing, when there are clearly homophobias in the plural. It also, with its image of a homophobic personality—who is the authoritarian personality—obscures the "choice of prejudice" problem. Are all homophobic people prejudiced not just against homosexuals but against all out-groups, as the authoritarian personality was said to be? Are there no people who focus their hatred on homosexuals and are, so to speak, satiated, or who hate homosexuals more, or more intensely, than any other group? The construction of a homophobic personality also stands in the way of any reflection on how different types of characters might be differently homophobic. Pursuing this line of inquiry is one of the purposes of the remainder of this book, but I want to set forth a brief sketch here to indicate the possibilities.

Study of homophobic character types has never been part of psychology or psychoanalysis, but it has a brilliant literary tradition that dates from the turn of the century. Marcel Proust's characterology is probably the best known example, but the most succinct is the novel *Young Törless,* published in 1906, by the Austrian writer Robert Musil, who began his work in 1902, when he was twenty-two. Freud had just issued his *Three Essays on the Theory of Sexuality* (1905), but it seems unlikely that the *Essays* influenced Musil's provocative, and for the time shockingly explicit, depiction of four military school cadets caught up in a web of exploitative homosexuality. Musil's text thus makes an excellent source for looking at how male adolescent homosexuality could be analyzed characterologically before the category "homosexual" was widely known and before psychoanalytic interpretations and later social science completely overshadowed its territory. The text also shows that sometimes the best path through accrued layers of definition and study of prejudice is back to the beginning, especially if there is a characterologist of genius there. Musil's intricate, meditative portraits show homophobia in operation—three different kinds of it.

Every character who has the opportunity in the novel to acknowledge that homosexuality is common among youths and in boarding schools does so. The characters consider it shameful to engage in homosexual acts, but not ruinous, and not a sign of constitutional inversion, degeneracy, or homosexual identity. Among the four aristocratic cadets at the center of the novel, only one is a homosexual by the modern identity definition. This is Basini, a slender, beautiful, effeminate boy whose father died young and whose widowed mother has become somehow impoverished, or at least too preoccupied to attend to her son. Basini incurs debts among his classmates and steals money to cover them. When an imperious, manipulative, self-serving youth named Reiting discovers Basini's crimes, he blackmails him, demanding Basini's servitude in exchange for his own silence. Thrilled by his conquest, Reiting draws two of his friends, Beineberg and Törless, into his pleasure in tormenting Basini. First Reiting, then Beineberg, and finally, Törless, engage in sex with the boy whom they profess to disdain. Their sexual practices reveal their motives and characters as clearly as do their modes of tormenting him.

Reiting came to the academy from a complex family. His father, "a strangely unsettled person," had mysteriously disappeared, leaving the impression that he had been living incognito and had an extended family elsewhere.[11] Reiting "expected that his mother would make him acquainted with far-reaching claims that he would in due course put forward; he had daydreams of *coups d'état* and high politics, and hence intended to be an officer." A "tyrant, inexorable in his treatment of anyone who opposed him," Reiting constantly intrigues, sets people against each other, shifts alliances, "reveling in favors and flatteries obtained by extortion, in which he could still sense the resistance in his victim's hate." With charm and winning ways, Reiting, a classic narcissist, practices ambitiously for the day when he will, on a larger stage, be Napoleonic. He boxes to harden his body and callous his hands.

Beineberg, whom Reiting had defeated in a contest of wills and then taken as an ally, lacks grace or charm but is formidably composed and gifted "for arousing antipathy against those who incurred his disfavor." Musil presents this youth's mother as a lady of great external propriety with a penchant for secretive adultery; his father, an eccentric officer, has retreated into asceticism and passed along to his son his fascination with Buddhist philosophy. The parents represent sensuousness and spirituality, split off from each other. Beineberg, exaggerating and distorting his father's proclivity into a weapon for dominating people, spins philosophical webs like a poisonous spider. He venerates sages and holy men who, according to his account, discover through meditation their soul's connection to "the great universal processes." But the would-be sage also mocks anyone who feels compelled to be moral, to show pity for fellow humans; he hopes to overcome any such inhibition in himself. He plans to succeed entirely in "beholding his own soul" by sacrificing Basini and destroying in himself any trace of pity he might feel for the boy. Törless, who possesses great but inchoate insight into people, has always found Beineberg somehow icy and prurient and realizes that this triumphal plan is a terrible "flight of fantasy." Beineberg is an obsessional magical thinker, sadistic.

Törless, whose adolescent "larval stage" is Musil's chief study, finds Beineberg frightening in part because his cruel enthusiasms have a cer-

tain contagious quality. A boy of subtle mind and sensitivity, a ruminator
and a future intellectual, Törless is disturbed by his own reactions to
Reiting and Beineberg, whose friendship he has sought because he
wants to put on their power, their assertiveness. He has stalled in a
paralysis of confusion, indecision, self-doubt; he constantly feels in himself a split between his rational mind and some darkness of sensual
thoughts, unwanted sensations, sexual excitement that he—to his terror—associates with three figures: his mother; a lower-class prostitute
named Bozena, who lives in a disreputable tavern near the academy;
and Basini. He develops a passion for Basini and, despite himself and
over great resistance, succumbs to it, allowing himself to be seduced by
the boy. He is the passive one, briefly, and then he repudiates his lover,
scorns him, in the classically hysteric manner—repudiating the lover
represses the desire he feels for his mother.

Törless's ruminating focuses on Basini. He must find out what Basini
has suffered, exactly and precisely what has been done to him, how he
feels. Basini cannot oblige this riveting curiosity about his feelings—he
is a shallow boy, quite unintrospective, a creature who has made his way
on obsequiousness—but he does tell Törless how his persecutors behave. The Napoleonic Reiting takes his slave to the attic hideaway which
is the novel's brothel. "Mostly I have to undress and read him something
out of history books—about Rome and the emperors, or the Borgias,
or Timur Khan . . . oh, well, you know, all that sort of big, bloody stuff.
Then he's even affectionate with me . . . And then afterwards he generally beats me." Beineberg requires the boy not to provide aggrandizement but to become split, with part of himself sinking into a primitive, animal-like state—the very image of Beineberg's own divided
psyche in which affect and intellect are separated as though by a wall:
"First he gives me long talks about my soul. He says I've sullied it, but
so to speak only the outermost forecourt of it. In relation to the inner-
most, he says, that is something that doesn't matter at all, it's only external. But one must kill it. In that way many people have stopped being
sinners and have become saints . . . He makes me sit and stare into a
prism . . . [The] surface of my soul is to go to sleep and become powerless. It's only then he can have intercourse with my soul itself." Beineberg makes Basini imitate a dog, a pig—on the assumption that in a
former life the boy had been these animals—and sticks pins in him to
see what effects his experiments have on the boy's body. Basini says his
tormentor is "beastly." Later, Beineberg reverses himself and tries to

paralyze Basini's saintly part with hypnosis, so that he can find himself with the sensuous sinner. Beineberg makes Basini—body and soul—into a simulacrum of himself and then manipulates Basini, has his own obsessional symptoms on him. Musil, in a later comment on his youthful novel, noted quite explicitly that the aesthete Beineberg was a Nazi precursor.

Törless, so endlessly curious, an explorer who cannot really let himself know what he finds out, has a strange reaction the first time he is present, overhearing but unable to see in the darkness, as Reiting and Beineberg—together—persecute Basini, attacking him, tearing his clothes off, whipping him, raping him. Törless remains mute and indifferent, but a desire wells up in him. "Then the desire came more strongly, trying to draw him from his squatting position down on to his knees, on to the floor. It was an urge to press his body flat against the floorboards; and even now he could feel how his eyes would grow larger, like a fish's eyes, and how through the flesh and bones of his body his heart would slam against the wood." As he imagined himself in a position to be passively penetrated, this desire was "like a tremendous surge of blood going through him, numbing his thoughts."

After Törless, floundering in his ambivalence, finally rejects Basini and extricates himself from the morass of this cruel episode, Musil interjects a passage about Törless's future. He becomes "exclusively concerned with heightening [his] mental faculties" and eschews "voluptuous and unbridled urges." But he does not forget Basini; he simply splits off the episode, transforming it, as he explains: "Of course I don't deny that it was a degrading affair. And why not? The degradation passed off. And yet it left something behind—that small admixture of a toxic substance which is needed to rid the soul of its overconfident, complacent healthiness and to give it instead a sort of health that is more acute, and subtler and wiser." Looking back, he sees that he made use of his memory; it acted upon his creativity with the force of another life, one that he no longer needed to live explicitly.

Each of the three adolescent persecutors used Basini to act upon and to rid himself of or control his own homosexual desires. To Reiting, Basini was nothing. He toyed with Basini to feel his own power, reassure himself of it, and then he discarded him. Beineberg, who imagined himself split into an impure and a pure, spiritual self, rid himself, cleansed himself, of his impure self by displacing it onto Basini, making him "animal" and then protecting himself against the animal's attack with obsessional rituals. Törless, by contrast, scorned Basini but also assimilated him, containing Basini inside himself as a residue, the locus of his sensuality. Basini was the girl inside Törless, who at the end of the novel appears aloof, fortified by his ordeal, able to control his sensuous feelings about his effusive, overprotective mother because he has identified with her and assimilated her passivity in the form of Basini, and also able to be more like his strict, upright, manly father. Basini has served him (as did the lower class prostitute Bozena) in the hysterical manner as a substitute for his family figures, on whom he can have his family-related desires without threat of violating the incest taboo.

Musil offered portraits of the three character types I study in the remainder of this book and showed each in his relation to a homosexual target. Beineberg, the obsessional type, exhibits prejudices against people whom he identifies as, on the one hand, dirty and polluting, and, on the other hand, shrewdly able to accumulate wealth, intellectual, and conspiratorial. His victims are commercial and educated peoples, in one way or another clannish, who exist as "strangers" or interlopers, itinerants or middlemen. The Jews are the archetypical victim group of obsessionals, but homosexuals can be hated in this way, too—especially Jewish homosexuals. When homosexuals are thus hated, their "degeneracy" is emphasized. They debilitate everything and everybody they touch, which can mean, as far as male homosexuals are concerned, that they feminize (by anally penetrating) or castrate. Financial power is attributed to them. They bankroll politicians, buy up media, infiltrate political parties and government agencies, and gain control—if admitted—over military men; worst of all, they teach, transmitting their way of life to innocent children. Now, they carry AIDS and they are being punished by that disease for their diseased state, a punishment that should proceed apace because they have begun to infect the heterosexual community.

Quite different are homophobes like Törless who need to have homosexuals as or among their servants or second-class citizens, who need to keep homosexuals "in their place." Keeping a person or a group in their place is the activity of the characterologically hysterical, and the activity means—fundamentally—making them available for actual or fantasy sexual service. The most common service homosexuals are needed for is acting out the oedipal desires that those prejudiced against them will not admit in themselves or cannot act upon for themselves. Homosexuals provide a masquerade. "They" can love people of the same sex, and "we" can punish them for it. "They" can do what is forbidden, and "we" can be the good ones by signing over our forbidden wishes to them. But meanwhile "we" can enjoy their loving vicariously, watch them on pornographic films, imagine ourselves as their lovers, even perhaps sojourn or experiment with them and then return to our world, "forgetting" that we ever left or that we did what we did. It is very important, then, that "they" live nearby but not in our world; they should have the servant's quarters of a subculture, say a bar culture, where they can be a secret. Homophobes of this sort do not want to eliminate homosexuals, they want to exploit them.

People of basically narcissistic character organization, like Reiting, need to be with people whom they consider like themselves, who can mirror them and reinforce the lineaments of their identities. In both homophobic and nonhomophobic cultures, they form same-sex peer groups that are as crucial to their identities and their social orders as their families are—often more crucial. But in homophobic cultures, such groups derive additional structure by being defined as nonhomosexual. Men's groups, teams, clubs, military units, and so forth allow their members safe homoeroticism if they can be demarcated clearly from homosexual groups; their groups can even contain homosexual activity if there is a border. Psychologically, what the same-sex peer groups give their members might be called genital supplementing. Men feel their sexual potency, their phallic power, augmented when they are with buddies; more than one penis is necessary to men whose ambitions are large but whose self-esteem is not secured inwardly. They expand, so to speak, to be the equals of their fathers. Women, too, feel supplemented and defined as nonhomosexual in their groups, but they also tend to merge with their mothers through such groups as much or more than they use the groups for individuating from their mothers.

Distinctions made along characterological lines provide a particular lens on the forms homophobia takes at any given historical and cultural moment. The American debate during the course of 1993 over homosexuals in the military can be seen, for example, as resulting in a compromise psychologically happier for hysterical homophobes than for any other type. Homosexuals may remain in the military, available for actual or fantasy sexual service, but must be secret, closeted. For obsessionals, this compromise is a horrible opening of the door to infiltrators, an invitation to rapists, and for narcissists it is a dreadful blurring of boundaries, a defeat for the project of establishing self-definitional spheres. Similarly, among the many American antigay legislative initiatives recently taken by homophobes, some, like the one in Oregon, which attempted to revoke laws banning antigay discrimination, look like the work of obsessionals: they are aimed at alleged homosexual conspiracies and at means by which homosexuals infiltrate nonhomosexual communities and schools. Other initiatives, like the one in Colorado, which focuses on housing discrimination, serve the more limited hysterical purpose of keeping homosexuals in their place. It seems clear that the Oregon proposition lost in the 1992 election because it was too extreme, too obsessional, too fascistic, for large numbers of homophobic Oregonians, people who hate homosexuals but nonetheless want the individualism that they subscribe to for themselves legally protected—an individualism that permits, as it were, their duplicitous actual and fantasy lives.

Drawing prejudice subtype distinctions along characterological lines, of course, presumes a theory of character and character formation as well as a theory about how individuals' characters intersect and interact with social conditions. Hoping that I have been able to suggest by sketching the homophobias how this prejudice (or complex of prejudices) reveals, more than any other, the inadequacies of any approach to prejudices that is not characterologically grounded, I will turn now from criticizing existing theory to providing this alternative.

# II

## Starting Again: Prejudices—in the Plural

# II

# 6

## "Social Character" in
## Search of a Theory

Up to this point, I have been analyzing a fifty-year history of theoretical work on prejudice and suggesting how this history has obscured the prejudices. Now, I want to be unfashionable and go beyond deconstruction to offer a reconstruction. But I have administered no questionnaires, conducted no surveys, and interviewed no victims and no victimizers. This is a work of theory, influenced negatively by the map I have drawn of overgeneralizations, questionable assumptions, dead ends, and areas needing a new look, and guided positively by elements of psychoanalytic theory and various sorts of anthropological, social, and political theory that I will outline. I refuse two overarching, organizing ideas: first, the notion of prejudice as one; and second, the related tendency to focus on a single prejudice, without making comparisons to others or to extrapolate from one prejudice to others. This tendency particularly characterizes writers who are victims and who begin from their experience.

At the same time I eschew the two types of theorizing that have become hypostatized entities: individual-level theory and societal-level theory. I avoid the most general claim of postwar social psychologists—that there exists a single authoritarian personality which can justifiably be called the prejudiced personality and which is the product of authoritarian families or societies. But I also avoid its Charybdis: the sociological claim that there is a single list of preconditions—economic, social, po-

163

litical, culture-normative—that will inevitably produce a society riven
with prejudice. It seems to me that only overgeneralizations flow from
those who look for a single source or locus of prejudice in a prejudiced
personality or in a prejudice precondition, which can, then, be im-
printed on individuals, inculcated or taught or transmitted in the bosom
of families by some vague process like "socialization."

## Personalities and Cultures

Questions about prejudice are, however, inextricably interwoven with
questions about relations between individuals and groups. Reading this
complex of interweaving, mediating terms requires linkages. In my
opinion, these were most interestingly charted by a range of theorists—
psychologists, sociologists, and anthropologists—who conducted before
World War II what were then called "culture and personality" studies.
Some of the prewar theorists practiced "ethnopsychoanalysis," the term
used by the Hungarian-born, French-raised, and American-educated
George Devereux, although few were actually psychoanalysts as he was,
and no one but Devereux extended the prewar work by actually con-
ducting analyses in a multiplicity of cultures and languages. In general,
the prewar social scientists wanted to escape bifurcating individual-level
and societal-level theorizing, and they would all have subscribed to the
conviction that the Harvard sociologist Talcott Parsons presented later,
in 1952:

> Psychoanalysis, in common with other traditions of psychological
> thought, has naturally concentrated on the study of the personality of
> the individual as the focus of its frame of reference. Sociology, on the
> other hand, has equally naturally been primarily concerned with the
> patterning of the behavior of a plurality of individuals as constituting
> what, increasingly, we tend to call a social system. Because of historical
> differences of perspective and points of departure, the conceptual
> schemes arrived at from these starting points have in general not been
> fully congruent with each other, and this fact has occasioned a good
> deal of misunderstanding. However, recent theoretical work shows
> that, in accord with convergent trends of thought, it is possible to bring
> the main theoretical trends of these disciplines together under a com-
> mon frame of reference.[1]

When feminist theorists in the 1970s looked back to this aspiration
toward a kind of unified field theory for the social sciences, they pointed

out that while Parsons and others had emphasized means and owner-ship of production in the traditional Marxist manner, they had left out of that account reproduction, women's particular contribution to la-bor—the making of laborers—and social organization. Feminists pointed out that the psychoanalysis Parsons and his peers worked with was uncritically "phallocentric." Quite rightly, they thought that the culture and personality theorists paid too little attention to gender is-sues, that sexism was not part of their inquiry. The alternative that even-tually came out of the feminist critique incorporated a range of theories indicating how gender roles are reproduced in families—how mother-ing is reproduced between mothers and daughters and how more public roles are handed on to boys, along with their society's sexism. These theories stressed the preoedipal mother-child bonds and childhood so-cialization. "The family"—often much too abstractly construed, even when the qualifiers "Western," "nuclear," and "middle-class" were added—was the key mediating term between individuals and societies.

Although feminist theorists have criticized the older culture and per-sonality assumptions, they have also worked with the notion that had been central to the tradition—"social character."[2] In its simplest ver-sion, "social character" refers to the single collective character shared by all members of a particular society—it is like a dye that tints all in-dividuals alike or the language that they have in common. This may make sense for some single families and for some homogeneous and small or isolated tribal or ethnic societies (what are technically called *Gemeinschaften*), but it is inadequate for more complex, pluralistic, and extended societies *(Gesellschaften),* which are constantly shifting and re-generating identities (that some members subscribe to and others do not). In complicated modern societies, many social characters prevail in different subsocieties and regions, local and translocal institutions. Peoples' experiential loci are groups defined by class, religion, lan-guage, and region, as well as societal *ethnos* (however that may be de-fined); they also reach beyond their backgrounds to form new group-ings. At particular historical moments—especially moments of crisis—a dominating set of social character traits may emerge and, over time, color large segments of the society, making some individuals feel at-tuned to the dominative configuration and others alien or alienated.

From the perspective of individuals, the same point can be made by saying that, particularly in times of crisis and change, societies shift so that individuals of one character type will have more chance to flourish, to gain power and exercise influence, than individuals of another character type. Complex societies normally resemble adolescents—full of contrary and conflicting traits, full of impulses of contrasting and often quite incompatible types—but they can rigidify quickly, eliminating or silencing people, repressing traits, becoming monolithic and entropic, until a revolution breaks them up again or until they deteriorate. And complex cultures also affect adolescents more than they affect any other group, because adolescents are in developmental terms maximally prone to influence, changeable, given to forming identities in and through identifications with the people around them. Both the older culture and personality theorists and their more recent feminist appropriators studied cultural influence primarily with reference to early childhood and child-rearing methods and thus missed the intersection of greatest volatility, adolescence, as they missed the possibility that changes do not require a full generation to pass into adult personalities, that personalities can be dramatically and quickly influenced by cultures and then in turn exert influence on cultures.

Looking at culture and personality dynamics in this complex way, we must add plurals in both places—to speak always of cultures and personalities. Societies have social characters, not a single social character; and any given society is made up of people of different character types, each of which will have complex relations with the social characters available—available, that is, in ascendant or descendant, waxing or waning, modes. But this way of looking at cultures and personalities dynamics also presumes a way of assessing both individual character and social character. It presumes two characterologies, one for what the sociologist David Riesman called "the more or less permanent socially and historically conditioned organization of an individual's drives and satisfactions—the kind of 'set' with which he approaches the world and people" and one for the part of this character "which is shared among significant social groups and which, as most contemporary social scientists define it, is the product of the experience of these groups."[3] My approach also presumes that a complex reading of the individual-social character dynamism can be developed. In this chapter and throughout this part of my reconstruction, I explore these possibilities.

Some historical reflections on the culture and personality tradition will show what is still useful in it. For one thing, it distinguishes between two different kinds of prejudices. Some prejudices are the order-producing mechanisms or mechanisms of defense that relatively established societies make available to their members. These prejudices lie ready-to-hand for people to select from, appropriate, and wield, each according to the needs of his or her individual character type. But individuals use other prejudices to order themselves into groups, to enact their desires—the sources of their prejudices—and to secure their identities with groups that are being established or are in a wished-for state. These two types of prejudice—the ready-made, off-the-rack ones and the rough cut ones that people tailor to their own configurations as they look for kindred spirits—I have called, respectively, ethnocentrisms and ideologies of desire.

Group-perpetuating ethnocentrisms and group-creating ideologies of desire involve and unite individuals differently. But these differences have not shown up in studies of prejudices because assumptions about individuals and groups that have congealed into clichés block the view. I see two quite distinct ways to consider the kinds of relationships or "fits" that exist between an individual's character (or personality) and a society's character (or culture). The first is the way presumed by all discussions of socialization (including the autonomous norms explanation of modern racism). The method tries to show how a society's culture puts its stamp upon the individuals who make it up. Culture produces personalities of its type. The guiding assumption is that a society, though it may comprise individuals of many and diverse sorts, will also have a prevailing social character type, a predominating type, in which even very diverse individuals may share to a certain extent. In this view, prejudices are part of the culture that gets stamped on individuals. A second approach focuses not on societies as they exist and perpetuate their cultures by socializing or acculturating individuals, but on individuals, in their peculiarities and types, as they band together and form societies. It emphasizes the kinds of groups that individuals of a given sort would be likely to desire, to establish, and to organize for the satisfaction of their desires and needs. Sociology and anthropology, of course, usually take the first route, but the second is a road relatively less traveled—social psychology has ignored it. I will come to the latter possibility, but first I want to track how the former was articulated in the culture and personality tradition.

The first approach, though developed by the pioneering American anthropologists of the 1930s in the culture and personality tradition, was in fact as old as Herodotus and had been for centuries the basic approach on which imperialists based their empire-building strategies, using culture and personality insights to assess the weaknesses of their opponents and prepare for the integration of the peoples they conquered into their empires.[4] In the 1920s the school around Franz Boas at Columbia University freed this type of work from the heritage of modern imperialism, which held that different "races" produce different cultures, the superior (Caucasian, European) ones, of course, making superior cultures. Boas and his school simply found no evidence for the idea that "race" somehow determines sociocultural patterns. But, having shown the falsity of the idea that biological heredity explains the differences between the social characters of two societies, and having exposed the racial thinking underlying that idea, the destroyers of race theory as a theory of social character, did not have a way to explain observed differences in social characters.

Edward Sapir and Boas's student Ruth Benedict set the comparative study of basic or ethnic personalities on a psychological footing. Sapir suggested that psychological concepts could be used to characterize whole cultures—so he spoke of introvert and extrovert cultures, for example. Benedict referred to "patterns of culture" rather than cultures as a whole, and she used a different psychological dichotomy—Apollonian and Dionysian. She contrasted cultures in which an intellectual approach to life is accompanied by low emotional affect and those in which high emotional affect and ecstatic experiences dominate. The Pueblo Indians, particularly the Zuni, served Benedict as ideal Apollonians, as they are tribes dedicated to formal rituals, but she did not find the Dionysian type to be so clearly illustratable.

Many anthropologists questioned the methodological wisdom of Benedict's inference of individual personalities from psychological characterizations of cultures as a whole—her idea that a culture is a personality writ large. Critics noted that a few broad cultural elements will be common to all of the members of a society, but each society will also have special segments or subgroups—gender groups, class groups, occupational groups, and so forth—with their own cultural specialties, and it will also have traits shared by some individuals but not others, not all, or not even all in a subgroup. Each society, finally, will have individuals with individual peculiarities that are not shared with the other members of the society. Benedict wrote about cultures in the way that early Greek theorists of individual character had written about character—in terms of single dominating traits. She assigned a trait like megalomania to a "pattern of culture," and thence to all members of a society, as characterologists in the tradition of Theophrastus had for centuries spoken of the "megalomaniac man," or the "avaricious man," or the "phlegmatic man."[5]

Benedict's work, although it eventually seemed even to its appreciators too simple, was trailblazing, and the anthropologists who learned from it made it much more complex and comparative. In *The Individual and His Society, Character, and Personality* (1939), Abram Kardiner and Ralph Linton, for example, avoided the single trait approach and looked at diverse traits and also at diverse groups within societies, attempting to study them with data—largely absent in the ethnographies available to Benedict—on child-rearing techniques. They focused on the general atmosphere in which the children of a given society are raised, however, not on specific child-care techniques or the details of when and how, say, weaning takes place, because they could see no direct "item for item" correlations between techniques and later adult character traits. But a general atmosphere, they argued, whether "permissive, affectionate, indifferent, hostile or whatever" establishes in a child a "series of anticipations . . . which later will influence the manner in which he will register and experience all the new situations that arise."[6]

Let me illustrate this developmental approach with the anthropologist Ralph Linton's description in his *Culture and Mental Disorders* (1956) of the "ethnic personality" predominating in a Native American tribe, the Comanche, which was dedicated to war and organized around its warrior group—a group with clearly shared characteristics:

> [The] average Comanche man was very much the sort of person one could expect Comanche culture to produce. Of course in every culture there are "saints," who come closer to living according to the ideal patterns of the group than the normal individual ever does. Thus, there was an occasional Comanche who spent all his time on the warpath and got most of his satisfaction from killing people. But even the average Comanche was a thoroughly aggressive, self-reliant individual, because as a child he was subject to a steady build-up, in which at each stage of his development he was given tests which were within his ability. The Comanche were careful never to expose the children to disappointment through failure, to reward them steadily for success in their tests and never to make them feel rejected or inadequate in any way. The result of this training was a curious lack of fear . . . This

attitude pervaded the whole Comanche way of life and, as a result, they were highly successful people. Interestingly enough, this attitude also carried over into an almost complete indifference to survival after death and expressed itself as an almost complete lack of mythology concerning future life.[7]

In Comanche culture, Linton pointed out, the ideal Zuni or Hopi man—"docile, ritually controlled, unemotional," Apollonian in Benedict's terms—would be a deviant. And Comanche culture, in fact, created a role for men who were "deviant" in the direction of the Zuni or Hopi ideal. Such men could refrain from warrior duties, wear women's clothing, assume women's roles, take part in women's activities—play the role called *berdache,* an institutionalized transvestitism involving homosexual activity and even homosexual marriage.

Linton's portrait of the Comanche typifies the kind of work done most brilliantly by the group for whom Abram Kardiner, a member of the New York Psychoanalytic Society and later of the Columbia Psychoanalytic Society, was the chief psychoanalytic theoretician. This group proceeded by isolating the basic institutions or forms of life in a society, which are inculcated through the child-rearing atmosphere, describing the shaping of individuals, and then indicating how individuals produced for themselves secondary institutions or "projective systems," like their religions, that reflected their experience and also became part of their means for shaping their young. The ethnographic materials generated by the group, which gave special attention to child rearing, were supplemented by two innovations—detailed life histories of individuals and Rorschach projective tests given to a cross-section of the society being studied.

The most thorough application of the Kardiner group's theory and method was carried out by Cora Du Bois, whose study *The People of Alor* (1944) showed how a "basic personality" characterized by suspiciousness and distrust, dissatisfaction, bursts of aggression, and inability to form enduring bonds could become the norm among people who, as infants, had been left behind with siblings while their mothers (under a system that rigidly divided labor along sexual lines) worked in the fields and gardens. Alor children were hungry the better part of each day and constantly confused by parents who behaved toward them with marked inconstancy of affection, inconsistency in discipline, and deceit. Girls grew up into women who resented maternal responsibilities (and thus behaved toward their children as their mothers had behaved toward them), and boys were driven to search for a wife who would be an energetic mother and provider, a type the society could not produce. The religion of the Alor centered on making food sacrifices to ancestral deities, but the society carried out its rituals in a desultory fashion, not expecting that attention to the gods would be rewarded, so people offered their deities no permanent homes or artful effigies. Among the Alor, who resembled in many ways people whose childhoods have been spent in ill-run orphanages or foster-care systems, oral deprivation and instability in object relations were handed down from generation to generation in the medium of the "social character."[8]

Linton's comparative work prepared him, in his last book, to generalize about the ways in which societies influence people and to classify these influences under three broad headings. People are, first and foremost, affected by what others do to them—most crucially by the techniques of child care and child training to which they are subjected and by the attitudes or emotional tones (harder to explore) that shape those techniques. Second, they are shaped by what others teach them informally and formally (in schools or educational institutions); finally, they are influenced by their observations of how the people around them behave, individually and comparatively, which provide the basis for their imitations but also for their appreciation and their criticism.

Linton's scheme shows that, as it evolved, the culture and personality tendency grew more developmental. Individuals are not shaped by the society in which they live all in one blow in childhood; society affects them differently at different moments of their childhood, youth, and adult stages, as they interact with its human representatives and its institutional modes. By contrast, as I indicated, one of the great weaknesses of the 1970s feminist culture and personality appropriation was that the developmental approach largely disappeared. Feminist theorists became focused on very early childhood, on the preoedipal period and the establishment of gender identity, to the relative neglect of the oedipal period and to the complete neglect of puberty or adolescence. George Devereux elucidated the problem with this emphasis in 1951, twenty years before the problem became specific to feminist theory:

> The effort to understand the basic personality *primarily* in terms of *baby* and *infant* care techniques is a futile one. In stressing almost exclusively the experiences of the preoedipal stage of psychosexual development, one tends to disregard the very crucial experiences of the oedipal period, and, *a fortiori,* of the pubertal period, during which

the oedipal conflict is once more faced and, in many cases, more or less successfully resolved. Indeed, the oedipal and pubertal stages of life are of special significance for the adjustment of the individual to society, since the manner in which the Oedipus complex comes into being and is resolved determines to a large extent not merely man's manipulation of his culture, but, above all, the nature of his relation to other human beings, *as real persons and not merely as sources of purely narcissistic preoedipal gratification.* In addition, it is self-evident that, as the child matures, the segments of the culture pattern mediated to it through cultural experience expand rather rapidly. Thus the child becomes increasingly capable of seeing—or, at least, of effectively sensing—the cultural forest behind the trees of discrete, atomistic experiences with individual cultural traits. In other words, only the broadening of the child's cultural experience enables it to detect the pattern, ethos, value system, means-ends schema, etc. which give a meaning and a structure to his discrete experiences . . . Only after the child is old enough for these early impressions, expectations, rules, etc. to acquire a meaning and reveal a pattern, can they be *accepted*—though with certain pregenitally determined distortions—instead of being merely *endured,* and only then can the human beings who reared it become *persons,* instead of remaining "partial objects" which are merely sources of narcissistic gratifications, or of blows to the infant's self-esteem.

It is therefore felt that the decisive force in personality formation is the *ethos,* which gives meaning to discrete culture traits, rather than the individual culture traits, e.g., training techniques, themselves. The determining force of the latter depends primarily on the extent to which they reflect the over-all *ethos* and pattern of the total culture. This means that the basic personality is formed *primarily* during the oedipal and pubertal periods, *whose resolving eliminates or sublimates earlier pregenital traits and urges.*[9]

The complex, multifaceted culture and personality approach that this passage describes was largely developed by anthropologists who were not looking at societies that resembled the United States of America at midcentury. They were looking at societies that they, generally, appreciated for their greater simplicity or their relative lack of industrialization and exposure to advanced capitalism. They were often drawn to cultures less puritanical than they felt America to be. Margaret Mead's *Coming of Age in Samoa* (1928) set the standard for this trend. Though not particularly psychoanalytic and without the techniques that developed only in the next decade in Kardiner's seminar, Mead focused on child rearing and adolescent sexual mores.

But World War II marked a transition in American culture and personality studies, as America itself became the focus. Anthropologists studied the country with the tremendous sense of urgency that at the same time permeated work on antisemitism and prejudice in general, like *The Authoritarian Personality*. Nearly fifteen years after *Coming of Age in Samoa*, less than a decade after the Great Depression, and in the middle of the war, Margaret Mead herself clearly felt this urgency. Her portrait of America, *And Keep Your Powder Dry: An Anthropologist Looks at America*, written in 1942, just when the bombing of Pearl Harbor had jolted America into the war, was part of a government-sponsored project to help Americans understand themselves as they moved into their new role in international affairs. The book contained many interesting reflections on immigrant heritages, but it concentrated on the American nuclear family—by which Mead meant the middle-class white family—and its intergenerational love story. American parents, Mead argued, particularly those jarred by the depression, urged their children to achievement, to be better and do better, to win their share of the American dream. Children were rewarded with parental love for being competitive and conventional or conformist—and punished for failure by having that love withdrawn. She saw people emerging who subscribed to a new Puritan ethic; they were the overachievers, guided by very little in the way of ethics. Mead's student Geoffrey Gorer, an Englishman, took up this theme in *The American People*, a portrait of Americans as hungry for love, untrusting in love, afraid of being alone, and completely addicted to joining groups and elaborating complex dating rituals—anything to keep the search for love and approval going. Incessant entrepreneurial and erotic activity, promoted particularly by pushy American mothers, was the ideal for men, but also for women, and passivity was detested—particularly by men in the form of effeminacy and homosexuality. Everyone in these books suffers *for* their insecure loves and *from* performance anxiety.

As the culture and personality tradition in anthropology developed during and after the war, its developmental complexity nearly disappeared, to some extent because of the sort of alarm and social prophecy apparent in Mead's popular work. Anthropologists assumed that even a society as complex and full of subgroupings and subcultures as America could have a single social character, a "national character." The middle class stood for the whole, without status distinctions or concern for racial minorities. The earlier Kardiner-Linton emphasis on child-rearing styles and attitudes in the preoedipal and oedipal years, the great concern with puberty and puberty rites, the focus on ego development, all gave way to a focus on social conformity—the very focus of *The Authoritarian Personality*.

At its worst, the culture and personality tradition descended into facile analogies between individual and social pathologies, a trend that appeared most clearly as a pathologizing of prejudice. For example, the sociologist Red Bain distinguished "social neurosis" from "social psychosis," on analogy with the distinction between neurosis and psychosis in the domain of individual psychology.[10] Like an individual neurosis, a social neurosis is characterized by rigid, compulsive, irrational, maladaptive behaviors. But these behaviors are less severe than those typical of social psychosis—the antisemitism of the Nazis or the racism of the American South—where there is no sign of pangs of conscience and where the distortions of reality are violent. A social neurosis can, over time, become a social psychosis: "The neurotic anti-Semite is put on the defensive, has to 'excuse' and 'explain' his conduct, has to compensate for his guilt feelings, and is thus driven to more and more violent 'vicious circle' expressions of the neurosis." It is guilt, and guilt alone, that drives the social neurotic antisemite to more and more extreme, psychotic behavior. Eventually, a whole society is characterized by its prejudice pathology, to which everyone conforms.

The emphasis on social conformity in this tradition did not, however, always end up in this kind of pathologizing. And in one work, *The Lonely Crowd* (1950), David Riesman and his collaborators Nathan Glazer and Reuel Denny richly articulated it. "The way in which society ensures some degree of conformity from the individuals who make it up" or the society's "mode of conformity," Riesman argued, is its clearest distinguishing feature and the society's most typical members are the ones who conform in the prevailing way. But modes of conformity change over time and no one mode rules a society completely. The overachieving, conformist type that Margaret Mead and Geoffrey Gorer had described was, in Riesman's view, one type among others—he was an "other-directed" conformist, quite a different creature from an "inner-directed" follower of the Puritan ethic who might live next door to him.[11]

The emphasis placed on "mode of conformity" related to the common postwar sociological opinion that the success of American and European social conformity was so great that conformists had become the prevailing social characterological type. Indeed, sociologists felt that in Nazi Germany the conformist type—as the authoritarian personality—had recently been raised to the level of social madness. Anxious studies like William Whyte's best-selling *The Organization Man* (1956) appeared one after another. Many of the conformist characterological traits that Whyte emphasized were charged by Erich Fromm to the "market-oriented personality," who was known to the neo-Freudian culturist-psychoanalyst Karen Horney as "the neurotic personality of our time." This man—and he was always a man, very little was said about women—was a salesman of his own personality, a commodity, a hungry being needing affection, afraid of solitude, bent on oral gratification. He avoided conflict, stifled his aggression, and glad-handed his way through life, without moral values but with dedication to *quid pro quo* deals. Studies of nonconforming misfits also abounded, and these focused on two groups: bad juvenile delinquents or rebels without causes, and artistic or creative, autonomous adult (white) men. Many argued that intellectuals are the quintessential adult nonconformists, an argument carrying the implicit claim that a particular social function being an intellectual, and a particular type of activity, critical thinking, are the keys to good nonconformity.

"In each society . . . a mode of ensuring conformity is built into the child, and then either encouraged or frustrated in later adult experience," Riesman asserted. To examine this integration of conformity, Riesman and his colleagues took a key psychological concept from Freudian psychoanalysis—that of the superego. People conforming to social norms are people whose psyches are organized to obey superego commands. In other words, Riesman and his associates shifted the culture and personality tradition's emphasis away from child-rearing attitudes toward the ways in which societies influence their children "through the parents as transmission belts," and specifically through the children's way of internalizing parental commands in their superegos.

Psychoanalysis had provided the social sciences, Talcott Parsons argued, with "an enormous deepening and enriching of our understanding of motivation," to which the central contribution was "Freud's discovery of the internalization of moral values as an essential part of the structure of personality itself," that is, as the superego. This discovery

had its complement, Parsons felt, in the work of the great French sociologist Émile Durkheim. "Durkheim started from the insight that the
individual, as a member of society, is not wholly free to make his own
moral decisions but is in some way 'constrained' to accept the orienta-
tions of the society of which he is a member."[12] Moral rules constrain
people by virtue of their authority—and not by coercion or force—and
this presumes that the rules have been internalized as the superego, as
part of the personalities of the members. In effect, a society's conformists are those in whom the superego, socially shaped, dominates,
whereas nonconformists are people of underdeveloped superego or of
superegos tuned to values other than those prevailing in the society
around them.

From Riesman's more historical point of view theories like Freud's
and Durkheim's were both descriptions and reflections of a period in
the history of social character in Europe and America. These were men
who explored what Riesman called inner-directed conformist social
character, by which he meant a mode for securing not just behavioral
conformity but conformity to commands inculcated by elders in children. Inner directions are goals that guide a person even when he or
she is exposed to conflicts among diverse traditions and values. The
"Protestant ethic" that Max Weber described is such a mode of inner-
direction. This and other types of inner-direction, Riesman stated, fundamentally differ from the earlier "tradition-directed" social character
typical of smaller, preindustrial, precapitalist *Gemeinschaften,* where
change is very slow, where values or social norms—tradition, in general—form a "tight web" around and among the people. Where there
are few if any conflicts among diverse, competing traditions and subgroups within the society, traditions rule indisputably, as they did among
the Comanche.

Riesman hypothesized that the socioeconomic transition underway in
the mid-twentieth century—which he described as a transition to societies of lower birth rate; more separation of the fewer children from
their family contexts; greater abundance, consumerism, and leisure;
and increased contact among diverse nations, races, and cultures—
would bring about a new social character, the "other-directed." In new
conditions, "other people are the problem," and this is a situation fundamentally different from that encountered by the inner-directed types,
who had struggled during the relentless advance of capitalism, bearing
the burdens of limited resources or long work hours, assuming the com-

plexities of survival as workers or domination as owners of the means of production.

People for whom other people are the problem live in a service-oriented economy; they engage with the world around them through the "media," a sheen and screen of words and images; and they are experts in socialized behavior, adjustment to others, adaptation to circumstances, and sensitivity to the latest and hottest trends and fashions. Being able to manage relations with other people—not abiding by internal standards—is the mark of successful living, and the peer groups and contemporaries (not the parents) with whom an other-directed type is engaged are the locus of life. So, as Riesman argued, the psychoanalyst of (perhaps also *for*) the other-directed type is not Freud but the American Harry Stack Sullivan, who superimposed upon Freudian foundations a portrait of people being socialized in their peer groups and learning "interpersonal relations."

Nowhere in his book did Riesman explicitly raise questions about whether there are prejudices typical of the different social character types. But he obviously thought that the other-directed type, whose problem is other people, was a type organized for tolerance. Tolerance, of course, means not lack of prejudice but, rather, dedication to getting along, developing flexible, frictionless relationships—even with groups that, a generation before, were beyond the pale for an other-directed person's inner-directed parents. The inner-directed are, in Riesman's account, made for ethnocentrism and the celebration of the "narcissism with respect to minor differences" that Freud held as the mark of groups asserting their identities. The other-directed will call for tolerance not as a matter of principle—say, in accordance with the American Creed—but as a matter of getting along practicality. They are, however, because of their adaptability and lack of principles, also susceptible to being manipulated by political groups that do have clear prejudices and an agenda for discrimination.

Riesman's three types were fluidly conceived, with great historical and theoretical richness. They are like three evocative line drawings: (1) of groups primarily oriented by shared experiences from the past as embodied in rules and rituals, (2) of individuals in groups primarily oriented by the internalized past, located in the superego, and (3) of group-seeking individuals relatively without past, oriented by their sense of the present and their immediate gratifications. Riesman carefully reminded his readers that none of his three types of social character is to be found in purity. They are intermixed in any given society, as they were in the midcentury America Riesman described, with its tradition-directed rural native and immigrant groups, its inner-directed European urban immigrant groups, and its emergent other-directed middle-class urban professionals (those known to sociologists as the "new middle class"). Groups of different types may engage one another and their sense of the prevailing norm in a vast "characterological struggle." Similarly, in individuals the types may coexist, perhaps in a struggle, with one having greater weight than another at different stages of life or in different social contexts. There is no single entity called "society" capable of calling a social character into being or stamping it on individuals. Riesman managed, that is, to avoid the simplistic notion that there is such a thing as *the* American national character.

One consequence of Riesman's approach, as he made clear, was that he felt it supported his most fundamental criticism of *The Authoritarian Personality*. The Adorno group, he argued, had assumed that "authoritarianism in character structure breeds and is bred by authoritarianism in social structure," while Riesman's own analysis showed something quite different: "I suggest that, in America and England, the Puritan [inner-directed] character, which qualifies in many ways as 'authoritarian,' actually helped foster a democratic social structure under given conditions of seventeenth century life; conversely, the pliable 'democratic' [other-directed] personality can be molded and made use of, under other social conditions and institutions, in developing a rigid and authoritarian society."[13] There is no simple or static link between character and society, Riesman insisted from his historical and sociological perspective. Different social characters can, under different conditions, shape or be shaped by different social structures. This insight is, I think, the great advance made by Riesman beyond *The Authoritarian Personality* and also beyond the national character reduction of the culture and personality tradition.

In overcoming the mechanical causal theory built into *The Authoritarian Personality,* however, Riesman dropped the concern with prejudice that had motivated that book. Riesman seemed to feel that he was witnessing a transition to a social character beyond previously known forms of prejudice—certainly beyond the kind of antisemitism that had so intruded on the lives of Adorno and his group. Other-directed people gravitate toward or away from others on the basis of peer group norms, popularity, aesthetic preferences, fashions. Theirs is a kind of ethnocentrism for people who float in and out of their *ethnos,* connected only to its most superficial and changeable dimensions. In the 1950s, when Riesman and his contemporaries were promoting culture and personality studies, they analyzed as the main socioeconomic phenomena the affluence and leisure stemming from changes in the nation's economy, for it looked, then, as though the American Dilemma, the traditional problem of racism, was about to be erased by desegregation legislation, the war on poverty, and the welfare state. Culture and personality studies did not focus on how cultures promote racism or are promoted by racism in individuals. So there was no tradition of inquiry into how racism functions in a personality (or personalities) to give a psychological dimension to the 1970s studies of cultural norms as part of modern racism (the tradition which, as I noted before, construes cultural norms as autonomously functioning, independent of personalities).

This silence on the topic of prejudices can be seen very clearly in the next—the third—phase of the culture and personality approach. Christopher Lasch's work epitomizes this phase, as Lasch tried to delineate a social character like Riesman's other-directed type but reconceived for the 1970s and—in a mode of prophecy—the 1980s. "The narcissistic personality in our time," the type invoked in Lasch's *The Culture of Narcissism* (1979), is other-directed but not a conformist, not a promoter of good feeling and feeling good. The narcissist is an exploiter of others, a person who presents an affable surface but in fact ruthlessly pursues possessions and position. A far cry from the teamplayer, the company man, this person has learned to play organizations to individual advantage. He or she (again, the emphasis fell on men) is the incarnation of self-promotion and manipulation, even annihilation, of others. This is the Me who came to be charged in the early 1980s with typifying the "Me Decade."

In the culture of narcissism, Lasch argued, racist ideology is unnecessary, as all racism is *de facto,* part of the general exploitation of everyone by everyone else. He described not "modes of conformity" but "modes of exploitation":

> In the United States, the transition from Theodore Roosevelt jingoism to Woodrow Wilson's liberal neocolonialism already spelled the obsolescence of the older ideology of Anglo-Saxon supremacy [associated with imperialism]. The collapse of "scientific" racism in the twenties and thirties, the integration of the armed forces in the Korean War, and the attack on racial segregation in the fifties and sixties

marked a deep-seated ideological shift, rooted in changing modes of exploitation. Of course the relation between material life and ideology is never simple, least of all in the case of an ideology as irrational as racism. In any case, *de facto* racism continues to flourish without a racial ideology. Indeed it is precisely the collapse of *de jure* racism in the South and the discovery of *de facto* racism in the North, sheltering under the ideology of tolerance, that distinguishes the most recent phase of the race problem in the United States. The ideology of white supremacy, however, no longer appears to serve any important social function.[14]

In Lasch's view, *de facto* racism, institutionalized racism, modern racism, is simply a mode of exploitation by narcissists. There are no racists, there are only narcissists who exploit everyone, anyone. Historical precedents and cultural norms may direct a narcissist's exploitation of African Americans, but nothing in his or her narcissism per se demands an African American victim. Ironically enough, the narcissist's victims resemble the identity-less scapegoats needed by the authoritarian personality. Prejudices are simply weapons *de facto* in the hands of people involved in a war of all against all. In effect, Lasch's analysis simply put concern for prejudice right back where it was in the early 1950s—all prejudices are the same, there is only prejudice, and there is but one dynamic underlying prejudice. But the one dynamic had become narcissistic hatred.

I have been outlining, in effect, three cultural moments in the history of culture and personality studies. The first, in the 1930s and early 1940s, tended to focus on child rearing and to present individuals as libidinal beings whose egos, as they developed, brought them a type and measure of control—the type and measure of regulation the social character of their societies called for. It studied the "ego versus id" dynamics of societies, the ego and libido economies of societies.[15] It is this period that has been echoed and transformed in feminist theory—although feminism emphasizes object relations to the neglect of libido, as the Freudian drive theory taken for granted by the early anthropologists fell out of favor among the feminists. The second phase, in the late 1940s, the 1950s, and on into the 1960s, more in sociology than in anthropology, focused on modes of conformity. Societies produce different sorts of authority structures, internalized versions of authority, and value systems. And in the third, still reigning version, narcissism has been the key concept. Developments within psychoanalytic theory gave impetus to and took impetus from the culture and personality work, first as ego psychology emerged to complement theorizing based in the instinctual drive theory, then as ego psychology rigidified into various kinds of theories about ego adaptation and lack of adaptation in psychosis, and finally as concern with narcissism grew in the 1970s.

These distinct moments in the history of culture and personality study, it seems to me, should be understood not as three competing versions of how to do such study—to be weighed on their merits and chosen among—but as three registrations of a changing American society and changing social characters within that society. The founders of the personality and culture tradition were living in and reacting to European and American societies in the throes of a vast transition. They were societies becoming more and more libidinally regulated—even in the crucial domains of child rearing and education of the young. And thus they were societies becoming institutionally equipped to instill and reflect values and prejudices in a new way.

In the first period of culture and personality studies, societies of the sort Riesman called "tradition-bound," the societies of the Comanche, the Alor, and the Samoans were thought to present dynamics that could be found in more complex forms in European and American societies— as though these societies were adults in comparison to the tradition-bound children. The idea was too simple, but it did reflect the correct perception that enmeshment in the past and a process—I would say a hysterical process—of eroticizing the past in both the conservative and the rebellious trends of "modernism" were pervasive. The turn of the century had been not only the era of hysteria but the era in which psychologists and psychoanalysts explored hysteria as the typical psychic configuration of the era, most obviously for women as they were regulated in their "separate sphere" of domesticity. But the hope that the dynamics of modernizing societies could be extrapolated from comparisons with tradition-bound ones simply collapsed when the methods of the early culture and personality theorists were brought to bear on complex multicultured, class-stratified and status-differentiated, industrialized European and American societies. Theorists of "national character" persisted, but their provocative, interesting results met great and justified skepticism.

In the second period, culture and personality theorists were reacting explicitly to American and European commercial cultures in which

competition and drive for success and wealth flowed across class boundaries and in which conformity was held to be the key to success. They
were looking at a society in which the psychic habits of the expanding
commercial middle class reached out into other milieus, helped by new
technologies, carrying a message from the children of the depression,
who had grown up and into a period of boom. Conformism, wary caution, and expectation of disaster, the message went, should go along
with achievement. The culture was basically obsessional, an updated,
technologized version of Puritan obsessionality. In the third period, the
theorists were reacting to a huge outburst in the 1960s against authority
in all its forms and a quick, violent embrace of deregulation, social anarchy, and cultural revolutionary upheaval, a heyday for the other-
directed.

These periods in culture and personality study show vividly how culture shapes the study of itself and also how the study of it reveals the
prevailing and subsidiary social characters (in the plural). But the emphasis in all these periods of study was always on how societies and
cultures instill values and shape social characters—the emphasis set in
the first period, developed in relation to non-European cultures. The
other side of the dynamic, how people of different character types
might, under different conditions, come together and exert, in concert,
an influence on surrounding groups and on the prevailing social character, to reinforce it or to change it—this was not revealed. David Riesman moved in this direction with his notion of "characterological struggle," struggle among social character types—among tradition-directed,
inner-directed, types. But he could not grasp the dynamics of group
building; he was concerned only with group socializing, group influence, and group production of conformity with established norms and
modes.

In terms of prejudices, the early culture and personality theorists were
able to formulate clearly different ways in which groups transmit prejudices to their young, by means of their child-rearing techniques, their
socialization processes, their educational institutions. They transmit
"group prejudices," meaning prejudices that most (or a majority) of
the members of a group hold in more or less the same form, for more
or less the same purposes, whether these groups be defined primarily
along ethnic, religious, linguistic, or class lines. They are available to all
members of a group, regardless of their individual character types, although they will be most congenial to those who most embody the pre-

vailing social character or ethnic character. The prejudices are simply part of the culture, like religious beliefs and practices, values, common ideals; they are the group's norms and purposes translated into statements about other groups that are not part of these norms, groups outside the *ethnos*. And those norms and purposes relate to the perceived welfare of the group—that is, the prejudices serve the group's competitive aspirations, its dominance over neighbors or its hope of dominance, and, generally, the maintenance of the group's identity and the group's narcissism. In small, coherent societies of the sort Riesman called tradition-directed, group prejudices *may be the only prejudices needed*—the group's traditional norms and purposes define it and define all its out-groups.

But it is very important to note that the culture and personality approach, in all its later variations, continued to operate on the assumption that all prejudices will be like those of tradition-directed societies and therefore directed against out-groups. This is the Allportian assumption, the equation of prejudice and ethnocentrism. With this assumption, the central theoretical problem becomes understanding how one society generates one sort of social character and another a different sort; plurality within the society is not considered, and neither is prejudice on the part of one segment of the group toward another, toward subgroups, or toward minorities. If a group shares a social character, there can be, really, no *internal* "other" social character. Riesman grappled with this problem as he spoke about conformity and then tried to understand how groups of nonconformists would arise and as he considered characterological struggle.

The culture and personality theorists obscured the key distinction between group prejudices or ethnocentrisms and prejudices common in a group but held by the individual members in quite diverse forms, for quite different (and more individually multifarious) purposes, and potentially directed at a segment or segments of the group.[16] Prejudices of this second sort, which I call ideologies of desire, historically begin to appear in highly articulated and "scientific" forms when that type of individualism and individuality Riesman identified as inner-direction has had time to appear and grow complex. They do not initially help hold the group together and further its group purposes; rather, they are group creating (either subgroup creating or transgroup creating) and legitimating; they call into being a fantasy group either alongside an existing group or where no self-identified group was before. Socially, they operate in much the same way as founding legends and national myths—they give people a common story, a way to define themselves as kindred for purposes that do not arise out of their historical relatedness, whatever that may be. People who have a prejudice in common in this sense construct each other as kindred—they give themselves mythical group names. What they have in common, they say, is invisible; what they have in common is what directs them inwardly (in the depths of their souls, they say).[17]

In the mode of ethnocentric group prejudices, people appeal to their common history as, say, Comanche or Alor. They may also claim their identities and be identified at different levels—they belong to an extended family, a tribe or ethnic group, and of a nation all at once. But their identity claims do not involve projecting themselves, creating themselves as (for example) Aryans or whites. The prejudices that subscribers to the designation "Aryan" came to have in common had diverse functions psychologically. Indeed, the functions their prejudices fulfilled were as diverse as the subscribers' individual developmental stories, and the forms of their prejudice were as diverse as the limited number of existing paradigmatic developmental stories the subscribers represented. A particular function and a particular type of person and story can, however, dominate in the group once it is called into being and established. For instance, those who called themselves "Aryans" at midcentury in Europe concentrated on cleansing their emergent group of anyone they designated "Semites" (again, the word has no historical accuracy, it is a fiction), and they were dominated in this enterprise by people whose characters could be described as cleansing-oriented. Cleansing came, then, to be central to the social character of the group.

## Ethnocentrisms and Ideologies of Desire

Let me use this quickly drawn distinction to begin elaborating on two kinds of prejudices—drawing in more detail exactly the sort of distinction precluded during the second and third phases of culture and personality studies and, more generally, during the long preoccupation in social science since the end of the war with how to transcend the incongruities between individual- and societal-level, psychological and sociological, explanations. As already noted, I call group prejudices, those shared in more or less the same form by members of an existing group, particularly a tradition-directed, relatively homogeneous group, "ethnocentrisms." This name indicates clearly the practice of putting ones own *ethnos* or group (however one defines it) at the center of the world, or the culture, as well as at the center of one's attention, and it encompasses negative judgments toward one out-group, or toward a few, or many, or all out-groups. Ethnocentrisms come, that is, with differences of degree and scope that will vary over time and changing circumstances for any given *ethnos*.

The term "ethnocentrism," as I have indicated, has been used since *The Authoritarian Personality* to designate in-group hatred of or claims to supremacy over out-groups; it has been used as a synonym for prejudice in general. What this vague usage has meant, I think, is that the second species of prejudice, the one that supports wishes for and inventions of a group and a group identity, has been obscured. This wishful type of prejudice is, in fact, so seldom distinguished from the first that it has never acquired a name of its own. I use the name "ideologies of desire," but I am also going to coin a name that can be used to capture the contrast with "ethnocentrism." To avoid using any familiar word—to prevent false familiarizing or falling into clichés or focusing too quickly on any one form—I am going to call an ideology of desire an "orecticism," from the Greek word *orektikos,* meaning desirous or pertaining to the desires. An orecticism is a worldview shaped by a desire, a desire that has produced an ideology or articulated itself into an ideology. The prejudices that I consider in detail in this book—antisemitism, racism, sexism, and the homophobias—are in almost all their modern forms orecticisms, not ethnocentrisms.[18] Because the distinction I want to draw between ethnocentrisms and ideologies of desire or orecticisms is unfamiliar, I am going to build it up piece by piece and draw the distinction in different planes. Later I will provide concrete examples of the two kinds of prejudice and of the ways in which they, in reality, transgress my conceptual distinction, either blurring or transforming one into the other.

First, as I began to suggest, the "we" of ethnocentrics has a referent in the world and a history, whereas the "we" of orecticists is more of a fantasy, a daydream. The orecticist dreams that he or she belongs to a group that has always existed, that is more ancient than any other, which may even be the source for all others—but at the very least is dependent on no others for its existence. At the same time, the orecticist demands an origin myth showing that the group dates from prehistory. As there is no logic to the need for originary power, the orecticist is undisturbed by needing both a claim to eternal existence and an origin myth.

The "Aryans," to return to my earlier example, were a wished for group—a *Volk,* a people—for many Germans at the turn of the century. After Kaiser Wilhelm II had been enlightened about the Aryans by reading Houston Stewart Chamberlain's tract *The Foundations of the Nineteenth Century,* he ruminated to the author in a manner quite typical of an orecticist who has discovered the means to formulate his longing:

> Our stifled youth needed a liberator like yourself, one who revealed to us the Indo-German origins which no one knew about. And so it was only at the cost of a hard struggle that the original German Aryanism which slumbered in the depths of my soul was able to assert itself. [You have come] with a wave of your magic wand to create order where there was chaos and light where there was darkness. You explain what was obscure, you show the way of salvation to the Germans and to all the rest of mankind.[19]

This statement has the sweep that characterizes orecticism: a wish is formulated, often with magical, charismatic help, and it divides and organizes the orecticist's immediate world, then his larger world, then the whole world, the cosmos.

The "Caucasians," as another example, are also a group—called a "race"—imagined with the help of distorted nineteenth-century philological research. In the area of the Caucasus Mountains, "racially pure" speakers of Indo-European languages were said to be the model for the "whites" living in other parts of the world. People who have never heard of the Caucasus Mountains seize upon an imaginary purity and construct conquering fantasies with it.

An ideology of desire requires a guiding past, a past that will be the future, but emphasizes the future in a vision relatively free of boundaries. The orecticist focuses not on once-existing or existing entities but on something that will be "supra"—supranational, for example, in the era of nation-states. Ethnocentric people, by contrast, are much more oriented toward the present, and when they evoke the past it is for the sake of a restoration in the present of that past and not for the use of that past as a foundation for some larger and more powerful entity (although their ambitions may grow in the course of their struggles). Restoration is a fundamentally different hope than expansion or limitlessness.

Ethnocentrism is a modality of inclusion, a centripetal complex of wishes and values and behaviors. It depends upon already existing group identifications and promotes them. Ideologies of desire, by contrast, are exclusive. They magnify differences, taking physical and cultural variations that in and of themselves do not constitute differences in social organization, mores, or culture and turning them into *essential* differences. Such centrifugal and expansive ideologies whirl outward, casting off the Other as they go. Similarly, each supremacist imaginary group requires as its opposite, its opponent, an imaginary group that is *quintessentially* non-Aryan or non-Caucasian or nonmale, and absolutely identifiable as such, and much pseudoscience may be expended asserting that a noninteractive, absolute definition is possible.

Ethnocentrists assert the centrality of their group and find other groups—some special others or even all others—wanting. They are comparatists. Their formulas read, "we are cultured, they are barbarians," "we are pure, they are corrupted," "we are strong, they are weak." But the orecticists want to push their others beyond the borders of comparison—their formulas read, "we are human, they are animals," "we are spirit, they are dead matter," "we are powerful, they are nothing." The ethnocentrist's center connects to a circumference by fields of force; claims and counterclaims are recognized and the whole is rough and tumble. But the orecticist demands an outer darkness—at least in public statements of position. And the orecticist always calls for choice, ultimate commitment, in apocalyptic accents like these: "The human race awaits the founder of a new religion and the struggle approaches its crucial phase, as in the first year of our era. Once again humanity has the choice between Judaism and Christianity, between commerce and culture, between woman and man, between the species and the individual, between non-value and value, between nothingness and divinity; there is no third kingdom."[20] In a manner typical of orecticists who center themselves in antisemitism, the author of this invocation, Otto Wenninger, an Austrian, extended his axis of hatred outward to the cosmos. He moved from Judaism and commerce on to women, then to the vague trinity of threats—species existence, nonvalue, nothingness—which he imagined as undermining to his individuality and uniqueness, to his tightly bounded and exactly defined self.

The world of the ethnocentrist has gradations; the categories of the orecticist are relentlessly dualistic in either horizontal or vertical or historical-evolutionary terms. The X are going to push the Y out into the outermost darkness; or the X are going to rule over the Y absolutely; or the X are going to leave the Y behind in future cosmic triumph. It is important to acknowledge quickly, however, that ethnocentrism sustained for many years and fortified by violence—by loss and mourning and bitterness and guilt—can gradually support a way of life indistinguishable behaviorally from the way of life of orecticists. "We" and "they" become separated by walls in fact—areas of towns and cities and countries are walled off, peoples are reorganized and ghettoized—and categories for speaking of them rigidify. Exchanges of revenge become ritualized. But, as many analysts of ethnocentric tribal and national wars have noted, more commonly than not they become recessive (not extinct) with two generations—exhaustion overtakes the grandsons if not the sons of the first generation ethnocentric combatants.[21] Ideologies of desire last longer, reach deeper.

In situations where ethnocentrism is prolonged in violence and violently institutionalized, people who are by character orecticists attach their needs and their categorical schemes to the evolving divisions, and the evolving divisions fortify them in their psychic habits. The same kind of assimilation takes place in the other direction when ethnocentrists are caught up in situations characterized by predominance of one kind or another of orecticism. But ethnocentrism does not, in and of itself, imply violence or entail legitimation for violence. It is aversive—it says "stay away," "stay out" to others—but it does not contain the denials of similarity, the refusals of shared humanity, spiritual life, or aspirations, that characterize orecticism and that encourage and legitimate the beating, mutilating, and killing of people whose humanity has been disparaged or denied.

Ethnocentrism, on the contrary, very often can coexist with some kind of religious or philosophical commandment that ethnocentrism violates, to the shame—in their quieter moments—of ethnocentrists. They believe "Thou shalt not kill" or that all people are the children of their God or that human life is sacred or that in the cycle of cosmic revolutions souls transmigrate, so they know at some level that when they act on their prejudices they are sinners, defilers, disappointers of their Father, or that those they hate may be housing the souls of their relatives. A God must be called upon to forgive them, or their creed must be preserved to show their children their better selves. Often, an *ethnos* will include a subgroup of priests or prophets, jesters or intellectuals, poets or shamans, whose official or semiofficial function is to remind the group that its hatred of its neighbors is wrong or self-destructive.

Thus ethnocentrists can assume a larger perspective and feel shame for their prejudices. Orecticists feel guilt, and then repress their guilt *with their prejudices.* One of the key functions of their prejudices is precisely to repress their guilt. Often unconsciously, without acknowledgment, they reproach themselves for being faulty, unworthy, evil people, but they keep this knowledge ineffectual by elevating themselves over others, to whom their secret faults are attributed. They project their forbidden desires onto others, who become their scapegoats—to use the terminology of the "projection theory." Their desires, guiltily repressed or guiltily projected, clamor anyway and require constantly renewed efforts of repression or projection, making their ideology grow in rigidity and in scope and their commitments grow more desperate.

This distinction can also be put in terms of modes of aggression. Ethnocentrists displace onto other people or peoples aggression that generates in their own psyches and within their own group, thereby relieving the group of internal tensions and hostilities. Displacement solves the problems of ambivalence that are inevitable in children with relation to their parents and siblings, in family groups, in groups of family groups. Love within the group can flourish if hatred is ejected, dissociated from the loved figures. Ethnocentrism is primarily a group-preserving mode of prejudice. Orecticists, however, tend to project hatred rather than to displace it. A "they hate me [us]" replaces an "I [we] hate them," which may well have grown up on the wreckage of an "I [we] love them." Hatred that has been projected is then felt by the projector to be coming from the outside, from the group that received the projection.

Orectic projection involves much more dynamism than ethnocentric displacement, which usually has the effect of creating a fortress mentality, a fixed barricade against the hated others. Groups that receive a projection of hatred are imagined as aggressors, and the projector both barricades and attacks. Prejudices reflecting projections are felt to be necessary defenses, as natural as deflecting a raging fury or warding off a blow. In elementary, psychologically paradigmatic terms, displacements of aggression seem to be patterned on defenses that arise first in and with children's experiences of their own bodily products, particularly their feces, as objects that can receive hatred or aggression they do not wish to direct at their loved ones. Accordingly, the most elementary

charge of the ethnocentrist becomes "they smell different"; their enemies are stinking, disgusting. Ethnocentrists cannot (as the German id-
iom goes) *riechen* other groups—they cannot stand them and literally
cannot smell them.[22] Ethnocentrists operate like dogs sniffing their way
down the street, and they also come as close as humans are able to come
to the doggy virtue of having little ambivalence, which, as Freud once
remarked, means just loving their friends and biting their enemies. But
projections, which have quite diverse contents, more often have their
roots in oral, anal, and phallic experiences in which aggression is expressed much more actively and directed at *others'* bodies, not at the
prejudiced person's own body products or by means of them. Orectic
enemies are then imagined as active devouring, gobbling up, polluting,
penetrating, castrating (or castrated), or rapacious (or crippled) beings,
monstrous whether as animals or as superhumans.

Appeals for tolerance directed at the two kinds of prejudiced people
fall, then, on two very different kinds of ears. In a frenzy of hate or a
pitch of feuding, an ethnocentrist may be deaf to any appeal for tolerance and claim that a moment of peace would simply allow the enemy
time to kill. But, over time, and especially over a time of relative peace
and prosperity for them, ethnocentrists can modify their prejudices,
particularly if they are listening to voices within their community that
call for a larger perspective. They are inhibited not by the complexities
of ambivalence, only by their needs for revenge. Orecticists are more
recalcitrant because their prejudices *are* their defenses—against acknowledging their wishes and against their own guilt feelings, the voices
of their superegos. Living without their defenses would presuppose both
that what they have needed to defend themselves against—their internal
enemies, whom they find represented in the external world—no longer
threatens them, and also that they have not become over time incapable
of living without their defenses, as certain neurotics cannot live without
their neuroses. Orecticists easily can, and often do, adopt the language
of ethnocentrism in conditions that do not sanction expression of their
prejudices—they put ethnocentrism on as a disguise, and they may even
believe it. They become, for example, the modern racists studied by
contemporary social psychologists and alluded to by Christopher Lasch
as "*de facto* racists." Or as modern antisemites they speak of the Jews as
an ethnic minority with disproportionate power and special prerogatives, not as an invidious international conspiracy. Sexism, because it is
directed at gender and not at a group defined as such, does not translate

or ameliorate into ethnocentric categories, but most sexists have a conventional language for acknowledging—rather than denying—sexual difference in a mode of polite disparagement: *Vive la petite différence!* They adopt categories of ethnocentrism—"men and women speak different languages."

These distinctions between ethnocentrism and orecticism, let me note again, are not matters of degree. Ethnocentrists may be practitioners of what Freud once called "the narcissism of minor differences," but this does not mean that orecticists are *more* narcissistic or concentrate on *larger* differences. Group prejudices or ethnocentrisms, shared alike by all members of a group, *are* the group's narcissism. But people who group together, sharing prejudices for different reasons and purposes, serve first and foremost their own individual narcissisms. The mechanisms of prejudice in the two cases are fundamentally different, even if mutually reinforcing in fragmented, continuously violent societies, and even if, as in the case of modern racists, one type cloaks the other in the same person. The two types, too, may become entangled if they exist side by side, drawing their adherents from the same population. In the former Yugoslavia, in the new state of Bosnia, there are Serbs now, for example, who view themselves as involved in a kind of ethnic war with Croats—the current revival of a war that reached a horrible pitch when it was embedded in the Nazi's race war two generations ago. But this ethnic war, which is really intraethnic, as both groups are South Slavs, is also going on in the context of a far more lethal and drastic ideological war against the Muslims, a war initiated by some Serbs, using the Nazi vocabulary about cleansing (called "ethnic cleansing" now) once directed at their own grandparents. This war is expansionary—it has a call for "Greater Serbia" behind it, like the Nazi call for a pan-German Reich—and its means are genocidal (concentration camps, mass rape centers). The ethnic-cleansing Serbs view the Muslims as antisemitic Germans viewed the Jews, that is, as a more educated, commercially successful group of latecomers or foreigners who have benefited from the economic disaster of Yugoslavia's demise.[23]

Let me add another layer of distinction, returning to conditions far short of this kind of inflammation of war. Ethnocentrists think stereotypically. Stereotypes are—as the derivation of the word from the printing process known as stereotypy indicates—molds or patterns of evaluation set down upon the world regularly, invariably, monotonously.

Walter Lippmann, who popularized the sociological use of the word "stereotypes" in 1922 in his book *Public Opinion,* said of them:

> They are an ordered, more or less consistent picture of the world, to which our habits, our tastes, our capacities, our comforts and our hopes have adjusted themselves. They may not be a complete picture of the world, but they are a picture of a possible world to which we are adapted. In that world people and things have their well-known places, and do certain expected things. We feel at home there. We fit in. We are members. We know the way around. There we find the charm of the familiar, the normal, the dependable; its grooves and shapes are where we are accustomed to find them. And though we have abandoned much that might have tempted us before we creased ourselves into that mold, once we are firmly in, it fits as snugly as an old shoe.[24]

Lippmann had a clear sense of how a stereotype system organizes self-understanding: "it is the guarantee of our self-respect; it is the projection upon the world of our own sense of our own value, our own position and our own rights. The stereotypes are, therefore highly charged with the feelings that are attached to them. They are the fortress of our tradition, and behind its defenses we can continue to feel ourselves safe in the position we occupy." This phrase, "the fortress of our tradition," really captures how stereotypes focus ethnocentrism.

Stereotypes are neither fantasies (like those used by orecticists for attributing wished-for positive or negative qualities where such qualities do not exist) nor idealizations (denying defects where such defects do certainly exist). They are not mental actions we take to make people fit our wishes and needs better than they would without our help. Rather, stereotypes are crystallized expectations; they are related to the world as we expect it to be when we wake up in the morning, not to the world as we think it *ought to be* or as we *wish* it were. Stereotypes are the record of our self-proclaimed realism. But our realism, realism of the possessive "our," has nothing to do, of course, with truth. An ethnocentric stereotype is no more true than the statement of expectation "the sun will rise tomorrow," which is earthocentric.

It is stereotyping, not orectic projecting, that is indicated by definitions of prejudice formulated to take into account cognitive content and affective valence, definitions that stress the literal meaning of "prejudice," *prejudgment,* deriving (as noted before) from the Latin *praejudicium* and having the same stress as the German *Vorurteil.* For example, "we might define prejudice as an aversive or hostile attitude toward a person who belongs to a group, simply because he belongs to that group, and is therefore presumed to have the objectionable qualities ascribed to the group." This definition of prejudice in general, which is—by my scheme—accurate only for ethnocentrism, fails to grasp that stereotyping is a form of relaxation. Relaxing through meditation means emptying the mind, whereas relaxing through stereotypical thinking requires filling the mind to such capacity that a novelty cannot penetrate. "The fortress of our tradition" is the self-respect of sleepwalkers.

Orecticists, by contrast, think more dynamically, more futuristically. They do not create molds and then fit those molds onto their experiences, setting them onto the world they encounter. Rather, their entire experience is colored with restlessness and a feeling that things are not—not yet—as they should be, could be, ought to be. They work constantly, in fantasy or in fact, at getting their world to conform to their visions, the images of their desires. The instrument of their work is their imaginary group, the group they bring into being by wishing it so. They are always hammering away at the hot metal of their hopes for "us."

Another major distinguishing characteristic of orecticism is that it focuses and refocuses on bodily differences "scientifically" (that is, pseudoscientifically) generalized. An ethnocentrist will hate the smell of his or her enemies but not bother to rationalize that smell on "racial grounds." He will note the differences of religion that separate him from his neighbor—or the differences of cultural heritage and historical experience; or matters of value, custom, and mores; of habits of the mind or heart—but the ethnocentrist does not charge all these differences to physical or anatomical differences. The ethnocentrist does not argue that intelligence is a function of "racial" characteristics, or that morality is a function of "blood" or sexual-anatomical differences. The orecticist does, however, believe—desire—that race is fate, that anatomy is destiny, that superiority is biological and heritable. And this belief is to be embodied in laws, not just circulated informally or handed down from generation to generation as folk wisdom.

According to the orecticist, laws (and thus political discrimination) should inform everyone that different races should not interbreed, that the "inferior" sex should not be allowed to leave the domestic sphere in order to work or to vote, and so forth. Ethnocentric prejudice ranges widely—it can focus on any one or more of a plethora of group characteristics—but orectic prejudices are monodirectional: they always move from the body to other group characteristics, which are said to derive from the body. Pierre van den Berghe, who, as I noted before, is one of the few theorists to distinguish clearly between ethnocentrism and racism (the only kind of orecticism—to use my term—that he considered) observed in *Race and Racism* that ethnocentrism is universal, while racism is not: "only a few human groups have deemed themselves superior because of the content of their gonads."

An ethnocentrist says of a hated group or groups: "they have always tried to take over our land," "they believe in X god, not ours," "they do not value X," "they wear X, even on sacred occasions," "they eat X, which is forbidden," "they have an old alliance with our enemies." The person who says, "they are an inferior group, and their bodily X proves it," or "they are impure, because of their bodily X," is an orecticist. Similarly, an ethnocentrist says "in this struggle, our group will prevail," while an orecticist says "our group will be supreme throughout the world, and everywhere the others will be humiliated, controlled, eliminated, with a definitive attack on their corrupt [corrupting] or evil or animal *bodies*." The orecticist must mark his victims bodily, in one or more of the typical ways. Each type of orecticism, I will try to show in detail later, has its characteristic ways of marking. Each must identify its victims unequivocally, brand them or show control on and over their flesh, and violate them or get inside their bodies.

Ultimately, no matter how grandiosely or imperialistically orecticists extend the reach of their power, they do not abandon the original goal of their ideology of desire, which is to protect their intimate, bodily assertion of control and to fortify the private spheres in which they originally exercised such control. World conquest goes hand-in-hand with preservation of control over all the details of bodily life. Orecticists cannot be satisfied to exercise power or enjoy the prerogatives of power, their "others" must be marked, literally, on the areas of their bodies that signify the type of dominance desired or on symbols for those areas. The tortures (in deed or in word) that they devise are as rigorously related to the bodies of their victims as the punishments in Dante's Inferno are to the nature of the sinners' sins. If it is genital potency that offends or allures or both, the genitals must be marked or mutilated; if it is brainpower that is threatening and envied, there must be brain washing and thought control. If "they" are "shitting" on you, you should drown them in their own shit—which is why, as Primo Levi reported from Auschwitz, the camps were known to their Jewish victims as *Anus Mundi*.

As a further key difference between ethnocentrism and orecticism, note that the orecticist is aware—not consciously or explicitly, but nonetheless aware—that the Other against whom hatred is directed is also loved, needed, desired, envied. Orecticists are aware—again, not usually consciously—that they have placed a part of themselves in the group they are against. They have, for example, found in that group (as they construct it or imagine it) the power they feel themselves capable of and desire. The famous czarist forgery called "The Protocols of the Elders of Zion" portrayed the Jews as a group organized for world conquest—for just the world conquest Nazi readers of the forgery desired for themselves. They read in this text formulas for their own future. In another type of orecticism, racists find in the group that they construct—the Negro "race"—the phallic power they wish for themselves. The more conscious orecticists are of their bond to the group they projectively construct, the more unrestrained—and, often, the more violent—they are in keeping their knowledge from becoming truly conscious. When racists manage to convince themselves that they are not racists, thus putting away all knowledge of their love, they settle for subtle institutions, they do not need apartheid.

There is also, I think, a final way in which ethnocentrisms are different in kind from ideologies of desire or orecticisms. The two kinds of prejudice have different effects upon their victims in several areas. Because ideologies of desire are focused so relentlessly on the bodies of their target groups and articulated with claims of natural inferiority and evil, and because they involve partial identifications and thus disorienting messages of love-and-hate, rejection-and-envy, they are able to undermine the confidence or self-esteem of their victims much more deeply than ethnocentrisms. Psychologically, this is because the ego is, as Freud once put it, first a body ego; it develops from and with a child's body image. Pleasure in one's body and its functions is experienced—or not experienced—before the more complex structuring that comes as identifications with parental figures and images develop and as the pleasures associated with group identifications, familial and extrafamilial, emerge. A child who receives the message that there is something awful about her skin and that of her parents receives a message far more intimate, elemental, and frightening than one who learns that she and her group are involved in an ethnic feud, a long-simmering tribal conflict, a "turf" dispute, a national rivalry, a religious controversy. The ethnocentric message comes with a kind of rough equality built into it, regardless of the actual power differentials of the groups: "they hate us and we hate them." The "us" offers protection, definition. But the protection that can be offered by a racially persecuted group, even one in which group identity and pride are celebrated, is defensive: "they hate black-skinned people, but we know black is beautiful." The temptation to use the aggressor's tactics is enormous and understandable—"white-skinned people are inferior"—especially because it can make up for time spent identifying with the aggressor's aggression.

The research generated in the 1950s by Kenneth Clark and others on the effects of racism on African American children has often been questioned and often been disputed. But, even though specific research situations yield different results, there has emerged a rough consensus that African American children, even those from families and neighborhoods where African American culture is celebrated, tend during their first elementary school years to express preferences for being white or for playing with white dolls when given a choice between a white and a dark-skinned toy. This expressed preference does not last in supportive contexts, but its very existence reflects a kind of prejudice that is different than ethnocentrism—one that induces identification with the oppressor or with the oppressor's prejudice. And the same point can be put the other way around. In studies of children's attitudes toward their own ethnic groups and nations, empirical research consistently shows children preferring their own group or nation, regardless of whether or not in strictly cognitive terms they know what a nation is. Affective ethnocentrism precedes cognitive ethnocentrism in these results. Younger children tend, also, to evaluate other groups and nations according to the ethnocentrisms of their own *ethnos*. Nevertheless, as the British psychologist David Milner has reported in his *Children and Race* (1975), the results of this kind of testing in Israel produced a two-tiered result. Two groups of children were tested, one of "Oriental" origin, one of European origin. The Israeli children showed a higher preference for Israeli people than children of almost any other national group had for their nationality. But both the groups of Israeli children preferred Israeli children of European origin, who were generally lighter skinned. The children, that is, reflected both the marked Israeli national consciousness, their group's ethnocentrism, and the "racial" or orectic prejudices within Israeli society against Sephardim.

Women who experience sexist attitudes and behavior and male and female homosexuals who are the targets of homophobia also know that they are experiencing something other than ethnocentrism or hostility to them as an out-group. They are not, of course, "out-groups" in the way that members of two tribal or ethnic or national groups are to each other. Girls and women live in the same families, the same communities, with boys and men; homosexuals are the children of heterosexuals (except for the very few contemporaries who have become the children of homosexual partnerships). The experience of being the denigrated part of a familial in-group—of being the Other to one's familiars, one's relatives, literally—has quite a different impact on ego formation and self-esteem than being an out-group to someone else's in-group. It is usually not in childhood but at puberty, as reproductive sexuality becomes possible, that the familial experiences of women and homosexuals become the prototypes, in their own feelings, for what they experience later. They are, also, well aware—even if not in a way that they can articulate—that the prejudices against them are prejudices of disidentification and fear: they hear "there is nothing of you in me" (no femininity, no homosexuality). So these prejudices deny the sense of commonality—including in-group solidarity—without which it is very difficult to be anything other than disoriented. Victims of sexism and homophobia often respond, thus, by creating alternative families. They look for or establish relationships that have parent-child ingredients, sisterhoods and brotherhoods; they may prefer same-sex separatist groups or communes or extended families.

The experiences common to members of groups that have been the targets of ideologies of desire, not just of ethnocentric prejudices, can be described generally with terms developed by Hannah Arendt for European Jews at the turn of the century. Orectic prejudices push their victims either to separate or to situate themselves in relation to the perpetrators in psychologically complex ways. The second alternative, the most commonly undertaken, produces marked psychological types because the victims are generally woven inextricably into the prejudiced societies. Arendt noted:

> The behavior patterns of assimilated Jews, determined by [their] continuous concentrated effort to distinguish themselves, created a Jewish type that is recognizable everywhere. Instead of being defined by nationality or religion, Jews were being transformed into a social group whose members shared certain psychological attributes and reactions,

the sum total of which was supposed to constitute "Jewishness." In other words, Judaism became a psychological quality and the Jewish question involved a personal problem for every individual Jew.[25]

Typically, there appeared a parvenu Jewishness or Jewish social character, characteristic of Jews who wanted to be successful in the terms permitted them in non-Jewish society, and who became servile and aggressive, accommodating and greedy, in their quests. But this type's opposite also appeared. Pariah Jewishness characterized Jews who refused assimilation but who also stayed away from Jewish society as well as from the fashionable or powerful non-Jewish circles. Pariahs, Arendt observed, are striking for their "humanity, kindness, freedom from prejudice, sensitiveness to injustice," while parvenus often develop versions of their oppressor's prejudices—including those against themselves (thus becoming "Jewish self-haters"). A third type, sometimes overlapping with the pariah, is what might be called a definitional activist, a reformer within the prejudiced society—the prewar Zionist, Civil Rights activist, feminist, or gay rights activist, people whose mission it is to create *group* (not individual) means of responding to orectic prejudice. Politically, they seek equality before the law, while culturally they work to achieve control over the definition of their group, to wrest that control away from the ideologically prejudiced.

## Methodological Implications

I have been distinguishing ethnocentrism from orecticism along five broad lines. The former is prejudice against real groups, and the latter against imaginary or constructed groups; one is present-oriented and restorative, while the other is sweepingly set on the future. Of the two, only orecticism is oriented toward the body and characterized by constant body referencing; and only orecticism involves partial identification with the group or groups against which prejudice is directed. Finally, the effects of the two kinds of prejudice on the ego formation and self-esteem of people, especially children, in their target groups are very different. These lines of difference also indicate, I think, why the different kinds of prejudice require different sorts and orders of study.

When ethnocentrism exists without being intermingled crucially with orecticism, when it is relatively pure, it can be approached initially with comparatively simple psychological assumptions. But it calls for intricately elaborate sociological work, because—to put the matter in stark terms—ethnocentrism involves real groups. Real groups have real histories, real social traditions, real economic habits and contexts, real political structures. The psychological assumptions of the 1930s culture and personality theorists about how Comanche culture produced the Comanche warrior, how the culture of Alor produced the people of Alor, were adequate to those societies, even if in application the theorists too often pathologized or took a mechanical approach. Orecticism, however, initially demands a complex psychological description, which must precede any effort to follow orecticists into public domains and, then, to study what their meeting with the public domain means for them and they for it. Indeed, the full-blown ideologies of desire that have had such horrendous effects in public domains during the twentieth century were typically brewed and concocted offstage for long periods before they surfaced, before they had the institutional life that history and sociology must study. They developed secretly before they intersected with existing ethnocentrisms, coloring those ethnocentrisms—helping "Jew hatred" become "antisemitism," or racial thinking become racism, helping censure of homosexuals as sinful become homophobia against homosexual acts and identities—and bringing the ethnocentrisms to the point where they became psychologically much more complex.

I am going to follow this methodological rule of thumb in the next chapter by launching a multifaceted psychological—largely psychoanalytic—investigation of character types given to ideologies of desire. More precisely, I look into the types of ideologies of desire that different character types characteristically employ. This inquiry will leave in suspense the suggestion I have made to the effect that orecticisms have flourished with particular strength and danger in the historical conditions of the West since the late nineteenth century, when, for example, a key distinction emerged between ethnocentric Jew hatred, which is ancient, and the antisemitism for which the German writer Wilhelm Mahr coined the word "Antisemitismus" in 1879. I will come back to develop this type of historical inquiry in Chapter 10, after I have set out a characterology.

# 7

## Character Types and
## Their Ideologies of Desire

The culture and personality theorists who developed notions of social character did not develop individual characterologies, even though they clearly acknowledged that people do have individual characters, which David Riesman defined as "the more or less permanent socially and historically conditioned organization of an individual's drives and satisfactions—the kind of 'set' with which he approaches the world and people."[1] As a result, Riesman could not ask how a person of one individual character type or another would fare in a society where, say, other-direction of social character prevailed. What he did speculate about was how a person of inner-directed social character would be out-of-step in a society where other-direction of social character prevailed. He could see only struggle among social character types, not struggles between individuals of different character types and the social character types. But it is this second sort of struggle, I want to suggest, that could, if carefully analyzed, link the suggestive culture and personality tradition with the topic it did not directly take up—prejudices.

### Theory of Character Types

Psychoanalysis might have provided Riesman with a theory of character types to coordinate with his own theory of social character, but he would have had to search it out, for there was no text by Freud containing such a characterology. The main gesture Freud made in this direction was a short essay called "Libidinal Types," published in 1931, although there were precursors to this systematic piece, especially "Neurosis and Psychosis" from 1924, which was an offshoot of *The Ego and The Id* (1923). But Freud's late essay went beyond any of the ways he had talked about character earlier.

In his early work, Freud had started out suggesting a characterology related to the instinctual drives, and many of his first associates responded by producing descriptions of oral characters, anal characters, phallic characters. Beginning in 1914 Freud had, second, distinguished narcissistic people of self-directed libido from object-directed, other-loving people, and he had linked this scheme with a contrast between people with masculine mental characteristics and people with feminine mental characteristics (whether male or female). Third, he and his colleagues had also considered characters dominated by a specific trait or a specific fantasy (those "wrecked by success," those considering themselves as exceptions). Similarly, they had written about characters dominated by a specific component instinct (the masochistic character) or a specific mode of instinctual discharge (the impulsive character). But his late essay on libidinal types makes it clear that for Freud the three character types associated with the three psychic agencies (id, superego, and ego) and keyed to the three major forms of the psychoneuroses—hysteria, obsessional neurosis, and narcissistic neurosis—were the most fundamental.

In "Libidinal Types," Freud first considered erotics, who are dominated by their ids and their quests for love; then obsessionals, who are dominated by their superegos and the (largely negative) commandments emanating from their superegos; and finally narcissists, who are organized by and for their egos and their egos' relations with the real world around them. To this day, no psychoanalyst has proposed a character typology that is as well grounded theoretically, as economical, or as encompassing.[2] Freud's scheme looked like this:

| *erotics* | *obsessionals* | *narcissists* |
|---|---|---|
| hysterical traits predominate = id dominated | obsessional traits predominate = superego dominated | narcissistic traits predominate = ego dominated |

But Freud's late efforts to think systematically about character remained without much influence, and as soon as Freud's followers began to develop characterological studies on his foundations, controversies arose. Some in the small original Viennese psychoanalytic group, for example, welcomed Wilhelm Reich's *Character Analysis* when it was first published in 1933. But others thought that Reich's work rested on too narrow a base of libido theory and was too tied to a sexual liberationist program, a vision of "sex economy" that would permit the "orgiastic potency" that Reich glorified as the goal of life, the content of mature character, and that, as I noted before, Reich considered the antidote to the prejudices organizing "the mass psychology of fascism." Still others thought that Reich's socialist political vision had led him to overdraw his portrait of how bourgeois capitalistic societies warp character development and forbid "orgiastic potency." But Reich's work did provide an important, and suggestive, elaboration of Freud's incipient theory of character by indicating how important types of defenses are to character formation and by showing how hysterical, obsessional, and narcissistic traits can consolidate into characters of these three forms.

Freud and Reich would have agreed on the general relation between character types and pathologies. Character traits are formed in reaction to the types of conflicts that can lead to pathologies, if uncontained by being transformed into character traits. That is, becoming hysterically psychoneurotic and developing an erotic or hysterical character are two different routes, one pathological and one relatively normal. Usually, a hysteric, suffering from one bodily symptom after another, will eventually become incapacitated. But hysterical defenses that become woven into an erotic or hysteric character can be tolerable, functional, in a person's life; the defenses are both more hidden from view (including therapeutic view) and more built into the fabric of a person's activities. To take another example, an obsessional character may, on the one hand, put such traits as discipline, orderliness, cleanliness, retentiveness, and stubbornness to use in a work situation where these are virtues. In developing such traits, he or she has reacted to internal conflicts that reference strongly to the anal stage and that involve intense guilt. An obsessional neurotic, on the other hand, will be crippled by symptoms that make it impossible to work—recurrent ideas that block intellectual activity, compulsive acts and rituals that are paralyzing. A narcissistically neurotic person may have grandiose, megalomaniac fantasies that make a realistic perception of possibilities for action impossible, and that produce constant debilitating oscillations in levels of self-esteem, but a person whose narcissism is characterological may have sweeping ambitions that are key to achievements or forceful leadership.

In the manner of the future culture and personality theorists, Freud made some suggestions about how the three character types behave in social and cultural settings. Freud's erotics, wanting to be loved and fearing loss of love, involve themselves in (or, more passively, get drawn into) relations of dependency. They are, like David Riesman's other-directed types, oriented by their need for love and approval or acceptance. The obsessionals, who heed the voices of their past as they have internalized them and identified with them, are conservative. These are Riesman's inner-directed people, but they are also the people who, under particular kinds of historical circumstances, can evolve into authoritarian personalities. And, as far as the third type is concerned, Freud noted that narcissists, independent, aggressive, active, loving rather than wanting to be loved (or wanting to compel love by being loving), can be leaders, cultural innovators, futurists—and he might have added that, if they are unable to succeed as leaders, they are submissive to narcissistic leaders, taking their sense of themselves from others, borrowing strength. In the home that is his castle, a narcissist who might be unable to lead in larger arenas reigns as a Man over his wife, whom he experiences as a part of himself.

In his clinical studies Freud also indicated the ways in which the various character types present themselves in the little social setting of the psychoanalytic process. Clinicians can get a feel for their patients' character structures by observing how their patients habitually behave toward them as analysis progresses—a process that also gives clear indications of how the different types relate to the people around them, including the people against whom they hold prejudices. The character types and the related neurotic types—in which the character types appear as caricatures—are condensed in analytic situations. Hysterical characters typically find it hard to stand the frustration of the analytic situation, particularly their "transference love" for the analyst, which must be unrequited. Moved by the love or love-and-hate they feel for the analyst, which grows out of or represents the early childhood loves they have forcefully repressed, they try to seduce or cajole or otherwise force the analyst to engage the revived early love and to enter into a personal or sexual relationship. Their main line of defense is repression, and it is often manifest by silence in sessions. Hysterics and hysterical

characters are also given, in the course of therapy, to changing symptoms. When one symptom dissolves under the effects of the work, another takes its place, as has happened in the course of the hysteric's
illness over time.

Obsessional characters, by contrast, do not develop new types of symptoms or change transference manifestations as the therapy unfolds.
They are constant, and they typically stay as they are by isolating their
words, which they often have in profusion, from their affect, their emotions. They go on and on, round and round, offering intricately and
conscientiously detailed accounts of their lives, their recurrent ideas,
their routines, without feeling, unable to feel. Most clinicians have to
fight their impatience and the temptation to interpret the obsessional's
words, in which unconscious thoughts and wishes may lie nearly exposed, as long as the words are so empty of affect. The interpretation
will not connect—it will be heard, even repeated and used, but it will
not touch the patient. As Freud once remarked, obsessional resistance
to analysis pursues "Russian tactics." The patient leads the analyst into
danger by accepting all interpretations, only to ambush the treatment
eventually by making it clear that all acceptance has been "under the
mental reservation of doubt."

Narcissistic characters may also be untouched by interpretations, but
this will be because they have refused or been unable to enter into the
transference. They want to love according to their images of perfect
love and they want to be loved according to their images of perfect
loving—which they did not have, and which they fear the analytic situation will not provide. They may consider the analyst unapproachably
omniscient, or they may be afraid to offer the analyst any opportunity
to prove with an "incorrect" interpretation that he or she is not an
omniscient being but a frustrator, even a castrater or attacker, a woun-
der. In this second mode, they may defensively disparage the analyst,
charging worthlessness, complaining about the analyst in much the
same mode that they use to express their prejudices—the analyst is inferior, too "feminine" (for males, but also females), uncultured. The
analyst does not, at any rate, exist as a real person, and this may also be
true of the other people in the narcissist's life, who are only extensions
of the narcissist.

As they accumulated clinical experience, Freud's followers added
elaborations of the character types and manifestations that he had suggested, while they worked to incorporate his later suggestions into ear-

lier characterological frameworks, like the instinctual drive scheme of oral, anal, and phallic characters. Key to this project was the insight, developed by Anna Freud in *The Ego and the Mechanisms of Defense* (1936), that the ways in which the ego defends against threats from the instincts (the id), orders from the superego, and challenges from the outside world are the crucial ingredients of character. But it was really not until Anna Freud published her *Normality and Pathology in Childhood* (1965) that psychoanalytic research produced a developmental theory adequate for undergirding a characterology of the sort Freud had suggested. What Anna Freud contributed was an organizing notion, as elegant in its simplicity as her father's three-part scheme, that a person's character, which is consolidated (though not finally, and not necessarily even firmly) in late adolescence and early adulthood, is the sum of his or her developments across a range of different lines. The "developmental lines," as she termed them, include the ones first traced by Freud and the many elaborations added by Anna Freud herself and others, particularly the child analysts of her generation:

- the libidinal line through the oral, anal, and phallic-genital stages and the component instincts associated with these—particularly sadomasochism with the anal stage and voyeurism and exhibitionism with the phallic;
- the object relations line from part-object to whole object preoedipal mother love through a negative Oedipal (same sex) relation and on (usually) to a positive Oedipal (opposite sex) parental love and then to identifications with parental figures outside the immediate family;
- the line leading from egolessness or symbiotic merger with the maternal figure through separation and individuation and on to ego strength;
- the (closely related) line of narcissistic development from primary narcissism or ego love and autoeroticism to mature love of others on the basis of secure self-esteem;
- the line of superego development from internalization of external figures and their superegos on to moral independence;
- the line of defense development that goes from earliest defenses such as regression and turning aggression on the self through projection and repression and to such complex defenses as intellectualization and sublimation.

Anna Freud added to this list a number of physical developmental lines with great emotional and mental implications:

- a line from autoerotic play to play with things and with others and on to enjoyable work;
- a line from inability to care for oneself or complete bodily dependence to weaning, body training, and varying degrees of independent management;
- a line from physical passivity and relative immobility to the exuberant joy in motion of toddlerdom to physical gracefulness and athleticism.[3]

Anna Freud and her colleagues also studied the cognitive developmental lines for speech, conceptualization, logical ability, speculative capacities, and so forth, but the most important explorers of this domain have been Jean Piaget and those who followed him in the creation of modern cognitive psychology.

In Anna Freud's view, a person's character can be read like an orchestral score—each instrument's part has a life of its own, but each is also a part within the whole. She did not, however, apply her developmental lines to the domain of characterology per se, performing the orchestration she had implied. But she and her associates did produce something quite similar, to which they gave the name the Diagnostic Profile, a way of systematizing intake and interview information to arrive at a diagnosis and treatment recommendation. A profile can show how some people develop evenly and harmoniously along the various lines, some develop unevenly—with strengths in some areas, weaknesses in others—and some remain relatively immature either altogether or in one or more areas.[4]

In general, this multifaceted developmental scheme registers the way in which psychoanalysis since Freud has moved away from schemes that too rigidly assign either pathologies or characters to specific stages of development. In both pathologies and characters, overlapping of stages is common. The greater flexibility, which is certainly welcome, does mean, however, that the field for applying Anna Freud's work to characterology is quite open. And within psychoanalytic writing on characterology, there is also little work on the relations between normal character types, character disorders, neurotic types, and psychotic types. In the remainder of this book, I will assume that there are spectrums or continuums of three sorts:

1. people with obsessional traits—obsessional characters—obsessional character disorders—obsessional neurotics—paranoiacs[5]
2. people with hysterical traits—hysterical characters—hysterical character disorders—neurotic hysterics—dissociative psychotics (including multiple personalities)
3. people with narcissistic traits—narcissistic characters—narcissistic character disorders—narcissistic neurotics—schizophrenics

I will also argue that children develop character traits, but that character forms or congeals only in late adolescence. Some people will remain at the level of having traits and not reach any habitual or characteristic way of acting and reacting, any characteristic way of harmonizing or at least regularizing through their ego agency the demands of their ids, their superegos, and the external world. Others may reach a habitual mode that is dysfunctional—a "character disorder." A particular pathology, neurotic or psychotic, can produce in a person a constant or a recurrent sabotaging of character formation (including dysfunctional formation), but the disruptive neuroses and psychoses will share ingredients or elements with the character formations that they disrupt or prevent. A hysteric, to put the matter differently, is a person whose neurosis does not allow the consolidation of a hysterical character, but whose neurosis may, if it deepens and is increased by further traumatization, give way to a psychosis. In such a case, the splits in the hysteric's psychic life, the products of repression, grow so unbridgeable that the hysteric becomes divided into, as it were, sealed psychic compartments, separate selves (as in multiple personality disorder).

Using the concept of developmental lines to approach the basic character types, we can bring together the various facets of characterology. We can say, for example, that hysterical characters are dominated by their developments along the libidinal and object relations lines—by their love lives—and particularly by the power their oral and genital desires and their preoedipal and oedipal objects have in them, over them, defying their defensive efforts at repression. Obsessional characters are dominated by the defenses they mobilize around their most frightening passive desires—particularly desires associated with or represented by passively enjoyed anal stimulation or anal fantasies, including those that reflect regression from phallic dangers. These are characteristically complex defenses that isolate affect, dampen or carefully control and assign roles to emotions, identify with aggressors. Their characters are like fortresses and their superegos are either very strong, even rigid, or persecutory: they punish themselves as they try not to punish others, and when they do punish others, they also punish themselves. Narcissistic characters are most shaped by the developments that their egos and especially ego ideals have undergone, either to achieve real ego strength or to achieve that unpredictable semblance of strength that is megalomania. Like obsessionals, they find it difficult to be passive; but they characteristically defend themselves by activity (as conversion of passive experiences into active strivings) or by using their passivity in an active manner. They operate by contending with reality, not by fortifying themselves.

The character types can have the same symptoms, but the symptoms will be differently constituted for each. Rather—for example—than speaking of depression, it makes greater clinical sense to speak of hysterical depression or obsessional depression or narcissistic depression. Mourning for lost love and feelings of abandonment, analsadistic rage unexpressed and turned on the self, deflated self-esteem—these are all forms of depression, each characteristic of a character type. Similarly, hysterics, obsessionals, and narcissists can all have phobias, but their phobias will be developmentally different and take different forms (in relation to objects or to situations). Hysterics commonly fear situations or objects that represent forbidden (incestuous) loves or sexual organs or acts; obsessionals fear polluting, infecting, disrupting, disorderly objects; narcissists avoid situations where they will be cut down. Diagnostic classifications based on types of symptoms—as is the scheme in the *Diagnostic and Statistical Manual* of the American Psychiatric Association—are not really characterologies, and they are of no help whatsoever in studying prejudices, which are not symptoms (as so many individual-level social psychological theories assume) but—at a deeper level—defensive processes.

As these quick sketches imply, in order for a developmental theory of character to be connected with a theory of social character, a bridge is needed. This, I will argue, can be built by reconsidering the mechanisms of defense outlined by Anna Freud in *The Ego and the Mechanisms of Defense* and then integrated into *Normality and Pathology in Childhood*. In the earlier book, Anna Freud had speculated that there is also a developmental line of types of defenses, from the earliest and most primitive to the most ubiquitous, repression, and on to the most complex and thickly armoring, intellectualization and isolation of affect.

People of different character types feel differently threatened by their own conscious and unconscious impulses, by their own developed strictures and guilt, by people or forces they encounter in their worlds, and they defend themselves differently, consciously and unconsciously. Using this insight, we can define prejudices by saying that they are the reflections in attitudes toward groups (and individuals as members of groups) of characteristic modes (usually complex modes) of defense.[6] Prejudices are social mechanisms of defense.

Just as the psychoanalytic literature gives little indication how the range from normality to psychosis is constituted, and how it might be, in a given individual's life, traversed backward or forward, so the literature on prejudices contains little about how prejudices function in characters, in neuroses and in psychoses. But it seems to me that the prejudices espoused by a normal obsessional character are milder, more coherent, less wild versions of those espoused by paranoiacs—that there is here, too, a continuum. The patient studied, for example, by Nathan Ackerman in "Antisemitic Motivation in a Psychopathic Personality" (1947) sounds like a horribly caricatured and dangerous version of the "normal" antisemites interviewed for *The Authoritarian Personality*.[7] Prejudices do not, I believe, presuppose pathology; they are—unfortunately—produced by normal people, and they often help normal people maintain their (relative) normality, as mechanisms of defense help normal people control their impulses, regulate themselves, balance the conflicting agencies of their psyches. But in psychotic people prejudices are part of the psychosis. The paranoid's Jews may have no point of contact with real Jews, while the obsessional character's Jews do.

Anna Freud's schemata make it very clear that within the broad defense-using types there are infinite variations, as Freud's three libidinal types, he stressed, are seldom to be found in pure form. No two people could possibly pass through the multitude of developmental lines in the same way, and there is no such person as the developmental paragon, the perfectly normal person. There are not even perfect specimens in developmental terms of the broad character types. Freud had, in fact, suggested that the mixed types in his scheme—erotic obsessionals, obsessional narcissists, narcissistic erotics—are much more common than unmixed ones. Taking these caveats into account, Freud did set out broad outlines that offer important indicators of how people may relate to others in their societies and to the shape of their social characters, while Anna Freud provided the specificity that is crucial for avoiding single-stage or single-factor emphasis, for criticizing notions of development that are too global or extrapolate too far from one sociocultural context, and for assuring that discussions of adult character consider childhood and adolescence. As Kenneth Kenniston noted in 1971, considering Anna Freud's work as the key step beyond the culture and personality work of the 1950s:

> Historical conditions which may stimulate development in one sector of life may well fail to stimulate it or actually retard it in other sectors. For example, many social critics today argue that a narrow kind of cognitive development is over-stimulated in Western societies at the expense of affective and interpersonal development, which are in turn retarded. Freud believed that precocious sexual development tended to retard intellectual development . . . Thus if we are to compare different historical epochs or different cultures from a developmental perspective, we must not merely compare how they define the overall stages of life and study the extent to which individuals actually pass through these global stages, but we must examine specifically how a given cultural and historical context affects each of many specific subsectors of human development.[8]

In the following three chapters, I extend my reflection on character and social character into a discussion, first, of developmental lines typical of various characters and their prejudices; second, of types of societies that promote and inhibit different types of character and social character; and, third, of psychosocial or culture and personality developmental types. But for the moment, I want to continue character-type sketching based on Freud's "Libidinal Types" and Anna Freud's theory of developmental lines. (These frameworks seem to me to encompass the important contributions from other Freudians, from Melanie Klein to Jacques Lacan, which I will take into account as I go, and also to be broad enough to apply across cultures.)

## Obsessional Characters and Their Prejudices

People with obsessional traits or characters are regular or rigid in routines, well organized and dedicated to devices of organization, habitually punctilious and punctual or at least habitual in spending time (even if this means habitually late), usually neat, aversive to dirt, and efficient, but sometimes (particularly in adolescence) studiously sloppy, laboriously disheveled, given to living in a chaos that only they consider ordered. People of this type can be mentally lucid and orderly, but they often take to constant intellectualizing in the sense that they run things over and over in their minds, brooding, repeating phrases, repeating stories, talking quickly and emptily. They may become fixed on certain mental acts (like counting, list making, scenario creating) that have the function of defending them against or warding off unwanted thoughts. But they are also made nervous by their mental acts. Else Frenkel-Brunswik, for example, asked a group of young women who had scored very high on a scale measuring antisemitism "what would drive a person nuts?" and the women replied, either little irritations from without or "ideas which keep running in your head."[9]

Obsessionals may rely on an *idée fixe* to organize themselves or become wound up in a superstitious or mystical or pseudomystical ideational system and organization. They are also ceremonial and may have neurotic ceremonies that "magically" protect them, like hand washing and other forms of germ fighting and cleansing or checking (to see if the door is locked, the stove off, and so on).[10] Often they are mystical in relation to the past, treating traditions as protections and talismans or—in the New Age manner—drawing eclectically on ideas held to be both venerable and pure or unsullied, as the character named Beineberg drew on Buddhism in *Young Törless*. Sometimes obsessionals keep disturbing questions of truth or morality at bay by making them into legal or technical questions, as they keep important decisions at a distance by breaking them up into smaller and more technical parts. They can, then, be uncertain or indecisive or vacillating without giving the appearance of being so. They can also maintain appearances by becoming engrossed in semantic disputes and logic chopping, thriving on complex interpretations of doctrines, commentaries upon commentaries, citations upon citations, in arcane or very academic language.

When obsessionals take up a project or a task, they devote themselves to it with constant activity. Their manner is often labored—and they give much attention to the amount of effort they are expending, as though a task not requiring great effort would not be worth doing. Their labor seems like a form of self-punishment, and they often reproach themselves explicitly, admonishing themselves for failures and mistakes as well as for wasting time or money (or both, for they often subscribe to Ben Franklin's conviction that "time is money"). Some obsessionals will talk to themselves admonishingly, as though their bad conscience had to have, literally, a voice. Once they take up a task, they do not put it down; they persist, even going on stubbornly well past the point that they themselves would, in their rationalistic accounting mode, designate as the point of diminishing returns. They find it difficult to admit defeat and will go to great extremes of either denying the costs of their imperviousness or presenting those costs in bloodless, abstract forms (offering "body counts," for one horrible example, rather than records of deaths in battles). One might apply the following Weberian description of the Puritan spirit to a typical obsessional:

> For this spirit displays an untiring activity, a boundlessness of grasp, quite contrary to the natural impulse to enjoyment and ease, and contentment with the mere necessities of existence; it makes work and gain an end in themselves, and makes men the slaves of work for work's sake; it brings the whole of life and action within the sphere of an absolutely rationalized and systematic calculation, combines all means to this end, uses every minute to the full, employs every kind of force, and in the alliance of scientific technology and the calculus which unites all these things together, gives to life a clear calculability and abstract exactness.[11]

Along with their tendency to identify with their tasks or projects or causes, obsessionals tend to identify with particular roles or social categories. They need to be able to designate themselves as "an X" (whether this is a religious group, a profession, an ethnicity, a gender). When they have assigned themselves a role, they feel secure in carrying out what they take to be its requirements. They know how to behave, which rules to follow, what proprieties are in force; they have standards, criteria for judging success and failure. Usually they are not, however, ostentatious in their roles, and they eschew any theatricality (of the sort that appeals to hysterical characters), often going so far as to sweep into their prejudices any people they judge to be given to self-display or ostentation (particularly of wealth). The obsessional tendency to identify with a role or embrace an identity (as in "identity politics") can go to the point of self-caricature. Theodor Adorno, for example, analyzing the character traits of the men who used American radio during the war for broadcasting antisemitic fascist propaganda, noted that there was a certain play-acting quality about these agitators. But they were not impostors—they did not play at being someone else; rather, they were self-caricaturists.[12] The same quality is obvious in many of today's fundamentalist broadcasters and self-appointed values-preserving pundits, both those who use pure, proper language and those who like to indulge scatology, the sewer and bathroom language so common among adolescent obsessionals. Such agitators often prefer radio, rather than television, because radio feels to them less overtly exhibitionistic, even if it is very exhibitionistic; they are a disembodied voice, and thus—in a delusional way—free of their bodies. This self-caricaturing quality baffles those who are not excited by it and leaves them unsure about how to judge such agitators (as, currently, journalists are unsure how seriously to take the clownish and vulgar Russian antisemite Vladimir Zhirinovsky).

Many obsessionals choose to wear uniforms or otherwise make themselves indistinguishable in appearance from others who share the same identity or role. Codes of appearance, dress conformism, also allow for a degree of sanctioned exhibitionism. Similarly, sanctioned and efficient aggression, channeled into precise forms, is tremendously appealing, as obsessionals need to keep their aggression in check. Keeping to their obsessional routines can give them a sense of unostentatious superiority; the routines, as Freud once remarked, flatter the obsessional's self-love "by making him feel that he is better than other people because he is specially cleanly or specially conscientious."[13]

Some obsessionals are collectors, others hoarders, and others accumulators of money in secretive ways (some alternating periods of penury with periods of largess), and most psychoanalytic characterologists link this kind of trait with childhood anal retention and expulsion—manipulation of anal functions designed to control others, to be in command of situations that are threatening. Freud cited three character traits as typical of obsessionals—cleanliness, obstinacy, and parsimony—and found these anal characteristics exaggerated in obsessional neurosis, which can tend into paranoid anxiety about dirt, about loss of control, about robbery or other forms of being depleted or, most persistently, can lead to paranoid fantasies (in both males and females) about being anally penetrated or raped.

Obsessionals are often attracted to large bureaucratic institutions where they can be both lost in the crowd and enormously powerful in a small sphere of activity where they can treat people like scum, dirt to be cleaned up, or like uncivilized children. Academics not infrequently need both the obsessional routines of schools and a "captive audience" of students whom they think of as in need of shaping up, mental laundering. Mental hospitals, old age homes, homes for delinquent adolescents, and prisons attract people as employees who want to be able to lord it over those they can call messy and messed up; their scenes are out of *One Flew over the Cuckoo's Nest* and their main dramatic quality is *Schadenfreude,* pleasure in their victims' misfortune. Their pleasure often focuses on humiliations they are able to bring about in the domain of their anal fixations. They relish making their victims feel shame over their bodily needs by regulating their toilet use with passes and schedules, depriving them of any provisions for their modesty, getting them to dirty themselves, engaging in all kinds of what the Italian chronicler of Auschwitz, Primo Levi, called "excremental coercions." Obsessional institutions are essentially organized around just such coercions—a condition that so jolts the sensibilities of the victims and shames them that they cannot find the words to protest it.

In the more paranoid reaches of obsessional fantasies, a dimension usually deeply repressed in obsessional characters and obsessional neurotics leaps out. Freud noted it in his study of the paranoid Dr. Schreber—a wish to be the opposite sex. Schreber's desire to be a woman was the expression of (and the form for) his desire to be passive, to enjoy passive pleasures.[14] All that the obsessional hopes to ward off—all unacceptable and dirty desires, usually of an anal or sadomasochistic sort, often connected with this deeply hidden desire to be the opposite sex—are attributed to people or forces in the world that are malignant, intellectually formidable, and aggressive. The "others" are dirty, nasty, assertive, and attacking, and there is little distinction among them along gender lines; the enemy women are construed as attackers and penetrators as the men are (and thus the women are, in a stereotypical formulation, the "Jewish American Princess," a pushy, castrating bitch-woman).[15] The lack of gender distinction among the victims connects to the obsessional's own desire to be the opposite sex, which is always a desire to be passive (even in women who desire to be male, the desire is to be a passive male).

Initially, the socially directed defense mechanism most frequently resorted to is displacement: obsessionals purge themselves of polluting thoughts and desires by displacing them onto others, who then are experienced as dirtying and assertively polluting.[16] Their ideal is a self filtered of all impurities, all temptations, an imperturbable, perhaps even saintly self that cannot be attacked. Similarly, their work ethic keeps out of bounds all tempting states of relaxation or spontaneity that could allow them to be swept away, overwhelmed or overstimulated.

(Certain forms of Prohibition behavior are obsessional—they aim not at alcohol per se but at intoxication.)

Putting unacceptable desires and ideas onto others results in a blockage and avoidance of introspection. Obsessionals direct intellectual effort out at the others, whose aggressive activities and plots and machinations need constant attention. Consequently, they can little say how they feel about anything, and they tend toward understanding their thoughts and feelings as under outside control to a dangerous degree. On the surface, they may appear free from self-reproach and guilt—but that is because their prejudices allow them to displace their guilty feelings onto others, blame others, and tell themselves that they have been sabotaged, that someone else is making them unhappy. The more paranoid they are, the more likely it will be that the ones making them unhappy or hurting them are the ones whom they most envy and want to be like—even love. When unable to displace their guilty feelings, they constantly complain of their own inadequacies—they should do this or that, they say; they must get organized and be more disciplined, less wasteful, more productive, more able in relationships; they should be better, more considerate, more self-sacrificing, and so forth. If only they could be good, they lament. Unable to displace blame, in a defeatist mode, they may say that they never will be happy, that they are bad people, whom no one should or could love.

But obsessionals also need to relieve themselves of the harshness of their self-critical, self-chastising superegos and the most taxing of their superegos' demands. These they displace onto others as well, and usually onto the same others as have had to absorb their forbidden anal and sadomasochistic desires. The same people who are called dirty will be charged with being of huge intellectual power. They are powerful enough to run the world, to constitute an international conspiracy, to have a monopoly on shrewdness for amassing wealth. These others are nearly omniscient, which makes them the best people from whom to learn how to be omniscient. Envy colors the hatred directed at the hidden powers.

Whether id-related, superego-related, or (usually) both, the obsessional prejudices are marked by their tie to aggression (specifically, to anal sadism), as the hysterical prejudices are by their tie to sexuality. Obsessionals construe their enemies as enormously aggressive—they invest them with their own aggression—both physically and mentally; their enemies are physically intrusive and mentally insinuating—they get inside in every way possible, they are parasites in the bodies and minds of the prejudiced, like science fiction "aliens." When the enemies are construed in this way, any feature of love or compassion in them has to be suppressed. The Jews, for example, become the "chosen people" of a vengeful God, a God totally without mercy. The Jews will do unto their enemies what they have done in obedience to such a God—they will circumcise and castrate—for this is what their aggressive God requires of them.[17]

Obsessional prejudices involve, to put the matter another way, hatred of hatred. Love is suppressed in the obsessional and lovingness is suppressed in the enemy. The obsessional then becomes someone who can subscribe to the self-understanding Joseph Goebbels, the Nazi propaganda minister, achieved after he let himself be penetrated completely by Hitler's person and ideology: "I, however, want to be able to hate . . . Oh, I can hate, and I don't want to forget how. Oh, how wonderful it is to be able to hate."[18] Particularly in the face of defeats, the obsessional can subscribe to a motto like the one Goebbels created for the Germans after their humiliating loss to the fearsome Russian "Red Wave" to their East—"Hatred our duty, revenge our virtue."

This psychological feature of the obsessional prejudices has been understood by analysts of antisemitism, but usually in historical terms. Maurice Samuel argued in a widely read call to resistance, *The Great Hatred* (1940), that the Nazi "antisemitic hallucination" was a quite different thing from "anti-Jewish sentiment," "the ordinary variety of racial, religious and economic bitterness," because it involved a constant "obsessional exaggeration" of Jewish power and Jewish capacity to mobilize both capitalists and communists for their international cabal. Why, Samuel asked, was the "diabolization of the Jew" so acceptable in different classes, conditions, and countries? Why had antisemitism become the core of all fascist revolutionary movements? He answered that antisemitism was the vehicle for horror of Christ the Jew, the Prince of Peace, the figure who represented "the diminution and elimination of force as the basis of human relationships." The force-worshipping Nazis were, fundamentally, fighting against the worldview of peace, which Jesus the Jew, inheritor and propounder of Mosaic law, represents or could represent for both Christians and Jews, who are—or should be—people of a single tradition. Antisemitism is "Christophobia." And antisemites, in Samuel's view, were, by attacking the Judeo-Christian tradition in which they themselves had been raised, attacking the possibility of love and peace in themselves.[19]

In less symbolic terms, the obsessional's aggressive "great hatred" is of an aggressor construed as a penetrator. In the obsessional mode of prejudice, the aggressors are a problem, and a solution for the problem must be found. The matter is intellectually set up, set out. The enemy people represent or carry penetrating impulses or strictures (they are related to the id or to the superego), and they must be gotten rid of. The obsessional gets rid of them in thought, by types of thinking or intellectual modes of defense, in manners which are later—if social and political conditions encourage it and leaders like Hitler articulate it as a political ideology—translated into action. Most commonly used is the defense known as undoing or what Freud called *ausgeschehenmachen,* "making unhappened," that is, making the past itself nonexistent. More than simply ignoring the past, this defense magically eliminates it, leaving a blank in memory. The equivalent social mechanism of defense would eliminate a people from the historical record, either by physically eliminating them or by destroying their history, or both. Similarly, isolating involves severing a happening from any emotion connected with it, cutting any ties it has to associations, and, as it were, dropping it off in mental space so that it does not enter into thought processes—out of sight, out of mind—and so that it generates no emotion in memory. The social equivalent of isolation ghettoizes or exports a people so that their history of connection and any history of appreciation or fascination with them are severed and they are made pariahs. At the same time, history can be rewritten, so that a people with a history suddenly has none, or the historical relationships between peoples no longer exist, or actions taken against a people disappear from memory and the historical record. In the current forms of antisemitism, like denial of the reality of the Holocaust—a form of undoing—it is the very history of antisemitism itself that is being denied.

When prejudiced, obsessionals are set against the very others they have used to cleanse themselves of frightening desires and to contain their superegos. But obsessionals do not, so to speak, stare at these others with a mixture of repulsion and attraction; the others become like trash containers that have to be emptied—the others must be gotten rid of. In mild forms, obsessional prejudice says "Keep Out," *Juden Verboten.* But at its most extreme, obsessional prejudice is annihilating or plans for annihilation: the others must be cleaned away and even evidence of them destroyed. (It is no accident that the phrase "nuclear holocaust," which named the way in which international Communism might be destroyed, came into use in America in the early 1960s, after the genocide against the Jews in Europe had been named the Holocaust.) His prejudices give the obsessional the feeling of being purged; they are a guarantee of his moral purity. Thus—to cite a chilling example—Himmler could say in a well-known speech of October 4, 1943: "Most of you know what it means when 100 corpses are lying side by side, when 500 lie there or 1,000. Having borne that and nevertheless— some exceptional human weaknesses aside—having remained decent [*anstandig*] has hardened us . . . All in all, we may say that we have accomplished the most difficult task out of love for our people. And we have not sustained any damage to our inner self, our soul, and our character."[20]

No matter what the intensity of their desire to eliminate the others, obsessionals are dedicated to classifying and marking the people and groups against whom their prejudices are directed, for they must make sure that their enemies are identifiable, that they cannot hide in a crowd, or—worse—infiltrate the obsessional's own group, spreading their pollution through sexual contact or intellectual takeover. Sciences of classification have to be developed. Symbolic insignias designed—*they* must wear a Star of David, a pink triangle, a numerical brand. Files must be kept. And very little distinction is made between the sciences (pseudosciences) of classification and mystical systems, numerology. Obsessionally prejudiced people typically find secret police forces and espionage agencies congenial, normal—as though these were their own minds writ large.

As social theorists, obsessionals entertain visions of social life in which distinctions disappear. At the most extreme, this means that all people deemed distinct, all rejected or unassimilated people, must be "disappeared." But many types of social arrangements can fulfill the distinction-destroying need, from communistic ones that are meant to eliminate class differences and private property to capitalistic ones that are meant to make it possible for anyone who works hard to move upward, into the dominating class. The psychological motive behind the obsessional's convictions could be expressed as "no one should be forced to be passive in relation to someone who has more power, authority, possessions, wealth." Even when obsessionals are fatalistic, as they often are, the fatalism has as its psychological content an elimination of distinctions. Anxiety about being overwhelmed, rendered ineffectual or inactive or passive, is key. Both males and females often express such anxiety in frightening fantasies of anal attack or rape or, in a more disguised form, in fantasies of people sneaking up from behind and stabbing them in the back.[21] Similarly, both devoutly desire a leader figure who can be construed as not attacking but impervious, as part of the attack prevention, as a fortress for the prevention of chaos, confusion, disorganization. The leader is, so to speak, the Great Obsessional— he *is* his followers on a scale that makes them feel more secure than any action of their own ever could. He is the one to whom the obsessional can submit without feeling penetrated, attacked—so the submission is ecstatic, the *innocent* fulfillment of a great and greatly forbidden desire.

The desire to be in control, or not to be controlled, that is so strong in obsessionals can make them leap contradictorily over their desire to eliminate distinctions, so that they, as controllers, have the distinction of being better at organizing and setting policy. Sartre once referred to antisemitism as "poor man's snobbery" because he thought antisemitism was indigenous to the lower middle class, flourishing particularly among farmers who had no tolerance for citified dealers in unreal property like money. But he completely missed with this formulation the kind of snobbery that antisemitism is—the snobbery of self-declared social reformers, people who think that they, and they alone, can make the world as it (morally) ought to be. They are people who divide the world rigidly into good and evil, pure and impure. And they form groups only with others who are good, with a leader who is Good.

## Hysterical Characters and Their Prejudices

People with hysterical traits and characters are restless and questing, always in relationships (in reality or in fantasy), often seductive, in person or through surrogates, often vain or at least very concerned with appearances and attractiveness. The hysterical character will use his or her body to make an impression or attract attention—by erotic display, by physical fitness exhibition, by decorative costuming, or by being ill. He or she is, in turn, impressionable, easily struck by the way others use their bodies. (As the old joke goes—for every exhibitionist there is a voyeur, and every exhibitionist can also be that voyeur.) If obsessionals are people whose minds have lives of their own, making them almost disembodied, then hysterical people are those whose bodies have lives of their own. Their bodies symbolize their minds.

Generally, the hysterical character relates to the world impressionistically, never focused on anything or anyone, but simply attracted or repulsed. Pleasure and displeasure are like cognitive modes for hysterical people, who have little interest in facts or knowledge per se and are often uninformed and naive. They react to other people immediately, without being influenced or deflected by inquiry; they entertain no complications and perceive no shadings. Correlatively, they are usually romanticizers, sentimental and given to idealizations and nostalgias for childhood ways.

Hysterical people are emotionally hungry and may act upon this hunger in literally or metaphorically oral ways—by eating, by assimilating or taking in or engaging everything and everyone greedily, by enjoying endless conversations for their atmosphere of conviviality and intimacy, or by being without boundaries, merged in ways that echo their childhood mergers with their mothers (which may have been full of frustration and anger and not in any way blissful). They launch relationships with great emotional display, energy, theatricality. Disappointments always come, leaving them enraged and despairing—sometimes with the feeling that the rage has boiled up from an unknown source, burst out of nowhere, taken over. Another round of hungry emotional display and effort to capture attention follows, and these ups and downs, mergers and explosions are felt by others as exploitative and manipulative. Hysterical types are usually completely surprised by the disruptive consequences of their behavior, asking "how could this have happened?" when relationships self-destruct. (Similarly, patronizing racists, after they have been "good" to their Old Black Joe or their talented young "boy," are completely startled to find themselves hated.)

Hysterical characters give the impression of play acting, being theatrical, because they are not able to gauge their feelings or say how they really do feel, although they experience themselves as bundles of feelings (unlike obsessionals who numbly cannot find their feelings). The emotions that seem to take possession of the hysterical are sometimes split off and assigned by them to another self, another half. It follows that people of this type often live some form of double life, go in some form of disguise, or engage in some form of imposture—they play both sides of themselves. They may, for example, have an adult self and a child self. Or they may have a good side and a bad side, a chaste side and a lascivious side. And they often think of their lives as conflictually parsed into masculine and feminine elements, work and love dimensions (one of which, usually their work side, will seem to them their good and chaste area). They often fear being found out, discovered, their disguises penetrated and their complex sexuality revealed. They unconsciously understand the people they are prejudiced against to be capable of exposing them, and this is especially so if they live in proximity to their victims—for example, if their victims work for them, particularly in domestic capacities, or if they engage in sexual relations with their victims. They will often be convinced that their victims have a kind of animal intuitiveness, which is alluring but frightening because it can penetrate secrets and reveal hypocrisies.

The mental style of hysterical characters, in addition to being vague and impressionistic, without the attention to detail that so characterizes obsessionals, is full of fissures. Hysterical characters can seldom render a full story—they tell an aspect, a part, whatever suits their needs of the moment, engaging in what might be called unintentional lying. They make contradictory statements without being aware. Whatever they find threatening or disturbing in a situation they repress, while emphasizing the opposite. Freud noticed this proclivity in the hysterics he studied, and he even linked it to the development of prejudices. Writing about a patient known as Dora, who lived in an archetypal hysterical milieu, that is, a family in which sexual manipulativeness and secrecy about relationships was the hypocritical norm, Freud noted that she had certain trains of reproachful thoughts that she constantly reiterated as though she were possessed by them ("I can think of nothing else"):

> Reflection will suggest that this exaggerated train of thought must *owe its reinforcement to the unconscious.* It cannot be resolved by any effort of thought, either because it reaches with its roots down into unconscious, repressed material, or because another unconscious thought lies concealed behind it. In the latter case, the concealed thought is usually the direct contrary of the supervalent one. Contrary thoughts are always closely connected with each other and are often paired off in such a way that the *one thought is exaggeratedly conscious while its counterpart is repressed and unconscious.* This relation between the two thoughts is an effect of the process of repression . . . This process I call *reactive reinforcement* and the thought which asserts itself exaggeratedly in consciousness (in the same way as a prejudice) and cannot be removed I call a *reactive thought.*[22]

The prejudices of hysterical characters are such hyperconscious, reactive thoughts. They think "I hate them" and repress the contrary "I love them"; their "I don't want to be near them" keeps from consciousness their "I want to be near them." This is a different type of defense than obsessional splitting of idea from affect, experience from emotion. Hysterical people are not unemotional or rigidly in control; they are— so to speak—half-emotional, or half-aware of their emotions.

Hysterical characters feel themselves to be more refined and less sexual than the people against whom their prejudices are directed. And it is always crucial to them that their others be lower, which means designated as the coarse ones, the more sexual ones. The classification keeps the hysterical characters separated from their own sexuality—it is assigned elsewhere, either to their own split-off self or to the objects of their prejudice, or both. In other words, a hysterical character's self-reproaches are cast onto his or her "lower" self or onto the Other in the form of reproaches. Freud noted that "a string of reproaches against other people leads one to suspect a string of self-reproaches with the same content."

If the hysterically prejudiced person both forms an other self and finds a group against whom to direct reproaches or prejudice, then there is a bond between these two sorts of split-off sexuality. In the guise of the lower other self, the hysterical character can, for example, visit with the hated group, go among its members, have sexual relations with them—and often never acknowledge or even actively deny the visiting, the mingling, the sexual relations. An upstanding citizen can go to a brothel and then "forget" the episode when at home with his unsullied wife. The central chapters of *The Autobiography of Malcolm X* form a casebook about white visitors to Black Harlem who actually visit their own fantasies. The hysterical prejudices are prejudices of "keep them in their places," and it is crucial that those lower places be both elsewhere and nearby, so they can be visited in fact or fantasy.

The objects of hysterical characters' prejudices are—in one way or another, literally or symbolically—domestics. They live in a distinct part of the household, whether in fact or fantasy or social theory or myth, whether in a familial, community, or national household image. Prejudiced hysterical characters find it necessary to have servants—and these come from the lower classes or from groups that have been acquired explicitly as slaves or servants, or, in colonial contexts, from the colonialized. When the hysterically prejudiced are upper class, descriptions like this fit them:

> Theirs was an aristocratic, antibourgeois spirit with values and mores emphasizing family and status, a strong code of honor, and aspirations to luxury, ease and accomplishment ... [They] typically recoiled at the notion that profit should be the goal of life; that the approach to production and exchange should be internally rational and uncomplicated by social values; that thrift and hard work should be the great virtues; and that the test of the wholesomeness of a community should be the vigor with which its citizens expand the economy.[23]

Eugene Genovese wrote these words in 1965 about Southern planters who rejected Yankee obsessionality and enterprise, but an adapted version of the description could also be applied to the lower-class whites of the region, who constructed an even lower class out of members of their own group ("poor white trash") or from the group they, too, construed as naturally slavish (the Negroes). Hysterical prejudices are conducted in the medium of dominance and submission, masters and slaves, and the characters of hysterics are themselves hierarchical: hysterical characters have intrapsychic masters and servants quarters, double lives. Class prejudice and race prejudice are interconnected in complex ways sociologically and historically, but psychologically they connect through the human need, most acute in people of the hysterical type, for persons on whom to set *down* a burden—a burden of desire and self-reproach.

The social theories hysterical characters adopt most frequently involve a vision of the family as the center of the world. This may be the theorist's own family or his organization conceived as a family, or it may be the region or nation as a family, or it may be the family of (most of) mankind—the scope varies. But the family always has a definite hierarchy in it, with a distinct lower rank in which the victims of prejudice live or to which they are naturally assigned. One group rules in a hierarchy that is "natural" and that is justified and rationalized in theories steeped in pseudoscience—not theories of the mystically and mathematically universalized variety so appealing to obsessionals, but those of the crudely biological. The ultimate hierarchy in the family, even more fundamental than whatever obtains between men and women, is the one between parents and children. All such theorists of the family have been children, and all build their theories upon that experience, making sure that a spot below the one they themselves occupied is accounted for—there is a lower class or race that serves even children. This vision makes it possible for the theorizers to remain respectful of the adults, of the mother's care and particularly of the father's law. Passivity in the face of the fathers is a virtue, as is respect for ancestors, traditions, and traditional familial ways of life. Prejudiced hysterical characters, as hierarchicalists, view with horror challenges to the hierarchy. Revolution is anathema, as is any outside interference in the organization of the family, particularly any form of abolitionism that criticizes prejudices in the family against the lower group. Invoking "family values" invokes natural hierarchy.

For a hysterical character to be cast by force or by accident into the role of a servant causes trauma. To be physically injured (especially in conditions—like wars—which require delusions of invulnerability as a condition of functioning), to be dispossessed, or to be threatened with downward mobility—these represent a fall into the lower depths, the split off realm. Many clinicians observed during both world wars that the number of diagnosed male hysterics in European and American populations increased dramatically.[24] Fear of injury, often felt as fear of castration, was the main contributor to the upsurge—as can be seen currently in America as fear of violent crime galvanizes the traits of many hysterical urban cowboys and opponents of gun control. A rebellion by the servants has the same meaning: if the servants step out of their place, the masters and mistresses may fall into it. But if rebellions, revolutions, and outside interference are the key challenges in political terms, the most profound and intimate challenge, the quintessential act of transgression, is intermarriage between the higher and the lower. Marriage represents equality for the lower partner and thus destroys the main theme of the hysterical character's prejudice—"they have a place and they must stay in it."

Objection to intermarriage, however, usually covers or keeps out of view the reality of life within the hysterical character's own family; it obscures whatever the degree of sexual traffic over stated borders, particularly as the family fathers and brothers develop liaisons with the women of the lower group. The family that hysterical characters idealize is one in which this reality is repressed—it is a sexual economy of looseness under the aegis of moralism or puritanism. (As I will note later, where "miscegenation" is the norm and not considered illicit, the hysterical prejudices do not flourish, a situation obvious to historians of the course of Negro slavery in Brazil, as opposed to that in the American South.) As hysterical characters repress or deny their own sexual desires, they also deny those of the parental generation—especially if these desires overlap, if there occurs sexual manipulation or incest or abuse between the parental and the child generations.

The hysterical type manifests neurotic symptoms known as conversion symptoms or somatizations—bodily expressions or symbolizations of psychic conflict, which may range widely from disturbances of eating and gastrointestinal functions to disturbances of sexual function and which may shift over time, one being succeeded by another or combined with another. People of hysterical character also often produce bodily configurations—they sculpt their bodies into shapes that represent responses of conformity to or rebellion against social conventions of physical beauty or propriety—without necessarily making themselves ill or debilitating their internal organs. When this hysterical type is severely disturbed, however, much more serious symptomology appears: depression (sometimes in combination with another "side," mania), and extreme splitting or dissociative shaping into different physical-mental selves (the so-called multiple personality), especially if there has been a history of trauma, including very early experiences of seduction, abuse, or loss of place in the family hierarchy.

An old controversy continues within psychoanalytic theory about whether the symptomology typical of hysterics and the traits typical of hysterical characters should be described in libidinal terms as oral or phallic. On the one hand, hysterics display the inconstancy in object relations that is said to be a manifestation of "oral character"—the vacillation between loving (in the mode of merger with or identification with, even incorporation of, the beloved) and angrily, impatiently rejecting either the beloved or other people as ungratifying, inadequately mothering. On the other hand, hysterics are not fixated at the oral stage; they have reached the phallic-genital level, and Freud always stressed that their main mode of defense, repression, presupposed the degree of ego development characteristic of children far beyond the oral stage. Hysterics seem to genitalize or treat as genitals many parts of their bodies, their fantasies are ceremonies of genital worship, and Freud even spoke of hysterical attacks as themselves "an equivalent of coition"[25] But, at the same time, hysterical people will often refuse to look at genitals (especially of the opposite sex), expressing great modesty, or showing reactions of disgust, sometimes phobias. In either mode, the genitals fix their attention.[26]

In psychoanalytic work after Freud, a rough consensus slowly arose to transform this controversy into a classification. Elizabeth Zetzel, in summarizing this trend, has argued for the existence of subtypes of hysterical characters—sometimes called oral and phallic, or "bad" and "good," or infantile and adult. The oral hysterical character usually has a complex background of inadequate mothering and deprivation in early childhood, sometimes to the point of sexual or physical abuse, and is quite unstable, given to extremes of exhibitionistic and provocative behavior. The phallic hysterical character comes from a less deprived background, has experienced more secure relations in childhood, and is better able to sustain adult relationships, as well as to succeed in work. The two types of hysterical characters are developmentally different, although their somatic symptoms may be similar.[27]

Especially in social situations where males are raised for life in the public sphere and females for life in the domestic sphere, hysterical characters (of both types) and their prejudices have quite gender-specific forms. Men, for example, have the latitude to act violently on their prejudices, which implies acting outward and usually targets the sexuality of their victims. Their scope for action accords with their tendency to externalize affects, a tendency that is probably reinforced by the externality of their genitals and the ways in which their phalluses become associated with acting, not being acted on. Rather than conversion symptoms on their own bodies, they frequently have their symptoms on their victims' bodies. They do not become impotent if they can diminish the sexuality of the males in their victim group—to the point of castration, emasculation—in order to keep the victims in their place and away from the perpetrator's women. They enhance their sexual power with weapons and they deny the victim males weapons or military training (or, in more democratic times, they make them into the expendable "cannon fodder" of their desegregated armies). They humiliate the victim males by taking their women as mistresses (not wives) and making sure that any children of these unions fall to the lower class or group. Prejudiced female hysterical characters, by contrast, devote themselves to preserving the hierarchy of classes and groups in the arenas where they can act. This may involve such tactics as overworking their victims, being ill and demanding care from their victims, requiring praise for their refinement, or compounding their victims' servitude with philanthropy—binding their victims with a rope of generosity in addition to their chain of servitude.

Such differences in possibilities for action between males and females have always been particularly significant among hysterical characters because such characters are particularly susceptible to cultural influences and able to sense or assess those influences, to register them like changes in psychic and social weather. The hysterical character's symptoms and actions easily take on the features of his or her milieu. By imitating, adapting, and playing to expectations in an exhibitionistic mode, the hysterical character relates to his or her audiences in the terms each audience requires. And this process is, of course, gendered along the lines of the audience's expectations. When hysteria was intensively studied at the turn of the century, the received opinion was that the vast majority of hysterics were female—the neurosis had, after all, been known since antiquity as a disease of the *hysteros,* the womb, and thus of women. But as the great French neurologist Jean-Martin Charcot and others presented cases of male hysterics and described them in the terms used for females, the common opinion receded somewhat. Among clinicians, if not more generally, it has been well known for a century that both male and female hysterical characters tend to behave in imitative ways.[28]

Anthropologists studying hysteria cross-culturally always indicate that it is, of the classic neuroses, the one most directly under cultural influence. Small, close, ingrown communities—minicultures—increase the incidence and greatly influence the form of hysterical behaviors (as they increase the incidence of incestuous behavior). Females in an all-female cloister, convent, or school can take on one another's symptoms by a kind of contagion, so that hysterical symptomologies like eating disorders become "epidemics." Similar phenomena can be seen in army basic training camps or in fighting units, as in athletic teams and gangs. The male group, then, acts out a prejudice as a unit, a little mob; for example, they have a "gang bang" upon lower women or a "gang bash" upon lower men, or they organize a lynching or a torturing. Prejudices, viewed as the manifestations of hysterical character—and, in hysterics, as woven into symptoms—can be passed around in such small groups like tics. As the anthropologist Ralph Linton once remarked: "Hysterical phenomena are everywhere very decidedly culturally patterned. In fact, if one knows a culture, one can predict what form hysterias are going to take in that society—or pretty nearly so. This is the strongest possible argument in favor of the thesis that, whatever the etiology and dynamics of hysteria may be, its symptoms are extensively and intensively shaped by culture.''[29]

Usually, those with hysterical prejudices fix on one group that they, consciously or unconsciously, designate their servants. They are, then, conservative, not wishing to disturb the hierarchy of their world. But if social and political conditions shift so that their victims become less accessible—they move out of the house, for example, because having servants or having slaves is no longer acceptable or feasible—the hysterically prejudiced adapt. They either change the mode of their prejudice or they focus on a new group. Denied one outlet, one "symptom," they find another, a pattern that allows different forms of hysterical prejudice—and violence—to wax and wane in a society. (Similarly, such specific expressions of the hysterical prejudices as phallic-supplemental gun carrying wax and wane.) Class prejudice and race prejudice psychologically connect in this way, as well: the lower-class position can be filled by a racial group or a cultural group or an age group, or many other groups. Children and adolescents of prejudiced people's own families can become victims—child abuse victims—to a greater extent when childlike others are less accessible. Many intrafamilial child molesters operate with an ideological prejudice that children do not have minds, memories, or sexual feelings and thus are a blank space where feelings can be put—they will not be hurt. The child must be "other" for an incest barrier to be overridden, ignored.

Common clinical knowledge also indicates that hysterical characters exaggerate their sexual roles—they act more like impostors than the self-caricaturing obsessionals do. In reference to conventional behaviors for their societies, they are exaggeratedly masculine or exaggeratedly feminine, most commonly according to their biological sex (the macho man, the coquettish girl-woman), but sometimes cross-sexually (the ultrafeminine man, the ultramasculine woman). Ultramasculine men, who play at Don Juanism or take up adventurous, pioneering, risky activities and recreations, who go in for paramilitary organizations and gun collecting, or who engage in exciting criminality—thus qualifying for the diagnostic label "antisocial"—are not infrequently hysterical characters. The members of fraternal orders and gangs whose prejudices are manifest in violent words and deeds are, also, not infrequently hysterical characters. Ultrafeminine women who cluster into exclusive sororities of various sorts, particularly those dedicated to no external or socially useful purpose, are often what might be called collective hysterics. As noted, their sororities exhibit virtually contagious hysterical conversion symptoms—if one has an eating disorder, all do—and trademark costumes and gestures (ways of giggling, verbal quirks, and accents) travel through the group like rumors or gossip. So do prejudices. It has often been noticed that some people, upon moving into a region with a common prejudice, will take on the prejudice even if it was not part of their upbringing. These people are likely to be hysterical characters.

Both male and female hysterical characters tend to rely heavily on projection for defending themselves against their libidinal and aggressive impulses—they unconsciously make over or transfer to others their impulses. When they are prejudiced, as I have noted, they have projected their desires onto the objects of their prejudice, the others have become an image of their forbidden or frustrated desires. But this means that the others, while classified as forbidden, are also alluring, as the drives they bear are still alluring (which is not the case with the people who become the vessels for obsessionals' displacements, who are judged disgusting and repellent). Hysterical types projectively identify with the people who bear their projections; they are bound to them, like doubles, even while they fear that the victims may reveal or expose them.

The hysterical character marks his or her victims with the signatures of the projected desires. If those desires are predominantly oral, the others are experienced as voracious, with big mouths and lips; they are childlike, eternal sucklings, and the women have full breasts. If those desires are predominantly anal, the others are dirty, shitty, smelly; they make their homes filthy and they soil public places; despite episodically explosive energy, they are lazy and shiftless. (Obsessionals also attribute many of these anal features to their victims, of course, but people of hysterical character do not, simultaneously, expunge their victims as clever, wily, and shrewd conspirators.) If the hysterical person's desires are phallic, the others are experienced as phallic—the men have powerful penises, the women are masculinized, viewed as wearing the pants, being matriarchal like the women of the Moynihan Report on the "Negro Family." Similarly, the others' aggression is experienced as phallic—they carry phallic weapons like guns, knives, or spears; they break and enter; they are rapists (if male), or they can steal phallic power (if female).

The prejudiced acts of hysterical characters really or symbolically attack the power that they feel their victims have for getting too great a share of life's satisfactions—that is, life's erotic satisfactions, usually either oral or genital. The discriminatory acts deprive the victims of their erotic partners (chiefly by breaking up families) and of their phallic power. The acts are humiliations, not eliminations (as the obsessionals' most violent acts are); they are designed to keep the victims "in their place" in terms of pleasure goods. In summary, the hysterical prejudices reflect hierarchical worldviews: they make or keep other people lower, inferior, not so much in moral terms as in terms of their capacities for getting satisfaction. Their alleged raw erotic drives are denigrated, and their talents for "civilized" nonerotic (especially intellectual) work are denied. The hysterical prejudices often resemble in form sibling rivalries, and they are often articulated in family terms—the lower people are infants, children, boys, girls, brothers, sisters.

## Narcissistic Characters and Their Prejudices

Of the character types, the narcissistic is the most complex to discuss within the framework of psychoanalytic theory, because narcissism is such contested theoretical and clinical terrain. First, confusion came from Freud's use of "narcissistic neurosis" in contrast to "transference neurosis," a distinction made to indicate that the neurotics who are able to form transferences in analytic therapy—that is, hysterics and obsessional neurotics—are treatable in a way that the narcissistically neurotic, perhaps close to psychotic, are not. As psychoanalysts after Freud have found means to reach the narcissistically neurotic, and to understand their special sorts of transferences, this distinction has been obviated and the term "narcissistic neurosis" has become obsolete. Second, narcissism is difficult to discuss in terms of characterology because narcissism is part of every character type, pure or mixed, in two senses. Most simply, everyone has a degree of self-love (without which a person would commit suicide in one way or another). More complexly, everyone begins life in a condition (both fetal and neonatal) of biological immaturity or what Freud called *Hilflösigkeit* (helpless dependency) on a caretaker, usually the mother, which, for the child, is also a state of self-sufficiency in the sense that the child does not have to go outside the womb or the womblike maternal embrace to fill its needs. The condition of primary narcissism, pure operation of the pleasure principle, which Freud compared to "a bird's egg with its food supply enclosed in its shell," inevitably ends.[30] After this fusion has been disrupted, the child and later the adult seek to recover its nirvanic pleasures, its feeling of "there is no other" (no disappointment, no outside, no difference, no rivalry). Those psychoanalysts who follow Freud hold that narcissism, both as a primary state and as a nostalgic desire to return to the primary state, is universal.[31] They would also conclude, considering the domain of prejudices, that all prejudices (ethnocentrisms as well as ideologies of desire) involve narcissism, all are framed as "me [in my nostalgic unity] versus you," "we [in our sameness] versus them." That is, Freudian analysts note that all people have trouble tolerating differences.

The psychoanalytic theory of primary narcissism presents newborns in a condition of being undifferentiated from others, symbiotic with the mother, and thus full, so to speak, of unused libido or libido not yet directed outward toward people or parts of people (breasts, for example) experienced as not-me. The ability to love people experienced as separate and constant beings in their own right is not yet developmentally possible. But, beyond this agreement, theoretical paths diverge. Some analysts stress the rage that infants feel as they experience their caretakers as separate, not always available, frustrating and—most pathogenically—inconsistent, sometimes attentive, sometimes negligent, or falsely loving, narcissistically loving the infant only as an extension of themselves. The developmentally crucial narcissism is, then, the one that appears as a defense against this rage and aggression; rather than self-love, it is withdrawal into the self for avoidance of destruction. Freudians call this retrenchment "secondary narcissism."

Other theorists put more stress on the continuation of primary narcissism in everyone and its normal function as a regressive refuge, reparation, and restoration, while a child grows up and apart. Margaret Mahler, for example, described "the entire life cycle as constituting a more or less successful process of distancing from and introjection of the lost symbiotic mother, and eternal longing for the actual or fantasied 'ideal state of self,' with the latter standing for a symbiotic fusion with the 'all good' symbiotic mother, who was at one time part of the self in a blissful state of well-being."[32] A particularly important elaboration on this theme has been offered by the French analyst Janine Chassequet-Smirgel, whose work I will consider in detail later, for she has explored Freud's idea that infant narcissism normally translates into an ego ideal, which is the image, modified over time, of the narcissistic bliss and well-being and of parental omnipotence or ability to satisfy all needs, an image that guides all the ego's later quests for love and work.[33] As both the nature of narcissism as a pathology and the nature of normal narcissism are vexed topics, for the moment I want to make a sketch that is general enough to leave the complexities aside.

Narcissistic characters are ambitious and oriented toward a future when longed-for goals will be achieved. But this ambitiousness can take two very different forms. One builds upon confidence in individual achievement and attainment of power, while the other stems from lack of confidence in individual power and willingness to achieve power by submitting to another's power, by joining or just imagining a group, enjoying reflected glory, living in the light of other people's celebrity. Some narcissists lead and some follow: the former exhibit a grandiose sense of self in contrast to the latter's tendency to idealize and "grandify" others, with whom they then ally and usually identify themselves.[34] (These types may be, respectively, more masculine or more feminine when the sexes live in relatively distinct private and public spheres.) Both types have a strong need for praise and approval, and both live with attenuated forms of this need by believing that the future will vindicate present efforts, or that appreciators will arrive later (even posthumously). They win independence by being able to postpone the gratification of their ambitions—an ability that heightens their sense of themselves as superior beings, beings with a long view. Their self-enforced independence may also have grown out of childhood curiosity and an exploratory engagement with the world that was frustrated—and eventually made stronger—by misinformation or deception. Their independence is laced with skepticism and distrust of others' views or reliability.[35]

Narcissists of all sorts have built up their character traits or characters on unreliable foundations. Although independent, they depend greatly on the praise and attention (even negative attention) they can get from others. Their dependency manifests itself in different ways, however. Some cannot bear to be alone or to have the source of their applause and appreciation out of sight or unavailable. Others prevent disappointments by staying aloof, uninvolved, distant, perhaps wrapped in arrogance—they actively fight their dependency. Criticism plunges some narcissists into depression, as it feels like rejection, while others take criticism well because they imagine that it will make them stronger if they can assimilate it. Generally, narcissists have some kind of exploitative streak in their loving: they make use of the people they love for the maintenance of their self-esteem. Similarly, in the domain of prejudices, narcissistic prejudices involve making use of the targets for the maintenance of self-esteem. Self-esteem can be regulated by various kinds of relationships—loving ones, hating ones, worshiping ones, denigrating ones—as long as the others in these relationships are usable, controllable and manipulable or, psychodynamically speaking, as long as they can be experienced *as parts of the narcissist's self.* Should the others make declarations of independence, they are useless. Should a loved one be unable to read the narcissist's mind, or should the hated one turn out to have a truly superior mind, the narcissistic system breaks down.

The leader narcissistic types also take the initiative in love, wanting to love more than to be loved or, more accurately, wanting to be loved (and praised) for their loving. This may mean that they have transformed the need to be loved into something attenuated and delibidinized, having translated all passivity into activity. They are often active as lovers, expressing themselves either directly or in a sublimated mode like intellectual activity, depending on whether they are—to invent labels—narcissists of the body or narcissists of the mind.[36] When they are body narcissists and directly active as lovers, narcissistic characters tend to describe sexual partners as of another type, another class, a different sort of being altogether, while experientially, unconsciously, they relate to their partners as like themselves or part of themselves. To use a phrase made common in the 1960s, they treat their partners "as objects," which means as themselves or as parts of themselves. They prefer partners who are somehow undefined, absorbable, moldable, sometimes rescuable. In men, the result is an attitude of exploitation toward women or girls or young boys (boys who are not yet masculine); in women, it is an attitude of exploitation toward men or boys or other women.

In both sexes, the exploitative attitude may render all specific kinds of prejudice unnecessary or irrelevant—the Other is, simply, the useful. People who are extremely narcissistic in bodily terms may pay little attention to differences of race, ethnicity, or class among their objects—the Other is purely and simply a body, which the narcissist considers similar to his or her own, even if of the opposite sex. (Differences of physical beauty and fitness, body type, and age may be more important.)

Narcissists of the mind, however, express their prejudices in the medium of mental abilities. Their prejudices are part of their defensive or secondary narcissism, their retrenchment in the face of frustrations in love and thwarted aggression. They are prejudiced against people they consider stupid, benighted, tasteless, or uncultured; they are intellectual or cultural elitists, and they relish the polemics that permit them to exhibit their superiority. They build a complicated edifice of differentness on top of an earlier denial of difference, pushing the object beyond the borders of difference. The Other is so different as to be, in effect, nothing. Especially attractive to such narcissists are religions that consign nonbelievers to some form of hell or cultural programs that insist on impermeable borders between advanced and underdeveloped people. Women are, in these cultural terms, mindless. What these creeds mean, fundamentally, is "no one here but us."

Generally, prejudiced narcissists focus on others who they feel threaten their narcissism and thus represent, so to speak, the possible competition. A variety of differences stand out. Narcissists can be racial supremacists, denying equality or recognition or freedom or acceptance to those of one or more other races. Or they can focus on people of different classes, functions, or professions, different characterological traits and abilities, different religious beliefs or cultural convictions. Or they can be elitists in a more generalized, vague way, taking on all comers. But at the bottom of their prejudices, or interwoven into them, will be an anxious reaction to sexual difference—a reaction that is especially noticeable or undisguised among those whom I called body narcissists, the ones who tend to minimize (or not care about) all other differences. To males of this sort, all inferior others are feminine or effeminate or effete; to females, the inferior others are either masculine or feminine, depending on whether the prejudiced female identifies herself femininely or masculinely.[37]

To males, the great bodily sign of difference is lack of the phallus. For them, the primary narcissistic state, before difference, is also the state in which the omnipotent, all-providing mother is phallic, like them and like the omnipotent father. As the mother becomes a distinct person, by failing (inevitably) to be the omnipotent, always available, symbiotic mother, and as the child gains the experience, reluctantly, that not all beings have the phallus, the mother becomes dephallicized. We could summarily render this psychic equation as follows: being disappointing = being other = being castrated. Women disappoint men, both in the sense that the mother proves less than omnipotent and in the sense that mere women are what men are left with after their disappointment. The narcissistic prejudices both keep this disappointment from becoming conscious and perpetuate it.

People who are narcissistic in mental terms tend to interpret bodily differences, especially the fundamental phallus/no phallus difference, as mental differences and often go on expansively to identify mental processes with the course of history. The mental narcissist, extrapolating from microcosm to macrocosm, takes his or her own mind and moment in history as a model and finds it difficult to appreciate differences realistically, especially differences that bespeak the superiority of an Other or the Other's ability to do something beyond the narcissist's inborn possibilities or acquired capacities. Denial of difference, typical of bodily narcissists, is often a key mechanism of defense for mental narcissists, too, and it is predicated upon the earlier conversion of bodily experiences into mental experiences, passivity into activity. But just as common is their unrealistic assertion of difference, their exaggeration of differences or claim that there are essential differences when there are only relative ones. But this assertion of difference, as I noted, ultimately serves the purpose of denial, for it sets the Other, the different, outside the narcissist's species or kind, beyond the point of being threatening.

To control this inability to appreciate and tendency to fear differences, the narcissist associates with the similar, the like-minded, valuing peer groups as much or more than family or ethnic groups and often attributing to the different ones envy for or emulation of the narcissist's own associates, the peer group. The peer group is the "I" made "we," and it is, thus, a substitute for the lost condition of nirvanic oneness with the mother. The "male bonding" of narcissists recreates their mother bonding; both are *homo*erotic. Such groups do not declare sexism or cultural elitism as their purposes as racist or antisemitic groups declare the Blacks or the Jews their enemies. They speak of values, traditions, and standards, which they must protect, without specifying their opponents as a group; it turns out, of course, that women (or, more recently, the feminists) are the real source of the decline and fall of all they hold dear.

Unlike obsessionals, narcissists turn to groups not for a role or an identity but for a feeling of merger. They thus tolerate poorly differences and disagreements in their groups and tend to ostracize dissenters, sending them to the outer darkness where all "others" live, making women out of them. This configuration of traits with regard to peer groups becomes especially neurotic when it grows up around an early grievous loss or hurt, a "narcissistic wound" (in Freud's phrase) that the narcissist has experienced as a decentering, a fall from parental affection or favoritism, a loss of prerogatives, or (more dangerously) an end to (fantasized) omnipotence. Narcissism, under such conditions, is expressed as a strong anxiety about bodily intactness or mental integrity, a strong fear of bodily injury or maiming, of aging, diminishing brain-power, amnesia, insanity. The others, the objects of prejudice, then seem like agents of destruction, not of penetration and persecutory pollution in the obsessional manner, but of disintegration or castration.

Inability to appreciate difference may well stem from a universal human characteristic, insofar as everyone is to some degree narcissistic and the difference between the sexes is universally experienced—unlike ethnic or racial differences. I quoted before George Devereux's remark: "The fact that mankind is made up of males and females has never been accepted as an *irreducible* fact, which just happens to exist. It was experienced both as an intellectual challenge and as a source of anxiety as far back as human records—including myths—go . . . [E]ach human being was and is perplexed by the fact that another being, congruent in nearly every respect with his (or her) self-model, should, in one respect—sexuality—be so different."[38] But the characterologically narcissistic person either disavows or denies this irreducible fact, or exaggerates it to the point of denial.

Thus the discriminating acts of prejudiced narcissists focus on the realities, signs, or symbols of difference. They deny difference—but in various ways. Most frequently, they convey the message that the others are in no way comparable to them—and thus not fit for doing what they do, living where they live, and so forth. This form of narcissistic prejudice can resemble the hierarchy-making of hysterical characters for whom the others are lesser, lower, and rawly or archaically sexual. But it is denial that can be seen operating in this kind of denigration, not hysterical projection. Narcissists may also exaggerate the differences, saying (for example) that men are essentially this way and women essentially that way, so that there can be no comparison. This mode, which classifies types, resembles obsessional intellectual ghettoizing or dualistic compartmentalizing, but its purpose is preservation of narcissistic sense of intactness rather than purification or elimination. There is no obsessional splitting off of affect, no cold-bloodedness; intactness may be celebrated. In a third, and more delusional, even psychotic form, narcissistic prejudice conveys the message that the others are not really there, which is a way of saying that the differences are not really there, which may mean at the most archaic level that women really do have the male phallus, but it is hidden.

Narcissists may use the defenses most common in obsessional and hysterical characters—displacements (sealed off with intellectualizations) and projections—but their chief mode seems to be disavowal or denial. They do not shift out of themselves unwanted desires or project forbidden impulses; they relate to a real people in the world but in the mode of (unconsciously) denying that those people are other, or denying the marks of otherness. In this sense, they are not like ethnocentrists, who assert actively that "they" are other than "we." The group narcissism of ethnocentrists functions in this positive way—it sets "we" over "them"—but the narcissism that makes itself manifest so fundamentally in prejudices like sexism and cultural elitism is a negation. There *are no others,* only us. The world is unisex or monocultural.

By contrast, the narcissists who are followers, who have been in some way defeated in their individual narcissistic quests, may feel that the target group—for men, paradigmatically, the group "women"—over which they want their own group to exalt is actually, or once was actually, superior. Male narcissists of this sort act on the idea that the anatomical features and reproductive capacities that women have, which men do not have, must be either strictly controlled and treated as masculine property, or in some way damaged, hidden, "castrated." Psychologically, female characteristics can be introjected to feed a man's fantasy that he is somehow a man-and-woman or that he is capable of pregnancy, but practically, she must be owned and controlled. More successful narcissists, who are more independent and individualistic in their thinking, may content themselves—as Freud, unlike so many Freudians, contented himself—with superciliousness toward women. Women who are characterologically narcissistic may envy the phallus, or they may deny difference intellectually: with a theory of all-embracing sexuality, pan-sexuality, or androgyny, for example, or by claiming to be in some way male as well as female—perhaps by having a "masculine mind" or by being able to play all the sexual parts in their sexual dramas. Or they may deny difference in the mental narcissistic manner by exaggerating it with a theory that men and women are essentially different. Women's arenas for denying difference are usually private, however, as they have not traditionally commanded the power and armory of public sexism.

The role of narcissism in male sexism is perhaps clearest in the masculine type known as the Don Juan. Psychoanalysts have had no trouble claiming that this type is in search of his mother, that he looks for her in every woman and finds her in none. But Otto Fenichel has also argued persuasively that the Don Juan's "Oedipus complex is of a particular kind," that is, heavily shadowed by preoedipal features:

> It is dominated by the pregenital aim of incorporation, pervaded by narcissistic needs and tinged with sadistic impulses. In other words, the striving for sexual satisfaction is still condensed with the striving for getting narcissistic supplies in order to maintain self-esteem. There is a readiness to develop sadistic reactions if this need is not immediately satisfied. . . . His sexual activities are primarily designed to contradict an inner feeling of inferiority by proof of erotic "successes." After having "made" a woman, he is no longer interested in her, first because she, too, has failed to bring about the longed-for relaxation, and second because his narcissistic need requires proof of his ability to excite women; after he knows that he is able to excite a specific woman, his doubts arise concerning other women whom he has not yet tried.[39]

The Don Juan of love is often one and the same person as the so-called Don Juan of achievement, a man who finds no success in his work sufficient and moves restlessly on from one task, one cause, one career, or one big deal or salary range to the next. He can never do enough, survey a large enough domain, create enough important cultural products, or make enough money. If he is, so to speak, as large as the world, and if he has dreamed the American Dream or written the great American novel that is as capacious as the country, then she can be no threat— she is nothing.

## Mixed Types and Mergers, with a Note on Classism

The obsessional, hysterical, and narcissistic types of ideologies of desire can be considered in their distinctiveness, but it is just as important, of course, to look at how they overlap. For example, it is immediately obvious that people of all three character types can be prejudiced against people of color—but the prejudices will not mean the same thing or take the same forms of discrimination or violence. The hysterical white man's hated black man is a sexual threat, usually a phallic threat (and, less commonly, an oral or an anal threat); the obsessional white man's hated black man is an anal product who must be eliminated; and the white narcissist's hated black man is a nonwhite effeminate person who has some real or fantasied claim to distinctiveness, perhaps even superiority. Similarly, all three types can be prejudiced against Jews, but differently. The hysterical character wants to cut down to size any Jew who is a phallic being, while the classic antisemite, an obsessional character equivalent to the Adorno group's authoritarian personality, wants to eliminate a Jew who is both a filthy nothing and a secret world-conquering conspirator. The narcissist's Jew is either effeminate or one of the chosen people or the cultural elite, that is, a person who can be construed as making a competitive claim to preeminence.

Sexism is everywhere, as narcissism is, but different character types have differently organized sexisms—though no type will make sexism as central to their ideology as the person of predominantly narcissistic character. For hysterical characters (most obviously for males, but also for females) women are either hugely maternal or overwhelming, devouring, and overly potent as they "wear the pants" and, Amazon-like, threaten castration. For obsessionals, women are impure, sullied creatures, oversexed, aggressive, and corrupting. Both the hysterical character and the obsessional operate narcissistically when they exhibit sexism, but the narcissistic character thinks more generally and centrally in sexual terms of us and them.

In developmental periods of heightened narcissism, people of the various character types are more prone to flagrant sexist acts and to acts against homosexuals who are construed as disturbing to sexual definitions, who are transgressive (most frequently, this means males who are "too female"). Most attacks on homosexuals are conducted by males in their late teens and early twenties, just when they find assertions of their own masculinity most necessary for identity consolidation. They seek out strong men to borrow phallic power from, good buddies to make a fortress against women with, and "faggots" to taunt or attack. By striking contrast, prejudice against women and homosexuals is not needed in the preadolescent latency period, which exists in societies, like our own, where older children are sent not directly into adult roles but into schools. A "moratorium" stage characterized by little internal or external pressure or permission to attempt mature sexual activity, latency requires relatively few prejudices.[40] "Separate spheres" of activ-

ity will do. Most eight-year-olds need education for tolerance less than
their parents do.

People of any character type who have been traumatized or narcissistically wounded may respond by elevating themselves over others, restoring their sense of themselves and their integrity—physical and emotional—by triumphing over others. The group to be triumphed over
will be chosen on the basis of the type of compensation needed. But
male homosexuals serve this purpose well for males of any character
type who feel their allure or their potency has been jeopardized, who
need to say that they are real men in comparison to those "female"
men. People of hysterical, obsessional, and narcissistic characters who
can agree on little else can agree on the unnaturalness of homosexuality, or at least agree that there must be a sexuality that is unnatural
(so that their own can be certified, by contrast, as natural).

Homosexuals are all-purpose targets, but other groups that cut across
racial, ethnic, and gender lines can also be all-purpose targets. As I
noted, adolescents play this role. Currently in America, they play it almost as frequently as adolescents did in the 1950s, when the nation was
in a great stir about the urban gangs and juvenile delinquency of the
"shook-up generation," and in the 1960s, when student politicosexual
revolutionaries and countercultural groups like the hippies created an
even greater stir. Now "Generation X" absorbs the characteristic derogations assigned by the various character types.

Any group that bears the designation "class" also cuts across racial,
ethnic, and gender lines. And there exists a term, "classism," to indicate
class prejudice—but it is a problematic concept. In the 1970s, as Black
feminists tried to show how important issues of race and class are in the
lives of Black women in order to convince white feminists that sexism
was not their only or their main problem, the term "classism" was popularized. It had a history, of course, within Marxist theory, where it
meant that differences in class are the origin of all prejudices, none of
which would exist in a future socialist world. Current usage of the word
is very vague. It is used sometimes for prejudice against people because
of their class, sometimes for prejudice that manifests itself in punishment by poverty or perpetuation of class differences. It seems to me that
classism in the second use is part of every type of ethnocentric and
ideological prejudice, not in the sense that it causes these prejudices
but in the sense that it flows from them: those who are derogated are
also punished with being kept from ownership of the means of produc-

tion, denied education and achievement, put in the worst jobs, paid less, and so forth. But those who are in the lower classes are also used in the same way that people of color are by those (particularly hysterical types) who need victims conceived as servants and domestics. Lower-class people of color are, so to speak, twice qualified, and qualified in fact not in fantasy if the race-class prejudice exercised against them comes from people whose domestics they have actually been and whose children they have raised. And lower-class women can find that their class status is used as a sign of the inferiority alleged of them by mental narcissists. Furthermore, the "proletariat" or the "lower classes" can be the object of obsessional prejudice: *they* are dirty, underhanded, devious, and connected to an international conspiracy—call it Marxism, Bolshevism, Communism—that is trying to take over the world. In other words, classism does not exist as a prejudice unconnected to others; it is always a feature of another prejudice, a mode of discrimination for another prejudice, or a form that an ideological prejudice can take.

But there is also a kind of classism that resembles ethnocentrism. When social classes are set and stable over generations, membership in them being determined by birth not acquisition, they operate like tradition-bound tribes: they produce relatively single-trait or dominant-trait social characters, and they can be compassed in a few adjectives, as can, for example, the suspicious distrustfulness of the orally deprived Alor or the self-assured assertiveness of the narcissistically supplied Comanche. Thus, aristocrats are bred to be disdainful, although the degrees of their *noblesse oblige* are quite variable. The basic technique is to have the children raised (and the males sometimes sexually initiated as well)—often lovingly, but always with a degree of dangerous resentment and bitterness—by the very people they are to disdain, the servants. Aristocrats' class prejudice is not xenophobic; they do not disdain strangers, though they distrust intimates and intimacy, for intimacy itself is dangerous. But, over time, the aristocrats become more and more prone to hysteria and hysterical prejudices—they become like the Southern plantation owners who had their children raised by their slaves. Among the lower classes, prejudices against the upper classes develop more as distance diminishes and resentment gives way to envy and hate. As the psychoanalyst Robert Waelder remarked: "David Hume has pointed out that envy seems to appear only when the distance between ourselves and those really or allegedly more fortunate is small enough that we can compare ourselves with them. One envies one's contemporaries, hardly one's elders . . . There is little if any envy of the rich in the feudal era. Class hatred is thus a consequence of diminishing class distance."[41]

In conditions of great and rapid social change, however, when class distinctions dissolve or get reconstituted on a new basis—and become defined by wealth or property and not birth—then class prejudice will reflect the process by which a class is being invented. This second kind of classism involves class members inventing themselves in and through the class and its prejudice—and it is, thus, suited to be interwoven with ideologies of desire. Tracking the class prejudices of the nineteenth-century European bourgeoisie requires, then, a chronicle like Thomas Mann's *Buddenbrooks,* a saga of generations, as the class members rise out of the ranks of those they must learn to hate. They, too, are raised by those who are going to be the victims of their hysterical class prejudices—but they are going to have to turn on their own kin, who wished them where they were going. Their prejudices unite them as a class and sweep them forward, futureward. The upward-moving families start out strong, prolific, and optimistic, raising children who are robustly self-serving, and become eventually enervated, full of neurotics and black sheep, deviants from their own increasingly rigid, moralistic standards. They begin by hating "upward" at the aristocrats they have supplanted to bring themselves into being—the aristocrats are effete, cunning but castrated beings, armed only with old (or Jewish) money; and they continue by hating the lower classes whom they fear will supplant them in the future—the revenge of the ancestors.

What these various overlappings of prejudice types imply, further, is that some people of each character type will actually be the people hypothesized by those who believe in the prejudice is one or generalized attitude argument. They will be prejudiced against almost any one person who is not them. Any person or group can be caught in the narcissist's net just by virtue of being not-me, not-us, although, as I argued before, the narcissist's ideology of desire will not show up on inventories and questionnaires as clearly different from an ethnocentrist's isolationism toward all directions at once. The more paranoid an obsessional is, for a second example, the more generalized will his prejudice appear to be—although, if it is examined closely, the group that most clearly connects to his anality will be at the center of the circle of his prejudices. In psychological terms, the main reason the authors of *The Authoritarian Personality* could conclude that they had discovered the single prejudiced personality type from which prejudice radiates in all directions is that they had discovered the one character type that does tend to draw all out-groups into the center of its prejudice—the obsessional with narcissistic traits.

Anyone who explores antisemitic literature carefully will find that when antisemites say they hate blacks, their racism reveals itself as an ancillary attitude. They will hate blacks for secondary reasons, perhaps because they believe that the blacks are controlled politically by the Jews, their real enemies. The definition offered by the American paramilitarist that I cited in the Introduction illustrates the derivative nature of antisemites' racism: "A nigger is a Jew turned inside out." He means that the dirty, fecal Jew is really behind, or inside, the nigger. Strategically minded antisemites, further, will hate Blacks because the X hate Blacks and the antisemites wish to win converts to antisemitism among the X. (Hitler was quite aware that many Americans would appreciate him for his display of racism against the American Negroes who competed at the 1936 Olympics in Berlin.) Finally, antisemites may—as many American neo-Nazis do—hate Blacks because they have learned from white racists to attach the power of racism to their own main cause, for the sake of political expediency.

Even though it is often combined with other prejudices, the anal, antipollution, purgative language of a true obsessional antisemite is always distinctive, as this sample from the White Aryan Resistance hotline (circa 1990) conducted by the American neo-Nazi Tom Metzger demonstrates:

> Hello, this is Tom Metzger, La Cesspool Grande, and this is White Aryan Resistance. All you worthless bastards in the House and Senate, what are you up to now? What's your beloved Pentagon porkbarrel going to do for you now that the phony cold war is being flushed down the toilet? What other ways are you planning to destroy white working people in the USA? You jerks cry out about quality of life, natural resources, and animal habitat being destroyed, but did you ever stop to think that if you quit allowing every squalid lottery player to enter the country we might have all these great things? Stop bringing in all these Asians and make room for national parks. Boxcar a few million Mexicans and central Americans south of the border and watch the streets get cleaner overnight. On another issue, you mutton-headed bureaucrats, why do you allow the Jew Mossad secret police full freedom to spy on Americans from the seventh floor of the Jew Anti-Def-

ecation [*sic*] League right there in front of you? You don't let any other
country do it. You chicken-shits worship the Jews so much you must
have holes in the knees of all your pants.[42]

Here the standard broad-stroke isolationist attack on immigrants, concentrated on people of color, forms just part of a more general compulsion to purge the country of the dirt and corruption that prevent
"great things" from happening, particularly for the benefit of the pure
but powerless ordinary people. Metzger is a White Aryan, but the emphasis is on Aryan.


Individuals may hold a mixture of prejudices for different reasons, fulfilling different needs. But so, too, do organizations, at any given moment and over time. Character-referenced distinctions among the prejudices can, I think, throw some light on how and why organizations that
purvey the various prejudices mix them and also change targets over
time. Before studying the historical conditions that promote the various
prejudice types in succeeding chapters, I want to indicate here how an
organization can, at different times, be dominated by people of different character types and how the prejudices purveyed change and merge
and mix accordingly. The story of the twentieth-century Ku Klux Klan
will serve as my example and set Tom Metzger's antisemitism in its context.

In 1915 a group of Georgians reconstituted the Ku Klux Klan of Reconstruction days, which had been a white supremacist organization
designed to restore "law and order"—the old white supremacist order—and repulse an invasion of Southern territory by Northern car-
petbaggers, Union League organizers of freed Negroes, and radical Republicans. The new Klan's founder, William Joseph Simmons of Atlanta,
was a joiner, an advocate of fraternal organizations, and a member of
the Masons, the Knight Templars, and other secret societies, who spoke
in the romantic, indiscriminate style of the hysterically prejudiced, focusing on sibling and paternal relations: "I believe in fraternal orders
and fraternal relationships among men, in a fraternity of nations, so
that all people might know something of the great doctrine of the fa-
therhood of God and the brotherhood of man." He had learned of the
Reconstruction Klan from his father, who he alleged belonged to the
first Klan, and from his Negro mammy. The Negro woman put her
charges to sleep, according to his memory, with exciting tales: "I can

remember how old Aunt Vinny, my black mammy, used to pacify us children late in the evening by telling us about the Kluklux.'' In his twentieth year, after reading a book about the old Klan, Simmons had a vision that echoes the ingredients of his childhood bedroom scene. "On horseback in their white robes [the Klansmen] rode across the wall in front of me, and as the picture faded out I got down on my knees and swore that I would found a fraternal organization that would be a memorial to the Ku Klux Klan.'' He was terrifically excited by the task of being a memorializer, a creator of fraternal family, the filial servant of powerful men.[43]

Simmons intricately structured the revived Invisible Empire as the old Klan had been, with layers of offices and jurisdictions flowing down like a genealogical tree from the great father, the imperial wizard. In his first several years as the imperial wizard, Simmons struggled to recruit members, control the organization, and design regalia, including the notorious costume—the peaked hood and robe, all in white. He invented the strange motto "Non Silba Sed Anthar," meaning "Not for self but for others" in a concoction of Latin and pseudo-Saxon. Withstanding adversity and always short of money, Simmons presented himself in his knightly mission: "During all this time of dread and darkness, I virtually stood alone, but remaining true to the dictates of unsullied honor, I steered the infant organization through dangerous channels and finally succeeded in making good.'' But his child—this child of his father's Klan, who was, as it were, himself, and who was on a quest presented in an image of vaginal penetration, a return to the (Negro) mother source—did not begin to grow until professionals were brought in to advertise and recruit.

In 1920 the Klan hired organizers who built up the ranks by appealing to every prejudice. In addition to the white supremacy inherited from the original Klan, they offered nativism for American ethnocentrists; they also offered antisemitism and both fortified the regulations forbidding female membership in the Klan and created ladies' auxiliaries. More important than any other single prejudice for many of the Klan chapters of the Midwest and West was anti-Catholicism.[44] Anti-Catholicism was a mode of obsessionality particularly important in areas such as Oregon, where few Negroes or Jews lived, where the public was generally well-educated, and where economic threats were seen as coming from without. Klan literature charged the Catholic Church with thought control, mind pollution, and division of loyalties (asking Americans to be loyal to "the dago of the Tiber," the Pope), but it is interesting to observe that Klan leaders construed Catholics in ways straight out of the book of antisemitism. They recruited "escaped nuns" who went on lecture tours to inform Klansmen about Catholic priestly lustfulness, orgies in convents, and the Catholic practice of putting illegitimate babies in special leather bags and throwing them in furnaces. They peddled themes of sadistic perversity and infanticide—the old European antisemitic chestnuts, the staples of obsessional prejudice.

The Klan under Simmons had been a Southern family affair. Chiefly a monument to the original Klan, it made its chief prejudice racism—it was, as Simmons said "the reincarnation among the sons of the spirit of the fathers." The growing Klan of the 1920s attracted community morals keepers, operating by ostracism, boycotting, blackmailing, and "night-riding" episodes that ended in tar and feathering, whipping, branding, and emasculating of morally offensive citizens, both Negro and white. A typical handbill originating in Indiana divided the world in the obsessional manner into two parts, the good and the evil, represented as a vast conspiracy:

> Every criminal, every gambler, every thug, every libertine, every girl ruiner, every home wrecker, every wife beater, every dope peddler, every shyster lawyer, every K. of C. [Knight of Columbus], every white slaver, every brothel madam, every Rome controlled newspaper, every black spider—is fighting the Klan. Think it over. Which side are you on?

The professionalization and growth of the Klan brought publicity, including a congressional investigation in 1921. "Congress made us," Simmons announced gleefully, as supportive letters poured into the Atlanta headquarters from around the country. He had proudly reasserted before the congressmen his paternity, or rather maternity—the Klan, he said, is an "infant organization, and if any person on earth should have control of the conduct and nourishing of the baby, the mother should"—but it was his professionals who capitalized on the publicity.[45] The Klan leadership grew wealthy, lived lavishly, created sex scandals (one Indiana leader was tried for murder after a woman on whom he had forced sadistic practices died in suspicious circumstances). But they also worked feverishly to found new branches. Simmons, a heavy drinker and a gambler, a man whose main motive was potency enhancement and supremacist adventure, was not up to the challenge of his success or the pure living his obsessional Klan colleagues prescribed (and did not much practice). A dentist from Dallas, Hiram Wesley Evans, emerged via a carefully staged palace coup as the growing organization's leader.

Evans was a reformer. Out went all self-serving sexually tainted professionals, the corrupt big spenders, and the drunken wizard; in came clean zealots and Prohibitionists who denounced Klan terrorism and insisted, instead, on Klan involvement in electoral politics. The central national Klan leadership became more autocratic—or tried to, often against much local resistance. "Americanism" became the central credo. From an organization in the hysterical mode, the Klan had finally transformed fully into one in the obsessional mode. And then it deteriorated—a victim of its own transformation and of the changing social conditions in the country. Under Evans membership declined—from more than 4 million Klansmen in 1924 to only 1.5 million in 1926— even though some political clout was gained, particularly when the Klan opposed the 1928 bid of a Catholic, Alfred E. Smith, for the U.S. presidency. By the depression, however, hardly 50,000 members remained.

The expansion of the Klan had resulted from its ability to tap all of the prejudices that surged up in American society in the wake of World War I. The Klan was isolationist, opposing immigration, favoring deportation of aliens, rejecting the League of Nations. It adapted its white supremacy convictions to the new condition of the Negroes—to their exercise of citizenship in joining the U.S. Army's segregated units, to their emergence as wage earners in the Northern cities where millions emigrated, to their cultural prominence as writers and musicians, to the creation of a "Black bourgeoisie" (in E. Franklin Frazier's phrase). The Klan stressed how "uppity" the Negroes had become and how easily their new condition allowed them proximity to whites—especially to white women. And the Klan, like Hitler's National Socialist Party, could point to the internationalizing of economic life and to the Russian Revolution as evidence of the secret power of the Jews. The speeches of antisemites like Gerald L. K. Smith and Conde McGinley were reprinted in Klan newspapers, and the "Protocols of the Elders of Zion" circulated among Klansmen. But Klan professionals also learned to target particular prejudice groups. In the West, they galvanized anti-Japanese feeling, in the Southwest, anti-Mexican. They supported anti–French Canadian groups in New England, anti-Catholic ones in the Midwest, anti-alien and antisemitic ones in New York. In the Deep South, however, the central cord always remained anti-Negro, and it always remained tied to the typical hysterical intraracial sexual issues, as was apparent in 1923, when only the Southern Klan members, and none from the North or West, asserted in response to a writer's inquiry that defending "the purity of womanhood" was one of their crucial ideals.[46]

The Klan's expansionist program—"chameleonic," as one commentator rightly called it—did not presume that all prejudiced people are prejudiced in all ways. Rather, it presumed that all prejudiced people have a lead or central prejudice but can make alliances with those of a different focus because all draw sustenance from a common critique. The Klan addressed the common grievance of its membership by being nostalgic and preaching against the "modernism" ushered in with World War I. The recruitment professionals in the Klan harped on the decline in church membership, the laxity in moral life, the overflow of private life into public places—women going to bars and smoking, teenagers carrying on sexually in parked cars, contraband liquor being sold on the streets—as evidence of the decline of the West, the deterioration of civilized family values (in the current phrase). Local Klan chapters acted as moral detectives, organizing raids on the homes of adulterers, boycotting businessmen who abused their female employees, running dope pushers and bootleggers out of town. Violence was common, and it generated a good deal of opposition—not just from victim groups, but from Americans who opposed extralegal vigilantism and terrorism.

Ultimately, when Evans reigned in this expansionist program and cleaned up the organization, the Klan lost its internal momentum. Factionalism within local groups abounded as leaders scrambled for the spoils of the expansionist period, while Klan members found little to bind them together ideologically. The Klan became defensively nationalistic, predominantly ethnocentric, and was, thus, indistinguishable from the multitude of other local Americanist groups. "We believe that the pioneers who built America bequeathed to their own children a priority right to it, the control of it and of its future," Evans announced blandly, focusing his ire on unassimilatable groups or groups of immigrants that in any way refused to adopt American values. Typical of the lackluster ideology was this assessment of the Jews, whom Evans thought of as less of a threat than other unassimilatable groups: "For one thing, [the Jew] is confined to a few cities, and is not a problem at all to most of the country. For another thing, his exclusiveness, political activities, and refusal to become assimilated are racial rather than religious, based on centuries of persecution. They cannot last long in the atmosphere of free America, and we may expect that with the passage of time the serious aspects of the problem will fade away.'' This kind of talk, so realistic in manner, or at least without irrational overestimation of Jewish conspiratorial power, could not draw antisemites. It had none of the obsessional prioritizing so obvious in a remark made by the imperial wizard of the early 1960s, Robert Shelton: ''I don't hate niggers, but I hate the Jews. The nigger's a child, but the Jews are dangerous people. All they want is control and domination of the gentiles through a conspiracy with the niggers.''[47]

The Klan of the late 1920s was redundant—it offered nothing that was not available in other social or political organizations and churches, which did not engage in the violence that had little appeal to the stolid middle class—but it was also visionless. It provided defensive nationalism and ethnocentrism, but it had none of the futuristic expansionism that made Hitler so appealing. John Mecklin, a sociologist writing in 1924, could see the problem clearly then: ''Were the Klan more closely organized and animated by a more definite and comprehensive program it might become a force to be reckoned with in national life. There is, however, little danger that the Klan as a whole will ever be able to utilize all its strength in a political or social program. This is due to the essentially local nature of the Klan, its singular lack of able and statesman-like leaders, its planless opportunism, and, above all else, its dearth of great unifying constructive ideals. In the language of Freudianism, the Klan is essentially a defense mechanism against evils which are more imaginary than real. It is for this reason negative rather than constructive in its influence.''[48]

During the late 1930s and 1940s, when Germany was America's enemy, Klan groups in the South generally refused any association with the ''un-American'' Nazi groups and German-American Bund. In the North, there was more sympathy. And after the war alliances sprang up among various northern Klan groups and the antisemitic National States Rights Party and the American Nazi Party, all sharing the conviction that the Jews were tied to international Communism, which had emerged as the central obsessional enemy of not just the Klan but the country. Robert Shelton, a fervent antisemite, promoted these Klan affiliations with antisemitic groups. His policy was continued in the 1970s and 1980s, when the Klan affiliated with the Aryan Nations, the Order, Posse Comitatus, and the Christian Identity movement, all of which agreed about the threat posed to America by the Zionist Occupational Government (ZOG) in Washington, D.C. Matt Murphy, imperial counsel for the United Klans of America, announced shortly before his death in 1965 that he could prove that a group of "international Jew Zionists" had had control of the U.S. government for the past forty years.[49] Meanwhile, anti-Catholicism declined to the point where Klan groups in the 1960s were accepting Catholic members, and David Duke could proclaim by 1975 that half his Louisiana Klansmen were Catholic. Similarly, Duke was happy to invite women, including his wife, into the Klan and into leadership positions. The leader of the Southern Knights had said clearly in 1957, "the fight today is against integration, communism and federal controls," and neither the power of Rome nor the power of women had to be singled out in that fight as it was waged obsessionally throughout the Cold War.

Some units of the Klan, however, did not need affiliation with antisemitic groups to sustain themselves. These groups sprung into renewed action on the day proclaimed in Klan literature as "Black Monday," the day the Supreme Court announced its decision in *Brown v. Board of Education.* The original ideology of the Klan—white supremacy—came back in full force, pushing aside all of the prejudices that had accrued to the Klan for recruitment and political alliance purposes. Concomitantly, since 1954 many Klan antisemites had come to prefer their own groups to the Klan, especially in the South, where racism never budged from the centerpiece of Klannishness. Tom Metzger, for example, was born a Catholic, started out his career in bigotry with the John Birch Society, and left, disillusioned, when he found out "you could not criticize the Jews." He joined David Duke's Knights of the KKK in 1975, working along the Mexican border with armed, blackshirted KKK men who searched out and beat up illegal Mexican workers. But he broke with David Duke and briefly organized a unit, California Knights of the KKK, which focused on harassing Vietnamese refugees in San Diego, whom he accused (in obsessional style) of entrepreneurial conspiracies to take away white people's jobs. Then, after a stint in electoral politics, he came back to his initial concern and, founding the group eventually called White Aryan Resistance (WAR), turned his attention to his chief prejudice, antisemitism. Like Shelton, Metzger was always convinced that Blacks were only a threat because they were pawns for the ZOG in its effort to take over the American government. And, as I noted before, Metzger, like Shelton, consistently conveyed his analysis in the crude anal metaphors typical of antisemites. The Negroes, Shelton had indicated, are just a by-product of the Jews—"Negroid is like hemorrhoid: they're both a pain."[50]

David Duke, by contrast, was and is a racist in the old Ku Klux Klan mold, with some adaptations to the new conditions of the Blacks and some accommodations to the more muted racist rhetoric typical of American politics in the last several decades. He calls for racial separation and outlines geographical areas that could be assigned to the white and nonwhite peoples of America. But in 1975, he incited his Knights of the KKK without disguise in hypermasculine rhetoric: "We say give us liberty and give them [the Blacks] death. There's times I've felt like picking up a gun and going shooting a nigger. We've got a heritage to protect. We're going to do everything to protect our race."[51] In the hysterical mode, he is an impostor figure, a man who enjoys a double life, even to the point where he has written under pseudonyms a sex manual for women (full of advice about non–family values practices to enjoy with married men) and a guerrilla warfare manual for Blacks (full of deliberate misspellings for its supposedly primitive readers). Duke, who comports himself in his political life as a clean-living business-suited good boy, keeps a pornography collection that, according to a defector from his circle, features films dedicated to white girls having oral sex with Blacks.[52]

The Klan in the era of the Civil Rights movement and since never regained the numerical strength it had in the 1920s, but it persists in a multitude of shifting local organizations. Recent losses in legal battles have undercut the national organizations financially, but the local Klan groups have had a great deal of recruiting success, particularly among the young, who are attracted to both Klan youth groups and the affiliations these have with neo-Nazi skinhead groups. The basic Klan message remains white supremacy, but there is much talk about the ZOG that controls the African Americans and all other "mud people" (nonwhites).[53] And, in keeping with a general movement on the American right, current Klan propaganda contains extensive antifeminism and homophobia. The slogan that feminism is a "Jew-dyke conspiracy against the White Race" catches the syncretistic flavor of the current moment, packaging, as it does, so many prejudices in one phrase.

Like all groups on the current American far right, the Klan targets adolescents in its recruitment drives. It uses the old hysterical appeal—the Klan is a family, an alternative family life to the unsatisfactory one at home. This approach is very different from Tom Metzger's most recent political turn, to recruit apolitical or even antiracist skinheads associated with big-draw heavy metal bands for the WAR ranks. His idea, in the obsessional antisemitic mode, is to create a grand conspiracy to attack the Jewish conspiracy. "Tom Metzger's hope," the Center for Democratic Renewal reports, "is that the skinheads will become educated racists like he is and that they'll penetrate into the military, the government, all aspects of life, until they can seize power."[54] The Klan groups and WAR appeal to different sorts of adolescents who have had different histories, and it is to these various typical adolescent and childhood developmental courses that I turn in the next two chapters.

# 8

# Origins and Developmental Lines:
# Children and Prejudice

Theorizing by social psychologists and sociologists about social character could not progress until the idea that character is hereditary or instinctual had been met and surpassed. Nature and nurture, biology and environment, had to be given at least equal weight before the contributions to character of culture—in the broadest sense of the word—could be compassed. In the domain of studies in prejudice, the same development slowly came about—twice: once with respect to prejudice itself, and once with respect to victims of prejudice.

Social scientists had to argue that prejudice is not innate or instinctual just as they had to argue that charging a racial or ethnic or sexual group with innate inferiority *is* prejudice. Until the late 1920s and early 1930s the notion that races fall into a natural hierarchy in terms of abilities (particularly intelligence) and accomplishments was so taken for granted that Anglo-American statements about the inferiority of Negroes, Asians, and southern European immigrants were viewed not as examples of prejudice but as manifestations of an inborn classificatory radar, an innate sense of race. People were also routinely said to be endowed with an instinctual feeling for their own kind and a biologically rooted fear of strangers. Social psychology studied the psychology of the various races, not attitudes toward the races or prejudices.

## Learning Stages

When social scientific attention shifted away from "race psychology" to studies in prejudice, questions about how prejudice is learned dominated. Research focused on children, both in family contexts and in schools. In American social science, Bruno Lasker's *Race Attitudes in Children* (1929) provided the first major psychological attack on the double innateness idea to be organized around study of children.[1] On the one hand, this study set patterns of concern in place that have not—to this day—shifted. First, Lasker concerned himself only with white racism. Race prejudice was the central and the model prejudice, just as it was, again, in and after the heyday of the Civil Rights movement. He did not connect or compare race prejudice to antisemitism, the prejudice that came to be called sexism, or ethnic prejudices. Second, Lasker concerned himself only with childhood, not with puberty or adolescence—so that the later preadult years fell out of the picture of prejudice study. This tendency to focus on childhood was reinforced by the fact that scientific study of adolescence, although it began at the turn of the century, did not really gather momentum until the late 1950s when "alienated youths" and non-conforming juvenile delinquents became a social concern in America and Europe.

Lasker's study, on the other hand, raised valuable questions about how children's attitudes had been described and studied during the dominance of "race psychology." Lasker reviewed, for example, all of the considerable evidence that young children have fear reactions to people who differ from themselves—say, in skin color—and noticed how conceptually jumbled the data became when interpreted:

> The existing confusion on the nature of first exhibitions of fear in children in the presence of certain phenomena is simply due to faulty observation; and the controversy as to whether certain fears are instinctive or acquired might quickly yield to agreement if there were a sufficient body of accurate and complete data . . . All observations made carefully and over a sufficient length of time suggest that it is unprofitable to study race attitudes apart from other aspects of child psychology. If most of the noticeable reactions of small children to race are fear reactions, as seems to be the fact, we shall do well to acquaint ourselves more thoroughly with the nature and causes of fear in childhood.   (pp. 8, 10)

Lasker, in effect, admonished social scientists to make the acquisition of race attitudes or prejudice a topic within a socially and culturally oriented developmental child psychology. And by the early 1950s that transition had come about. Kenneth Clark could announce confidently in *Prejudice and Your Child* (1955): "Social scientists are now convinced that children learn social, racial and religious prejudices in the course of observing, and being influenced by, the existence of patterns in the culture in which they live."[2]

Mary Ellen Goodman, author of *Race Awareness in Young Children* (1952), referred to the abandoned position of innatism as a belief in a "prejudice unit-of-personality," some ingredient of personality that produces prejudice or predisposes one to prejudice, some unit that—by this moment in American history—was widely evaluated negatively as a "bad seed," as though prejudice resulted from bad breeding. "What we are dealing with is not a simple matter," she cautioned. "It is a complex set of causes, lying behind a complex set of ideas, habits, and feelings."[3] There is no bad seed, handed down to children, that can be extirpated to create "racial democracy," Goodman's ideal.

The transition from hereditarily focused race psychology to studies in prejudice learning involved a rejection of instinctual unit-of-personality antipathies. But it also involved a complex and ambivalent adoption of Freudian psychoanalysis. On the one hand, study of children and developmental psychology in general had been decisively shaped by Freud's work—in the very notion of developmental stages of the ego and the very idea that prejudice might be learned in childhood and then have an influence throughout later life. On the other hand, Freud's instinctual drive theory was associated with both the doctrines of hereditarians and the specific claim that prejudice is instinctual—exactly the notions rejected by Lasker and those who followed him. Lasker himself confused Freud's instinctual drive theory with the general doctrine of instinct that had been used by the discredited American proponents of race psychology.

The result of the simultaneous rejection of Freud's instinctual drive theory and acceptance of his ego developmental scheme is obvious in Goodman's pioneering *Race Awareness in Young Children*. She provided an enormous amount of material gathered from five years of observational work in three nursery schools, where she had worked with 103 four-year-olds, 57 Negro and 46 white, and many parents and teachers. About a quarter of the four-year-old children had already developed strong systems of preference relating directly to skin color (and less directly to other physical characteristics like hair texture). All of the children were clearly aware of racial differences, and among both the Negro and the white children, white skin was considered superior. Goodman carefully correlated her observations to stages of ego development, focusing a great deal of attention on issues of self-esteem or (among the Negro children) lack of self-esteem. In this emphasis, she agreed with Ruth Horowitz, who in 1939 had argued Freudianly that the beginnings of race consciousness should be understood "as a function of ego development."[4] But Goodman did not relate the development of racial attitudes to libidinal development, although she acknowledged that childhood sexuality was just as complicated an area of development as racial awareness.

Again and again, as Goodman noted that parents and teachers were shocked to find out from her that their children and students were so aware of racial differences, she drew a key connection: "Precocious sexuality shocks them and so does precocious raciality."[5] Among the adults Goodman and her staff interviewed, ignorance—or denial—of children's racial attitudes was the norm, and Goodman consistently charged this oblivion to prudery. "There is a prevalent feeling among our parents that race, like sex, is a rather hazardous topic and one best left alone, at least so far as the children are concerned. They feel so partly because both topics rouse their own emotions." But her clarity about the adults in her observational world did not lead Goodman to take sexuality or libidinal development into account in her study of the four-year-olds.

Goodman's ego-centered approach, with its courageous if limited frankness, did, however, leave her optimism intact. Any theory of innate or instinctual race attitudes seemed to this generation of progressive researchers to imply that prejudice was natural and thus ineradicable, irreversible. They rejected Freud's instinctual drive theory because it was associated—mistakenly—with the instinct doctrines of race psychology, and attention to libidinal development went out the research door with the theory. As a result, non-Freudian—or rather half-Freudian—child study was left a strangely abstract business. It filled up with images of social learning that later lent themselves very well, in the 1960s and after, to cognitive learning theorists because they were almost free of any notion that children have desires or that their prejudices have affective content and emotional dimensions. Faulty learning seems quite a correctable condition.

There are now many works available on prejudice learning as a cognitive matter, including the book I examined in Chapter 1, Frances Aboud's *Children and Prejudice* (1988). Much of the research done as the cognitive approach reached its apogee has been ably summarized by Phyllis Katz in "The Acquisition of Racial Attitudes in Children" (1976), and the cognitive approach itself has been placed in a larger theoretical social science context by John Duckitt in *The Social Psychology of Prejudice* (1992).[6] But, to my knowledge, there has been only one study written from a Freudian developmental point of view, which neither Katz nor Duckitt mentions. Like these surveys, however, Marjorie McDonald's Freudian *Not by the Color of Their Skins* (1970) deals only with race prejudice, or more specifically skin color prejudice.[7] McDonald posits "skin color anxiety" as a normal—this does not mean *instinctive*—component of development that can become woven into and inseparable from, either normal or pathological courses of development unless it is defused, discharged, and detached from the conflicts typical of the various developmental stages.

In the remainder of this chapter, in reviewing the various types of child study literature on prejudice, I will give a picture of the kind of developmental study that points to the three character types—and thus prejudice types—that I suggested and presented preliminarily in the last chapter. The lack of attention in the child study literature to Freud's instinctual drive theory and the lack of appreciation of the way in which drive components are laced into overall character development has allowed researchers to continue to speak of prejudice in the singular and prejudice as only a cognitive matter when they try to show how children acquire prejudices. Even Marjorie McDonald herself, the Freudian child analyst, operated with the Allportian general concept: "All forms of prejudice have certain common characteristics in the mechanisms which form and maintain them. The uniqueness of a particular prejudice is usually marked by the superficial manifestation of its content (racial, religious, etc.)."[8] Differences are superstructural, commonalities are structural. But the doctrine of common features, when held by child psychologists, also produces a characteristic image: there is a single trait of prejudice in children—not given from birth, but acquired early—that grows up over time into a single full-grown plant. There may be no inborn bad seed, but there is a single type of socially constructed weed.

A linguistic problem largely explains why Freud's instinct theory was left out of account in Freudianly influenced child study. In the six passages in all of his writings where Freud used the German word *Instinkt,* he made comparisons with phenomena that can be observed in the animal world, like instinctive recognition of dangers. He defined the word as "inherited mental formations." But he was not convinced that inherited mental formations exist in humans as they do in animals.[9] Children, for example, do not recognize dangers as animals do, so they need a protecting adult nearby (20:168). But, if humans do have some kind of instincts comparable to those of animals, they must, Freud argued, "constitute the nucleus of the unconscious" (14:195).

> It is hard to dismiss the view that some sort of hardly definable knowledge, something, as it were, preparatory to an understanding, [is at work in small children]. We can form no conception of what this may have consisted in; we have nothing at our disposal but the single analogy—and it is an excellent one—of the far-reaching instinctive [*instinktiv*] knowledge of animals.
>
> If human beings, too, possessed an instinctive endowment such as this, it would not be surprising that it should be very particularly concerned with the processes of sexual life, even though it could not be by any means confined to them. This instinctive factor would then be the nucleus of the unconscious, a primitive kind of mental activity, which would later be dethroned and overlaid by human reason, when that faculty came to be acquired, but which in some people, perhaps in everyone, would retain the power of drawing down to it the higher mental processes.   (17:120)

Freud's caution about *Instinkt* was not known to his American and English readers in the 1930s, however, because when they read "instinct" in their translations, they were reading about *Trieb,* not *Instinkt.* Freud never used the word *Trieb,* which would be more accurately rendered "drive," to indicate any primitive mental activity like the recognition of danger so obvious in animals. *Trieb* meant, rather, a continuous stimulation or excitation arising in human organs and pressing upon the mental capacities for some kind of work ("an instigation to mental activity" as he said once, 20:200). Such internal stimulations cannot, like external stimulations, be escaped by retreat or flight; they must be either gratified or repressed. The *Triebe* are continuous drives or pushes or pulsions that can be represented mentally, consciously or unconsciously, but that themselves never come to consciousness. Translating *Trieb* as "hormone effect" would avoid the confusions of "instinct" and be accurately suggestive, if not technically accurate because *Trieb* is a wider, less strictly biochemical concept.[10]

Freud used the technical word "libido" for the energy of the sexual drive, which he at first distinguished mainly from hunger (an instinct), as sex and hunger had always, in the entire history of psychology with which he was familiar, been acknowledged as the great animators, the great movers and shakers of people and animals. Libido has, Freud always noted, aims and objects—ends and means. Generally, the aim of the sexual drive is pleasure as satisfaction, relief of tension, but intermediate, diverting, or alternative aims can provide the route to satisfaction. The object is that part of a person's own body or that fantasized Other or that external person in which or through whom the aim is attained. Originally, Freud held, drives do not have predetermined objects—they find them, gain them, in the quest for satisfaction, and they may change them over time, as a child changes from seeking satisfaction in the mother's breast to seeking it in thumb sucking to seeking it in food, kissing another person, and so forth. There is always, he argued in the 1920s, a degree of variability in people between on the one hand their sexual anatomies and physiologies, their developed sexual mental attitudes (their sense of themselves as masculine or feminine or some mixture), their aims and on the other their objects—there is no formula, no simple fixity, among these dimensions.[11] No psychologist has ever made a stronger contrast to the doctrines of hereditarians than this argument.

Any external visible, touchable area of the human body, including any part of the skin or the skin as a whole, and any internal organ can become an expressive area for the sexual drive, but certain areas characteristically have the quality of high erotogenicity because they are related to the major organic needs (nourishment, defecation, urination, discharge of sexual tension) and because they are important in children's relations with their surroundings and their loved ones (technically called "objects"). The mouth, through which a suckling infant receives nourishment and is bound to the breast of the mother or nurse, is the first characteristically erotogenic zone. The anal zone becomes particularly important as children become aware that they produce feces out of their bodies and learn to keep themselves clean. The ure-thral-phallic zone (a general term covering the girl's clitoris and the boy's glans penis) takes center stage when children experience and ac-knowledge sensations in their genitals (which they may associate with urination), when they come to enjoy exhibiting themselves and mastur-bating, and when they explore the differences between adults and chil-dren's genitals and between the genitals of the two sexes. Oral, anal, and phallic stages form, as Anna Freud once put it, "the inborn, ma-turational base" for the broad developmental line that leads from de-pendence on maternal care to early adult ability to be emotionally and materially self-reliant.[12]

As a child reaches puberty, these independent sources of excitation and satisfaction become gradually secondary to the pleasures that the biologically mature genitals afford. Then the sexual drive's aim is release of "sexual substances" (genital swelling and tension, and sperm in the male) and the sexual object is another person. But the early discovered sources of excitation and gratification do normally continue to play a role in mature sexual pleasure, especially as they are involved in sexual foreplay. Any of these zones may become particularly important to a child and then to a mature person if the pleasures they afford are par-ticularly intense, or particularly conflictual, or associated with particular fantasies. They may, therefore, become sites for fixation (that is, play a major role in all future pleasures) or for regression (be the sites from which pleasure is sought nostalgically when other avenues are blocked or forbidden).

But the significance of the zones themselves for any individual cannot be understood without the corresponding development of object rela-tions and emotional and material self-reliance. On weaning, a child's early pleasure in nursing gives way to autoerotic pleasures like thumb sucking, and also often to an intense erotization of the skin as that which the mother continues to hold, stroke, cleanse, after the weaning takes place. Anal pleasures such as retaining a stool, enjoying the release of one, or playing with one, though autoerotic, are closely tied to their effects on the adults around, who may react anxiously to retention or to messing, and who very often (especially in hygiene-conscious or an-ticorporeal cultures) stigmatize "waste products" as dirty or disgusting. Pleasures arising from urination, exhibiting the genitals, or masturbat-ing are also autoerotic but inseparable from fantasies of other people and other peoples' actions and reactions. As I have noted, Freud posited a normal stage ("primary narcissism") of transition from predominantly autoerotic pleasures to pleasures involving other people directly, and he emphasized that this stage of narcissism or love of the pleasure-giving whole body and the developing ego is crucial to a child's ability to love others, to turn outward what has been concentrated on his or her own body and developing ego. This stage, like the erotic-libidinal stages, can also be, however, a site of fixation or regression, as it is in narcissistic character developments and in narcissistic pathologies.

In a child's developmental sequence, different ingredients that may coalesce later into prejudices come into play at different times, in different contexts. Marjorie McDonald, building on work by Rene Spitz and others, observed that infants are able to differentiate color, including skin color, by the second half of their first year and also noted that many have, at about eight months, what is known as "stranger anxiety."[13] Children who have reacted relatively indiscriminately toward people other than their caretakers begin to react to others as *not* their caretakers, *not* their mothers, because they are able to cognize their mothers as distinct and special to them and also as apt to disappear, be lost to them, unavailable. A mother can go away, and a mother's love can be lost. Frustration teaches anxiety. A mother's existence in the web of a child's narcissistic fantasy can be disturbed—the child's sense that the mother lives, so to speak, inside him or her is disproved by her absence, her unavailability, her frustrating actions. A child who is developing the notion that there is a border—literally at the child's own skin or at the mother's—between the child and the mother, a child who is anxious about strangers, may at the same time be especially sensitive to differences in skin color and, to a lesser degree, skin texture, as one of the signs of separation and difference. Discovery of skin differences "either comes at a time when the skin is highly invested and the ego functions are barely developed, or else it comes after the skin (oral) phase and *reawakens* the invested memories of this early period."[14]

For children in whom the oral stage—with its preliminary differentiations of self and other, its preliminary ego development—remains strong and conflicts remain unresolved, skin color anxiety can become merged with frustration and separation anxieties. Children, for example, whose object relations continue to display the features common to the oral stage—complete merging with some people and angry, explosive intolerance of others who are perceived as not adequately gratifying—can manifest their feelings in food fads as well as people fads. Like their people preferences, their food preferences can be organized along color lines—they eat only white rice or bread (not dark) and reject anything not covered in white sugar. There are good and bad people, good and bad foods, good and bad colors. If such faddishness continues and is reinforced over years, it can become part of the hysterical trait complex or character that is especially marked by inconstancy and volatility in love relations. Dark skinned children living in white-majority or white dominated cultures often display an early preference not for dark but for white colors, a preference they leave behind later unless it is reinforced in their milieus. Their white preference can, in adverse circumstances, develop into a split-off "white" or good self.

Children raised by biracial couples, children with a nurse not of their own color, and children who live in truly color-integrated environments learn color difference as an integral part of the world they are coming to know as not-themselves, as separate and on the other side of their skin. Theirs will not be *stranger* anxiety, but it may be anxiety about the differences among loved ones—particularly if those differences are problematic to the adults. Children raised in relative segregation may be startled by their first experience of color difference and have to be reassured so that color difference does not jar their normal narcissistic sense of their own bodily integrity.

Children who do not have the opportunity to experience people of a different color at the time when their own sense of themselves as separate, skin-bordered beings emerges, and when their skin is highly libidinized as the body part through which the mother is loved and loves, may have more difficulty integrating the differences later. James Baldwin described well the extreme case in an essay he wrote after living for several brief periods in a remote Swiss village where none of the children had ever seen a black man. The children in the village shouted *Neger! Neger!* at him in the street; they wanted to touch his hair, and they were astonished that his color did not rub off on them. "In all of this, in which it must be conceded there was the charm of genuine wonder and in which there was certainly no element of intentional unkindness, there was yet no suggestion that I was human: I was simply a living wonder."[15]

Children in the anal stage or still working through its excitements and the common adult prohibitions on its pleasures are particularly concerned with brown, with darkness, and with the association between dirt and feces and skin color. Light-skinned children will often touch the skin of darker children and call it dirty or wonder as the Swiss children did whether it will rub off on them and dirty them. Dark-skinned children sometimes think of their own skin as dirty, particularly if they have had no encouragement to think otherwise. The common association of brown skin and feces is not hidden. Goodman, without commenting, gives a clear example of how a child's anal anxiety can be read into his observation of color difference and suffused with the aggression characteristic of the anal stage. A white four-year-old, looking at a picture of a brown-skinned boy, grew alarmed: "He's black! He's a stinky little boy.—He's a stinker—he sh——! Take it away! I want another little boy!"[16]

Some psychoanalytic commentators, Lawrence Kubie for example, find this kind of reaction endemic not just to the anal stage and its afterlife, but to the more general phenomenon of body shame, which may be accentuated in the anal stage as a child is taught cleanliness, often in a shame-inducing way. He asks why body shame and hostility focus on pigmentation and answers:

> We know that in the beginning children have no such derogatory feelings about themselves. They delight in nakedness and its free display. They delight in all the apertures of the body and in all body products. They like the feeling, the sense of movement, the warmth, the smells and tastes of their own bodies and . . . products, and they have the same joy in the bodies of others. They know no hierarchies of dirtiness, leading from that which is so clean it can be taken into the mouth to that which is so filthy that it cannot be touched, looked at or named or thought about even to oneself and not even in solitude and silence. The child picks up or "learns" this contrast between "clean" and "dirty" in subtle ways. Like the caste system of Indian culture, he develops a caste system for his body: with untouchable or unmentionable body parts and products, parts that he must neither touch nor mention nor look at nor think about nor even have words for, so he makes up slang substitutes. This is associated with the fact that the apertures and also hairy places of the body are more darkly pigmented than is the rest of the body's surface, and that all body products, except tears, have some degree of color, flavor and odor. Without our ever intending to do this, we teach the toddler to feel that his body is an animated, mobile, more or less symmetrical dirt factory.[17]

Like most psychoanalytic commentators, Kubie emphasized the child's projection onto others of its body shame: "Thus out of the defense against the initial concept of an untouchable 'I' with untouchable, unmentionable, unthinkable body parts comes the concept of an untouchable 'You.' " But Kubie did not note that in the oral and anal stages, or in regression to them, children often display something else: a fear of contamination, which implies a projective identification and a fear of incorporating, bringing into their own bodies, what has been judged dirty or corrupting. Bruno Lasker's extensive collection of examples includes one of a five-year-old white boy who backed off in fear from a Negro child saying "Look out, little black child, don't breave your black bref on me!"[18] Displacement outward of a frightening feeling or a frightening fantasy seems a more characteristically anal stage defense; rejecting incorporation of a projected fear by withdrawal is more oral.

The anal phase is also characterized by vacillations between activity and passivity—the activity being often tightly connected to aggressive rebellion against training and to the overall body mobility and the enormous joy that children who are graduating from crawling to walking usually take in their freedom. Cross-culturally, in all social strata, from the exhausted adult point of view, the designation the "terrible twos" captures the trials of this period, writ as they are in motion and aggression. Many children develop at the same time rudimentary sexual theories that feature anal products as babies or babies being born anally like feces. Images of sexual intercourse formed from observing people or animals often revolve around anal penetration and mounting, and little boys as well as little girls can identify with the one being penetrated, particularly if this reinforces great pleasure in passively retaining and actively expelling stools. Associations between dark or feces colors and anal eroticism as a kind of proto-intercourse can greatly influence later race attitudes, though, on the surface, they appear to relate to phallic sexuality. These associations especially affect people with many obsessional character traits, including the three—stubbornness, cleanliness, and parsimony—explicitly linked by Freud with anal eroticism.

McDonald stated in *Not by the Color of Their Skin:* "In the phallic phase the skin color difference and genital difference can become confused, so that castration anxiety and skin color anxiety now take on a complex relation to each other."[19] But she also carefully recorded that in the Cleveland nursery school where she and her staff made their observations on children between the ages of three and seven, the number of anally tinged racial conflicts they observed far outnumbered those revealing phallic conflicts, a result that surprised her "because our culture seems to place so much stress on sexual dangers and conflicts as an important basis for our current racial problems."[20] She interpreted the surprising result as evidence that the therapeutic approach of the nursery school had helped the older (phallic-stage) children achieve a significant severing of their sexual conflicts from their conflicts over skin color. The children had achieved "an advanced stage of psychological racial integration." She might also have noted that in the late 1960s, when she was collecting her observations, African American culture was asserting "Black is beautiful," which helped many children of color avoid stages of color dislike or work through them with less than the previously usual damage to self-esteem, and which made it harder for white children to look down on Blacks.

The surprising result could also be explained by the preoccupation that phallic-stage children have with sex differences and with differences between their own genitals and those bigger ones of their parents and other adults. Strong phallic narcissism, as I indicated before, tends to minimize all differences except *the* difference of genitalia. Skin color distinction can be put into the service of intense sexual exploration and curiosity. Also, as McDonald's study only dealt with children, she did not have an opportunity to observe how skin color distinctions become erotically charged in adolescence, with the upsurge then of libido. Often, the anal stage association of black skin with dirt and feces is transcended in this libidinal upsurge, overtaken by phallic concerns, so that skin color distinctions are genitalized. This development does not occur in antisemites, as I will explain later.

Despite her overall result, McDonald did observe behavioral correlates of phallic conflicts, particularly in the Black children, who had the double burden of dealing with their own intrapsychic, developmental issues at the same time that they were reacting to the skin color anxiety of the (majority) white children. The Black boys tended to identify dark skin color with femininity, and to avoid the Black girls, as though fearing contamination and emasculinization. Both Black boys and girls tended to identify their hair with phallic power and to be anxious when they got haircuts or when comparisons with the white children's long, straight hair came up. McDonald's book was published in 1970, when the Black Power fashion of up-standing Afros was well known in urban nursery schools. The current fashions for equating power and hair are, of course, more diverse and multicultural—African braiding and beading, Jamaican rastas, tall flattops and intricate hair-carved sign systems.

Particularly if their environments give them opportunity, children in the phallic stage also tend to play out their oedipal conflicts in the medium of color. They can, for example, associate the sexual activities of their parents—so exciting, so jealousy-arousing—with nighttime, darkness, and, by extension, dark-skinned people. More specifically, dark-skinned people can be associated with rivals whom a child wants off the scene. McDonald observed a five-year-old white girl who exiled from her dollhouse the Black girl dolls, so that she could claim for herself the exclusive attention of the white father-figure. She sent away, that is, all siblings and her mother in the medium of the Black dolls. A Black boy of the same age took to criticizing his father's very dark skin while he was trying to win his mother's attention. He succeeded in enraging his father and disrupting the family by playing out his oedipal rivalry in the medium of "colorism." A white South African six-year-old provided the psychologist John Duckitt with a typical example of how oedipal castration fear can be represented by Blacks—one from a South African atmosphere completely lacking any of the therapeutic approaches in McDonald's nursery school. The white boy was explaining why he could not have a Black doll present at his pretend tea party and resorted to an image clearly learned from adults: "If I have to sit next to one of these I'll have a nervous breakdown."[21]

The children in these examples are old enough to be strongly influenced by their parents' attitudes and by their experiences in school with other childrens' and adults' attitudes. Research done in the 1930s as American social science shifted away from race psychology, like work done in the early 1950s, stressed the importance of direct parental instruction in transmitting racial attitudes—probably for the simple reason that such direct parental instruction typified practices in the American South and North. But Allport's *Nature of Prejudice* marked a shift of emphasis. It gave more weight to indirect socialization and toward studying prejudice as something that is as often—so Allport put it—"caught as taught."[22] This tendency to be more nuanced in discussing how parents influence children also resulted from the baffling failure of empirical study after empirical study to produce strong correlations between parental attitudes and children's attitudes. Some studies even indicated—flying in the face of one of the most commonly held opinions of the general public—that the correlation between parental attitudes and children's attitudes is quite weak.[23]

As John Duckitt has pointed out, trying to determine whether direct or indirect learning is the more important for children of around five is methodologically very complex and really makes sense only if historical and social contexts are taken into account. Direct instruction is an important and powerful way for children to be inculcated with a prejudice when the prejudice is the norm—that is, in segregated, overtly and uninhibitedly racist societies. Indirect learning is more important in integrated societies where racial equality is preached, if not widely practiced, and where direct instruction is socially unacceptable.

But even this refinement does not reveal much about *how* attitudes are transmitted. And it does not show anything about how transmitted attitudes are woven into children's developing desires and object relations and theories of sexuality. Unfortunately, the cognitive literature gives no help on these questions, although it contributes in other ways. As I noted in Chapter 1, a consensus has emerged among cognitively oriented empirical researchers that indicates three broad stages in acquisition of prejudices. Frances Aboud reports in *Children and Prejudice* that children below the age of three to four are most influenced in their development of racial awareness by "affective processes such as emotions and needs" (such as fear of strangers), while children of three or four and on up to about seven are most influenced by their perceptions of their own and others' appearances and behaviors. In this second stage, differences in appearance—like skin color—are important to a child but not connected in the child's mind with personal qualities or identities. Appearances and behaviors define groups, not individuals. Children may take skin color into account but think that a person can change skin color and thus change group. When children do evaluate groups and differences in this three- to seven-year-old stage, those who are majority whites tend to find whiteness preferable. So do many children of color—although the cognitive researchers agree with McDonald that this tendency among minority children generally diminishes after age seven.

An empirical consensus, moreover, indicates that all children develop cognitive abilities at about age seven which allow them to rely less on appearances for their understanding of the world. They grow to understand that peoples' ethnic identities are constant. Appreciating people in their individuality becomes possible as they recognize different points of view, note that others have preferences different than their own, make comparisons, and think abstractly. Most empirical studies demonstrate that prejudice or negative evaluations of out-groups diminish in children over seven. But this development takes place, except in unusual cases, only in the absence of social forces that actively teach prejudice. Children over seven are more influenced by prejudiced people in their families and surroundings than younger children, who cannot cognitively appreciate the lessons of prejudice. When familial and social forces do begin to play a larger role in older children's lives, enormous variety comes into the attitudes and evaluations and prejudices formed.

This developmental scenario does not, as I noted, take intrapsychic factors into account, and it explicitly leaves "affective processes such as emotions and needs" out of the picture for any children over age three or four. From a psychoanalytic point of view, the empirical evidence suggests that children who have passed the pitch of their phallic and oedipal period are able, in their less drive-dominated latencies, to direct their attention to other people in and of themselves, not as players by projection or displacement in the children's oedipal dramas. But it also suggests that the intellectualizations that accumulate in the latency period—intellectual products that reinforce and elaborate defenses developed in the oedipal period—are likely to involve prejudices, especially if these are being actively taught in the environment. Most empirical researchers agree that ethnic prejudices and prejudices against groups not visually distinguished by skin color or sexual characteristics—most Jewish populations, homosexuals—appear only in children aged ten or eleven. From a cognitive point of view, these groups require cognitive appreciation of invisibles and values, while from a psychoanalytic point of view these prejudices are second-order defenses and defenses more in the realm of intellectualization. In the scheme I am developing, they are the defenses more typical of obsessionals than of hysterical characters.

Those who study the cognitive stages of prejudice development concur that race awareness—meaning, specifically, skin color awareness—precedes awareness of group differences that are less visual or not apprehendable perceptually. But there are no studies of, for example, the development of antisemitism in childhood. This may well be because antisemitism only appears after children have passed the classification "children," and moved on to "preadolescents." But the fact remains that studies of race awareness and race prejudice have dominated the whole domain of "children and prejudice," setting the patterns for study, and that the cognitive approach has eliminated any questioning about transformations of prejudices from childhood to latency to puberty and adolescence. On reflections of this sort clinical literature has more to say. But, despite a good deal of clinical material on antisemitism dating from right after World War II, clinical cases by psychiatrists, psychologists, or psychoanalysts in which racial prejudice is a key or even a salient ingredient are very rare. The ones that do exist tend to confirm the close association of phallic stage, oedipal conflict, and color consciousness, while they raise many questions about what kinds of factors turn color preference into fully articulated or actively pursued racism.

## Case Studies: Three Faces of Hysterical Prejudice

In "A Consideration of the Etiology of Prejudice" (1957), the psychoanalyst Brian Bird presented "a young hysterical girl" (aged nineteen, presumably a child during World War II) who was suffering from "phobias, mostly of bodily disease, and overwhelming attacks of unheralded anxiety." In the course of her therapy, the young woman, an inveterate romantic daydreamer, developed a transference to her analyst that she found very threatening. She covered her romantic fantasies about her analyst with a layer of hostility and then felt exposed when the hostility was analyzed and began to recede. At that point in the analysis, she, a Jew dedicated to a vision of racial equality, began to fantasize that Negro men were making advances toward her. She expressed hatred for Negroes, charging them as a race with inferiority and lack of sexual control. This outbreak of racial prejudice, Bird suggested to her, was a way of controlling her own impulses—particularly toward her analyst—by assigning them to the Negroes, projecting them. As she worked with this interpretation and accepted it, the prejudice "evaporated."

In this case racial prejudice was not learned *directly* in childhood. In a more intricate fashion, the young woman had developed the idea that she herself "looked very Jewish and perhaps even Negro," while her mother and older sister, whom she envied, were lighter and not Jewish-looking. The mother and sister also were not—as she felt her father was—uncouth, coarse, ugly, and unsuccessful. The analysis revealed a complex relation between her prejudice against her father (and against herself because she was like him) and her prejudice against male Negroes: she was better able to function when she was feeling prejudice toward Negroes, when her aggression was directed outward (as it had also been several years earlier in a transitory period of antisemitism). In effect, her prejudice against Negroes served her as a defense against self-reproachful depression. Her self-depreciation, she found, reflected her mother's critical attitude toward her. But more fundamentally it rested on her combination of love, hatred, envy, and fear of competition with regard to her mother and older sister, and on the love disguised by denigration she felt for her father. Her bout of racial prejudice protected her from the intense feelings associated with these preoedipal and oedipal entanglements.

Bird's case study clearly shows racism as a type of what I have called hysterical prejudice. But, just as clinical work on hysterical characters and character disorders has evolved toward a consensus that there are two distinguishable subtypes, oral and phallic, so there also seem to be two distinguishable forms of hysterical prejudice. Without being acknowledged as such, they were described in Richard Sterba's article of 1947 "Some Psychological Factors in Negro Race Hatred and in Anti-Negro Riots," a piece he wrote on the basis of analytic work with white males during the time of the 1943 race riots in Detroit.

In the first part of his article, Sterba noted that several of his patients who had had intense rivalries with their siblings reworked those rivalries in their dreams, with Negroes playing the roles of the siblings. One violent Negro hater, for example, dreamed of being on a small raft in a harbor and seeing a big boat approach. Some Negroes jumped out of the boat's portholes, and the dreamer drove his raft toward them and crushed them against the side of the boat. Sterba, interpreting the dream as the man offered his associations to it, perceived the boat as the body of the man's mother and the Negroes as his siblings, being born from her. The dreamer destroyed the Negroes as he had wished to destroy each of the five younger siblings who had come into life and disturbed his relation with his mother.

> The attitude of [racists] toward Negroes mirrors exactly the attitude of the older child toward his sibling rivals: Negroes should be kept in their place, as inferior members of a social group to which they are hardly allowed to belong. They are considered immature, incapable of development, and eternal children. Every attempt at, or actual achievement of a Negro is resented with furious anger and with fear. The reaction of fear is noteworthy, and in its nature is very similar to the fear of dethronization which the older child experiences with re-

gard to his growing rival. Every attempt is made to prevent the Negro's integration into the social structure of the white . . . The greatest horror is therefore expressed about intermarriage, because this would really mean complete acceptance in the family.[24]

Racism as sibling rivalry, then, takes the form of discrimination—exclusionary practices—which unconsciously means crushing Negroes into poverty or lack of any kind of threatening (love) achievement.

Racism as renewed and redirected sibling rivalry uses both male and female Negroes, Sterba pointed out. He also noted that it involves people acting as individuals. In both these ways, it contrasts to the type of Negro hatred manifest in group or mass psychological violence, including riots, against Negro males only. In males, this kind is, psychologically, an outbreak of father hatred, which Sterba described in terms similar to those used by the sociologist Pierre van den Berghe to present the "paternalistic racism" typical of plantation and colonial contexts.

> Negro hatred had its origins in the South, where many white children were and are brought up by a Negro "mammy," toward whom they often develop feelings like those toward a mother. Due to the development of the Oedipus complex, the male Negro is then naturally brought into the position of the hated father. The South furnishes the classical example of the race riot in the form of lynching. The rebellious sons unite against the hated father substitute with the aim of killing and castrating him. The inhumanity, cruelty and brutality with which they proceed reveals the origins of this conduct in the most primitive and barbaric layers of our minds, where it is otherwise buried in the unconscious and is brought forth only under the mass psychological conditions of the riot. The fact that the [anti-]Negro riot regularly breaks out through the rumor that a Negro has raped a white woman confirms our opinion about its patricidal origin. Almost without exception the riot is then the revenge for the alleged sexual assault upon a white woman by a Negro.

Sterba's description alludes to the idea, developed by Freud in his speculative culture studies like *Totem and Taboo,* that in current all-male groups such as hunting lodges or army units men reenact a primeval rebellion of sons against father—the group psychological form of the Oedipus complex. This particular Freudian notion, with its corollary of phylogenetic inheritance, is interesting to speculate about, but it is not necessary to appreciate the observations in Sterba's article. He commented, for example, "that among the most embittered participants in

the race riots in Detroit were adolescents, many of Southern origin."
These youths, Sterba thought, were experiencing the typical adolescent
second stage of their oedipal rivalries with their fathers, when "new
currents of sexuality" called for "a more disguised form." The disguise
was race prejudice.

Sterba did not note the difference in childhood stage-reference of
the two kinds of hatred he described, but it seems obvious that the
first—the sibling rivalry renewal—echoes early separation experiences
and oral greed, not wishing to share the maternal body or breast. But
the second—the patricidal reenactment—is oedipal, phallic. In effect,
Sterba described "oral" and "phallic" versions of racism in males.
Bird's case, detailing the hysteric's rivalry with her sister and her feeling
of being frustrated by and criticized by her mother, also resembles the
first type, which (as I suggested before) may be the commonest type of
hysterical racial prejudice among women, particularly among women
who define themselves in an exaggeratedly feminine way and thus forbid themselves the active, conventionally masculine modes they may
desire. Female hysterical characters and women with hysterical character disorders are much more inclined to conversion symptoms and depression than are males of either the oral or the phallic sort. Males more
frequently engage in risk-taking behavior, in their recreational activities
or their jobs, and present their hysteria or hysterical traits in antisocial
or delinquent forms or in forms that are legal but excitingly violent,
like gun toting and hunting. As two recent clinical commentators have
indicated, a male hysteric's "sociopath-like behavior may be confused
with the true sociopath; however, the hysteric will show splitting of his
personality. The underlying dependency in many of his anti-social acts
will seem exaggerated and bizarre, in contrast to the true sociopath,
whose actions and personality are more integrated and, in one sense,
more mature."[25]

We can discern a third sort of hysterical type and prejudice not included in Sterba's survey. In this type, a hysterical personality and prejudice are overlaid with obsessional features. As Freud noted many times,
particularly in his long case study of the patient called the "Wolf Man"
in 1918, obsessionality almost always grows out of hysteria: it supervenes
in latency, when defenses generally take intellectualized forms and
when prejudices develop that require intellectual skills not available to
children. T. C. Rodgers presented a male patient of this type in "The
Evolution of an Active Anti-Negro Racist" (1960).

This man had grown up in the 1920s as the only child of upper-middle-class Southern parents, both obsessional, who kept Negro servants, including a nurse who was the patient's "mammy." The patient's mother had toilet trained him very early, with many prohibitions on anal pleasures and a strict taboo on masturbation, but he associated his Negro nurse with a milder regime. As an adult he treated his nurse with great leniency in comparison to the retaliatory obsessional way he treated his widowed mother. He tenderly loved the black woman, but he was terrified of black men.

Rodgers's therapy with this man, who was severely inhibited in his sexual life (which was confined to "degraded" women) and also thwarted in his work life, slowly uncovered his strong hatred and fear of his father. It also became clear that in his dreams and fantasies the patient represented his father by the nurse's Negro husband and by aggressive phallic signs of this man (in one dream he was beaten by a black cane; black bull's horns were prominent in another). The patient deeply feared anal rape by Negro men. But he also strongly identified with the Negro men who were, he fantasized, waiting to attack his mother. Stirred up by his therapy, he elaborately protected his mother from the fantasized Negro attackers, and eventually he became an outspoken advocate of capital punishment for Negro criminals. Finally, when he abandoned his therapy, he took up active work in the White Citizens Council, a racist group specifically opposed to miscegenation and the "mongrelization" of the races. He turned his passive fear of rape into a frantically active aggression against the alleged rapists (and, insofar as he also identified with the rapists, he controlled himself with threats of punishment).

Rodgers's patient certainly learned prejudice from his parents when he was a child, and he clearly remembered specific later instructions, like the ban his father laid on any contact with the girls in "nigger town," who, he was told when he was seventeen, all carried venereal disease. But he worked these instructions into his individual—though not at all untypical—system of obsessional anxieties and defenses. Rodgers indicated that the patient's obsessional defenses, along with his conscious association of Negroes with forbidden and dangerous sexuality, dated from his adolescence, but Rodgers could not in this brief therapy find out much about the patient's childhood symptomology. The kind of hysterical symptoms that usually precede and undergird an obsessional neurosis were, however, apparent in the man's somatizations—

his general body rigidity (hypertonicity), impotence, and "hysterical bowel." More important, the patient's anus was "genitalized"—his phallic desires were primarily passive, and he was identified with his mother in his desire for—and terror about—anal penetration. That is, he had the typical obsessional desire to be the opposite sex. If this man had grown up in a society where antisemitism was common, he might have made a good antisemite, but as it was, he constructed the available Negro "fathers" as his attackers. He could retaliate only through a legal organization, not in the reckless, rioting way more typical of oral and phallic hysterical characters and also quite typical of the hysterical Ku Klux Klan of the 1920s, which could be characterized as a kind of lodge dedicated to hunting Negroes.

## Case Studies: Obsessional Fortress Building

I have charted three subtypes of hysterical characters and their prejudices—those directed primarily at siblings in competition for the mother, those expressing patricidal desires, and those defending against paternally related homoeroticism. The cases suggesting these subtypes were undertaken by different analysts, working independently of one another and in different periods. The study of racism contains nothing like the multiple-case, comparative work undertaken after World War II to analyze antisemitism.

I have mentioned before the most extensive exploration of antisemitism through case studies, a volume in the Studies in Prejudice series called *Anti-Semitism, an Emotional Disorder,* by Nathan Ackerman and Marie Jahoda. Using material from psychoanalytic treatments of sixteen men and eleven women, they made a composite description and offered some reflections on common childhood developmental factors.

The two authors made clear at the beginning of their work that the antisemites they studied could not be assigned a single diagnostic classification. They also indicated, however, that they had found a proclivity along the obsessional-paranoid axis among their subjects. "We find a preponderance of character disorders, a smaller number of psychoneuroses, including four cases of obsessional neurosis, one case of paranoia, and a number of less precisely defined disturbances."[26] They described numerous features typical of obsessional characters. The antisemitic patients were indecisive and doubt-ridden in both their relationships and their interests. They were "under continuous apprehension of injury to their integrity as individuals." Their self-esteem was damaged but the damage was denied. They were social conformists but restless and rebellious in groups for fear of submissiveness. On the one hand, they showed enormous fear of passivity, including sexual passivity, and compensated with aggression, incessant activity, and pursuit of power or money or recognition. On the other hand, they also avoided situations where they had to be directly confrontational. They maintained, instead, a general attitude of being opposed, being against, hating. "These people are not only against the Jew; they are against themselves and everyone else. They are notoriously 'against.' The reliance on attitudes of both avoidance and opposition subserves the primary defense pattern of substituting aggression for anxiety."

These antisemites attributed the two sets of characteristics they shared—the great sense of vulnerability, inferiority, and isolation, in combination with aggression and incessant activity—to the Jews. They projected upon the Jews both stereotypical images of weakness—outsiderdom and injury (including the symbolic castration of circumcision)—and stereotypical images of strength. They saw Jewish strength in powerful networks and financial clout, not sexuality. And in this projection the patients resembled the antisemitic people interviewed at the end of World War II by Bruno Bettelheim and Morris Janowitz. Those subjects also spoke always of Jewish economic power, not sexual power. Bettelheim and Janowitz observed that American antisemites seldom accuse Jews of sexual prowess in any form, not even in the from of perversity, and that they also very seldom object to Gentile-Jewish miscegenation or intermarriage. "This stands in sharp contrast to an important element of European antisemitism and antisemitic agitation, which stressed the Jew's supposed sexual immorality."[27] (It might be speculated that America, a nation which, unlike the European nations of the World War II period, included a large Negro population and had accumulated centuries' worth of experience with racist fantasies of Negro sexual potency, did not need for its Jews to play this role.)

Several of Ackerman and Jahoda's antisemitic patients reported the kinds of beating fantasies that Freud discussed in his paper of 1919 "'A Child Is Being Beaten,'" that is, fantasies in which the patient reported seeing a Jew being beaten and identified with the Jew. But, in a manner I consider typically obsessional, they immediately turned this passive identification into its opposite and identified with the attacker.

The deep-seated identification with the Jew's symbolic weakness, his crippled, castrated state and his subordinated defenseless position, is denied because of its danger to the integrity of the individual's self and his social position; in its place there is substituted an identification with the attacker, in order to avoid being victimized and also to draw strength from the identification. Thus the Jew, at one and the same time, stands for the weakness or the strength of the self; for conscience, which reproaches the self for its deficiencies and badness, and also for those primitive, forbidden appetites and aggressions which must be denied as the price of social acceptance.

Ackerman and Jahoda noted that their subjects, although very different in terms of sex, age, background, and religion, shared two features of family context. First, their parents were like the parents encountered so frequently by *The Authoritarian Personality* group—strict, rigid disciplinarians who did not always stop short of physical beating as they compelled their children into conformity and submissiveness. The children responded with obedience but also grievance and great reservoirs of unexpressed aggression. Further, "in several cases, the fixation of anal character traits can be traced back clearly to severe, early toilet training which was made a test of the parents' approval and affection." Second, in all the cases the parents themselves had a hostile relationship, vying for dominance and quarreling. The children were inhibited from secure identifications with either parent. Identifying with the weaker one meant being weak and vulnerable; identifying with the stronger one meant joining the oppressor's camp and becoming part of the battle against the weaker one. In structural terms, these incomplete or insecure identifications meant the antisemitic patients were characterized by ill-formed or faulty superegos. And they all also shared a noticeable instability of conscience and lack of overt guilt feelings. "Examples of this abound in our cases. There is the wealthy business man who cheats his newspaper dealer out of small change; the mother who neglects her small child because she feels like going out for a walk; the woman of forty who does not know whether to approve or disapprove of anything unless she first asks her mother, etc."[28]

Another common and related family pattern, which appears repeatedly in the psychoanalytic literature on obsessionality, features children who, viewing one of their parents, usually the mother but sometimes the father, as a burdened, overworked, illness-prone, fragile, inconsistent, even martyred figure, become that parent's protector. If the other parent is absent or is viewed by the child as an inadequate protector, or even as a source of danger, the effort to take on the protecting role intensifies, fueled by the feeling that the unprotecting parent can be eliminated as a rival. Often the unprotecting parent gets cast as an active aggressor and protection against this aggressor parent is mounted— even while the missing protection continues to be desired. Meanwhile, the child works beyond his or her means managing and ordering the life of an adult who seems to need protection. Reaching for pseudoso-lutions, the child can invent rituals of caretaking and stick to them re-ligiously, or invent self-berating, self-reproachful thoughts and think them over and over, or develop excessively "good" behaviors meant to solicit love and convince the parents that the child is not bad. Repetitive actions and thoughts can also constrain and banish aggressive wishes— especially death wishes—against the parents who cannot, in their op-posite ways, be parental.[29]

The child or adolescent who overmanages and overthinks begins to feel empty and without identity or takes temporary refuge in temporary identities. The conformism of the obsessional often stems from a habit of identifying or forming partial identifications with the people who come along. The child or adolescent becomes first this one and then that one, adopting with each identification that person's mannerisms, accent, style—and prejudices. But it can also turn out that the person who is unable to establish in childhood or adolescence a relationship of normal dependence with parents or family looks outside the family and finds such a relationship on what terms are available. Often this means submitting to someone (often mistaking exploitation for loving attention) or joining a group and obeying the group leaders and rules. The prejudices of the authority figure or of the group then become part of the child's and adolescent's management rituals. The pattern can be seen in many studies of Hitler Youth.

Ackerman and Jahoda pointed to a type of faulty superego in their antisemitic population that is common among obsessionals and that the contemporary French analyst Bela Grunberger has called a "pregenital superego" and described as a "precociously formed superego which is based not on the introjection of complete objects but on their educative function. It pertains to a training role, which is represented in the un-conscious by the introjection of an anal phallus as a part object."[30] Translated from psychoanalytic French, this formulation means that the antisemite's superego comprises partial identifications, commands and

prohibitions, and "shoulds," rather than rounded, full identifications
with parental figures; and these commands and prohibitions are assimilated as were the commands and prohibitions that constituted the antisemite's toilet training and, in general, disciplining, so that the commands and prohibitions are experienced as patriarchal-sexual power
taken in or intruded anally. The antisemite's morality is, thus, formulaic—perfect manners and impeccable execution of orders will matter
to the antisemite much more than right and wrong, or they will, as I
noted before of obsessionals in general, take the place of questions
about right and wrong. Ideas and formal practices, too, are cut off from
affect by the defenses described before as undoing and isolation. Guilt
feelings are displaced onto the victim, so that the antisemite does not
feel them and feels, instead, coldly numb, empty. In this sense, it was
not surprising that Adolf Eichmann at his trial in Jerusalem could accurately state Immanuel Kant's Categorical Imperative and regret that
he had not followed it but express no remorse whatsoever for the mass
murders he organized. Hannah Arendt chose to call this characteristic
formulaic morality and cold-bloodedness the "banality of evil."

The image patterns typical of the fantasies and dreams presented by
Rodgers's mixed hysterical-obsessional patient in his brief analysis can
be seen—with changes in the *dramatis personae*—in the antisemitic fantasies and dreams that Ackerman and Jahoda report. They are staples
of antisemitic literature. To show this, and to offer an application of the
case study method, I want to turn briefly to what is certainly the most
influential work of the twentieth century by an antisemite, Adolf Hitler's
*Mein Kampf.* There, the standard antisemitic image pattern is present—
but it has to be read out, or through, Hitler's political vision. I will
interpret that vision as though it were a portrait of Hitler's psyche, in
much the same way as Rodgers's patient's dream of the black-horned
bull was of his.

Stripped down to its essential ingredients, its core content, the guiding ideology of *Mein Kampf* looks like this: The motherland—in *Mein
Kampf,* Hitler spoke of Germany always as the motherland ("beloved
mother . . . the young Reich")—must grow because its self-sufficiency
depends on growth. It must grow to the East, into Russia, on contiguous
continental land, not to overseas colonies, for Germany's land base for
eventual rule over the world must be wide and firm, like the base of a
pyramid. The motherland must be able to feed and supply her own

people, take care of her population, which must increase. Germany has historically suffered at the hands of her enemies because she has been a land of mixed racial stocks, which has meant that she never had the unity, the organic evolutionary thrust, the herd instinct, to achieve supremacy and to take revenge upon her past predators and ancient enemies. Her Aryan stock should be promoted with a policy encouraging the pure Aryan young to breed and discouraging racial pollution. Germany's pure stock must also be preserved from spiritual corruption, and this means corruption by the false god of the modern world, money, by international finance, and by any economic ideology, capitalistic or socialistic. Behind all of Germany's enemies—her external foes and her internal impure elements—stand the Jews, who aspire to world conquest racially and spiritually. They are the blood poisoners and the money idolaters, and they must be expelled or eliminated.

Above all, Hitler conveys an image of autarky and activism. Germany must never depend on others and must never be passive, which means penetrable by outside others or pollutable by inside others. It is a fortress image. Even though the ultimate goal is world conquest, the impulse is isolationist. It fairly screams, "Do not enter!" The world will be controlled from the base of the great Reich; tentacles of power will reach out from a closed state. To keep this autarkic realm pure, and thus strong and aggressive, internal corruption and waste must be removed. Dirty people and dirty ideologies of money must be evacuated. The cleansing takes place by identification with the power of the imagined attackers: the beaten country rises up and is the beater.

Interpreted as a psychic image, a vast blow-up of Hitler's feeling about himself, a portrait of himself or (to use Freud's term) his unconscious "endopsychic perception" of himself as the German motherland, the image says: I am my mother, beaten, passive, and penetrable, but I will—by force of will—masculinize myself and not be, as it would be evil to be, this female. No father, no male, will force himself on me, enter my anus, or beat me, and I will grow big, strong, and able to put my evil out onto them. No Jew—no "emasculating germ" as he called the Jew—will survive, much less triumph. His motto might well have been the one created for the Hitler Youth: "Youth shapes its own destiny."

As every one of his psychologically inclined biographers has noted, Adolf Hitler was deeply tied to his mother and, as an adolescent, at war with his father, a violent drunkard who seems to have beaten his much younger wife—and thus provided his son with opportunity to identify with the beaten mother or the beating father, or both. Ostensively, the son's battle focused on the father's demand that the son prepare for civil service, not for art school. When Hitler's father died abruptly in 1903, the fourteen-year-old son lived with his mother. Until her death from cancer in 1908, the son was weak, stalled and listless, unable to pursue the art school route left open, directionless. Then, at the beginning of 1909, when he was twenty, he left home and went to the site of his father's civil service career, Vienna, to try to make his fortune as an artist, the career his father had forbidden him. He had no success whatsoever and drifted through four years of abject poverty and struggle for survival. In Vienna, he encountered for the first time a large Jewish population and waves of antisemitism. "At home, as long as my father lived, I cannot remember that I ever heard the word [Jew]." "I detested the conglomerate of races that the . . . capital manifested . . . among them Jews and more Jews. To me the big city appeared as the personification of incest."[31]

Hitler biographers usually read this striking image—"the personification of incest"—as a clue that Hitler conflated his incestuous desire for his mother with the Jewish traffic in prostitutes that he described so frequently and with such horror in *Mein Kampf:* "an icy shudder ran down my spine when seeing the Jew for the first time as a cool, shameless, and calculating manager of this shocking vice . . . But then my indignation flared up." Hitler is seen as a projector of incest guilt onto the Jews, those corrupters of Aryan racial purity. Or, along the same lines, he has been interpreted as a youth who projected his oedipal rivalry onto the Jews, who fought his father in the form of Jewry. Erik Erikson has offered the diagnosis "hysteria" because Hitler acted out his oedipal rivalry so grandiosely, with such imposture on the great stage of the world.[32] But it seems much more likely that Hitler identified with the prostitutes and feared the predations of the Jews—that his passive shudder was followed by aggressive indignation according to an old habit of obsessional defense. For it is fear and anxiety that are palpable in his descriptions of Jewish male sexuality: "the black-haired Jew boy, diabolic joy in his face, waits in ambush for the unsuspecting girl whom he defiles with his blood." As Bela Grunberger comments generally about antisemites: "The anal struggle in toto is projected onto the Jew. Not only as regards dirtiness and all forms of money but also all forms of aggression and treachery, culminating in the paranoiac fear of anal penetration. . . The anal components of sexuality are also projected upon the Jews—lewd monsters who rape innocent German girls in order to pollute the race."[33]

## Why Can't a Woman Be More Like a Man?

The psychoanalytic clinical literature does not contain cases focused on sexism as a development in and from childhood. Psychoanalytic theory has been for most of its existence too sexist to focus on sexism either as a symptom or as a character trait, in the sense that many behaviors and attitudes that would constitute sexism from a feminist point of view have qualified as ego syntonic or culturally syntonic among analysts. Nevertheless, within the history of psychoanalytic theory and case literature, sexism—under the labels "misogyny," or "denigration of women"—has been investigated, and those investigations fall into roughly two periods. The first period, dominated by Freud's ideas, concentrated on male oedipal castration anxiety. (Even the early critics of Freud's views on female psychology, such as Karen Horney and Ernest Jones, focused on the "phallocentrism" of Freud's theories, by which they meant the castration anxiety displayed in those theories.) The second period presupposed several decades of work in which the preoedipal period in males and females received the attention of critical or dissident Freudians, and it related sexism to difficulties in the processes of male children's disidentifications with their mothers and to narcissism. The approach I am taking here to the narcissistic prejudices draws on both psychoanalytic epochs.

Any number of passages from Freud's work could be offered to demonstrate the ingredients of his view, but I think this one from his essay on Leonardo da Vinci (written in 1910) is particularly instructive:

> Before the child comes under the dominance of the castration-complex—at the time when he still holds women at full value—he begins to display an intense desire to look, as an erotic instinctual [*triebisch*] activity. He wants to see other people's genitals, at first in all probability to compare them with his own. The erotic attraction that comes from his mother soon culminates in a longing for her genital organ, which he takes to be a penis. With the discovery, which is not made until later, that women do not have a penis, this longing often turns into its opposite and gives place to a feeling of disgust which in the years of puberty can become the cause of psychical impotence, misogyny and permanent homosexuality. But the fixation on the object that

was once strongly desired, the woman's penis, leaves indelible traces on the mental life of the child, who has pursued that portion of his infantile sexual researches with particular thoroughness. Fetishistic reverence for a woman's foot and shoe appears to take the foot merely as a substitutive symbol for the woman's penis that was once revered and later missed; without knowing it, 'coupeurs de nattes' [perverts who enjoy cutting off females' hair] play the part of people who carry out an act of castration on the female genital organs.   (*Standard Edition* 11:96)

Freud anticipated that this passage would be met with the disbelief that it has, in fact, prompted, so he followed it with an elaborate disquisition showing adoration of the genitals as common among those who have not ruined their appreciation with civilized ideas about the genitalia as shameful. Ancient androgynous deities whose sculptural and pictorial representations are mistakenly called hermaphrodites are, he explained, females with a penis, not beings with the characteristics of both sexes. They are females, with full breasts, to whom a penis has been added.

What Freud was stressing in this and similar passages was the male child's narcissism: the child who assumes all beings are like himself and disparages the woman when he discovers she is other. And in his later work, Freud extended this theme by suggesting that children create an "ego ideal" while their primary narcissism still reigns, employing its materials, which are fantasies of parental omnipotence. This ideal comprises a wish or a composite of wishes, the image of what the child wishes to be and to have. An image of the omnipotent and phallic mother takes up residence in the boy's ego ideal, as does one of the omnipotent father. Through the course of life, and particularly in adolescence, the ego ideal is modified by its encounters with reality, including the reality of the mother's genital condition as well as of her necessarily frustrating unavailability and her alliances with other people, including the father, who are rivals. Or, if the ego ideal is not modified by reality, its persistence helps occasion the ego's divorce from reality. An unmodified ego ideal becomes implicated in the sometimes debilitating waxings and wanings of self-esteem that characterize narcissists. The depressed narcissist, his self-esteem lost, suffers from the gap between the ego ideal and his self.

Among his early colleagues, no one followed Freud more seriously on this line of thought about narcissism than Wilhelm Reich, who interpreted Freud very literally and under the aegis of his own (perhaps quite narcissistic) celebration of normative heterosexual genital "orgiastic potency." He set a kind of standard with passages like this one about phallic-narcissistic characters from his *Character Analysis* (1933)

> Phallic-narcissistic men show a high erective potency, although they are orgiastically impotent. Relationships with women are disturbed by the contempt for the female sex which is rarely lacking. In spite of this, [such men] are highly desired sexual objects because in their appearance they show all the traits of masculinity. In women, the phallic-narcissistic character occurs much less frequently. The definitely neurotic forms are characterized by active homosexuality and clitoris sexuality; those who are genitally healthier are characterized by great self-confidence, based on physical vigor and beauty . . .
>
> Typically, analysis [of men] reveals an identification of the total ego with the phallus, in women the fantasy of having a penis; also, a more or less open display of this ego . . . The frustration of genital and exhibitionistic activity at the height of their development by the very person [of the opposite sex] toward whom the genital interest is displayed results in an identification with that person on the genital level [and a need for sadistic revenge] . . . In such men, the sexual act has the unconscious meaning of again and again proving to the woman how potent they are; at the same time it means piercing or destroying the woman, in a more superficial layer, degrading her. In phallic-narcissistic women, the leading motive is that of taking vengeance on the man, of castrating him during the act or of making him impotent or of making him appear impotent.[34]

Reich was here focused on the oedipal stage, imagining first a time of disillusionment about the mother's phallus and then a period of men identifying with their mothers, women with their fathers, in the course of further frustration of their narcissistic and genital-exhibitionistic desires.

But this strand of elaboration on Freud's view of male narcissism as the foundation for derogation of women disappeared from psychoanalysis over the next decades. It was replaced by the idea that men derogate women *because* they view them as castrated beings, not because they first imagined them as phallic and then were disillusioned, or because they enjoyed exhibiting in front of them and then were frustrated when they did not win them, besting the father, with this exhibiting. The emphasis that Freud put on the boy's and the man's fantasy that

women really do have a penis has, in fact, been so difficult to accept
that even psychoanalysts pursuing Freud's understanding of the roots
of sexism will not concentrate on it.

For example, Harold Blum, in an exposition contained in a volume
he edited called *Female Psychology: Contemporary Psychoanalytic Views*
(1977), claimed in awed tones: "Freud's genius uncovered the universal
unconscious fantasy of men and women that women are castrated. This
fantasy pervades institutions and social attitudes and becomes a ubiquitous myth structuralized as a 'cultural force.' Freud first analyzed the
fantasy, but did not discuss in depth the sociocultural influence exerted
by the fantasy of a castrated, inferior female." Repeating himself, Blum
pushed the point: "Freud's discovery of the castration complex was an
extraordinary event in the history of ideas, and an extremely important
discovery for the 'liberated' sexual and social role of women. For the
first time there was a scientific understanding of the contempt and derision toward women based upon overdetermined, irrational unconscious fantasies. Both boys and girls and their parents unconsciously
regarded the female as castrated and, therefore, inferior." Viewing
Freud as a liberator, Blum could conclude only that it was paradoxical
that his liberating discovery coexisted with a view of the "female as
having a diminished and constrained libido, a weaker and masochistic
sexual constitution, an ego with an incapacity to sublimate and a tendency toward early arrest and rigidity, a relatively defective superego,
and incomplete oedipal and preoedipal development"—that is, with a
view of the female as, *in fact,* not in irrational fantasy, castrated.[35]

Male castration anxiety, in Freud's understanding, is the male's anxiety that what has happened to the woman could happen to him. The
"castrated woman" fantasy, to say the same thing differently, is a product of disappointed or disillusioned narcissism, and it reflects the anxiety this disappointment lets loose. The boy concludes, trying to control
his anxiety: If there really is a being who is castrated, she must be less,
inferior. But it certainly seems unlikely that Freud's discovery of castration anxiety or his achievement of conscious knowledge that the castrated woman is a fantasy would have prevented him from making and
accepting a portrait of women as castrated. Putting castration anxiety
into a theory does not automatically entail relief from castration anxiety,
healing of the wound. Intellectual discoveries, as Freud himself knew,
do not heal. They offer a new venue for fantasies, they are a sublimation.
Neither the fantasy of the castrated woman as inferior nor the discovery

that the fantasy is a fantasy has power to give relief equal to restoration of the original fantasy of the phallic woman, paradise regained. Indeed, fantasizing the castrated woman, whether consciously or unconsciously, would only keep alive for the male the ominous possibility of his own castration. If sexism consisted only of the claim, vastly institutionalized, that men are superior and women inferior, then the fantasy of the castrated woman could sustain it. But if sexism must do more, if it must *relieve* male castration anxiety, then the fantasy of the castrated woman cannot sustain sexism—on the contrary, it undermines it.

For a male, restoring the original fantasy (or restoring the original condition of primary narcissism) is the route that feels reparative. He can develop many ways to recreate the phallic woman of the nirvanic past—and to connect her new forms with the original fantasy. The original fantasy that women are omnipotent and have a penis, even if reality or science ''proves'' it wrong, never disappears; it only becomes part of the ego ideal.

Freud considered fetishism one of the chief modes of reparation. The male finds the missing female phallus in, say, an article of clothing, which operates as a token of the female phallus, and he worships it, basks in its power. It is magically able to restore the phallic woman. But even this solution, Freud saw clearly, has its limits. It does not entirely still the fetishist's anxiety, and he will usually express that anxiety by behaving toward the fetish in a mixed manner—worshipful but also castrating. He will do unto the fetish what he still fears may be done unto him. In 1931 in the essay ''On Fetishism,'' Freud explained the behavior of the *coupeurs de nattes* more complexly than he had been able to in 1910, when he had not yet elaborated his views on narcissism:

> In very subtle cases the fetish itself has become the vehicle both of denying and of asseverating the fact of [female] castration . . . It is not the whole story to say that he worships it; very often he treats it in a way which is plainly equivalent to castrating it. This happens particularly when a strong father-identification has been developed, since the child ascribed the original castration of the woman to the father. Tender and hostile treatment of fetishes is mixed in unequal degrees—like the denial and recognition of castration—in different cases, so that one or the other is more evident. Here one gets a sort of glimpse of comprehension, as from a distance, of people who cut off women's plaits of hair—in them the impulse to execute the castra-

tion which they deny is what comes to the fore. (*Standard Edition* 21:157)

This same ambiguity in the fetishist's behavior could be looked at in another way. Because the restoration of the original fantasy, the primary narcissistic condition, is so uncertain—reality keeps intruding—the second-order or reparative phallic woman fantasy is seldom without an ingredient of aggression. The phallic woman of the restorative fantasy can be an aggressor, unlike the original blissfully nurturing omnipotent maternal phallic woman. The restorative fantasy woman is, then, less maternal, more of a knife wielder, a castrater. It is thrilling to a man to imagine her loving him or being loved by him, in all her power—she restores his omnipotence—but she is also dangerous and could turn on him. In many current Hollywood films, the classic solution to this dilemma appears: a phallic woman who gets out of hand and threatens a "fatal attraction" is killed off by a maternal woman (a mother of children) or she destroys herself. Generally, the phallic woman causes so much anxiety that she is almost always understood as violent and castrating, a view that overlooks her original blissfully empowering function. (There is a theoretical reason, too, for this emphasis, which I will come to shortly.)

Finding a fetish is only one reaction to the disillusionment of discovering sexual difference. Another mode of reparation would be homosexuality, which can, of course, come about by many other developmental paths as well. The path most to the point here involves a man's effort to find a man who is "feminine," that is, a female partner with a penis—like the phallic mother. Such a partnership means, as well, that the frightening "castrated" genitals of a woman can be avoided (as they are, in various ways, by all types of male homosexuals and by many heterosexuals who avoid the female genitals by being impotent or by engaging in practices that do not involve the genitals or that allow them to be "blind" to the genitals, for example having sex only in the dark or only from the rear). The homosexuality of the Greeks was of this sort, as older men sought in younger men "feminine" partners whom they could educate into adulthood, into a secure masculinity—giving unto the young what they had given unto themselves as a defense against anxiety.

Homosexuals and fetishists (who may by their fetishistic route be heterosexual, after their fashions) have very clear strategies for restoration of the phallic woman fantasy and for dealing with castration anxiety, even if it is not clear why they came to their particular strategies and not others. But the most mysterious case is neither of these—it is the "normal" man. As Freud noted: "Probably no male human being is spared the terrifying shock of threatened castration at the sight of the female genitals. We cannot explain why it is that some of them become homosexual in consequence of this experience, others ward it off by creating a fetish, and the great majority overcome it" (*Standard Edition* 21:154). How do the great majority overcome it?—particularly if developing a fantasy of the castrated woman and denigrating her offers no solace and only keeps the anxiety lively?

The most common method, the one adopted by Freud himself, creates not fetishes—tokens of the female phallus—but images of the phallic female *as an existing being*. The ancient androgynous sculptures of goddesses, like the Egyptian Mut, with both (maternal) breasts and a penis are the archetypes. Freud's own psychoanalytic theory includes images of women who are not, or are no longer, castrated. There are the mothers who, Freud explained, get a penis by having a male child, by fulfilling the equation of penis and baby that exists in the female unconscious. Some kind of mother-with-son image like Freud's is, I think, the "normal" man's reparative image: a woman who has a baby has a penis. To put the fantasy from the son's angle: a mother is restored to her phallic condition by her son, by his existence. He is his mother's happiness, her pride and joy—and thus she is, once again, his nirvanic happiness.

As Thomas Laqueur has shown in enormous historical detail in *Making Sex: Body and Gender from the Greeks to Freud* (1990), from ancient Greece until the seventeenth century, images of the female as a being with a phallus dominated medical and more general knowledge in Europe. Women were said—adamantly by Galen, the "father of medicine"—to possess genitals exactly like the male genitals except inside the body rather than outside. In what Laqueur calls the one-sex theory, the woman's vagina was a penis, her ovaries the testes, and so on down to the last details. Her orgasm was just like his orgasm, except internal; and conception was thought to be impossible without an orgasm, as it is impossible without ejaculation. At the same time, women were held to be inferior, less perfect, lacking in sufficient body heat to descend their genitalia or to produce male-standard spirit and rationality. This tradition denied and simultaneously asserted difference, particularly on

the mental plane, in the realm of secondary or defensive narcissism—
the assertion of difference marking the incomplete success of the nostalgic denial of difference, like the fetishist's castration.

Laqueur offers cultural explanations for this phallic woman and for
the amazing tenacity with which she survived centuries of medical research that was, in such a graphic way, blind to the appearance and
structure of female genitals. Similarly, he offers cultural explanations
for how a shift finally came about. He discusses, for example, how the
clitoris, which had been there all along, was acknowledged. But de-
phallicizing women was not simple, and the clitoris was promptly called
a homologue for the penis, a female penis, sometimes despite the assertion of a vagina-penis. Movements for equality during the Enlightenment, Laqueur argues, at last brought about a two-sex theory in which
women were no longer imagined as failed or less-than-perfect men, in
which they were granted a sexuality and genitalia of their own.[36] *Making
Sex* has no psychological explanation for the normal (medical) man's
phallic woman, but she does seem to be the Freudian phallic woman,
who can, as much as possible, restore in the boy his undisturbed primary
narcissism, his fantasy of the phallic woman, the imagistic source of his
ego ideal.

But such images can also be found in contexts with less of a medical-
theoretical orientation. Indeed, this woman whose partner is the little
man born from her genitals and now standing by her, her pride and
joy, is omnipresent. She is there whenever men create images of women
who feel unfulfilled without male attention, women who cannot live
without men, women who are weak without men, or women who fade
or swoon away when men leave them. She is there being protected by
him, being completed by him. She is no longer the inferior castrated
woman but the woman who needs a man to be herself—her phallic
self—to be a natural woman, to fulfill her womanly nature, and thus to
be not different. She is there, the preoedipal and oedipal mother, loved
by her son. She is there, the goal of his sexism both in the sense that
she is his nostalgic destination and in the sense that every mere woman
is not *her,* is less than her as well as threatening to him.

The ban upon incest, taking various forms but universally promulgated, signifies that this reparative fantasy could easily prompt the ultimate action—the son could become the mother's lover, penetrating her
with his penis, impregnating her. So the fantasy of the phallic mother
often takes a shape that shows strong respect for the incest barrier. *She*

is a virgin, never penetrated by any man, and he is a baby Jesus sitting on her lap or a crucified Christ draped across her knees in a pietà. He must not grow up to become his father's rival, for this would renew the very threat of castration that the image of the mother-son unit assuaged. In this safe fantasy, the son stays always what he was as a baby, a child— the apple of his mother's eye. He stays wrapped in a narcissistic cloak, his very existence a wonder.

Or, if his fantasies challenge the incest barrier, a defensive fantasy arises in which the son rescues the mother, a fantasy actually meaning that he gives her a child—one like himself, that is, conceived on a narcissistic basis. The boy, now identified with his father, has taken his father's place and fathers himself.[37] Similarly, if the incest barrier is breached in behavior, in sexual practice and object choice, it will have to be on a denial basis: the man will have to split his love, giving one part over to a woman who, like his mother, can be loved but not desired, and giving the other part over to a degraded woman, a sensual, lower-class, "fallen," or more darkly colored woman, who can be desired but not loved. He loves dissociatively, half as a boy, half as a man, or, as Freud put it, half out of the affectionate current of his childhood love and half out of the sensual current of his postpuberty desires. Here, narcissism meets the hysterical mode of prejudice typical of racists and classists.

This path of Freud's thought implies that the prejudice called "sexism" is the ego's social mechanism for defense of the ego ideal from modification by reality or for restoration of the fantasy of the phallic woman. Sexism is the preservation of narcissism by social means. The same conclusion might be translated into affective terms by saying that sexism is the social means for avoiding the shame of falling short of the ego ideal. But these implications have never been developed. Freud's studies of the ways in which men derogate women to make them the not-mother have been, along with the fantasy of the castrated woman, the main strands of his work used to interpret sexism. Even those who have used these two strands, however, have not gotten behind them, developmentally underneath them, to the territory of original narcissism and the phallic mother fantasy and thence to the reparative sequels. There has been little emphasis on the idea that a fantasy which restores the phallic mother also reinforces the son's original narcissistic position, the very position in which he assumed that all creatures are like him, with a penis

like his. The circuit closes: the fantasy of the mother with her penis-son
is a fantasy in which the penis-son is encouraged not to grow up, not to
leave his infantile narcissism, not to overcome the psychic position that
gave rise to the fantasy of the phallic mother in the first place. But this
man—this man forever a young man—was the one whose existence
called forth the second period of psychoanalytic effort to understand
sexism (not, of course, under the title "sexism"), the period in which
investigation of narcissism has loomed large in the theory and practice
of psychoanalysis.

The inception of this period can be seen in the case material published in 1954 by Peter Blos, an Austrian émigré to America who made
a specialty of adolescent analysis. Many features of Blos's cases were
quite specific to that moment in American history and to the milieus of
the conformist middle class, to a period when middle-class families were
pervasively engaged in the project of assuring for their children a future
of speedy upward mobility and grand fulfillments of the American
Dream. These were the sons Margaret Mead invoked as the bearers of
the American "national character" in *And Keep Your Powder Dry* (1942).
But at a deeper level, Blos's cases transcended time. Young men in
whom "exalted self-expectations figured dominantly" were operating
"under the influence of parental ambition and narcissistic overevalua-
tion." When adolescence—inevitably—brought challenges to their ego
ideals, blows to their ambitions, and defeats, they responded by desperate attempts to make good. Prolonging their adolescence, they tried to
retain the illusion that their lives really were going to unfold along the
scintillating lines imagined for them by their parents and built into their
own ego ideals. Being unable to tolerate living without the self-image
that they had created and that had been created for them, they stayed
emotionally tethered to it:

> One might say of these young men that their great future lies behind
> them when they reach the threshold of manhood; nothing that reality
> has to offer can compete with that easily obtained feeling of elation
> and uniqueness which the child experienced when he was showered
> with maternal admiration and confidence. Both mother and child—
> for reasons of their own—have persistently overlooked the child's early
> failures, inhibitions, nervous habits or feminine exhibitionistic traits.
> The sanction of the parent nullified the significance of failure; the
> child came to substitute narcissistic aggrandizement for reality mas-
> tery. Fantasy never became distinctly separated from reality-directed

thinking. The sense of time has become affected by the constant substitution of the past for the future and, in addition, by the vague belief that a lucky break could accomplish what ordinarily in a man's life will take years to achieve.[38]

Blos noted that boys who, being identified with their mothers, do not enter into oedipal rivalry with their fathers—indeed, who may look on their fathers with versions of the mother's pity and contempt—must conduct their adolescent rebellion, if and when it comes, against her. They must disidentify with her. But the great temptation is to persist in closeness and identification with her, enjoying all the narcissistic gratification that position carries. A boy will be greatly aided in his strategy by a cultural atmosphere full of messages that success will come with a lucky break, not long years of effort; that elation can be restored quickly with a big business deal or a grand enterprise, with a trip to the casino or the stock market, or with a drink or an aggrandizing snort of cocaine. He will be ready to believe messages that tell him his next lover will be the one who gives praise and adoration in the right (unreal) form—the maternal form.

Blos was studying a particular phenomenon—prolongation of adolescence on narcissistic grounds—in a particular social context of absent or remote fathers and ambitious, pushy mothers denied fulfillment of their own in sexist societies and seeking it through their sons. But he heralded a development in psychoanalysis that has, in the course of a generation, moved the science away from Freud's emphasis on castration anxiety and the Oedipus complex into an emphasis—often exclusive—on preoedipal mother-child bonds. Many who subscribe to the newer psychoanalytic emphasis consider all disorders with preoedipal roots narcissistic disorders, just as the reigning normality and pathology in the present cultural moment in the West is narcissistic, as Lasch argued in *The Culture of Narcissism*. This stretch of psychoanalytic history, identified in this country with the names Heinz Kohut and Otto Kernberg, the former having put his exploratory lens on normal narcissism and the latter having analyzed pathologies of narcissism, is much too complex for quick summary. It is a stretch of history—like so many others in psychoanalysis—that eventually produced a *reductio ad absurdum* in the field, the sweep and jargonization of which can be illustrated by a statement in which an analyst at the Menninger Clinic asserts that there are basically two sorts of children and adolescents in the world.

There are those who have been well cared for in their preoedipal years by a "good enough mother" (who has obeyed this analyst's sexist prescription that she stay at home to care for her child full-time) and those who have not, that is, the narcissistically disturbed.

> [While] oedipal-type conflicts and rivalries certainly appear during the latter part of a child's preschool years, the healthy child, possessed of a sound, nascent self-identity resulting from an optimal balance of interdigitated growth and dependency needs, proceeds to deal with these conflicts and rivalries with little or no personal and interpersonal perturbation. Of course, such balance is achieved as a result of the child's mutual attunement with an empathic, good enough mother and a healthy father who both nurtures the mother and provides for the child's ongoing separation-individuation ... The same may be said of the period of adolescence, the regressive-recapitulative features of which were classically cited to support the long since discredited view of the adolescent as a turmoil-ridden, even normally psychotic victim of untrammeled instinctual drives unleashed by surging and shifting hormones and the psychological effects of frightening bodily changes.[39]

When this kind of simplistic and narcissistic (as well as sexist) thinking of "us versus them" became typical, a part of the avenue within psychoanalysis for understanding narcissism—not to mention narcissistic prejudices—closed off.

Moreover, the part of that avenue that remained open changed character. Analysts began to see the phallic mother as, from the beginning, a frightening, dark figure, not an object of nostalgia at all. The omnipotent preoedipal phallic mother, then, is a fantasy creature born out of the male child's fear of a castrating, penetrating mother who takes advantage of his weakness and vulnerability. According to the theories of Melanie Klein, the phallic woman is the male child's aggression against his mother projected, and she is also his mother as a being who has (he imagines) orally incorporated his father's penis in intercourse. From the beginning, she is a witch with a broomstick, and his developmental task is to overcome his fear and anger, reconciling himself to the inevitability of frustration.[40] In other words, this approach to narcissism exclusively emphasizes frustration and aggression and learning to control or make reparations for aggression. No paradise is there to be lost, even though the images of raging frustration do imply a prior condition of satisfaction.[41]

To my knowledge, the only psychoanalytic theorists of narcissism who retain the original Freudian emphasis on primary narcissism as a condition of satisfaction and omnipotence that is the goal of all future nostalgic narcissistic desires are Janine Chassequet-Smirgel, Bela Grunberger, and Joyce McDougall, all working in Paris, independently of the various French schools, including the Lacanians. In *The Ego Ideal* (1974) particularly, Chassequet-Smirgel emphasizes the role in development of the child's ego ideal, his or her image of "narcissism lost," of the time when the child *was* his or her own ideal. The ego ideal is projected onto others in the course of development and, normally, onto the father by the male child, for whom being like the father represents the only fulfillment of the desire for return to the mother that is possible or permissible.[42] For the female child, who also desires return to fusion with the mother, the ego ideal can be projected onto the condition of motherhood, in which she can experience a reunion with her mother in a way that is socially sanctioned (as homosexually choosing a "maternal" lover is not in many societies).

If the male child's projection does not take place, and the boy remains tied to his mother and specifically to the original narcissistic fantasy of her as phallic, then his sexuality will remain pregenital. In this understanding, perversions, of which fetishism is the paradigm, are fixations, narcissistic attachments that cannot be given up. Similarly, if the girl's projection does not take place, she will remain fixed on fusion with her mother without being propelled toward her father, without the typically feminine—typically bisexualizing, one might say—condition of having her eroticism "run counter" to her ego ideal, her father love against her narcissistic mother love.[43] In both sexes, the strength of the nostalgic pull toward lost narcissism colors the whole of development, especially because development itself is, normally, desired by those who are able to project this nostalgia forward, to make maturity the condition of paradise regained.

A view like this, although it emphasizes heterosexual normal development, also stresses the enormous variety of ways in which children emerge from their early symbiosis, their initial dependency, their internal "narcissistic milieu." It thus stays away from recent psychoanalytic efforts to divide the species into the narcissistically disturbed and the normal, or those who are forever enraged at their frustrating mothers and those who get over it, making reparations for their aggression. But the complexities of this view also point up how difficult it has become to entertain the idea that many paths diverge from the elemental human experiences of discovery—"she is not me, she is not always available to me, she is not all-powerful so neither am I, she and he are a couple that I am not in, and [for males] she is not like me." Similarly, it is difficult to entertain the idea that there are many ways in which humans try, always unsuccessfully, to deny or rearrange the results of these discoveries. But these difficulties within psychoanalysis itself seem to me a manifestation of the very problem under study. That is, the primordial nostalgic sexism of "we are all alike here," the sexism sustained by fantasies of a phallic mother who is omnipotent *and empowering*, not castrating, is usually obscured by layers of later developments. The developmentally second-order sources of sexism in defense mechanisms of disavowing or denying the continually obtruding reality of difference (and thus castration) preponderate, just as mental narcissisms have built up in complex layers over body narcissism, obscuring this experiential core. Psychoanalytic theory reflects the situation by emphasizing how infants experience difference, not how they long nostalgically for sameness.

Interestingly, within feminism, which also deals almost exclusively with the preoedipal period, it is the psychoanalytic emphasis on separation-individuation in object relations terms, but not the corresponding focus on narcissism, that has had the greatest influence. Among American feminists, as I noted in Chapter 4, the main "origins and development" explanation for sexism has centered on the male child's preoedipal process for separating from his mother, individuating and disidentifying with her, and eventually identifying with his father. It is assumed that the boy disparages his mother and her femininity to establish his own male identity as different. This process, then, becomes the habit of his lifetime, which he shares with all other males as they build patriarchal institutions. He embraces difference.

The feminist focus on the object relations, separation-individuation strand of child development theory, and the correlative disinterest in male narcissism largely results from the very phallocentric theorizing feminists have been working to illuminate. Women characteristically misinterpret male narcissism because it is so unlike their own, and their own has been little explored precisely because, in psychoanalysis, it has been interpreted as a fallback position. When a woman discovers that she does not have the penis and develops penis envy, so this explanation goes, she lavishes attention on her own body, making the best of what she has, even going so far as to treat her whole body in fantasy as a phallus. Men worship phalluses and women worship perfect female figures (by whatever standards prevail). Their children, however, particularly their sons, can relieve women's lack and make object love possible for them. Women overcome their defensive narcissism in motherhood.

This idea is, I have suggested, part of the male reparative fantasy of the phallic mother. Clinically, it does seem that there are women whom it fits quite well, but that does not in any way justify universalizing the script. On the contrary, if all human beings, as Freud himself believed, start off as incarnations of primary narcissism or ego libido, unable as yet to recognize the mother as an other or attach any of their libido to objects, then female infants must, like males, begin with the fantasy that all humans are like themselves. They would not originally develop the fantasy that all humans have a penis but would create the fantasy that all humans have female genitalia (insofar as the female genitalia, which are so much more hidden than the male, are apprehended by the girl).[44] For example, a female child might fantasize on a narcissistic basis, with reference to her mother, who is like her, that there is a perfect femininity—most basically, a perfect female body (not a phallus-body). Such a fantasy might then, for just one developmental example, be the ground on which she later narcissistically sought a female lover incarnating the perfect femininity she wished for herself.

Again, following the analogy between girls and boys: a girl's discovery of sexual difference, her encounter with the reality of male penises, would, then, be a wound to her narcissism, too. And her response would, analogously, be to deny the reality of the penis or, later, to disparage the penis as inferior. But Freud's interpretation of the female child's experience leaves out the possibility that she might create a reparative fantasy that does not include the phallus. He assumed that females, discovering the penis, feel immediate envy. They do not deny the reality of the penis for a time and then slowly accept it; immediately, they believe the evidence of their senses. Why? In his late essays on female psychology, Freud gradually came to the recognition that for his ideas about female penis envy and his ideas about primary narcissism (including female primary narcissism) to make sense together, one would have to assume that before she made the acquaintance of the penis, the girl was a disappointed creature, that she had already felt that she was inadequate, so that discovering the boy's possession could, then, *explain* her inadequate state: "Ah, it is that which I do not have, then I want it." She would have to feel that the penis is the organ, owned by her father, needed to win her mother's love: "So, it is that which wins her, then I want it." The condition that brings her disappointment and causes her to seek an explanation is called by Freud "loss of love." She suffers not castration anxiety but anxiety over loss of love—her mother's love, which she feels she loses on weaning, in the oral stage, or in being trained, in the anal stage. But even this hypothesis does not explain why she does not respond to loss of love, to her own raging frustration, with a reparative fantasy of omnipotence and perfect femininity.

In psychic and social circumstances in which female children are not wanted or are considered second best—which, in Freud's view, they would be by any mother who wanted a penis-son, and by any father who found the existence of penisless creatures anxiety producing—feeling inadequate in some unspecified way could easily be *la condition féminine*. When sexism reigns in a family and a society it means, in a female infant's life, that she is inadequate, and it makes fantasies of adequacy hard to create. This is a powerful, and often accurate psychosocial portrait. But it omits the possibility that a girl might come to the experience of sexual difference as many boys do, that is, without any sense that she was inadequate in gender terms, without prior narcissistic wounding precisely over her anatomy, if she had had the fortune to be wanted as a girl, well loved in her femininity by her mother and her father. Such a girl might then deny the penis, view it as a detachable part, or take pity upon the boy for having such a piece of equipment (a pity often noted in the Freudian literature but interpreted as a reaction formation covering up her envy). She would be a female chauvinist.

We must be careful to distinguish female chauvinism from sexism in women. When women are sexist in the sense of denigrating women or worshiping phallic power—not chauvinistically elevating women over men but participating in male sexism—they, too, may be sustained by a fantasy of a phallic woman. They may restore their sense of power and adequacy in the male manner. Narcissistic fantasies created in this way to assuage narcissistic pain resemble the one described in the autobiography of a 1960s revolutionary aptly titled *With the Weathermen*. Susan Stern, who had attached herself to the male leadership of the Students for a Democratic Society and lived in the light of their celebrity, felt loved and admired by the males for her fervor and recklessness. In an "acid frenzy" she painted on her wall "what I wanted to be somewhere deep in my mind: tall and blond, nude and armed, consuming—or discharging—a burning America." The mural depicted "an eight-foot tall, nude woman with flowing green-blond hair, and a burning American flag coming out of her cunt!"[45]

The fantasy of the phallic woman is not an original fantasy for a woman, but it can be reparative for her, as for the boy. It does not, however, restore her to her original condition or psychic position and it need not be, ultimately, a fantasy of a phallic *mother*. If she fantasizes a phallic woman, she may be attaining the penis she envies. And it could be enjoyed in the mode of "I am a phallic woman" or "I love a phallic woman" (the first could be enjoyed by a "masculine" heterosexual or homosexual female, the second by a "feminine" homosexual). Her body may, in her fantasy, be a phallus, perhaps her father's, which allows her to win her mother as he did or in competition with him.[46] She could, however, fantasize "I am a phallic mother" or "I love a phallic mother." For a woman, the fantasy that a male child is a penis could mean that she herself will get a penis through the child (Freud's idea about what a woman wants) or that she can take him from another woman. In other words, the phallic woman fantasy can take many forms and have many meanings for women, supporting sexism or female chauvinism in many ways, while it seems to be rigidly singular for men.[47] For him, it always means, at bottom, "she is like me [and there is no castration]."

My proposal—that the narcissistic fantasy of the phallic woman is at the motivational core of the many layers and forms of sexism and has been since the incipit of the sculptures with breasts and penises that Freud described—is, so to speak, more Freudian than the Freudians. As I have noted, discussions of sexism—no matter what their provenance—always emphasize male assertions that women are different and, by implication, inferior. Correlatively, an assertion that women are the same appears to support equality. Even the image of the phallic woman could be construed this way: giving the woman a phallus would thus be like giving her the vote or any other instrument or emblem of equality. It looks like antisexism in a patronizing mode—"you, too, can be a man, so we will all be equal." But creating fantasies to restore the original fantasy of the phallic woman does not give women male power or make them into spear-wielding Amazons, equal in phallic assertiveness. It alleviates male castration anxiety and restores male supremacy in the sense that the original fantasy promotes—namely, there are only males here. The phallic woman is a "male," but not an enemy male, not a rival, not a paternal figure. She has the phallus, but not *phallic* power, for her phallus is not her own: it is the male's, it is *the male himself*. She is the female whose "maleness" ultimately depends upon her son; he controls it. And *that* control is the core of sexism.

Exercising that control, a man dictates the conditions of female reproduction. The dictation reveals the primal fantasy. In the present debate about abortion, for example, many people who call themselves "pro-life" assert that a fetus (at any stage after fertilization) in a woman's body is a little person, which should be so precious and so sacred to her that the thought of destroying it—aborting it—should fill her with horror and shame. She should not be allowed to entertain such a thought, much less to act on it with a rationale that she cannot care for a child, cannot afford a child, cannot give to a child resources she must give to other children or to herself, cannot love the child because it was conceived against her will. My argument implies that men who urge their vision of the fetus upon pregnant women are identified with the fetus.

If control over the female, sustained by and serving a controlling reparative, nostalgic fantasy, is the motivational core of sexism, then social control of women's bodies and particularly their reproductive functions—their function for producing men, as it were—should be the site for marking the intersection of this psychological exploration and the wider sociohistorical arena of sexism. I will try to make this connection after adding one more building block to the psychological analysis—a look at how sexism and the other orectic prejudices consolidate in adolescence.

# 9

## Adolescence and the Aims of Hatreds

The case literature available for studying the origins and developments of the various prejudice types suggests that adolescence is the key period for the conversion of incipient prejudices into fully articulated prejudices and acts of discrimination or violence. But following the suggestion implicit in these cases is not an easy matter. Amazingly, the vast recent literatures on adolescence, nonpsychoanalytic and psychoanalytic, do not make prejudices a developmental topic. This is so even though almost every report on prejudice involving vandalism (against property) and violence (against people) notes that those most frequently involved are aged fifteen to twenty-five. Social psychologists, sociologists, and more recently cognitive scientists have simply assumed that prejudices are acquired in childhood and then, without alteration, translated into adult life. Many psychoanalysts make the same assumption, as the child analyst Marjorie McDonald did when she chose not to consider prejudice among adolescents.

Authors of books with titles like *Adolescent Prejudice* study the prejudices of adolescents, of course, but not *developmentally*. The crucial psychosocial questions go unposed.[1] In the stages of adolescence, with their developmental tasks, what becomes of the prejudicial attitudes children have acquired in the service of their efforts to resolve stage-specific childhood conflicts? Do childhood attitudes directly support later prejudices, or do they become transformed in the transformations of pu-

299

berty? How do prejudices serve adolescents? What social forces and social opportunities influence prejudices developing in adolescence?
How? Although the existing case literature on prejudiced adolescents
is especially thin, it does, nonetheless, point to some directions for considering these questions, and I will set off by summoning from it two
patients of the immediate postwar period. One is, in my terms, a man
whose prejudices are obsessional; the other's are hysterical. Comparing
their stories will help us explore how prejudices can prevent accomplishment of the developmental tasks of adolescence or provide pseudoso-
lutions to them. I have considered orectic prejudices as social mechanisms of defense; here I want to consider them (to put the same
approach in slightly different terms) as social means to solve—uncertainly, precariously, usually self-destructively, always harmfully—the dilemmas of adolescence.

## The Developmental Tasks of Adolescence

The psychoanalyst Robert Lindner, author of a popular collection of
five cases called *The Fifty-Minute Hour* (1954), worked in an American
prison during World War II. There he encountered a young man he
called Anton, an agitator who styled himself after Hitler, even imitating
the dictator's appearance and gait.[2] Anton had left home as a fourteen-
year-old, fleeing an abusive, alcoholic father and escaping the seductive
attentions of his lonely, sickly mother. (He certainly did not know it,
but Anton was also living out a version of the Reich chancellor's familial
configuration—the abusive father, the abused mother seeking protection and compensation in love from her son.) Even though Anton left
home, he stayed emotionally completely within the orbit of the hateful
father and the seductive mother. In a first stint in prison for robbery,
he encountered a bogus minister who instructed him in organizing,
taught him "about power and the magnetism of the big lie, about the
little seed of rottenness in everyone's soul that—with proper care—
could be swelled to bursting." Once they were released, the boy and his
cynical mentor assembled a group of dispossessed, unemployed, bitter
men, equipped them with brown shirts and boots, and sent them out
to desecrate synagogues, break up union meetings and political rallies,
and recruit youngsters with displays of paramilitary drill and bravado.
Anton himself became the leader of this group when he was barely
twenty. He produced a "scurrilous newspaper," harangued over the

radio, and stirred up mobs of marchers until, after Pearl Harbor, he was picked up by the FBI while he was in the process of writing an editorial urging the Japanese on to victory over America.

During his imprisonment for his agitation activities Anton ended up in Lindner's care. Deprived of the adulation his swaggering public performances had brought him, and deprived of the aggression outlet his fascist activities provided, Anton began to suffer from nausea and blackouts. The murderous rage he had been able to vent on working for the defeat of his country and of the international Jewish conspiracy was then all internal. He was terrified enough of dying to accept psychotherapy from Lindner, who was intrigued by the opportunity to analyze an agitator, a "psychopath" (as he called Anton). What Lindner discovered in his patient was a profound ambivalence toward his brutal father—a desire to murder him and a desire to be cared for by him, "caressed." Anton strongly identified with his passive mother and had fantasies of being sexually attacked by the father as she had been. He satisfied this homosexual current in the fascist group and in the anonymous, brief homosexual affairs this basically ascetic obsessional carried on in an indifferent manner and with (homophobic) contempt for homosexuality. He was locked into his conscious opposition to his father, which he acted on in compulsive fascism, compulsive universalizing hate, first focused on the patriarchal Jews and then expanded. When he and his substitute father-figure (a harsh but also caressive father) founded the fringe fascist party, it provided, in Lindner's words, "everything for which the psychopath could ask: a whole world to hate, in extension of his primary hatred of his father; targets on which to exercise brutality and revenge, both as expressions of identity with the father's strength and dominance, and in retaliation for the hurts of childhood; symbolic trappings and uniforms reminiscent of cherished infantile wishes and proclaimers at the same time of the homosexualism beneath the hypermasculine pose."

Lindner sensed clearly one of the key differences between childhood prejudicial attitudes and adolescent prejudices: adolescents form affinity groups, which supply them with both a field of action and a kind of second home. If they need more than ethnocentrisms that affirm an already existing familial or ethnic or racial group, they use their ideological prejudices for group formation, as they exercise their characterological affinities or find their like-charactered peers. In Anton's case, as in the case of obsessionals generally, the formed group is the means

for the first home to be attacked. The enemy group and the original
family become identified—the Jew is the father. Children can, of course,
become obsessional, but articulated obsessional prejudice seems to require the adolescent ingredient of a gang or group, a brotherhood, a
secret society, or a youth club. The idea that the Jews (or any other
obsessional target group) are filthy arises without group membership,
but the idea that the enemy is organized in a secret society, a conspiracy,
is supported by group experience and involves a displacement of the
guilt-inducing homoerotic, antipaternal, rebellious excitement of group
experience. In Anton's case, which is a typical one, the self-defining
attack on the father also covered for his desire. He retained, most importantly and debilitatingly, his intense fear of being confused or overwhelmed—fundamentally, of being passive, expressing a passive desire.
Lindner could not, for example, hypnotize him; Anton would jolt himself awake just before succumbing to hypnosis, saying that he had a
vague feeling of a body near him, threatening—and this turned out to
be an image of his father. In the analytic transference, Lindner, a Jew,
fell heir to the fear and hatred of the father, from which Anton's antisemitism derived. He fearfully expected—and also desired—his Jewish
analyst to trick him, sneak up on him from the rear, penetrate him.

Anton's fascist behavior vividly contrasted with the behavior of Lindner's Communist patient, Mac, who was a study in dependency and oral
fixation, a man who had put on the Communist Party like a dramatic
role, seeking in it restitution, justice, and a vast equitable distribution
of goods that would heal his very individual pain, and finding in it an
outlet for his rivalrous aggression. Mac was an orphan, whose mother
had died giving birth to him and whose father, a remote man, died in
World War I. He was raised by two women—a wet-nurse who made her
breast abundantly available to him, spoiling him and creating a deep
dependency, and a step-grandmother who dismissed the nurse when he
was three, took away every one of his childhood pleasures, treated him
harshly, and made him feel that he was a dirty nuisance and a bother-
some boy. He had, to use the shorthand of Melanie Klein's analytic
categories, a good breast and a bad breast; or, in the terms I will develop
later, he had the hysteric's typical two-tier, two-mother, family.

Behind Mac's women stood the towering figure of the grandfather,
whom Mac admired but found awesome and frightening. As an adolescent, after this grandfather died, he fled from his home, aware that his
rage against his step-grandmother might lead him to harm her. His chief

defense was and remained flight, from familial figures he raged against but also, more deeply as his life unfolded, from any love object—like his wife, whom he alienated with his inattention. He was sexually impotent with his wife, and it became clear during his treatment that he feared being dependent on her as he had been on his nurse, his true maternal figure. His adolescent flight from the mother figure became the model of his life flight. He did not, like Anton, attack his family in the medium of his target group; he needed a group where he could reconstitute the family, have it as he wished it. (On the level of politics, this difference has an analogy I will detail later: obsessionals are state destroyers, hysterics are state appropriators.)

The Communist Party, which Mac joined after roaming around the country from job to job, gave him an education and made him feel like he possessed secret, powerful knowledge—more powerful than anything his grandfather possessed. He knew the secrets of history. But the party also gave him, Lindner stressed, a way to contain his rage at his step-grandmother, his frustration and his feeling that she had stolen his nurse from him. He could be angry in a cause. "The Party, then, was Mac's neurosis." And it served him well through the war, until in the early years of the Cold War it became, like so many American institutions, stingy, overdisciplined, routinized, demanding of him a self-denying, unnourishing regime like his step-grandmother's. The party became too obsessional for Mac, and—unconsciously—he began to turn on it, disillusioned. He continued to espouse its line and to fight for social justice, but mechanically. Lindner first met him at a meeting during which Mac was arguing adamantly for putting a Negro on a panel that was considering issues of socialized medicine. The Negroes had to be represented, he insisted, although he had no names to suggest. The Negroes were, in his conception, like himself—outsiders, victims of the system. His advocacy was eventually revealed to be patronizing, based not on any understanding of the Negroes or real concern for them but on reflexive resentment of the capitalists, the ones responsible for the frustration of his wishes. He was not a democrat but a hierarchical man, imagining the bottom of the hierarchy becoming the top.

Freudian psychoanalytic theory as it had been translated into American training institutes operated in both of Lindner's cases: the patients' Oedipus complexes were determinative in their developments, and their sexual lives—Anton's homoeroticism and asceticism, Mac's impotence—were key sites for therapeutic work. That is, the cases reflected failures on the two developmental lines to which Freud had given the name "transformations of puberty" in his *Three Essays on the Theory of Sexuality* (1905). In that text, Freud had established that adolescence is the stage in which the libidinal developments and the oedipal config-uration of childhood are reactivated and recapitulated. During the re-capitulation, mature sexuality should be achieved and extrafamilial love should become possible. But neither Anton nor Mac was able to enjoy sexual relations in which—to follow Freud's terms—a person outside the family takes the place of the child's parental and sibling oedipal loves, and in which genital sexuality comes to dominate over and or-ganize the sexualities, the autoeroticisms, associated with early devel-opmental stages and their erotogenic zones—oral sexuality, anal sexu-ality, phallic sexuality.

Lindner's theory and therapy also registered, however, the develop-ments that had taken place in psychoanalytic work on adolescents after Freud's first formulation. Freud's description was so clear, and so force-ful, that it took some time for his followers to question it. Questioning had also been significantly inhibited by a very powerful and systematic paper offered by Ernest Jones in 1922, his one and only contribution to the topic of adolescent development and one apparently not based on any clinical experience. In "Some Problems of Adolescence," Jones made Freud's suggestions about the relationship of recapitulation be-tween adolescence and infancy into a formula, a "general law."[3] He made a detailed case for the claim that "the individual recapitulates and expands in the second decennium of life the development he passed through in the first five years," and that "stages are passed through on different planes at the two periods of infancy and adoles-cence, but in very similar ways in the same individual." Jones's sweeping claim was then repeated in the literature without either proof or dis-proof.

During the 1920s, however, a more complex picture and a growing catalog of adolescent types was being built up from detailed clinical social work and from study of adolescent productions—particularly di-aries and literary creations—done by Siegfried Bernfeld and Willy Hof-fer in Vienna. Similarly, August Aichhorn's therapeutic efforts with ju-venile delinquents and the experiments with adolescent analysis made at the psychoanalytic clinics in Vienna, Berlin, and Budapest set new standards for research. In 1923, Bernfeld took a stand opposite to Jones's with this remark:

> Adolescence is less well understood from the viewpoint of psychological and sexual development than childhood. One of the reasons for the insufficiency of scientific literature on this period of life is to be found in the great multiplicity of phenomena in this age. Adolescence manifests itself in various areas: physiological, psychological, and sociological. Confronted by the enormous variety of individual, social, cultural, historical and physical differences in the group, one is tempted to question the validity of classifying all these manifestations under the one heading of adolescence.[4]

The systematic study of this adolescence, the multidimensional one, proceeded slowly—it did not really gather momentum until after World War II—while the theoretical leap made by Jones continued to be quoted, especially by analysts of adults who had no experience with child or adolescent therapy.

The first revision or change of emphasis with respect to Freud's theory came from his daughter, Anna Freud, who stressed in *The Ego and the Mechanisms of Defense* (1936) that when the Oedipus complex is revived in puberty it operates in conjunction with an ego that "has dimensions, contents, capacities, dependencies different from those of childhood."[5] She argued that the strength of the ego in adolescence in comparison to its strength in childhood explains why two particular mechanisms of defense against instinctual urges, asceticism and intellectualization, characteristically become prominent in adolescence. Asceticism results when the ego declares instinctual gratification completely out of bounds; it deals with the instinctual upsurge of puberty by refusal, suppression, and attack on the instincts, although it often suffers from relapses because this effort overtaxes its resources, so that bouts of indulgence interrupt the periods of asceticism. Intellectualization is manifest in the capacity of adolescents for seemingly endless abstract discussions, philosophical arguments and debating, and tedious arguments with family and school disciplinary figures over the finest details of rules, regulations, and requirements. Adolescents who employ asceticism and intellectualization—often in conjunction—are on constant high alert to temptations issuing from their own desires and from their environments.

In adolescence, defenses like asceticism and intellectualization primarily function to keep childhood love objects—parental and sibling love objects—at a distance or to break ties with them. Because mature sexuality becomes a possibility in adolescence, the incestuous nature of these childhood loves shifts dramatically: the possibility of their becoming "real," being acted upon, shifting out of the domain of fantasy, looms (and, from the side of the parents, the sexuality of their adolescents is also challengingly alluring and frightening in ways that it was not in childhood). In Anna Freud's words: "The libidinal cathexis of the [love objects of the individual's preoedipal and oedipal past] has been carried forward from the infantile phases and was merely toned down or inhibited in aim during latency. Therefore, the reawakened pregenital urges, or—worse still—the newly acquired genital ones, are in danger of making contact with them, lending a new and threatening reality to fantasies which seemed extinct but are, in fact, merely under repression."

The resurgence of sexual urges lies behind one of the phenomena of adolescence noted by all clinicians—and marveled over by most parents who generally have needed to forget their own adolescence: the changeability of adolescents. They move quickly from one mode to another of presentation (they dabble in dress signals, hairstyles, speech patterns, and accents), swap routines or regimes (they are disciplined, then slothful, healthy, then unhealthy), shift habits of interaction (politeness, boorishness, and aloofness are all possible), leap emotional levels (from intense to laid back to apathetic), and so forth. Alliances and friendships are made and abandoned, crushes come and go, authority figures and educators are splendid one day and dictatorial the next. Value systems are as unpredictable as spring weather: adolescents are religious and then atheistic, socialist and then capitalist, they champion the underdogs and then want the underdogs to lie down, go away, be more responsible. They declare themselves without prejudices and then express prejudices without compunction. Across the different kinds of changes, a single process is reflected—a process of identification.

As adolescents try to separate themselves from their infantile love objects, to break their ties to their parents and siblings, they pull back emotionally and delibidinize these ties. Moving in the direction of their primary narcissism, adolescents become like small children who are not yet fully able to love people whom they know as distinct from themselves, who are not yet of a piece or in any way stable in their identities. Both small children and adolescents relate by assimilating themselves to their objects, taking on everything from manners and gestures to habits and emotions. But adolescents are, more than children, prone to engage in this identification process in relation to groups (or to a group or gang experienced as a large person) as well as to individuals. Their thoughts and actions and feelings and desires are imitative; they *are* who they love, and they *become* who they love. And they are convinced that unless they adapt themselves to the wishes of their loved ones—to the preferences and predilections, the views and values—they will not be loved. In social terms, they are conformists. In psychodynamic terms, they are reconnecting themselves again by identifications to a world from which they have withdrawn into their narcissism.

As far as prejudices are concerned, two consequences follow from this normal dynamic of retreat to narcissism and identification. First, adolescents, particularly males whose behavior is culturally reinforced, are, by developmental definition, sexist in their same-sex peer groups. When Gordon Allport noted, without explanation, that boys in the fourth grade reject girls, he was observing this attitude.[6] Their peer groups are their social means for denial of sexual difference, their "no one is here but us." Second, and more generally, adolescents frequently assimilate the prejudices of those whom they love in the mode of identification, either individuals or groups. They make something like a preliminary step in becoming prejudiced. At this stage of acquiring a prejudice, the prejudice becomes available for other functions. The prejudice (or prejudices) become part of the ego and superego; they are built in and have greater or lesser meaning and charge depending on the importance in the adolescent's psyche of the love objects of which they were once a part, and depending on the use to which they can be put as these infantile identificatory loves give way and object loves outside the family present themselves. It can be said as a general rule that the more dependent an adolescent has gotten on prejudices (especially the developmentally typical sexism) for self-definition, the less able he or she will be for object love. Anton's case shows clearly how a bigot becomes too attached to his bigotry to love.

The transition to loves outside the family is complex, and the transition period often quite prolonged. Frequently progress requires autoerotic activity—another revival of early childhood—as a kind of "trial action" for sexual activity with others.[7] Most adolescents' masturbation is accompanied by fantasies, usually unconscious, that are variants on a central or organizing masturbatory fantasy first constructed in childhood: "the fantasy that contains the various regressive satisfactions and the main sexual identifications."[8] An extensive psychoanalytic literature exists on the central masturbatory fantasy, in which the influences of the fantasy on developing sexual identity as well as on adolescent dreams and daydreams, make-believe activities, and behavior generally have been studied, but no effort that I know of links masturbation fantasies with the kinds of sexual fantasies that routinely organize the various types of prejudices: obsessional fantasies of anal penetration, hysterical fantasies of phallic hypersexuality, narcissistic fantasies of phallic women, and so forth. Occasionally, however, this theme does arise in the literature, and it is clear that the adolescent's central masturbation fantasy, which may be entertained in lieu of actual masturbation, contains or epitomizes his or her emergent sexual identity. The role played in the fantasy by various victim groups reveals how prejudices become anchored in a developing sexual identity and character.

Victor Eisenstein, for example, analyzed a Jewish-Gentile couple's adolescent son, who had an obsessive hobby. The boy made thousands upon thousands of drawings in an effort to control his masturbation and to master his fear (mixed with allure) of turning into a girl and becoming penisless. In many of these drawings the figures who threatened (and allured) him with anal penetration were Nazis in uniforms and regalia. But this same boy also spent many months of obsessive activity making himself a Nazi uniform, cutting and sewing it, fitting it with lead buttons he cast himself, so that he could identify with the same Jew-hating Nazis that he feared.[9]

Prejudices become part of an adolescent's superego as well as part of the transforming erotic activity that the superego must regulate. This complexity accounts for a typical feature of early adolescent prejudice, its highly projective nature. Projection is a defense that makes its initial appearance in the course of children's superego development, their internalizing of parental images and criticism, when it is used to send outward onto other people any desire or deed that the child has felt or committed and been guilty about—any offense the building superego condemns. If the child feels that his or her libidinal or aggressive feelings for parents or siblings are "wrong," then he or she attributes the feelings to others. Adolescents, operating in this early childhood mode, use prejudices existing in their surroundings to sign over the unacceptable feelings not to an individual close by but to a whole group, even a group beyond personal acquaintance. *Those* people are curious and love to look; *those* people want to hit and hurt; *those* people have dirty thoughts. The result is a great deal of intolerance for other people and indignation at their attributed faults. Many a twelve year old, in this phase of superego development, measures *all* people, including family members, against a strict standard and finds most of them bad and false. The world has good people, with whom the young adolescent identifies, and bad people, who do what their youthful condemners have done but do not want to feel guilty for.

In some young people, the development of the superego goes no further. They remain intolerant in this projective manner. The typical next developmental step of coordinating the superego's standards and the ego's understanding of its own feelings and actions does not take place; the superego's critical judgment is not turned inward, so that the ego does not have to feel the unpleasantness and guilt that are to some degree built into moral maturity. As they grow older, such people represent the extremes of intolerance within their character types. Their opposite numbers are those who suffer constantly from the inward turning of their superego. Especially in an obsessional manner, but also in a narcissistic manner, they can be debilitated by guilt. Such people, who cannot attribute blame elsewhere, even when it is deserved, take the sins of the entire world—their own included—upon themselves. These are the totally unprejudiced self-sacrificing savers of the world, who may actually end up being perceived as prejudiced by members of victim groups because, in their willingness to suffer and their unworldly inwardness, they often misunderstand other peoples' needs to fight their own battles and do their own suffering.

The specific features of the superego in adolescence also open another path to the acquisition and projective use of prejudices. Existing in the adolescent superego, the parental figures are still invested to some extent with libido because they remain connected to the parental figures in actuality, who are still libidinally invested. The process of delibidinizing the superego has to be gradually completed—and this is a task of adolescence. In the course of normal development, adolescents tend to take up this task by alienating themselves from their own superegos, which are put under partial repression, while they strive to achieve independence from parental figures. But this leaves the adolescent without the superego's full help to deal with the libidinal upsurge and growth of sexual possibilities that come in puberty. Many turn to powerful individuals and peer groups for help in regulating themselves; they obey group norms.

An adolescent ego needs the support of the regulatory superego, but if it can get this support from a group, the superego can be disregarded. If a group's ideals provide a kind of external superego, and the group's activities provide gratification, an individual adolescent can be induced to submit to the group even to the point of a total relinquishing of older values and norms. An adolescent may go through a dramatic change with this kind of obedience, and such a change may be closely tied to the changing that goes on with shifting identifications. Prejudices that are part of the group's constitution are assumed by both means. But those prejudices that are substituting for the superego tend to be more entrenched, less capable of being replaced, than those that come with shifting identifications. The prejudices that substitute for the superego are also more deeply woven into consolidating characters, particularly in the case of obsessionals, whose superego needs are comparatively great. Hysterics, so given to being disillusioned in love and dissatisfied, even with their own superegos or substitutes for their superegos, change groups and norms more than other character types. They are like Mac, who gave up on the Party when it became to him rule-bound, bureaucratic, and unnourishing; it no longer supplied his need for a superego imperative that said, in effect, the meek shall inherit the earth. Narcissists notoriously do not last long in groups: whether they lead or follow, they always need great support and appreciation and more space for their activities. "A man's home is his castle" captures very well one of the key dynamics of sexism—the narcissistic sense of entitlement, of deserving a title—but it is obviously not fitted to be a group's slogan. Sexists do not, therefore, construct a worldwide mystical group of themselves—the Males—that is comparable to, say, the Aryans or the Whites. Their groups are local and immediate, a kind of castle guard, usually with a specific purpose or agenda.

The processes of identification and of finding substitutive superego functions are complex, and they add layers to the superego of childhood, which was itself not a simple product of a severe upbringing, as though it had been stamped into a child with harsh treatment or beatings, as many descriptions of the authoritarian personality assume. Child analysts have argued since the 1920s that two extreme types of upbringing promote rigidity in the superego—one harsh, one overindulgent. Antisemites like Anton, however, are very frequently the children of a parent of each sort, or more generally of parents at war with each other (see Jahoda and Ackerman's research, cited in Chapter 8). Hysterics are frequently raised by an indulgent nurse or mammy and a more remote biological mother. Narcissists typically have a narcissistically involved parent (usually the mother) and a less involved one. In adolescence, superegos (in obsessionals, often the formulaic "pregenital superego" described by Grunberger) become the vehicles of tradition, complexly reflecting the ways in which parents tailor a discipline-and-punish regime to the challenges of maturing adolescent sexuality. Freud pointed to the parents' behavior:

> Whatever understanding their ego may have with their superego, they are severe and exacting in educating their children. They have forgotten the difficulties of their own childhood and they are glad to be able now to identify themselves fully with their own parents who in the past laid such severe restrictions on them. Thus a child's superego is in fact constructed on the model not of its own parents but of its parents' superego; the contents which fill it are the same and it becomes the vehicle of tradition and all the time-resisting judgments of value which have propagated themselves in this manner from generation to generation . . . the past, the tradition of the race and of the people, lives on in the ideologies of the superego, and yields only slowly to the influence of the present and to new changes.[10]

But a child's own assimilation of the parents' superego is also indirect, and one who cannot defend himself against a severe parent or take revenge for a punishment suffered may identify with the parent, as "he takes the unattackable authority into himself." This is what Anna Freud called "identification with the aggressor" or with the aggressor's aggression. The superego then also represents the child's own hostility toward the parent, which increases in adolescence if ties with the parents still cannot be broken. Adolescents are then aggressive in the mode of the aggression they have endured; they do unto others as has been done unto them.

At the other extreme, a severe superego can be the product of overindulgent parenting. Children and adolescents who are loved indulgently (even seductively) often cannot turn their aggression on their loving parent or parents because their love forbids them to—as Mac's forbade him to turn on his nurse. Outward expression of aggression may be renounced, and the aggression turned inward, or the aggression may be turned inward when no gang is available to pull it outward.

Inward aggression reinforces the superego and increases its hostility toward the ego. From such a development can come commitment to high ethical standards, doctrines of universal love, and aggressive pursuit of social justice, accompanied by a great deal of self-reproach and punishment for failing these ideals. People who become what Freud called "moral masochists," that is, people whose self-punishment is in the medium of morality, tend to draw others into their self-critique: no one is good, everyone is a traitor. Cynicism is the generalizing prejudice of the smotheringly loved.

Although he was not always consistent in his terminology, Freud stated that while a child is forming a superego he or she is also forming an ego ideal on the basis of glorification of the parental figures and on the basis of its infantile feelings of omnipotence—feelings dating from before the inevitable fall into frustration that comes when an infant experiences the mother's unavailability and her regulations. As I noted before, the ego ideal is all the child worships and wants to be; it is a narcissistic guiding light.[11] In adolescence, although the core of the ego ideal (made up of glorified parental identifications) remains, other figures accrue to it—especially teenage idols and celebrities, gang and political leaders. And the adolescent has the developmental task of modifying the ideal to bring it into line with—or at least in touch with—what is realistically possible, so that the ego ideal can remain a goal-providing agency without constantly inducing shame and depression because it cannot be followed. A person who is always falling short of internally set goals, unsatisfied with any achievement, any praise, any partner, is a person who can easily turn to a prejudice to blame the shortfall on others or to attribute the shortfall to others. The prejudice then certifies that the others are no more (and probably much less) able to live up to the ideal. These are tactics especially common among narcissistic characters, the model sexists.

Of the developmental tasks specific to adolescence, the breaking of infantile object ties is central and it is the one that seems to be most clearly connected to the development of prejudices. I have indicated some general modes of separation and individuation, but there are specific modes that seem to be typical of particular emergent characters. Of these specific modes, flight is the simplest. Some adolescents sharply and suddenly withdraw their libido from their infantile love objects and turn the libido—project it—onto people outside the family: parent-love substitutes, idealized leaders, friends of the same or the opposite sex, or gangs of one type or another. This shift of direction may be accompanied by actual flight—leaving home—or by a state of being at home like a stranger. And it may be accompanied by a release of formerly repressed libidinal and aggressive wishes that are then acted out with the extrafamilial people, harmlessly or injuriously, in sociable or asocial forms.

This kind of flight defense—a variant on simple repression—is typical of individuals tending toward the development of hysterical character traits. Like Lindner's Mac, the Communist, they specialize in splitting—not splitting of the ego, but splitting of love objects into good and bad, acceptable and not acceptable, and their lives are made up of love flights and pursuits, in fact or in fantasy. They have variants on the good nurse and the evil step-grandmother, or they develop affections for pure people and lusts for debased ones. In addition, they are often fickle, moving back and forth between representatives of their splits, and even more often their bodies are friezes of conversion symptoms, impotence or frigidity being frequently among them.

When adolescents take flight from their families into a peer group or gang, they tend to recreate there—as Mac did—a family. They do not use this family to attack the one they have left; they use it to satisfy the erotic and aggressive wishes that could not be satisfied in the first. They use the new family to rectify the unjust distribution of love resources of the original family. Sibling rivalry is translated into war with another group or gang, the target of prejudice. The oedipal figures who were unavailable become available, without the incest barrier being crossed. Mother figures who are distant from the mother are obtained—as the group, for example, obtains prostitutes or seeks out supposedly debased women in a victim group. Father figures who can be fought with are found in a victim group (a feature shared with more obsessional organizations).

To break off from infantile love objects the adolescent can also convert into their opposites the feelings he or she has for the parents. "This changes love to hate, dependence into revolt, respect and admiration into contempt and derision," Anna Freud observed.[12] But, because reversal of affect represents no real motion outside the family, because it leaves the underlying object ties untouched, this defense—this "compulsive opposition"—brings nothing but suffering and requires constant reinforcement in the form of more hostility, more sullen or contemptuous behavior, often more self-destructiveness, or even a switch into the opposite mode, compulsive obedience to authority. If the reinforcement fails, the adolescent may, in a paranoid fashion, displace all the hostility he or she feels onto the parents, so that the parents become persecutory figures. Or the hostility may be turned inward, fueling self-destructive, self-doubting, and self-critical behavior. This manipulation of affect, which implies great intellectual efforts to control the affect and to erect rationalizations in order to keep control, is typical of individuals who are tending in the direction of obsessional character organization. They cannot give up control, of themselves and whatever features of their environment they can master. The objects of such a person's prejudices will be representatives of or stand-ins for the persecutory figures, outer or inner, as the Jews were for Lindner's Anton, the fascist.

Even more serious in their consequences than flight and compulsive opposition, according to Anna Freud, are two further specific defenses, more typical of individuals tending toward a narcissistic character organization. An adolescent who, having withdrawn libido from the parents, cannot turn it on new objects outside the family, turns it inward, investing it in his or her own body, ego and ego ideal. The manifestations of this maneuver are huge ambitions, grandiose schemes, delusions of grandeur, or grand visions not of power and triumph but of suffering and self-sacrifice in order to save the world. If libido is invested in the individual's body or body ideal, hypochondria may result, or (to note a development more common since the late 1960s) some form of rigid, extreme routine of physical fitness or body sculpting. Prejudices serve a person of narcissistic grandiosity and rigidity as means to ward off challenges—the target groups are shown to be either no different and thus unchallenging or so different that they are beneath contempt and beyond challenge.

More ominously, an adolescent whose anxiety over object ties is especially strong may escape them by regression in all parts of his or her personality. The boundaries of the ego become permeable, and the objects may be drawn into it (a process of identification), or the ego may become involved in projections that obscure the difference between the internal and the external world. Such efforts, toward delibidinizing the objects, may reduce anxiety, but they also create another anxiety at the possibility of what Anna Freud termed "emotional surrender, with the accompanying fear of loss of identity." Prejudices serve someone in this condition, which can verge on the psychotic, as an identity—they encompass the emptiness and provide a magic circle of definition. "I hate, therefore I am."

The extreme narcissism as a defense that Anna Freud described is a heightened variation on the narcissism that I called a feature in all adolescents, a feature of both defenses against instinctual urges and defenses designed to break object ties. Self-love makes a kind of restitution for renunciations of urges and losses of object love, and self-love can, thus, imply sexism as a renunciation of the different, the Other. And many adolescents form relationships—especially same-sex friendships—on the narcissistic basis, so that, for example, they have difficulty forming friendships with those they consider different, out of their clique, or not on their wavelength for some reason (unless they can construe friendship with the Other as self-enhancing or self-flattering as those who are out to save the world often do). Their prejudices are narcissistic barriers. The exquisite sensitivity to every detail of bodily change, the "vanity" of adolescence, is partly for the sake of the opinion of others but also partly—often largely—a manifestation of narcissism. Along these same lines, it is certainly no exaggeration to say that the images of adolescence itself that adolescents have are part of their narcissistic defenses. Construing and describing themselves as a homogeneous generation, a group, is a feature of their narcissism (as their parents' construction of them as a group is a feature of the parents' narcissism). "The problem of generations" that the sociologist Karl Mannheim described—known more recently as the generation gap—is a narcissistic "us versus them" formation.[13] Trust no one over thirty.

In much more extreme forms, adolescent narcissistic prejudices are modes for self-restoration—they restore the self by saying, in effect, that the others do not exist as others. As I noted in considering the childhood antecedents of sexism, this form provides a restoration far more effective than claiming that the others are wanting (no better than us, no more supplied) because the latter claim merely implies that such a deficient state is there to be fallen into. Deficiencies of body or mind stand as a threat to the prejudiced person—he, too, could be such a victim. Adolescent boys tend to form cohesive peer groups, and these say, in effect, "we are all males here." Adolescent girls also form all-female groups, but they frequently turn on one another—a divisiveness that is reinforced by competition for males. In early adolescence, boys notoriously work to stabilize their peer groups, while girls are usually more changeable and move from one esteem-enhancing best friend to another, cutting out former best friends as they go.

Male adolescent peer groups organized for sexual conquest are usually interpreted as societies for the denigration of girls, which they are—but only by consequence, not by sexist (unconscious) purpose. Boys who gather together in the manner of the Los Angeles Spur Posse, a gang made famous in 1993 when the members' game of recording their rape and harassment "scores" was exposed, are boys who perform, first and foremost, for one another. Their conquests allow them to say to their buddies, "my penis is powerful and intact," and be affirmed, "so are we all powerful and intact." Several of the Spur Posse's fathers, too, were pleased by their sons' show of virility and power, becoming part of the circle. Gang rape has the same function of phallic enhancement or multiplication of phalluses as do other forms of rape—like date rape—if the rapist's report to his peers about his exploit is the centerpiece of his behavior, the motivating piece. The multiplication of phalluses is most graphic in group masturbation scenes, which may not involve women at all. But the phenomenon is also obvious in combination with exhibitionistic performances like those Harrison Salisbury described in *The Shook-Up Generation* (1958), a book about postwar Brooklyn gangs. "The 'circle jerk,' or mass masturbation, is a common sex activity. Groups of as many as twenty Rovers join in such a ritual on a summer evening in a deserted public park. Sometimes a boy and a girl may give an exhibition in the center of the circle while group masturbation goes on."[14]

To Anna Freud's catalog of specific (and I would say character specific) defenses deployed in adolescence to break object ties, her colleague Peter Blos added a complex and crucial item. Blos noted that one of the features of the adolescent revival of the Oedipus complex, which marks it off as quite distinct from the Oedipus complex of childhood, is that in adolescence, as Blos put it, "polarities of masculinity and femininity reign supreme." In most American cultural circumstances, adolescents—unlike prelatency children—can seldom tolerate well the state of bisexuality, cannot enjoy it in the mode that Freud once called "polymorphous perversity," pleasure in all the erogenous zones and any and all sexes of objects.[15] An oedipal child does not usually feel any contradiction in loving both father and mother, the same- and the opposite-sex parent, in the forms known as the positive (opposite-sex) and negative (same-sex) oedipal relations. When a child's Oedipus complex dissolves, or disappears from view, as latency begins, it is, however, usually the positive form that is resolved, especially in boys, while, Blos argued, the negative form (same sex) awaits resolution in adolescence. To break this same-sex object relation, adolescents may employ what Blos calls the "oedipal defense." By this he means that they engage in heterosexual fantasies and behaviors defensively, to cover or to block the original homosexual object relation or whatever substitutes for the original have come from ties to other same-sex adults or peers. According to Blos, "since the resolution of the negative Oedipus complex is the task of adolescence, the coming to terms with the homosexual component of pubertal sexuality is an implicit developmental task of adolescence."[16]

The "oedipal defense" can influence any of the prejudices, but it is, of course, specifically at play in prejudice against homosexuals, which crescendos in adolescence. Hypermasculine and hyperfeminine behaviors designed to forge an identity have as their corollaries prejudice against homosexuals, who represent the feared possibility—as they did for Lindner's Anton, whose ambivalent negative oedipal tie to his father was so strong, so unresolved. Beating a homosexual is like beating down a possibility in the self, from the past. Similarly, many object choices of adolescence have exploitative dimensions that make them, in effect, sexist. A young man uses a young woman to prove his manhood; a young woman uses a young man to prove her womanhood.[17] Each may, unconsciously, also be borrowing a location for forbidden desires—he can put his feminine dimension in his girlfriend, and she can put her masculine dimension in her boyfriend. Similarly, each may be unconsciously taking on the other's desired characteristics—he may be against his conscious wishes taking on her femininity, and she may be against her conscious wishes taking on his phallic power. But these unconscious processes go on behind the scenes of proof of manhood or proof of womanhood.

Once we acknowledge the differences between childhood and adolescent defenses that Anna Freud and Peter Blos explored, we must abandon the idea advanced by Ernest Jones that adolescence simply recapitulates childhood step by step on a higher plane. It becomes apparent that the notion that the Oedipus complex is simply reactivated or recapitulated in adolescence does not allow enough room for psychic change—for transformations of personality. Ushering in postwar work on adolescence, the analysts Heinz Hartmann, Ernst Kris, and Rudolf Loewenstein noted in 1946: "We feel that the potentialities of [the personality's] transformation throughout adolescence have for some time been underrated in psychoanalytic writings." Blos, who often used Anna Freud's evaluation—adolescence is a "second chance"—as his touchstone, said in summary:

> The resourcefulness of the adolescent ego allows it to cope with the revival of infantile object relations in consonance with bodily maturation, thus bringing the state of infantile dependencies to a close. This achievement usually, if not always, contains rectifications and resolutions of conflicts or immaturities carried forward from the infantile period to adolescent level. In this sense, we speak of adolescence as a "second chance." This normative developmental advance is forfeited whenever the child fails to acquire the appropriate ego differentiation or ego supremacy during the latency period.[18]

Blos's assessment, of course, puts a great deal of the burden for achieving ego strength on the years when families and school systems make their first alliance, the years between about six and ten, which are cross-culturally and transhistorically the elementary years of formal schooling. But it also has critical implications for therapy: "Considering adolescent therapy, it follows that latency ego deficits often demand our attention above all else, even though sexual and dependency conflicts occupy the forefront of the behavioral and mental stage. While such conflicts are real enough, they have to be scrutinized as to their defensive aims which push these conflictual, typically adolescent themes into the forefront of the patient's awareness." Adolescent storm and stress or the lack of storm and stress need to be interpreted defensively.

Blos's assessment suggests that, as far as prejudices are concerned, they will be strong in inverse relation to the ego's strength. Prejudices, among other things, make up for ego deficits. The ego may be unable to tame the resurgent pubertal id, or it may the lose the contest with the newly consolidating superego, or it may be overwhelmed by the demands of a reality unrealistically—narcissistically—conceived. Prejudices can operate as props or diversionary tactics. They say: it is not your own desires that threaten you, it is *those* hypersexual people; it is not your own superego that persecutes you, it is *those* hostile and persecutory agents of a superpower; or, it is not you who are full of unrealistic, grandiose wishes, which set you up as the standard for measuring everyone, it is *those* people who insist on being other than you and challenging your world-system. But the more the props are used, the harder it is to play on without them.

## Prejudices and Adolescents' Political Opinions

Although prejudices have not been a particular focus for social scientists studying adolescents developmentally, there has evolved, along with the current interest in cognitive development, a literature on adolescent cognition and, particularly, on adolescent morality and political conviction. I have made some suggestions in reviewing the psychoanalytic literature about adolescent development and prejudice types—to which I will return; but I want now to set these suggestions together with a look at what has been learned in recent empirical work on adolescents' political imaginations and political cultures.

Jean Piaget was among the first psychologists to try to analyze the specific qualities and capacities of adolescent thinking, and his many successors have created a rich portrait. In 1971 Joseph Adelson produced an important summary of how adolescents develop political imagination, and various studies have been published since.[19] Adelson's most provocative general conclusion was that of all the factors influencing the development of political cognition or imagination, age (developmental stage) was the most important—more important than sex, intelligence, social class, or community and national political context. Context—particularly family context—did, however have a large influence on the degree of interest taken by adolescents of various ages in politics or in the political realm, The more interest at home, generally, the more interest in an adolescent. But degree or intensity of interest (and accumulation of information and opinions) and ability to reason or cognitive development were *not* related.

Early adolescents (aged twelve and thirteen) simply reason very differently from later adolescents (aged fifteen and sixteen). The younger ones lack capacity for abstract thought, which is clear when they personalize concepts (the law is, for them, the police officer) and when they fail to think in terms of societies or communities of people, considering only individuals, themselves or those close to them. As they mature, adolescents are able to some degree to put political matters in historical perspective, although real historical sense remains rare (even among adults). But older adolescents can usually imagine the future better than they can imagine the past. They can think in terms of consequences, imagine results, weigh costs and benefits, and they can operate in a conditional mode—if this, then that—while being able to come at questions from different perspectives.

As budding psychologists, younger adolescents believe that people do things because that is the way they are. People commit crimes because they are criminals. Young adolescents see few nuances: people are either good or bad. But twelve-year-olds also believe firmly in human tractability. Older adolescents appreciate the complexity of human motivation, becoming able to take circumstances and contexts into consideration, but they also conclude—to one degree or another, depending on their optimism—that people resist change just as they resist education, rehabilitation, and authority. The capacity for distinguishing between surface behavior and intentions—for charging hypocrisy—that historians have long noted as so characteristic of adolescents, particularly in postwar and postcrisis contexts, is cognitively an achievement of middle adolescence. Early adolescents do not often realize that people frequently say one thing and do another, intentionally or unintentionally. Many adults find this insensitivity to hypocrisy to be "innocent," but it is actually the product of unquestioning surety that people are of two types, good and bad, often combined with the further surety that the majority are bad. From a psychodynamic point of view, as I noted before, early adolescents are the great projectors onto others of their own felt badness.[20]

Adelson, like many other child and adolescent psychologists, noted that younger adolescents are bloodthirsty—again, regardless of sex, intelligence, or education, specifically political education at home or at school. They are eager to see people sent to jail; they embrace the death penalty, spy networks, and police informers; hidden cameras strike them as excellent devices for catching people out in their misdeeds; and they think of laws not as guidelines but as constrictions, punishments. Adelson spoke generally of "a pervasive authoritarian bias" in early adolescence, which he attributed initially to twelve-year-olds' preoccupation with human wickedness. "They see men as tending naturally toward the impulsive and anarchic. They are Hobbesian—it is the war of all against all. They do not seem to have much faith in—or perhaps they do not cognize adequately—the human capacity for self-control, or the demands of conscience."

In more psychodynamic terms, Adelson was describing how the inner world of the early adolescent (the adolescent emerging from latency)— composed of the ego's battles against the id, negotiation with the superego, and search for inner control—is read onto the outer world. At age twelve or so, as psychoanalysts note, the early adolescent undergoes a reactivation of the object loves of infancy, and the ego has to cope with this resurgence, using the strengths gained in latency. And, as Anna Freud stressed, early adolescence is a period of intensely increased egocentrism and narcissism as the process of breaking object ties begins and libido is drawn back into the self and sometimes into heightened focus on the body (and thus to hypochondria-like manifestations and somatic symptoms). The early adolescent whose ego has been learning police tactics has, as Adelson put it, "an ingenuous belief in the goodness and justice of authority. . . His first inclination—and his second and third—is to support any law, even when he is not altogether clear about its purposes." He has no appreciation for dissent, no understanding of minority rights. The ego is the center of the world.

Early adolescents of all character types tend to gravitate toward being the authoritarian personality. "[The] child's authoritarianism can be seen to stem from a certain conservativism of mind, which leads him to view values and institutions as fixed and immutable. . . The young adolescent does not spontaneously entertain the concept of amendment. If you suggest to him that a law is not working out as expected, he will likely propose that it be enforced more rigorously." It is not, again to speak psychodynamically, until the "second individuation" process begins that this conservativism of mind, this undifferentiated exercise of ego strength, breaks up. Latency and early adolescence can cover over the distinct lineaments of emergent character. In latency, however, as I noted in the last chapter, prejudices are not salient. Self-policing dominates. In early adolescence, prejudices appear, but in an undifferentiated way. Early adolescents willingly put into their "bad" category anybody whom the people in their surround, from whom they have still not separated, suggest that they so classify. Similarly, they take seriously the attitudes of their peer group, especially the group's sense of who is "in" and who is "out."

Older adolescents, the political reasoners, have to one degree or another launched upon or even gone a good distance with the project of breaking object ties and moving out of the family. But the narcissism of early adolescence does not end—it simply changes form. "The libido which [the adolescent] withdraws from the infantile object is turned on the ego and the self, resulting in the increased narcissism which so regularly follows on the breaking of infantile object ties. It also goes into the idealizations of abstractions and moral and ethical values and concepts, for example, or into asceticism, religious beliefs, philosophies, and intellectuality in general."[21] The cognitive developments of later adolescents draw their energy from the breaking of object ties that goes on simultaneously.

The kind of striving that Adelson described is, of course, much more likely to take place if an adolescent has a long period of preadult time to pursue it, that is, if he or she is in the major institution in American and European societies for what Erik Erikson called "psychosocial moratorium," the university. The university prolongs adolescence and provides time for the extremes of subjective experience to tend toward middle ground, for ideological choices to be made, for realism in views and commitments to emerge. Cognitive abilities are not necessarily any greater among university students, but prejudices tend to be more attenuated.

When Adelson turned his attention to political ideology rather than capacity for reasoning, he noted that families and their interests had a profound influence on the American, British, and German adolescents he studied. Adolescents from families that fused religion and politics—fundamentalist families, for example—believed that politics should be in the service of good order and reduction of human wickedness. At the opposite end of the political spectrum, adolescents from liberal families were moved by visions of restitution (social justice for the oppressed) and atonement (guilt was the common denominator—other people's guilt, or their own). In cognitive terms, the conservative families operated in an early adolescent manner, an authoritarian personality manner, making judgments of good and evil and doling out punishments, and the liberal families operated cognitively in a late adolescent manner, making relativistic judgments, taking circumstances into account, focusing on social justice.

But Adelson could articulate these styles only at a great level of generalization. Beyond the two basic developmental types of ideology, another and more diverse array of ideologies stood out from Adelson's research. These three forms of ideology, which emerged recurrently and to some extent cut across the general conservative-to-liberal axis, were an unexpected research finding:

[There is a] politics of dependency . . . in which the imagined and described political world is organized around the idea of government as a succoring parent and the citizen as a receptive child. [Second,] there is a politics of envy, resentment, dominated by the conviction that the high and mighty unjustly retain the world's resources for themselves. And there is [third] a politics of power, in which we can discern a preoccupation with domination and control. These themes—guilt, dependency, envy, power, and no doubt others—seem to emerge from an interaction between salient values in the child's milieu and certain dispositions in personality. When felt strongly enough they order the political perceptions and provide a framework for the organization of ideology.

The three ideological forms Adelson pointed to have implications for the way in which prejudices are maintained, cast, or justified as part of an overall view, that is, for the way in which prejudices are ideologies of desire. Adelson observed, for example, distinct social characterological trends among the German, British, and American teenagers he and his staff interviewed. The politics of dependency was a German specialty, much more common or salient in this group of interviewees than in the other two. Above all else, at least a third of the German teenagers openly feared chaos and confusion and viewed political arrangements as bulwarks against anarchy, rootlessness, perplexity, and disagreement. They did not (as a majority of the British did, and as most early adolescents in all three cultures did) view human beings as by nature primed for a war of all against all, but they did see incipient confusion everywhere.

An impressive number of the German adolescents thought that their government should be under the leadership of a strong man. The strong leader would prevent arguments and disagreements and, above all, keep the country from being disunified and weak in the face of its enemies. Even when they supported a party system, a substantial number (about 30 percent) of the young Germans saw it as a means of inhibiting conflict, not as a means for expressing political opinions. As Adelson rightly remarked, the German youths were not authoritarian in the manner typical of early adolescents cross-culturally—they did not want to dominate or bully. "To the contrary, they seem to see themselves as weak, child-like and inept, and they yearn for the strong, comforting hand of a benign and vigilant leader. Offered it, they will follow." They also, as their responses show—although Adelson does not remark on it—saw themselves as enormously vulnerable to being overwhelmed, confused, and violated by their external enemies; and this is precisely the motif so obvious in the young Hitler's redemptive vision of a country united inwardly and protected like a fortress against penetrating external aggression.

Among the British, the predominating ideological style was the one Adelson termed the politics of resentment and envy. He stressed the pronounced orality that appeared in most of his British interviewees' responses. They constantly spoke about laws, for example, as protection against people stealing from each other, particularly stealing food. (Theft was their archetypical crime, whereas American adolescents concentrated more on murder.) The British teenagers' analyses of human nature followed this theme: "People steal because they are greedy—that is, they are voracious, insatiable, unsatisfied by what they have. Or they are consumed by envy—that is, they cannot abide the prosperity of the other in the light of their own deprivation. Or they are truly deprived—that is, poor and in want. Or they are merely self-indulgent—unwilling to work as the rest of us must, they take the easier path of theft." The British teenagers thought that government should provide for the people, justly, fairly, and equitably, but they also considered the political leaders corrupt and hypocritical, willing to deprive the people of the things that they permitted themselves.

This is a politics of the sort described in Richard Sterba's essay on white attitudes during the Detroit race riots of 1943. It is a vision of sibling rivalry—a politics dominated by the fear that others are going to get more, more parental love, more goodies. Antiracism as a view of fair play may very well cover—but not cancel—the attitude, as it did in the following statement from a fifteen-year-old British girl, which should be read in the context of the tremendous increase during the early 1970s in immigration to Britain from the Caribbean, Africa, and the Indian subcontinent:

> I'd like darkies to be accepted because they're not as bad—I don't think they're as bad as they're made out to be. Some are very nice and then again there are some who are horrible. I think they're more nice than horrible. Try to get on with them, you know. They're nice to talk to sometimes. I think they should be accepted because after all they're no different really, except for the color of their skins. The only thing I don't like about them is the way they come over here and in a few days—well, before they've been over here very long, they seem to have got a good job, and they've got a great big car and they've got loads

of clothes and it just seems a wonder how they get them—those jobs—just like that as they come over.

Adelson's portrait of the American teenagers shows many of them as exemplars of his third type of ideology, the one organized around questions of domination and control. But their preoccupation was quite specifically with a tension between community, which all extolled as an ideal, and individual aspiration. Would the community good control and dominate over individual pursuits? How can politics produce harmony between competing individuals or competing groups, including minority groups? "All voices should be heard, all interests accommodated whenever possible. The wish to reduce differences within the community is seen in its strongest form in the emphasis on equality." Egalitarianism prevailed. In the psychodynamic terms I have been developing, the young Americans were moved by the imperative "we are all alike, and no one should be different [especially not sexually different]."

Adelson found the American egalitarianism basically reassuring. "But there is a fly in the ointment. Beneath the generally optimistic view of government, we find some real tensions, involving the potential collision between equally prized values—individualism and the public good. Some of the time the American handles this conflict by a kind of denial." Thus the American teenagers seemed to expect a magical reconciliation of the conflict, assuming the problem would go away as long as everyone just contributed to the concert of aims. If, in a more ominous vein, individualism ran rampant in the form of crime, antisocial acts, and willful opposition to the public good, then the public good would have to be asserted with a heavy hand. "The outlaw haunts the American imagination." This is the politics, in the terms that came widely into currency in the 1970s, of narcissism, or of narcissists fearing themselves, or of individual and individualistic egos struggling to situate themselves vis-à-vis reality (in the form of the social, the community and its good).

## Defining Adolescence: Prejudices as Puberty Rites

Adelson's research suggests that different prejudices serve and are supported by different general structures of political conviction, which emerge in adolescence, and that these, in turn, relate to group—in his study, national—social and political histories. Social character is reflected in both prejudices and political convictions more generally. In Chapters 10 and 11, I take up directly the matter of how the three character types I have been sketching, and the three conviction types Adelson outlined, are produced in and influence various social and political contexts.

But here I want to show how adolescence itself has been constructed in a complex weave of prejudices, political convictions, and social and political histories. As individuals or in groups, adolescents themselves, drawn together by prejudice affinities, have been the most intense bearers of prejudices, but they have also been, as a group and within victim groups, the target of prejudices. We must examine why, among all sorts of prejudices, adolescents (the ones newly arrived at mature sexuality) so frequently become the targets and the foci within the victim groups.

As an example of what I mean, let me cite a typical turn of the century American pseudoscientific racist claim about the "Negro race": "It was a race the children of which might with favoring circumstance show an intellectual development equal to white children up to the age of thirteen or fourteen; but then comes a diminution often a cessation of the intellectual development. The physical overslaughs [*sic*] the psychical and they turn away from the pursuit of culture."[22] This opinion reflected the widely shared and wildly argued notion that at age fourteen "the physical brain of the Negro reaches its maturity, and nearly all that can be done for a generation must be done by methods suited to the children."[23] When scientists began to study intelligence with IQ tests, they found that the average scores of Negroes actually declined after about age twelve or fourteen, and the biological explanation for the decline lay at hand in the earlier racist literature. This kind of prejudice against Negroes and Negroes as adolescents meshed perfectly with the underlying anxiety that Negroes (especially males) at puberty would be sexually out of control. That anxiety reverberates through a racist tract of 1957 with the unabashed title *Close That Bedroom Door!*—a response to the prospect of integrated high schools:

> Our daughters, under the school integration mandate, are now forced into proximity with the sexually undisciplined Negro adolescent, day after day in school buildings, held prisoner in these buildings under the Compulsory Attendance Law, terrified into silence and conformity by sweeping injunctions and by the sight of armed tanks on their playing fields, intimidated by the spectacle of their natural protectors,

their brothers and fathers, being hauled off to jail for even daring to speak against this infamy . . . our helpless lost daughters, afraid to stay at home, afraid to be delivered to those bold, black eyes, black hands and blacker sperms, our daughters who now from the earliest grades must become accustomed to the sight and odor of the Negro, so that what comes later will not seem so strange, so wrong. How well the Negro leaders understand the weapon of Proximity! Especially when used against the inexperienced captive white girl![24]

Adolescents can be feared as primitively sexual and unrestrainedly violent (especially if they are lower class or black, as in these racist examples) and thus fitting targets for hysterical characters, but they can also suit obsessionals if they are considered con artists and hustlers who are always trying to get something for nothing, to take advantage and cheat older people out of money, jobs, prestige. As for narcissistic characters, they find adolescents particularly disturbing because they resent adolescents for having their lives before them, for being full of possibilities, energetic, beautiful, creative—for possessing what narcissistic people desire for themselves.

To many people of all character types adolescents are frightening in their ambiguities of identity (particularly if they are homosexual), their boundary-challenging amorphousness, their mockery of adult authority. In complex modern industrial and postindustrial societies, adolescents belong to one of three groups (or groupings) encompassing people of both genders and all races and ethnicities that can become targets of the different types of orecticisms. As I noted in Chapter 7, these groupings are of class, sexual preference (primarily homosexuals but also bisexuals and various kinds of "deviants"), and age (primarily adolescents but also the aged). The literature on adolescence abounds with all of the forms of prejudice—as do the current daily newspapers, where violent inner-city youths and pregnant teenagers are the two most discussed subgroups. And it is quite possible that social scientists do not make the prejudices of adolescents a topic not only because they focus on the prejudices of children but also because their own prejudices *about adolescents* guide them to other questions.

In the 1970s, the other big question that guided research was, simply, What is adolescence? The social science literature on adolescence had, at that time, a kind of growth spurt under the press of a unique phenomenon: the adolescent-led cultural revolution of the 1960s, the stu-

dent rebellion that coursed through North and South America and
Western and Eastern Europe. In the history, anthropology, and psychology departments of American universities this question was particularly important, although as work in these disciplines multiplied, they
grew farther and farther apart. Historians focused on the problem of
origins: When did adolescence begin? Is adolescence a modern phenomenon? Anthropologists, building on work done by the Franz Boas
school in the 1920s—like Margaret Mead's *Coming of Age in Samoa*—
asked if adolescence is universal: Does it have different forms in different cultures? Meanwhile, psychologists pondered an issue closely related
to the one about universality: Is adolescence necessarily a period of
*Sturm und Drang*? The question itself was meant to refute the psychoanalytic theories of Anna Freud and others who held that adolescence
is *normatively* a period of upheaval.

The historians' debate was initially complicated by the lack in their
conceptual arsenal of a clear distinction between puberty and adolescence, a distinction that might have come into view if contemporary
feminist articulation of the distinction between sex and gender had echoed in the historians' camp. "Puberty" refers to the processes of phys-
iological and anatomical maturation that result in physical adulthood,
characterized by reproductive capacity unavailable earlier. Puberty can
be defined in terms of these maturation processes and, more loosely,
in terms of chronology. "Adolescence," like "gender," refers to a process of social construction. Adolescence is all of the ways in which puberty is lived, understood by those who live it, understood by those who
have already reached adulthood, and all the ways in which puberty is
situated in society's institutions for schooling, for divisions of labor, for
cultural production, and so forth. Adolescence reflects the sum of prejudices directed at puberty in any given societal time and place. Where
that sum of prejudices is small, there is little in the way of adolescence,
and where it is large and complex, adolescence is focal to societal self-
understanding and self-regulating.

The word "adolescence" became widely used after the mid-nineteenth century because it filled a need created by a great demographic
and socioeconomic shift. During all the many centuries of societies
based on large agricultural enterprises and promotion of large populations to provide the labor for these enterprises, women—organized as
wives, that is, domestic laborers in patriarchal orders—raised children
who, as soon as possible, became laborers and, as soon as possible after

that, became producers of children themselves. Children were viewed and treated as little adults, and physical maturation, puberty, implied availability for adult labor and readiness for reproduction. But, wherever urbanization and industrialization slowly changed the means of production, families gradually shrank in size as childbearing was condensed into a few years of a wife's lifetime rather than stretched over the better part of her maturity. European and American children, after a period of transition in which they labored in industry as they had labored on farms and in which child labor legislation had to be forged to protect them, no longer went into the labor force as soon as possible, as women no longer started childbearing in their late teens. Instead, the young became "adolescents."[25]

While some historians (particularly the feminist historians writing the story of "gender") told versions of how "adolescence" and its related stage of life concepts came into being, dissident voices noted that there had been adolescents before the Industrial Revolution. And it certainly is the case that groups of young people—usually boys—had been educated outside their homes in preparation for labor long before the modern period. In urban centers during the Renaissance, for example, where guild apprentice systems absorbed the labor of boys who were not children, youth groups formed and special ceremonies were established to contain the youthful exuberance and excess of these groups.[26] In Puritan America, elders in communities expostulated on the particular dangers of adolescence, that time of life when unruly desires most assiduously do the devil's work. But it was only in the late nineteenth century that large portions of the youth populations of Europe and America—both girls and boys—went to school, for longer and longer periods, outside their family homes, in the public domain. Indeed, the addition of girls to the ranks of adolescents is one of the clues that adolescents were a social novelty.

As is often the case in historical debates, between two extremes—between those who said that adolescence was unknown before the mid-nineteenth century and those who responded with examples and arguments to show that adolescence is ancient—lies a position that does greater service to a complex issue: it shows what is new in modern adolescence, and it shows what features of adolescence—features closest to and most reflective of puberty—subtend all the different ways in which adolescence has been socially and culturally organized. The definition of adolescence that I offered before (as the sum of social prejudices directed at puberty) could be reformulated for historiographical purposes: the more widely and forcefully—one might also say the more anxiously—the transformations of puberty are shaped by social institutions, the more there is a distinct social category "adolescents."

By the *fin de siècle* in Europe and America, then, "adolescence" had become the word of choice to designate the social construction of the period between childhood and leaving school to go into the workforce (for boys) or into the ranks of child producers (for girls). From that point on, adolescents became progressively more distinctive, and their societies became progressively more like subcultures. They had this in common with another group of people who received a revised designation in the late nineteenth century and became, once designated, more distinctive as a group and more and more like a subculture. As I noted before in discussing the homophobias, the homosexuals, meaning people said to be of exclusive homosexual preference, emerged as a group in a deeply anxious and largely medical discourse that called them not-heterosexual and meant by that abnormal, deviant. There had, of course, been homosexuals before the designation arrived, but there had not been a social concern with homosexual behavior as a disease—not just as a sin and an abomination—defining certain people as exclusively oriented to the same sex and completely other than heterosexuals.

Preparing adolescents for their future as laborers and as procreators, on a scale unknown in the history of puberty and adolescence, was a combined task for parents and professionals, who shared the belief that adolescents must be supervised and controlled. They conceived the adolescent who was to be supervised as a naturally wild, conflicted creature who needed education. The adolescent boy particularly resembled the hypersexual primitive peoples that imperialism was then subduing for the great good of bourgeois global commerce. Some theorists of the period even made this analogy part of their program by subscribing to a Darwinist view in which adolescents recapitulated the adolescence of the human race, which had been manifest in the migrations of primitive peoples, the spread of *Homo sapiens* across the planet—migrations that could still be seen, lingering on, lagging behind in the march of civilization, in the colonialized world. The great turn-of-the-century architect of this view, G. Stanley Hall, had written a gigantic two-volume work called *Adolescence* (1904), in which he extolled the adolescent as the one in whom the adolescent genius of the species is on display, in whom there is a natural exuberance of contrary forces. The phrase *Sturm und Drang* was Hall's importation from German Romanticism, and it meant for him that adolescence comes straight out of Goethe's *Sorrows of Young Werther,* that is, a volatile mix of hyperactivity and inertia, sociability and egotism, exalted religious humanism and childishness, which education should contain (particularly in its sexual manifestations) but not cut off. Adolescence, in Hall's view, should be as prolonged as possible and exploited to the full for a rich future adulthood—so he put its end at age twenty-five or thirty.

Hall's ideas had enormous influence on the vast range of youth-directed organizations and activities that grew up in the first decades of the American Century. They informed church groups, which agreed with Hall's notion that adolescence is the period par excellence of religious conversion, thus the period when the church had to exercise special vigilance to receive and foster converts. Hall's ideas spread in schools and boys' clubs, where active participation and conformity were the twin goals, where group spirit and loyalty to teams were inculcated. They also informed the characteristic American deep hostility toward intellectuality and support for product-directed, vocational work and conventional Christian spirituality. Adolescents were not supposed to think too much. They were to be cheerfully obedient—perhaps not as cheerful as their British counterparts, but just as obedient; and perhaps not as obedient as their German counterparts, the children of wartime defeat enrolled in the *Jugendbewegung,* but just as studiously cheerful or at least not permitted to be morose. They were also to be fundamentally passive, although in team contexts the boys were to be good fighters.

Into the beginning of the twentieth century, youth organizations took the form, in America, of clubs like the Young Men's Christian Association, the Boy Scouts, and the Girl Scouts and, in Europe, of the *Jugendbewegung* organizations. But by the end of World War I the high school was emerging as the center of adolescent culture in America, each high school a complete little social world, dominated—then as now—by organized athletics. By this time, few schools remained that were not age-graded, for everywhere the consciousness had grown that there are not just "ages of man" in the sense depicted popularly in seven-paneled prints, but also *developmental* stages that make it inappropriate for twelve-year-olds and seventeen-year-olds to be in the same classes or even the same schools.

It has often been noted that American adolescent girls at the turn of

the century were assigned to the "separate sphere" of female domesticity along with their mothers. That is, they took part in this period's
exercise of patriarchal control (now called sexism) that was necessary
to keep middle-class women who were not required to produce large
families from thinking that they might do something public with their
nonmaternal time. Girls were certainly discouraged from public roles
or work or service outside the home. But turn-of-the-century middle-
class American girls were educated—often privately—to a degree unknown before. Even cultivated European visitors to our shores, like
Freud, usually so contemptuous of American culture—while admiring
of our political traditions—noted that American middle-class girls were
much better read, more lively in conversation, and more artistically and
musically instructed than any other group in the population. This contradiction—from the point of view of patriarchal power and sexism—
points to the key feature of adolescence in this period. Control of sexuality was its centerpiece—and if cultivation could do that, well, fine for
cultivation. The goal was refinement, not empowerment.

As the historian Joseph Kett has rightly noted, these girls were "the
first adolescents" in the modern sense of the term.[27] They were regulated to prevent what was known anxiously at the time as "precocity."
This meant that their sexuality and their reproductivity were under strict
control, and that sexuality and reproductivity were ideologically soldered together—sex was only for reproduction. By the time these girls
came into high schools in great numbers after World War I, the lineaments of their control were already drawn and only needed reinforcing
in the public domain. At the same time, masculine precocity was less
strictly regulated—boys were permitted more leeway for sowing wild
oats—but the same ideological insistence on linking sex and reproduction obtained. Masturbation was considered as damaging in boys as ren-
egade heterosexual activity was in girls. G. Stanley Hall, who confessed
in his autobiographical writings that he was tormented by the temptation to masturbate, made control of masturbation the essence of his
programs for young men. Early physical maturation among young men
was, correspondingly, looked upon as a liability, even though it was recognized that early maturation had its benefits for athletic achievement.
There is a kind of historical rule of thumb that can be applied to the
adolescent institutions of the early twentieth century: the greater the
felt danger of puberty (the more explosive sexuality is expected), the
more education is called to the rescue—specifically, education for self-

control or, if self-control is beyond reach, submission to authority. To put the matter baldly, by reinforcing the idea that puberty is explosive, education of this period promoted hysteria and then got progressively better at promoting obsessionality.

Claude Lévi-Strauss once remarked that anthropology came into being as a critique of European imperialism overseas. By the late 1920s in America, it had evolved into a critique of the middle class's other great control activity—control over adolescents. Particularly the research group that had formed around Franz Boas at Columbia University focused a great deal of attention on adolescence—specifically, on rites of passage—and concluded that adolescence is not everywhere the same. They emphasized this message because they wanted vantage points, examples of diversity, with which to call into question what adolescence had become in America: a form of regimentation or, rather, regimented confusion, the quintessence of unnaturalness. The Boasian anthropologists criticized obsessional education.

The anthropological critics of the 1920s judged the several decades of American efforts to shape and mold adolescents in specifically adolescent organizations and subcultures to have produced the very storm and stress, the very upheaval, these efforts had been meant to contain and assuage. As American educators and youth workers tried to make adolescence universal in the United States—as universal as compulsory public education was becoming—the anthropological critics argued that such universalization was the route to deadening mediocrity in combination with great increases in maladjustment and neurosis. As the liberators challenged the anxious regulators, a debate began that has captured the ambivalence toward adolescence still so deeply characteristic of our national culture.

The anthropological arena for debates about adolescence opened when Franz Boas's twenty-three-year-old student Margaret Mead—by Hall's standards, an adolescent herself—landed in Samoa in 1925. Her report on the people she studied, *Coming of Age in Samoa*, published in 1928, had a clear mandate, which Boas himself set out in the book's preface:

> In our civilization the individual is beset with difficulties which we are likely to ascribe to fundamental human traits. When we speak about the difficulties of childhood and of adolescence, we are thinking of

them as unavoidable periods of adjustment through which everyone
has to pass. The whole psychoanalytic approach is largely based on
this supposition ... The anthropologist doubts the correctness of
these views, but up to this time hardly anyone has taken the pains to
identify himself sufficiently with a primitive population to obtain an
insight into these problems ... The results of [Margaret Mead's]
painstaking investigation confirm the suspicion long held by anthropologists, that much of what we ascribe to human nature is no more
than a reaction to the restraints put upon us by our civilization.

Margaret Mead's own sense of her contribution was less theoretical and
more pragmatic and reformist.[28] She felt that the Samoan young people
whose lives she had described could teach Americans that "adolescence
need not be the time of stress and strain which Western society has made
it; that growing up could be freer and easier and less complicated."
Mead has been accused of romanticizing the Samoans, but she carefully
drew her balance sheet. Although she argued that the Samoan lack of
complication meant "less intensity, less individuality, less involvement
with life" than could be found in any sector of Western society, she
clearly felt that the Samoans provided many lessons in how to produce
freedom in and for puberty—or how to avoid that Western construct,
"adolescence."

In the terms that historians had set out, what was missing in Samoa
was any period designated as prelabor and presex. As children of four
of five, Samoan girls and boys joined in their villages' work routines, the
girls specializing in child care, the boys in food gathering; there was no
time after infancy in which they did not do some work, and there was
no schooling that was not directly related to the community's tasks. Girls
and boys both became sexually active as soon as they were physically
able, that is, at puberty. Sexual relations were quite casual, involving no
great intensity of feeling and no exclusivity; the only rules concerned
certain social or class barriers that were not to be traversed and certain
official men and women who were supposed to be too busy with community affairs for the playfulness of the multitude. Mead reported that
the Samoans had no idea that sexual activity should be connected to
reproduction—indeed, when Christian missionaries brought this idea
to the islands, the people simply rejected it.

In more psychological terms, Samoan families were not nuclear. On
the contrary, Mead found them to be so openly arranged and so completely extended that children moved about from one adult to another,

one household to another, whenever there was a need for them to do so. Any conflict between parents and children was resolved by moving the children over to another caretaker. Infants were cared for by all the adult women in their surround and by any girls aged seven or over. They were then separated into strictly segregated sex spheres until puberty, when sexual activities brought them back into contact—but without puberty rites of any sort. Neither the pubescent girls nor the boys had any desegregated experience that would have led them to view their lovers and future mates as individuals, in their individuality. Their friendships, too, were strictly regulated along kin and class lines, with the leading and executive families of the village living quite apart from the ordinary folk. Social categories, not preference, determined friendships. In Mead's assessment, these factors meant that the Oedipus complex as Freud had described it simply did not exist—specialization of emotion was not possible.

Mead's Samoans provided one of the key examples for a generalization that developed in anthropology over the next two decades—the anthropological equivalent of the generalization that adolescence exists in societies to the extent that they are apprehensive about puberty and to the extent that puberty seems to call for regulation and control. Societies, according to this new anthropological rule, have elaborate and rigorous puberty rites, rites of passage, to the extent that they are apprehensive that mother-child bonds are too strong to dissolve without ceremony.[29] Societies in which mothers have exclusive care of their children and keep their children, particularly their sons, very close—sometimes removing themselves sexually from their husbands for a long period after birthing, sometimes continuing nursing for years—are societies that ritualize separation at puberty and forcibly, sometimes drastically, certify their young people's sexual identities. They make youths, particularly boys, undergo physically arduous tasks; they isolate girls at menarche; they may scar, make incisions in, or bind the genitals of both sexes. Modern societies have only vestigial puberty rites of the sort so salient in child-centered earlier or less modernized societies. But this does not mean that there is no closeness that needs to be overcome—no deep, usually unconscious object ties that need to be broken, in psychoanalytic terms. Puberty rites, on the contrary, take quite different forms. And they may take the form of ideological prejudices, both those directed at adolescents to control them, regulate them, certify their identities, and those directed by adolescents at others for the purpose of achieving or consolidating their own sexual and social identities. Orectic prejudices are the functional equivalent of puberty rites in Western or Westernized developed societies.

Mead put her heaviest comparative emphasis on the absence in Samoan society of heterogeneity in religious and value systems, in standards for sexual and marital behavior, in groups advocating causes and offering self-images, in ideas and ideals (which, in our culture, are not only diverse but contradictorily held by any given person). Heterogeneity means, in Western societies, that choice is the defining activity of adolescence so that all groups, religious and sectarian, see adolescents as their main field of influence and focus on getting them to make the right choices. But no Samoan young person would ever be battled over, pulled in different or opposite directions by the beliefs and practices of family members or community members. No young person would have to go on the kind of identity quest considered a necessary feature of adolescence in America circa 1928, celebrated in the 1960s (and especially celebrated in psychoanalytically informed anthropological work under the influence of Erik Erikson), and transformed as the decades have passed into a lifelong project that simply commences in adolescence. No one would have needed an ideological prejudice to become a self.

Educational schemes for prolonging adolescence like those proposed by G. Stanley Hall were, Mead saw clearly, schemes for postponing the time of choice in adolescence until the influence of education had, in effect, predetermined the choices. By raising the working age, raising the mandatory schooling age, protecting children from controversies, and making sure that they had no sex education or knowledge of birth control, educators were hoping to create homogeneity where there was none. Mead's own progressive solution was not postponing choice or trying to predetermine it, but educating for it.

> Education, in the home even more than in the school, instead of being a special pleading for one regime, a desperate attempt to form one particular habit of mind which will withstand all outside influences, must be a preparation for those very influences . . . The child who is to choose wisely must be healthy in mind and body, handicapped in no preventable fashion. And even more importantly, this child of the future must have an open mind . . . The child must be taught how to think, not what to think . . . Unhampered by prejudices, unvexed by

too early conditioning to any one standard, they must come clear-eyed to the choices that lie before them.

The liberationist anthropologists of Mead's generation who explored adolescence cross-culturally came again and again to this theme—adolescence would engender less storm and stress if the intensity of parental and societal investment in shaping and molding, in making homogeneity out of heterogeneity, were reduced and tolerance and open-mindedness promoted. Less-prejudiced people would appear if less prejudice were vented upon the young in their adolescence—both in the sense of teaching them prejudices against particular groups and in the larger sense of prejudicing their identities. The antiprejudice chorus was joined in the 1950s by a rank of sociologists who turned their attention to life in American small towns, suburbs, and cities and who took as their great theme alienation, the consequence of a society in conformity overdrive. They chronicled the "shook-up generation" of adolescents after World War II who conducted desultory and nonpolitical rebellions—they were "rebels without a cause"—in street corner gangs. Then a group of commentators followed the adolescents of the late 1950s into their high school lives and wrote fervidly about the mediocrity and deadening routines of the schools. But the critical, liberationist voices suddenly quieted in a wave of wartime fervor for conformity and 1950s renewal of homogenization efforts. The return of the repressed, the 1960s generation that came bursting out of this postwar and Cold War confinement was, in a sense, a generation of anthropologists. And some of them, the apolitical sheerly cultural revolutionaries of the hippie commune–building varieties, were actually inspired to become Meadian Samoans—to have no prejudices, to love everyone or, at least, everyone under age thirty.

This rebellious generation of the 1960s in Europe and America made overt, direct, and undisguised expression of ideological prejudices "politically incorrect." The rebels had discovered—without intending to—the deep connection that exists between sexual repressiveness and the ideological prejudices (in contrast to the ethnocentrisms, which are not similarly tied to sexual repressiveness). The slogan they attached to this discovery had a specific source in Vietnam War protest but made a broader statement—"Make love not war." Although they often followed the deeply ingrained habit of assuming that all prejudices are the same and analogizing the generational prejudice they experienced to race prejudice by writing tracts like *The Student as Nigger,* they did not miss the challenge their sexuality, and the sexual revolution, posed.[30] So they could also break mental habits and grasp that they were the targets of cross-ethnic, cross-racial, cross-gender prejudices—prejudices drawn together by being targeted on adolescents as a group. Youths of privilege, encouraged by their upbringing to be prejudiced, and youths of traditionally targeted groups were all lumped together as rebels and charged with being international Communist conspirators (or lacking patriotism, in the case of Vietnam War protesters), charged with racial traitorousness, or charged with transgression of sexual roles and disrespect for traditional marital (heterosexual) values.

Progressive behaviorists of the 1950s had fostered the great hope that prejudices could be alleviated by changing institutions; that attitudes would change if people could be brought into contact with one another; that integration and equal opportunity legislation would spell the end of not just segregation and social injustice but prejudice as well. In the 1960s and early 1970s, however, the rebellious generation disregarded the behaviorist ideals of social science and embraced the belief that the social equivalent of the adolescent's breaking of object ties with the oedipal family would have to take place before prejudices would ever abate. Its leaders saw personal autonomy and sociopolitical power in and for oppressed groups as the preconditions for change. Outside universities, among the rebellious young intelligentsia, antisemitism was once again (as it had been in Reich's *Mass Psychology of Fascism*) understood as a function of the sexually repressive discontents of Western civilization. Black militants spoke a language of sex therapy in books with titles like *Look Out Whitey, Black Power Gonna Get Your Mother!* Women's groups did "consciousness raising." All turned to schools, not as places where different groups were legally compelled to meet, but as purveyors of curricula that became the battlegrounds of the cultural revolution. Multicultural education came to mean both assertion of the traditions of oppressed groups and education about prejudices, against prejudices; it was assumed that until the oppressed groups could assert themselves, until they had power, prejudices against them would not abate. Victims of prejudice charged themselves with growing up and breaking the bonds that kept them in the houses of their oppressors.

Members of this rebellious generation were the first to grasp, uncertainly, unanalytically, the conclusion that the only adequate defense of target groups is power. They also began to see the complex psychodynamics of specific prejudices, especially racism and sexism, although they did not advance further comparatively or systematically. Their insights have had almost no effect on social scientific study of the prejudices, but they have had tremendous impact on the popular culture, virtually assuring a great defensive backlash, a renewal of all the prejudices, and a widespread rejection of the liberal perspective represented by Mead's *Coming of Age in Samoa* (including efforts to prove that her anthropological fieldwork was biased and distorting). Such backlashes have strongly attacked African Americans and other peoples of color, feminists, and homosexuals in the last twenty years. I will consider these currents and cross-currents of prejudice in Chapter 11, after constructing, in the next chapter, an outline of how the various types of prejudices are socially shared.

# 10

## Shared Prejudices, Societal Styles

I argued in Chapter 6 that it is just as methodologically suspect to psychologize society as it is to sociologize individuals. The first fallacy presumes that a society can be understood as a large diagnosable individual. We might say that the society is paranoid or that it has a superego (say, a class of elders, a judicial system, or a constitution), an ego (perhaps executive and legislative functions), and an id (usually some driving passion, like making war or acquiring money). The second fallacy treats an individual as no more than a function of or player in a group, as only a tablet on which social order is stamped. Intrapsychic processes become products of social imprinting, as though the unconscious were the society at large beamed into an individual's brain.

But, while it is certainly incorrect to analyze or to diagnose a society either as though it were a large individual or as though it existed independently of the individuals who make it up, these are not the only ways to apply the insights of psychology or psychoanalysis to a society.

### Making Group Portraits

It seems to me quite reasonable, for example, to speak of groups that have come about as a union of (predominantly) obsessionals, of like-minded obsessional characters, or to speak of societies that promote obsessionality or even paranoia and of societal orders that allow obses-

340

sionals or paranoids to move into positions of prominence and influence. It also seems quite reasonable to speak of historical conditions—social, economic, political, cultural—that tend to encourage or hamper the development of obsessionality or paranoia. Any given group will contain a certain number of paranoid people—very few in some instances, many in others—and historical lines of development will sometimes keep them marginal and other times help them achieve "normalcy." A society in which obsessionality has become "normal" generally has an obsessional leadership and a sufficient number of followers to color the society's customs and institutions, so that the society, in turn, offers them the protective coloration of, so to speak, institutionalized obsessionality. When the American historian Richard Hofstader spoke of the "paranoid style" in American politics, he was talking not about a society—America—that was diagnosably paranoid, but about a tendency in American history for certain conditions to bring about a "paranoid style" in some important American subgroups or subsocieties. There are always Joseph McCarthys, but they become powerful Congressional leaders only under certain conditions. Adolf Hitlers die without historical trace unless conditions allow them—and they are able to help conditions help them—become Reich chancellors.

If a notion like "societal character" is to have any validity, then, we must give up the idea that societies at any given moment in time have a single, identifiable social character or that all individuals in a society share a social character. As I suggested in Chapter 6, these ideas might make sense for some fairly simple, homogeneous, and small or isolated societies (what are technically called *Gemeinschaften*), but they are inadequate for more complex, pluralistic, and extended societies *(Gesellschaften),* where the analogy between individual character and societal character does not hold well. In complicated modern societies, many social characters prevail in different subsocieties, regions, and local and translocal institutions. There is no such thing as "the culture of narcissism." But at particular historical moments—especially moments of crisis—a dominating set of social character traits may emerge, affecting the whole society, making some individuals desire to connect with the dominative configuration and making others feel alien or alienated.

Particularly in times of crisis and quick change, individuals of one character type will have more chances to flourish, to organize groups, to gain power, and to exercise influence, than individuals of another character type. The dominative character style will have the greatest influence on adolescents because, for the developmental reasons already mentioned, they are the ones who are most organized by their identifications and the ones whose superegos are the most malleable. A societal style does not have to translate over a sustained period into child-rearing methods in order to influence younger people or to become deeply woven into the society's educational institutions, as the first psychoanalytic culture and personality theorists held. The story of the Hitler Youth, for example, shows how, in a matter of less than a decade, a markedly obsessional style—a kind of caricature of Prussianism— could be inculcated in a large segment of a generation.[1] A generation that had suffered wartime deprivations in childhood, that had sustained so many losses of fathers and brothers, was ready in adolescence to idealize a leader like Hitler and heed the nostalgic vision of order, simplicity, security, and triumphalism that he offered.

As I noted before, considering culture and personality dynamics in these ways requires plurals in both places—cultures and personalities. To pursue this pluralizing now, I am once again going to leave aside the kind of prejudice that I call ethnocentrism and focus on the field of orecticisms or ideologies of desires, which my distinction between ethnocentrisms and orecticisms was meant to open up. I do not think that ethnocentrisms differ fundamentally in their psychodynamics, although the roles of given factors—like religious controversies, economic histories, immigration patterns, and ties to neighboring imperial *ethnoi*—obviously produce differences among ethnocentrisms. But differences among ethnocentrisms can be compassed in sociological and historical terms, and they do not require the intricate dialectic of psychological and sociological-historical analyses necessary for orecticisms, which differ in psychic origin and development.[2]

In this chapter, I present in social and political terms the three types of orecticisms—obsessional, hysterical, and narcissistic—that I have been studying psychologically and developmentally. I describe social and political conditions and purposes that bring these prejudices to the fore, in which they operate as galvanizing ideologies and organizing ideas. The types of groups that become the targets of the different ideological prejudices provide the clearest clues to their psychosocial functions. Thus my discussion of the prejudice types begins with a general portrait—a general group portrait—of the victims as they appear in the rhetoric of each prejudice. I will turn in the next two chapters to the prejudices themselves, portraying them generally in psychosocial terms and offering illustrations.

## The Paranoid Style in Politics

The obsessional prejudices are directed toward groups that are imagined or constructed (and may, to varying extents, actually function) in the following ways:

1. The groups are considered clannish or separatist and seem to organize into units that are tightly bound internally by complex (allegedly incestuous) interbreeding. They are imagined as extremely regulated, even if those regulations are envisioned as promoting behavior much more dangerous and provocative than any the obsessionally prejudiced person will admit to. The target groups are also imagined as tightly bound internally by means of elaborate communication systems, customs, and languages (in the broadest sense of the word) that are hard for outsiders to understand and thus resemble codes or ciphers.

2. People in these groups appear in some way archaic, ancient, or able to draw strength from simplicity and sacrifice for the benefit of the group; they are ritualistic and formalistic, usually in modes that barely disguise a violent, invidiously murderous and sexually perverse mentality. Their leaders are ruthless and cunning, brainy.

3. The groups' close and ritualistic social structures are understood as male-dominated and patriarchal; their women are nearly invisible, always obedient, and, even when they are felt to be lascivious or promiscuous, imagined as somehow veiled, hidden. The sexual practices of these people are dirty (and this often means, explicitly, anal).

4. The people affiliated with these groups are imagined to be concentrated in domains of enterprise that allow them to infiltrate other groups easily or exist as liminal figures between groups. They are itinerant traders, commercial people, technologists, service providers; in sociological terms, they are "middleman minorities." Such people are without traditions of being on the land, or, at least, they are known for not being worshipers of the land; they are spiritually, other-worldly oriented, or they are nomadic or stateless, or they are in some way rootless or deracinated. Both their infiltrative activities and their wandering way of life are aided by (or produce) their smallness of stature, their wiry physiques, their somewhat "feminine" lack of athleticism, but also their dangerous trickiness.

5. These people are seen as dedicated to world conquest in subtle ways—by thought manipulation, by purchasing influence, by producing perverse literatures or degenerate art, by concentrating their energies in educational institutions that make their children particularly shrewd and competitive. They are connected by their internal communication networks to vast, far-flung subsidiaries or agencies of their relatives or fellow believers; their ideology or religion, conveyed over their networks, is their strongest weapon. Often they are known as descendants of great civilizations of the past—so they are considered highly literate—and this distinguishes them fundamentally from groups that are considered backward and primitive (like those which hysterical prejudices target).

6. These people are felt to be uncanny in their capacity to see into the future and prepare themselves for taking advantage of developments; they produce prophets, priestlike figures, fortune-tellers (these especially in groups with only magical, not material, power—like the Gypsies), prognosticators, and also trendsetters. They are people who fulfill their own prophecies or make others do so, for example, pundits who control communications media and make reality conform to their versions of it.

7. These people are considered filthy, in the senses already implied—invidious, perverse, wily—but also in the sense of filthy rich, acquisitive, greedy for money or for property as well as for influence; they gain their power, too, as filth does—by spreading through the elements (through water, through air) like germs, sickness, pollution, poisons, insects, vermin. Such people are the incarnation of impurity, and relations with them—especially sexual relations—would be deeply corrupting, corrupting internally, in the blood. (Taking the last three characterizations together, it can be said that these people are both terrifically intellectual or full of spiritual strength and terrifically materialistic—and there is no felt contradiction here, as they are so totalitarian in their striving for control.)

Typically, people with obsessional prejudices take as their scapegoat group an immigrant group (or an established immigrant population which has received a recent infusion from a new wave of immigration) that takes a middle position between a dominating group and a paternalistically dominated group—between white Europeans and their colonial laborers, between upper classes of birth or wealth and their working classes, between a dominant and a dominated "racial" group, between elite and mob in more cultural terms. The middle-stratum immigrant group, which is or becomes a merchant or trader group, is not a landholding group and not connected to surviving paternalistic institutions. It is blocked from landholding and assimilation by the group above, while it receives from the group below a portion of the resentment that its members feel but cannot directly express against the ruling group or the government. So, in America, the white Protestant elites have been antisemitic "downward," and the white working classes and urbanized, ghettoized black communities have been susceptible to antisemitism "upward." Similarly, white middle class people have been anti-Asian (Japanese, Korean, Vietnamese) "downward," and lower-class whites and inner-city blacks have been susceptible to being anti-Asian "upward."

Those above and those below the middleman target group construe it as a monolith, despite the many differences within it of class, language, and culture and the variations or sects in its religion. The group is portrayed as clannish and tribalistic, defined by its tendency toward endogamy, which may be as much a function of its position in a sea of hostility as of the endogamous principles that inform its traditions. The group is also portrayed against the background of its imagined ancient past, and any divisions within its traditions are ignored as the skillfulness and literacy that ancient past implies are emphasized. Animosity is directed toward the Jews, the people of the Old Testament, the "People of the Book." Or, in East and South Africa, it is directed toward the Asians, pointedly known as the Jews of Africa. The Asian populations are from India and Pakistan, speak a multitude of North and South Indian languages, come from diverse class and caste backgrounds, are Hindu and Muslim and Christian, and so forth, but a common Indian or Asian civilization is attributed to them. In Indonesia and Malaysia, the Chinese are similarly regarded as a monolithic group descending from one ancient civilization. None of these peoples are construed as backward or primitive like the Africans.

The East and South African construction of the Asians, which began when Asians were imported as an indentured laboring population and continued when they became freed people and entrepreneurs, is being echoed currently in Great Britain—on the model of the formerly British colonies of Africa. Prejudice among whites in Britain has two main directions, against African immigrants, mostly from the West Indies, and against Asians, mostly from Pakistan and India. The Africans have become the equivalent of the indigenous colonialized populations of East and South Africa, while the Asians serve as the middleman population. The West Indians are imagined in the hysterical "black" manner: as primitive, childish, lazy, unreliable darkies. But the Asians are imagined in the obsessional manner: as eager to take over business operations, crafty, underhanded, shrewd, unhygienic, filthy and growing filthy rich, particularly because they rely for their success on their clan connections and they reproduce at a rate higher than the rate among white British citizens. A recent commentator on the British scene noted that in the public rhetoric of law and order, so common since the 1960s and exacerbated after the urban rioting in 1981, "the Afro-Caribbean population [is] increasingly being seen as instinctively 'anti-authority' and their youth as responsible for a growing incidence of street crime, whilst the Asian community [has fallen] under a general suspicion of harboring large numbers of 'illegal immigrants.'"[3] Police practice against Afro-Caribbeans tends to focus on stop-and-search operations on the streets, but police actions against Asians involve moving into Asian homes and workplaces to prove abuse of immigration controls. The blacks, in other words, are rioters, and the Asians are crafty infiltrators, filling the country with a network of their kin. The same kind of breakdown of stereotypes exists in present-day Germany, where the black African population receives the hysterical prejudices and the immigrant Turks, along with "economic refugees" from Eastern Europe, construed as more "Jewish" and entrepreneurial, experience the obsessional prejudices.

The confrontation between capitalism and Communism in the 1950s produced the major twentieth-century variant on this group portrait of the obsessional target, which features a middleman class serving as the scapegoat for economic competitors' anxieties. This variant came about in conditions when two nations, the United States and the Soviet Union, already imperialist, vied for dominance in a supranational realm (conditions quite unlike those obtaining when the Nazi movement was seeking to reach beyond the state to a supranational form). American anti-Communism focused on an imagined infiltrator group—usually located right in the government, for example, in the State Department—spearheading the conquest ambitions of a huge monolithic group, the Communists, looming offstage. On the other side, the capitalists were thought to have established a beachhead for their conquest ambitions with a spy network. The contests played out on the level not of ethnic or racial groups but of supernational entities, and the competitiveness was both economic and ideological.

As these examples indicate, the targets for obsessional prejudices vary, but the initial form that obsessional prejudices themselves take is similar everywhere. The obsessionally prejudiced feel a desperate need for protection against the infiltrating and polluting conspiracy they have imagined. The protections have all the marks of obsessional ceremonials: they are repetitive and rigidly adhered to; they are presented publicly with a peculiar pedantry, with a plethora of lists, "hard" evidence vaguely invoked, scientific and scholarly trappings; they must be revised ceaselessly (becoming more and more drastic) because they are never totally effective; they are rationalized down to the most minute detail. Obsessional protections are carried out with enormous stress on precision and efficiency (even if they are not, by outside standards, in any way efficient).

The obsessionally prejudiced divide the world and groups of people into completely distinct categories, categories with impermeable boundaries. There may be many categories, but, at bottom, the scheme will be Manichaean: there exist only the good (pure) and the evil (impure). Thus in the race ideologies that such people embrace, human beings are not one species but a plurality—an absolute rejection of the Enlightenment idea of common humanity—and the most important rule for these plural species is that they should have no possibility for infiltrating one another. Sexual activities across the designated barrier or miscegenation is the ultimate evil; eugenic race purity the ultimate good, especially for the single ultimately good species. Although rarely noted in studies of race ideology, this obsessional racialism differs quite significantly from that embraced by people with hysterical prejudices. Hysterically prejudiced people believe in inferior and superior groups, but they forbid only *upward* miscegenation. Putting superior "blood" into the inferior groups (by concubinage or rape, from males to females) is not forbidden until competition from the inferior group becomes fearsome and has to be contained. But the obsessional is a totalitarian isolationist of blood, as well as of other products that can flow across group divisions to penetrate the isolate, pure group. Obsessionals combat penetrating ideas, for example, with rigorous censorship and rigorous assault upon "common humanity" Enlightenment rights, like the right of free speech.[4] In general, it can be said of obsessionals that they tend politically toward isolationism and separatism, and this is true even when separatism is a response to actual (as opposed to imaginary) persecution by a conspiratorial and imperialistic group.[5] Obsessionals also want, however, to extend the sphere of their own society's domination, and a titanic struggle between the fortress mentality and the imperial impulse always exists.

Ultimately, or in the ultimate logic of obsessionality, the only protection against a creeping worldwide conspiracy is eradication, extermination, even to the point of destroying any evidence of the destruction.[6] Anything less means that the conspiracy can regenerate, regroup. Obsessional prejudices carry genocidal impulses in them. But if eradication remains a fantasy or is not possible, the next best strategy is containment, which means in some manner putting a ring, a boundary, around the conspiratorial people. They can be deported to a settlement on the other side of a natural barrier; they can be ghettoized; allies can be commandeered to constitute a fortress of groups around them. But containment can also be carried out by an imitation of the conspiratorial enemy's methods—methods of communication, coding, infiltration.

More generally, the obsessional prejudices involve not just fear and hatred but admiration and envy of the conspiratorial group's methods and of the aspirations for conquest attributed to the group. The intelligence that is frightening is also inspiring; the wealth and power that are threatening are also desired. Of all the types of prejudices, the obsessional prejudices are the most ambivalent. And the ambivalence appears as ambivalence does in paranoia—the group that is feared as corrupting and destructive is also the group that is, without acknowledgment, unconsciously, the most alluring.

This ambivalence manifests itself in doubt and indecision, so doubt and indecision have to be ruthlessly curtailed—and this is one of the key functions of leadership in a group where obsessionality is rife: the leader must never waver, never turn back, never reconsider, never be anything less than hard, steely, a beacon in any darkness. People outside of the group may find the leader fanatical, but the followers feel the leader's rigidity as—to use metaphors that are psychoanatomically precise—their backbones, their sphincter control. In the language of gesture, obsessional people invent ways of demonstrating in front of their leaders that require feats of muscular clenching and releasing—like the Nazi goose-step march, many other forms of parade drill, and various forms of ceremonial saluting and bowing. Hypertonicity is the obsessional mode of dependency.

Obsessionally prejudiced individuals and groups display what the American historian Richard Hofstader called the "paranoid style."[7] Hofstader's word "paranoid" refers to what I have been calling obsessional, but he used the term neither in a clinical sense nor to delineate a psychopathology: "It is the use of paranoid modes of expression by more or less normal people the makes the phenomenon significant." In my understanding, however, the more or less normal people who are given to the paranoid style are of a specific characterological sort—they are obsessional. Paranoid expressions are the means by which obsessionals displace out onto the world the battle they feel in themselves between their bad desires and their moral strictures, their wishes and their warning lights, their fantasies and their "Thou shalt not's," their ids and their superegos. Obsessionals use paranoid mechanisms, but only the most severely obsessional people become fully—psychopathologically—paranoid.

Hofstader was the first theorist of prejudice (a designation he would not have given himself, for he wrote as "an Americanist") to recognize that a number of prejudices—antisemitism among them—share the paranoid style and to offer a general characterization. The distinguishing characteristic of this style, he noted, is that it organizes around an image "of a vast and sinister conspiracy, a gigantic and subtle machinery of influence set in motion to undermine and destroy a way of life." All of history is imagined as being moved by "demonic forces of almost transcendent power" that no mere political opposition could stop; "an all-out crusade" is required, and it will usually adopt the methods of the enemy conspiracy.

The paranoid spokesman sees the fate of this conspiracy in apocalyptic terms—he traffics in the birth and death of whole worlds, whole political orders, whole systems of human values. He is always manning the barricades of civilization, constantly living at a turning point: it is now or never in organizing resistance to conspiracy. Time is forever just running out. Like religious millenarians, he expresses the anxiety of those who are living through the last days.

As Hofstader rightly observes, the paranoid confronts a totally evil enemy, who must be fought to a finish, not compromised with, not negotiated with. "Since the enemy is thought of as being totally evil and totally unappeasable, he must be totally eliminated—if not from the world, at least from the theater of operations to which the paranoid directs his attention." The futuristic world-embracing sweep of the paranoid's ideology is obvious, but it is important to recognize, as Hofstader does, how perilous the future is felt to be. *If* the enemy is vanquished, there can be a Thousand Year Reich.

But Hofstader also understood that the dichotomizing thought of the paranoid, the division of the world into absolute good and absolute evil, goes along with the element I designated ambivalence. The paranoid's enemy is "on many counts a projection of the self: both the ideal and the unacceptable aspects of the self are attributed to him." The paranoid imitates his enemy's powerful capacities and techniques and also attributes to his enemy his own licentiousness and violence ("the fantasies of true believers serve as strong sadomasochistic outlets"). To use the language of the 1950s anti-Communist campaign in America, a paranoid can say "the only good Red is a dead Red" (in a sadistic mode) or "better dead than Red" (in a masochistic mode) while constructing a secret police worthy of combating the Red secret police in an apocalyptic duel.

After reviewing a panoply of American nineteenth century religiously tinged crusades against Masons and Catholics and then comparing them to the post–World War II crusade against Communism, particularly in its McCarthyite form, Hofstader noted that in social terms the paranoid style is not a constant:

> The recurrence of the paranoid style over a long span of time and in different places suggests that a mentality disposed to see the world in the paranoid's way may always be present in some considerable minority of the population. But the fact that movements employing the paranoid style are not constant but come in successive episodic waves suggests that the paranoid disposition is mobilized into action chiefly by social conflicts that involve ultimate schemes of values and that bring fundamental fears and hatreds, rather than negotiable interests, into political action. Catastrophe or the fear of catastrophe is most likely to elicit the syndrome of paranoid rhetoric ... In American experience, ethnic and religious conflicts, with their threat of the submergence of whole systems of values, have plainly been the major focus for militant and suspicious minds of this sort, but elsewhere class conflicts have also mobilized such energies. The paranoid tendency is aroused by a confrontation of opposed interests which are (or are felt

to be) totally irreconcilable, and thus by nature not susceptible to the normal political processes of bargain and compromise.

People without access to or marginalized in normal political processes are particularly inclined to find their "original conception of the world of power as omnipotent, sinister, and malicious fully confirmed" when they fail in an effort to influence the political process. They go for leaders who are outsiders, who are not products of normal political processes, who may even be converts from the enemy camp (and thus intimately apprised of enemy secrets and techniques).

Hofstader's description is very compelling, but it seems unlikely to me that a paranoid disposition is mobilized into action in a crisis in the manner that Hofstader indicated. I think he has shown the second of a two-step process. Paranoid (in my terms, obsessional) dispositions are always in action, always defending against outbreaks of desire, but what does happen episodically is that a crisis ruptures the fragile balance in obsessionally prejudiced people and sets in motion a frantic *recuperative* activity. A trauma, to speak clinically, can so heighten a paranoid's (or obsessional's) anxiety that his characteristic defenses and ceremonials do not function and a new, more thorough defensive effort has to be instituted. Methods grow more elaborate, violence becomes more common, more completely technologized and rationalized. And, most important, the obsessional becomes desirous of a group—only a group can counter the threatening conspiracy "out there."

People with obsessional prejudices, when they do establish organizations and mass movements, need these to be structured to make them feel just like the other people in the organizations or movements. They are happy to wear uniforms that make them uniform; to march in step; to submit to orders and disciplines; to be relieved of decision making. They exhibit a self-less type of mass psychology: more precisely, they attempt to get rid of parts of the self that are impure and pledge the remaining cleansed self to absolute purity as represented by the organization. A hysterical type of person wants to establish or join groups for the enhancement of his or her power and becomes fired by involvement as achievement of an expansive, more powerful, even wilder sense of self. But obsessional people seek the group's perfectionism, and they are quite capable of being swept away coldly, that is, in a rush of logic. As early as 1929, Adolf Hitler saw as the "great thing" of the Nazi movement the fact that individual men (as he said) "have outwardly become almost a unit," with nearly identical ideas and even facial expressions: "Look at these laughing eyes, this fanatical enthusiasm and you will discover how a hundred thousand men in a movement become a single type."[8]

The people most prone to seek a group's perfectionism are those who have been disenfranchised, cast out of or excluded from any kind of group. In recent history, this has meant primarily surplus people, the mass of people who have no places in their societies and are detached from their traditional kinship settings by processes of immigration, urbanization, resettlement, economic disaster, unemployment. But it can also mean alienated or disillusioned intellectual or professional people, people whose obsessionality has been functional for their education and advancement but who then find themselves without a sense of place, a containing or structuring surround, and without direction, in an intolerable (to them) social and political randomness and disorder. Masses and elites that have nothing otherwise in common can find that the same ideology and the same organizing leadership unites them, relieves them of their rootlessness; the same apocalyptic and redemptive vision gives them a common future. They are relieved by it, enthused by it, feel swept into place by it, and they are glad to be all alike, uniform, in a historical process that asks no thinking of them but gives them the comfort of an obedience that does not feel passive to them.

In obsessional movements and regimes, symbols of order are not symbols in the usual sense; they are order made sacred. Hofstader astutely observed that in nineteenth-century American crusades against Masons and then against Catholics, religions provided the venues. Toward the end of the century, however, the crusaders began to mix their "fortunes with American party politics." These nineteenth-century crusades resembled ethnocentric quarrels, replete with xenophobia, until the enemy groups were said to be taking over American politics—until Protestant crusaders alleged that Catholics, for example, were doing things like causing the depression of 1893 by starting a run on the banks. At the turn of the century, Catholicism ceased to be a religion coming to America in waves of immigrants and became a disease lodged right in the heart of America, a religion become political. At the same moment, antisemitism flourished in America for the first time, with the allegation that Jewish financiers stood behind the government.[9] The kind of crusade needed to counter such a threat was surgical, rational in the extreme, to any extreme.

For an obsessional prejudice to emerge as a commanding social force it must galvanize a widespread feeling in a society that the political institutions are corrupt. As in America, in late-nineteenth-century Europe hostility to the state and the political parties vying to control the state apparatus combined with the idea that a group—the Jews—had a special hidden power in the state. Hostility toward the government or toward government interference in life, will go along with a conspiracy theory— the government is really a front for Jewish power, or for the secret agents of a foreign power, or for the values of a sinister "cultural elite," and so forth. Conservative political theories that stress the importance of keeping governments limited and restrained are well designed to lay the political ideological groundwork for conspiracy theories. In some circumstances the government itself may be the chief focus of obsessional prejudice, and various different groups and forces may be conceived as ruling the government from behind the scenes.[10]

Obsessional prejudices flourish in reaction to what Hofstader called crises of value, but it seems to me that these are specifically crises of value *in relation to economics,* when the economic foundations of ways of life seem to be at stake. The nineteenth-century religious versions of these crises were, so to speak, crises about God's economy, about how "the Protestant ethic and the spirit of capitalism" were, in combination, to be preserved. But at the turn of the century and in the twentieth century, while the role of religion in individuals' and societies' existences has been so ceaselessly under question, political-economic values have more often been the key sites of crisis. The precipitating condition for obsessional prejudices to become public forces or rallying points might be generally designated "depression and disillusion."

In the context of an immigrant society like the United States, the depression experience usually entails fear of increasing waves of immigration that are expected to make the economic situation even more precarious. Thus increases in antisemitism in this country have correlated with increases in immigration, culminating during the last years of World War II, when there was a spike upward in polls registering antisemitism and, despite the fate of European Jewry, tightened immigration regulation.[11] Similarly, in Western Europe in the 1980s and 1990s, during the most intense movement of refugees that has taken place since World War II, xenophobia and resurgent antisemitism go together.

An economic depression, felt psychologically as depressive, comes to stand in an obsessional's mind for passivity and vulnerability; it represents the way in which the world has become hostile; it represents what Oswald Spengler in *The Decline of the West* called *Weltangst,* fear of the world. Being stripped of money becomes equated with being stripped of one's most intimate and private property, of one's body products—to speak in terms of the psychoanalytic libido theory, of one's feces. It may also represent being deprived of one's most secret envious desires, specifically desires to be of the opposite sex: for men, to be able to be women with female reproductive capacities; for women, to be able to be men.[12] The loss of money or economic security is felt as a violation, a rape, which exposes these secret desires, gives them an absolutely forbidden fulfillment, or hints that they are ultimately impossible to fulfill, inducing raging frustration. The conspiratorial group that becomes the object of the obsessional's prejudice in these circumstances is charged with having penetrated walls of security, breached all defenses, turned all activity into passivity; and the reply, in the medium of group action, must reestablish walls, restore activity, and institute law and order on a total scale. What is valued is activity and productivity, and what is feared is passivity or parasitism, which the targets of obsessional prejudice are said to induce. Thus Henry Ford, for example, constantly reiterated in his antisemitic writings the basic contrast between "creative Industry" and the parasitic, passive "international Finance" that threatened it.

When the prevailing mode in both individual and public worlds deserves the designation "depression," and when depression continues over a prolonged and painful time, many people find themselves without capacity to follow their own "Thou Shalt Not" internal voices. Forbidden desires clamor. And then a rescuer in the form of a leader who has an explanation for why the world is as it is, a conspiracy theorist, has tremendous appeal. He says: "The whole political system is rotten, and the X have caused this rottenness." He offers isolationism as a remedy, like a kind of quarantine, which will aid eventual world conquest or attainment of superpower because it is a husbanding or recontrolling of resources and a process of purification. People feeling threatened imagine relief from immigration barriers going up, trade barriers rising, exclusions and quotas and standards being established in all areas of institutionalized life. The United States today provides another example: this kind of value-crisis obsessionality targets the Japanese, who are seen as taking over the American economy and influencing political processes. The chief mode of obsessional response is longing for the outsider leader—a Ross Perot, who is a brilliant businessman and a conspiracy theorist, a clownish agitator of paranoid style given to launching investigations that will reveal the rottenness of the system and the true causes of that rottenness right here among all the elected representatives in Congress, all the corrupt politicians in the pockets of foreign lobbyists.[13]

Most periods of depression and disillusion provide conditions for obsessional prejudice to crystallize in disparate groups and among obsessionals who are not group-minded, but they do not encourage obsessional prejudice across groups and throughout a population. There are clusters of obsessional prejudice. Then, when the conditions abate, the public obsessional phenomena recede with them or generalize to encompass a new victim group. This scenario applies to the burst of antisemitism in the 1890s in America and to the period after World War II, when a peak of antisemitism was followed by a decline and a refocusing of obsessional prejudice onto domestic Communists, particularly (in the McCarthyite ideology) the elite, Ivy League Communists lodged inside the American government.[14] But what happened in Europe in the wake of the 1870s depression was quite different. What might be called a respite from anxiety occurred at the turn of the century, from the 1890s until 1910 or so—a *belle époque*. But the generation that had spent its childhood in the late 1870s depressions then spent its young adulthood in World War I and its parenting years in the Great Depression. The children of this cohort grew up during World War I and then came to adulthood in the depression. The conditions were cumulative: they reinforced the deepening paranoid style, and they gave no disproof of the paranoid economic visions espoused in so many social and political groups. The widespread feeling was that the social fortresses of the nation-states had simply collapsed.

I am going to trace this European story briefly, focusing on the paradigmatic obsessional prejudice, antisemitism, with the help of Hannah Arendt's *Origins of Totalitarianism,* a book that is not informed by psychoanalysis and also not Marxist. I have chosen this version of the European story because it is so resolutely political, which means that it focuses on the ways in which antisemitism *becomes political,* the ways in which (in the terms I have just developed) an obsessional prejudice metamorphoses into hatred of governments and conviction that "the government'' (the obsessional's own) is being taken over and undermined. The key condition for an obsessional prejudice to turn lethal, for its genocidal logic to be set in motion, is, I think, the linking of the target group with the government, the linking of the prejudice with government hatred. (This link to government hatred distinguishes modern antisemitic conspiracy theories from those which, as Norman Cohen showed in his *The Pursuit of the Millennium*, have been typical of Jew hatred since the Middle Ages.)

In the first part of *The Origins of Totalitarianism*, called "Antisemitism," Hannah Arendt drew a careful distinction of kind between Jew hatred as it appeared in the West through the period of the Enlightenment and antisemitism in the nineteenth century, during the rise of imperialism. But she also drew a firm line of degree between *fin de siècle* antisemitism—antisemitism used as a weapon and a rallying point, an ideology, by political parties—and the antisemitism that grew up after World War I, which was fully and clearly articulated as an ideology quite different from "rampant nationalism and its xenophobic outbursts." Fully developed antisemitism, which grew out of an antisemitism first used as a political instrument in a nationalistic context, was an ideology for the destruction of all merely national political forms.

Arendt made these distinctions because she refused to accept any easy answers to the question, Why the Jews? She was struck by an anomaly. The Jews, a relatively small population group, declining from the apex of their early-nineteenth-century financial influence on the states emerging from Continental empires, a group without political power or territory, ended up the target of Nazi destruction. How did the "seemingly small and unimportant Jewish problem" come to have "the dubious honor of setting the whole infernal machine in motion?"[15] Following her question, Arendt did two things rare in postwar studies in prejudice: she explored thoroughly the history of the Jews, that is, she acknowledged that the victims had a story, too, and were not simply a scapegoat out-group or the latest generation of an eternally hated people; and she realized that understanding a prejudice requires taking seriously what the victimizers say about the victims, attending to the exact way the prejudice is expressed, no matter how incredible and horrible the expression may be.

Arendt's story told of the transformation of Europe from a continent of absolute monarchies into diverse nation-states in republican or constitutional monarchy forms.[16] Relatively homogeneous or single-nation populations like the French made the transition to nation-state organization first. But nation-states of the French sort did not emerge in Russia, Austria-Hungary, or much of southern Europe, especially in the Balkan peninsula where no firmly rooted, nonmigratory, emancipated peasant classes lived, and where territorial boundaries had shifted about for centuries with mobile populations dispersed into small dialect-speaking units or tribes. The modern states that succeeded the absolute monarchies rendered all nationals equal before the law, as citizens. The aristocrats thus lost their hereditary privilege as the ruling class, and the oppressed received a guaranteed right to protection; the remains of feudal hierarchies ultimately disappeared. After the absolute monarchies, no class succeeded to the aristocratic role of being identified with the state. This division between the aristocracy and the state allowed the emergent nation-states to stand successfully above all classes and relatively independent of particular class interests. But it also meant that, without a particular class for an ally, the nineteenth-century state governments set themselves up as huge business enterprises, quite apart from the enterprises of the bourgeoisie, who kept their businesses resolutely private and fueled the development of capitalism. Financing for state enterprises came from the one group ready to participate—the elite or privileged Jews, who became state bankers as they had once been financiers to royal courts. "With their credit and international connections," Arendt noted, "they were in an excellent position to help the nation-state" (p. 17).

Nation-states guaranteed political equality but not equality of social or economic condition and opportunity. As class societies based on wealth and type of work grew up, political equality became, in effect, only equality before the law. An individual's status was defined by class position and relation to other classes rather than by position in the state or the state's apparatuses. The only exceptions, Arendt argued, to this general status-definitional rule were the Jews, some of whom were wealthy financiers identified with the state and some of whom were economically disadvantaged:

> The Jews did not form a class of their own and they did not belong to any of the classes in their countries. As a group, they were neither workers, middle class people, landholders, nor peasants. Their wealth seemed to make them part of the middle class, but they did not share in its capitalist development; they were scarcely represented in industrial enterprise and if, in the last stages of their history in Europe, they

became employers on a large scale, they employed white-collar personnel and not workers. In other words, although their status was defined through their being Jews, it was not defined through their relationship to another class. Their special protection from the state
(whether in the form of open privileges, or a special emancipation
edict which no other group needed and which frequently had to be
reinforced against the hostility of society) and their special services to
governments prevented their submersion in a class system as well as
their own establishment as a class. Whenever, therefore, they were
admitted to and entered society they became a self-defined, self-pre-
serving group within one of the classes, the aristocracy or the bourgeoisie.   (pp. 12–13)

The European states that turned to business enterprises without the
cooperation of their bourgeoisies produced, particularly in the 1870s,
disasters and much corruption. Depressions ensued in many states. Citizens who had invested in such ventures as the Panama Canal project
were ruined and deeply resentful of the Jews, whom they perceived as
responsible for the states' blunders. In the late 1870s, just before the
word "Antisemitismus" was coined in Germany, the first specifically
antisemitic political parties formed. Conservative nobles made alliances
in these antisemitic parties with lower-middle-class people who had been
ruined in the state scandals. Together these traditional enemies hoped
for the death of the European nation-states and envisioned new supranational entities that would be based on what Arendt called tribal or racial
ideologies. But these supranationalist and antisemitic parties did not
explode into prominence at the end of the century. "By the turn of the
century, the effects of the swindles in the seventies had run their course
and an era of prosperity and general well-being, especially in Germany,
put an end to the premature agitations of the eighties. Nobody could
have predicted this end was only a temporary respite, that all unresolved
political questions, together with all unappeased political hatreds, were
to redouble in force and violence after the First World War" (p. 41).
    In the last two decades of the century Arendt noted, Jews in particular
experienced a "Golden Age of Security." But the hostility toward the
state and toward the Jews of the citizens who suffered in the state business disasters did not bode well. This is Arendt's summary of the situation in which political antisemitism arose:

   Just as the Jews ignored completely the growing tension between
   state and society, they were also the last to be aware that circumstances

had forced them into the center of the conflict. They never knew how to evaluate antisemitism, or rather never recognized the moment when social discrimination changed into a political argument. For more than a hundred years, antisemitism had slowly and gradually made its way into almost all the social strata of almost all European countries until it emerged suddenly as the one issue upon which an almost unified opinion could be achieved. The law according to which this process developed was simple: each class of society that came into conflict with the state as such became antisemitic because the only social group which seemed to represent the state were the Jews. And the only class which proved almost immune from antisemitic propaganda were the workers who, absorbed in the class struggle and equipped with a Marxist explanation of history, never came into direct conflict with the state but only with another class of society, the bourgeoisie, which the Jews certainly did not represent, and of which they were never a significant part. (p. 25)

But hostility toward the state had to metamorphose fully into aspiration to transcend and replace the state before the ideology of antisemitism could metamorphose into an ideology calling for destruction of the Jews. The transition came with the end of the European solidarity and commitment to a "balance of power" among sovereign nation-states in Europe. The transition required imperialism, which Arendt understood both as the extension of bourgeois capitalistic development overseas or across continents in a limitless grab for wealth and power, and also as an attitude of supranational limitlessness, lawlessness, rule by decree—complete abrogation of the rule by law attempted by the nation-states. As the bourgeoisie overcame its traditional distance from politics and created state enterprises that carried excess capital and superfluous workers beyond Europe, it also justified its expansion with an ideology of race. Similarly, as "Continental imperialists" in Russia and Germany tried to unify their dispersed peoples—the Slavs or the Germans—in political (rather than economic) expansions beyond their nation-state borders, they, too, appealed to supranationalist ideologies of race: pan-Germanism, pan-Slavism. In Arendt's opinion, the Continental imperialisms, conducted by "pan-movements," contributed more directly than overseas imperialisms to the formation in Austria, Germany, and Russia of large groups of people who thought in racial terms, who longed to submerge themselves in a *Volk*, and who felt the soul of a people in their individual souls.

The antisemitism of particularly the German pan-movement was, Arendt argued, an antisemitism of envy. The pan-movement believers in Germanism recognized in the Jews a people who professed to be what the Germanists wished to be—a chosen people, a people claiming to be unique and better simply by virtue of their birth, their membership in a society that was not a nation, not a state like any other. "It seemed that the Jews were the one perfect example of a people in the tribal sense, their organization the model the pan-movements were striving to emulate, their survival and their supposed power the best proof of the correctness of racial theories" (p. 242). Without any appreciation of the historical specificities of Jewish life or religion, the pan-movements' leaders achieved a simple "insight": the Jews, they knew, had divided the world into two camps, themselves and all others, and this made them the one people whose claim clashed with the claim of the pan-movements themselves. There cannot be two messianic peoples, two chosen peoples. In this turn-of-the-century period of imperialist envy of the Jews, the famous forgery called "Protocols of the Elders of Zion" appeared and purported to present the Jewish ambition for world domination. This ideological antisemitism—legitimated by the "Protocols" pamphlet—did not sustain political organizations until after World War I, but it was enormously important as a type of antisemitism quite distinct from the one apparent in France during the Dreyfus Affair or in the earlier antisemitic parties of the 1870s, because hatred of the Jews was, for the first time, "severed from all experience concerning Jewish people, political, social or economic, and followed only the peculiar logic of an ideology" (p. 472). It became an obsession.

The next key moment in the development of antisemitism came when the pan-movements turned totalitarian. As economic dislocations radiated like a wake after the upheaval of World War I, leaving more and more people stateless or alienated from their states and from political parties, which they had never felt represented by—that is, as the masses grew—they gathered themselves into political movements like National Socialism. They were lured with propaganda full of both state hostility and doctrines of historical necessity—of inevitable race triumph in Germany. Arendt repeatedly cited social atomization and extreme individualization or social alienation as the preconditions for mass movements:

> Masses are not held together by a consciousness of common interest
> and they lack that specific class articulateness which is expressed in

determined, limited, and obtainable goals. The term masses applies only where we deal with people who either because of sheer numbers, or indifference, or a combination of both, cannot be integrated into any organization based on common interest, into political parties or municipal governments or professional organizations or trade unions . . . The chief characteristic of the mass man is not brutality and backwardness, but his isolation and lack of normal social relationships . . . [Or, in other terms:] the radical loss of self-interest, the cynical or bored indifference in the face of death or other personal catastrophes, the passionate inclination toward the most abstract notions as guides for life, and the general contempt for even the most obvious rules of common sense.   (p. 316)

In Germany, antisemitism focused the Nazi vision of racial purity—the Jews, like all inferior peoples, were obstacles to purity. But it also channeled Nazi political energy—the Jews, secret manipulators of the state, were the conspiratorial world power standing in the way of the Nazi's world triumph.

The most efficient fiction of Nazi propaganda was the story of a Jewish world conspiracy. Concentration on antisemitic propaganda had been a common device of demagogues ever since the end of the nineteenth century, and was widespread in Germany and Austria of the twenties . . . Not one Nazi slogan was new—not even Hitler's shrewd picture of a class struggle caused by the Jewish businessman who exploits his workers, while at the same time his brother in the factory courtyard incites them to strike. The only new element was that the Nazi party demanded proof of non-Jewish descent for membership and that it remained . . . extremely vague about the actual measures to be taken against Jews once it came to power. The Nazis placed the Jewish issue at the center of their propaganda in the sense that antisemitism was no longer a question of opinions about people different from the majority, or the concern of a national politics, but the intimate concern of every individual in his personal existence; no one could be a member whose "family tree" was not in order . . . Nazi propaganda was ingenious enough to transform antisemitism into a principle of self-definition, and thus to eliminate it from the fluctuations of mere opinion.   (p. 358)

In general, ideological prejudices convert into lethal modalities at the moment when prejudiced people institutionalize their desire or envy by demanding of themselves and their group proof of their freedom from contamination by the group or groups they desire or envy and thus hate:

when racists must be racially pure, sexists without feminine traits, homophobes without perverse desires. But Arendt made her point in political, not psychological, terms by stressing that in totalitarian contexts such demonstrations presuppose mass movements and give the masses exactly what they lack—identity. The propaganda and required tests of purity "gave the masses of atomized, undefinable, unstable and futile individuals a means of self-definition and identification which not only restored some of the self-respect they had formerly derived from their function in society, but also created a kind of spurious stability which made them better candidates for an organization" (p. 312).

It is important to note that Hannah Arendt, unlike all those in the Marxist tradition, including the Adorno group, pointedly did not attribute political antisemitism in any of its stages of growth to one class—the bourgeoisie or the lower middle class. She stressed how antisemitism had appealed to the "mob" of people who had dropped out of any class ("the refuse of all classes") in the economic upheavals of the late 1870s and been swept into overseas imperialist ventures; but she also noted how many of the elite of intellectuals who had been disillusioned and embittered in World War I subscribed to the notion of a Jewish world conspiracy. And the masses, those rootless and disconnected people who had never belonged to any organization before the totalitarian movements magnetized them, were not class members either: they were guided by no visions of limited class interests and checked by no identifications of their enemies as class enemies. In Arendt's understanding, twentieth-century antisemitism was an ideology not of an *ethnos* defending against an out-group, but of disparate people defining themselves; not a prejudice serving as a pretext for passion-dominated people to nurture their passions, antisemitism was a lure for passionless people to lose themselves in a group and a vision of history.[17] And, most important, it was ultimately directed, in the medium of the Jews, against the state, against government, against governance conceived of as interfering and ruinous. A violent hostility toward the government resulted in a replacement of that governance with a control of totalitarian sweep. This is the logic of obsessional prejudice—to fight control conceived of as coming from without, infiltrating, polluting, with a fortress, a factory of countercontrol.

Finally, Arendt turned her attention to the function and dimensions of antisemitism that are revealed when a totalitarian movement is in power. Unlike the antisemitism typical of the pan-movements and that typical of mass movements becoming totalitarian, the antisemitism of a totalitarian regime explicitly and without pretense aims for extermination. The Nazis expelled Jews, thus exporting to other countries the consequences of their policies, as well as suggestions for emulation. But they also moved the Jewish populations remaining in Germany and the lands to the east into ghettos and eventually into concentration camps. In the camps, the ideology calling for race purity by fabricating a race was put into practice. Not only the Jews as a people, but everything that their vitality and specificity and ingenuity represented had to be flushed away: "The camps are meant not only to exterminate people and degrade human beings, but also serve the ghastly experiment of eliminating, under scientifically controlled conditions, spontaneity itself as an expression of human behavior and of transforming the human personality into a mere thing, into something even animals are not" (p. 456). The Nazis pursued this ideological goal without regard for its practical consequences on the German economy or the German war aims, and without regard for any morality or legality, private or public. In this hideous context, antisemitism was the leading step in an assault that would have, if the war had developed differently, gone on to eliminate all imperfect "Aryan" populations in the Third Reich and as far beyond as the Nazis could have reached.

## Hysterical Dramas on the Stage of the World

Let us turn to the constructed features of the individuals and groups at whom the hysterical prejudices are directed.

1. The groups are seen as organized into extended and complex families or tribes in which relations of power are highly sexualized or depend upon sexual arrangements, exchanges of favors and swapping of partners, bargaining, and so forth; the paternity of children is often in doubt.

2. People in these groups are imagined as primitive and lazy; they live from day to day and give no thought to the future; their lives follow seasonal rhythms like those of the plants and animals, to which they closely relate—they are wild and bestial. If they gain power it is through their sexuality, their seductiveness, their population growth—they breed like rabbits. But they may also be construed as childlike and innocent, presexual. That is, both adult (parental) and child (sibling) sexual character are attributed to them.

3. The societies these people compose are imagined as either female dominated (matriarchal) or laced with female influence and power. Their women, while openly sexual and very sensuous, are also overbearing and intensely caregiving as mothers, exercising an alluring ("mammy"-like) or threatening mother power. (This aspect implies that if a person who is prejudiced against a group constructed in this way has sex with one of these women, it feels like sex with a "fallen" or debased, but compelling, mother figure). The women of this group are often construed in fantasy as phallic women or as women with great breasts.

4. Such people concentrate in lowly laboring positions, because they are serflike or slavelike by nature and can make their livings only from their physical strength. They are artless and unintelligent, without spiritual accomplishments, or with gifts for only nonliterate arts like music. Their men should be tamed into being beasts of burden; their women should be in domestic service or sexual service, or both.

5. They are capable of harm (leaving aside the physical threat that their strength implies) in the medium of traditional magic—curses and uses of plants and animals, witch-doctoring and shamanism, never miracles of technology or invention, never futurology. They deal voodooistically in the production of potency and impotency.

6. Such people have an uncanny feeling for hidden currents of nature, for natural forces; they can guide others—less attuned to nature—through dangers and they can predict in the manner of almanacs. Their insight, however, is primitive and libidinal, and they resemble *idiot savants*. Thus their insight is itself dangerous, susceptible to reeling out of control.

7. People of this sort are often dark, even "black" in color, or else they have (if they constitute an ethnic or class group) physical features distinguishing them clearly from those who are prejudiced against them. Whatever the distinguishing physical characteristics, they are associated in the minds of the hysterically prejudiced with genitals; the distinguishing characteristics are genitalized. When the people in these groups are dark, their skin color marks their inferiority (not as the impurity an obsessional imagines, but as spiritual and moral inferiority). It is their curse, signaling their existence at the margins of the human race: expelled from history (they have no story worth telling) and from culture (they are imagined as illiterate), they reside at the ends of the earth (from which they may, at one time, have been imported toward

the "center" or the metropolis for labor). The curse under which these people are imagined to live is often conceived in sibling terms—they are the people of Ham, they are the benighted brothers in relation to a father or mother figure.

The form that hysterical prejudices take reflects the need that the hysterically prejudiced feel to be sexually powerful and to overcome their feelings of being deprived of sexual gratifications, their jealousy toward others who they think are getting more satisfaction than they are getting. The prejudices express competition and rivalry for pleasure, formulated often in oral terms but most frequently in phallic terms. The victims of hysterical prejudices in one way or another become reduced to their genitals; their genitals are synecdochic. The physical features that distinguish them get drawn into the genitalizing image systems—hair, body hair, skin texture, facial shape, and so forth are taken as signs of their sexuality.[18] The prejudices appear in images and acts of genital domination and, more generally and politically, of mastery and enslavement.

The hysterical prejudices, sexual and sexualized, take quite different forms among men and among women, unlike the obsessional prejudices, which have similar manifestations in men and women. This need for sexual power sometimes connects with the third group of orectic prejudices, the narcissistic, which reflect a need to feel sexually intact, defined, and distinguished, a need to have sexual boundaries intact and sexual organs unattacked. Hysterical prejudices—racism, for example—overlap with sexism when they are aimed at women, and when aimed at women they are often fetishistic, as some forms of narcissistic prejudice are. But the hysterical prejudices emphasize power and potency and convey jealousy as the main emotional current.

There seem to be two main forms for these prejudices: an offensive one that involves cutting another group down or mutilating it, and a defensive one that involves self-inflation and self-enhancement, which may mean either disguise of inadequacy or compensation for inadequacy. These two forms are not usually disconnected. Men who, for example, mutilate a man by castrating him may, in fact or in fantasy, be taking his phallus into their own possession, for their own empowerment. Hysterical prejudices directed at males have to do with finding a supplementary penis. (They share this characteristic with a certain type of homosexuality, latent or manifest, which also involves finding a sup-

plementary penis by finding a buddy or pal who can help out, particularly in defending against dangers of castration. Under certain social
conditions, the buddy or helpmate can be a peasant or lower-class man
or a person of color, a Sancho Panza or a Tonto.)

Obsessional prejudices express striking ambivalence, combining hatred of the Other with love, admiration, or envy. But hysterical prejudices, with all their reversals, reveal striking dynamism. The phallic
power that people prejudiced in this way want they have first to create:
they project it onto or attribute it to a group, and then they strip it away
or steal it. It is not that they simultaneously both love and hate, find
alluring and find repulsive. It is that they cannot live without their others
because from these people they get their power supplement. They are
addicted to these people and therefore far less frequently than obsessionals tend toward genocide. They must feed on their enemies, so they
cannot eliminate them, although in their cruelty they often do kill large
numbers.

Most psychologically minded (not cognitively minded) commentators on white racism think that whites attribute to blacks—particularly
white males to black males—their own sexual wishes; that they simply
project their unacceptable desires onto blacks, who then become the
sexually powerful ones. In fact, this account seems to be only part of
a much more complex story, usually told only by victims.[19] But its motivational level has sometimes been approached by "white sociology,"
as it was by Charles Herbert Stember in a book called *Sexual Racism*
(1976). Stember made one of the few analyses to begin from the guiding psychological assumption that a feeling of *deprivation* subtends
deep, and often violent, hostilities. He used this assumption to argue
that all prejudices are one, conflating, for example, antisemitism and
racism. Disregarding that Allportian direction of his work and his focus
on white men acting against black men, we can see that Stember clearly
asked the key question: What is it that whites—the privileged group—
feel deprived of? In nonplantation, industrialized modern settings,
they may feel threatened to some degree by economic competition
from minority males, but this perception, Stember argues, can hardly
account for the emotional violence of racism. His exploration, then,
depends on another psychological assumption: that male sexuality
(outside stable, loving relationships, that is, in situations of pursuit and
competition) revolves around pleasure in conquest and "defilement"
of the female.

In conquering her, he rips away the mystery and ethereal quality that surrounds her; he brings together the polarized parts, reducing the "higher" [spiritual side of her] to the "lower" [genital part]. To perceive her as experiencing animal pleasure provides a further increment to the defilement experience. This may be more important to the male than ego gratification. A certain amount of satisfaction lies in merely exposing her, demonstrating that she really has sexual parts. Thus the perennial male fascination with nudity and strip tease: seeing the woman so "reduced" is to approach the sensation of sexual conquest itself.[20]

Men are, in Stember's view, degraders of women, they are all the Henry Millers and Norman Mailers of Kate Millett's *Sexual Politics*. Moreover, minority males, if they are able to conquer a majority female, are maximalists of defilement pleasure, because they experience themselves as coming from a socially designated "low" condition to her "high" purity.

The minority male's pleasure in conquest of a woman from the majority group—the black man's pleasure in obtaining a white woman—has an intensity, a charge to it that is unavailable to the white man.[21] A white man conquering a white woman who is above him in class, or who is especially desirable in relation to the prevailing cultural norms of beauty, approximates to the minority male's achievement, but he cannot equal it. The white male's mythological constructions of black male sexuality—the images of Negro phallic power, animal lust, and rapaciousness—signal the jealousy and resentment over the black's defilement pleasure, and they also reflect the white male's anxiety that white women really desire the black's aggressive sexuality. In the cultural web in which interracial sexuality develops, the interplay of projections and perceptions, Stember argues, white women often do respond to the idea or the image of black men as sexually powerful and as powerfully wanting them.

Stember's analysis, depending as it does on the assumption that male sexuality inherently manifests the desire to conquer and defile (while female sexuality, accordingly, manifests the desire to be taken, to be conquered), focuses on male assessments of who gets most *defilement* pleasure. All men aim for and compete for the woman—the majority woman—who is constructed as having the most purity to loose, while relegating to second place all other women, especially those of the minority. This analysis too narrowly makes one kind of jealousy (over defilement pleasure) subtend the whole phenomenon of racism or even of prejudice in general, but it does point to the domain of jealousy and rivalry that had been identified, for example, by the psychoanalyst Richard Sterba in his descriptions of the male white racists he analyzed, the ones who dreamed of Negroes taking sustenance from the mother like sibling rivals or besting the dreamer in his pursuit of the mother like a paternal rival.

It is not necessary to assume that the pleasure racists feel deprived of is defilement pleasure. Hysterically prejudiced people recreate their family configurations in social terms, with the victims of their prejudices playing the roles of the ones who got more erotic goods generally or substituting for the mother (for men and women) or the father (for women), who was the source, the font, of erotic goods. They feel deprived of preoedipal and oedipal satisfactions, and they construct ways to get these that circumvent or avoid violating taboos upon such satisfactions. For the hysterically prejudiced, the others represent the family displaced downward—deidealized, rather than idealized as in the "family romance" that Freud described, where mothers and fathers become queens and kings, figures of great power and grace.[22] Since the others are displaced downward, which means out of the domain that falls under the incest taboo, they can become servants or slaves.

Both men and women use splitting devices to avoid oedipal anxieties in their sexual relationships. Men commonly split their love choices, taking as lovers only women who are low-born, immoral, dirty, or other in racial or ethnic terms, that is, women who do not resemble the moral and pure mother, high-born in fact or in fantasy, whose successor they take as a wife. With women who resemble the mother, as the wives they choose must be, such men are distant, even sexually impotent. This kind of split would be reinforced in societies that also reinforce the theory common among children that sex is something dirty and immoral involving a violent assault upon a virginal, disinvolved mother by a rapacious, hurtful father.[23] The choice would also be reinforced in prejudice-ridden societies which already have a great supply of images of rapacious, hypersexual others.

Males who imagine the pure mother as an assault victim in sex avoid assaulting a maternal figure, but they do not avoid assaulting a non-maternal woman. Indeed, such an assault can seem legitimate and in accord with their identification with their fathers.[24] They can, however, even more thoroughly absolve themselves of guilt for their desires by denying that they are in any way engaging in the satisfaction of their desires: all sexual behavior is attributed to the hypersexual others—*they* are the paternal attackers, or *they* are the male adolescents with sexual desire on their minds. Males then view males of the lower group as competitors for the mother, in the form of siblings or paternal figures, and they punish them. They administer direct punishment to the competitors' bodies, often in the form of sexual mutilation. But they can also assault their competitors' sexual prerogatives indirectly, exercising control over lower groups by breaking up their families. This indirect technique, so central a feature of plantation racism in the American South, keeps lower men away from both the pure women and their own women. Creating all-male labor units or isolating lower males in institutions like prisons has a similar effect, particularly if the lower males will be sexually humiliated in those institutions (for example, by being raped in prison).[25] Appropriating money for prison building is one of the most acceptable current American forms of racism. But lower men can also be humiliated by rape of their women or abuse of their children.

Girls do not frequently have the opposite of the hysterical male's sexual theory, which would explain sex as a violent act by a mother on a father, although images of females biting or cutting off penises are certainly reported in analytic cases and occasionally in sensational court cases. Usually, they seem to have the same fantasy as the male child. They also imagine that a dirty father rapes or assaults a pure mother (and a violent mother can, then, be a revenger for violence suffered). If they identify primarily with their mothers, they set themselves up in fantasy as women who are raped or assaulted by hypersexual men. In the purest racist variant on this fantasy, the attacker is a man who is quite different in appearance from the father, so the father's identity is protected and the incestuous nature of the fantasy concealed. The substitutive male must be without refinement, education, professional status, or any other characteristic that would disqualify him for the role of sexual attacker and rapist, pure and simple. He must not have any "good father" characteristics. The criterion for selecting will be, as Malcolm X noted in describing this racist variant in his *Autobiography*, "the blacker the better." Women whose inclinations and identifications are masculine or bisexual—as is often the case among hysterical characters—respond as boys do to their parents' sexual lives. Out of their own bisexual tendencies, they identify with both figures in this scene. They identify with their fathers and treat their lovers, who must be other—immoral, impure, low-born, unlike the mother—as though they were feminine, whether they are male or female. Competitors, too, in the form of black women—construed as women who have phallic power or as women who are sexually loose and easily able to command male attention—are drawn into the racist image system.

People prone to the hysterical prejudices organize their lives into separate spheres; they lead, more or less egregiously, double lives. They are, for example, men who like to live in what they think of as normal family contexts, with wives and children toward whom they behave conventionally well. They act as models—insofar as they are able—of family rectitude and often of religious conservatism. At the same time, they have another life in a semisecret club or organization where they are wild, unrestrained, bound to and energized by other men. These clubs do not, like the secret societies that obsessionally prejudiced people frequent, provide purification and release from guilt: they assuage anxiety about potency. Some men of this sort, who are bisexual or homosexual, acknowledge and need to acknowledge the homoeroticism of their club, but most heterosexual men insist upon the buddy-buddy nature of their group. Other men locate their second life among women, with prostitutes or concubines, whom they visit sometimes alone and sometimes in the company of other men. These women are generally of a lower, darker, or subservient group. Armies often serve the nonmilitary function in societies of structuring into late-adolescent men's lives both the male club and the organized use of "other" women—and the army unit is, then, the model for clubs ex-servicemen establish later in their lives. Whether the second life takes place with men or with women or with both, it enhances potency. This enhancement may involve simply the vicarious power of being with men who are powerful, but usually it also entails both power with women (which may mean power over women or power by being with women who have phallic power) and power to take women away from other men. For white men, the purpose is especially well served if the women are women of color and the men who are bested are men of color to whom great power has been attributed.

Women who have lived in conditions that made it impossible for them to divide their lives into a private sphere and a public (or at least nondomestic) sphere have divided it within the household sphere permitted them. Often their unrestrained life has been imaginary or vicarious, constructed with the aid of stories or (in literate societies) romance novels or (in advanced technological contexts) radio and television soap operas. The other life may center on an adulterous affair (with a man or a woman). Or it may be largely unconscious, a matter of fantasy, sometimes irrupting in illness—especially hysteria among the mental illnesses. When women have had people in their domestic service, their second life has organized around the second family, either in terms of an adult sexual and illicit affair in regressive forms such as being a "baby"—a child—to a lower-class or colored maternal figure. Darker or lower-class women can also be construed by women who are hysterically prejudiced as caretakers more available than their own mothers were—available for hire, but not for too much hire, too much salary, lest they seem to be giving their care only for money and thus to be failing the fantasy that they are more warmly and spontaneously mothering than the biological mother. The same kinds of dynamics can be built up with male and female servants who are not people of color— the second life can be played out along class lines alone, for example, in Lady Chatterly's manner—but it is heightened when color prejudice is at work.[26]

The most obvious mental characteristic of the hysterically prejudiced is hypocrisy. Their hypocrisies run along the lines of their psychic splittings and repressions. Gunnar Myrdal emphasized the hypocritical nature of American racism, its "shameful shortfall" between the American Creed of equal opportunity and flouting of that creed, but he was not the first to make the point. Samuel Johnson, for example, had responded to the revolutionary calls for liberty emanating from the South in 1776 with the wry query: "How is it that we hear the loudest yelps for liberty among the drivers of Negroes?" Racists entertained and presented contradictory convictions without conscious hypocrisy. Post–Civil War segregationists alternately insisted, for instance, both that Negroes preferred segregation and that it was necessary to use the harshest means to keep them segregated. The closer discussion came to the most anxiety-producing topic, miscegenation, the more irrational the arguments became. John Morgan, who urged so vehemently that all whites innately felt "race aversion" for all Negroes then said that white men could modify their aversion when it came to Negro women of "wealth, character, abilities, accomplishment and position" or when moved by considerations "of a baser sort."[27] White men, that is, can have high class Negro women for high-class reasons and low-class ones for low

(sexual) reasons. But white women, he insisted, would never counte-
nance marriage between a white female and a Negro male: "the snows
will fall from heaven in sooty blackness, sooner than the white woman
of the United States will consent to the maternity of negro families."
The fundamental hierarchicalism of the prejudice is apparent in the
metaphor—heaven must be white, as the white woman must be immaculate; interbreeding can only go down.

To my knowledge, no one has done an analysis of what might be called
the hysterical style comparable to Hofstader's analysis of the paranoid
style. But many of the studies of "mass psychology" that stem from the
work of Gustave Le Bon actually analyze the mass psychology of hysteria
and not mass psychology in general. This tradition does not fit the
obsessional crowd, which is chained to the charisma of a leader who
provides the meaning of life, the logic, the value system, the images
of purity and cleansing, the mystical channeling and ordering that
eliminate uncertainty and doubt. Obsessionals march in file and speak
with one voice, or, when they go wild, attack shops and other economic
sites, while hysterical characters surge, pulse, behave orgiastically, build
to climaxes, and want bodies. Obsessionals in a crowd happily loose
their individuality and all the guilt that individuality entails, while hysterics gain power, grow bigger, feel themselves swell up to the macrocosm of the crowd. The hysterically prejudiced are potential rioters. And
their readiness for riot behavior reflects the greatest social fear of the
hysterically prejudiced: that the ones who are to be kept in their places,
kept down, low, will revolt. They construe their victims' leaders as fire-
brands, men who whip up passions and advocate violence (including
the violence of rape). Violence against the victim mob and its leaders
is phallic and aimed at passions—they should be shot, bludgeoned with
sticks, cattle-prodded, genitally mutilated. Then the violence between
groups becomes imitative, as hysteria is imitative: an eye for an eye, a
beating for a beating, a white body dragged from a truck in reply to a
black one that was dragged from a car (as in the Los Angeles rioting of
1992 in response to police officers' being acquitted of beating Rodney
King).
    The hysterical prejudices are not manifest, as the obsessional preju-
dices are, in activities marked by efficiency, precision, pedantry, and
selflessness. Supremacists in the hysterical style are more likely to be
vulgar and exhibitionistic; they are the id speaking and commanding

attention. They do not invent exquisite tortures, models of engineering and know-how, or design assembly lines for death; they use the phallic weapons they use for hunting to go after people they have classed as animals. They bring home trophies; they do not destroy the evidence of their violence. Their heroes are wild men, social mavericks, frontiersmen, tricksters who are able to heat people up and create enthusiasms, but they may also need to present themselves in their split manner as gentlemen, men of tradition and refinement, who have to switch into another mode—a disguise, like the Klansman's hood—to act on their prejudices against the lower others.

The aggressive actions in groups of the hysterically prejudiced are clues to the social need that these prejudices fill, as their sexual behavior reveals their individual psychic needs. Psychologically, as noted, the victims fill the need for alternative families—both for substitute oedipal partners who are parental but not familial, not under the incest ban, and for substitute siblings who can be despised without harm to real siblings. But socially the victims supply the need for a specific kind of labor: they support from below the life and the lifestyle of those who rule over them. They do "despised but essential labor," labor the prejudiced will not do themselves because doing it would make them feel lowly, beastly, and unclean.[28] They do whatever the rulers, by reason of religion, custom, and mores consider dirty and fleshly—caring for the sick, carrying corpses, slaughtering animals, removing or cleaning any kind of garbage.[29] This is obvious when the victims are domestics, but it also applies when they are channeled into menial service and custodial jobs and even when they are relegated to labor that literally or figuratively keeps them low—under loads, bent over, in the bilge, down the mine shaft—or like beasts of burden. As hysterical prejudices grow from the limited, familial settings (like plantations) where they have their origins out into broader arenas, the victim group is made into not a laboring class but a caste. From a caste, members cannot rise, cannot escape—they are never to be anything but the lower part.

The term "caste" has had a complicated social scientific history, full of disputes about whether it should be reserved for the most elaborate caste system in the world, the one on the Indian subcontinent, where there is an "untouchable" ultrapariah caste but also a vast network of groupings that are sealed off by descent regulations and endogamy. The most illuminating way to use the term, it seems to me, is to follow Pierre van den Berghe and distinguish caste societies—whole societies divided into rigid endogamous groupings, the two clearest instances being India and apartheid South Africa—and societies containing one or more stigmatized, endogamous caste groups. Among the latter would be Japan (the Burakumin) and the United States (the African Americans). In both caste societies and societies with castes, the caste strictures—the stigmatization, the laws forbidding marriage out of the caste—function to keep the caste available for its labor. Again, the hysterically prejudiced do not, like the obsessionally prejudiced, think in terms of eliminating their target group; they need them. And they dissolve the barriers of caste with the greatest reluctance—as the history of the Civil Rights movement shows, and as the current debates over affirmative action, which is a caste-breaking strategy, show again.

I want to turn very briefly to a historical reconstruction comparable to the one Hannah Arendt offered for European antisemitism—that is, one neither psychoanalytic nor Marxist but focused on political factors—to demonstrate with the specific example of American racism how people with hysterical prejudices become organized and their prejudices institutionalized.

C. Vann Woodward's *The Strange Career of Jim Crow* (first published in 1957) presents vividly the contours of American—particularly Southern—racism. From his account, the formula emerges that racism takes different ideological and institutional forms according to the degree of the racists' fear of their victims' revolutionary capacity. On plantations, the lives of the planters and their slaves were governed by house rules and etiquettes (rather than formal caste laws) that allowed for great intimacy and contact within a context of total authority and rigid hierarchy, which was enforced in some cases with rapacious or punitive violence against individuals. Episodic slave rebellions occurred, but after Emancipation fear of revolution escalated:

> The temporary anarchy that followed the collapse of the old discipline produced a state of mind bordering on hysteria among Southern white people. The first year a great fear of black insurrection and revenge seized many minds, and for a longer time the conviction prevailed that Negroes could not be induced to work without compulsion. Large numbers of temporarily uprooted freedmen roamed the highways, congested in towns or cities, or joined the federal militia. In the presence of these conditions the provisional [state] legislatures established by President Johnson in 1865 adopted the notorious Black Codes.

Some of them were intended to establish systems of peonage or apprenticeship resembling slavery.[30]

When this period of anarchy wound down and order was restored—at the expense of Negro employment opportunity—the Black Codes lapsed. Negroes, whose votes were needed by vying political parties, entered into the political life of the recovering South, often in alliance with hard-pressed lower-class whites of the Populist movement. But, after a prolonged agrarian depression in the 1880s and 1890s, a period of economic frustration and social deterioration, support for Negro educational and political goals withered and white fear of the Negroes increased, often artificially whipped up: "In Georgia . . . a sensation press played up and headlined current stories of Negro crime, charges of rape and attempted rape, and alleged instances of arrogance, impertinence, surly manners, or lack of prompt and proper servility in conduct. Already cowed and intimidated, the race was falsely pictured as stirred up to a mutinous and insurrectionary pitch."[31] "Negro atrocity stories" and stories of how the Populist movement was giving Negroes a real political base helped create the atmosphere in which mob violence against Negroes escalated and lynching increased in the South.

> In their panic over the [Populist] rebellion, the New South leaders relinquished their last claim to responsibility linked to the Old Order. Abandoning their commitment to moderation in racial policy, they turned politics over to racists. In the name of white solidarity and one-party loyalty, they disenfranchised the Negro and many lower class whites and unleashed the fanatics and lynchers. In their banks and businesses, in their clubs and social life, as well as in their inner political councils, they moved over to make room for increasing delegations of Snopeses. In place of the old sense of community based on an ordered if inflexible hierarchy, they substituted a mystique of kinship, or clanship, that extended the familial ambit spuriously to all whites—and to such Negroes as had mastered and sedulously practiced the Sambo role to perfection.[32]

As white racism grew more strident around 1900, and used social Darwinist theories to provide its rationalization, Jim Crow laws for separation of the races in everything from public waiting rooms and toilets to sports arenas were passed throughout the South. Disenfranchisement was pushed further and further, over only feeble objections by federal authorities pledged to uphold the Constitution. Whereas the postwar

Black Codes had been defensive, the segregationist, supremacist legislation of the turn of the century was ferociously aggressive: it did more
than establish a caste—it pushed the caste down. A commentator noted
in 1911: "Its spirit is that of an all-absorbing autocracy of race, an animus
of aggrandizement which makes, in the imagination of the white man,
an absolute identification of the stronger race with the very being of the
state."[33]

This was the moment in the politics of American race relations when
racism, particularly as practiced by an alliance of gentry and "Sno-
peses," moved from being a weapon in party battles to being state doctrine. Such a sequence of caste formation followed by state racism never
came about, by contrast, in Brazil, where the slave population was absorbed to a degree by "miscegenation" into the white population. Although many Afro-Brazilians were and are in the laboring classes, and
racism certainly exists, the racial interbreeding that was so extensive
during the plantation period never ceased, never fell under a caste ban.
In South Africa, however, the equivalent of the sequence of caste formation and state racism was accomplished in 1948. The Afrikaaner Nationalist Party, an ethnic party, won the national elections, ending forty
years of coalition governments in which Afrikaaner and English whites
had shared the political and economic profits of rule over a majority
African population, which the whites had restricted through a "migra-
tory labor system" to domestic service and dirty jobs in industry, particularly diamond and gold mining.

The South African example shows clearly the direct relationship that
exists between the severity of miscegenation legislation and caste creation and the severity of the later state racism. As European settlers
moved into South Africa, a period of sanctioned miscegenation produced the mulatto group known as the Cape Colored. But this came to
an end in the late nineteenth century, with the ascendancy of the Boers'
Calvinist morality and the Boers' fear of being populationally overwhelmed by the Bantu tribes. A resounding rhetoric of damnation
backed the rigid ban on miscenegation. Later, the apartheid policy hammered existing colonial discriminations—in landholding, in labor, and
especially in marriage law (an Immorality Act had been passed in
1927)—into a system of rigid and impermeable barriers under state
administration. Enfranchisement was limited for Black and Colored African men, first to electing minimal white representation and then to
electing African representation to a puppet parliament, while for Afri-

can women it was denied. The state gained totalitarian powers of control by arrest, seizure, detention without trial, censorship, exiling, and so forth, while it practiced murder and torture with impunity.

The Afrikaaner minority, imbued with a sense of itself as an indigenous, not a colonial European or settler, group—"the white tribe of Africa"—celebrated itself as a long-sufffering and heroic, knightly, family or clan, tested against the perils of life at the extremity of a vast primitive continent. Afrikaaners shared the conviction that the African majority would, if not tightly controlled, rise up and destroy or force into emigration all the whites. Their aspiration was not—like the Nazis'—to expand across the continent or to become supranational; and they had no equivalent of contiguous Aryan populations to unite with. Like the American Southerners', their conception was upward, vertical, hierarchical. They saw no limits to their supremacy or to the debasement of the nonwhite castes (Colored, Asian) and particularly the African caste they created. Despite (or perhaps because of) the presence of many antisemites among the Afrikaaners, the party did not stop at appropriating for the Afrikaaner people the biblical designation "chosen people."

The American and South African cases, particularly if considered in contrast to Brazil, show the key sociopolitical moment in the development of racism: responding to a deteriorating economic situation and fearing the overthrow of the "natural" hierarchy, the racist group expands its political base and becomes aggressive about turning the state into a national household in which the dominative relation between masters and servants is legally reestablished on a grand scale. The nation is the biggest plantation; patriotism is the racism of the mythic family. The white supremacists find each other; they feel themselves kindred, a people.

## World-Historical Narcissism

The narcissistic prejudices are, fundamentally, prejudices against reality. They deny, disavow, or attempt to alter what is, and they repudiate facts, specifically facts of difference. Ethnocentrism builds on a narcissistic foundation in the sense that an ethnocentric person measures all others by the standard of himself or herself, a standard generalized to "us," the identity group, the group identity. But ethnocentrism also underlines and accentuates differences—it says *we* are not *them*—and relieves the in-group of any intragroup hatreds by displacing those outward. Comparison is desired, and the resulting negative image of *them* is relished; comparison is not, in and of itself, something threatening or frightening that must, ultimately, be abolished. The narcissistic prejudices, by contrast, deny differences, even though they may, in their behavioral manifestations, seem to accentuate or exaggerate differences. If a difference can be properly exaggerated—the Other pushed beyond the pale of humanity—then the difference is, in effect, denied, as the Other is no longer in the realm of comparison.

A description of how narcissists construct their others cannot be made in the same way as descriptions of how hysterical and obsessional characters construct their others. Those characters assert salient characteristics of appearance or mentality, declaring *they* are primitively sexual, or *they* are shrewdly avaricious. But the narcissist ultimately denies defining characteristics. So the narcissist must accomplish the trick Søren Kierkegaard captured in a joke in *The Concept of Irony*—he must portray an elf wearing the magic cap that makes him invisible. This group construction is complex: it asserts difference in order to deny it and negate the others. By contrast, the obsessional's others are both envied and despised, loved and hated, so that the obsessional must resort to a literal and brutal negation if the tension is ever to be stilled. And, by further contrast, the hysterical person's others are rivals for love who have been loved and may be loved again, so that the hysterical person must, to still the tension, split himself or herself. But the narcissist denies first—denies reality—and then has to retreat to assertion of difference because reality will not be denied. The negation that succeeds denial must be indirect, perhaps symbolic. It is accomplished in the realm of what I have called mental or cultural narcissism.

These distinctions imply for my analysis that one cannot make a general sketch of the group characteristics of the narcissistically prejudiced person's victims. I am going to begin, instead, with a historical approach, using one of the most provocative, wide-ranging, synthetic works in the rapidly growing, scintillating library of women's history. Gerda Lerner's *The Creation of Patriarchy* (1986) focuses on the societies and civilizations growing and intertwining in the Near East between about 3000 and 600 B.C.E., the period during which, she argues, a complex process brought about the establishment of patriarchy. Like Arendt's *Origins of Totalitarianism* and Woodward's *Strange Career of Jim Crow*, this is a theoretically self-conscious history with many dimensions—economic, social, and to some degree psychological—but with a guiding thread of political analysis, as its trajectory comes to rest on the process of state formation.

Gerda Lerner, one of the pioneering historians of women who began to reshape her discipline in the 1970s, realized quite clearly that, although studying the origins of patriarchy requires avoiding patriarchy's rationalizations, it also requires clearing the path of feminism's compensatory theories. She understood that feminist visions of a primary matriarchal period in human history had been created for the sake of the future, guided by the conviction that if matriarchies had existed, then patriarchy was not a natural, inevitable, incontrovertible condition. There is as yet no anthropological or archaeological evidence for either a particular matriarchal society or a matriarchal period, Lerner argued, although it seems clear that many different kinds of social arrangements have existed and currently exist that could be described as matrifocal, matrilocal, or matrilineal, and that some women have been consorts to the powerful and thereby held in high esteem in certain societies and under particular circumstances. But women have not, in any yet known place or time, ruled, in the sense of having political power over males, making the decisions, or, most fundamentally, formulating the rules governing sexual conduct and reproduction.

What can be said confidently from the anthropological and archaeological record is that the most egalitarian relations between men and women, those of a "separate but equal" sort, exist in conditions of what Lerner calls "economic interdependency." In hunter-gatherer societies, "A woman must secure the services of a hunter in order to be assured of a meat supply for herself and her children. A hunter must be assured of a woman who will supply him with subsistence food for the hunt and in the event the hunt is unsuccessful . . . Such hunting/gathering tribes stress economic co-operation and tend to live peacefully with other tribes. Competition is ritualized in contests of singing and athletics but is not encouraged in daily living."[34] Generally, only in horticultural societies, often located in ecological areas where animal breeding is not feasible, have women made decisive contributions to the economy. But even under such circumstances women have not had controlling political power.

In hunter-gatherer and horticultural societies, women had and have total responsibility for infant care. As Lerner and many others have argued, this responsibility marks the first sexual division of labor. The

necessity for it derives from the needs of human infants, who, among
all the animals, are the ones least equipped at birth for independent
survival. Human mothers give birth when their infants are at a greater
stage of immaturity than those of other primate mothers; they bear
naked babies in need of constant warming, babies with the relatively
small heads—and thus brains—necessary to accommodate the birth ca-
nals of upright, two-footed women. The human brain does more developing outside the womb than that of other animals, so it is more susceptible to influence from its extra-uterine social world, but it is also
less able perceptually to discriminate at birth between "I" and "other."
Mother and infant compose, as psychoanalytic theory has always postulated, a symbiotic unit. The mother has complete power. And, for the
sake of a tribe, living in harsh and precarious conditions, letting the
mother exercise this power exclusively is the route most conducive to
group survival.

Lerner notes, quite rightly, that the conditions of life and sexual division of labor in hunter-gatherer and horticultural societies would have
fostered both women's competence in their domains of reproduction
and cultivation and a sense in all, women and men, of awe at female
reproductive and mothering power. It is this awe, she thinks, that is
expressed in the multitudes of molded, carved, and painted images of
females—mother-goddesses—that have been found all around the Mediterranean basin. "The life-giving mother truly had power over life and
death. No wonder that men and women, observing this dramatic power
of the female, turned to the veneration of Mother-Goddesses" (p. 40).
And it is such awe, Lerner reasons, that would have made it more difficult for boys than girls to find or be provided with ways to separate
themselves from the mother's power. In the modern, industrialized,
nuclear family described by Nancy Chodorow and other feminist interpreters of psychoanalytic theory, boys separating from their mothers are
socially empowered to establish their identities by disidentification,
while girls, less separated, are encouraged to engage in the "reproduction of mothering." Lerner's hypothesis, both social and psychological,
is that in the earliest societies the situation was reversed.

> In civilized society it is girls who have the greatest difficulty in ego
> formation. I would speculate that in primitive society that burden must
> have been on boys, whose fear and awe of the mother had to be trans-
> formed by collective action into identification with the male group . . .
> The evidence from surviving primitive societies shows many different

ways in which the sexual division of labor is structured into societal institutions, which bond young boys to males: sex-segregated preparation for initiation rites, membership in same-sex lodges and participation in same-sex rituals are just some examples. Inevitably, big game hunting bands would have led to male bonding, which must have been greatly strengthened by warfare and the preparation necessary to turn boys into warriors. . . The ego formation of the individual male, which must have taken place within a context of fear, awe, and possibly dread of the female, must have led men to create social institutions to bolster their egos, strengthen their self-confidence, and validate their sense of worth.   (p. 45)

The institutions for dividing labor and creating male bonding established within the contexts of hunter-gatherer and horticultural societies were, most historians and anthropologists agree, crucially different from those that came about in the next developmental stage, with sedentariness and agriculture. A process began when militarism came to be characteristic of expanding hunter-gatherer tribes, increasingly engaged in intertribal warfare: warrior groups within tribes exercised authority over women and children and also over other men within their tribes. When large agricultural enterprises became the norm, this authority grew into control over exchanges of women between tribes. "Exchange of women" between tribes is the phenomenon that Claude Lévi-Strauss and many who have followed him have identified as the first and main social cause of female subordination.

The exchange of women between tribes signifies that women had come to be recognized as a tribal resource by a ruling elite. Women became, then, a kind of property—the model property if not the first private property, the basis for future forms of private property.[35] The more women a tribe had, the more it was able to reproduce and extend its labor force with children and adults. In the emergent agricultural societies, the size of the labor force was key, and increases in production, along with stabilization of production over seasonal changes and the possibility of surplus production, depended completely on increases in reproduction. So it was women rather than men who were exchanged between tribes; men had rights in women that women did not have in men.

Out of the expansion and slow reorganization of agricultural communities came the "urban revolution," the rise of cities out of agricultural centers and the rise of city-states out of cities. Vast processes of class division—usually along the lines of farmers and herders versus managers, who were temple or priestly elites—and vast enterprises of resource control had a profound impact on women's roles. Lerner agrees with anthropologists like Rayna Rapp who highlight the conflicts that came about during the urban revolution between older forms of kinship organization and newer forms of class organization: "In prestate societies, total social production was organized through kinship. As states gradually arose, kinship structures got stripped and transformed to underwrite the legitimacy of more powerful politicized domains. In this process . . . women were subordinated with (and in relation to) kinship" (p. 55). Of course, the women of elite, and eventually royal, families, had privilege within early state contexts. They were often their husbands' deputies or emissaries to neighboring powers. But their sexual roles and reproduction were strictly—more and more strictly as written codes came into being—controlled.

Women without privilege—either women of the lower classes or women acquired by war and conquest—were completely regulated to serve the expanding new production mode. The subordinate status of women, Lerner argues, served as the model for another subordination institution that came into being with the pastoralism and agriculture that gave rise to cities and state formations—slavery.

> The "invention of slavery" involves the development of techniques of permanent enslavement and of the concept, in the dominant as well as in the dominated, that permanent powerlessness on the one side and total power on the other are acceptable conditions of social interaction . . . Historical evidence suggests that [the] process of enslavement was first developed and perfected upon female war captives; that it was reinforced by already known practices of marital exchange and concubinage.   (p. 78)

In the intertribal wars of developing agricultural communities, men were generally not taken captive. Male captives require large investments of manpower and resources for their control and supervision, so male slavery presupposes either already existing large labor forces or techniques for control other than human guards, or both. Females, more physically vulnerable, bereft of any of their own males who might try to free them, removed from their homes, dishonored with respect to their families of origin, and sexually abused or raped and forced to bear their captor's children, could be brought into the despairing, hopeless condition that led to acceptance of their slavery.

The techniques developed for control over slave females, which centered on asserting sexual prerogatives and using sexual violence provided the model for male slavery when that developed. A male slave could be, it was discovered, deprived of his sense of his own autonomy by being abused, by suffering the abuse and rape of his own women by his captors, by being separated from them, having his family life destroyed, his children taken away. Humiliation, in other words, was understood to be a matter of symbolic castration. "By subordinating women of their own group and later captive women, men learned the symbolic language in which to express dominance and create a class of psychologically enslaved persons" (p. 82). As the institution of slavery developed, literal castration, too, was understood to be symbolically a womanization.

> Castration as a form of punishment for crimes and, later, as a means of fitting slaves for harem service, was widespread in ancient China and Mesopotamia. The practice led to the development of political eunuchism in China, Persia, ancient Rome, Byzantium, Egypt, Syria and Africa. [It] illustrates the need for the visible marking and marginalization of persons in order to designate them as permanent slaves, and [shows] the use of sexual control in order to reinforce and perpetuate a person's enslavement.   (p. 82)

Techniques of subordination, resting, ultimately, on techniques for controlling sexuality and reproduction, were a—if not the—*sine qua non* of the growth of states from their archaic forms into centralized kingships and eventually empires. Control over women and slaves was exercised within patriarchal families, which were organized into the grander patriarchal family of the state.

> From its inception, the archaic state was organized in such a way that the dependence of male family heads on the king or the state bureaucracy was compensated for by their dominance over their families. Male family heads allocated the resources of their society to their families the way the state allocated the resources of society to them . . . From the second millennium B.C. forward control over the sexual behavior of citizens has been a major means of social control in every state society. Conversely, class hierarchy is constantly reconstituted in the family through sexual dominance. Regardless of the political or economic system, the kind of personality which can function in a hierarchical system is created and nurtured within the patriarchal system.   (p. 216)

In *The Creation of Patriarchy* Lerner, drawing on the work of many scholars, has shown how the social and legal arrangements for subordinating women were woven into the foundations of the archaic states of the Near East. They were elaborated in those states' structures but also rationalized and extended in the medium of their culture creations. This long era of state formation was also the period—the German philosopher Karl Jaspers called it the Axial Age—in which the major civilizations of the Near East (but also of India and China) produced the philosophical and religious systems that have, ever since, generally shaped their descendants' cultures and specifically shaped their understandings of gender. A vast transition has been mapped: from cultural production in which mother-goddesses figured prominently; to polytheistic religions in which female deities with specialized sexual and reproductive functions appeared as companions and complements to male deities with specialized "public" functions (gods of war, of craft, of seas and shipping, and so forth); and finally to systems in which a chief patriarchal deity rules, as first among equals or, in the Hebrew religion, as *monos*. Monotheism, as it developed among the Hebrews, brought with it what Lerner calls "the revolutionary idea of intolerance toward other gods and cults," particularly those associated with fertility. Periodic prophetic revivals during the two hundred year history of the kingdom of Israel led to persecutions against the cults of Baal and Asherah. "The bull cult was outlawed, and the concept of fertility was more firmly affixed to Yahweh by Hoseah's metaphor, which transposed the covenant idea by turning it into Yahweh's marriage with Israel, the bride. The prophets, in their inspired preaching, equated the sinfulness of Israel with 'whoring.' Thus patriarchal sexual metaphors became firmly embedded in religious thought" (p. 161).

Gerda Lerner tracked across two and a half millennia a process in which the subordination of women became first the foundation of family life with its division of labor along sexual lines; then the constitutive and exemplary domain of legally codified and regulated, state-sanctioned control over reproducing and producing (slave) populations; and finally the referent and reason for vast religious and metaphysical systems. She detailed a process, to put it summarily, of accumulation and layering: from the paterfamilias, to patriarchy, to patriarchalism; from the private to the public to the cosmic; from body narcissism to cultural narcissism. In psychosocial terms, patriarchal family, state, and religious systems are the manifestations of male narcissism, which dictates that there shall be no sexual difference, that reproductive activity is, essentially, ultimately, male activity.

This historical process provided and continues to provide the social matrix within which a similar process is recapitulated individually. Recognition of sexual difference, which involves recognition of the natural division of reproductive roles, is refused: she cannot be not-us; her awesome life-giving, pleasuring power must be appropriated, enchained, made dependent, restored to the "narcissistic milieu," made once again part and parcel of male omnipotence. The fantasy of her as phallic that was once incorporated into treasuries of stone and terra-cotta goddesses, hard flesh that can be handled, is translated into more abstract and disguised modes. She, for example, is imagined as made of the flesh of man, the rib of Adam. She is a phallus, she has a phallus, he is her phallus. When, under the weight of familial organization, her difference does not disappear, it is controlled legally, exploited, and then, when even that repression does not silence the difference, the male is made the solitary divinity, the ultimate source of all creativity and reproductivity, the universal category. As the male is universalized, she is metaphysically erased. In individual terms, the process is denial, repression, reaction formation, more reaction formation. When the narcissistic system breaks down, when it will not hold, violence against women results. The desperate effort to control her with beatings, rape, mutilation, and murder, is an effort to restore her again to her state of being no different.

Obsessional prejudices are, ultimately, antistate; they aim at suprastate entities like world conspiracies. People with hysterical prejudices want to universalize "natural" familial hierarchies in the state; they use the state as the institution of the prejudice. *Apartheid* is the logical end of racism, and the racism in a state can be judged by how closely it approximates *apartheid,* by whatever means—economic, social, political, or legal. States are instruments of sexism, as cultural institutions (including religious institutions) can be, and they are imagined by sexists as ultimately in the hands of higher divine or divinized forces "like me." But, while racists imagine the state as a family writ large and seek to use its institutions and laws for keeping their victims down, sexists imagine the state as the ultimate securer of family order and family values, the protector of families.

# 11

## Constructing Ideal Types

In 1971, C. Vann Woodward reflected on the controversy that had grown up around his book *The Strange Career of Jim Crow* and its claim that segregation had really begun not just after the Civil War but at the turn of the century, following a period of confused and acrimonious experimentation in American race relations. Such a controversy could go on and on, he noted, continually sprouting new branches pro or con in relation to a topic like the origins of segregation, which depended on a prior agreement about how to spot—how to define—an "origin." "What is needed," he said, "is a theory, a model, perhaps a typology of race relations that would conceive of the historical problem of segregation not as one of dating origins at a point in linear time but of accounting for the phenomenon in whatever degree it appears."[1]

Woodward observed that some historians have argued that segregation evolves step by step over time—an idea that does not account for its periods of dormancy and outbreak—while others have asserted that it has a cyclical pattern, an idea that leaves all causal questions in abeyance. Some have argued that there is a specific precondition for segregation, namely, industrialization, but this approach does not deal with the opposite evidence, which suggests that industrialization, when it comes to an unindustrialized but racially ordered region—like the American South—takes place along racial lines. The variety of theories simply reinforced Woodward's feeling that the more appealing models or theories were comparative and typological. He himself made some steps in this direction, drawing on Max Weber's reflections on *Idealtypen* and the work of sociologists and anthropologists, but in 1971 typologies were not in favor in the social sciences and they have been even less so in the deconstructionist days since.

A comparative and typological approach to prejudices can, however, meet a number of problems that have beset the study of prejudices since the end of World War II. How can the waxing and waning of prejudices, their changes in form and degree, be accounted for? How can the persistence of prejudices through all these changes be accounted for? In my view each of the major prejudice types—obsessional, hysterical, and narcissistic—has a typical developmental course in psychosocial terms in which ebbs and flows, progressions and regressions, appear predictably for reasons that can be formulated. Each of the prejudice types has junctures at which it becomes especially dangerous, either in terms of violence or in terms of deeper entrenchment in the social and political fabric of a society. And each has a particular kind of resistance to change or eradication. We cannot consider what is to be done about the prejudices without grasping these kinds of patterns.

## Obsessionality Becomes Political

As I noted in reviewing Hannah Arendt's analysis of antisemitism, at two key moments European, and particularly German, antisemitism took its Nazi form and became the ideological centerpiece of Nazi action and aspiration. The first came in the 1880s, when political parties for the first time organized around antisemitic platforms. The second came after World War I, when the antisemitic National Socialist Party aimed at conquest of the state with supranationalist intent, that is, with the intent of destroying the state apparatus and the political realm while becoming—to use the party's own paranoid construction—an international conspiracy. Every group that hated the state could hate the Jews as the perceived owners of the state; the National Socialist Party galvanized and channeled this hatred. Only in the history of Nazism has this second step in the transformation of antisemitism ever been fully taken. It is certainly not the case, as Jean-Paul Sartre wrote right after World War II in *Anti-Semite and Jew,* and as many apprehensive observers of antisemitism during the postwar period have argued, that "antisemitism leads straight to National Socialism."[2] On the contrary, the developmental road of antisemitism resembles a double helix—an intertwining of social and political strands, ethnocentric and orectic, ideological strands, in a spiraling back and forth.

The developmental dynamic of antisemitism—and of the obsessional prejudices generally—involves a legislative or political institutionalization that splits off and may eventually destroy completely a previously existing social relation. An individual obsessional who feels enviously compelled by a love object will be made panicky by his or her love and will split the love feelings off, displace them outward or bury them, erecting on top of them a containment wall of undoing ceremonies, only to be, finally, haunted by the love object, expecting it to come back, imagining it as attacking, usually attacking from the rear. So obsessionals in a society suppress a socially alluring, even fascinating, group living in their midst, in—so to speak—their society's very bowels, its very business and banking innards. All kinds of unacceptable desires are displaced onto this alien group, including the uncomfortable moral strictures that the members of the society chaff under. This group may have been kept at a distance for long periods by social discrimination, but if that distance lessens, if the discrimination gives way to allure and envy, then it has to be put back in place by other means—by political means. The juncture at which antisemitism becomes political and focuses on state hatred compares to the juncture in individual obsessional development represented by the continued influence of the anal stage—the point of depressing loss and disillusionment later becomes the regressive flash point of aggressivity and sadism.

Again, in more psychodynamic terms, the growth of political antisemitism indicates that the love and fascination side of the social ambivalence needs suppressing and the hate side needs enforcing. The political and legal means enforce the hate, legitimate its pursuit, provide the images—like the international conspiracy image—for the hate's enactment. The process has a gendered dimension as well: the most hated and feared ingredient of the obsessionals' gender identity—passivity before an attacking patriarchal figure (which means feminization for males)—is refused by refusing, attacking, the group that embodies that patriarchal assault. At the same time as the threat of being feminized is removed, the hard, tough masculinity and discipline of the fortress society is preserved. I have already described the context in which this whole dynamic unfolds: real or feared economic depression, the generalized feeling throughout the society, across classes, that economic security no longer exists and that the government has contributed to or even brought about the crisis. The fortress of society is being penetrated and undermined.

The key dynamic of obsessional prejudices involves two movements: first, envy-producing allure and closing of social distance followed by social discrimination, followed once again by allure—an oscillation of ambivalence; and, second, a political reaction to these changes in social distance—the less social distance, the more political discrimination or segregation (physical distance) or assault. Political discrimination thus becomes an obsessional ceremonial erected to keep a distance in place, to keep an allure under repression. For its allure, the target group must be blamed and politically branded. This model, obviously, requires arguing (as Arendt did) that social antisemitism, which had throughout the nineteenth century seeped into almost every social grouping in most of Europe, is different from antisemitism that has become political. In European history, the two types of antisemitism have, to her understanding, different roots. They grew out of exactly opposite aspects of Jewish emancipation: "political antisemitism developed because the Jews were a separate body, while social discrimination arose because of the growing equality of the Jews with other groups."[3]

Arendt certainly saw that the two antisemitisms are related, but she argued that their relation is not a matter of degree: social antisemitism does not grow greater and greater until it converts into or produces political antisemitism; social antisemitism is not a prelude to or a rehearsal for political antisemitism. Arendt took it for granted that political equality, when it is achieved, entails an increase in social discrimination among groups in the polity. When groups have lost their political difference, their power difference, they distinguish themselves in the social domain and become socially ethnocentric. "It is because equality demands that I recognize each and every individual as my equal that the conflicts between different groups, which for reasons of their own are reluctant to grant each other this basic equality, take on such terribly cruel forms." This analysis implies that as political antisemitism declines, social antisemitism increases, and vice versa. There is, in short, a relation of inverse proportion between the two, thus the Jews "always had to pay with political misery for social glory and with social insult for political success."

Arendt gave as the most extended example of her formula the situation in France during the Dreyfus Affair, which she presented as a decrease in social discrimination during intense political antisemitism followed by an increase in social discrimination when the outburst of political antisemitism had passed. "The main point about the role of the Jews in this fin de siècle society is that it was the antisemitism of the Dreyfus Affair which opened society's doors to Jews, and it was the end of the Affair, or rather the discovery of Dreyfus' innocence, that put an end to their social glory . . . [Social] interest in the Jews subsided as quickly as did political antisemitism" (p. 118).

As background for this analysis of France in the period of the Dreyfus Affair, Arendt offered an analysis of the Jewish salons in Berlin at the turn of the eighteenth century, before the emancipation of the Jews of Germany began. The partial emancipation achieved between 1807 and 1812, which was equivalent to a decrease in political antisemitism, meant a rise in social antisemitism. This change brought to an end a period of social glory when salon hostesses like Rahel Varnhagen, the biographical subject of Hannah Arendt's first book, had provided meeting places for Jews and Gentiles, aristocrats and middle class intellectuals, scholars and military men, poets and actors. Personality and talent were all that mattered in these milieus, where Jews were treated by Gentiles as harbingers of a new era of humanity, as exemplars of a new humanism in which all distinctions among groups would be submerged. The great mass of Jews who were not exceptions to the norm of Jewish life or exceptional as personalities or talents, were quite unaffected by the largess bestowed on the elite. And the elite, after this brief period of social glory ended, were forced to maintain their exceptional status by exceptional achievements that distinguished them from the mass of their fellow Jews. Social discrimination brought in its train fissures within the Jewish communities.

Mid-nineteenth-century Gentile Berliners developed toward Jews a peculiarly ambiguous attitude, a compound of fascination and exclusion, and German Jewish intellectuals developed a peculiar double consciousness of superiority over ordinary Jews, which meant denial of their community connection, along with accentuation of their Jewish exceptionality. The political progress of emancipation meant nothing to the intellectuals, struck as they were by the social misfortune it brought. Jews were identified and identified themselves less by "race" or religion than by a typical psychological quality: "For them the Jewish question had lost, once and for all, all political significance: but it haunted their private lives and influenced their personal decisions all the more tyrannically. The adage 'a man in the street and a Jew at home' was bitterly realized; political problems were distorted to the point of pure perversion when Jews tried to solve them by means of inner experience and private emotion'' (p. 65).

Nearly a century of bourgeois expansion separated the Berlin salons from the growth of antisemitic parties in the 1870s and 1880s. In Arendt's view, the whole time was most importantly characterized by progressively diminishing attention to public life and to political questions and by progressively increasing boredom and preoccupation with matters private and psychological. The trajectory was fully visible, she held, in the Dreyfus Affair because antisemitism in France was on an earlier schedule than in Germany and in Austria. It never turned completely lethal because it never connected with supranationalism.

The French Jews had been granted political equality in the wake of the Revolution, and thus social antisemitism—the backlash, as it were—was entrenched throughout the nineteenth century rather than building up after the emancipation acts in the period 1807–1812 or after the revolutions of 1848, as happened in Germany. Paris never had the opportunity to be a hub of Jewish sociocultural achievement of the sort that Berlin was from 1890 to 1910. But France was the scene for a smaller and shorter Jewish renaissance with the remission of social antisemitism during the intensely politically antisemitic Dreyfus Affair. Nothing like a salon life occurred again in Germany until after World War I, when Hannah Arendt's generation of young Jews went to German universities in record numbers and received the education that eventually made them so valuable to America when they were forced to emigrate. German political antisemitism after World War I focused on allegations that the Jews had been complicit in Germany's military defeat, as that of the Dreyfus period had focused on accusations that the traitorous Jews had infiltrated France's military.

In Arendt's analytical scheme, the basic distinction between social and political antisemitism correlates with a distinction between crime and vice. In *fin de siècle* France and in post–World War I Germany, the Jews were attacked politically as criminals and military traitors while they were embraced socially as exotic agents of vice. Social fascination with vice fitted completely with the diminished concern for public life that Arendt held to be typical of bourgeois society—''a victory of bourgeois values over the citizen's sense of responsibility.'' The bourgeoisie stayed away from politics, attending to private enterprise and finding vice exciting, particularly in the person of Jews, but also of homosexuals, both groups being viewed as antidotes to boredom and as sources of passion. The mob of déclassé people produced by the bourgeoisie's economic ventures could wish death to the Jews openly, while the bourgeoisie, without objecting to the mob, nonetheless found the Jews fascinating. In Germany, this ambivalence was the bourgeoisie's heritage from the beginning of the nineteenth century, when bourgeois Germans had loved the salon Jews and then rejected them. Arendt speculated that this ambivalence, reinforced during the 1920s, another period of Jewish cultural flourishing, was what later made the bourgeois Germans in their Nazi days so barbaric toward the Jews—they were extirpating part of themselves as they were exterminating the Jews. The Nazis were destroying the remnant of their earlier social acceptance of the Jews in a fury of political antisemitism.

Arendt's formula—where political antisemitism increases, social antisemitism declines, and vice versa—pointed up just what the Jews, and anyone who cared about them, could not see in the historical contexts Arendt studied. They felt most secure in periods of minimal social discrimination, but this security—for example, at the turn of the century—blinded them to the more ominous antisemitism. Conversely, when the Jews felt most anxious, in moments of intensifying social antisemitism, they failed to realize the importance of the political gains that could, in such circumstances, come their way. They did not value political emancipation enough or realize that legal protection was the only protection worth the name.

The kind of distinction that Arendt drew between the lesser of two evils, social antisemitism, and the greater, political antisemitism, is quite foreign not just to the consciousness of the nineteenth- and early-twentieth-century Jews whom she called naive, but to contemporaries who have been taught by the Holocaust never to underestimate what antisemitism can lead to, where its logic points. A paragraph from a memo that Arendt drew up soon after the end of World War II would make most victims of ethnocentric social discrimination shudder: "It should be borne in mind that whether a person does or does not like Jews is of little interest. If, however, somebody maintains 'we fought this war for the Jews,' then his statement assumes importance. The person who declares 'Jews want to dominate the world' is clearly an antisemite; the same is not necessarily true for people who prefer not to share a hotel with Jews, or even declare that Jews are greedy."

In Arendt's view, social discrimination of the sort she noted hardly even qualifies for the title antisemitism, and in practical terms her view implies that if such discrimination appears alone, without political antisemitism in its background, it should basically be ignored. At the very least, it should not distract anyone from the important political signals. Again, no one should assume that social discrimination, gradually heated up, leads to political antisemitism. If such a causal chain did exist, social discrimination would have to be fought full force to prevent its worsening into political antisemitism. The relation between the two, a relation of inverse proportion, actually implies that—to put the matter crudely—social discrimination is not bad in and of itself. The Jews (or any target of obsessional prejudice, I would say) are safer when they are just being snubbed and socially insulted than when people think they are a political force. The closer antisemitism gets to being just another ethnocentrism, the less dangerous it is.[4]

In the prewar twentieth-century American context, the only group organizing around an image of invidious international conspiracy—an obsessional ideology of desire—that had any social and political possibility to become a mass movement appeared in the 1930s. Father Charles Coughlin, who started out as a radical monetary reformer, briefly supported Franklin Roosevelt but then formed the Union Party to make a bid against Roosevelt in the 1936 presidential election. This electoral effort had little success, and Coughlin withdrew. Returning to politics in 1938, working for a nationalist movement on the model of Juan Perón's in Argentina and Getúlio Vargas's in Brazil, Coughlin openly and vehemently preached antisemitism. He argued that the Jews were responsible for the prolonged depression and, in various polls, between 15 and 25 percent of the respondents expressed support for his attacks. But his actual following, which came mainly from the urban working class, poor rural people (many of them Catholics), and the unemployed, remained limited. He did not reach deeply into the lower middle class as the European fascist parties did, but—like Perón and Vargas—stayed tied to his proletarian base.

Interestingly, when asked about his antisemitism, Coughlin admitted that he had learned that "Jew-baiting won't work here. Fascism is different in every country."[5] In fact, antisemitism has never had in the United States anything like the impact on popular politics that it had in Europe. Class position, party commitments, and beliefs or values have been more important in determining political allegiances, and the strong commitment to democratic institutions dampens somewhat the potential for antistate *political* antisemitism to develop. No political emancipation of the Jews specifically fostered political equality and thus increased social antisemitism, and only a relatively weak tradition of social antisemitism exists. Instead of a long history of religious persecutions, we find a history of political protections against religious persecutions.

In American history, moreover, there has been such a strong strain of anti-Negro prejudice that it tends, as I have remarked before, to take up the more sexualized features of antisemitism. Generally, in a highly diversified immigrant society there are so many groups that can be targeted that the generalizing obsessional prejudices quickly become diffuse. As a result, a typically American paranoid style has developed in which the style matters more than the particular target group. There is something like the passion for hatred itself that Sartre (for reasons of his own philosophy) attributed to the antisemite. As the social critic Seymour Martin Lipset reflected in 1962:

> The object of intolerance in America has never been as important as the style, the emotion, the antagonism and envy toward some specified other who is seen as wealthier, more powerful, or, particularly, as a corrupter of basic values. The Jew, like the Wall Street banker, has been a symbol on which the intolerant could hang their need to hate what is different, or what is powerful, more wealthy, or better educated. Basically there is some undefined segment of the population that responds to the need to hate, not to a specific target.[6]

During the Cold War, however, a specific target did come into play. Joseph McCarthy propounded the image of an international Communist conspiracy lodged in Washington. He capitalized on not an existing economic depression but the deep fear of one among the insecure lower and lower middle classes who had lived through the depression and war. In the late 1940s, harangues about domestic Communists in the form of Ivy League elites infiltrating the government appealed to recently marginalized people, those still without political influence although usually registered as Republicans and opposed to the Democratic Party. These were people who were anxious to maintain their visions of upward mobility, their American dreams. Like Father Coughlin, McCarthy garnered support predominantly among the urban and rural lower classes (more among Protestants than Catholics), but he also appealed to small self-employed business people. All of these people, in the years after the depression, were defensively concerned with keeping what they had achieved and resentful of any ideology—like Communism—that they perceived as a threat to their opportunities. In addition, McCarthy's demagoguery could call upon almost two decades' worth of strong anti-Communist feeling in America, when year after year polls showed more than half the respondents wanting the Communist Party outlawed.

Generally, however, historians agree that although the McCarthyites all subscribed to isolationism, anti-communism, and economic conservatism, the most clear common denominator among them was the authoritarian personality, a pronounced intolerance for ambiguity and propensity for bigotry.[7] They needed to hate—in my terms, they needed a blameworthy enemy perceived as attacking them. One sociological study presented the typical McCarthyite as "conformist, agreeing that there are too many 'oddballs' around, that the 'good' American doesn't stand out among his fellow Americans, and that children should not develop hobbies that are rare or unusual . . . He expresses a more misanthropic social outlook, concurring with the statement that 'people are out to cheat you' and that there is 'wickedness, cheating and corruption all about us.' " Among well-educated people, who as a group were less susceptible to McCarthyism than those with grade school educations, the McCarthyites scored high on the authoritarian scales developed by the Adorno group. Jews were not, however, swept into the anti-Communist net by any McCarthy followers other than those who believed that Jews tend to be Communist. Jews served as McCarthy's prominent aides and allies, and many among his followers were willing to support Jewish political candidates. By contrast, the extreme and virulent anti-Communism of the John Birch Society in the 1950s appealed predominantly to *nouveaux riches* concerned to protect America from income taxes, welfare, trade unions—all kinds of conspiratorial institutions judged to be subversive of individual initiative. It had little appeal to the economically deprived and would have remained completely marginal except that its well-heeled Republican backers were able to buy influence for it.

Although the McCarthyites and the Birchers had some political success in cleansing institutions of "un-American" fellow citizens, they had no movement behind them. They had limited impact on the political process, and they could appeal to no frightening dynamic of a hated (and envied, loved) group growing too equal, too intimate, too penetrating. Recently, obsessional prejudice has returned in a new shape with, I think, the same limitations. Political neoconservatism grew in the 1980s, with the usual ingredients of anti-Communism and protectionism for making "fortress America." Japanophobia, really a prejudice against the Asian American middleman minority, surged dramatically. But Japanophobia lacks, as yet, a claim that the Japanese are taking over (rather than just lobbying) the U.S. government, and it has not yet been exploited to the full by political figures who espouse it, like Ross Perot, whose constituency does not yet include a broad spectrum of the masses, the economically depressed and psychologically disillusioned.

The American anti-Communist activities of the 1950s and since did not congeal into movements because they were embedded in a completely novel obsessional phenomenon, one without analogue in European history. The images purveyed by McCarthy and his like of Communists penetrating the government (particularly the State Department) and the universities, were a piece of a much greater, wider American anxiety about the country as a whole being penetrated by Soviet bombs or missiles. After the Japanese bombing of Pearl Harbor, which shattered the idea that America is a land mass protected by two oceans from foreign military penetration, and with the terrifying prospect that another nation could develop the capacity to do unto America what had been done by American bombs to Dresden, Hamburg, Tokyo, and, even more ominously, Hiroshima and Nagasaki, American public opinion was galvanized by frightening scenarios of vulnerability that even the Allied war victory did not dispel. Much McCarthyite activity focused on protecting American atom bomb secrets from conspiratorial enemies, who might be able, then, to turn these aggressive weapons on U.S. cities. When the Soviets began atomic testing, the United States responded with massive weapons production and stockpiling—obsessional weapons hoarding, with vast national military bureaucracies involved in counting and increasing, improving, the weapons. In typical obsessional style, the way to fight a threat of penetration was to make a national fortress out of the very weapons of penetration.

American (and European Allied) concern with nuclear weapons has waxed and waned somewhat since 1945, lessening when test ban and disarmament treaties have been negotiated, escalating again in the crises represented by U.S. or Soviet invasions or threats of invasion in contested areas; and it has taken somewhat different forms as various strategists have offered different descriptions of how "national security" can be achieved. But in the history of the nuclear era, perhaps the vision that most clearly captures the "genocidal mentality"—as the psychohistorian Robert Lifton has named it—propelling nuclear weapons production is the Strategic Defense Initiative (SDI), also known as Star Wars. In this mid-1970s fantasy, later endorsed enthusiastically by President Ronald Reagan, and once again part of Republican defense policy in 1994, the United States will become a fortress that no foreign missile can penetrate; a "nuclear shield" will, in President Reagan's typical sexual metaphors, render enemy nuclear weapons "impotent and obsolete."[8]

Robert Lifton and others have pointed out the many similarities between the "genocidal mentality" of the Nazis and the "genocidal mentality" of the U.S. and Soviet military strategic planners and theorists recommending to citizens strategies for *Living with Nuclear Weapons* (1983), as the title of one Harvard study put it. Lifton has stressed a sequence of psychological characteristics or psychological defenses that are typical of people whose totalizing ideology could be called "nuclearism." He offered a catalog for a general type—as general as the authoritarian personality—with no connection to any characterological typology, but the features closely resemble those I have termed obsessional:

> "Dissociation" or "splitting" is a separation of a portion of the mind from the whole, so that each portion may operate to some degree separately from the other. "Psychic numbing" is a form of dissociation characterized by diminished inclination or capacity to feel, and usually includes separation of thought from feeling. "Doubling" carries the dissociative process further with the formation of a functional second self, related to but more or less autonomous from the prior self. When numbing or doubling enables one, with relatively little psychological cost, to engage in and sustain actions that cause harm to others, we may speak of "brutalization."[9]

Lifton portrayed the nuclearist planners as normal professionals who developed a capacity to think one way at the office and another at home, to split their planning processes off from any emotional or affective level, to develop an "Auschwitz self" that could imagine a nuclear holocaust without horror—by, for example, calculating species "survivability" in a scenario involving "only" 500 million deaths.

With the onset of the nuclear era, obsessional prejudices featuring groups that have gotten inside a state and are controlling or ruining it, groups that need to be eliminated for a suprastate entity to come into being, exist alongside—and overlap with—prejudices that feature the enemy striking with weapons.[10] These prejudices—in their nuclearist form, a novelty in human affairs—contain and set the terms for the more traditional sort of obsessional prejudice. Thus it is not surprising that, since 1989, as the immediate threat of a nuclear attack has receded, antisemitism has burst forth again in the former Soviet Union, along with other forms of ethnic conflict, many of which take quite obsessional forms. Many Russians feed and echo Vladimir Zhirinovsky's nationalist agenda laced with antisemitism. The traditional "Protocols of the Elders of Zion" is once again widely in circulation, and the Jews are being once again accused of taking over the country's agencies and media (recently an antisemite charged that newspapers were being written in "Gulag Hebrew" rather than Russian, for example).[11] In America, obsessional prejudice of the more traditional sort is also on the rise. Espoused by Pat Robertson, presidential candidate in 1992 and leader of the Christian Coalition, it permeates his best-selling book *The New World Order*. But both Christian Coalition members and the military, which seems less preoccupied with nuclearism in its daily routines or planning, have as their chief current obsessional prejudice not antisemitism but homophobia.

As efforts by Pentagon officials and officers to purge the armed services of homosexuals escalated in the "new" post–Cold War military, they were greeted with counterefforts by homosexual rights groups and their political allies to change military policy. This contest continues to be played out within a larger context of conflict supplied by an incipient movement. Drawing its population from Christian (Catholic and Protestant) fundamentalism, this movement promotes family values and seeks primarily to protect the fortress of the American family from people and ideas that are penetrating into its very heart. It alleges that a conspiracy of feminists (particularly abortion rights feminists) and gay liberationists is undermining the country. Of course, these groups have a long history as targets of ambivalent social fascination and discrimination. The movement has, characteristically, gathered force with a recent decline in social discrimination against women and then homosexuals, which is what has provoked the present strong political reaction—a backlash.

Robertson's Christian Coalition typifies the new organizational shape of obsessional prejudice. A group dedicated to electing its candidates to local political offices and school boards, it wants the Republican Party's platform to reflect its view. It works to keep gay people from becoming what they threaten to become—the predominant political or state-controlling force in the country, the leaders of a conspiracy against "traditional family values." "I don't care if you believe in evolution or creationism," says one of the coalition's leaders, "either way, homosexuality is unnatural for government to be sanctioning."[12] Another precinct activist (male) told an interviewer what brought him, for the first time, to political work: "I finally understood that I was in someone's cross-hairs. The things I believe in and that are important to me, I felt were being targeted. It's like when I was in Vietnam. When someone was targeting you, you knew." The bullet of the hidden homosexual conspiracy is about to get this man from behind. Another (female) added: "Obviously, in the last twenty years since they wrote their homosexual agenda, they have had a methodical plan. That's why we had to wake up." The phrase "the homosexual agenda" appears again and again in coalition literature, and the usage implies that there exists a document in which this agenda is written, like a "Protocols of the Elders of Zion."

The Christian Coalition is not radical, these precinct workers insist. They are trying to hold the line on the country's existing values, or as one described the organizers with unintentionally scabrous humor: "They're running around trying to put their fingers in the dikes." The fortress imagery does, however, often give way to typical expansionary antistate ambition. The Reverend Don Wildmon, a leader in the drive to force the National Endowment for the Arts to refuse funding to "obscene" arts projects, is an important figure in the Coalition on Revival (COR), a spin-off of the fundamentalist Southern Baptist Convention. His ideal is a Christian fundamentalist state, and his avenues of attack involve abolition of public schools, the Internal Revenue Service, and the Federal Reserve System. "Biblical law" is to be imposed on American society, which is to become "the Kingdom of God." A faction of COR called Reconstruction advocates stoning to death of homosexuals and also, revealingly, of incorrigible adolescents—a program that acknowledges how closely tied adolescent rebelliousness and homosexuality are in the minds of obsessionals.[13]

These fundamentalist organizations have a much broader constitu-

ency in terms of region, class, and employment status than the antisemitic religious groups of the 1930s did. They draw the contemporary
masses—the economically depressed, psychologically disillusioned,
unemployed, and politically unrepresented. A national leadership exits;
many local elected offices and school board seats have been won; the
homosexual agenda has been successfully attacked in the courts, particularly on matters relating to homosexual families, like adoption and
"spousal" benefits, and through anti–gay rights legislative initiatives.
These activities put the development of antihomosexual prejudice on
the level reached by European antisemitism when antisemitism became
a party program in the 1880s. Proposals for purging the country of
homosexuals—that is, for genocide—are still the work of fringes within
these organizations, but it may well be that the AIDS epidemic, widely
interpreted among fundamentalists as a scourge directly from God, is
already supplying this "cleansing" facet of the obsessional program—a
medical tragedy obviating the need for a manufactured tragedy.

Homosexuals and women who deviate from traditional family roles
are the current reigning targets of obsessional prejudice, it seems to me,
because this form of prejudice has become, as a result of the 1960s
sexual revolution, so much more overtly sexualized than it was at
midcentury. The sexual desires and fantasies organizing obsessional
prejudices have been brought closer to the surface of individuals' consciousnesses and more into public display, public discourse, public representation. Economic realities are still alleged by the obsessionally prejudiced to be under the control of entrepreneurial and middleman
minority groups—the Jews, the Japanese, sometimes immigrant groups
represented largely by business and professional people, like the Indians
and the Arabs—and homosexuals are drawn into these orbits when, for
example, they are said to be major financiers of political campaigns or
major players in Hollywood or the media generally, or when propaganda sheets stress the high average income of gays. But the specifically
sexual dimension of the prejudice is frequently isolated and aimed at
homosexuals exclusively. They are the ones who will, so a strong current
of obsessional prejudice now says, destroy the U.S. military with their
form of pollution or "disease," which is sexual preoccupation. "With
openly gay and heterosexual personnel together," wrote two Marine
officers on the *New York Times* op-ed page, "sexual tension would fester
24 hours a day in deployed military units and ships. Romantic interests,
even if unconsummated, would shatter the bonds that add up to unit

cohesion."[14] Discussions of "gays in the military"—almost always focusing on gay men, while lesbians are, in fact, just as frequently victims of discrimination—reverberate with the classic obsessional theme: units being broken into, anal rape. In bunks, in showers, in foxholes, in ship holds—the potential rapists are everywhere.

The sexualization of the obsessional prejudices—which amounts to putting the forbidden libidinal side of the prejudice into the foreground and the superego side, with its shrewd international conspiracy, into the background—is a very complex matter in fundamentalist contexts because puritanism is the norm. Homosexuals in addition to the other items on their alleged agenda supposedly try to sexualize the culture. They are responsible for the pervasiveness in contemporary life of sexual images, explicit sexual language, pornography. One of the key marks of all of the prejudices in their contemporary forms is that they hold their victims responsible for the conditions that govern the existing forms. The prejudices are more overtly sexualized, and the sexualization is the work of the gays, of Hollywood (and whomever may be thought to control it), of African American sports and entertainment figures who have no morals, of wild feminists, of perverse rap lyric writers and gender mocking adolescents. Accusations of sexualization can be launched in any and all directions, but the sexualization of the prejudices themselves, and of prejudiced people, is forbidden discussion territory. Each of the types of prejudices is currently caught in its variant of this dilemma.

## Paternalism, Competition, and Crisis: Metamorphoses of the "In Their Place" Prejudices

The moment that determines whether a given manifestation of obsessional prejudice is going to be widely institutionalized and turn coldly violent comes when the target group is said to be in control of the government or to be the government. The state itself is, then, targeted, and its demolition is in the service of a suprastate goal, an expansionary vision (although making the state pure and fortifying it may be undertaken as the necessary step before expansion, so that the obsessional vision appears nationalistic, not supranationalistic). The ambitions of the hysterically prejudiced are not expansionary in this way, and they do not focus on governments and conspiracies. Their ambition is, as it were, vertical. The superior group will triumph in a spiritual ranking, a

moral hierarchy. The emphasis is on supremacy in a very literal sense—
the inferior are to be in their place and the superior in theirs, which is
on top. Hysterically prejudiced people may be relatively without imperial ambitions and focused, instead, on their family homesteads, their
locales and regions, like pre-emancipation Southern racists who wanted
the Old South to remain as it had always been—only with greater economic viability thanks to slave labor. The hysterically prejudiced view
governments, whether local or imperial, not as agencies of betrayal but
as systems of order that can be commandeered to enforce or reinforce
discrimination, to embody and conserve supremacist values. State racism is the ideal.

A typology of the hysterical prejudices has to be set on a vertical axis,
as it was by the most systematic sociological contributor to the typological study of race relations, Pierre van den Berghe. In the late 1950s,
drawing on Max Weber's work, van den Berghe had offered a basic two-
part typology that he later revised and elaborated in a comparative study
of Mexico, Brazil, the United States, and South Africa called *Race and
Racism* (1967); then he returned to this typology with a more sociobiological approach in *The Ethnic Phenomenon* (1981). Van den Berghe
suggested that in the paternalistic systems of closed societies *(Gemeinschaften)*, which use social distance to define status, two castes obtain,
masters and slaves. The dominant group, usually a minority, considers
the majority it rules to be childish and irresponsible but remains benevolent as long as the inferior ones stay in their place (although horrible violence may be meted out over perceived violations of the rules).
All kinds of etiquettes and ceremonies keep that place clearly defined.
But miscegenation and concubinage cross the line, especially when the
offspring fathered by upper-caste males can either be taken into the
females' lower caste or come to form a kind of intermediary caste of
their own. Such intimacies, because the social distance is so carefully
maintained, do not threaten the certainty of the hierarchy (the status
differences) except in lower-class milieus where lower class dominators
are both despised by their class superiors and uncertain of their prerogatives over those they consider their inferiors (the dominated caste).

This model of paternalistic relations has run primarily along race lines
in Western slave plantation societies—in the United States, the West
Indies, Brazil—and in hacienda systems throughout Central and South
America. It was the norm as well in the colonial settings of Africa and
Asia. But it has also existed in racially homogeneous societies. Among

black Africans, for example, in Central Africa (now Rwanda) the tall, athletic Tutsi, viewed in the nineteenth century by Belgian colonializers as more European, kept the Hutu, a shorter group, as serfs, and that relationship, more ideological than ethnocentric, stands in the background of the current struggle for state power. From a broader perspective, paternalism is also structurally indistinguishable from late feudalism. This similarity is a very important point, because it indicates that in societies without racial differentiation, class differentiation supplies the psychic and social needs of the hysterically prejudiced. Serfs can be the paternal figures and also the rival siblings; serf women can play the role of the non-mother and can be loved (conquered or submitted to) without arousing anxiety about incest; and the serf group can do the despised but essential labor that supports the ruling group's domesticity. Serfs and peons share with racial castes all of the standard hysterical accusations—they are dirty (and their dirtiness is associated with darkness, swarthiness), sexually loose or hypersexual, irresponsible, lazy, childish, primitive, and so forth.

In terms of intellectual history, as well, we find a striking similarity between late feudal and paternalistic arrangements: for race ideology had its origin in the reaction against the breakdown of the European class system. The claim that there are different species—called races—of humans and not just one humankind was issued in book after book during the years between 1848 and the publication of Darwin's *Origin of Species* in 1859.[15] Rationalistic conservatives who interpreted the revolutions of 1848 as the clearest possible sign of Europe's deterioration promoted the notion of race plurality. These theorists saw the European middle class under dire threat—as dire as the threat to the upper class had been in the wake of the French Revolution in 1789—and they proposed to explain the upheaval and offer a prescription for the future. Race theorists produced many variations on the idea propounded by Georges Cuvier that there are three races, the Negroid, the Mongoloid, and the one suited to triumph in Europe, the Caucasian, whose isolation from one another should be prescribed to avoid the inevitable decline that race intermixing brings. A class uprising—not a racial uprising, and not overseas colonization per se—precipitated this hysterical reaction, which in effect asserted natural hierarchy in the face of growing equality and egalitarian ideas.

Van den Berghe based the second part of his typology not on social distance and its intellectual rationalizations but on physical or spatial

distance. The ruled race is forced to live elsewhere, not on the plantations or in the houses of the rulers. In this type, which van den Berghe
called competitive race relations, there is direct competition for jobs
and for roles between freed slaves, or people who have been able to
leave their lower caste situation, and the lower classes of the dominant
group. Class lines begin to cut across race lines as the boundaries of the
lower caste are broken or dissolved (by an emancipation or by a less
dramatic evolution). The dominant (white) lower classes join the dominant upper classes to form a "*Herrenvolk* democracy" from which they
jointly exclude the rising, increasingly competitive (dark) race or caste,
now known to its competitors as "uppity," aggressive, too assertive. The
*Herrenvolk* democracy seeks, in effect, state racism—racism woven into
the structure of the state it controls. Within the *Herrenvolk* democracy,
the lower classes become, however, trapped by their anxiety about the
rising competitors—they so strongly want to be superior to the competitors that they submit to the authority of the upper classes, thereby
preventing any assertion of their own class interests and also perpetuating their tendency to vote their prejudices rather than their economic
needs.[16] During the years of segregation, working-class whites in the
South had among the worst wages, hours, and conditions of any laborers
in the country. The upper classes have discovered that they can keep
their own lower classes in place by advertising the threat posed by the
new competitors.

In a *Herrenvolk* democracy the relatively benevolent paternalistic des-
potism of the dominant groups gives way to bigotry, violence (in mobs,
not by individuals), and organized resistance to racial advancement.
Racial ghettos are created with strict taboos against crossing ghetto lines
for miscegenation. The competitors are not to receive any genetic help
upward from the dominant class or any increase in the "white blood"
of their labor force. As Woodward noted, commenting on van den Berghe's typology, in Southern American history the evolution from paternalistic to competitive race relations took place first in the cities of the
antebellum South, where segregation also first developed after the Civil
War. In the Southern cities diverse populations mingled as they did not
in rural areas; free people of color, many of them well off and well
educated, were much more numerous in the cities than elsewhere in
the South, and much more threatening to poorer whites. The paternalistic caste system was not—and never had been—securely in place.

Woodward presented this Southern situation in its economic dimension, but it was very well understood by patrician Southerners in its fundamental sexual dimension, its relation to the possibility of an entire exploitative and hierarchical way of life being disrupted. Thus, for example, the dean of the Department of Education at the University of Mississippi, Thomas Bailey, spoke about the importance of race prejudice in a democracy:

> Extirpate race prejudice in a democracy and social communion and intermarriage are bound to follow. One of the reasons why the Northerners fail to understand this is their aesthetic antipathy to the Negro. Most Southerners like individual Negroes that "keep their place"—and I daresay the Negroes like all primitive folk are likable. The Northerner is protected from social communion and intermarriage by his feelings; the Southerner is protected by what he calls his principles—the superiority of the whites and such.[17]

Prejudice, social distance, if it erodes, must be reinforced politically and legally, because the two peoples—masters and slaves—are too intimately connected; they do not have the alleged Northern "aesthetic antipathy" and sheer ignorance to rely on.

Van den Berghe's typology shows the two key features of hysterical prejudice—the way in which the victims fulfill both a family need and a labor need—in their interactions. But he declared himself unable to pursue the psychological dimension and referred his readers to the work of the psychoanalytically oriented commentators. Woodward, meanwhile, noted that van den Berghe's effort could be compared with the typology offered by the Englishman Philip Mason in *Prospero's Magic: Some Thoughts on Class and Race* (1962), a work indebted to the French psychoanalyst O. Mannoni, whose *Prospero and Caliban: The Psychology of Colonialization* was also a primer for Frantz Fanon. Mason's typology, which he developed using his experiences living in England, India, and the West Indies, blends sociological and psychoanalytic perception in a threefold scheme. He considered, first, a "stage of certainty" in race relations, a stage, like van den Berghe's paternalistic one, in which "a slave is a slave and can be sold, but you can eat with him, talk with him, travel with him . . . [T]he key to this stage was that the relationship was accepted on both sides."[18]

Mason's second stage, which again resembles the developmental course suggested in van den Berghe's typology, is characterized by the absence of acceptance: the ruled group challenges the rulers, and status uncertainty spreads as competition becomes the norm. This is a stage of "challenge and rivalry." Bitterness and resentment grow among the ruled. Racial barriers become rigidified, reinforced, even impermeable, "and this means that the top people are frightened." Mason summarized the transition:

> So long as there is a formal and in extreme cases a legal, distinction between the status of persons who consider themselves to belong to different groups—whether they are divided by class or by race—they can often mix on a personal level with easy relaxation. But as the formal nature of the difference diminishes, so the dominant groups tend to put up barriers and personal relationships deteriorate . . . Before emancipation, Tom Sawyer and Huckleberry Finn thought it wicked to help a runaway slave to escape, but were not at all embarrassed by eating with him; sixty years later, their judgments would have been reversed.[19]

The developmental line from paternalistic to competitive race relations, which can be adapted to class relations as well—or to the transition from feudal estates to classes—is the most common one. But there are important variations. First, not all societies that are organized for paternalistic race (or class) relations evolve toward competitive relations or complete such an evolution. In van den Berghe's comparisons, Brazil stands as an example of paternalism modified but not fundamentally outgrown. The African slaves in Brazil were one of a number of groups that were brought into a system of personal domination and remained in it. The Brazilian planters had no fear of competition from their former slaves, and they did not set up any barriers after the decline and abolition of slavery; they assumed, rather, that the patterns of domination characteristic of the slavery era would persist, and they largely did. Widespread miscegenation entailed the inertia in the paternalistic form. Racial hatred and intolerance of the segregationist sort were not developed in the upper classes, where the old authoritarianism and social distance kept racial inequality in place. Furthermore, the upper classes actively kept their hegemonic peace by working against any racial hatred that appeared among lower-class whites or immigrants.

Nevertheless, not all societies characterized by competitive race relations have a history of paternalism. As a second variant, consider mid-nineteenth-century America, where the strongest opposition to slavery and the most vehement anti-Negro prejudice came in the states of the West and Northwest where there had been no slavery. What the working whites of those frontier areas feared was a wave of Negro labor, either slave labor (before emancipation) or freed labor. Race relations, in this context, were a matter of pure class relations—with the Negroes in the role of an immigrant group. In such a context, the immigrant groups that later filled "Negro domestic roles," as immigrants from Mexico and Latin and South America do now, also inherited hysterical prejudice in its competitive form. California is now the flash point of anti-immigration racism.

A third important variant is represented by situations in which the transition from paternalistic to competitive race relations takes place only very slowly. Woodward argued that in much of the South after the Civil War, paternalism stayed in place. After the Civil War, Southern whites faced the prospect of Negroes with the franchise, with land distributed to them by interfering Northern political operatives, and perhaps with arms. They reacted with an "initial fright and hysteria" but soon realized that attitude was unwarranted. The Northerners were much too racist themselves, the Southerners discovered, to persist in their transvaluation of values, and the former slaves were not going to forget their "place," forget all the social distance that had existed for so many decades. In the agricultural South, paternalism remained the norm, so much so that when Jim Crow legislation did begin to establish new barriers toward the end of the century, the upper classes often denounced the laws as unnecessary constraints on the docile, well-behaved Negroes.[20] The lower classes had concocted these laws, the patrician argument went; and to many of the gentry, the "poor white trash" and "crackers," not the submissive Negroes, seemed to be the people to be feared on streetcars, to be sent to the backs of buses. In effect, according to Woodward, once segregation in the South was put in place, it became an extension of, not a replacement of, paternalistic racism. It provided legal means to keep social distance and to allow older forms of dominance-submission behaviors to be carried forward, at least until the Civil Rights movement brought fundamental changes to the South's institutions and ushered in the more fully competitive race relations that exist now.

The paternalistic and competitive forms of race (and class) relations could also be described more psychodynamically as the forms in which the antipaternal and antisibling forms of the hysterical prejudices are, respectively, incorporated. Paternalism is directed primarily against the

projectively "paternal" male victims, and it involves both exaggerating
and then attacking their male sexual power and forcibly taking their
women away from them (while obtaining nonmaternal, nonincestuous
"mammy" or whore figures for the ruling males). Competitive relations
are directed against uppity younger sibling rivals who threaten to take
away satisfactions in the national family. But, as I noted in sketching
subtypes of hysterical prejudices in Chapter 8, there is also a third psychodynamic variant, sharing some features with the obsessional prejudices, that involves construing the victim group's males as attackers of
males as well as rapists of females and ambivalently wanting them and
warding them off. This third variant seems to correspond to a third stage
of race (and class) relations proposed by Philip Mason.

Mason went beyond van den Berghe's twofold scheme to outline "a
stage of crisis." This stage comes about chiefly because those whom
Mason called "the top people" decide that their welfare demands they
make concessions; it seldom results directly from a revolutionary movement or insurrection—though threats and actions from below may focus the minds of the top people. The form the stage takes, then, depends both upon how the top people act and upon how their actions
are received. "They may resist change till the last or they may accept it
grudgingly and too late, step by step, making just the concessions which
would have been acceptable *last* time. And the people to whom concessions are being made may suddenly reverse the whole process and re-
gurgitate what is being fed to them."[21] A stage of crisis entails confusing
tendencies because the concession makers give with one hand and refuse—often unconscious of what they are doing—with the other, and
the subordinates act out of both their history of suffering and their
pride. Generally, when concessions are first offered, the subordinate
group embraces assimilationism. Their expectations rise, their dreams
are given public voice—but the resistances of those who are conceding
their privileges also grow. In America, movements for separatism or
rejectionism have arisen periodically, in the wake of disappointments.
The "Back to Africa" movement led by Marcus Garvey spread rapidly
in the 1920s, when Negroes hoped—in vain—that their wartime efforts
would win them recognition. Similarly, the Nation of Islam flourished
in the 1960s when the Civil Rights movement won many victories but
was handed many false promises as well. Especially when political and
economic separatism are not feasible, cultural rejectionism takes hold,
as the movement called Afrocentricity is doing currently. To the top

people, rejectionism looks like uppity ingratitude and stands as proof that the subordinates are irresponsible, overdemanding—in short, not subordinates.

In a stage of crisis, Mason argued, the oppressed oscillate between accepting concessions and rejecting them, while the top people, each in his or her own way, obey a law of contrariness: "Different people will react in different ways [to threatened loss of privilege] and there will usually be a reaction between conscious and unconscious, one compensating by regression for any advance in the other."[22] A calculated concession to equality will be countered with an unconscious move to put things—people—back in their place; and the opposite may be the case if acts of discrimination and violence arouse guilt and new versions of the fear for the future that prompted concessions in the first place. To the consternation of everyone, greater relaxation and integration between groups and greater tension and segregation develop side by side, as do white envy for black beauty or athletic (read sexual) prowess and contempt for blacks who are said to be "culturally deprived." As the middle class becomes somewhat integrated, the lower class becomes more wretchedly segregated—segregated into abject poverty. And it is in relation to the new ghettos that the figure of the black rapist, the attacker so well known in paternalistic contexts, arises anew. In the new form of sexualization of racism, the rapist is now the out-of-control black teenager, "wilding" on the streets and in the parks, carrying a gun in his high school. His counterpart is the promiscuous black teenager who bears children for welfare checks. It seems to me no accident that the figures of black hypersexuality are now adolescents, for adolescents generally represent the prevailing great crisis of confidence in America— what will become of Generation X, the group supposedly without values, corrupted, degenerate? Adolescents are the group in which the adjectives of the obsessional prejudices and those of the hysterical prejudices meet in this time of economic turmoil and near-depression.

Mason did not note it, but one of the most striking features of a stage of crisis is the extent to which the oscillations of the former masters and those of the former slaves become tied to each other—as in families, communication between one unconscious and another is intense, and all parties react to one another's desires and histories as they come out of repression and speak. African Americans feel acutely—"hypersensitively" whites say—the repressed sexual desires and the outgrown paternalistic institutions of the whites each time these rise up anew from under layers of conscious progress, each time they are sexualized anew. Extremist African Americans mirror the now "politically incorrect" racism of the whites with their own "racism," an assumption that the whites are everything the whites once publicly said the blacks were— evil, devilish, stupid, undisciplined. Extremists even use the language of theory, casting whites as "melanin-deprived." At the same time, whites feel, often in bewilderment, the rage and prideful rejection of people who resent patronization and tokenism and self-serving progressivism as thoroughly as their ancestors resented Jim Crow. In a stage of crisis, race relations follow the unconscious law of talon that I mentioned before—a symbolic eye for a symbolic eye, an unconscious rage for an unconscious rage. If the blacks will not take "our" (white) welfare and improve themselves instead of having more babies and perpetrating violence, then they deserve their poverty—after all, no one gives a break to the hard-working people who pay the taxes.

This unconscious law of talon has made the current American disputes about affirmative action, where the competitive type of racism that resembles sibling rivalry focuses, particularly acrimonious. Middle-class white youth on college campuses, for example, frequently express their fear of economic downward mobility through complaints about special treatment given to African Americans. "They" don't deserve to be here (admissions standards were lowered for them); they get all the scholarships, all the attention, say white students, sounding pathetically like small children begging for parental affection.[23] The African Americans, rightly offended by such episodes, declare that they would rather live apart from the whites, in their own residences, where they feel comfortable among their own kind. They are thus able to trouble the liberal consciences of the white officials, who believe in integration but do not want to dictate housing arrangements, enforcing integration as their predecessors once enforced segregation. The situation simmers.

Whether the stage of crisis will give way slowly, painfully, to a true multicultural society could be said to depend upon the extent of the regressions that come about during it. If the layers of paternalistic and competitive racism that lie in repression under its troubled surface are frequently and forcefully revisited, to the point of becoming reinstituted, then the crisis will not cease; it will just change emphases as social contexts evolve.[24] In Europe, for example, where the underlying paternalistic and competitive types might better be called colonial and post-colonial, the stage of crisis is changing emphasis dramatically because of the influx of Third World migrants, refugees, and asylum seekers, who provide the cheap labor and do the usual cleanup and domestic service jobs. But the latest racism is pan-European, not just national, and it has emerged along with the concept of Europe as a political entity and the expansion of multinational companies.

In racist states, in America or in Europe, the signs of regression are clear enough. If legislation won by the Civil Rights movements is reversed—particularly in the sphere of voting rights and (in Europe now) immigration and nationality legislation—and if programs designed to compensate for past injustices are destroyed, then political regression is in process. The key moment in racism's development, the appearance of state racism, is reinvoked, and the ultimate logic of it, as noted before, is *apartheid*. If the rhetorics of paternalism and competitive racism begin to appear in public and in private, especially if little hue or cry meets them, then social regression is in process. Unlike the complex, inversely proportional interplay of social and political forms that characterizes the obsessional prejudices, the forms of the hysterical prejudices are linear. They progress and regress along a developmental line that could be called (as far as the dominant group is concerned) "learning to love without using the Other as a substitute family." Or in James Baldwin's haunting words to his fellow Americans: "White people in this country will have quite enough to do in learning how to accept and love themselves and each other, and when they have achieved this—which will not be tomorrow and may very well be never—the Negro problem will no longer exist, for it will no longer be needed."[25]

# 12

## The Body and Soul of Narcissism

The narcissistic prejudices, particularly those based on body narcissism, as I have noted before, closely relate to the hysterical prejudices. The bodily narcissistic prejudices are almost a mixed type—and it may well be that they best serve people of the mixed libidinal type that Freud had designated erotic-narcissistic. Among the paternalistic societies where racism has flourished, colonial Brazil presents one of the clearest examples of this mixed type in prevalence, as the enormously influential works of Brazil's national historian, Gilberto Freyre, show in luxuriant detail.

*The Masters and the Slaves* (1946) presents the Brazilian slaveholding plantation owners in their Big Houses as dedicated to procreation, to the creation of their own labor supply. Miscegenation, considered to be a service to the state and the economy, was not even frowned upon by the Jesuit fathers who looked after the slaveholders' souls. The Big Houses of the Portuguese planters, whose ancestors had, of course, been ruled for seven centuries by the Moors, a dark-skinned people of high civilization and polygamous traditions, were full of the mixed-race children—first Luso-Indian, then Luso-African. Freyre appreciatively called the patriarchs "unbridled stallions." And these stallions raised Portuguese colts who were also paragons, pushed by their fathers, and often their mothers as well, into precocious sexual activity. At age nine or ten the sons donned men's garments and acquired adult vices: the acqui-

412

sition of syphilis and its scars on their bodies marked their coming of age.[1] Precocity was demanded of daughters as well, and they typically married at twelve, thirteen, or fourteen to men three times their age. The white women aged quickly in the climate and under the harsh childbearing regime and the "morose, melancholy, indolent" lives they led.[2] Old women by the time they reached thirty or forty, they contrasted with the mulatto and Negro women, who stayed more healthy and aged less quickly. The white women, whose lives were so controlled and circumscribed by their husbands' dictatorial powers, hated their husbands' mulatto and Negro concubines and often expressed their feelings violently.

Freyre had a certain admiration for the Portuguese stallions, but he was also keenly aware that they reduced their lives to their preoccupation: "In the case of the slave owner the body became little more than a *membrum virile* . . . Slothful but filled to overflowing with sexual concerns, the life of the sugar planter tended to become a life that was lived in a hammock." He wrote even more succinctly: "There is no slavery without sexual depravity."[3] In his later work *The Mansions and the Shanties* (1963), Freyre drew the conclusion made obvious by the historical development of slavery and then emancipation in a context where extensive miscegenation blunted the future development of competitive racism (except in the biggest cities): "We Brazilians liberated ourselves more quickly from racial prejudices than from those of sex." "The inferiority of women" took the place of "the inferiority of race."[4]

This kind of developmental judgment, of course, sidesteps altogether any questioning about how sexism and racism relate or compare when both flourish or when one diminishes (particularly as directed at males) and the other stays on. It also obscures the difference between the prejudices directed at slave women and those directed at the slaveholders' own women. Both of these might be called "sexism," but this usage would obscure both the similarities and the differences between the two prejudices. Basically, what the narcissistic prejudices (especially in the bodily narcissistic form) and the hysterical prejudices have in common psychodynamically, and what shows them in their overlapping and intermingling so easily, is their focus on marking—branding in some literal way—the body of the Other. But the brand is not the same in the two cases. The victims of hysterical prejudice are branded as servants or slaves; the brand means ownership for labor and it means control over sexual functions for the "safe" (nonincestuous, nonfamilial) satisfaction of desires rooted in the oedipal stage. The victims of narcissistic prejudice are branded not only for ownership and reproductive control but also, in the bodily narcissistic form, for the establishment of sameness, the denial of difference, in service to a nostalgia rooted preoedipally, in the primary narcissistic oral stage. These are two distinct routes to sexual power: the hysterical route is a kind of theft of (phallic) power attributed projectively to the male others and a dominance over a nonincestuous mother figure, while the narcissistic route is nostalgic, restorative of a primordial paradise lost in which phallic power was the single condition—one might call it monophallicism. Sexist-racism, furthermore, reaches its logical development in state racism, while narcissistically based sexism is a phenomenon primarily institutionalized in families of different types. States, of course, can support sexism as it is institutionalized in families, but the key moments in the development of sexism are not antistate (as with the obsessional prejudices) or state appropriating (as with racism).

Before constructing a psychosocial typology of sexisms of narcissistic sorts, I must first acknowledge that when contemporary feminists discuss "sexism" they do not usually make a distinction between prejudice directed at in-group women and prejudice directed at women of a "racial" or class out-group. The trinity sexism-racism-classism implies that women who are the victims of racism and classism are also the victims of sexism, whereas I think that this is so only if the racism directed at lower-class or dark females is called "sexism" or if the word "sexism" refers to prejudices men of color direct toward women of color. I would prefer, given my emphasis on the narcissistic basis of sexism, to keep the word "sexism" for prejudice directed at women of the same kind, specifically of the mother's kind. The prejudices men have toward women who are mother and toward those who are not-mother and can thus be (nonincestuous) substitutes for the mother are quite different. To the latter I give the name "sexist-racism" (or "sexist-classism"). As I will suggest later, if we can maintain this distinction between in-group sexism and out-group sexist-racism, we will see one reason why communication and political alliance building among women of different groups is so difficult—they do not all suffer from the same sexism.

I also want to acknowledge that, among (white) feminists who construct sociopolitical theories of sexism with the aid of psychoanalysis, as I am going to do, an orientation quite different than mine prevails. Beginning with the pioneering work of Margaret Mead, feminist social scientists, particularly those in anthropology and sociology and more recently in object relations psychoanalysis, have focused on how men's and women's personalities are socioculturally constructed. The approach entails showing that there are no universal, biologically based differentiating personality characteristics and then presenting the various types of sociocultural conditions in which men's personality characteristics prepare them for oppression of women.

In any society multifarious ingredients contribute to the shaping of men's and women's personalities. The degree of a society's complexity, how a society's economy is organized and its labor divided along sex lines, family type and size and how the households are organized, whether children are raised to work as children or only when they reach physical maturity, and whether child-rearing practices imply continuity or discontinuity in children's developments generally—all of these modes and factors produce sex role differentiations, large or small. But, from the several generations of feminist cross-cultural studies of these modes and factors that have succeeded Mead's *Male and Female* (1949), two key generalizations pertinent to the forms of sexism have emerged. The first is that all children are raised primarily by women. No society normally assigns child care, after the birth process, to men, although in many child-care arrangements older female children and women other than the mother perform the mothering. So both girls and boys are first socialized by women.

The second generalization is that, comparatively, the young male's socialization is more complex and more uncertain than the young woman's, because he moves from the world of women to the world of men and male labor as a child or an adolescent. His identity will build upon a process of differentiation from his mother and other women, while the girl's will build upon assimilation or identification, an inherently more stable process. His identity will be "achieved" while hers will be "ascribed"; and his may have to be continuously achieved or proven, as his capacity for reproduction has to be achieved in sexual potency, while hers can be enacted even if she is unwilling or frigid. There are exceptions, but generally the more a society differentiates female and male roles and personalities, the more complex the boy's transition will be and the more likely it will be carried out by means of puberty rites

or male gangs with a ritualistic cast that destroy—more or less strenu-
ously and violently—the female socialization in him, his earliest personality layer.

Theoreticians who put their interpretive emphasis on the male's differentiation from a maternal matrix in which the girl remains (more or
less), look for the key to sexism in the process of differentiation. Differentiation entails some form of rejection of women and feminine
traits, but this rejection is conceived in terms of sex roles and gender
identity—it is basically a sociological theory. Among psychoanalysts,
Karen Horney has most clearly supplied a corollary psychological theory. She has argued that boys feel toward their mothers a deep dread
based on the power she has over them to satisfy or frustrate their infant
needs and reflecting the fact that it is her body toward which their first
aggression, spurred by frustration, is directed. When their fathers later
exercise control over them, it is a more "actual and tangible, less uncanny" dread that boys feel toward them, especially because this father
dread is not mingled with fear of the father as a different kind of being,
a fear that damages the boy's self-respect or self-esteem. Throughout
their lives, according to Horney, men express their "dread of women"
indirectly, either by worshiping women as glorious creatures who could
not possibly be dreadful or by disparaging women as poor creatures,
not even worthy of being dreaded. Psychologically, they seek all kinds
of ways to extirpate any early feminine identifications, or to suppress
the feminine side of their bisexual identifications, while culturally they
seek all kinds of ways to secure male power and prerogative and to
reduce in status and contain female activities.[5]

From this gender differentiation theory, which is a synthesis of sociological cross-cultural comparisons, elaborated with sociological psychoanalysis, a basic typological guideline emerges. Derogation and dread
of women will be greatest in conditions (or will increase in conditions)
that most stringently separate male and female spheres, place little value
on functions males and females share or participate in together, and
assign child care exclusively and in an isolating way to women. Derogation, that is, flourishes in conditions that make the males' transition
to the male sphere and to masculine identifications most difficult and
conflictual. For example, if the males in a society are absent from the
domestic scene much of the time—whether because they go off on hunting expeditions or because they commute by train to their offices in the
city—their sons will be more likely to derogate women. If the society is

organized for discontinuity between childhood and adulthood—if it has a long nonworking, nonprocreating interval, a long period that can be designated "adolescence"—this, too, will increase the likelihood of male identity confusion and derogation of women. In short, egalitarianism and maximal similarity in sex and gender roles will be correlated with minimal male sexism.

But this theoretical approach to gender differentiation yields quite another sort of guideline for evaluating what sexism means to women. The same conditions that produce male identity conflict and thus foster sexism *can* support a coherent and strong female identity. Matrifocal societies in which men are largely absent or irrelevant and in which women's roles are valued and entail a good deal of economic and social power give women many sources of self-esteem other than child rearing. Mothers have no need to keep their children in isolated units, no need to keep their daughters or their sons in a state of dependency that makes it difficult for children of both sexes to develop their abilities. But even in societies that devalue women's roles and confine women to a segregated sphere, women can develop communities among themselves that sustain and support them. The sexism of the household and social institutions does not have to produce low self-esteem in young females if their identities are securely developed in their mother's and kinswomen's company. In general, whether male sexism is destructive of women's self-esteem and produces conflicts in their gender identities depends on whether the form of the sexism permits female communal life. In answer to sexism, when a public oppositional politics is not at issue, women have an alternative in what might be called psychosocial separatism—a separatism supported by the way in which women's gender identities are shaped in female relations. The feminist theorizing that has recently accompanied this kind of separatism stresses the differences between male and female modes of relating and communicating.

This theoretical and sociological picture of gender differentiation emphasizes the male's mother as a frustrator and an Other. Girls, too, of course, experience frustrations, but the rage and aggression that a male child develops as he is frustrated are mobilized and used in the course of his differentiation from his mother, who is experienced by him as other and who is aggressively derogated. The theory presumes that a boy can experience his mother as other, which would mean that his primary narcissistic image of her as like himself had already given way and been shattered. From the Freudian point of view, this feminist interpretation focuses on a boy's secondary narcissism—his effort to win out over others, assert his supremacy, after his reactions of anger and fear have disturbed his primary narcissism. But from the object relations point of view in which this gender differentiation theory about why men derogate women is posed, there really is no primary narcissism for either sex. All infants start out in a relationship with their mothers. The boy's relationship becomes problematic as he differentiates. The theory cannot feature a mother who is omnipotent (and phallic for the boy) or a merger with her that is blissful; it does not appreciate nostalgia, desire to return to the womb, or the womblike primary narcissistic matrix.

If the Freudian theory of narcissism that I have been drawing upon in the preceding chapters is to be the base for constructing a typology of sexisms, then the key site for reading the forms of sexism in a society must be not male differentiation from the mother and from female socialization but, rather, the existence and institutionalization in the society of narcissistic nostalgia. This approach provides three advantages. First, a narcissism-based theory can meet the main criticisms of the gender differentiation theory that have been raised by socialist feminists. They have pointed out that gender differentiation does not imply male domination—just because males must disidentify with or dread their mothers does not mean that they must dominate women. Further, the claimed universality of mothering and male disidentification gives no attention to the very different forms that male domination takes, for example, in distinct types of families or in precapitalist and capitalist societies, in the prestate and state formations Gerda Lerner studied.[6] The typology I am going to suggest should meet these calls for clarification about what need male *dominance* supplies and for greater historical attention to forms of dominance. Second, gender differentiation theory, particularly when it incorporated Horney's work, provided some analysis of why sexist imagery is so full of contradictions—simultaneous derogations and elevations of women, charges that they are biologically inferior offered in combination with paeans to their moral superiority, assertions that they are like men combined with claims that they are different (and either inferior or superior, or both). Nevertheless, gender differentiation theory cannot be thorough on this topic because it lacks a theory of male narcissism. Finally, the theory treats sexism in isolation from other prejudices and does not recognize it as a type (the fundamental type) of a larger category, the narcissistic prejudices, and this means that no connection has been drawn between sexism and cultural elitism.

To the two basic forms of sexism I distinguish I give the shorthand names "sameness sexism" and "difference sexism," or "one-sex sexism" and "two-sex sexism." They have developmentally distinct origins psychologically and historically, but once they both exist they do not appear in completely discrete individual or social forms. Sameness sexism, the developmentally earlier form, is always underneath, playing into the developmentally later difference sexism, although the lower layer is not immediately apparent to the reconstructive clinical ear or historical eye, particularly in times, like our own, in which difference sexism is the only sexism discussed and in which difference sexism exists in a baffling, complicated form.

Sameness sexism arises directly out of nostalgia for primary narcissism and takes predominantly what I have been calling bodily narcissistic forms. Its main purpose is to deny sexual difference or to assert sameness—to say that women really are men, even if failed men or imperfect men. The claim that women are inferior men makes the point that sexual difference has been perceived and reality has intruded on primary narcissism; the claim that women are men then denies the perception and extrudes reality. Historically, sameness sexism marks the disappearance of the conditions in which goddess religions flourished: prepatriarchal conditions in which men imagined women as awesome, omnipotent birth-givers, omnisexual creatures with both big breasts and penises. The era of goddess worship, the era in which the votive objects that fascinated Freud were manufactured, is the era of the phallic woman fantasy before it needed reinforcement, before *she* had to be other. Sameness sexism protects access to the original fantasy, asserts it, with an element of fear included—*she* may be harmful, a Medusa, with penises all over her head. And, in social terms, what sameness sexism emphasizes is male control over paternity and thus kinship relations in general. All children, the future laborers in agricultural ventures and the future breeders, belong to men. Patrilineality, accompanied by the theory that the woman contributes nothing to a child but the womb as an incubator, and often accompanied by commonly practiced pederasty (sex between an older male and a younger male, a 'woman' with a penis), keeps female reproduction from having any meaning of its own. In effect, sameness sexism says "men reproduce."

The later form of sexism develops as the earlier structure of fearful denial gives way. As women keep stepping out of their definitions and the reality of sexual difference keeps reintruding, the denial defense is strained, so a reaction formation or secondary line of defense is needed. The careful historical and anthropological reconstructions of the history of patriarchy that Lerner and others have synthesized and summarized are—if the terms I am proposing are followed—histories of how these reaction formations keep archaic denials of female sexual difference in force. In social terms, arguments for women's equality and the phenomena of women as creatures with their own lives, motivations, and public possibilities bring about the greatest uncertainty. Too much reality disturbs the fantasy structure. And the secondary line of defense, the secondary narcissism, the backlash, takes the form of assertion of difference to such an extent that the Other is pushed beyond the human realm or the realm—for example, the public realm—defined as the one that is essentially human. Women, confined to the domestic sphere, are then said to be essentially different from men. Dephallicized, they become "feminine" as strictly opposed to "masculine." And they are the ones who reproduce—indeed, they have no other task in life than to reproduce. Men and women inhabit different cultures in this cultural narcissistic form, which lends itself to elaborate cultural histories of female inferiority. Cultural histories of female inferiority provide the basis for more general cultural elitisms that condemn the Other as effete.

In European history, the most dramatic shift away from sameness sexism toward difference sexism came about with the movements for equality in the Enlightenment, spurred on by the French Revolution. This shift also coincided with the vast transformation of economic and social forms that is called capitalism. In precapitalist societies, agricultural enterprises and household labor (in what are sometimes referred to as disaggregated households) were the norm, whereas capitalism is marked by industrial development and industrializing of agricultural enterprises that put the bulk of laboring outside households, in public realms, where labor can be organized around wage relations. In the period of transition, the population in Europe grew staggeringly—it leapt beyond the harsh constraints that farm life, with its backbreaking routines and lack of hygiene, had put upon it. People died in their fifties rather than in their thirties. Then, as capitalism expanded and industrialization advanced, European households grew smaller, for children had to be supported on wages; no longer contributors to family work as farmhands, they became adolescents before they went into the work world. Correspondingly, women became more and more confined to the domestic sphere, and control over female reproduction increased. Marriages were arranged and reproductive customs—including age at marriage—fixed. In general, during the last two centuries population booms have been followed by assertions of reproductive control—and it is only recently, under the impact of feminism, that the question of who will control reproduction has been effectively advanced politically. Throughout the nineteenth century in America, males asserted control; after the post–World War II population explosion, reproductive control emerged as the crux of feminist struggle, so that stopping legalization of birth control and abortion became central to stopping women's liberation.

Control of reproduction (not of paternity per se, but of the number of children and the conditions of women's service to the children, the conditions of motherhood) is the centerpiece of difference sexism. It is the main project when women have been acknowledged to be not-men and when reproduction has been assigned to them as their reason for being. As I noted before, Thomas Laqueur's *Making Sex* has documented how this acknowledgment appeared in the history of science and medicine as the two-sex theory, the theory that women have genitalia which cannot be understood as inverted male genitalia. Similarly, women make their own contribution to a child—they produce the eggs (discovered in the eighteenth century) that descend from the ovaries on a schedule (discovered in the nineteenth century), a schedule controlled by the hormones (discovered in the 1930s). Although scientists conceded that women have their own type of orgasm, and not a shudder of their interior penile shaft, the female orgasm was not really explored scientifically until William Masters and Virginia Johnson began their work. But before these advances could be made, the two-sex theory denied that there is such a thing as a female orgasm, or that women have sexual desire or take pleasure in sex. The stereotypical passive and numb Victorian woman was the first cultural product of the two-sex theory—precisely she was so controllable reproductively, fitted so well the image of saintly motherhood. Modern institutions that separate male public and work spheres from female reproductive or motherhood spheres rely on the assertion, in extreme terms, of the difference between the sexes.

It was also precisely this woman, so artificially understood as feminine, whom Freud had in mind when he asserted his new version of the one-sex idea: all libido is masculine. He knew this feminine woman as a hysteric, a woman whose desire had been warped by social institutions dictating that women should engage in sex only for the sake of reproduction. One-sex theories have always been associated with appreciation of female desire, even if that desire is (narcissistically) conceived as masculine or like the male's, while two-sex theories, paradoxically, appreciate female difference but not female desire. Two-sex sexism always tends to push femaleness beyond the realm of the human and into nothingness—so the female becomes so different from the male that she cannot feel desire at all. Freud did not deny female desire.

In societies where sameness sexism and bodily narcissism reign, pederastic homosexuality (representing sexual desire for a male who is not yet a man, a phallic-woman man) is usually common, as are fetishistic practices and institutions. Cultures in which men normally and typically have sexual relations with other, usually younger men, while they father children with wives who are kept in an almost servantlike condition, are cultures organized for paternity assertion or for the production of large families of heirs and continuers of family enterprises. The servantlike condition of the childbearers is reinforced by physical, often fetishistic, constraints on their bodies, although the constraints may not look or be interpreted as such by anthropologists or culture commentators. For example, among the most striking of sexist practices is foot binding, which was acceptable among upper-class Chinese until the beginning of this century. Over a period of years, a girl's toes would be forced back under her feet until the feet resembled clenched fists and she was unable to walk on them—she was hobbled. One author has come up with a simple and catchy rationale for this practice: "Why must feet be bound? / To prevent uncivilized running around."[7] The ditty captures the cultural prejudice—women should not be allowed to move in male territories of social and political activity. But its underlying meaning appears if the bound foot is considered as a fetish, which, as noted before, Freud defined as a man's token of the female phallus. In Chinese pornographic art, the open space in a bound foot is frequently represented as an entryway for a penis. A foot encasing a penis, a foot-fist enwrapping a penis, is, in effect, a female genital with a penis. She who cannot run around and is kept in the male's house and fantasy is the phallic woman.

The bodily narcissistic prejudice tries to restore the phallus to a woman, thus denying the reality of her sexual difference; the mental narcissistic prejudice of two-sex sexism recognizes difference and tries to eliminate it by derogation, by saying, "she is castrated." But when mental narcissism supervenes, it may also mean a direct attack on the phallic woman. The phallus that she has been given in fantasy is ripped away (analogously to the way in which the oversized phallus a racist has attributed in fantasy to a "lower" or "darker" male person is ripped away). When this attack is carried out bodily, when it is a mental or fantasy construction translated into bodily terms, the means is something like clitoral excision—her phallus is cut out. At times, this practice has been justified both as a way of keeping women from having an erectile organ that could be used in lesbian coitus (as a homophobic practice) and as a way of preventing female masturbation or, more generally, female pleasure. But it seems to me that its most sexist meaning is on the narcissistic level: the practice says, "she is castrated." It makes the phallic woman into a feminine being, the Other, in an act of raging disappointment; it says, "she is not us." It is a means of asserting control over her as only a reproductive being.

But expressions of narcissism on women's bodies are never simple, they always involve the layering so characteristic of sexism—a layer of assertion of sameness under layers of assertion of difference. In the case of genital mutilation, there are two main forms: clitoral excision (complete, or of the tip or sheath) and infibulation, which is frequently practiced in combination with clitoral excision and involves in some way sealing off the vaginal canal—by sewing the labia together or by putting a ring through the labia. Infibulation, although it has sometimes been interpreted as a means for preventing masturbation, is usually interpreted as a means for preserving virginity or keeping a woman from being penetrated by anyone other than the man who owns her and has the right to have her opened for his own use. Infibulation, then, is cited as a support of patriarchy, of control over paternity. This is likely the case, but many anthropologists who have studied infibulation note that societies practicing it have theories about the female phallus and believe that infibulation keeps that phallus inside. They subscribe to a theory, like the Greco-Roman theory outlined in Laqueur's *Making Sex,* which holds the female genitals to be a phallus turned inside out, a phallus pointed inward. Behind the castrating clitoral excision, then, lies a practice for keeping the phallic woman intact—an assertion of sameness behind an assertion (on the mental narcissistic level) of difference.

## Forms of Sexism and Forms of Family

In the postwar history of Euro-American feminist theory, the most complex intersection of "radical feminism" and "Marxist feminism" has come over the family. Radical feminists like Kate Millett advanced the claim that the family is the structure in which sexism is created and perpetuated. Any Marxism, they argued, must, if it is to be foundational for feminist theory, be reformed to focus on the family and reproduction, not just on types of production and class conflict. Marxist feminists have replied that the family is an abstraction both ahistorical and universalist. For the family and reproduction to be integral to Marxist theory, careful work on the various and changing forms of the family must be done, relations between oppression of women and other forms of oppression must be considered. It seems to me that this complex debate grew up and has continued because no correlation between forms of the family (including forms of marriage) and forms of sexism has been offered. The principle for constructing such a correlation has been missing. I want now to consider the typological distinction between one-sex and two-sex sexisms with this debate about the family and its possible resolution in mind.

When one-sex sexism, an expression of bodily narcissism, preponderates, reproduction is thought of as male and paternity (manifest in patrilineal descendent lines) is emphasized in social arrangements. In terms of family structure and marriage form, polygamy is the norm. Polygamy was the type of marriage that evolved in the course of the story that Gerda Lerner told in *The Creation of Patriarchy*. Polygamy pervaded the whole region of the so-called Fertile Crescent, much of India, China, and Japan, and also most regions with a process of urbanization and class stratification of the sort Lerner described. In such societies, class hierarchies (and slavery systems) grow up along with a kind of sex slavery or ownership of the bride that is marked by both requirements on a bride that she be virgin and a "double standard" for her male owner's sexual activity. Her condition has to assure his paternity; his prerogatives assure that he is maximally reproductive. The wealthier the man, the more wives and concubines he can have; but such societies also support brothels to accommodate less wealthy, unpaired males, as they support the kind of contingent or opportunistic homosexual activity that is common wherever the average male's sexual outlets are limited (in this case, because the wealthier men control so many of the women).

But polygamy can, of course, be interpreted in a number of ways other than the historical one Lerner offered. From a sociobiological or economic perspective, polygamy maximizes the reproductivity of a man who can afford many wives—for one penis and many wombs is, so to speak, the most efficient reproductive arrangement. Psychologically, however, polygamy most elaborately and powerfully fulfills the reparative male narcissistic fantasy and provides the reality of a kind of omnipotent mothering to a man—one man and many wife-mothers is as much a utopian scene for a nostalgic as one man with his all-providing mother. (For this reason, societies in which assertion of difference, two-sex sexism, reigns, and which tend to be monogamous, are terrifically prejudiced against polygamists—as most Americans are against the Mormons and against Muslims—since they represent a blissful condition that has been given up.)

Polygamous societies might also be described as maximally phallic-narcissistic. Phallus worship is normal in them, and all kinds of phallic action are celebrated—so all kinds of penetration are tolerated (although being penetrated is not acceptable for a male). In the *machismo* cultures of such societies, active homosexuality is not despised. Lesbian activity, however, is usually thought disgusting; it is kept strictly away from public domains and left to the seraglio because lesbian sex is not phallic or nonphallic. Similarly, oral sex is looked down on, while anal sex is not, as attentive observers of Greek vase painting have long noted. Anal penetration is actively, phallically assertive; but fellatio cedes control to the partner's mouth—it is more phallically passive, and it is closer to the dangers of castration represented most forcefully by images of the *vagina dentata*.

Polygamous societies do not tie sex and reproduction together by an ideology that requires sex to be in the service of reproduction. Such an ideology appears only in contexts where—to put the matter in economic terms—one man has only one official woman with whom to reproduce, so each pregnancy has great meaning. When sex and reproduction are not thus soldered together, both men and women are understood to have sexual desire, comparable orgasmic experience, and sexual needs that can be satisfied in many different ways. Sex is taught. Men teach boys, as pederasts, and women teach boys and sometimes girls, too, as did Sappho on Lesbos, at a school in which girls were prepared for their future sexual and domestic lives.

Within the Judeo-Christian tradition, marriage to a virgin bride evolved from polygamy into monogamy, and from what is sometimes called "noncompanionate marriage" into "companionate marriage." Sexual repression was—as Freud long ago sighed—required. In the Muslim tradition, this evolution did not come about, and Muslim societies remained polygamous, less repressive of sexuality per se, that is, less puritanical and more tolerant of homosexuality and other nonprocreative practices. Other societies, of course, like that of the Japanese, evolved toward monogamy without a Christian basis, and these are usually more tolerant of homosexuality—having remained more tied to their polygamous pasts. Similarly, many regions where Christianity prevailed retained a great deal of both their polygamous and their polytheistic pasts, so that their official monogamy retains a heavy imprint of the characteristic earlier features—tolerance for contingent and pederastic homosexuality, a great deal of phallic narcissism or *machismo*, and so forth. Catholicism in Latin and South America, for example, is much more one-sex sexist than Catholicism in Northern Europe or North America, as the great Mexican poet Octavio Paz, in *Labyrinth of Solitude*, has shown in luxuriant detail and in his own terms.

In the terms I am developing, evolution toward monogamy is evolution in the direction of "female reproduction," which means acknowledgment of the woman's role in reproduction and of her reproductive difference. Sexism does diminish in such an evolution—but only one-sex sexism. It is reasonable to argue—as many Christian historians of Christianity partisanly do—that Christianity made marriage less sexist, but it is crucial to acknowledge that by granting women certain protections and rights the church diminished only one-sex sexism. Marriage based on choice rather than family selection both reduced the power of clans and kinship groups—from which the church and the European states benefited—and gave women some say in their destinies. The early church seems also to have made its offer of some official power to women a selling point for potential converts from pagan and Jewish communities. By forbidding adultery, the church tried to promote partnership between wives and husbands, who were encouraged to treat their wives as sisters. By forbidding divorce, the church also gave women protection against being abandoned without alimony by their husbands and losing their children to their husbands, who under Greek and Roman law owned all children and owed no support to their often impoverished ex-wives. By forbidding infanticide, the church protected female children and assured that shortages of women would not encourage men to engage in nonmarital sexual practices.

These challenges to one-sex sexism show clearly, however, the two-sex sexism or mental narcissistic nature of the Christian monogamy system: it assigned women the role of mothers and allowed their reproduction to be regulated by males; women received the private sphere for their own, and they were not to be educated or cultivated beyond the level necessary for them to be companionate to their men. Their purpose was to be different from men, and a text like Mary Wollstonecraft's *Vindication of the Rights of Women* (1792), which contained a clarion call for female education, did not suggest that women should in any way question the definition of their difference or the "grand duty" of child care, which is "annexed to the female character by nature." Female reproduction—under male control, but not representing a fantasy of male reproduction—was chartered, even though the one-sex view of female reproductive equipment still largely dominated medicine.

In such a system, unmarried women have no function and spinsters experience enormous prejudice. Similarly, lesbians are seen to have shunned the only definition of woman—mother. It is not lesbian sexual practice that is despised—it is usually thought to be nonexistent, because female desire in general is not acknowledged—but lesbian un- or antimotherhood. Whereas phallic-narcissistic cultures are cultures of contempt for nonphallic practices, the mental narcissistic cultures are cultures of contempt for ideological renegades, women who do not abide by the rules. Only in a mental narcissistic culture does the idea and image of homosexuality as a way of life and an exclusive preference arise—for in cultures that measure by the phallus, only the great categories "phallic" and "nonphallic" matter, not "heterosexuality" and "homosexuality."

As capitalism developed, bourgeois women had less and less to do with household productivity, which was slowly eliminated in favor of the public economic sphere, so reproductivity became their sole function. But the situation was different for working-class women and women involved in the spread of imperialistic commercial ventures, whether overseas from Europe or across the continent in America. Working-class women remained closer to the conditions typical of polygamous families, which assert paternity over children who are going to labor for the family. Women associated with imperial ventures often worked in more precapitalist conditions, in productive households, operating like their men, that is, assuming management over domestic servants but also over ranch hands, field hands, and so forth. The sexual division of labor blurred, as it generally does in situations where women are in short supply and men must compete for them—which gives women a certain degree of power, including control over their own reproductivity.

By the time bourgeois women in mid-nineteenth-century Europe and America had created suffrage movements, the Christian monogamy system was showing great strain. A vast population of women existed who were without role except as mothers and who developed female worlds in their households for the companionate ideal that their husbands, working outside the house, did not provide. Many such women turned to what might be described as "companionate lesbianism" (like the nonsexual Boston marriage). Further, both the church's ban on divorce and its ban on nonmarital sexual practices created great problems—women whom the ideal of companionate marriage failed were trapped, adolescents who engaged in masturbatory sex stood condemned as degenerate or insane, and homosexuals became outlaws. As for divorce, most of the Protestant churches relented, so that regions of America (not including the South) under the influence of Puritanism recognized divorce long before England did. But most women were much too economically dependent on their husbands to consider divorce.

The truly great test of the Christian system came in the twentieth century, however, when the ideal—never more than an ideal—of companionate marriage was challenged on one front by the entry of married women into European and American work forces in large numbers and on a second front by the wide availability of relatively effective contraception. Women leaving home to work and women having the means to control their own reproduction have ushered in—to admix with all the earlier forms—a new form of sexism.

## Sexism Here and Now

Any assessment of sexism in contemporary America needs to be made with a sense for the various types of sexism, for all the types exist in our society, side by side, confusingly, chaotically.[8] There is what I have called the sexist-racism of those hysterical types who split their object world into madonnas and whores and assign the whore role to a not-mother woman of a darker color or lower class (or to an in-group adolescent). There is bodily narcissistic one-sex sexism, with its phallus worship, its focus on paternity and expropriating reproduction for males. It exists in the form that flourishes in the polygamous societies of other parts of the world, especially agricultural societies that are industrializing but still precapitalist, and it is to be found among groups that are actually polygamous—Muslims, for example—as well as in groups that tend toward the new form of polygamy, serial monogamy. There is two-sex sexism of the sort that is typical of strictly monogamous, virgin bride societies, featuring emphasis on female difference, located in her reproductivity, which is strictly controlled and wrapped in an ideology of motherhood. This form, which also features disparagement of female mental and cultural abilities (cultural elitism on a sexist foundation), thrives in conservative religious milieus—Catholic, Protestant, Jewish—and among political conservatives who invoke family values. Single-issue sexists, particularly opponents of abortion, usually come from this kind of background. The public program of such sexism concentrates on ways to keep married women either out of the work force altogether or in subordinate positions in the work force, so that they do not lose their sense of difference.

As women have entered into the public sphere in greater numbers, other forms of marriage and the family have become more important in European and American societies. For example, the virgin bride system is quite different than the system that has survived into the modern world most strongly in Scandinavia—and in the pages of *Coming of Age in Samoa*. Known variously as Nordic marriage, "night courting" (in Denmark), or "bundling" (after it was imported during the seventeenth century to New England), this is a betrothal system. Breeding partnerships begin not with a marriage but with a betrothal. Each spring, young males court unpaired females by coming to spend the night in their farmhouse dormitories. The companionate pairs that form announce their betrothal to their families, and then, if a pregnancy results, a marriage is arranged. Marriage marks the all-important ability to create a family—an ability that means much more than any permission to bring a virginity to an end and that reflects a great deal of sexual egalitarianism or lack of emphasis on establishing paternity. The young women choose their partners in this system, even though they live within patriarchal social and political institutions, but they also assure their own importance and independence in the child producing.

In American social history, a marriage form like the Nordic has operated in rural areas, particularly in the West, and particularly during the era of Western imperialist settlement, when women were in short supply. Similarly, a Nordic form has operated in segments of the working class, particularly among immigrants from Scandinavia and Eastern Europe, and in other groups or subgroups that place much stress on encouraging fertile partnerships to keep an extended group going, as opposed to encouraging motherhood to keep an individual man's family going. The Nordic system also, in effect, operates currently in liberal middle class America, where young unmarried adults decide to live together, an arrangement that may begin in college dormitories rather than in family quarters. Although the experiment is not undertaken for testing fertility, it is not uncommon for such couples to marry after a desired pregnancy is achieved. In the Nordic system, sex is not part of the "male reproduction" that is typical of the polygamous virgin bride system nor is it part of the "female reproduction" that is typical of the monogamous virgin bride system (particularly where there is a cult of motherhood). Sex is, on the contrary, detached from reproduction until it serves reproduction. And this is the existing (that is, not utopian) situation that most frees women from one-sex and two-sex sexism. The contemporary Scandinavian countries are certainly by every measure of opportunities, rights, and protections for women the most advanced countries on the planet, and segments of the privileged American and European middle classes approximate to their structures. By the same token, the Scandinavian countries are more tolerant of homosexuality than any others in Europe, confirming the often documented link between sexual permissiveness and education and such tolerance.

Both the Judeo-Christian virgin bride system and the Nordic betrothal system are organized for pairing, for nuclear families, rather than for an extended kinship family. Many African tribes, by contrast, both patrilineal and matrilineal, comprise extended kinship units, and many African American families have a similar organization as a legacy of the complex and tragic interaction of slavery with the African practices imported to this country along with the slave populations. On plantations, children resulted not from marriages but from relationships that were completely under the masters' control. Children could be taken from their parents, sexual partnerships could be broken by selling one or both the parents, and slave women could be used by the masters and their sons for their own reproduction. Slaves too old to work in the fields, usually the women, formed an extended kinship unit and did the child rearing. Currently, the external pressure on African American families comes from poverty and competitive racism rather than from plantation owners, but the coping strategy, with its old African roots, is similar: women work, and child care is done by old aunties and grand-mothers. Males are attached to and proud of their children, but they often do not live in the same house with them or their mother and grandmother (particularly if welfare structures make it financially more beneficial to the mothers for the fathers to live elsewhere). Women have more potential for control over their own reproductivity in this system than in any nuclear family system—although that potential is more of-ten than not thwarted by poverty, poor medical care, lack of education, and violence.

The same adverse social conditions promote homophobia among Af-rican Americans. Tremendous stress is put on producing children "for the sake of the race" (a phrase common in early-twentieth-century Af-rican American texts), and both gay male and lesbian relationships can be judged on this basis to be a kind of betrayal. Similarly, because there is such a high mortality rate among young African American men—they are the population group most likely to fall victim to homicide, for ex-ample—and such a high rate of incarceration, males are in short supply, so the conditions that promote male contingent homosexuality do not exist. (Similarly, child molestation is much less frequent in African American households than in the general population.) Psychologically, as well, men who have been the victims of racism, with its assaults di-rected specifically upon their masculinity, its emasculating parricidal and sibling rivalry dynamics, will often respond with various kinds of hysterical hypermasculinizing, including homophobia. Under siege and threatened with economic disaster, African Americans, as noted, are prone to obsessional prejudices against merchant groups—Jewish land-lords, Korean grocers, Chinese service networks—and they may extend this to homosexuals, who they perceive as taking up public policy atten-tion or infiltrating political processes and seizing control, particularly in cities where they are numerous and well organized.

The sexism of many African American males, especially those raised in matrifocal extended kinship settings, tends to be more of the one-sex, bodily narcissistic variety than of the two-sex, mental narcissistic variety. Outside the suburban black middle class, which is psychosocially organized in ways comparable to the white middle class, the African American extended family structure resembles polygamy more than monogamy as far as the males are concerned. Men often have more than one household (rather than more than one wife in a household) and children by a number of women. But, for the reasons just noted, they do not frequently practice pederasty. They frequently do, however, idealize a woman—black or white—who is androgynous and has some type of phallic quality. In her most recent incarnation, she is rap music's "gangsta bitch": tough and assertive, a mirroring twin, but also big-breasted and nurturing and adoringly available.

Different societal subgroups and minorities have different prevailing sexism types—of which the prevailing African American urban type can stand as an example—but there are also certain features of the sexisms that extend across boundaries of race, ethnicity, and class, often beginning in a privileged middle class and radiating outward, propelled by streams of advertisement and telecommunications.[9] As every commentator on the current American scene has noted, across all classes but especially the middle class young people are marrying later; more women are having children as single parents and not marrying at all; many untraditional household groupings are emerging; and the divorce rate is over 50 percent. Particularly among young adults, sexism is becoming more detached from specific family contexts and forms, specific arrangements for reproduction, and floating through private and public contexts. But, at the same time, a growing number of traditionalists are promoting the restoration of monogamous households with women in the reproductive role, and a growing number of women and children are experiencing domestic violence, both of which are in part reactions to the amorphousness of the current family. A pattern known as "serial monogamy" is growing more common, although it might more accurately be called "postmodern polygamy," as it features both women and men taking children—or responsibility for children—and thus custody connections with their previous spouses from one marriage to the next, bringing about complex linkings and mergings of families. In diverse ways, not just the forms of marriage but the forms of the family are becoming more amorphous, so that the patterns or correlations of sexism type to marriage and family types are breaking down or overlapping.

From this shifting scene emerges a clash of fantasies, a variant on the "battle of the sexes" created by current social conditions that allow much more public scope to women's desires. Both male narcissism and female narcissism are being expressed in new ways, and the ways conflict. Most important among men is the phenomenon that I referred to in Chapter 9 as prolonged adolescence. Men who have been narcissistically promoted by their mothers (and often by their fathers as well) expect both a kind of attention from women that continually recreates the maternal promotion and, more deeply, conditions that keep in place their maternal ideal—the omnipotent, all-supplying woman who is like them. Their expectation rules no matter whether the mother's narcissistic attention was constant, unpredictable, or cold and aloof, no matter whether she was overempathic, inconsistently empathic, or unempathic, because the main ingredient of the child's experience was of not being allowed to grow as an individual and to individuate because he was in the service of his mother's needs. His mother, then, could be the stereotypical middle-class suburban mother of the 1950s in her one-family house devoting herself full-time to her children, or she could be that woman's daughter, a mother of the 1970s juggling family and career, wanting her children to be both perfect and perfectly adapted to her schedule. Men who prolong their adolescence (or their childhood into adolescence) are both very dependent on others (especially women) for appreciation and very frightened of commitments or dependency. They move from situation to situation in their search, Don Juans of nostalgia, whereas men of other eras and places might have found satisfaction (and been sexist) via polygamy or via monogamy combined with pederasty or prostitution or other forms of extramarital sex.

Most influential among women is the phenomenon of female narcissism going public, becoming part of feminist consciousness (in the broadest sense, not necessarily as a political position). More and more women, particularly of the middle class, hold up as an ideal a form of reproduction that is neither the paternity-centered male reproduction nor the female reproduction enforced by the private sphere, but what might be called shared reproduction. This form means not just shared parenting—equal responsibility for children and for maintaining the household in which children are being raised—but male emulation of female capacities. Psychologically, it is female narcissism asking, "why can't a man be more like a woman?" or "why can't he be mothering?" (to the children and to me). The ideal, that is, expresses a fantasy that the primary narcissistic bliss of the woman with her mother will be recreated in the marriage; a fantasy that has never been expressed historically in a marriage form.[10] Male sexism, in such a context, incorporates resistance to the ideal, which can take many forms depending on how and to what degree a man feels the ideal as a challenge to his own nostalgic ideal of narcissistic bliss restored. A man who prolongs his adolescence—and his reliance on his mother's attention and nurturing, his fantasy of her as like him—is not a good candidate for supplying nurturance to a wife.

Contemporary conditions favor splits in consciousness. In one example we see a man who supports or tries to support women in their quests for equal participation in public spheres and their visions of equal responsibility at home, winning praise for his efforts, while he simultaneously (often quite unconsciously) works to hold the lines of traditional discrimination in place so that his women will remain the mother—his mother. He may compromise by making her a public mother: she must be a mother at the office or a mother in her elected office or a maternal officer. He may disguise his ambivalence by participating in a male consciousness-raising group where he can be praised *by men* for his sensitivity to women. Contemporary conditions also favor female chauvinism and all kinds of theories that show women's superiority over men, their greater gifts for relatedness, their sensitivity and sensibility, their unrationalistic and humane moral standards. The rhetoric of empowerment obscures female narcissism, with its conflicts over dependency and independence. A woman may end up unintentionally helping to assure with her attack upon male self-esteem that a man who can satisfy her ideal will not be able to reach adulthood. The dilemmas of assimilation known to all minorities are hers—she does not wish to make her critique so strenuous that men are even further damaged, but she wants them to change.

The prevailing acrimonious mixed-up American sexism, neither one-sex nor two-sex, is nightmarish and makes contemporary daily life very wearing. Polls show teenagers looking futureward as the present scene would lead one to expect: boys desiring restoration of the old regime in which men rule homebound women happily ever after; girls saying that they are preparing themselves for careers because they must be able to take care of themselves, since divorce is so common and men are so unreliable.[11] All that can optimistically be said about a stalemate in which men want women to be like them and women want men to be like them is that, should this *actually* happen in ways that would be pleasing to all concerned—not a threat, not a deracination, not a deprivation of identity—the conflict of narcissistic desires could become a complementarity. Fortunately for men and women, there are men and women whose lives—and whose experiences of prejudice—have prepared them to be pioneers in such a psychosocial possibility. These are the ex-"homosexuals," the homosexuals who have leapt over their assigned category, whose history I will sketch below.

## The Homophobias in Their Contexts

As I have been indicating, different forms of sexism, of family life and attitudes toward reproduction, of economy, of religion, correlate with different attitudes toward male and female homosexuality. The history of homophobia is embedded in a wider history of socioeconomic and political circumstances and a wider history of the family and sexism. But some general patterns can be extracted from the correlations and related to socioeconomic and political events. To construct a thorough typology of homophobias, cross-cultural study is crucial, but to show what cross-cultural study can yield I will focus my attention first on European and American history in the three periods when antihomosexual campaigns have been most intense. These three periods, which appear with similar outlines in the works of the current generation of historians and practitioners of Gay Studies, are quite different, reflecting distinct characterological norms as well as incomparable socioeconomic conditions and cultural moments. There is no linear developmental course for the homophobias—different circumstances give rise to different forms of homophobia.

In the near-decade between John Boswell's pioneering *Christianity, Social Tolerance, and Homosexuality: Gay People in Western Europe from the Beginning of the Christian Era to the Fourteenth Century* (1980) and David Greenberg's encyclopedic *The Construction of Homosexuality* (1988), a sea change came over the history of homosexuality. It shifted ground from work designed to recover a history little and not well told to work focused explicitly on how homosexuality has been construed in history and by historians and anthropologists. The shift represents the beginning—but just the beginning—of a realization that there are homophobias (plural) in need of study, not just one sort of homophobia. And it marks also the beginning—but just the beginning—of some clarity about the types of homosexuality that have existed and do now exist, as well as the types of definitions of homosexuality, whether by acts (or

aims or behaviors), by preference in object, or by psychological characteristics or role or identity (by self-identification). It is now widely
recognized among historians and other students of homosexuality that
pederasty (in the sense of transgenerational homosexuality, usually engaged in by married men) is not the same as transgender homosexuality
(in which men take up female roles and females take up male roles),
and that neither of these is the same as the homosexuality of contemporary self-identified homosexuals (which is less tied to fixed sex and
gender roles and might be called "egalitarian homosexuality").

The burgeoning and brilliant field of Gay Studies has already
achieved a clear agreement that there are three key moments in European (and American) history when prejudice against gay people flourished. Viewed from the most illuminating angle for describing prejudice
types, we could refer to three moments when periods of relative tolerance ended: (1) the abrupt cessation (circa 300 C.E.) of the Greco-Roman era in which (predominantly pederastic) homosexuality had been
celebrated; (2) the collapse of the nearly six century Christian period
(700–1300) in which homosexuality was widely, although not officially,
tolerated; and (3) the late-nineteenth-century destructive end of the era
ushered in by the French Revolution (1789–1850), in which homosexual activity was protected by a rank of egalitarian legislative initiatives.
The most violently repressive periods of antihomosexuality have come
in reply to flourishing homosexual practice—but of three quite different sorts.

As I have noted, during the Greco-Roman era pederasty was normal
for most male citizens with sufficient wealth to sustain both their households and their protégés. What prejudice there was focused on acts that
transgressed the well-understood boundaries of the pederastic relationship. In the Greek and Roman texts that present normal homosexuality,
one finds an obvious and direct correlation between what I have been
calling same-sex sexism or bodily narcissism and prejudice against any
kind of activity that is viewed as nonphallic. Nonphallic activity included
both passive male homosexuality—being penetrated while acting like a
woman—and all sorts of lesbianism except for the lesbianism that was
specifically initiatory or pedagogical, which could accurately be called
"sapphism," as it was the sort practiced in Sappho's girls' preparatory
school on Lesbos.

But passive male homosexuality was usually considered a much more
serious offense than female homosexuality, for it involved a renuncia-

tion of the phallus—a "castration," not a lack—and its consequence was felt to be powerlessness or unreliability in public affairs, a lack of virtue horrifying to the polis-minded Greeks. Young men who were receptors of the phallus but did not transgressively feminize themselves, however, were celebrated on narcissistic grounds, as Aristophanes adoringly celebrated them in Plato's *Symposium:* "Those who love men and rejoice to lie with and be embraced by men are also the finest boys and young men, being naturally the most manly. The people who accuse them of shamelessness lie; they do this not from shamelessness, but from courage, manliness, and virility, *embracing what is like them.* A clear proof of this is the fact that as adults they alone acquit themselves as men in public careers." (192A, italics added). In the most diverse societal contexts where pederasty is normal, and always where it is incorporated into puberty rites, a young man who receives the phallus or the semen of an older one is held to be empowered and helped to become a man himself by the phallic borrowing or infusion.[12]

Starting in the third century of the common era, as the Roman Empire declined, laws of the phallus-centered sort were enacted against same-sex male eroticism, bringing to an end the era of "Greek love" that the Romans had so creatively extended. The Theodosian Code of 390 C.E., for example, explicitly targeted "all persons who have the shameful custom of condemning a man's body, [by] acting the part of a woman's, to the sufferance of an alien sex (for they appear not to be different than women)." This passage represents the "female," receptive, male homosexual as the initiator of the shameful custom (the model may be temple prostitution). The theme of the "alien sex" of passive homosexuals is also common to the whole homophobic tradition that descends from *Leviticus* and the Old Testament passages in which the Hebrews made into law their frantic effort to distinguish themselves from the Canaanites, a people who practiced fraternal polyandry (a plurality of brother-husbands to one wife) and among whom homosexual love was as common as it was fraternal. The Canaanites had a culture in which establishing paternity was clearly not a priority—which horrified the Hebrews, who were striving to retain their traditional culture in a new land and to preserve both the remembrance of their ancestral ties and the purity of their lineage (the importance of which for them is obvious in the story of Esau's selling Jacob his primogeniture). It was the Canaanite sex goddess Ashtart, known to the Hebrews as Kadesh (meaning holy), who particularly had to be repudiated. She represented

sex as detached as possible from concern with paternity. Her name, for
example, was given to temple courtesans of both sexes—and "kadesh"
is the word translated with such contempt in the King James version of
the Bible as "sodomite."

Nothing so ethnocentrically "nationalistic" or group preserving motivated the Christian homophobia of the third through sixth centuries
C.E. The earliest Christian writers, including the strenuous Paul, were
homophobic as part of their generalized, and fanatical, asceticism or
antisex attitude. They did not seek, as the Hebrews did to keep a kingdom on this earth but instead anticipated one in the next world; Christians were, as Paul said (1 Cor. 7:35) to "attend upon the Lord without
distraction." Their asceticism, which included renunciation of sexual
activity in heterosexual marriage as well as any kind of extramarital practice, was part of a world weariness and despair that swept around the
Mediterranean as the Roman state, once a monument to civic virtue,
became more and more tyrannical, casting its citizens back on private
codes and otherworldly religious mores and interfering in all public
manifestations of morality. By 300 C.E., when the state began to fine
passive homosexuals and deprive them of their inheritances, as well as
forbid the gay marriages that Romans had enjoyed, Christian writers
were defining absolute moral standards. These were all that remained
in Rome by the time the state had disintegrated under attacks by the
"barbarians" from Northern Europe with their militarized cultures.

Generally, highly authoritarian regimes promote a homophobia that
has an obsessional cast even while it is narcissistic.[13] Rule-bound and
intrusive states support rule-bound and prescriptive moral communities
that engage in thought reform as a normal activity. In psychological
terms, the asceticism—including that of the Christians—that became so
common as the tyrannical Roman state clamped down on its citizens,
looks like an extreme reaction to the earlier bodily narcissistic celebration of the phallus and location of self-esteem in phallic activity; it is the
opposite stance, a repudiation. Paul made an explicitly narcissistic call
for celibacy—he set himself as the standard: "you all . . . be as I am
myself" (1 Cor. 7:7). Eventually, phallic activity was renounced totally,
and self-esteem located in spiritual or mental life, in control over worldly
desires and corrupt flesh, where it then had to be obsessionally reinforced and wrapped in rules. This was Augustine's route, as he repudiated his youthful homosexuality and took up the two-sex sexist or mental
narcissistic form of homophobia: no man should allow himself to be

used as a woman is used because "the body of a man is superior to that of a woman as the soul is to the body." "There is nothing," Augustine noted in a completely two-sex sexist manner, "which degrades the manly spirit more than the attractiveness of females and contact with their bodies."[14] In this context, homophobia seems only the continuation of sexism by other means.

Paul's Christian celebration of celibacy lacked, in his lifetime and during the early years of Christianity's development, state institutional enforcement, but it had triumphed in Rome by 390 c.e. when Theodosius issued his code. In the next century, however, a different kind of homophobic atmosphere began to appear in the Christianizing empire, as is clear in the way the Emperor Justinian (in his *Novella* 77, dated 538 c.e.) imagined homosexuals as powerful secret agents whose acts were magically destroying the stability of his realm: "for because of such crimes there are famines, earthquakes, and pestilences; wherefore we admonish men to abstain from the aforesaid unlawful acts, that they may not lose their souls." Here, the mode has become more characteristically obsessional. But this kind of obsessionality was not the prevailing mode in Christian Europe until after the fall of the Roman Empire (except in parts of Spain, under the Visigoths).

The intolerance of homosexuality that characterizes mental narcissists in monogamous settings, particularly in the context of monotheistic religions that are antisex like Judaism and Christianity, has a developmental logic tending to move away from a focus on the nonuse of the phallus by the "female" male lover and toward the persistent obsessional topic of anal penetration as a fearsome, disorganizing threat. Homophobes of this type condemn not just passive or penetrated male homosexuals, but the act of anal penetration and homosexuality per se. Along with masturbation, both male and female homosexual practices are judged as nonprocreative sex and ruled deviant and sinful as such. The ultimate model for conduct is the Deity, who is nonsexual, unlike the gods of most polytheistic religions, some of whom are not just sexual but—as psychoanalysts say—polymorphously perverse, enjoying sexual relations with immortals and mortals of the same and the opposite sex. Antihomosexuality as a mode of obsessional prejudice is the prevailing type of antihomosexuality in milieus that are ideologically dedicated to either rigidly controlled procreation or celibacy.

In obsessional milieus, in accord with the generalizing tendency of obsessional prejudice, any other practices—like usury—that can be con-

strued (in the equivalences of the unconscious) as associated with forbidden anal pleasures are also forbidden. The objection made to usury
among the Romans and among the Jews (noted in *Leviticus*), which was
adopted by the Christians, was that it involved unnatural increase, that
is, increase involving no agency on the part of the money's lender: "usu-
rers violate nature by making money grow which would not increase
naturally," as a Christian commentator noted.[15] Money that just swells
up pleasurably of its own accord is out of control or, more accurately,
is frighteningly in control. Heresy, too, could easily become assimilated
to this way of thinking, for it penetrates into persons and groups and
grows there uncontrollably, taking over. Preservation of personal
boundaries, of doctrinal or ideological purity, or of commerce (in the
broadest sense, including both sexual and financial) are the linked
needs that account for the similarities in the developmental courses of
homophobia and antisemitism that have occasionally been noted by
historians. In his *Christianity, Homosexuality, and Social Tolerance,* John
Boswell observed:

> Most societies . . . which freely tolerate religious diversity also accept
> sexual variation, and the fate of the Jews and gay people has been
> almost identical throughout European history, from early Christian
> hostility to extermination in concentration camps. The same laws
> which oppressed Jews oppressed gay people; the same groups bent on
> eliminating Jews tried to wipe out homosexuality; the same period in
> European history which could not make room for Jewish distinctive-
> ness reacted violently against sexual non-conformity; the same coun-
> tries which insisted on religious uniformity imposed majority stan-
> dards of sexual conduct; and even the same methods of propaganda
> were used against Jews and gay people, picturing them as animals bent
> on the destruction of the children of the majority.[16]

But Boswell's observation rests on a vague claim that tolerance of variety
or difference—sexual or religious—links the courses of the two prejudices. He did not allow that the two might be in certain periods manifestations of the same prejudice syndrome. In part, Boswell's view was
blocked by his concentration on the charge that "the children of the
majority" are targets for both homosexuals and Jews, which is only one
facet of the psychology these two prejudices share.[17] But in greater part,
his view was determined by his assumption that European antigay prejudice has been the same in each of its three major flourishings.

To press this point, Boswell suggested that rises in antigay prejudice

and antisemitism were a function of deurbanization or regressive returns to the dark ages of rural conditions. He interpreted the fall of the
Roman Empire as a massive return to or devolution into the kind of
precity state or prepolitical rural conditions where kinship structures
dictated that homosexual relations had to be forbidden. "A very great
proportion of social and moral taboos in kinship-structured communities is directed toward regulating legitimate procreation and discouraging forms of sexuality which would complicate social organization by
producing persons with ambiguous claims to a position within the family. Such efforts usually bear little relation to superficially similar concerns which underlie sexual morality in politically organized societies,"
he explained.[18] Thus Boswell claimed that tolerance for homosexuality
is greater in urban settings that are "organized political units which
explicitly transcend kinship ties" and that emphasize not family justice
but more "abstract justice administered impartially by the state for the
welfare of all."

But there is nothing in cross-cultural anthropological literature to
support such a view.[19] As I noted before, homosexuality is very common
in kinship-structured (particularly polygamous) communities, especially
in its pederastic or transgenerational form, which is frequently woven
into puberty rites and manhood ceremonies. The societies most accepting and even celebrating of transgender or gender-exchanging homosexuality have been and are those in which there is a traditional role
for homosexuals, like the male and female *berdaches* among the Native
American Plains tribes, which permits men to live and work as females
and marry men and allows women to live and work as males and marry
women. These roles exist in kinship societies where both heterosexual
and homosexual marriages are polygamous and where the religious
traditions are "animistic" or organized around a concept of spirits animating alike the human and nonhuman worlds, as well as the male and
female bodies.[20] Such societies are culturally and religiously egalitarian
to an extent that certainly rivals, if it does not surpass, any egalitarianism
achieved in urban settings by political means.

Boswell's typology, nevertheless, quite rightly stresses that urbanization was the precondition for the production of distinct homosexual
subcultures in which not just the pederastic transgenerational and the
transgender but also other forms of homosexuality have flourished and
in which, eventually, people who identified themselves as homosexuals
appeared. After the period of the most intense Christian ascetic and

eventually obsessional prejudice against homosexuality had spent itself, that is by 700 C.E., an era of official church condemnation (more or less enforced in different regions) and widespread priestly practice of homosexuality set in. Most of the legislation against homosexuals was civil, and most of the control that civil and church authorities wished to exercise was against adultery (which could be construed as heterosexual or homosexual). Boswell's thesis about the relation between urbanization and tolerance holds well for the succeeding period, starting in about the tenth century, in which cross-continental trade and city life waxed in Europe: "The reemergence of a distinct gay subculture in southern Europe is almost exactly coetaneous with the revival of major urban centers, and the relation between the two was obvious even to contemporaries. It was also during this period that erotic passion—which had been almost totally absent from Western literature since the fall of Rome—suddenly became the subject of a large proportion of literature and seemingly the major preoccupation of feudal society."[21] The "courtly love" poetry of the early twelfth century was exchanged between men and men and women and women as well as between men and women.

Within the twelfth-century church, a vocal group of ascetics decried the growth of homosexual love and literature, particularly among clerics. An opposed contingent celebrated male friendships. The critical party spoke in the pure language of obsessionality, with images of pollution, penetrated fortresses of the body and mind, suffocation in filth, lost sphincter control. According to Saint Peter Damian in 1051:

> Absolutely no other vice can be reasonably compared with this one, which surpasses all others in uncleanness. For this vice is in fact the death of the body, the destruction of the soul; it pollutes the flesh, extinguishes the light of the mind, casts out the Holy Spirit from the temple of the human breast, and replaces it with the devil, the rouser of lust; it removes truth utterly from the mind; it deceives and directs it toward falsehood; it sets snares in man's path and, when he falls into the pit, blocks it up so there is no escape; it opens the doors of hell and closes the gates of heaven.[22]

But Saint Peter Damian's diatribe aroused no great interest in his pope, Leo, or in the contemporary synods. He was ahead of his time.

The usual social obsessional conditions created the context for obsessionality like Damian's to become the norm: successive generations experienced escalating economic turmoil and devastations of war and plague (the Black Death over a century *halved* the population of Europe). The dynamic, one I identified before as depression and disillusion, in this particular context might better be named Crusades and Inquisition. The Crusades, not all of which were fought outside Europe against the allegedly sexually perverse and effeminate Muslim enemies, drained resources (as state imperialist ventures would at the end of the nineteenth century) and tore at the social fabric, while the struggle for conformity in the church (eventually, the triumph of systematic Aquinian theology) redounded on all who could be called deviant, heretical, different. The sequence is one in which a great peak of social acceptance of homosexuals—the cultural renaissance moment of courtly love poetry that included homosexual love poetry—was followed by a political backlash, the second major homophobic period. The same can be said for the Jews, who participated as intellectual leaders in the so-called twelfth-century renaissance and then were hit with anti-Jewish legislation of the sort that, later, during the early nineteenth century, brought the brilliant Jewish salons of Berlin to an end.

The result for homosexuals can be read in the penal codes of the times. The main mode of punishment for homosexual acts (of the passive sort) shifts from castration to burning or other forms of whole body elimination like hanging with burial (the mode of punishment common in Greece and Rome for women who had violated sexual codes) or even burial alive (prescribed in an English code of 1300 called "Fleta"). The *Etablissements* of Saint Louis, the French code of 1270, is a transitional document, setting forth both narcissistic and obsessional punishment modes in an escalating series:

> He who has been proved to be a sodomite must lose his testicles. And if he does it a second time, he must lose his member, and if he does it a third time he must be burned.
>
> A woman who does this shall lose her member each time and on the third must be burned.[23]

Burning was the preferred punishment by the fifteenth century; hanging came in second. Both punishments were used frequently against men and women until the eighteenth century, when the Napoleonic Code swept away all punishments for consensual adult sexual activities in French dominated regions. In other regions, like England, homosexual behavior was punishable with death until the late nineteenth century

(1861 in England). The reforms inspired by the French Revolution did not, importantly, include Prussia, so a context of intolerance was left undisturbed there to become the background for the homophobia embodied in the Nazi codes.

In important ways, however, Nazi laws and enforcements differed significantly from the Prussian tradition. Coital acts between homosexuals were criminalized when Prussia assumed leadership of the German Empire in 1871. But during the Weimar Republic after World War I, these laws were not enforced, and Berlin became—like Paris and New York—a center for a vast and vibrant homosexual subculture. The Nazis reacted against this "degeneracy," particularly after the prominent homosexuals in Hitler's entourage, like Ernst Rohm, were purged. How "intellectualized" and totalitarianly obsessional their antihomosexual legislation was can be grasped immediately from the fact that they criminalized noncoital as well as coital acts—and not just kissing and embracing, but homosexual *fantasizing*. By 1942, *any* infraction was punishable with death, and the antihomosexuality program was firmly set in the context of the Nazi program for controlling reproduction and increasing the Aryan birth rate—creating the master race.

This eugenic and reproductive program reprised the features characteristic of precapitalist agricultural societies—striving for large families and clan *(Volkish)* empowerment through child production and control over paternity (the emphasis being not so much on virgin brides per se as on clan or racial purity and prevention of miscegenation). Similarly, the Nazis were, despite some of their public rhetoric about the importance of the church, anti-Christian or, more accurately, early Christian. Ideologically, they resembled ascetics of the early Christian period and of the Emperor Justinian cast of mind—a mixture of phallic-narcissistic features and growing obsessionality marked their attitudes toward homosexuals. Their ideology centered on Teutonic deities and pagan rites or festivals, while they invoked the purity of womanhood associated with Christian antisex traditions. Although monogamy was the official marriage form of Nazi Germany, the society, in effect, turned toward polygamy because Aryan males were encouraged to beget Aryan children with as many racially qualified women as possible—in or out of wedlock. Two other measures reveal the strongly phallic-narcissistic base of the reproduction program: first, although lesbianism was disapproved, there were no laws in Nazi Germany against lesbians; and, second, antigay laws were not enforced in conquered territories, on the theory that homosexual practices there would aid the Reich by weakening the unity of the new Reich subjects, fitting them for subservience.

In contemporary life, the only manifestation of obsessional homophobia that is as cruel in its conceptualizing and sometimes in its practice as the Nazi one comes from the far and fundamentalist right in America, although the current Iranian Muslim fundamentalist regime is also strikingly brutal (and very un-Muslim in this regard).[24] In the American precincts, the AIDS epidemic is routinely described as a scourge from God upon the homosexual population, a punishment for the homosexual lifestyle—a variant on the Nazi theme for enemy populations: let them be destroyed by their own homosexuality. But the AIDS epidemic has also brought forth all the usual bureaucratic obsessional devices: plans for quarantines, ghettoizing of homosexuals, restrictive immigration policies, and even a proposal from an exemplary obsessional intellectualizer, William Buckley, Jr., for branding HIV-positive homosexuals on their arms (like Jews in camps)—and, of course, on their buttocks as well.[25]

It is in quite a different kind of milieu that homosexuals—like blacks, like people of the "primitive" lower classes—are imagined as hypersexual, archaically libidinous and promiscuous and are defined by their sexuality. The third period of homophobic upsurge in European (and American) history came at the end of the nineteenth century, and it had a quality—a hysterical quality—distinct both from that of the obsessional periods for which ascetic Christianity was the main ideological conduit and from that of the outbreaks of phallic-narcissistic anxiety over homosexual passivity. These earlier forms focused on acts and did not go on to identify homosexuals as persons or, rather, a type of person, as the Hungarian physician Karoly Benkert did when he came up with the name "homosexual" in 1869, just a decade before Wilhelm Marr coined the word "antisemitism" and thereby connected hatred of "the Semites" to the "race theory" that was then sweeping Europe. "The homosexual" was also a kind of a race or a species in late-nineteenth-century hysterical homophobia.

According to the prevailing concept of the homosexual, he or she was a "third sex," a term in use in the mid-nineteenth century but made common parlance at the *fin de siècle* by the activist Karl Ulrichs and the psychiatrist Richard von Krafft-Ebing, who hoped to see homosexuality decriminalized on the ground that it was an innate condition, beyond the control of anyone suffering from it. A member of the third sex—Ulrichs even gave the subspecies a name, "Uranians"—was neither male nor female but either a "feminine brain in a masculine body" or a "masculine brain in a feminine body." By the medical and psychiatric standards of the time, being a member of the third sex was a perversion, a diseased condition. Contemporary historians of sexuality generally agree with Michel Foucault that widespread understanding of the homosexual as a perverted or inverted person was a novelty of the period:

> The nineteenth century homosexual became a personage, a past, a case history, and a childhood, in addition to being a type of life, a life form, and a morphology, with an indiscreet anatomy and possibly a mysterious physiology. Nothing that went into his total composition was unaffected by his sexuality. It was everywhere present in him: at the root of all his actions because it was their insidious and indefinitely active principle; written immodestly on his face and body because it was a secret that always gave itself away. It was consubstantial with him, less as a habitual sin than as a singular nature. We must not forget that the psychological, psychiatric, medical category of homosexuality was constituted from the moment it was characterized—Westphal's famous article of 1870 on "contrary sexual sensations" can stand as its date of birth—less by a type of sexual relations than by a certain quality of sexual sensibility, a certain way of inverting the masculine and the feminine in oneself. Homosexuality appeared as one of the forms of sexuality when it was transposed from the practice of sodomy onto a kind of interior androgyny, a hermaphrodism of the soul. The sodomite had been a temporary aberration; the homosexual was now a species.[26]

People who imagine homosexuals as split beings (part male and part female), and thus of a lower or lesser human type and who hate them as such, as monsters or deviants from the two norms of male and female, direct at them a variation of the "in their place" hysterical prejudices. This different species must be lower, inferior, and it must be kept in an inferior position, often with the help of general theories of degeneracy linking homosexuals to the criminal and the insane, even the congenitally poor and the drunken. The abnormal homosexuals are a group on whom internal images of primitive sexuality can be projected, and, as is typical of these prejudices, they are a group intimately intertwined, familially intertwined, with the people who hate them. Prejudiced people of this sort entertain ideas that out-of-control homosexuality is contagious in the manner of mob violence, as a frenzy, a sexually transmitted disease. Accordingly, all kinds of acts must be forbidden: late-nineteenth-century legislation, particularly in England and America, outlawed oral sex and mutual masturbation (even between married heterosexuals).[27] The hysterical prejudice asserts at one and the same time that homosexuality is transmissible and that the third sex is unnatural or monstrous, which would seem to imply that natural people are immune, protected by a barrier of species difference. The contradiction (or hypocrisy) in this fantasy system betrays the underlying assumption of sameness or shared desire. The hysterically prejudiced are themselves split beings—they are the ones who most fit the well-known general psychological claim that people who fear homosexuals fear the homosexual in themselves.

As I noted in Chapter 8, the hysterical prejudices take a number of different forms. Parricidal form (in males) focuses on eliminating figures constructed as paternal rivals for the "mammy," a (nonincestuous) maternal figure; a sibling rivalry form construes the inferior group as siblings who must be beaten in a competition for parental (particularly maternal) favor; and, finally, a more obsessionally tinged form targets the inferior group as a group of infiltrators whose sexuality is debilitating. Each of these variants has a particular manifestation in prejudice toward the homosexual.

The more obsessional form is the most obvious and in contemporary American life the one most involved in legal battles. Allegations about acts directed at children have always been a feature of obsessional prejudice: as the Jews have been accused of poisoning Christian children, and nomadic groups like Gypsies and Bedouins of kidnapping them, so various middleman minority (trader) groups have been charged with running child slavery or child prostitution or child pornography rings. The long history of the homophobias, too, is laced with charges that people (particularly males) who engage in homosexual activity are corrupters of children. But the charge leveled at modern homosexuals is quite specific—they infiltrate educational institutions to be able to abuse and molest children as well as to miseducate them about the immoral homosexual lifestyle. They become teachers, leaders of youth groups, camp counselors, and so forth. Study after study makes it clear that most—the figure usually hovers around 90 percent—incidents of child abuse and molestation are committed by heterosexual men on girls, the majority of the victims being relatives of the victimizers, but the evidence has no effect on the prejudice. One of the most virulent campaigns against homosexuals in American history, led in 1977 by Anita Bryant and concentrated in Florida and the new Old South (in the territory of plantation racism), went under the title "Save Our Children." This campaign stood in the background of the (unsuccessful) 1978 Briggs initiative in California, legislation designed to license dismissal from California's schools of all openly gay teachers and anyone who "advocates, solicits, imposes, encourages, or promotes" homosexual activity. Since that period, agitation about abuse and miseducation has tended to shift into the arena of homosexual parenting, but efforts in the schools continue as part of the fundamentalist Christian effort to take over local school boards and prevent any seepage of homosexual rights into school curricula.

Another facet of this obsessional-hysterical form is resistance to seeing any distinction between homosexuality and pedophilia. Pedophilia elicits a double standard. Many cultural manifestations of pedophilia that involve heterosexual men and girls—films like *Pretty Baby*, for example—meet with no criticism, while any comparable manifestations that involve homosexual men and boys are quickly condemned. Attacks on pedophilia are attacks on homosexuality—a tendency that makes it difficult to protect children from those heterosexual pedophiles who are most dangerous to them. Similarly, there is resistance to acknowledging that cultures other than our own do not look on pederasty (with youths) as equivalent to pedophilia (with children). Pederasty is still horrifying, particularly to phallic narcissists, if and when the younger sexual partner is feminized or feminizes himself; but it is horrifying to more obsessional-hysterical types because the younger sexual partner is conceived as an innocent who is corrupted or polluted (even if he is a street hustler). The hysterical modern assumption that if a person engages in homosexual acts he will become a homosexual—that acts produce preferences by contagion—reigns among people prejudiced in this way. For them, homosexuality is catching.

The sibling rivalry prejudice usually takes the form of envy that homosexuals are free to be sexual all the time: they have no responsibilities for children or marriages; they have no moral inhibitions about casual encounters and no inhibitions of any sort about sexual practices; they live in milieus that promote sexual contact and have designated institutions—bars, tearooms, bathhouses, festivals, sections of opera houses, theaters, college campuses—for cruising and pickups. Their lives are, so the image goes, organized for sex. Those who envy homosexuals and—to use Dennis Altman's term—"homosexualize" themselves in imitation, have created an urban heterosexual singles cruising scene modeled on gay bar culture.[28] But those who envy without outlet are more likely to take to gay bashing, a specialty of young men at the end of adolescence, who are usually both envious and unsure of themselves and thus hypermasculinizing. Among women, envy of lesbian sexuality involves specific features: this sexuality carries no threat of pregnancy, it is less disease-prone; it is said (by lesbians) to be more pleasurable than heterosexual activity; it is not sexist. Heterosexually identified women who enviously initiate experiments with lesbian sex can become homophobic; when they deny the envied desires in themselves and return to the straight world, they claim they have been seduced or used. That is, they follow the rule of envy—what you cannot have, you denigrate.

The form of hysterical prejudice that looks least likely to have a variant targeting homosexuals is the parricidal one, as no homosexual male would seem on first thought to qualify as a paternal rival for the love of anyone's mother or wife. But it is not uncommon for boys and girls to either fantasize or experience homosexual contacts with family or extended family members and to want, in response, to attack homosexuals. Boys who have been raped at home or in schools or prisons often become such attackers; and *any* homosexual will do as a surrogate. The attack mode may well be sexual—that is, the boy may master the trauma of having been homosexually abused by homosexually abusing. When the contact is a fantasy and not a fact, the father or a father figure can be in the desired lover's role, and guilt may then motivate attacking a homosexual.

There are also social contexts that resemble the two-tier ones of paternalistic racism and class prejudice, particularly in milieus where merged family or overlapping family arrangements are common and not rigidly organized along sex role lines. In these contexts, homosexual or bisexual men and women are sometimes intimates of heterosexual women, not in *ménage à trois* arrangements but either as sexual partners or as confidants, counselors, companions, special friends. The womanliness of such men or the manliness of such women and the pleasure that heterosexual women take in them can be furiously resented by heterosexual males or more generally by people who find the idea of something like a Bloomsbury Circle or a hippie commune transgressive

of their needed role ideas. Similarly, heterosexual men sometimes have
a male or (less frequently) female buddy who arouses the resentment
of their mothers or wives—but whatever erotism exists in these configurations is usually coded and undeclared. More and more often both
men and women who have married and raised families are turning in
their adult years to homosexual relations, either exclusively or bisexually, and their decisions often arouse storms of homophobic resentment
in their families and associates and in people whose fantasies connect
them with such family upheavals.

These phenomena of mixed, merged, or reconfigured families point
to two features of homosexuality within the last two decades in America
and Europe that are having an effect on homophobic attitudes. First,
even though most homosexuals value homosexual subcultures—and
many would say that life is only safe and sympatico in *their* districts—
there is more integration of declared homosexuals into workplaces and
predominantly heterosexual living places than has ever before been the
case. Fewer homosexuals have to live ostracized from their families of
origin. More homosexual parents have their children in public schools.
And what this means—as with racism—is that the prejudice that exists
is both reduced (in terms of overt behavior and legal discrimination)
and increased (in the sense that greater contact stimulates the intimate
sexual sources of the prejudice, resulting in more subtle homophobia
and more sexualized violence). On the fundamentalist right, the homophobic rhetoric of boundary breaking and values traducing escalates
with each advance in civil rights for gay men and lesbians. Each defeat
of "in their place" discrimination feels to the prejudiced like a revolution.

Second, as gay subcultures have become more visible, more self-as-
sertive, and more powerful economically, socially, and politically, the
third sex notion has decreased among homosexuals themselves, especially in the educated middle class. Except in small circles, homosexual
men have rejected pederasty as a type of sexual relationship, and
lesbians have thoroughly questioned (sometimes in the mode of par-
ody) the "butch" role that translated into behavior the third sex view
of lesbianism. The prevailing self-presentation among gay men is no
longer the "feminine brain in a masculine body," which resulted in an
effeminate man or a "transvestite with a very high-pitched voice."[29]
Many gay men cultivate their male bodies—they are avid participants in
the sports and fitness culture that their "fairy" predecessors scorned—

as they cultivate a "macho" attitude, although they embrace the exquisitely sculpted and youthful ideal rather than the beefy or tough look. Very short haircuts and very trim mustaches adorn the type the French historian Phillipe Ariès calls "the virile homosexual." Among lesbians a type has appeared who rejects the extremes of "butch" and "femme" for a center that is in one way or another negatively construed. Sometimes she wears discrete not-butch sports clothes, or she wears either her black leather pants or her miniskirts with her heavy black shoes, not-femme, and flashes her bright red lipstick à la Madonna. What these types "say" is that the straight world's third sex classification and, further, even the designations "homosexual" and "heterosexual" represent a narrowing of definitional possibilities and do not apply. The virile homosexual also says to the straight man, "I look like you"—an unsettling statement. And the androgynous lesbian with style, who is not frumpy or obviously self-hating, says to straight women, "I am just like you and more free and interesting." Both types also say, more generally, that there is a unisex, or perhaps more accurately a pan-sex, style pioneered by homosexuals that defies traditional categories of any sort.

But these types are also the public (and public relations) side of changes in private relations. Among contemporary homosexuals, the ideal type of comradely homosexuality invoked at the turn of the century—for example, by Walt Whitman—but seldom actually to be seen is becoming more common. This is a relationship, of short or long duration, premised on equality between the partners in terms of sexual roles, which are often rotated in the relationship, and sexual acts, which are less formulaically modeled on heterosexual acts of submission and dominance or reflective of older pederastic or transgender forms of submission and dominance.[30] The relationship is premised on shared responsibility for confronting homophobia as well as for compassionately helping when comrades are struck with disease—especially AIDS among gay men—or trouble for which "family" is needed. These gay male and lesbian types have prepared the way for the emergence of bisexuality as a much more common self-definition. More generally, there are many more people who, if they wanted to answer a social scientific questionnaire about their sexual identities, would now want to answer with sentences rather than a noun like "heterosexual" or "homosexual," just as there are many more people who find the old census categories of race and ethnicity inapplicable because they come from the multiculturalism of the bedroom that has rendered these categories too simple.

Generally, the more visible as groups and the more assertive self-identified homosexuals of the modern sort are, the more the forms of homophobia incorporate them and respond to them. Homosexuality that is taken for granted in a culture—as pederasty was in the Greco-Roman world and is in so many of today's non-nuclear families—or that is structured into a culture's accepted or even celebrated life-forms, as transgender roles often are, is either tolerated within declared limits, in set forms, or is criticized in fixed ways. But homosexuality of the modern identity-based sort changes and interacts with the culture more, just as it is more subject to prejudices that change, on the surface even if not at their psychic core. The homophobias are unpredictable. They wax and wane, are aggravated and soothed, stirred up and calmed, by a dense mix of factors, and they in their different types—narcissistic, obsessional, and hysterical, with variations—interact complexly on one another. But it certainly can be said, despite their supreme intricacy (which exceeds that of all the ideologies of desire), that there is one and only one clear address to them, as homosexual liberation organizations of all political sorts have agreed throughout the twentieth century. And that address is for homosexuals—regardless of how they interpret or define themselves and homosexuality—to be "out."

"Homophobia" was coined to point to the fear that homosexuals arouse, to the anxieties about homosexuality that homophobic people live with and take out on homosexuals. But the word was invented when homosexuals were as hidden in society as those anxieties were hidden in the unconscious minds of homophobes. The persecuted and distorted lives of homosexuals provided reinforcement for homophobia both because homophobes could conclude that deviants would be condemned to and stuck in that ultimately frightful space the closet, and because homosexuals were so invisible in their closet that they could be construed and constructed in fantasy by homophobes without a reality check. The slogan of the activist group Queer Nation ("We're here, we're queer, get used to it") captures the realization that the therapists for those who suffer from homophobia are the homosexuals. They, who are now one of the most self-reflective and self-conscious of groups—accustomed to the condition that made the gay writer Edmund White realize, "once one discovers one is gay one must choose everything, from how to dress, walk, and talk to where to live, with whom and on what terms"[31]—confront one of the least self-reflective and self-conscious groups, the homophobes. They who are "out" draw out of the unconscious minds of their victimizers the fantasies that cripple the victimizers, condemning them to fearfulness. As in any therapeutic process, cure comes after much heightening of the conflict and reinforcing of defenses, which only slowly disintegrate, after painful overcoming of resistance.

# III

## Current Ideologies: The Victims Speak

# 13

## Varieties of Silencing

Each type of prejudice can be explored as a psychosocial manifestation both of a prejudiced person's character and social character and of a group in which kindred characters have gathered and prevailed. But each type can also be explored as an effect on its victims. Victims take in the prejudices directed at them, are injured, and respond with confusion, acquiescence, or resistance in ways that tell a great deal about the prejudices. People's psyches take on the forms of the prejudices that envelop them, sometimes as invisible as the air, sometimes as opaque as a shroud. They also develop defenses appropriate to the prejudices. Victims sometimes hate themselves in the mode they have been hated and sometimes are able to protect themselves in a mode that registers their understanding of the attack and their desire to turn on others with versions of what they have experienced themselves. The oldest studies of "internalizations" analyzed Jews—"Jewish self-haters"—but there exist now large literatures on black self-hatred, women's self-hatred, gay self-hatred. Less well studied are the modes in which victim groups resist insofar as these reflect the type of prejudice the victim groups are resisting.

### Necessities of Resistance

A victim group's reply may begin as a reflex, but it usually develops as a carefully chosen sociopolitical weapon as well as a self-cure; it is

457

both a diagnosis of the oppressor and a therapy for the victims—although these purposes do not always permit simultaneous fulfillment. Zionism is the Jewish political reply to political antisemitism, thus the original twentieth century model for a national liberation movement. Elementary as it is to note, however, Jews do not use their political movement to say, for their self-respect, "Jewish is beautiful." People who are, as Fanon put it "outwardly determined," who have been assaulted directly for their appearance, say, "Black is beautiful." In colonial contexts, blacks may, as the majority or indigenous population, work for national liberation; however, in much of the New World they cannot point to a territory or a nationality but must struggle with the contradictions of a cultural nationalism and a political assimilationism, a civil rights movement. Either way, the political struggle involves leaving definitively the servant's quarters of the Big House.

In both the instance of the Jews and the instance of the African diaspora, the forms and histories of the prejudices set the terms for protest. The same phenomenon can be seen in the subgroups of the Gay Liberation movement, who direct their reply "Gay is good" primarily at religiously based attitudes about the evilness of homosexuality. But the most important and distinctive feature of this liberation emerged wherever its protest focused clearly on how homosexuality had come to be construed as psychologically or medically pathological or deviant. Those who have felt locked away in a category challenge the very terms of the prejudice, the territory of definition, sometimes with a mocking and uncloseted, exhibitionistic, appropriation of the oppressor's terms: "We're here, we're queer, get used to it."

Victims of prejudices that put them in a position, in a place, resist the prejudices, first, by rejecting the place; victims of those prejudices that classify or define resist the prejudices by dismantling the oppressive categories. This dynamic makes the hysterical prejudices of place and the narcissistic prejudices of classification very different from prejudices of the obsessional type, which have as one of their peculiarities their ability to baffle their victims and shame them into silence. The victims' common sense is outraged and their intellects are defeated, dumbfounded, by the cold intellectuality of the obsessional prejudices' defensive structures, by the sadistic, genocidal impulse in the prejudices, particularly when the prejudices are espoused by people who glorify rigor, cleanliness, and order. A tremendous intellectual effort is needed to reply to a prejudice that confounds the intellect while it shames and assaults in more brutal and bodily ways.

All the types of prejudices have in their operating modes ways for suppressing their victim's insights into the nature of their victimization, as well as for suppressing their victims' resistances. Some of these ways are apparent—as I noted throughout Part I—in the history of social scientific studies of prejudice; some, also, are apparent in the various types of theories of prejudice. In the chapters that make up this part of my study, I want to focus on what the victims of the various prejudice types have had to say about the prejudices, how they have resisted by analyzing their oppressors, how they have struggled against the prejudices externally and internally. Using literatures by contemporary victims, I will suggest how the victims have met the strategies of suppressing resistance or of entangling the victims in definitions characteristic of the various prejudices and of theories about the various prejudices. I will not, however, try to draw a representative picture or take a census; I will not survey the literatures. In my judgment, the spokespeople I turn to were or are particularly situated both emotionally and intellectually to be able to see and to concentrate on showing the particular qualities of the prejudices they experienced. Of special importance are the testimonies of people who have been the victims of multiple prejudices and of victims who have, at one and the same time, been victims for multiple purposes. Out of these testimonies, the outlines for a comparative approach to prejudices can grow—as, I hope, can a more secure theoretical basis for coalition building among victim groups.

## Undoing, Isolation, Intellectualization: Current Antisemitism from the Right

Anyone who wades out into the wide sea of literature on antisemitism by Jews will immediately see how stormy and full of disagreement it is. On the most elementary issues of definition, one finds nothing but controversy. What is antisemitism? Is it a religious prejudice? Is it peculiar to the Christians? Or is it a racial prejudice? Are the enormous number of different expressions that prejudice against the Jews has taken over the centuries and into the twentieth century variants of one prejudice or do they have different sources? Did anti-Jewish prejudice of the Middle Ages lead, by some inexorable logic, to Auschwitz? When did prejudice against the Jews begin—and what caused it initially? What causes and conditions reproduce it? In the twentieth century, what do the antisemitisms of Central European clerics, anti-Dreyfus French nationalists, German race theorists, Oxbridge snobs, and neo-Nazi skinheads have in common? What do the antisemitisms of Heinrich Himmler and Ezra Pound, Joseph Goebbels and Louis-Ferdinand Céline, have in common? These kinds of questions have motivated recent surveying and synthesizing efforts like the one reviewed in Chapter 2, Gavin Langmuir's *Toward a Definition of Antisemitism,* which did not so much answer the questions as restate them. It seems to me no accident that a prejudice that has as one of its key effects baffling of the intellect should have as one of its corollaries that its study has been full of intellectual bafflement.

It also seems unsurprising that explorations of a prejudice which in its modern form carries such hatred of states and makes allegations that the victims have a secret, conspiratorial power over states should be so relentlessly politicized. In current contexts, for example, two debates have served as political lightening rods. The first involves the question, "Is Zionism a form of racism?" This question, debated at the United Nations and enshrined there in a positive resolution, represents the old tendency to collapse distinctions between types of prejudice—it assumes that a nationalism and racism, an ethnocentric prejudice and an ideology of desire, can be dynamically the same—but it also makes a political attack on Israel and the United States, Israel's patron, because it does not ask directly, "Should Israel offer the Palestinian population displaced since 1948 territory for a state?" The second debate considers the question, "Is anti-Zionism a form of antisemitism?" The answer should be "Sometimes yes, sometimes no," but usually supporters of the State of Israel reply with an aggressive yes, while a counterattacking no comes from those, sometimes antinationalist or cosmopolitan leftists, who equate Zionism with fascism, ultranationalism, and religious chauvinism. Debates about antisemitism get tied to attitudes toward states and toward nationalism—but the agenda of the debates is always controlled by images of Jewish power; the history of political antisemitism is woven into them.

The terrain of antisemitism is turbulent, politicized. And when it comes to the vast literature on Nazi antisemitism and the Holocaust, the contentiousness escalates to extremes because, around the arena in which genuine scholars debate, antisemites carry on a supposedly intellectual fight against the Jews in historical or pseudohistorical writing.

The most horrendous political outcome of antisemitism, the Holocaust, has itself become a focus of the prejudice—*it* is being denied. A strand of historical so-called revisionism actually asserts that the Holocaust was not intended by the Nazis or did not happen. These antisemites assert that the manufacture of death in the Nazi concentration camp system and the numbers of its victims have been fabricated or grossly exaggerated by the Jews for political purposes. They allege an international conspiracy of Holocaust manufacturers, the latest international Jewish conspiracy, in their efforts to erase what sympathy the Holocaust has aroused for the Jewish people and the State of Israel.

Holocaust denial flourishes on the political right in Germany, in the far right parties of most of Latin American and European states—like Jean-Marie Le Pen's National Front in France—and in American neo-Nazi groups. In the political agendas of these groups, denying the Holocaust is a means for asserting that National Socialism was not—and is not—evil. National Socialism's redemptive vision has fallen victim to a Jewish plot. But Holocaust denial serves other purposes as well: it is a growing tendency in Japan, for example, where it incorporates the idea that America is a nation controlled by Jews bent on undermining Japanese business and fomenting Japan bashing. The obsessionality of Japan bashing in the United States has its counterpart in Japan, where the Jews are the culprits. In the cauldron of Middle East politics, Holocaust denial is a staple in anti-Israel propaganda, and it leads to the claim that the Jews, having generated sympathy for themselves with the myth of the Holocaust, then used this sympathy as a cover while they displaced and persecuted the Palestinians, establishing and extending the State of Israel.

To non-antisemites (or non–anti-Zionists), the sheer audacity of Holocaust denial is bewildering. Those not prejudiced against the Jews are startled to hear that, for example, the *Diary of Anne Frank* is being called a hoax and find it hard to believe that anyone would tell bald and unabashed lies about how the *Diary* was forged for profit and for the purpose of mobilizing sentiment in favor of the Jews. But the mechanism of Holocaust denial is not so surprising if it is viewed against the main psychic purpose of the obsessional prejudices, which is to make the victims out to be victimizers, enormously aggressive, sadistic conspiratorial conquistadors, penetrators.

Obsessional prejudice builds first in intellectual terms, it is a vast wish structure, an omnipotence of thoughts, a mode that says, "we must be all-powerful to defend against them." So Holocaust deniers are impervious to argument and scornful of the legitimate historians who try to expose their fabrications and show up their lies. But "lies" is not really the right word, for it presumes a conscious intention to mislead, and the deniers view their statements as leading toward what they hold to be the truth, the end justifying the means, the obsession producing a rigid mental state of conviction that is split off from any feeling for the victims or their history. For expediency's sake, some deniers do adjust their statements to contexts, trying to appear unfanatical, deploring the fanaticism of others—even of the Nazis. These deniers assume reasoned tones and stress that they are engaged in a public debate, in which their speech is protected by law (by the First Amendment to the U.S. Constitution). Their appeal to free speech baffles newspaper editors and talk show hosts into applying "equal time" guidelines to claims that are certainly not by any reasonable definition "opinions."

Those Holocaust deniers who speak in scholarly accents sound like another group, the revisionists who currently, in more academic contexts, question not the reality but the exceptionality of the Holocaust, making efforts to "historicize" it, that is, to approach it as a series of events in need of narrating like any other. Some advocates of this revisionist approach insist that a historicizing perspective will make it clear that during World War II the Germans, too, were victims, both because of what they suffered at the hands—under the bombs—of the Allies and because their actions were so guided by what they imagined the Bolsheviks would do to them if the Red Army penetrated into Germany from the East (Germany's metaphoric backside). When the threat posed by the Bolsheviks (often called "Asiatics," which reverberates with current fears of Asian business penetration) looms large in historical accounts, a conclusion like Ernst Nolte's usually follows: "Auschwitz is not primarily the result of traditional antisemitism. It was in its core not only a 'genocide,' but was above all a reaction born out of the anxiety of the annihilating occurrences of the Russian revolution."[1] In the manner typical of antisemites and the obsessionally prejudiced in general, Nolte has found a sinister, attacking group to blame for the Germans' trouble—but it is the Bolsheviks, not (overtly) the Jews.

This revisionist controversy has been reflected in many recent German ceremonies of commemoration for German civilians and soldiers who lost their lives in the war. In 1985, the revisionist program extended to the fortieth anniversary of the German defeat, with an invitation to

President Ronald Reagan to visit the SS cemetery in Bitburg, an invitation intended to convey the message that the Germans and the Americans, enemies to each other, had really fought in the common cause of the Western struggle against Bolshevism, against the Russians who had been for all of his adult life Ronald Reagan's "evil empire."[2] These ceremonies manifest a nostalgia for normalcy, for a Germany in which people acted for normal reasons of self-defense, for a Germany that could produce patriotic heroes: a comprehensible Germany. German antisemitism baffles even the Germans.

While the Holocaust is being denied by pseudoscholars, and a "historian's debate" *(Historikerstreit)* flourishes among more credible—if no less self-serving and ideologically motivated—scholars, another quite diverse group of intellectuals has emerged to argue that the Holocaust was so extreme and exceptional a complex of happenings that it cannot be represented in any existing form of discourse. Those who assert that the Final Solution, which the name "Auschwitz" represents, cannot be narrated in traditional historical modes are influenced by the current academic deconstructionist trend of finding all discourses inherently self-defeating and the fad for trying to write in a postmodernist style that avoids supposedly naive modernist claims to truth or verifiability. The sincerity of this "problematizing" seems questionable when it is affectless and intellectualized, when its authors show themselves caught up unthinkingly in the dilemmas of antisemitism (as I will argue in a moment that Jean-Paul Sartre was just after the war).

Others seem genuinely overwhelmed by the phenomenon itself. Their sincerity is shown in their concern for why the problem of narratability or representability arises with regard to the Holocaust—and has arisen for every generation since the war. First, it seems too horrifying to say in mere words or images that human beings are capable of the atrocities that all but the Holocaust deniers know were committed. Auschwitz crossed a line and made it impossible for anyone ever again to say such atrocities are "inhuman" in the sense of not committable by human beings. Furthermore, Auschwitz was state policy. A state apparatus, not a single leader or a group of perpetrators, engineered and eventually, and to one degree or another, involved an entire citizenry in the Holocaust—to the incomprehensible point of national self-destruction. An extermination program evolved that flew in the face of all utilitarian purposes, all other needs of the German people, the army, the war effort. This self-destructive state policy, moreover, reflected an ideology that seems, also, incomprehensible. Was Nazi antisemitism an outgrowth of Christian antisemitism or was it a revolt against both Judaism and Christianity and the principles the two religions hold in common? Is there continuity between this ideology and the Western tradition—and, if so, does that mean that the tradition always contained, and still contains, the possibility for turning lethal in that way? These are the turbulent questions of antisemitism's definition in its current form. Finally, in Auschwitz the actions and the ideology of extermination became normal; they became a way of life as murder became regular and efficient. Apocalyptic events happened day in and day out—and this, too, seems incomprehensible and unnarratable.[3]

Each of these stances toward the Holocaust—denial of it, historicizing of it, questioning its narratability—has arisen at a particular political moment and situation in Germany, in Europe, in America, in the Middle East, and throughout the world in which Israel is now a state among states. And each has further complicated the ways in which antisemitism is discussed and understood. But each of these stances also says that there is something in antisemitism itself and its effects that calls forth complex intellectualizations, from antisemites but even from non-antisemites, for antisemitic purposes or even for the purpose of exposing and combating antisemitism. Current reactions to the Holocaust keep tending toward silence and toward silencing the specificities of Jewish history and experience. Victims of each of the prejudice types testify that they have been silenced and their stories suppressed, but each silencing has its distinct form. The form of silencing distinctive to antisemitism (and to the obsessional prejudices in general) arises from the social defense mechanisms obsessionality itself characteristically employs. These I earlier identified as undoing and isolation, reflecting and being connected to typically adolescent modes of intellectualization and asceticism.[4]

These intellectualizing modes of Holocaust denial and revisionism and the insincere hyperconsciousness are continuations—to put the matter another way—of strategies for depriving the Jewish victims of any sense of themselves as active beings, capable of spontaneous action or mastering a trauma. Earlier, in the 1960s, a period of worldwide political activism among the young, this deprivation strategy took the form of a question: "why did you not resist—why did you go like sheep to the slaughter?" This question was put, for example, to Jewish survivors acting as witnesses at Adolf Eichmann's trial in Jerusalem, where Hannah

Arendt, reporting on the trial, rightly called the question "cruel and silly." But it is also, quite specifically, antisemitically cruel. It implies that protest, escape, and resistance were normally possible in Europe before and during the war, as the Jews were being subjected to legislation that cut off their livelihoods, to ghettoization, to being stripped of their resources and then deported—shocked and debilitated—to camps. And the question is meant to make Jewish survivors and their descendants feel guilty, as though the Jews were responsible for the fate that befell them. Such guilt or feeling of complicity makes mastering a trauma impossible, as all abusers of the defenseless or the young know.[5]

This question about why the Jews did not resist, when it is not posed with conscious malice and political purpose, stems from an ignorance—culpable in itself—of the key feature of obsessional prejudice in its most extreme manifestation: the disorganizing and disorienting of the victims. In the words of the Italian camp survivor and writer Primo Levi:

> Remember that the concentration camp system even from its origins (which coincide with the rise to power of Nazism in Germany) had as its primary purpose shattering the adversaries' capacity to resist: for the camp management the new arrival was by definition an adversary, whatever the label attached to him might be, and he must immediately be demolished to make sure that he did not become an example or a germ of organized resistance.[6]

The policies and practices of the camps, which immediately isolated each prisoner in a mass of the anguished, spiritually devastated, shamed, and humiliated people continued by more horrible means the existing policies for reducing people to inexpressiveness.

Both during rises of political antisemitism and in retrospective moments like the present one, when political antisemitism is being denied, expression is singled out for attack. The obsessionally prejudiced construe their victims as intellectually powerful—cunning, shrewd, in charge of cultural institutions—and they attack their cultural media at the same time that they attack them bodily, as trash or refuse or fecal products. (So, following the Nazi model, the Serbians are now attacking Muslim cultural institutions in Sarajevo and elsewhere while they are engaging in brutal "ethnic cleansing.") The victims are refused positions in universities or libraries, their literature and art are destroyed after it has been classified by some term like the Nazi's "degenerate art." The victims' expression in the broadest sense is sited, censored, decomposed. This silencing is part of the sadism of antisemitism, which aims right at the victim's need for speaking. To deny the Holocaust, to deny survivors' memories and stories, is, of course, to mine further the sadistic vein of preventing expression. It is the most extreme form of cruelty for survivors, who all shared in an anxiety that Primo Levi captured when he described why he wrote his memoir *Survival in Auschwitz* right after the war.

> I've had the feeling that for me the act of writing was equivalent to lying down on Freud's couch. I felt such an overpowering need to talk about it that I talked out loud. Back then, in the concentration camp, I often had a dream: I dreamed that I'd returned, come home to my family, told them about it, and nobody listened. The person standing in front of me doesn't stay to hear, he turns around and goes away. I told this dream to my friends in the concentration camp, and they said "It happens to us, too."[7]

The need to tell a story—an unbelievable story—and be believed, by a therapist, by family, by a larger public, by History, is the need to master (if not ever to overcome) the trauma, to make the world inhabitable again after it has been experienced as so malignant and so deadly. When an antisemite attacks the products of this need, the stories, the traumatizing is repeated, instituting another "final solution." When a historian says that this story is a story like any other, not unprecedented, the small comfort that the mantra "Never again!" offers is undermined. These acts induce the feeling that this horror could happen again and is not an anomaly in human affairs. Similarly, but without the explicitly antisemitic motivation, someone who declares that the Holocaust is beyond narrating, that it is too horrible and immense and inhuman for words, makes, inadvertently, a version of the concentration camp policy of isolating prisoners in groups where they had no common language, punishing them with linguistic isolation.

Primo Levi understood that the need to tell is also proportional to the extent and to the manner in which the assault has been made beyond telling, made incomprehensible. The Nazis made no effort until their last days to destroy the documentation of their administrative massacre; on the contrary, they filled archives with their lists, their plans and preparations, their executive orders and reports. But precisely this routinized accounting for horrors is what made their intentions and actions unaccountable. The rage for order astonished the victims and suggested, slowly, the insight that the Germans were doing unto the victims a hideously extreme version of what they had done unto themselves and their society in the years leading up to the war. As Levi noted in *The Drowned and the Saved,* the camps stood at the end of a decade-long concentrated manufacture of obsessionality as a social character.

Levi's conclusion comes after a discussion of the camp practice called *Bettenbauen,* a system for making up the ragged camp bunks into neat, sharp rectangles, a system that *Lager* inmates were required to follow to the letter every morning of their precarious lives:

> For the SS in the camp, and consequently for all barracks heads, *Bettenbauen* had a prime and indecipherable importance: perhaps it was a symbol of order and discipline. Anyone who did not make his bed properly, or forgot to make it, was punished publicly and savagely. Furthermore, in every barracks there existed a pair of functionaries, the *Bettnachzieher* ("bed after-pullers," a term that I believe does not exist in normal German and that Goethe certainly would not have understood), whose task it was to check every single bed and then take care of its transversal alignment. For this purpose, they were equipped with a string the length of the hut: they stretched it over the made-up beds, and rectified down to the centimeter any possible deviations. Rather than a cause of torment, this maniacal order seemed absurd and grotesque: in fact, the mattress leveled out with so much care had no consistency whatever, and in the evening, under the body's weight, it immediately flattened down to the slats that supported it. In point of fact, one slept on wood.
>
> Within much more extended limits, one gains the impression that throughout all of Hitlerian Germany the barracks code and etiquette replaced those which were traditional and "bourgeois": the insipid violence of the "drill" had already by 1934 begun to invade the field of education and had been turned against the German people themselves. Those newspapers of the period which had preserved a certain freedom of reporting and criticism describe exhausting marches imposed on adolescent boys and girls within the framework of premilitary exercises: up to fifty kilometers a day, with knapsacks on their backs and no pity for stragglers. Parents and doctors who had dared to protest were threatened with political sanctions.[8]

The current assault on the victims' needs for storytelling, for mastering—needs created by the victimizer's actions—comes in the context of not just social-educational forms but also theories that represent the basic obsessional ideological pattern. The questioners of Jewish resistance mock the powerlessness of the victims by suggesting that they—the wily, connected, conspiratorial Jews—possessed the wherewithal to oppose their enemies had they but chosen to exercise it. The Holocaust deniers have invented a new international Jewish conspiracy—for manufacture of the Holocaust, for furthering Zionist or Israeli political aims, and so forth. The German historicizers have created an image of Germany besieged and about to be undermined or penetrated not by the Jews but by the Bolsheviks. They have, in a sense, reverted to the form of obsessional behavior and anti-Bolshevik ideology that, as Levi noted, was spreading through German society in the 1920s and 1930s, before Hitler's antisemitic version completely took over the role of ideological mainspring. These guiding ideas have reached the young neo-Nazis who currently attack Jewish business people and those immigrant "guest workers" who can be construed as like the Jews.

## Obsessional Theorizing from the Left

To elucidate this obsessional mode of silencing more fully, I consider how it operates in a work (like the contemporary work on narratability) meant to combat antisemitism, that is, in a work in which this mode of silencing operates against the conscious intention of the author. In such a context, the kinds of psychological and political assumptions that animate antisemitic works are present with the clarity of a photographic negative: because the picture is not there to distract, the outlines and the contrasts are clearer. This work, Jean-Paul Sartre's *Anti-Semite and Jew,* is also—not coincidentally, I think—the most quoted, anthologized, and republished single study within the whole postwar literature on antisemitism.[9] Nothing could make clearer the intellectually confounding character of antisemitism than the fact that the most widely read and quoted book about it is confounding. Sartre's book represents the way in which critiques of antisemitism from the Left have so often, by misconstruing the problem of antisemitism, offered solutions that exacerbated the problem.

Most theorists of antisemitism have understood that a fiction, "the Jews," serves antisemites as a scapegoat and as monster with which to frighten potential converts to antisemitism. When attacking the Jews, antisemites attach the characteristics they have displaced onto the Jews and made them represent. This understanding can lead to questions about why the Jews have been so frequently and disastrously cast in the scapegoat role, as it does, for example, in Otto Fenichel's rich essay "Elements of a Psychoanalytic Theory of Anti-Semitism." This essay, written in 1946 and included in one of the original Studies in Prejudice volumes, focused explicitly on the question, "Why the Jews?"[10] The Jews were peculiarly fitted to be the scapegoats of their non-Jewish neighbors, Fenichel argued, as Hannah Arendt did at the same time, because they had been forced into being a commercial people, not a landed people. They had been ghettoized and, until the French Revolution, both unassimilated and eager (in most cases) to preserve their separateness for religious reasons.

As a separate and clannish people, Fenichel continued (embarking on an analysis Arendt would not have agreed with), the Jews were suited to represent foreignness—both external and internal. They were exotic, but they could also stand for what is foreign in every person: "One's unconscious is also foreign," as Fenichel put it, and people need figures in the world onto whom that foreignness can be projected or displaced so that it does not rise up in internal rebellion. The Jews could stand for the primitive and archaic, and they did so especially well for the Germans because many of their customs and costumes signified an earlier period in German culture. Their language, Yiddish, seemed like an archaic German.

Fenichel suggested that desires known to all people—desires to murder, to revel in filth, to commit incest, to be debauched—could be attributed to the Jews as a foreign people. But the Jews could also represent guilt and vengeance for these same forbidden desires. Theirs is, Fenichel wrote, a "national character" easily associated with indirect aggression—that is, not aggression by means of armies and conquest, but aggression taken care of by a God who could be construed as vengeful against the Jews' enemies, a God of retribution. The Germans, suppressing any trace in the Judaic religion of love or compassion, viewed the Jews as a hostile people with a hostile God. Jewish customs, especially ritual circumcision, could be interpreted as prototypes for the punishments to be inflicted on the Jews' enemies—hence the many images of the Jews as torturers, abusers, kidnappers, well-poisoners, in short, castrators. In addition, the extreme patriarchalism of the Jewish religion and of Jewish family life could be interpreted by Gentile sons as threatening to their own phallic power and their own wishes to be the "chosen people" of a frightening father.

Unlike many psychoanalytic elaborators of scapegoat theories, Fenichel, who was a socialist, also carefully indicated that these elements of antisemitism—antisemitism on the instinctual drive level—would have remained fuel for antisemitic agitation but would not have developed into the Holocaust without external conditions promoting their most lethal dimensions. A "revolutionary mood" in the masses was such a condition, he argued, and antisemitic propaganda exploited it. Indeed, he suggested, the European property owning ruling classes used antisemitism to distract the working class and the masses from any political action or revolution to improve their condition. Hence, the Jews got the anger that might otherwise have flowed toward the ruling classes. So Fenichel's scapegoat theory, one of the most important produced on the émigré Jewish Left in America, was also a historical and social theory. And this dimension sets it in contrast to the pure scapegoat theory offered by Jean-Paul Sartre in *Anti-Semite and Jew.*

*Réflexions sur la question juive,* which Sartre began to compose in October 1944, was published in book form in 1946. The book's first section, which draws a portrait of the antisemite, had appeared by itself earlier, but the third section, which deals with authentic and inauthentic Jewish existence, had been held back at the request of Sartre's Jewish friends. Apparently, Sartre judged the situation in France to be calm enough by 1946 for a discussion of Jewish life—by a declared atheist. The complete text of Sartre's *Anti-Semite and Jew,* as the English translation of 1948 from Schocken Books was entitled, then appeared while Sartre was also writing about *négritude,* which he expounded and publicized (again, speaking for a persecuted group) in an essay called "Black Orpheus."[11] Sartre wanted to argue that Gentile Frenchmen could and should realize that solving problems of prejudice through socialism is in the interests of the majority, and he held that the same realization would lead European colonialists to give up their imperialist conquests in Africa and elsewhere. It is in the self-interest of the strong to recognize and reject the inequality that will, eventually, make them weak: "Not one Frenchman will be free so long as the Jews do not enjoy the fullness of their rights."

But Sartre's suggestion about how the Gentiles could solve their problem and save themselves would be costly—for the Jews. Socialism would permit the Jews to assimilate, and, assimilated, they would no longer exist as the Gentiles' problem. They would no longer exist as a distinct social group. But Sartre went quite beyond the general Marxist position on the necessary future "withering away" of religious groups by arguing that no "authentic" Jew would find this solution—the dissolution of the Jews as a group—strange, because no authentic Jew is Jewish for any reason other than to protect himself from the antisemitism that has invented the category of Jews. Sartre not only presumed to speak for the victims, he also told the victims that giving up their historical identity would be no loss for them.

Sartre considered antisemitism and white racism as two versions of the same problem of prejudice. In his most famous passage on the antisemite and his Jewish scapegoat he wrote: "The Jew only serves him as a pretext: elsewhere his counterpart will make use of the Negro or the man of yellow skin. The existence of the Jew merely permits the antisemite to stifle his anxieties at their inception by persuading himself that his place in the world has been marked out in advance, that it awaits him, and that tradition gives him a right to occupy it."[12] In this version of the Allportian assumption that prejudice is one, prejudiced people—all of them—have but a single need, which the pretexts of their prejudice help them to satisfy. "If the Jews did not exist the antisemite would have invented them."

All prejudiced people, Sartre argued, have a basic need to give up their freedom, to make a choice not to be free, and thus to choose life "on the plane of passion." *Anti-Semite and Jew* is a scintillating catalog of character traits in two columns, one for people who live on the plane of passion and one for people who live in freedom and reason. Again and again, obsessionally, Sartre stressed that the passionate are unchanging, impenetrable, impervious to experience. They are like stones, while the free and reasoning ones are open, flexible, welcoming to new experiences. The passionate refuse to examine themselves, to think about themselves, and they identify with the crowd of their likenesses while they are busy inspiring fear in the crowd of the "others" (whichever others are to hand). The passionate crowd is ordinary, mediocre, rooted in land and concrete property, distrustful of intelligence and of abstract property forms like money or credit. Their morality is inherited and inherited in a rigid, petrified mode: they believe in equality but only in their group, where they permit no distinctions of function to be recognized. They are a secret brotherhood, a "primitive society" embedded in but isolated from the larger community, which owes its existence to the very abstract principles, laws, and authorities that the primitive brotherhood finds abhorrent.

Prejudice appears here as a function of class embeddedness and class conflict, and when classes disappear in the revolution, so, too, will prejudice. To put this crude view in the crude terms that it shares with all forms of Manichaean obsessional thinking, Sartre saw two kinds of people, the good reasonable ones and the evil passionate ones, and imagined a future in which the conditions producing the evil ones (and all prejudice) would disappear. Again, antisemitism would have no existence in a society without classes and founded on collective ownership of the instruments of labor, one in which man, freed of his hallucinations inherited from an older world would at long last throw himself wholeheartedly into his enterprise—which is to create the kingdom of man. Antisemitism would then be cut off at its roots.

When Sartre turned to consider the Jew in an antisemitic situation, he stressed the individuality of the choice a Jew can make to live authentically or inauthentically. The inauthentic Jew is, basically, someone who wants to escape his situation as a Jew. He is hyperreflexive and cannot stop attending to himself; he has an inferiority complex; he lives in fear of conforming to the stereotype of Jewishness that he knows non-Jews entertain; he sees himself through non-Jewish eyes, as though he were a kind of perpetual witness to himself; he struggles for admission to non-Jewish circles while, in the privacy of his own circle, he adheres to his Jewish ways, so that he maintains a divided consciousness; he denies himself by living like a thing, a stone, or by becoming antisemitic himself, or by embracing universalist ideas from which all Jewish specificity or distinctiveness have disappeared.

Revealingly, Sartre did not say that the inauthentic Jew is a person of passion rather than reason. The earlier dualism does not apply to the Jews, even though there is an obvious overlap in the characterologies, particularly when Sartre considered the inauthentic Jew who is antisemitic or self-hating. The Jew who wishes to be a thing, a stone, cannot tolerate either himself or the authentic Jew, who is a rebel, an independent thinker, a free man. But the Jews, inauthentic or authentic, really fall outside the basic Sartrean dualistic characterology of passion versus reason. The man of passion, who will be an antisemite or a racist, shares some characteristics with the inauthentic Jew, but he is, as far as the preponderance of his character traits are concerned, the inauthentic Jew's opposite. He is sadistic, while the inauthentic Jew tends to be masochistic; he enjoys inspiring terror, while the inauthentic Jew is terrorized; he relishes his ordinariness, while the inauthentic Jew tries to distinguish himself in the eyes of non-Jews; he is a traditionalist, a conservative, a partisan of his group, while the inauthentic Jew tends toward denial of his group in social assimilation or intellectual universalism.

The difference between the dualistic characterology that Sartre offered for the non-Jews, antisemitic and not, and the one he offered for the Jews, authentic or inauthentic, stems from his basic conviction that the Jews are sheerly a construction of the antisemites. The Jews, in the situation the antisemites have created for them, are different. They are an ancient people, certainly, but they are, as Sartre put it, "not yet historical" in the way of, say, the French. "Until the nineteenth century the Jews, like women, were in a state of tutelage; thus their contribution to political and social life, like that of women, is of recent date." Such judgments would come as a surprise to anyone who had heard of the Old Testament or the Talmud. Anyone who had toured the sites of ancient Jewish cities or read the Kabbalah would be equally amazed by this remark: "the Jews cannot take pride in any collective work that is specifically Jewish, or in a civilization properly Jewish, or in any common mysticism." The Jews, really, do not exist—or exist only because of the particular historical situation of which they are a function, in which they are the antisemite's invention.

These claims, so outrageously dismissive, were in the service of a distinction Sartre wished to draw between modern antisemitism and premodern antisemitism, which he felt was directed at a people who were ghettoized, separate, and understood by Christians primarily as non-Christian or anti-Christian. Modern antisemitism presupposes the nineteenth-century emancipation of the European Jews, their assimilation and their secularization, their entry into "history" (which must mean Gentile history). So Sartre actually insisted that "the Jews who surround us today have only a ceremonial and polite contact with their religion." In Sartre's estimation, modern antisemitism is directed at a people who have no defining characteristics of their own; they are eminently constructible. Furthermore, as I noted, the authentic Jews, those who have refused to escape their constructed situation by assimilating, will be happy to assimilate when antisemitism has been destroyed by a socialist revolution. "Thus the authentic Jew who thinks of himself as a Jew because the antisemite has put him in the situation of a Jew is not opposed to assimilation any more than the class-conscious worker is opposed to the liquidation of classes." Any authentic Jew will be happy to give up his definition, the label "Jew" that the non-Jews have constructed for him, when all particular classes and cultures and religions have disappeared in the universal socialist future.

Sartre took the most extreme way to elaborate the idea that prejudiced people project ideas, images, needs, and fantasies onto their victims. But Sartre's book offered more than an analysis of the antisemitic tendency to construct the Jews as the Other, as a people with an existence only in terms of not-us. It in fact gave a demonstration of such a construction, an example of it. The entire text is written from a non-Jewish point of view, in the non-Jewish "we," the first person plural of people who can choose to live on the plane of passion or transcend to freedom, and it puts the fate of the Jewish "them" in non-Jewish, authentic, and freedom-fighting, socialist hands. "The Jew of today is in full war. What is there to say except that the socialist revolution is necessary to and sufficient for the suppression of the antisemite? It is for the Jews *also* that we shall make the revolution."[13] Socialist and Jew share a political solidarity: "we are all bound to the Jew, because antisemitism leads straight to National Socialism." But in Sartre's vision for the future, the solidarity of non-Jew and Jew is keyed to the end of alterity; it cannot be associated with a Jew defining himself as a Jew, much less fighting his own battle as a Zionist. In the socialist future, no one will need the Jew—or, presumably, the Negro or the woman. The Jews will be glad to give up their Jewishness, so there will be no Jews.

Sartre apparently had no idea how offensive his text would be to any Jew who did not live in anticipation of no longer being Jewish or did not consider Jewish life and culture outside of history, much less to any Jew who identified as a Zionist. He also had no idea that a socialist future in the sense of a classless society, a society of economic equality, could be a society of many religions (or ethnicities or gender identities). The logic of the argument is driven by the obsessional desire for all people to be one people, The People. And the logic has had its confounding appeal to Sartre's admiring readers precisely because the vision of equality has silenced all questions about how and why people identify in and with their groups.

Sartre's prescriptive hostility toward any identification other than "socialist," a group for everyone, indicates how much more extreme his obsessional prejudice was than the long tradition of hostility toward Jews on the Left. His is not the attitude toward the Jews that permeates the critiques of the eighteenth century English deists and French rationalists and finally the nineteenth-century Young Hegelians and Marxists for whom Judaism, as the root of Christianity, was the origin of a spirit that has corrupted and debilitated the modern world, a spirit that could only be combated with radical change and faith in progress toward a universalist future. Sartre did not make the argument Karl Marx had made that "the practical spirit of Judaism" had infiltrated and polluted Christian society to express itself, ultimately, as capitalism. He did not even give the Jews the dubious (that is, quite antisemitic) distinction of having such a historical role and corrupting spirit. The Jews are *only* the creation of the class-bound antisemites.[14]

Only when the Jews are in their antisemite-defined situation are they to identify as Jews and fight. As authentic fighters, they would be, Sartre argued, living refutation of both antisemitism and the position he labeled "democratic universalism." A subscriber to democratic universalism "recognizes neither Jew, nor Arab, nor Negro, nor bourgeois, nor worker, but only man—man always the same in all times and places."[15] In this view, the Jew should stop considering himself a Jew and be a Man protected by the Rights of Man or a Frenchman protected by French citizenship. But this change, in Sartre's dismissive terms, would mean that the Jew could not be authentic—could not choose to embrace his Jewishness for the time being against the annihilating policies of his enemies—any more than a worker could choose to band together with other workers to bring about the socialist future. Concrete existence, particularity, should not be willed away or assimilated away for the sake of universalism; rather, concrete existence should be *transformed* in the socialist revolution. According to Sartre, the authentic Jew can and should *freely* give up his Jewishness after his struggle has been won for him. But then his struggle is not for the civil rights of minorities in a nation-state or for the existence of a State of Israel: it is only for socialism.

Sartre's socialism was the intellectualized sort that, while attributing all antisemitism to class-based hatred, lent itself very well to Stalinism and to the antiminority (including antisemitic) policies that developed throughout the Soviet-dominated states of Eastern Europe after the war. In this worldview, all particular groups were perceived as creations and instruments of the class enemy—of capitalism, of fascism—lodged right in the People, infiltrating and inhibiting the socialist achievement like giant conspiracies. Now, of course, the suppressed minorities of the socialist states—especially in Eastern Europe—protest the authoritarianism of the antiparticularist Sartrean way of thinking, protesting in the streets they want named after their particular group heroes. But the enormous reactive assertiveness of the suppressed minorities' tribalisms and nationalisms is also fostering a renewed authoritarian spirit across the continent, where the obsessional rigors and rigidities of Communist life have been normal for decades. Some of this spirit grips tribal and national ethnocentrics, but it can also be seen in the form of ideologies of desire. In the name of imaginary or mythic national groups, floundering post-1989 central and new state governments are being attacked by ideologues seeking to extirpate state-owning enemy conspiracies and form pan-tribal or supranational alliances—to do unto neighboring others what was done unto them. "Greater Germany" and "Greater Serbia" are being invoked as entities that should be cleansed of all groups that appear—in the usual obsessional images—clannish, wily, and entrepreneurial, connected to networks of kinspeople in other lands.

## Primo Levi: On Fabricating a "Convenient Reality"

There are many ways to set about erasing a people's history, their narrated specificity as a people. The two I have been focusing on—the variations on Holocaust denial, revisionism, and theory of narratability, and the claim from the anti-Zionist Left and specifically from Sartre's existential viewpoint that the Jews are *only* "the Jews," a construction— define the present post-Holocaust moment of political antisemitism. These postwar manifestations of antisemitism show that there is a connection, a similarity, between the basic dynamic of the obsessional prejudices (especially antisemitism) and the dynamic of obsessional retrospection or rewriting of history, silencing. The "envy and blame" mode of prejudice correlates to the historiographical mode of "construct and eliminate." The common denominator is—to use a moral term—irresponsibility.

In the enormous literature on the Holocaust—now even with a bibliographic designation, Holocaust literature—no writer, it seems to me, was more alert as he wrote to the changing contexts of antisemitism in the postwar period than Primo Levi, whose writings I have been citing. From *Survival in Auschwitz* through *The Reawakening* to *Moments of Reprieve,* in many stories and essays and poems, and in his retrospective *summa, The Drowned and the Saved,* Primo Levi—trained as a chemist, rounded up with a group of Italian partisans in 1944 and shipped to

Buna—dedicated himself to the meticulous, cautious, reflective decant-
ing of his memories of the *Lager*. Because of his outstanding gifts among
the authors of Holocaust literature—rare analytical ability, emotional
precision, and literary power—I want to ask his books to speak here for
the memoiristic work of many survivors. And I want to focus on what
he focused on, the meaning of responsibility for others.

Like almost all Jews, particularly Holocaust survivors, who have tried
to search down into the psyches of their oppressors, Levi wanted to find
a single spring of prejudice. In the preface to *Survival in Auschwitz*, he
named the conviction he felt the oppressors of the Jews shared:

> Many people—many nations—can find themselves holding, more
> or less wittingly, that "every stranger is an enemy." For the most part
> this conviction lies deep down like some latent infection; it betrays
> itself only in random, disconnected acts, and does not lie at the base
> of a system of reason. But when this does come about, when the un-
> spoken dogma becomes the major premise in a syllogism, then, at the
> end of the chain, there is the Lager. Here is the product of a concep-
> tion of the world carried rigorously to its logical conclusion; so long
> as the conception subsists, the conclusion remains to threaten us. The
> story of the death camps should be understood by everyone as a sin-
> ister alarm-signal.

Levi understood that antisemitism is a dogmatic intellectuality, a logic
carried out to the maximum, an obsession obsessionally institutionalized. He took this dynamic as applicable to all prejudices, which it is
not. But his overgeneralization did not carry him past the specificities
of the dynamic because his emotional response to it was so restrained
and acute. He was not baffled by the antisemitic logic or overcome by
his own intellectuality, which was never of a dogmatic sort.

For example, when *Survival in Auschwitz* was published in German, he
told its German readers in a preface that he harbored no hatred for the
German people, for he believed that no individual should be judged by
the group he or she belonged to, and he understood hatred only *ad
personam*. However, he continued, "I cannot say I understand the Germans. Now something one cannot understand constitutes a painful void,
a puncture, a permanent stimulus that insists on being satisfied. I hope
that this book will have some echo in Germany, not only out of ambition, but also because the nature of this echo will perhaps make it possible for me better to understand the Germans, to placate this stimulus."[16]

The letters that Levi received in response to this discrete form of "research" taught him very little that he had not known already from observing the Germans who rounded him up and transported him to a camp near Auschwitz, the ones who manned the camp, its factories, and infirmaries, and the ones who fled before the advancing Russian troops in 1945. He noted again and again the recurring character traits, which he summarized in telling how his Italian camp mate Alberto negotiated his survival by manufacturing little colored tickets and trinkets to exchange for bread rations: "Alberto knows his Germans and the *Block-altester* are all German, or German-trained: they love order, systems, bureaucracy; even more, although rough and irascible blockheads, they cherish an infantile delight in glittering, many-colored objects."[17] During the National Socialist regime, it was precisely those qualities that so admirably fitted the Germans for their bourgeois existences as jobholders and family men, that allowed them to rationalize the developing brutality and horror of the totalitarian storm. Their sheerly private traits could be endlessly appropriated: the priority they gave to individual and family enterprise and security, their submissiveness to authorities whom they hoped would further their collecting of the trinkets signifying predictable daily routines, their very lack of the *civic* virtues, which demand responsibility for others who are not kin.

Levi thought that the postwar trials of Nazi officials also yielded a recurrent character portrait, emerging as those on trial were questioned about why they had done what they had done, and whether they were aware that they were committing crimes. In reflecting on the Nazis who appeared in the various docks, Levi sounded his most important analytical theme about the Germans, a theme that, translated into developmental terms, concerns the formation of the obsessional character and its fissuring along the lines between emotion and intellect, experience and protective construction, lived reality and functional *idée fixe*. This theme of Levi's is also one of his strongest rejections of the philosophical and psychological assumptions of the sort that Sartre articulated. Levi simply did not divide the world obsessionally into two camps—the reasoners and the passionate, the authentic and the inauthentic, people of good faith and people of bad faith—and he always emphasized that evil *evolves* in people, from childhood, from adolescence, as they encounter life's challenges and fail themselves, and as the social conditions that educate them change.

Expressed in different formulations and with greater or lesser arrogance, depending on the [Nazi] speaker's mental and cultural level, in the end they substantially all say the same things: I did it because I was ordered to; others (my superiors) have committed acts worse than mine; in view of the upbringing I received, and the environment in which I lived, I could not have acted differently; had I not done it, another would have done it even more harshly in my place. For anyone who reads these justifications the first reaction is revulsion: they lie, they cannot believe they will be believed, they cannot see the imbalance between their excuses and the enormity of pain and death they have caused. They lie knowing that they are lying: they are in bad faith.

Now, anyone with sufficient experience of human affairs knows that the distinction (the opposition, a linguist would say) good faith/bad faith is optimistic and smacks of the Enlightenment, and is all the more so, and for much greater reason, when applied to men such as those [Nazis] mentioned. It presupposes a mental clarity which few have and which even those few immediately lose when, for whatever reason, past or present reality arouses anxiety or discomfort in them. Under such conditions there are, it is true, those who lie consciously, coldly falsifying reality itself, but more numerous are those who weigh anchor, move off, momentarily or forever, from genuine memories, and fabricate for themselves a convenient reality. The past is a burden to them; they feel repugnance for things done or suffered and tend to replace them with others. The substitution may begin in full awareness, with an invented scenario, mendacious, restored, but less painful than the real one; they repeat the description to others but also to themselves, and the distinction between true and false progressively loses its contours, and man ends by fully believing the story he has told so many times and continues to tell, polishing and retouching here and there the details which are least credible or incongruous or incompatible with the acquired picture of historically accepted events: initial bad faith has become good faith. The silent transition from falsehood to self-deception is useful: anyone who lies in good faith is better off. He recites his part better, is more easily believed by the judge, the historian, the reader, his wife, his children.

The further events recede into the past, the more the construction of convenient truth grows and is perfected.[18]

Levi described here the slow process by which intellectualizations, undoings, and isolations—the typically obsessional defenses—cover over reality, accumulating like a palimpsest.

The habit of putting a construction in the place of reality is deeply connected to and grows out of the habit of attributing responsibility for events to others (externalizing and blaming) and out of the habit of attributing responsibility for events to a hidden conspiracy of others, a habit built up from childhood, from adolescence, but easily aggravated by years and decades of frightening or threatening events. In conditions favoring this kind of renunciation of personal responsibility, the self-inflicted species of loneliness and depersonalization, the habit of construing oneself as a passive victim while exaggeratedly fearing passivity and victimization, grows progressively more dangerous. A family or group or nation in which it is normal for everyone to say that someone else is directly or secretly responsible—a family or group or nation of the "paranoid style"—is, Primo Levi constantly emphasized, making potential totalitarians. They are all "the Germans" in social character, regardless of nationality. The strongest opposing tendency, he understood, comes from people who are pained at being told what to do and think, at being absorbed into rituals especially on a mass scale, and whose greatest pleasures derive from what Levi called "human solidarity." Such people, of curiosity and investigative passion, interested in other people, would likely be ashamed in conditions that made responsibility for others, human solidarity, nearly impossible:

> Few survivors feel guilty about having deliberately damaged, robbed, or beaten a companion. Those who did so (the *Kapos*, but not only they) block out the memory. By contrast, however, almost everybody feels guilty of having omitted to offer help. The presence at your side of a weaker—or less cunning, or older, or too young—companion, hounding you with his demands for help or with his simple presence, in itself an entreaty, is a constant in the life of the Lager. The demand for solidarity, for a human word, advice, even just a listening ear, was permanent and universal but rarely satisfied. There was no time, space, privacy, patience, strength.[19]

The hallmark of obsessional prejudice in literature by the victims of this prejudice type is that *they* feel the very shame that their oppressors, armored by the prejudice, by their convenient truths, *cannot feel.*

## Obsessional Prejudices among Victims

Primo Levi's frank comprehension of what obsessional prejudice can do to those who harbor it and to its victims—in daily life, and, *in extremis,* under *Lager* conditions—is borne out in the example and testimonies of victims of other forms of prejudice who, themselves, respond obsessionally. The emergence of the Nation of Islam in African American urban ghettos provides an instructive instance of the development of victim-group antisemitism from a social form into a political form, via the development of an obsessional organization.

In his autobiography, *Black Boy* (1937), Richard Wright candidly commented on Jew taunting as both a power game and a part of Christian religious obligation among Southern blacks before World War II. Wright met a Jew for the first time when he was nine years old, living in West Helena, Arkansas, and spending his precious few pennies at a Jewish grocer's shop.

> All of us black people who lived in the neighborhood hated Jews, not because they exploited us, but because we had been taught at home and in Sunday school that Jews were 'Christ killers.' With the Jews thus singled out for us, we made them fair game for ridicule.
>
> And when the baldheaded proprietor would pass by, we black children, poor, half-starved, ignorant, victims of racial prejudice, would sing with a proud lilt:
>
> > A rotten egg
> > > Never fries
> > > > A cheating dog
> > > > > Never thrives.
>
> There were many more folk ditties, some mean, others filthy, all of them cruel. No one ever thought of questioning our right to do this; our mothers and parents generally approved either actively or passively. To hold an attitude of antagonism or distrust toward Jews was bred in us from childhood; it was not merely racial prejudice, it was part of our cultural heritage.[20]

In the African American communities of the South and later the North, this kind of Jew taunting, with its ancient accusations about Christ killers, was taken up right along with Protestantism or Catholicism. But the religious ethnocentrism gave way to more politicized antisemitism in the North, wherever the Nation of Islam had influence. That is, it gave way in the context of an ideology of Black *supranationalism*, Black supremacy, and a proselytizing organization of an obviously obsessional cast. Muslim discipline, conveyed with a rhetoric of cleanliness and purity, has since the 1950s focused on strict patriarchalism—wives were and are required to be subservient to their husbands—a regime forbidding alcohol and drugs and prescribing diet, a scheduled and rule-bound daily order. The economic program of the Nation of Islam calls for economic autonomy for Black communities, and it requires an object of economic blame—the Jews. (The vision of economic autonomy and political separatism in fact makes the Nation of Islam much less dangerously antisemitic than the fundamentalist Christian Coalition, which aims at majority status and taking over the government, making it a Christian government and part of a new world order.)

Few Black intellectuals of the late 1950s and early 1960s appreciated the shift from anti-Jewish ethnocentrism to antisemitism, social to political antisemitism, because most were, like James Baldwin, under the impression that antisemitism, like racism, could be understood in terms of scapegoating. Baldwin articulated the formula of Sartre's *Anti-Semite and Jew* in an essay called "The Harlem Ghetto." "Just as a society must have a scapegoat, so hatred must have a symbol. Georgia has the Negro and Harlem has the Jew."[21] But this formula misses the specificity of Black antisemitism, as opposed to ethnocentrism, and it cannot catch the reasons why the Jews, and not just any handy group, fulfilled a need that intensified as the anti-integrationist supranationalism of the Black Muslims challenged the integrationist vision of the Civil Rights movement.

On a trip to Harlem in 1958, the Georgian-born African American historian Louis Lomax recorded his first experience with a street-corner Muslim orator, an experience he later turned into a TV documentary called *The Hate That Hate Produced*. In the Muslim's harangue, the classic antisemitic image system unfolded. First, he subtly suggested that the audience should be able to smell the Jews. They represent, they are, offal. Next he claimed that these offal-people can turn all they touch into gold, because they are part of a conspiracy of money. In archetypical bathroom titillation language, the orator built his audience's excitement. In strophe and antistrophe, he got them to groan and sweat, to climax in a moment of expulsion and pleasure—an "excremental coercion" (to use Levi's phrase). Unlike the painful coercion wrecked upon Jewish victims, this coercion through pleasure was meant to transform people from being the victims themselves of the endlessly painful, soul-wearying routine of the Hell's Kitchen sweatshops that the orator invoked. He assumed that blaming would transform them into an army of counterattackers.

"You work all day, eight hours a day, five days a week for forty-four dollars."

"That's right."

"And while you making forty-four dollars, Mr. Eisenberg is watching you sweat and grunt and he makes forty-four hundred dollars. Am I right or wrong?"

"You right; great God, you right!"

"Say on."

"Tell it like it is."

"Oh, don't worry brother, I'm going to tell it just like it is. I'm going to bring it right down in front so everybody can smell it!"

"Now—and watch this—you work all day for Mr. Eisenberg, you come back up here to Harlem and buy your clothes from Mr. Gosenberg."

"Yeah."

"You buy your jewelry from Mr. Goldberg."

"Yes."

"You pay your rent to Mr. Fineberg."

"Yes."

"You get borrowed money from a finance company headed by Mr. Weinberg."

"Yes, tell it."

"Now what you don't know is that Mr. Eisenberg and Mr. Gosenberg and Mr. Fineberg and Mr. Goldberg and Mr. Weinberg is all cousins. They got you working for nothing, and then they take back the little nothing you make before you can get home with it. That's how they get you in the economic locks!"

And with this the crowd breaks with wild, pained laughter.[22]

The Jews, in this image system, stand against Negro pleasure. They do so as employers, landlords, and merchants. But the orator's audience would also have known them as the people blocking the exit from the ghetto. Lomax cited a 1959 University of Chicago study which showed that more resistance to Negroes buying houses in the suburbs of Chicago came from the Jews than from any other white group. This resistance, Lomax commented, generously, was not a matter of prejudice but of Jewishness: "Jews in these gilt-edged ghettos opposed integration not because they hated or discriminated against Negroes; rather they were seeking to realize that element in their tradition which calls for togetherness."[23] Regardless of their motivation, the antisemitic image system of the Muslims' urban audiences drew in the Jews because they were felt to be the ghetto gatekeepers. They were the ones who constrained the Negroes and clamped down on their freedom and mobility.

The Muslim orators could also tap the conviction, growing year by year in the South and the North, that the Jews stood behind the old guard of Negro leadership. Antisemitism began to increase in Negro communities as the determinative intra-Negro revolt was building, as Lomax's fine history *The Negro Revolt* (1962) makes clear. A younger generation of Negro leaders sought to displace elders identified with the failed policies of Booker T. Washington—policies that called for "raising the race" by patiently accepting separate (and inferior) education and emphasizing Negro self-help. These elders seemed to many Negroes of the postwar boom period to be, like the Jews, gatekeepers. Members of a constraining paternal generation, they restricted the freedom and mobility of their own children.

The young Negro leaders, who called instead for freedom rides, sit-ins, boycotts, voter registration, demonstrations, and legal assaults on discriminatory legislation, also harshly criticized white philanthropy—including Jewish philanthropy—that they thought had bought Negro acquiescence in the manner so vividly described in Ralph Ellison's *Invisible Man*. Even liberal Jews who were political allies of the younger Negro leadership and active in Civil Rights organizations felt the sting of suspicion as a call went out for Black organizations to appoint Black leaders and, sometimes, to be open to Blacks only. The Muslims, although they were separatists and wanted no alliances with either the old or the new Negro leadership, realized that the moment was right to paint all white philanthropy as the white devil's work.

In the context of European antisemitism in the 1920s and 1930s, the Jews had been targets of hatred from those who called them plutocrats and those who called them Communists, those who saw them as agents of the old regimes and those who saw them as liberals. Similarly, the Black antisemites of the late 1950s could paint the Jews as Negro-bilking money grubbers or as false friends promoting false freedoms. The Jews could be hated for their tribalism and hated for their liberalism all at once. Antisemitism from the Right and from the Left used the same images, reflecting the same obsessions.

Since the early 1960s the Nation of Islam has made no shift away from the basic rhetoric of antisemitism. Some Muslims have adopted the current Holocaust-denying form of antisemitism. More revealingly, they also engage in an "original" and specific new chord of history rewriting.

A small number of African American scholars—pseudoscholars—with university appointments have asserted that Jews played a crucial role in the development of the slave trade in North America. They make the ridiculous argument that a minuscule Jewish population engineered a vast slave-importing operation—as a conspiracy. Although this typically antisemitic canard is part of the current mode of general antisemitism, which concentrates on the rewriting of history, it also reveals that whatever general consensus about the nature of white racism existed within the African American intellectual community through the ascendancy of the Civil Rights movement has broken down. Where there was theoretical unanimity about white racism, there is now great disagreement—and in the confusion new strategies of blame have arisen. This is another story of victims being silenced, and I will turn to it in the next chapter.

# 14

## On Resistance to Hysterical Repression

In *Toward a Definition of Antisemitism,* Gavin Langmuir noted that the literature on antisemitism, especially the Jewish literature, is full of stormy disagreements over even the most fundamental definitional matters. By contrast, anyone who reads what male writers (not social scientists) of the African diaspora have had to say about white racism cannot help noticing their unanimity. Despite differences of emphasis and differences that reflect historical contexts and community proprieties, the diagnosis is always the same. White racism had its origins in the slave trade and the "conquest of Africa," for which it served as the rationalization and sustaining ideology, but it developed into a sexual sickness.

### The Diagnosis and the Secrecy

American diagnosticians have shown that this sexual sickness has many dimensions, producing many guiding images. The image that looms largest conveys an attitude among white males (primarily) about the supposed lust that black males have for white women; this hypersexual image appears as the "black rapist." But white males also evince an attitude about black females, which appears as the "black whore." And white females share an attitude that finds expression as—again in shorthand—the "black stud." We also find the "black mammy or maid," a construction in which the sexual dimension is less obvious because she

486

is relatively, complexly desexed, as is the "black matriarch," a woman who has renounced men, a woman who is antisex and even phallic in her commanding role in the Negro family. These images, collectively, stand behind what one postwar British anthropologist—unusual then for his frank insistence that whites must come to understand the role of these images in racism—called "the intensity of emotional hatred against the Negro that we find in the United States."[1]

Whites usually refuse the sexual diagnosis, and they refuse it even more adamantly in times—like our own—when racist behavior frequently comes wrapped in layers of disguise and falls into the spheres of competitive racism. The sexual dimensions of racism, when they are mentioned, are assigned to the past, to the era of lynching and castration. They have nothing to do with modern racism, the claim goes; they have no relevance to a time when the majority of American whites profess to frown upon racism and when issues like affirmative action dominate the policy agenda. But whites advance this claim in the face of constant evidence that it is delusional. Take the recent story first reported in the *New York Times* under the ameliorating headline "Vestiges of the Old South." A high school principal in Alabama canceled his students' senior prom when he discovered that a dozen or so interracial couples planned to attend. The same educator reportedly informed one of his students, the child of a black mother and a white father, that she was a "mistake" of the sort that his action (with its message about miscegenation) was meant to prevent.[2]

But even when the sexual dimensions of racism were more commonly overt, before the Civil Rights movement, white interpreters refused to accept the diagnosis almost as unanimously as Negro commentators who were not professional social scientists insisted upon it.[3] Gunnar Myrdal, for example, who gave a good deal of attention to white fears of black sexuality and of miscegenation in *The American Dilemma*, argued nonetheless that the basic white desire is "to keep the Negro in a lower status," to promote inequality. Myrdal claimed that prohibitions on intermarriage reinforce this basic desire, as fears of Negro sexuality rationalize it. "The persistent preoccupation with sex and marriage and the rationalization of social segregation and discrimination against Negroes is to this extent an irrational escape on the part of whites from voicing an open demand for differences in social status between the two groups for its own sake."[4]

Most liberal antisegregationist theorists have followed this causal tack, as have many African American social scientists. St. Claire Drake, reviewing the postwar literature on racism, observed a strong strand of what he called ''neo-Freudian'' emphasis on the sexual fantasy structures underlying racism, but concluded that ''most black intellectuals do not rank this kind of explanation very high.''[5] The conclusion is justified for social scientists, among whom sociologists dominate, but it certainly is wildly incorrect as far as nonacademic African American writers are concerned. Academics and nonacademics agree that race theory initially grew up in America and in Europe as a rationalization for slavery. But the neo-Freudians go on to argue that, once in place, each New World slavery system in which white families had Negroes in their households as objects of sexual fantasy for generations of children and adults evolved a structure of sexual fantasy, one subtending all subsequent developments and rising into unmistakable view in sexualized violence against Negroes. The American slavery system brought about the condition in which Negroes, even after emancipation, had to live in and off of positions as domestics to individual white families and to play the role of domestics in images and mythologies of the national household. The sexual fantasy structure that is racism came to support and to undergird, not follow from, the economic realities; Negroes came to be kept in place for their sexual and fantasy services, because many whites could not live without these services, could not live without their images of the Negroes as sexual athletes and rapists, nurture suppliers and whores—the phalluses and breasts, skin and lips of the nation.

African American social scientists have rejected or downplayed the neo-Freudian view for two main reasons. First, the voices of African American women have had (as I will show in this chapter) so little influence on social science that social scientists have not—until quite recently—explored the interplay of racism and sexism. Second, more generally, the neo-Freudian view implies that racism is too deeply embedded for social engineering to reach beyond its manifestations, to reach its roots. As the South African psychiatrist Noel Chabani Manganyi noted:

> Institutional changes involving political, social and economic systems represent an essential beginning in the process of social change. To eradicate racism in the institutional life of a society it is not sufficient to demystify the unconscious ramifications involved in the fantasy social structure underlying such a system . . . On the collective level, the

difficulties of working through the fantasy social structure supporting racism raises many practical problems which society prefers to ignore.[6]

Resistance from white social scientists, by contrast, seems to flow much more directly from defensiveness. Outside the academic and policy circles where antipsychological conventions dominate, however, there have occasionally been white voices of dissent or of agreement with the consensus among blacks who are not social scientists. Many historians and psychohistorians, for example, acknowledge W. J. Cash's conviction that the foundation of white racism in the South was the white Southern idolization of white women in their purity—a key piece of the fantasy structure. He described the fear that pervaded the South as Reconstruction followed emancipation: "What Southerners felt, therefore, was that any assertion of any kind on the part of the Negro constituted in a perfectly real manner an attack on the Southern woman. What they saw more or less consciously in the conditions of Reconstruction was a passage toward a condition for her as degrading in their view as rape itself."[7] Academic commentators also acknowledge that even Myrdal's own research at midcentury showed that opposition to and fear of miscegenation was highest on the list of white concerns in the domain of "race relations."[8] And this result is repeated conscientiously—but almost always under the cover of Myrdal's conclusion that the sexual issue was a rationalization. "Time and again interviews in the Newsweek survey," wrote William Brink and Louis Harris in *Black and White* (1967), "brought out the ultimate concern over integrated housing: that it would lead to intermarriage."[9]

Most well-intentioned American whites, lacking experience of what such evidence means, or of how the white preoccupation registers in the daily life of Blacks, dismissed it again and again, finding it hard to credit even a white who took the unusual step of providing himself with experience. John Howard Griffin, a white journalist who darkened his skin and "passed" as a Black for a month could not get away from the evidence he recounted in *Black Like Me*. As he hitchhiked across Mississippi and Alabama in 1960, he was picked up at night—under cover of darkness—by white men who would not have stood near him in the daytime or in the presence of other whites.

It quickly became obvious why they picked me up. All but two picked me up the way they would pick up a pornographic photograph or book—except that this was verbal pornography. With a Negro, they assumed they need give no semblance of self-respect or respectability. The visual element entered into it. In a car at night visibility is reduced. A man will reveal himself in the dark, which gives an illusion of anonymity, more than he will in the bright light. Some were shamelessly open, some shamelessly subtle. All showed morbid curiosity about the sexual life of the Negro, and all had, at base, the same stereotypical image of the Negro as an inexhaustible sex-machine with over-sized genitals and a vast store of experiences, immensely varied. They appeared to think that the Negro has done all of those "special" things they themselves have never dared to do. They carried the conversation into the depths of depravity. I note these things because it is harrowing to see decent-looking men and boys assume that because a man is black they need show him none of the reticence they would, out of respect, show the most derelict white man. I note them, too, because they differed completely from the "bull sessions" men customarily have among themselves. These latter, no matter how frank, have generally a robust tone that says: "We are men, this is an enjoyable thing to do and to discuss, but it will never impugn the basic respect we give one another; it will never distort our humanity." In this, the atmosphere, no matter how coarse, has a verve and an essential joviality that casts out morbidity. It implies respect for the persons [that is, the *men*, not the women] involved. But all that I could see here were men shorn of respect for themselves or their companion.[10]

The white men who picked Griffin up assumed that he would give them the verbal pornography they requested, that he would play the pornographer's role. One man asked Griffin if he had a pretty wife, and if this pretty wife had ever "had it from a white man." He then explained that all the white men he knew craved colored girls, and that he himself had "had his way with every colored woman he had ever hired for domestic work or in his business." When Griffin refused to participate in this braggadocio—" 'Surely some refuse,' I suggested cautiously"—the man grew testy and announced his view that whites who put a bit of white blood into the Negro race were doing the Negroes a favor. Griffin was appalled:

The grotesque hypocrisy slapped me as it does all Negroes. It is worth remembering when the white man talks of the Negro's lack of sexual morality, or when he speaks with horror about mongrelization and with fervor about racial purity. Mongrelization is already a widespread reality in the South—it has been exclusively the white man's contribution to the Southern Way of Life. His vast concern for "racial purity" obviously does not extend to all races.

It is chiefly this "fervor about racial purity," shared by modern antisemites, that has led to the common idea that racism and antisemitism are variants of the same prejudice, "racism." But antisemites have never been known to try to improve the Jewish "race." Antisemites seek to exclude or eliminate their enemies, they do not patronize them, keep them in a place where they can continually use and humiliate them, make them the subjects of pornography, demand that they purvey the pornography, and then punish them for playing the roles assigned in the pornography. The dynamic of antisemitism is not the one so obvious in Griffin's account: the white men who wanted him as a pornographer fantasized that Griffin, and all Black men, enacted the perversions that the whites only fantasized or enacted only with Black women. Black people exist to provide the means for expressing forbidden desire—as they are made into the pornographers or the sexual subjects—and they are supposed to collude in the reestablishment of the repression. They are not to tell the white man's secret. It is not that the history of the blacks or their suffering is to be split off, excluded, or eliminated from the human record, but that their history is to be censored, distorted, and desexualized.

The black writers who have defied this ban have understood very clearly that the ban operates as sexual repression does, that it censors sexuality and implicates black sexuality by penetrating into the consciousness of the blacks, making it nearly impossible to think except in relation to, in reaction to, the projections of the whites. Racism, like all forms of hysteria worked out on the bodies of others, becomes to some degree embodied in the victims—and the less the degree, the more the projectors are frustrated, vengeful, and accusatory. The white projections, the rapacious "whitening" of the darker race, and the white secrecy can become entangled in black sexuality, which means supporting black fantasies of being white, being—as the psychiatrist Frantz Fanon put it—"lactified." The black poems and novels and memoirs and meditations that expound the secret are addressed to two audiences: to blacks, as a matter of sharing knowledge and affirming that the projections, the "lactification" desire, and the silencing can be resisted and thrown off like shackles; and to whites, as a warning—you cannot go under the cover of darkness.

## Frantz Fanon, His Own "Black Orpheus"

Many Africans and people of the African diaspora contributed to the diagnosis of white racism, participating as they did in the "double consciousness" and address to a double audience that had been described so powerfully at the turn of the century by W. E. B. Du Bois.[11] But nowhere is the diagnostic more clinically astute than in the lyrical, raging, cutting, digressive, reeling text titled *Black Skin, White Masks* (1952) that Frantz Fanon, then a twenty-six-year-old Antillean psychiatrist, working in Paris, created to cure himself, his people, and his oppressors.

In the postwar France that was so receptive to Sartre's existentialism and found his distinction between people of passion and people of reason Cartesianly self-evident, Africans from the French colonies were welcomed as students. The French certainly had had no hesitation about colonizing in the Caribbean or on the west coast of Africa, but they then characteristically divided their colonial populations into two sorts, those who remained in their culturally inferior native traditions and those who Frenchified themselves, those frankly named *évolués*. Being an *évolué* meant, in effect, having evolved beyond the body passionate—beyond blackness—into reason. Midcentury Parisian culture-keepers made exact distinctions among dark-skinned émigrés and expatriates from Africa, North America, the West Indies, Malagasy, Brazil—that is, they could truly see the blacks, they did not treat them as invisible people or censor their stories, as told in French. And they could appreciate black culture as a kind of exoticism, a cult of energy and rhythm, which they held up to rebuke other culturally inferior peoples—frivolous white Americans or staid, bourgeois Swiss, for example. To African Americans escaping racism at home to write or paint or dance in Paris, the French seemed ethnocentric and xenophobic, anti-American, rather than racist. Racism existed and supported the narcissistic French cultural elitism, but it did not require silence over sexuality—it required only cultural transcendence.

At first, the price did not seem excessive to émigrés like Frantz Fanon, and it allowed for a political-cultural movement, one that had been launched in 1934, when Leopold Senghor from Senegal and Aime Cesaire, like Fanon from Martinique, founded a review in Paris. *L'étudiant noir* became the vehicle for their guiding concept, their aspiration: *négritude,* a celebration of African intuition, rhythm, sentiment, and culture as beautifully not-European, not-rationalistic, not-technological, not-imperial; an assertion that all peoples in Africa and in the African diaspora were one; a protest against all forms of white supremacy, from slavery to colonialism; and an invocation of African socialism. The group of African, Caribbean, and American writers and artists lending their voices and their works to the *négritude* movement grew throughout the 1930s and survived the enforced quietude of the war years. In 1947 the movement gained a new forum, *Présence africaine,* and an enormously influential volume of poems was published in 1948. Sartre wrote the preface to this *Anthologie de la nouvelle poésie nègre et malgache.* A movement that had grown through a chorus of statements suddenly had a manifesto, Sartre's essay "Orphée noir," a white man's interpretation of *négritude* into Hegelian-Marxist categories, a plea for transcendence.[12]

Sartre's essay had two audiences. It presented and explained *négritude* to an audience Sartre assumed would be uncomprehending. The essay's opening is for these white readers: "What then did you expect when you unbound the gag that had muted those black mouths? That they would chant your praises? Did you think that when those heads that our fathers had forcibly bowed down to the ground were raised again, you would find adoration in their eyes?" Sartre moved back and forth between a "your" and an "our" in addressing his white audience, but with his other audience, his black audience, he moved on another plane. For interpreting *négritude* to the Negroes, he used the language of universalism. This was the same "we," marching out of the future, who had spoken in *Anti-Semite and Jew* and anticipated the end of all particularist histories and cultures, all Jewishness, all *négritude,* in the socialist revolution. Many Negro intellectuals heard this universalist "we" with mixed feelings, but political events ultimately directed the differences of opinion among them. By the time Frantz Fanon criticized Sartre in his *Black Skin, White Masks,* the *négritude* movement no longer existed as such—the politics of African national independence had overtaken it.

And Fanon had learned his dialectical lesson. *Négritude*—as later, in America, Black pride and still later Afrocentricity—is necessary for reversing white valuations, for saying that everything the whites despise in the blacks is beautiful. But blacks must realize, Fanon insisted, that the reversed valuations of *négritude* are still laid down by the whites. *Négritude* is still in reactive dialogue with the oppressors. Not reaction, but action must be the way of the future; liberation must be new creation—of black nations, black culture. Similarly, any theory of racism must begin with an analysis of how racism distorts black consciousness, and specifically *black* consciousness, not the consciousness of some unspecified victims. Exorcism is the precondition for a vision of liberation.

Fanon's odyssey, which went from rejecting the white patronage of socialists like Sartre, to the *négritude* movement, and on toward a theory of revolution, began for him during the war, when he was a soldier in the French colonial army in Martinique, serving with soldiers from Senegal. Most Martinicians, including Fanon, despised the Senegalese, adopting the French attitude that the Senegalese were culturally inferior barbarians, not *évolués*. Reflecting on this situation, Fanon realized that the Martinicians thought of themselves as white, or near-white, as well as culturally near-French. He had come upon the key concept of *Black Skin, White Masks,* which he wrote after the war, while finishing his internship in psychiatry. The concept is "dual narcissism." "The white man is sealed in his whiteness. The black man in his blackness." But the black man in his blackness must face a desire to be white that pulls him, or—if he has embraced *négritude*—that once pulled him, while the white is locked in a vision of white supremacy.

Fanon found much to admire in Sartre's *Anti-Semite and Jew,* which was also a study of dual narcissism, a reflection on the immobile, unfree antisemite, locked in his worldview, and the Jew who either accepts or struggles against the antisemite's image of Jews. But Fanon did not think that Sartre's analysis could be moved onto the territory of white racism as Sartre's scapegoat theory implied. Considering his own experience, Fanon angrily pounded out two arguments against Sartre, one psychological and one philosophical. Without even stopping to note that Sartre's scapegoat theory presumed that all prejudices are the same, as all objects of prejudice are pretexts, Fanon went straight for the implication of this assumption, which he took personally. What mattered to him was that Sartre's portrait of the Jew and of what prejudice could mean to the Jew was not true to a black's experience. He recalled Sartre's description: "They [the Jews] have allowed themselves to be poisoned by the stereotype that others have of them, and they live in fear that their acts will correspond to this stereotype . . . We may say that their conduct is perpetually overdetermined from the inside." And then he fairly shouted:

> All the same, the Jew can be unknown in his Jewishness. He is not wholly what he is. One hopes, one waits. His actions, his behavior are the final determinant. He is a white man, and, apart from some rather debatable characteristics, he can sometimes go unnoticed . . . Granted, the Jews are harassed—what am I thinking of? They are hunted down, exterminated, cremated. But these are little family quarrels. The Jew is disliked from the moment he is tracked down. But in my case everything takes on a *new* guise. I am given no chance. I am overdetermined from without. I am the slave not of the "idea" that others have of me but of my own appearance.[13]

Fanon failed to distinguish discrimination, upon which he thought the Jew's behavior might have some effect, from antisemitic policies, which could send a Jew to a gas chamber absolutely without regard for whether the Jew's behavior was or was not stereotypically Jewish. Antisemitic policies have as one of their goals to make it impossible for a Jew to be "unknown in his Jewishness." But Fanon was not thinking about how a yellow star makes a Jew visibly knowable and generic in his or her Jewishness. He was thinking only that Sartre, one of the white family, could not imagine being overdetermined from without.

The unspoken accusation echoes again in Fanon's philosophical argument. Sartre imagined the end of antisemitism in the advent of socialism, and in the essay "Black Orpheus" he imagined the end of racism in a postcolonial era of universalism. Both antisemitism and racism were moments in dialectical movements, destined to be lost in higher syntheses. Blackness can be transcended. And the blacks have made the first step in the synthetic direction when they retaliate against their white racist former master by creating an "anti-racist racism," by glorifying blackness. Fanon cited Sartre's vision:

> The Negro, as we have said, creates an anti-racist racism for himself. In no sense does he wish to rule the world: He seeks the abolition of all ethnic privileges, wherever they come from; he asserts his solidarity with the oppressed of all colors. At once, the subjective, existential, ethnic idea of *négritude* "passes," as Hegel puts it, into the objective, positive, exact idea of *proletariat* . . . In fact, *négritude* appears as the minor term of a dialectical progression: The theoretical and practical assertion of the supremacy of the white man is its thesis; the position

of *négritude* as an antithetical value is the moment of negativity. But
this negative moment is insufficient by itself, and the Negroes who
employ it know this very well; they know it is intended to prepare the
synthesis or realization of the human in a society without races. Thus
*négritude* is the root of its own destruction, it is a transition and not a
conclusion, a means and not an ultimate end.[14]

To this Fanon replied that Sartre, a "friend of the colored peoples" but
also a "born Hegelian," had awarded the Negroes a false prize: being
a transition, taking up a dialectical task set in advance by History. He
objected: "I am not a potentiality of something, I am wholly what I am.
I do not have to look for the universal. No probability has any place
inside me. My Negro consciousness does not hold itself out as a lack. It
*is* its own follower."

Universalism, Fanon realized, would be the fork in the road for the
Negroes and white friends of the Negroes like Sartre. These white
friends, whether in Hegelian terms or some other, would look forward
to the day when racism would cease and human harmony be achieved.
Some of the original exponents of *négritude* would find the prophets of
transcendent harmony appealing. Leopold Senghor did in 1961, when
he had become president of Senegal and discovered in Teilhard de
Chardin's "phenomenological synthesis" a way to reconcile "the necessity for living in our time and of remaining faithful to the spiritual
exigencies of the Negro-African civilization," that is, a way to "transcend
the contradiction of materialism and spiritualism."[15] But Fanon maintained that universalizing visions could proceed only from an intellectualization and denial of Negro experience. While Senghor was becoming a transcendentalist, Fanon was writing *The Wretched of the Earth,* which
became the torch of African national liberation movements and of
American Black nationalism.

Politically, universalism came to look to Fanon like imperialism continued by philosophical means. Universalism meant colorless, which
meant white. But in *Black Skin, White Masks,* he conducted his argument
with friends of the Negroes like Sartre in the medium of psychoanalysis,
not in the medium of political theory. He demonstrated why the whites
have not—perhaps even cannot—get over their racism. And to do this,
he examined the difference, as he perceived it, between racism and the
more curable disease that Sartre had analyzed, antisemitism. "Jean-Paul
Sartre has made a masterful study of the problem of antisemitism; let
us try to determine what are the constituents of Negrophobia."[16]

Fanon drew his key distinction between the psychology of the Negro and the psychology of the white toward the end of his book, after he tracked the evolution of Negro consciousness and his own consciousness through the moment of Cesaire and Senghor's *négritude* movement. The basic experience of every Negro, Fanon argued, is to be caught between a Negro family and a white society, to be torn and traumatized by moving out of his family and into a scene where inevitably "a white man oppresses him with the whole weight of his blackness."[17] The saving grace of this horror is that, for the Negro, the drama of race is never hidden and never repressed. The drama is there, before his eyes, and conscious. The horror does not make him neurotic; even if it leaves him with a feeling of inferiority, that feeling is not unconscious. "In him there is none of the affective amnesia characteristic of the typical neurotic" or the typical white racist. The Negro can always tell—or sing, or dance, or paint—his story.

The white drama of race is quite different: it is unconscious. White people are, as white psychoanalysis has so convincingly shown, first shaped by their families, not by encounters with the society and culture surrounding their families. They are people of the Oedipus complex, which, Fanon argued, does not exist among Negroes in the French Antilles in a form comparable to the one described by Freud. Specifically, whites are prone to phobia. They are "governed by the laws of rational prelogic and affective prelogic: methods of thinking and feeling that go back to the age at which [they] experienced the event that impaired [their] security."[18] That event, of course, is the frustrating anger-inducing absence of the mother or the loss of her to a sibling or paternal rival. But to this loss accrue secondary traumas associated with more or less imaginary attackers or sexual abusers. Whites are destined to be always loosing their beloveds, loosing love, on the model of their first losses. So these phobia-prone white people, according to Fanon, fear sexual theft and assault—white men by a male and white women also by a male. Their collective phobogenic object is precisely the Negro male: "the Negrophobic woman is in fact nothing but a putative sexual partner—just as the Negrophobic man is a repressed homosexual."

Again and again, Fanon stressed his central claim about the neurosis that is racism: "In relation to the Negro, everything takes place on the genital level." White men fear and are jealous of the Negro phallus, and white women both fear and desire the Negro phallus. For both the Negro generally represents the "biological," the historical past of uninhibited, animal sexuality, which the "jungle" Negro incarnates. "The Negro is the incarnation of genital potency beyond all moralities and prohibitions." As Fanon developed this basic theme, he added another diagnostic layer to it. He equated racism with masochism.

The white men who most fear Negroes need and love to be guilty over Negroes. They take the Negro's aggression and resentment and turn it on themselves; they allow themselves to be beaten or they masochistically enjoy participating in scenes or reading books in which Negroes make love to white women or kill white men. White men, Fanon asserted, understand Negro anger because they know that, in the Negro's place, enduring white racism, they would be just as angry. They act out their understanding in masochistic identification with the Negro—they imitate Negro jazz and blues, they sing Negro spirituals, they write novels in which whitelike Negroes ("whites in blackface") express their anger.

For white women, Fanon produced a variation of the portrait offered by two female psychoanalysts, Helene Deutsch and Marie Bonaparte, the two most elaborate theorists of feminine masochism. Girls have an active, aggressive phase of oedipal attraction to their mothers. The aggression of this stage, much of it directed toward the mother, is turned inward. As the girl's libido shifts toward her father, she wants aggression from him, too, and she is frustrated when he does not supply it. In her fantasy, the aggression she desires from her father is supplied by the Negro. She imagines herself being raped by a Negro male.

White men and white women have their individual psychologies, but "the unreflected imposition of culture" reinforces them. All whites share a culture in which "the Negro has one function: that of symbolizing the lower emotions, the baser inclinations, the dark side of the soul. In the collective unconscious of *homo occidentalis,* the Negro—or, if one prefers, the color black—symbolizes evil, sin, wretchedness, death, war, famine."[19] And it is this culture which the Negro encounters on leaving his family and with which the Negro enslaves himself. He, too, can become a Negrophobe, hating himself and his people because they are evil, base, dark. Interestingly, when Fanon set out his theory of "the unreflected imposition of culture," he presented the Negro as unconscious of the imposition, as neurotic, while he had earlier insisted that the Negro's race drama is conscious and that Negroes, not being children of the oedipal family, are not neurotic. The implication Fanon left unstated is that in this concept of cultural etiology whites are both individually and culturally pathological, while Negroes go crazy only in white culture, *from* white culture.

In his passages on "the unreflected imposition of culture," Fanon came closest to Sartre's *Anti-Semite and Jew,* and particularly to Sartre's portrait of the self-hating Jew. But in his passages on the Negrophobia of white men and women, he carefully contrasted the Negro and the Jew as objects of prejudice and rejected Sartre's scapegoat theory with its universalism.[20]

> If one wants to understand the racial situation psychoanalytically, not from a universal viewpoint but as it is experienced by individual conciousnesses, considerable importance must be given to sexual phenomena. In the case of the Jew, one thinks of money and its cognates. In that of the Negro, one thinks of sex . . . No antisemite, for example, would ever conceive of the idea of castrating the Jew. He is killed or sterilized. But the Negro is castrated. The penis, the symbol of manhood, is annihilated, which is to say that it is denied. The difference between the two attitudes is apparent. The Jew is attacked in his religious identity, in his history, in his race, in his relations with his ancestors and with his posterity; when one sterilizes a Jew, one cuts off the source; every time a Jew is persecuted, it is the whole race that is persecuted in his person. But it is in his corporeality that the Negro is attacked. It is as a concrete personality that he is lynched. It is as an actual being that he is a threat. The Jewish menace is replaced by the fear of the sexual potency of the Negro . . .
>
> When it is a question of the Jew, the problem is clear: He is suspect because he wants to own the wealth or take over the positions of power. But the Negro is fixated at the genital; or at any rate he has been fixated there. Two realms: the intellectual and the sexual . . . The Negro symbolizes the biological danger; the Jew, the intellectual danger.

Fanon's diagnosis of white racism as grounded in the mode in which whites want black sexuality—in which they want the pleasure of painful phallic assault—differs from the most well-known white psychoanalytic interpretation, the frustration-aggression theory of Dollard and his colleagues that I outlined in Chapter 2. In this theory, white men, subscribing to a Christian association of sex and sin, leave their women in sinless purity while they use Negro women for sex, but they also project onto Negro males their unfulfilled desires for their white women. The Negro male bears their frustrations and their aggressions. The Negro woman, accordingly, is sexualized. This theory focuses on white heterosexuality and splitting of heterosexual objects into a pure one (maternal, saintly) and an impure one (whorish). Fanon, though quite aware of this approach, did not follow it. His diagnosis focused on white male Negrophobia as a homophobia, and he has little to say about Negro women.

In the terms I developed in Chapter 8, Fanon emphasized the most obsessional and homophobic variant of the hysterical mode that is racism, not the competitive sibling rivalry mode or the paternalistic parricidal mode (which has more in common with Dollard's picture). This is not surprising given his context. The racism of the French colonies and of midcentury France, with its approval of exotic or *évolué* blacks, its emphasis on cultural assimilation, its intellectualizing, its relative subtlety, was more like modern racism in America than like either paternalistic or midcentury competitive racism. Among the black diagnosticians, the American who most clearly shared Fanon's view was James Baldwin, who wrote out of his experience as both a homosexual and a black, his life in America and in France, his cultural assimilation and his appreciation of black cultural traditions. For Baldwin, as for Fanon, the white sexual sickness that is racism reflects, always, under the most diverse conditions, white lovelessness, which Baldwin thought was more acute in America than in France. He described the "sexual despair" of white America, the lack of sensuality, as part of "an emotional poverty so bottomless and a terror of human life, human touch, so deep that virtually no American appears able to achieve any viable, organic connection between his public stance and his private life."[21]

In one characteristic passage, Baldwin reflected on a white Southern politician, a power broker, who, having drowned his inhibitions in alcohol, tried to pick Baldwin up in a newly integrated Little Rock, Arkansas, washroom.

> When the man grabbed my cock, I didn't think of him as a faggot, which, indeed, if having a wife and children, house, cars, and a respectable and powerful standing in the community mean anything, he wasn't. I watched his eyes, thinking with great sorrow, *the unexamined life is not worth living.* The despair among the loveless is that they must narcotize themselves before they can touch any human being at all. They, then, finally, touch the wrong person not merely because they have gone blind, or have lost the sense of touch, but because they no longer have any way of knowing that any loveless touch is a violation, whether one is touching a woman or a man. When the loveless come to power, or when sexual despair comes to power, the sexuality of the

object is either a threat or a fantasy. That most men will chose a woman to debase is not a matter of rejoicing either for the chosen woman or anybody else; brutal truth, further, forces the observation, particularly if one is a black man, that this choice is by no means certain. That men have an enormous need to debase other men—and only because they are men—is a truth history forbids us to labor. And it is absolutely certain that white men, who invented the nigger's big black prick, are still at the mercy of this nightmare, and are still, for the most part, doomed, in one way or another, to attempt to make this prick their own: so much for the progress which the Christian world has made from the jungle in which it is their clear intention to keep black men treed forever.[22]

## What Malcolm X Saw

An English edition of Fanon's *Black Skin, White Masks* finally became available in America in 1967, that is, not until a brief moment in American political and cultural history when an analysis of race relations focused on sexuality could get a limited hearing in the white world, even if it was presented in psychoanalytic terms. The Black diagnosis of white racism was permitted into the cultural mainstream in a burst of countercultural fervor, a cross-current of anti–Vietnam War protest and sexual revolution. The beginning of the period could be marked with Baldwin's *The Fire Next Time* (1962), and his *No Name in the Street,* published in 1972, from which I have been quoting, appeared at just about the end. *The Autobiography of Malcolm X* (1965) is perhaps the most well-known diagnostic work of the period, but it has, in the decades since its publication and particularly during the reception of Spike Lee's movie version, been drained of its revelations.

Malcolm X's *Autobiography* gave three analyses of white racism. One, available ready-made to Malcolm in the theology he acquired from Elijah Muhammad (the spiritual and organizational leader of the Nation of Islam), explained why whites are a race of devils. The other two Malcolm developed out of his own experience: his vision of sexual pathology and a Marxist manifesto on white greed. The Nation of Islam theory has been the topic of intense discussion because it is racist—it is what Sartre called "anti-racist racism"—and because it has continued to be injected into public attention by the Nation of Islam's leaders, who use it to support their antisemitism. Because it is so controversial, the white devils theory has proven ideally suited to block reception of Malcolm's own contributions: Malcolm was an extremist, a racist, therefore his analysis of racism should be given no credence. Similarly, when Fanon's *Black Skin, White Masks* appeared in print, his later firebrand work, *The Wretched of the Earth,* which he had in fact published earlier, was used to tag Fanon as a terrorist, as nothing but an advocate of violence. The analysis of white racism in *Black Skin, White Masks* even though it was made available could be discredited as the work of a fanatic.

In 1946, during the first of the seven years Malcolm spent in prison, convicted for armed robbery and withdrawing from drugs and from a hustling and scrambling life on the streets of Harlem and Roxbury, he was a bitter and angry man of twenty-one, known to the men in his cellblock as "Satan" because of his "antireligious attitude."[23] His brothers and sisters in Detroit, who had joined the Nation of Islam, tried to break through his callous, cynical protective shell. Two years later, after he had begun to listen to his brother Reginald's advice, Malcolm was more receptive to his family's new religion, which they insistently called the "natural religion for the black man." Reginald visited the prison and explained the Nation of Islam doctrine to Malcolm, starting with its basic premise that white people are devils. Malcolm reviewed his entire white acquaintance—"my head swam with the parading faces of white people"—and he began to agree and also to realize that the white devils had kept him and all blacks in ignorance of their history, their true identity. He understood that the whites had deprived their African slaves of any knowledge of their glorious African past just as they had deprived them of their true color by raping slave women and calling the mixed-race progeny the Negro. The whites had also forced on the Negro the Christian religion with its deluding stories about salvation in the next life.

   Malcolm was astonished when he reflected back on his reaction to the Muslim doctrine that Reginald communicated to him. He knew he had had a conversion experience, which he also knew was related to the Black nationalism that had been advocated in the 1920s by Marcus Garvey, whom Malcolm's father had followed: "I have since learned—helping me to understand what then began to happen within me—that the truth can be quickly received, or received at all, only by the sinner who knows and admits that he is guilty of having sinned much. Stated another way: only guilt admitted accepts truth . . . The very enormity of my previous life's guilt prepared me to accept the truth."[24] The truth that struck "Satan" was at once the truth of his own sinfulness and an explanation of it—he was the Satan the white man created, he was the devil's very own Satan. Malcolm was stunned, dazzled, and then stunned again when his sister Hilda visited and conveyed to him the part of Elijah Muhammad's teaching that Malcolm called the "demonology."

This complicated story began with a paean to a wise Black scientist living in Mecca who created an especially strong Black tribe, called Chubs, from which the American Blacks are descended. But it went on to present a discontented latter-day scientist named Dr. Yacub, who developed breeding techniques of a quite malign sort: he isolated a group of his Black followers on an island and laid down eugenic prescriptions for the progressive transformation of them into a bleached-out race of people, a white race. After six hundred years, this white race left its island and mingled with the Blacks still living in Dr. Yacub's original land, Africa. The Africans realized that these horrible people were a threat, so they rounded them up and deposited them in lands to the north, Europe, where they lived in caves, like savages. Allah then decreed that these people, led by Moses, would have a period of ascendancy and triumph lasting six thousand years. But when this period came to an end—as it was soon to do—some of the original African Black people, who had been brought to America, would lead the way in exposing the white people's history and overcoming them. Elijah Muhammad was destined to herald the Black triumph.

When Malcolm heard this tale from Hilda, he felt that it was meant for him, and it fueled his growing desire to ally himself with Elijah Muhammad. "Satan" wrote letters about his new-found knowledge to his old hustler and barfly friends in Harlem and Roxbury, and he wrote to white politicians, knowing that the white prison officials would also read all his mail. The whites, Malcolm began to realize, were the ones who would quickly recognize the demonology. If the prison officials did not censor his mail, "the real reason was that the white man knew he was the devil." The white people, after all, were the ones who had kept the Black people ignorant; the white people were the ones who already knew the truth, even if they would not admit it. His next experiments in prison confirmed this insight. He preached to his Black fellow prisoners, imparting to them his convictions bit by bit, giving them time to go through the kind of conversion he had had himself. And he started participating in debates where he could shock the white prisoners and officials by stating the truth they knew already, causing an uproar. "It was right there in prison that I made up my mind to devote the rest of my life to telling the white man about himself—or die.''[25] To Blacks, he stressed how empowering it could be to recover their history, to take back the stolen history; and to whites he stressed the coming end of the white hegemony.

Near the end of his life, when Malcolm had broken with Elijah Muhammad and traveled to Mecca, looking for the true Islam, he reflected back on his response to the Dr. Yacub story skeptically: "I was to learn later that Elijah Muhammad's tales, like this one of Yacub, infuriated the Muslims of the East. While at Mecca, I reminded them that it was their fault, since they themselves hadn't done enough to make real Islam known in the West. Their silence left a vacuum into which any religious faker could step and mislead our people.''[26] Disabused of the white devils story, Malcolm was left with his own analysis of white racism. He had a different explanation of why he had been receptive to the Yacub story: it was not his guilt for his sinful life, but his experience with whites, which lacked a redeeming instance of undevilish behavior. As he explained, looking back on his life as a hustler and his life as a minister: "Nothing in either of my two careers as a black man in America had served to give me any idealistic tendencies. My instincts automatically examined the reasons, the motives, of anyone who did anything they didn't have to for me. Always, in my life, if it was any white person, I could see a selfish motive.''[27] But the Yacub story also distracted Malcolm's attention from the main theme of his own analysis of white racism, which was not "racial." Embracing the myth of white racial degeneracy meant obfuscating the realities of white—and Black—psychology, which were too dreadful to contemplate without the obfuscation.

Malcolm's conversion to the Nation of Islam had taken the classic form of a withdrawal from sinfulness and a transcendental marriage to the church. He gave up not just pork and liquor and tobacco, but also a life based on sexual exploitation. Minister Malcolm married and had children by his Muslim wife, Betty, and he preached monogamy and sex only in the service of reproduction. Then Elijah Muhammad's promiscuity, and the paternity suits brought against him by his secretaries, drove the disciplined, purified Malcolm away from his savior, the guide who betrayed the guidelines. The language in which Malcolm recorded his break with Elijah echoes the earlier experience of being stunned that had been the beginning of his redemption:

I was in a state of emotional shock. I was like someone who for twelve years had had an inseparable, beautiful marriage—and then suddenly one morning at breakfast the marriage partner had thrust across the table some divorce papers. I felt as if something in nature had failed, like the sun, or the stars. It was an incredible phenomenon to me, something too stupendous to conceive . . . But I could not yet let myself psychologically face what I knew: that already the Nation of Islam and I were physically divorced.[28]

Malcolm had the years of his separation from white society, safe in his marriage to the Nation of Islam, to set in stark contrast to the years and worlds he described in great—and explicit—detail in the early chapters of his *Autobiography*. In this wartime world of Harlem dance halls, clubs, and brothels, Malcolm said, he "got my first schooling about the cesspool morals of the white man from the best possible source, from his own women," that is, from the prostitutes in the house where Malcolm rented a room. White men who could not be men at home with their hen-pecking white wives came to the brothel, Malcolm claimed, for a woman who could make them feel powerful: "More wives could keep their husbands if they realized their greatest urge is *to be men*." But most women, Malcolm concluded, torment their husbands at home and then cheat on them while they are at work or in the service: "there seemed to be a higher code of ethics and sisterliness among those prostitutes than among numerous ladies of the church who have more men for kicks than prostitutes have for pay."

When Malcolm began to work for pimps steering white men to their prostitutes, he continued his study of human nature. "And then as I got deeper into my own life of evil, I saw the white man's morals with my own eyes. I even made my living helping to guide him to the sick things he wanted."[29] Those who wanted Black women wanted, he thought, to be Black. They resembled the Black men—and Malcolm himself—who wanted to be white and needed a white woman to declare their whiteness to their Black buddies. "The white racist won't tell you it also works in reverse." Whites "just mad for Negro 'atmosphere' " rushed to the Harlem nightspots. What white people cannot get in their own homes and with their own kind, Malcolm thought, is what they go to Negroes for. "The white woman wanted to be comfortable, she wanted to be looked upon with favor by her own kind, but she also wanted to have her pleasure. So some of them just married a white man for convenience and security and kept right on going with a Negro. It wasn't that they were necessarily in love with the Negro, but they were in love with lust—particularly 'taboo' lust."[30] For the white men: "Harlem was their sin-den, their flesh-pot. They stole off among taboo black people and took off whatever antiseptic, important, dignified masks they wore in their white world. These were men who could afford to spend large amounts of money for two, three or four hours indulging their strange appetites." Malcolm was particularly amazed by white men in their sixties who liked to be whipped by a strong Black woman, and in general it impressed him that white men and women liked very dark-skinned Negroes, "the blacker the better."

Malcolm never saw white men going to white prostitutes, but he took white men to specialty houses where they could watch "a sleek black Negro having a white woman." "Was this the white man wanting to witness his deepest sexual fear?"[31] Malcolm was convinced that the basis of white male hatred of Negro males is jealousy and fear of Black sexuality: "most white men's hearts and guts will turn over inside of them, whatever they may have you otherwise believe, whenever they see a Negro man on close terms with a white woman."[32] He did not consider any form of white female racism based on jealousy and fear; he only cataloged modalities of white female lust for Negroes, and he thought (in quite a sexist manner) that all women are born betrayers, incapable of understanding or serving their men. Racism was a specifically male devilishness.

Malcolm told Alex Haley the story of his experiences in Harlem while he was still in the embrace of the Nation of Islam. But the final chapters of the book were told after his divorce, and after he had made his pilgrimage to Mecca and begun to formulate yet a third theory of white racism. In the all-male circles in which he traveled on his pilgrimage to Mecca, Malcolm was astonished by the "color-blindness" he encountered, and by the gracious civility shown him everywhere he went; he was converted to the idea of brotherhood as he had once been to the idea that whites are devils. "The true Islam has shown me that a blanket indictment of all white people is as wrong as when whites make blanket indictments against blacks."[33] He began to think that there is a devilishness deeper than racism, productive of the worst evil, racism, and all other evils: materialism and lack of true spiritual values. The basic ingredients of the Marxist analysis of racism as a function of capitalism and capitalism's imperialist advance into the Third World became Malcolm's last approach to racism, and he tested it as he traveled. He thought he could see, for example, the contrast between these true Muslim circles and cultures touched and corrupted by the capitalist West as soon as he entered Beirut on his way home. Falling back on the sexism that had always permeated his racism analyses, Malcolm saw in Beirut "how any country's moral strength, or its moral weakness, is quickly measurable by the street attire and attitude of its women—especially its young women. Wherever the spiritual values have been submerged, if not destroyed, by an emphasis on material things, invariably, the women reflect it. Witness the women, both young and old, in America—where scarcely any moral values are left."[34]

As he traveled in Africa and was treated like a statesman, Malcolm began to realize that American Negroes had to learn to think globally; they had to learn to understand themselves as Africans and to understand that there were Africans with the same interests and aspirations all over the world. "I said that just as the American Jew is in political, economic and cultural harmony with world Jewry, I was convinced that it was time for all Afro-Americans to join the world's Pan-Africanists."[35] He arrived, that is, at the basic premises of the postwar *négritude* movement and its socialism for Africans, its attack on capitalism and materialism. "What do you think is responsible for race prejudice in the U.S.?" Malcolm was asked in the last months of his life. "Ignorance and greed," he replied.[36]

## Mirroring Images, Hysterical Ideas

Like Frantz Fanon, who focused on white males and females creating the mythological Negro phallus, Malcolm perceived racism "on the genital level." But he saw a different range of phenomena, with different eyes. Fanon had written about the Negro male as a phobogenic object, feared and desired, particularly by passive, masochistic males and masochistic females. But Fanon did not consider at all what brings white men (or women) to black women; he considered only white male homosexuality and dread of homosexuality. He emphasized desire for and fear of Negro male potency. James Baldwin, although he spoke generally of white lovelessness, white lack of sensuality, also concentrated on white male envy and debasement of black men. What Malcolm saw, by contrast, was universal envy. Everyone wants what others have and wants to be what others are. The whites want blackness, black sexuality, and "taboo" pleasures; the black men want white power, money, prestige,

and access to white female purity. But Malcolm's outlook was heterosexual, and he focused on heterosexual desire and perversions. He thus
came close to Dollard's analysis of the white male's split of his objects
of desire into white (pure) and black (impure), but he did not confine
himself to talk about white frustration and puritanism. He took envy
and fear as his themes. Malcolm's conclusions could be summarized
with a passage by the African American sociologist Calvin Hernton, from
*Sex and Racism in America*, a book that came out the same year (1965)
as the *Autobiography*. Working the theme of white male projections,
Hernton wrote:

> Whether the white supremacist is sexually virile or not, he *fears* he
> is inadequate, and he feels guilty about his fear—he therefore says
> Negroes are oversexed. The racist *fears* his sexuality is sinful, immoral.
> He therefore creates, out of the Negro female and Negro male, objects
> of degradation upon which he can act out his own feelings of iniquity
> and vulgarity. The racist *fears* that the relationships between Negro
> men and women are healthier and freer than those between himself
> and white women. He also *fears* that black men can be better with white
> women than he is. He therefore transforms the white woman into a
> "lily lady," no longer a woman, but an idol, and he fills her with his
> paranoid fears of Negro men. And, finally, as he craves to maim the
> Negro, the racist acquires a false sense of superiority and justification
> for his action by imagining that the Negro is bent on deflowering the
> symbol of his guilt and inadequacy—"sacred white womanhood."[37]

These differences in diagnosis—and a wider sample of African and
African American male diagnostic literature would show other variants
as well—reflect differences in the diagnosticians' psychology, experience, cultural setting. Each brings into focus part of the whole of the
sexual fantasy structure that is racism; each concentrates on a form of
racism (although it is interesting to note how little attention is given to
the sibling rivalry form). None, however, focuses on black women's experiences, none even has the social consciousness about women that
had already been apparent in W. E. B. Du Bois's essay "The Damnation
of Women," published in *Darkwater, Voices from the Veil* (1920). Racism
appears in the 1960s Black male texts as predominantly, dominatingly,
a white pathology in relation to Black men. It is either a contest among
males over white women (as Malcolm and Hernton saw it) or a white
male homophobic structure (as Fanon and Baldwin saw it); among
white women, the diagnostic consensus goes, racism rests upon rape
fantasies.

Both the modes of exploration in these texts and the absence in them of consideration for the experience of black women reveal a great deal about the dynamic of white racism as it lodges in its victims' experiences. First, a pattern in these male writers' texts mirrors the historical course and the psychodynamic of white racism. Most African and African American male writers of the 1960s, of the period when the sexual sickness of racism was most insistently analyzed and spoken—to Blacks and to whites—follow a three part autobiographical pattern, one Fanon would have called Hegelian. The first part tells the story of the writer's youthful entanglement in desiring to be white and in trying to solve the problem of racism by subscribing to a universalist vision of some sort, whether the universalism of the Christian Church or the Black churches (in which Baldwin was a boy preacher), the universalism of socialism (as prescribed by Sartre, or as available in African socialist manifestos), or a political vision of integration and assimilation.[38] The solution, then, turns out to be a false solution, a false promise, a collusion with racism, and a second part brings a new endeavor—separatism. Whether of the cultural sort supported by a philosophy of *négritude* or (currently) Afrocentricity or of the more concretely economic and political sort recommended by the Nation of Islam (as, earlier, by Garveyism, the Back to Africa movement that Malcolm's father had joined), the separatism entails a change of life, a withdrawal from wanting to be white and from all corruptions of white culture, white commerce, and white sexuality. An ideology of Black supremacy may be envisioned (as it was by Elijah Muhammad but not by Garvey), or at least seen sympathetically. But eventually separatism, too, comes to seem bound up with white racism, to take its terms from racism, to be reactive, derivative. A third phase follows.

This is a phase of educating, and it depends upon the conviction, gained in the first two phases, that Blacks have an authority, an experience, a truthfulness, a resistance to racism's secrecy, that puts—and should be known to put—whites in debt. Black witnessing and truth telling then appears to be the only route to redemption for whites, the only cure for their sickness, as well as the mainstay of Black integrity and moral superiority. As Baldwin wrote in *The Fire Next Time,* after he had told of his renunciation of Christian universalism and his sympathy for but rejection of the Nation of Islam and its separatism:

> White people cannot, in the generality, be taken as models of how to live. Rather, the white man is himself in sore need of new standards,

which will release him from his confusion and place him once again in fruitful communion with the depths of his own being . . . The American Negro has the great advantage of never having believed that collection of myths to which white Americans cling: that their ancestors were all freedom-loving heroes, that they were born in the greatest country the world has ever seen, or that Americans are invincible in battle and wise in peace, that Americans have always dealt honorably with Mexicans and Indians and all other neighbors or inferiors, that American men are the world's most direct and virile, that American women are pure. Negroes know far more about white Americans than that . . . And one felt that if one had had that white man's worldly advantages, one would never have become as bewildered and joyless and as thoughtlessly cruel as he. The Negro came to the white man for a roof or for five dollars or for a letter to the judge; the white man came to the Negro for love. But he was not often able to give what he came seeking. The price was too high; he had too much to lose. And the Negro knew this, too. When one knows this about a man, it is impossible to hate him, but unless he becomes a man—becomes equal—it is also impossible to love him. Ultimately, one tends to avoid him.[39]

Put very simply, these stages on life's way reflect visions of living (hopefully as equals) in the white man's house, of living outside the white man's house, and of building a new house; visions of striving for equality of place, rejecting false promises of equality, and redefining equality. These stages also mirror the history of white racism in Europe and America. Enlightenment universalism, Enlightenment convictions about the family of mankind, the oneness of the human species, the ameliorating effects of advancing reason and science, were supplanted by race theory. White supremacy was a doctrine of race separatism, deeply conservative and stupefying—inducing a condition of mental debilitation, emotional hypocrisy, inhibition. A third phase, a reaction against such a separatism, represented by liberalism and what Myrdal called the American Creed, is an effort to return to Enlightenment values—to universalism. But this universalism seems pathetic and inadequate to the Black writers, both because it is a return to a rhetoric that disguised a reality of white hegemony and because it arises from no real appreciation of the psychosocial needs served by white supremacy, so it is constantly regressing into white supremacy. The Blacks' own third phase represents a revisioning, a search for something new, not a nostalgia.

Underneath the history of white racism, the 1960s Black diagnosticians and analysts could sense a psychological pattern. The tradition of the family of mankind could serve psychosexually a vast desire to encompass both races as well as all sexual possibilities, to be and have all the people and possibilities represented in the complex, two-tiered families and national family made up of rulers and ruled, masters and servants, living together and rearing children in intimate proximity, with the multiple mothering typical of class-mingled estates and race-mingled plantations. White supremacy, by contrast, represented for males a rigid masculine identification, a hypermasculinizing designed to suppress all unacceptable desires and make one object, the pure white woman, into the only acceptable object. It emphasized the threat to white women represented by Black men, while it covered over, kept out of sight, the white male exploitation of Black women, the nonincestuous mother figures in the household. Hyperfeminizing among white women would have the same effect of detachment from the complexities of multiple mothering (white and Black) and multiple available objects, including Black men, the nonincestuous fathers. Liberalism has been an obscurantism that has silenced the whole problem of sexual debasement.

Among Blacks, separatism or Black supremacy could also represent a drastic and defensive narrowing of sexual possibilities, a retreat from desires directed at whites and at being white, as well as a defensive assertion of masculinity in conditions where masculinity is threatened, literally and figuratively. Reacting against separatist programs, African writers looking for a new synthesis would envision partnerships made free from legal coercion or unconscious repetition compulsion and then imagine these as models for political partnerships—not assimilations or suppressions of blackness in whiteness, but partnerships. As Baldwin put the matter in his wry style: "Why . . .—especially knowing the family as I do—I would want to marry your sister is a great mystery to me. But your sister and I have every right to marry if we wish to, and no one has the right to stop us. If she cannot raise me to her level, perhaps I can raise her to mine."[40]

## Sexism-Racism-Classism

That so many African American women's texts begin with a taken-for-granted attitude of moral worth and access to the truth and involve no cathartic, self-asserting and racism-exorcising dialectical journey, speaks to the differences between racism's impact on men and on women. These differences are especially obvious in the torrent of works published by African American women in the last twenty years, a literary renaissance quite unlike the Harlem Renaissance or the Black Arts movement of the 1960s. In those movements, though African American women's literary productions reflected the general ferment, men's voices dominated. Women have dominated the literary renaissance of the last twenty years.[41] In this period black women's experiences have been most extensively presented, and a rich layer of feminist ("womanist," in Alice Walker's term) scholarship has tracked the library of novels, poems, memoirs, and new prose forms like the one the poet Audre Lorde called "biomythography." In this literature, what comes into view is black family life; not the odysseys of individuals trying to understand their experiences of racism and to come together in movements of resistance, revolution, and liberation. The women trace the complexities of intersexual, intergenerational, relational life under racism and the solidarity among black women that has existed since the slavery period. It was certainly no accident that this literature provided the strongest reply to the 1960s shift in the race relations policy of American white liberals. As the kind of thinking that informed Moynihan's report proliferated, bringing into new prominence old images of deviant black families, black matriarchs, and derelict black men, African American women countered with an outpouring of history writing and fictional historical reconstructions of Negro families in all their intricacy and resilience.

As African American women writers have represented the history of racism in this country, they have made its impact on black women their centerpiece. In a typical passage, the historian Darlene Clark Hine discussed the need for new histories of slavery:

> As slavery became deeply entrenched in southern states, and the prospect of securing fresh Africans disappeared after 1807 with the official end of the slave trade, slave masters knew that control of the reproductive capacities of black women amounted to the only sure way of maintaining a viable slave-labor population ... Perhaps the most daunting task confronting black women historians [in 1993] is to persuade students of slavery to see it as more than an economic institution. Slavery was also a sexual institution, and it was white male control of black women as sexual beings that shored up the patriarchal dimension of the system.[42]

The legacy of the slavery experience under conditions of competitive racism produced a particularly complex set of character traits and organizational strategies, as Hine concluded:

> It would be a mistake to see black women solely as victims under slavery. It is equally undesirable, however, to create myths of the superheroic black woman who stoically met every obstacle, endured total debasement, only to rise above her tormentors and captors. Black women in all eras understood the multilayered realities of their oppression and exploitation and developed an array of survival strategies and functional identities. On plantations and farms of all sizes and purposes, black women developed networks with each other, and where feasible, they embraced their own form of Christianity, crafted a distinct moral code, and fashioned permeable family boundaries that freely made room for blood relatives and fictive kin. The extended, flexible, adaptable black family is as much black women's invention as it is an African retention. In other words, part of the requirements for survival dictated that black women, when necessary, reconfigured and reimagined families, communities and themselves. Survival mandated that they develop private identities and worlds known only to their own.

The private identities of black women have been and are the source of their resistance to the sexual images of black women that—still—suffuse the culture, carrying on the racism that has its roots in the slavery era. As the essayist and culture critic bell hooks has summarized these images:

> Overall representations of Black females in contemporary mass media continue to identify us as more sexual, as earthy freakish, out of control . . . [But] running counter to representations of Black females as sexual savages, sluts or prostitutes is the "mammy" stereotype. Again, this image inscribes Black female presence as signified by the body, in this case the construction of woman as mother, as "breast," nurturing and sustaining the life of others . . . Despite the fact that most households in the United States do not have Black maids or nannies working in them, racist and sexist assumptions that Black women are somehow "innately" more capable of caring for others continues to permeate cultural thinking about Black female roles.[43]

The stance that Hine expressed and that hooks exemplified begins and ends in the third of the three stages so typically represented in African American men's texts: the problem of reenvisioning, coming to new definitions, is and has been the immediate female agenda. These women envision a world beyond racially and sexually stereotyped roles. In the words of the feminist critic Barbara Christian, the "main thread" apparent in contemporary African American women's literature has been the struggle "to define themselves rather than being defined."[44] The grounds for definition are built in, as the poet Nikki Giovanni made clear in her witty, mocking autobiography *Gemini* (1971), which has not a trace of anguished black male struggle over separatism and "place" in relation to whites and white culture: "We Black women are the single group in the West intact. And anybody can see we're pretty shaky. We are, however, (all praises), the only group that derives its identity from itself. I think it's been rather unconscious, but we measure ourselves by ourselves, and I think that's a practice we can ill afford to lose. For whatever combination of events that made us turn inward, we did." The pressures on black women are always understood as multiple, complex, and requiring a complex response. No partial or reactive mode of asserting her own definitions will do. Again, Barbara Christian:

> As poor, woman and Black, the Afro-American woman had to generate her own definition in order to survive, for she found that she was forced to deny essential aspects of herself to fit the definitions of others. If defined as black, her woman nature was often denied; if defined as woman, her blackness was often ignored; if defined as working class, her gender and race were muted. It is primarily in her expression of herself that she could be her totality. And a result of that expression is also the articulation of the interconnectedness of race, sex, and class as a philosophical basis for the pattern of dominance and hierarchy in their society.[45]

African American women have made it clear to the male diagnosticians of racism as a sexual sickness that focusing on the creation of the mythological black male phallus is focusing too narrowly. The women agree that a mythological phallus is created and attacked and appropriated for many reasons—among them the homophobia of whites males, the white male fear of projected black male sexuality, and the fantasies about black male sexuality typical of white women living in patriarchal conditions. But they stress that it is crucial not to leave out of the accounting how these dimensions of black male mythologizing have served the exploitation and mythologizing of black females. This fuller picture is necessary for resisting racism but also for understanding how the panoply of white racism has profoundly disturbed relations between black men and black women. By exploiting black women and purveying negative images of them, and by inducing hypermasculine defensiveness in black men, white racism has continued by means of cultural imagery the breaking-up of black relationships that crucially maintained the slavery system. This divided and conquered stance is the victims' manifestation of the hysterical splitting so characteristic of racism. In an era when white racism takes coded and disguised and indirect forms, nothing could be more satisfying to the white racist's psychic needs than to see black women and black men quarreling with one another, affirming white images of the black matriarch and the black stud.

This aspect of racism was stressed by black women writers but not, of course, news to black men. In general, however, men have responded that the induced quarrels should be kept out of public—white—view. They feel the story of black sexism should not be emphasized or made available for white use. In novel after play after poem, however, African American women have insisted on having the quarrel out, working it through, making it part of the project of achieving self-definition rather than definition by the Other, regardless of what white people make of it. Important conversions to this view have been made. Calvin Hernton, for example, acknowledged how he had overlooked black women's experiences in *Sex and Racism in America* and made reparations with *The Sexual Mountain and Black Women Writers*. But the charges from black males about black females as male bashers that greeted Ntozake Shange's play *For Colored Girls Who Have Considered Suicide When the Rainbow Is Enuf* in 1975 or Michele Wallace's *Black Macho and the Myth of the Superwoman* in 1979 have continued, although recently they have provoked efforts at dialogue and reconciliation like *Breaking Bread,* a conversation between bell hooks and Cornel West.

Few African American women writers call for separatism (except those who belong to the Nation of Islam), and thus few have moved from separatism into an educationalist stance like Baldwin's. That is, there is little expressed need to respond to white racism with an "anti-racist racism" or the equivalent of a hypermasculinization, a defensive sexual identity, and thus no struggle out of these positions. Much more frequently women express the view, "don't bother to try to educate the whites—they can read our books if they want education—we must continue to educate ourselves." They seek to keep the family together and the black community at the center of concern, with its identity (as Nikki Giovanni put it) "intact." So Audre Lorde could say sharply in a 1979 speech addressed primarily to white feminists: "Women of today are still being called upon to stretch across the gap of male ignorance, and to educate men as to our existence and our needs. This is an old and primary tool of the oppressors to keep the oppressed occupied with the master's concerns. Now we hear that it is the task of black and third world women to educate white women, in the face of tremendous resistance, as to our existence, our differences, our relative roles in our joint survival. This is a diversion of energies and a tragic repetition of racist patriarchal thought."[46]

# 15

## Feeling the Contradictions of Sexism and Being the Targets of Homophobias

The disappointment and annoyance with white feminism that Audre Lorde expressed so forcefully has preoccupied black, and Third World, and white feminist theorists in recent years. They have pursued the trinity of sexism-racism-classism from all kinds of angles in an effort to broaden feminism's theoretical base, include the diversity of women's experiences, and respond to African American, Third World, and other social movements or visions of social change. But, as the feminist theoretical agenda has been widened, an awareness has also spread that the sexism third of the trinity is itself not a monolith, that there exist sexisms in the plural.

### "The Two Faces of Feminism"

Through most of the period of second-wave feminism since the early 1970s, however, the sexism in sexism-racism-classism had been treated in the singular, so that the variants that I called sexist-racism and sexist-classism—which are directed by men of one group at women of another group, and which are characterized by splitting women into the chaste, maternal ones (of the in-group) and the unchaste, nonmaternal ones (of the out-group)—were not clearly distinguished from sexisms directed at in-group women. The prevailing assumption, on the contrary, was that white women and black women experienced sexism differently

517

because black women experienced racism and classism along with sexism while the white women of the middle class who devised feminist theory knew only sexism. (Similarly, lower-class white women assumed that what distinguished their experience from that of the feminist theorists was classism.) White women and black women were, without registering the phenomenon conceptually, experiencing different forms of sexism from white men and being cast in roles—the pure virgin versus the impure whore—that set them against one another. And the sexism that black women knew from black men was not of the sexist-racist variety, although it was and is decisively influenced by the oppressed position of black men in colonial, slave, and competitive racist social formations.[1]

Both the complexity of sexism itself and the complexity of its intersection with hysterical prejudices like sexist-racism or sexist-classism have led to the present troubled state of feminist theory of male dominance and oppression. A paradoxical theoretical state exists: there are many developmental layers and varieties of sexism, which have not been clearly distinguished, and there are, simultaneously, many explanations of sexism built up on the assumption that sexism is one thing. But sexism is also a prejudice cluster with a multitude of effects upon its victims, all silencing them variously as they have tried to tell its story, their stories. Unlike antisemites, sexists do not rewrite the history of sexism, continuing to confound and baffle the intellects of the victims, particularly by denying the culminating episodes of their victimization. Unlike racists, sexists do not repress the knowledge that the victims try to speak, treating that knowledge as they treat their own forbidden desires, the secret of which that knowledge reveals. As shown paradigmatically in the myth of Philomela, who was raped by King Tereus and then silenced by having her tongue cut out, sexists deny their victims any identity or story of their own. The victims must be as sexists say they are.

The victims of sexism feel the erasure of identity as isolation, as being alone and exceptional in their pain. Sexism, in its difference-denying narcissistic nature, acts against the possibility of solidarity among the victims. In its derivative forms that assert difference, sexism actively sets the victims against one another by making it impossible for them to hear the whole of their common story and also by weaving into the story of sexism the oppressions that women suffer *from other women*. On a theoretical level, sexism as a kind of narcissism draws into its own terms the theory—feminist theory—launched against it; in ways that are difficult for the victims to see, their own theorizing, their own explanations of sexism, get wrapped in sexism's theorizing.

In this chapter, I want to explore the current modalities of this theoretical level of the silencing. To do this, I will treat the "faces of feminism"[2] and consider again the history of feminist theory since the end of World War II. This time I view it globally as a history that began with a clear claim, articulated most forcefully by white, middle-class American feminists, that sexist oppression is universal, something that all women experience in common, which, as a common story, constitutes their sisterhood. In the course of a massive production of feminist analyses in Europe and America and throughout the so-called Third World, this clear claim gave way to a sense just as clear that the experiential differences among women divide them, that they do not experience in common one thing, sexism, and that they are not one group, a sex "class." To my understanding, this history shows a playing out in the victims' lives and theories of the developmental history of sexism itself, which I have described as moving from bodily narcissism to mental narcissism, one-sex sexism to two-sex sexism or sameness sexism to difference sexism. Sexism's psychosocial forms have been mirrored and condensed in the history of the victims' efforts to comprehend and resist. To see this narcissistic interplay, let us recall what some of the representative feminist theoreticians have written.

The postwar history of American feminist theoretical responses to sexism, eventually so torn by centrifugal forces, centered first on "sexual politics." American feminists of the late 1960s and early 1970s, deeply influenced by Kate Millett's book *Sexual Politics,* felt all women experienced the dynamic of sexual politics. Millett argued this idea with an encyclopedic range of analyses—psychological, sociological, anthropological, historical—but she set it out first in *Sexual Politics* with three quick takes of literary analysis designed to shock. In an ironic, detached, masterful and mastering tone, a tone that had no precedent in scholarly writing then, she purposefully and self-consciously fought the silencing of phallic power with its own instruments—analytical speech and cutting writing.

Opened up for Millett's quick probes was, first, a scene from Henry Miller's *Sexus* in which the narrator-hero "buggers" his best friend's wife Ida in the bathroom—taking her first in the bathtub and then, *après bagne,* spurred on by a little playful fellatio that she has offered eagerly, penetrating her from the rear. Her role in the activity is summed up in the comment "Not a word was spoken." Second, Millett took a scene from Norman Mailer's *The American Dream* in which the hero, having murdered his wife, goes to the live-in maid for a bit of bracing, invigorating, rapacious anal penetration, against her will. Not a word is spoken. Jean Genet's autobiographical *The Thief's Journal* provides the third scene. Armand, who is a bully, dominates his *marcione* (faggot) Jean after making a display of power—a rather pathetic one, in Jean's eyes, but terrorizing nonetheless—by whipping the air with his belt; then he sends the young queen off to pick up customers and bring the money back "intact." Millett read Jean Genet as the novelist who "unerringly penetrated to the essence of what heterosexual society imagines to be the character of 'masculine' and 'feminine.' " Masculinity is the brutal mastery of the pimp, while femininity is the queen's servitude, which is not even servitude in exchange for protection, but only that "intensity of humiliation which constitutes identity for those who despise themselves."

Each of Millett's vignettes exposed an ingredient of sexism. Miller's hero, who worships his own phallus and basks in the mindless adoration bestowed upon it by Ida, Miller's ideal bimbo, is really bound erotically to Ida's husband, his best friend, who possesses a penis of awe-inspiring size. In the medium of the silent woman's body, Miller's hero both buggers and triumphantly overpowers the absent male, appropriating supplementally his penis-power. Mailer's Rojack, who has always been troubled by his homosexual feelings, controls them, keeps them in repression, by killing off his much too masculine and castrating wife and then finding in the anus of a "lower" woman—for him a man who is not one, a mother who is not one—a source of life, a place he experiences as earthy and deathly but that nonetheless provides him a rush of vital power. Armand, who is a homosexual, and whose preference in sexual acts Genet does not describe, makes his woman who is not one cower with self-despising fear. Sexism means not only phallic narcissism and anal sadism but also—in these three instances—homoerotism.

Millett used the vignettes and the analyses to advance the claims about sexual politics that became central to that moment of American feminism. Sexual politics is not about men and women as biological beings nor about the two sexes; it is about power and power positions. There are masculine dominators and feminine dominateds—and the latter can be either female or male, but they must be voiceless. Their silence is the condition of and for their domination; they have nothing to say in it. Ultimately, Millett argued, women have nothing to say because the sexual dynamic they participate in is buggery—that is, it is between men. Female silence or erasure is the essence of "sexual politics at the fundamental level of copulation." Furthermore, copulation—sexuality and the expressions of sexual desire—is, quintessentially, the realm in which sexism can be read. Sexual relations condense and display human beings' power relations, particularly sexual acts that tend toward violence, battering, or rape. Since sexual scenes epitomize sexism, liberation must come through sexual liberation.

Millett claimed that because it defines the "primary human situation," sexism is the primordial prejudice: "sexual caste supersedes all other forms of inequalitarianism." As I noted in Chapter 4, Millett and many other theorists of her vintage argued that sexism could be understood on analogy with racism—that women were, so to speak, a sex-slave group. But once they established that analogy, theorists also felt it necessary to argue for the uniqueness and primordialness of sexism. As Simone de Beauvoir had taught, women are the Other in ways unlike any other group's alienation. Specifically, women live in families with men, which makes families the key organizations for perpetuating women's oppression. But it was the analogy with racism that helped theorists argue for the idea that women are *a group*—like the blacks.

Millett articulated the main ingredients of what came to be known as "radical feminism": a theory of sex-based male and male group (homoerotic) power, a focus on the sexual liberation of a sex class, and a catalog of charges against the family as the main vehicle for inculcating sexism generation after generation. This analysis had immediate and strong appeal. Although few of her generation put as much emphasis on homoerotism as Millett did, most of the radical feminist theorists she influenced understood that this emphasis did explain why men seem to be so oblivious to women, in bed, in social institutions, in theory. The attention of men is elsewhere—on other men; "they" are bound in their homoeroticism.

Translated into the terms I have been developing, the sexism on which Kate Millett focused her attention is the kind that I have called one-sex sexism or sameness sexism, the bodily narcissistic mode—although she came to her point without an explicit theory of male narcissism and certainly without emphasis on an assertion of sameness. She was describing homoerotic (in a sense, pederastic) men for whom women, as a group, exist to be used as sexual outlets and as reproducers of the family—the patrilineal and patriarchal family. The literary-sexual scenes that Millett represented, and in which she found the essence of sexism, all depict women as having no independent identity, no difference from men, and as only sites for male phallic display. Men are brutal masters, and women are only an "intensity of humiliation," whose role is to worship at the phallus and not to remind men by being nonphallic that the phallus is in any way vulnerable.

In focusing on sameness sexism, Millett created what might be called "sameness feminism" in response. By this I mean a feminism envisioning a future in which socially constructed differences between the sexes, ultimately differences of power position, would disappear. For this future to be ushered in, the site of social construction, "the family"— meaning the monogamous nuclear family in its American and European bourgeois format—would have to wither away, to be replaced by more communal forms, under socialism. Women would be relieved of their burden of motherhood in nuclear family settings, while "at the fundamental level of copulation" they would no longer be bystanders, vehicles for male desire, but have an autonomous position. In a document called "Sexual Politics: A Manifesto for Revolution" (1968), Millett argued that feminism should and would bring about free sexual expression and "bisex, or the end of enforced perverse heterosexuality."[3]

Radical feminism dominated the years between roughly 1968 and 1973, when American feminism burgeoned in American cities. But it gradually gave way to a type of feminism—usually called "cultural feminism"—that the radicals despised and viewed as reactionary.[4] Cultural feminism did not begin from the idea that differences between men and women are constructed in the nexus of the family and solidified as power positions, as rulership of one class over another. On the contrary, it began with the idea that there exist differences between men and women that are (in one version) biologically grounded or (in another version) so deeply constructed as to be virtually equivalent to biological givens. The characteristics that differentiate women from men, so cultural feminists argued, have been used by sexists to oppress women; but, if rightly understood and evaluated, they constitute women's peculiar virtues. Sexism is, basically, male envy and hatred of specifically female capacities, especially reproductive capacities, and the key mode of defense against this sexism is appreciation and celebratory embrace of those female capacities.

Cultural feminism came to the fore in the American Women's Liberation movement as the movement, despite its legislative successes, particularly the Supreme Court's 1973 decision on abortion, began to lose power. The main organizational and theoretical problem was factionalizing within women's groups along class, race, and particularly sexual-preference lines. Against the solidarity-promoting idea that women are a single sex class, the realities of female diversity came crashing in, and cultural feminism arose as a way to reformulate what women have in common.

The new formulation provoked a formidable array of criticism. To feminists of working-class background and to socialists, radical feminist sexual liberation had seemed apolitical, as the notion that "the personal is political" had seemed much too personal, too removed from practical matters of pay equity, workplace discrimination, lack of childcare, and poor working conditions. Much of the radical feminist dedication to criticizing "male" forms of institutional power—like the hierarchical nature of organizations—seemed irrelevant to those whose main concern was to get organizations to crack open their doors and distribute their wealth. African American women frequently charged that only middle-class white women could afford to worry about sexual liberation or have the audacity to insist that every woman ought to analyze her condition in the terms of sexual politics. Brooklyn's representative in Congress, the first African American congresswoman, Shirley Chisolm, famously summed up the common complaint by accepting the idea that not all housework should fall to women while distancing herself from feminism: "Everything else they say is baloney."[5]

To many lesbians, however, sexual liberation within heterosexuality held no interest and even appeared to them as a co-optation, a matter of "sleeping with the enemy" in a different way rather than fighting for liberation from what came to be called (in a phrase supplied by Adrienne Rich) "compulsory heterosexism." Feminists of all political persuasions were forced to reconsider their convictions when lesbian theorists began to insist that lesbianism is a choice and can be a specifically political choice to separate from men. In lesbian sexuality, they argued, women can be sexually free. The challenge to radical feminism from lesbian separatists was certainly the most deeply divisive challenge of the early 1970s, and it sent many movement activists in the direction of more liberal, reformist organizations undergoing less theoretical—and personal—turmoil.

This range of criticism only expanded as other groups of women came forward—particularly professional groups, including the academics who created Women's Studies in universities—and the liberal, reformist feminist organizations had to take more and more responsibility for keeping the movement going. The intensity of the criticism also reflected a shared feeling among the critics that they would not be helped by exchanging one form of prescription about how women should be for another—from radical women. Many factors contributed to this shared feeling, but I think that fundamentally the critics were rebelling against the radical feminist assumption "we are all alike" with its androgynizing vision of overcoming the power differences between the sexes. And this rebellious impulse was so strong that it obscured the contribution to analyzing the male sexist attitude "we are all alike" that radical feminism had been able to make precisely because it assumed that all women, commonly, are reduced to being not-women by sexism.

In effect, cultural feminists offered a vision of women being exactly what two-sex or difference sexism had always said they were—different, not-men; but cultural feminists then refused any tactic blaming women for their difference, castigating them, or judging them inferior. Beginning with a focus on difference sexism, cultural feminists also began with an assumption that women have an identity, which sexism then devalues as other. Their theory reasserted sexual difference and laid claim to a uniquely female way of living and being that could not be absorbed or assimilated into a male vision or a male mode. Cultural feminists credited all the discredited female capacities—for nurturing and caretaking, intuition and emotionality, intimate communication—just as the *négritude* movement revaluated the qualities and characteristics of African life and history. They sought to show male qualities—rationality, competitiveness, aggression—in their limitations and as the means for (if not the origin of) sexism. At their starkest, cultural feminists sounded like Elizabeth Gould Davis as she simplistically explained why women are *by instinct* the natural ecologists:

> Man is the enemy of nature: to kill, too root up, to level off, to pollute, to destroy are his instinctive reactions . . . Woman, on the other hand,

is the ally of nature and her instinct is to tend, to nurture, to encourage healthy growth, and to preserve ecological balance.[6]

Strategically, cultural feminism, with its focus on gender difference rather than on gender equality and the eventual elimination of the gender roles that consolidate male power, aimed at protection of female identity, "Woman." Not the family as the specific molder and shaper of gender roles, but the much more general institution of "heterosexism" is the means by which female identity is devalued. Those facets of the heterosexist culture that could be construed as assaults directly on the different female identity—like pornography, which excises any concern for feminine virtues—became central issues. As assaults on female identity, cultural phenomena like pornography also seemed to transcend differences among women of class, race, or sexual preference; every woman could see—it was hoped—that pornographic productions erase female difference. The bathtub scene in Miller's *Sexus* is not, from this point of view, about sexual power as the basis for all power, it is about denying Ida's womanhood and eliminating any space for female relationships or culture. Some of the most extreme proponents of cultural feminism viewed sexism as something created and sustained by the all-pervasive sex industry. They deemed everything "at the level of copulation" pornographic. In other words, cultural feminists proposed a counterrevolution to the sexual revolution—they blamed the sexual revolution for giving aggressive male sexuality a vastly expanded arena for oppression, for treating women as sexual objects, and for sexual violence.[7]

Cultural feminism did—and does—have a wide appeal. The antipornography campaign has even brought feminists into alliance with antifeminist conservatives. Emphasis on difference appeals to defenders of the traditional nuclear family (in America) and to women around the world who live in and wish to continue living in family and religious settings where differences in sex or gender roles are sanctioned, natural. Conservative (from the radical feminist point of view) women embedded in families of various traditional sorts and in patriarchal religious traditions, understand radical feminism solely as an attack upon difference, not as a vision of gender equality. As one of American antifeminism's chief spokeswomen, the syndicated columnist Phyllis Schlafly, said recently about a young woman's court case seeking admission to the Citadel, an all-male military academy: "This case has nothing to do with equal rights or sex discrimination or giving women the 'opportu-nity' to have a . . . Citadel education. It has everything to do with the feminist goal of eliminating gender diversity and turning America into an androgynous society." The case is about "a unisex view of the law of the land."[8]

But cultural feminism failed to address the problem that had led to it—the "we are all alike" in radical feminism, which had spurred fac-tionalism in the movement. It simply said "we women are all different from men." And two consequences arose. First, differences of class and race were said to be both superficial and the product of male social organization—used by men to divert women and obscure their solidar-ity. Thus the cultural feminist theologian Mary Daly wrote in *Gyn/Ecology* (1978): "Women who accept false inclusion among the fathers and sons are easily polarized against other women on the basis of ethnic, national, class, religious and other male-defined differences, applauding the de-feat of 'enemy' women."[9] And, second, this difference feminism led to a prescription *against* the sexual revolution just as formidable as the radical feminist prescription *for* the sexual revolution. Any trace of "masculine" behavior or sexuality in women—particularly any promis-cuity, male role-playing in lesbianism, sadomasochism, transsexualism— was branded.

Viewed through the lens of a theory of narcissism, sameness feminism or radical feminism is an assertion of female bodily narcissism. It pro-claims the "right" of female anatomy to be treated as the same, for male and female sexuality are basically the same, and it rejects any vision of female anatomy as lacking or less than male. Difference feminism or cultural feminism is an assertion of female mental narcissism, a cultural elitism. It highlights differences and proceeds to an evaluation of female superiority. Psychologically, these expressions of female narcissism op-erate differently than the expressions of male narcissism that compose the historical and social layers of sexism. Sameness sexism reflects a desired merger of the male with his (phallic) mother, while sameness feminism represents a rebellion of daughters against mothers, a break with the sexist sexual and moral order that radical feminists felt was most intimately and deeply reproduced in mothering. Difference sex-ism reflects a male's anxious repudiation of his frustrating, threatening, and dangerously different mother, while difference feminism, by con-trast, celebrates a female's bond with her mother, her sameness with her mother: it is a narcissism in the plural, "we" (mother and daughter) are not them, which fends off a perceived threat from males against the mother-daughter merger. As Mary Daly, for example, explained in *Beyond God the Father* (1973):

> The religions of patriarchy—especially the Judaeo-Christian tradition and its hideous blossom, Freudian theory—have stolen daughters from their mothers, and mothers from their daughters. . . Mothers in our culture are cajoled into killing off the self-actualization of their daughters, and daughters learn to hate them for it. If they begin to see, the pain drives them to their male analysts, who help them to understand that they must hate their mothers for not having destroyed them enough to erase the pain. Still, the destruction has not been complete, and women are beginning to dream again of a time and space in which Mother and Daughter look with pride into each other's faces and know that they both have been victims and now are sisters and comrades.[10]

## Feminisms and the Contradictions of Oppression

In the American feminist context, sameness and difference feminisms have been vying with each other throughout the last twenty-five years.[11] The positions are not metaphysical—like realism and nominalism, materialism and idealism; they are identity statements made into political ideologies. And they are identity statements made in reaction to sexism. Sameness feminism was constructed by women who experienced the phallic narcissism of men, ''at the fundamental level of copulation,'' as the center of sexism; they reacted to sameness sexism. Difference feminism was constructed by women who, while repudiating sameness feminism, which they considered prescriptive, reacted against the male difference sexism that insists women are other and inferior.

Feminism and many individual feminist theorists as well have been caught in a dynamic that resembles the one I noted as typical of African American male writers who moved from a desire to be white to an assertion of black otherness *(négritude)*, often entailing separatism and some form of antiracism racism, and then moved on to a more synthetic position like Black pride. But the third stage, what Fanon called active revolution, has not come about within or from within feminism, even though the sameness-difference debate has become so articulated that good histories and analyses of it now exist, calls for its overcoming have been made repeatedly, and it has been argued that the terms of debate obscure social and political realities that help keep the terms in place. As Carol Lee Bacchi has noted:

> "Sameness" and "difference" in some abstract sense . . . are not in dispute. In dispute is the nature of the social arrangements which inadequately cater for the personal side of people's lives. In dispute are the political and social values by which we choose to live. . . [The] sameness/difference framework does feminism a disservice since it mystifies these political issues. And so we would be well advised to avoid describing the movement in these terms. It is far preferable to discuss openly disagreements about strategies and political visions than to create the impression, first, that the problem is whether or not women are like men, and, second, that women must (or can) choose either to replicate contemporary male lifestyles and values or take responsibility for the world's caring work. The way to get beyond sameness/difference debates is to bring to the surface the political conditions which force women to these alternatives. The way to stop the "pendulum swing" between "same as" and "different from" is to confront the changes required to allow people to live fully human lives.[12]

The social and political realities that keep women and men from sharing fully responsibilities for and benefits from their lives and work certainly have been and are obscured by the feminist debate. But just bringing such realities to the fore would not move feminism beyond the debates. The static quality of contemporary feminist theory, matched now by a stasis in the American movement, reflects the way the forms of sexism, expressed through political conditions, bind theorizing. Such binding characterizes sexism but not the other prejudices to the same extent; it is a function of the bodily and mental narcissisms that animate the forms of sexism.[13]

In the past decade, since about 1985, the stasis in American feminist theory, the pendulum swing between the sameness and the difference theories, has been challenged by women with "outsider" and critical relations to feminism. Not surprisingly, women with multiple and complex identities, for whom *an* identity can be only approximately mapped out, have articulated an appropriately complex theoretical stance, off the pendulum course. These women organize their thought in terms of concerns that surround or cut across the division between masculine and feminine, the division central to both the sexisms and the feminisms that are bound up with sexisms. They reject the category "Woman," appealing for their rejection either to philosophical attacks on essentialism and ethnocentrism or to the dilemmas of practical feminist politics, or both.[14]

Beginning from the realization that not all women's experiences, including their experiences of sexism or the types of sexism that they experience, are alike, these theorists have sought a new common ground: not the "we are all alike" common ground of sexuality, not the "all women are different than all men" common ground of gender identity, but the multiethnic, multiracial, class diversified, sexually panoramic, kaleidoscopic terrain of "all women have some experience of sexism, in one or more of its forms and interlocking discourses, but their positions and experiences as often divide them as unite them." And this is, finally, a framework not determined by male narcissism and not determined by reactive female (mother-daughter) narcissism. Consider how Cherrie Moraga in *This Bridge Called My Back: Writings by Radical Women of Color* (1983) introduces herself and the others in the preface to her anthology:

> The theme echoing throughout most of these stories is our refusal of the *easy* explanation of the conditions we live in. There is nothing *easy* about a collective cultural history of what Mitsuye Yamada calls "unnatural disasters": the forced encampment of indigenous people on government reservations, the forced encampment of Japanese American people during WWII, the forced encampment of our mothers as laborers in factories/in fields/in our own and other people's homes as paid or unpaid slaves . . . Closer to home, we are still trying to separate the fibers of experience we have had as daughters of a struggling people. Daily, we feel the pull and tug of having to choose between which parts of our mothers' heritages we want to claim and wear and which parts have served to cloak us from the knowledge of ourselves.

## (Homo)sexuality and Culture

The homophobias are the prejudices that mean each contemporary gay man or lesbian has at least one before-and-after in his or her life. Each has a private moment of self-recognition—*this* is my desire, and it marks me as different, it means my membership in a hated minority. In the era of Gay Liberation in America, a growing number, although not yet a majority, also have a public before-and-after moment or process of "coming out," a public notice of the desire and an assertion of it. The "love that cannot speak its name" speaks first privately and then out loud—the public conditions being crucial to the fear or freedom the private speaking entails. Homosexuals differ from other minorities in having a site of cultural learning for sexual behavior that is distinct from, and often in opposition to, their familial site. The before-and-after of coming out marks the time when gay culture—in whatever form it is encountered or sought out—supersedes family-oriented culture as the main source of learning. In this sense, there is some gay culture for every gay person—although there certainly is not a gay culture that all gay persons would or could call their own.

In recent years, many gay men and lesbians have reached a third turning point as well, in which they have begun in some way to stand outside the declared and accepted identity—"homosexual"—as deconstructors, critics, and parodists enacting an antigeneric posthomosexuality. This third moment is theoretical, or perhaps it should more accurately be called stylistic or cultural—a moment of performance art. Like the feminists of multiple identity who have begun to dislodge feminism from its narcissistically dictated preoccupations with sameness and difference, the posthomosexuals both look critically over the history of resistance to homophobia and celebrate the complexity of their lives, imagining themselves and the world as beyond the great heterosexual-homosexual divide, in a plethora of identities that can be put on and taken off like costumes.

In this most recent phase of gay resistance, which coincides with the establishment of Gay and Lesbian Studies in European, Canadian, and American universities and with an enormous proliferation of gay cultural outlets, the basic understanding of the homophobias is shifting. A catalog of explanations for homophobia has been assembled through the twentieth century. The prejudice (always conceived as a singular thing) has been charged in Europe and America to the erotophobic Judeo-Christian religion; it has been explained, on religious or evolutionary grounds, as a product of the species' need to reproduce and reject nonreproductive ways of life. People have been said, on psychological grounds, to hate homosexuality from envy, from fear for their own sexual definition or fear of their own homosexuality, from having learned the strictures of authoritarian regimes or acquired in such regimes authoritarian personalities. Sociologists have pointed to modern conditions of population surplus or imbalance, regulation of sexuality, urbanization, and so forth. Each of these analyses assumes a place in a larger, or more general, conceptualization that has been growing under the influence of burgeoning libraries on the history of sexuality generally and of homosexuality in particular. Homophobia (still usually considered as a singular phenomenon) is now widely understood as the prejudice that has determined the content of the word "homosexual" and the words that preceded it—like "sodomite"—as designators of certain sexual acts, roles, and identities. And it is now widely acknowledged that periods in the history of homosexuality are marked by changes in the ways people engaging in homosexual acts or homosexual people have reacted to the homophobia directed at their acts or at them. The main reason analysts of homophobia still speak of homophobia rather than homophobias is that one form of homophobia—prejudice against men who are feminine or sexually receptive—has dominated, and still to a large extent does dominate, the discussion. The discussion is clued to interpretations of sexism. But, as homosexuality gives way to homosexualities, to a sense of the plurality and lability of sexual and gender identities, homophobias, too, will have their theoretical coming out.

A dialectic between sameness and difference underlies the resistances of gay people just as it does those of feminists, and it operates at the two levels I have called body narcissism and mental or cultural narcissism. Gay writers modulate back and forth over themes that revolve around the nature of their sexuality and their culture (or cultures) in relation to their sexuality. Because these themes look so different from male and female perspectives, I will consider the two perspectives separately, but first I want to speak generally about the dialectic as it became clear in the Gay—predominantly gay male—Liberation movement.

Among the American gay male intelligentsia, many have debated whether there is a "gay culture," a question that also has a before-and-after. Before, when most gay men were invisible, hidden, closeted, undeclared, there was what might be described as a culture of censorship. Gay cultural expression was self-censored or externally censored, and either way it became—as it departed the gay urban ghettos, left the bars for the precincts of majority culture—a culture of strategies for speaking without speaking, speaking in disguise or double entendre. It was this largely male culture that Susan Sontag famously compared to Jewish modernism: "Jews and homosexuals are the outstanding creative minorities in contemporary urban culture. Creative, that is, in the truest sense: they are creators of sensibilities. The two pioneering forces of modern sensibility are Jewish moral seriousness and homosexual aesthetics and irony."[15] But since the late 1960s, censorship, although it has continued, has not defined gay culture. As gay men have become more visible, and as external censorship has decreased, the diversity of the gay population has been accentuated, sub-subcultural groups have emerged, as have controversies among them. A deep political disagreement between culturally assimilationist gay men and culturally separatist gays runs through the whole period and into current books like Marshall Kirk and Hunter Madsen's conservative *After the Ball: How America Will Conquer Its Fear and Hatred of Gays in the 90s* (1989), which was issued—by a mainstream publishing house—to urge assimilation and to show how destructive gay political and cultural shock tactics have been. The book conjures an American melting pot able to melt even gays, and it instructs gays how to be just as properly bourgeois as the next heterosexual. The main impulse within gay culture, however, has come from those who oppose this kind of assimilationist reformism and articulate some kind of revolutionary vision, even if they do so along the sameness-difference continuum.

Particularly in the late 1960s, when the contemporary Gay Liberation movement emerged, European and American homosexuals tended to concentrate on showing the sameness of homosexuals and heterosexuals, as radical feminists did on showing the sameness of female and male "bisex." For their project, gay theoreticians adopted the Freudian—and specifically left Freudian, Reichian, Marcusian—notion that all humans start out initially bisexual or, as children, "polymorphously perverse" and then develop by a process of delimitation into people with distinct preferences in type of object and type of act. Gay people were, in this vision, sexual revolutionaries who could lead the way to a more general triumph over delimitation for homosexuals and heterosexuals, a vast and transmogrifying return to pleasure freed from "surplus repression" (in Herbert Marcuse's phrase) and from modern ideologies of sex solely in the service of procreation. "Liberation," wrote Dennis Altman in 1971 in his enormously influential book *Homosexual Oppression and Liberation,* "would involve a resurrection of our original impulse to take enjoyment from the total body, and indeed to accept the seeking of sensual enjoyment as an end in itself, free from procreation or status-enhancement."[16]

This Gay Liberation effort to assert sameness came as a response to many decades in which both heterosexual and homosexual theorists had constructed homosexuals as innately different—even as a "Uranian" third sex—and pathological. Rejecting any "anatomy as destiny" claim was part of the project of rejecting any pathologizing of homosexuality. Sex is sex, desire is desire—humans seek out other humans. Differences are, to use the theoretical terminology that evolved in historical studies of homosexuality, socially constructed, not essential.

In the 1960s and early 1970s American gay culture was usually understood as a culture—or a loose confluence of cultures—shaped by its starting point in turn-of-the-century essentialist definitions of homosexuals as biologically determined to their otherness. The culture was reactive, and what gays hoped for was a movement away from the reactions of self-denigration and self-hatred reflected in so many novels and memoirs of desperation, drunkenness, and promiscuity. They envisioned resistance as critique of imposed definitions and celebration of a unique "lifestyle," as gay writers worked to establish their equivalent of the feminist distinction between sex and gender: homosexuals are made, not born. Jean Genet acted as the patron saint of this critique—as Kate Millett had realized when she celebrated him as the writer who understood most thoroughly that "masculine" and "feminine" are not biological categories but power positions, identities, which both heterosexuals and homosexuals can assume.

But as gays emerged from the closet, especially during the Gay Liberation movement, of the 1980s, homosexual desire was revalued and homosexual culture celebrated as actively, not reactively, different. Gay theoreticians began to support once repudiated arguments for the biological innateness of homosexuality and to make claims for an innate gay sensibility. Like the historians of homosexuality who were called essentialists, these gay theoreticians posited an unchanging homosexual desire and a constant increment of homosexual desire in the human desire reservoir. Ten percent (the percentage Alfred Kinsey had estimated) of humans have been and will be homosexual, and their homosexuality predisposes them to specifically gay cultural capacities.

Much of the impetus behind this shift to the biological was pragmatic: if homosexuality is innate—the product of a hormonal configuration, a particular kind of hypothalamus, an aggregate of nerve endings—then no homosexual should be blamed for his or her condition. The conclusion says, "we were born this way, there is no choice involved, and thus no moral culpability." Particularly during the years of the AIDS epidemic, the doctrine that homosexuality is not a chosen condition has been used to combat the hideous idea that AIDS is a moral punishment. Parents can be reassured that they did nothing "wrong" to produce a homosexual son or daughter; therapeutic pathologizers can be assured that there is nothing to fix; religious condemners can be assuaged with the image of people who are not sinners but the sexual equivalent of pagans awaiting conversion, and capable of it. Of course, on this religious battlefront, the theorists of biological inevitability face the consequence that chastity is really the only way to be relieved of sinfulness by the religious definition. And they have to face the specter, as well, that biological theories have a history—in the histories of anti-semitism, racism, and sexism—of being employed eugenically, that is, to select out those who are born with a "defect." Determinist theories that are embraced for removing a stigma can be used for restigmatization.

Biological theories and the gay equivalent of cultural feminism have been rejected by all those within gay culture who have, in recent years, shifted into what I called posthomosexuality. The recently emergent actors have embraced social constructivism in its most extreme forms and returned to the sexual revolutionary impulse of the 1960s with a twist: it is not polymorphousness of sexual desire that is being conjured now but polymorphousness of gender identity and sexual role. Homosexuals and heterosexuals—as socially constructed—have in common that they have been socially constructed, and they could have in common, too, a revolution against their condition. Describing this stance, Ken Plummer, editor of an essay collection called *Modern Homosexualities* (1992) wrote:

> Processes are at work which recognize difference, relativities, changes: potential chaos yet enormous possibility. With these come the radical options for diverse and diffuse sexualities—the divorce from traditional religions, traditional family structures, traditional communities, traditional politics, traditional limited and restricted communication channels. The workings of modern homosexualities seem largely congruent with the contradictions of modernist culture, on the one hand displaying an obsessive uniformity in its organization and on the other displaying in its flux that "all that is solid melts into air." The homosexual is both rigid scientific discovery and diverse signifier of potential, plurality, polymorphousness.[17]

Posthomosexuality is celebrated by both gay men and lesbians, as it is celebrated in Gay and Lesbian Studies programs and conferences. But the merged story conceals a story specific to lesbian culture(s) now out of the closet and asserting difference.

It is the sexually experimental and challenging—sexually outrageous, critics would say—dimensions of gay culture that chiefly occasion the in-group gay political controversies over whether gays should aim at assimilation or not. Gay male culture is, more than any other minority culture in America, physical culture, body culture. I mean this not just in the obvious sense that making the body beautiful is a ubiquitous occupation and that fashion and body theater are celebrated ingredients of gay culture; I also intend the deeper sense that when male bodily narcissism is most self-consciously incorporated into the culture it is incorporated "gayly." "Gay sensibility," as Seymour Kleinberg claimed, "sexualizes the world."[18] Moreover, in motivation and effect, gay culture is men celebrating men and doing so in modes that involve explicit celebrating of the phallic mother rather than denigrating of women. Although such denigration is certainly not rare, it is secondary, derivative from and reversing the celebration of the phallic mother. As so many commentators on the American gay scene have noted, the gay cultural heroes are not males but strong, assertive, lovably exhibitionistic, self-mocking females who incarnate a triumph of artistic form over gritty, oppressive reality—especially actresses like Judy Garland, Bette Davis, and Mae West and singers like Maria Callas, idol of several generations of gay "opera queens." Men have less need for sameness sexism when they can *have*—or even *be*, imitatively, self-consciously—the phallic mother rather than unconsciously building compensatory fantasies of her or striking out at her in her capacity to frustrate and her fearsomeness.

The story of recent "lesbian culture" in America, by contrast, has been a story of ambivalence about sexuality and about grounding culture in sexuality or of creating an explicitly sexual or sexualized culture. Lesbian culture since the 1960s has been intertwined with feminism, so that it had a brief period dominated by the ideas of radical feminism, and a much longer period—still in course—dominated by the ideas of cultural feminism and by visions of "woman's culture." Lesbian cultural feminists set out to create all kinds of alternative institutions where the sexist or masculinist values that they held to be utterly destructive and antiwoman would not enter. They were the

main translators of cultural feminism into separate institutions, and
through these institutions they touched the lives of the many lesbians,
especially of the working class and of more socially conservative nonurban milieus, who were not connected to and even disliked the idea
of lesbian politics in any form. In the 1970s, an economy to employ
and serve women grew up—food stores, clothing manufacturers, professional services, bookstores, recording companies; similarly, newspapers, publishing houses, art galleries, spiritual centers, and music
festivals flourished.

The role that music and music festivals have played in lesbian culture
marks a key difference between gay male culture and lesbian culture in
the 1970s. There is no lesbian equivalent of the urban gay "opera
queen" who complexly, playfully attaches himself to opera and opera
divas, homosexualizing an existing cultural form, imitating its female
phallic figures, using it for sexual encounters. Musical festival culture
was and is a culture organized for bringing women together in a safe
space, wrapping them in bonds of womanly affirmation, overcoming
isolation, making choruses, providing a folk tradition, celebrating female—not male—artistry. Gay male culture, not having to be constructed as antisexist, was envisioned not as an alternative or separate
culture, but as one permeating—penetrating—the dominant culture;
the music festival, by contrast, is a separate world.

In reaction to the dominant chord of cultural feminist lesbian culture,
however, there arose by the late 1970s a subculture of radicalism, with
ties to the largely vanished, vanquished radical feminism of the late
1960s. Those who accepted the title "sex radicals" felt that cultural
feminist and separatist-leaning lesbianism was antisex or, as the slang
phrase had it "vanilla sex," because it accepted patriarchal constraints
upon female sexuality and espoused a puritanical family-centered ethics
that deprived lesbians and all women of the power that comes with
sexual freedom, sexual experimentation. The sex radicals took their
inspiration from gay male culture:

> They observed that while many women were busy in the 1970s building
> lesbian-feminist alternative institutions such as women-only living
> places and women's music festivals, their male counterparts were ex-
> ploring revolutionary sex; and they were convinced that it was an area
> that the lesbian sub-cultures, especially lesbian-feminism, had ne-
> glected to their own detriment. The women who saw themselves as
> lesbian sexual radicals thus went about the business of modifying gay

male sexual customs and institutions—which represented the essence of liberation to them—for a female community.[19]

The sex radicals were sameness feminists, but the male sexuality with which they felt identified was gay.

The emergence of lesbian sex radicalism reflects, also, a larger area of debate within lesbian culture that both distinguishes it from gay male culture and gives another indication of the specificities of homophobia directed at lesbians. Diane Richardson, writing in 1992, posed a question without equivalent in gay male culture: "Why as lesbians do we rarely talk about sex?" Her reply had a number of facets. For some, the silence is antidefinitional, a reaction against being defined only by sexual preference or only by some proof of kind or type of sexual activity, whether the defining be medical-scientific and pathologizing or feminist and depathologizing. For some the silence is a legacy of early 1970s debates within feminism that made many lesbians feel that lesbianism was perceived—as a matter of internalized homophobia—as bad for feminism, not pathological, but definitely threatening to the heterosexual norms accepted widely among nonlesbian feminists. Other debates among feminists, particularly over pornography, suggested that in a sexist society any kind of sexual activity, even between women, is corrupted with male-dominated ideas and practices. In a related vein, lesbians have wanted to avoid having any discussion of their sexuality be available for male voyeurism or exploitation of the sort common in pornographic novels and films featuring males who come upon and triumphantly interrupt a lesbian sex scene.

Behind the various ways in which lesbians have felt constrained in discussion of their sexuality by homophobic definitional discourses that emphasize their sexuality, there lies a paradox: lesbian sexuality has, at the same time, been denied. Lesbians are women who have sex with other women, but that sex is not really sex. This paradox prompts lesbians to question—as Richardson has with frankness—"what is sex?" She intended to attack the prevailing definition of sex, which is phallocentric or (in my terms) male bodily narcissistic: sex is penetration by the phallus, with penetration of the vagina construed as normal. By phallocentric definition, lesbian sex is thus not sex or is merely imitative (if a phallus substitute is used or one partner assumes in some way a phallic role). To this process of desexualization have been added various psychological theories about lesbians as women who desire not sexual

pleasure but mothering, whose relationships are recreations of or in-
vocations of mother-daughter bonds, presexual or asexual.

Lesbians, being both sexualized and desexualized in phallocentric
(bodily narcissistic) or sexist (mental narcissistic) definitions, have often
responded with silence. But they have also worked for various kinds of
redefinition. Lesbianism, to some, is a political stance against sexism,
against male supremacy. As Ti-Grace Atkinson famously said in the
1970s: "feminism is the theory, lesbianism the practice." Among lesbian
artists, the strongest current of assertion—of sex radical, female, bodily
narcissistic celebration—has come from writers like Monique Wittig in
France, who wrote her *Le corps lesbien* in recognition of the cultural silence on the theme of lesbianism: "Male homosexual literature has a
past, it has a present. The lesbians, for their part, are silent—just as all
women are as women at all levels . . . Only the women's movement has
proved capable of producing lesbian texts in a context of total rupture
with masculine culture, texts written by women exclusively for women,
careless of male approval. *Le corps lesbien* falls into this category."[20] A sea
change in lesbian fictions distinguishes those of the 1950s, in which
lesbians were typically isolated, punished, defeated or "cured" into heterosexuality, from those of the 1970s, in which lesbians were more often
healthy, successful, living in expanding and loving lesbian communities
and spiritually freed from confining religious traditions into woman-
centered goddess worship. But Wittig's work was even more ambitiously
transformative: she did not invoke communities within—even separately
within—a larger society; she wrote *ab novo,* as though there were no
beings but those defining themselves in her prose.

More recently, lesbians have made a posthomosexual effort at definition destruction, sometimes involving mockery of role playing, or role
exchanges or gender-bending dress meant to confuse and disguise
roles. This cultural moment is less optimistic and expansive, but it does
at the very least imply that every culturally self-conscious lesbian must
in some way consider the influences upon her of a heterosexual upbringing—both in the sense that she was brought up by heterosexuals
in sexist contexts and in the sense that she was brought up for heterosexuality. The word "heterosexism" often replaces "homophobia"
when lesbians seize the definitional terrain rather than just protest their
victimhood or protect themselves. Gay writers use "heterosexism," too,
of course, but it does not carry the same meaning of "phallus-centered-
sexism" for them.

Within the many currents that now make up American lesbian and gay male culture, the phenomenon so important to the many feminisms is also present. People of multiple identities are complicating the autobiographical or biomythographical picture, and this multiplicity frees the picture from the influences of sexism and heterosexism, from the unconsciously assumed cultural and theoretical tasks of fighting narcissisms with narcissisms. They are recognizing both that there are homophobias—in the plural—and that prejudices against homosexuals can be expressions of, or woven into, all types of prejudices.

Although they do not work with the typology of obsessional, hysterical, and narcissistic prejudices that I have been developing, current lesbian and gay male historians of homosexuality do often note, for example, that in the 1950s, when obsessional prejudice flourished in American society, directed primarily at Communists foreign and domestic, homosexuals were frequently imagined as conspirators undermining the fabric of American family values. They report that at the time, Edmund Bergler, a prolific psychoanalyst who did a great deal to promote the pathologizing of homosexuality among psychoanalysts, wrote a book criticizing the sex researcher Alfred Kinsey.[21] *Kinsey's Myth of Female Sexuality* (1954) conjured up a conspiracy in which homosexuals had duped Kinsey into providing evidence of the commonness of homosexuality so that under the cover of science homosexuals could spread their perversion throughout society, guiltlessly and efficiently. By resisting psychoanalytic cure, homosexuals were also proselytizing for their perversion. Similarly, Frank Caprio's *Female Homosexuality* (1954) suggested that lesbians were undermining the American social structure by promoting defeminization, man hating, and women's emancipation.

Current historians recognize this homophobia as the kind now most prevalent among religious fundamentalists who raise their own children with obsessional stress upon purity and conventionality and who promote conventional Christian or Jewish or Muslim marriage. Historians investigate fundamentalism's programs for elimination of homosexuals by turning them into heterosexuals or, more drastically, by ghettoizing them and killing them or letting them die of sexually transmitted diseases. Many cultural studies texts show how available images of homosexuals as men in women's bodies or women in men's bodies are used to purvey the typical obsessional themes: homosexuals are infiltrators, pollutants, wily commercial agents, and so forth. But current lesbian and gay male historians and novelists are also very aware that the man/

woman and woman/man homosexual images are most blatant in the kind of hysterical homophobia that combines with racism. As there is a difference between sexism and sexist-racism (or sexist-classism) that is not captured by considering sexist-racism as simply sexism plus racism, there is a homophobia that is not adequately illuminated by a category like homophobia plus racism. Homophobic-sexist-racism specifically attributes the "masculinity" of lesbians (and also the "femininity" of gay men) to blackness; it is blackness—equated with primitive sexuality—that creates perversity. In the image systems of whites, for example, the black lesbian is most frequently an aggressor, a Bulldagger or Bulldyker, a "Queen B," who takes white women as sibling or paternal competitors; she is the female black rapist. Even whites lured to Harlem by black culture, loving it, identifying with it, being empowered by it, conjure the black lesbian as a phallic-power creature—although she is less a knife-wielding attacker than a person whose pain or self-attack can be appropriated to give her white imitator power. Thus, for example, Carl Van Vechten's 1926 portrait of Bessie Smith in his appreciative tour book *Nigger Heaven:* "This was no actress; no imitator of women's woes; there was no pretense. It was the real thing: a woman cutting her heart open with a knife until it was exposed for us all to see so that we suffered as she suffered."[22] By contrast, in African American women's literature, the Queen B appears as a heroic figure, suffering and struggling, but with a *female* transformative power. She is most often a blues singer, on the model of Bessie Smith or of the many other singers who were more given to separatism and cross-dressing than Smith was, and her transformative power works through *women's* music. She faces—and analyzes—homophobic-sexist-racism as the white's dream, frightened or envious or both, about black phallic power.

The "Jew"-like homosexual (who may be Jewish) and the phallic black lesbian are examples of cultural images in need of more analysis. Studies in prejudices that draw together work on both the types of homophobia that target different homosexual populations and the types— obsessional, hysterical, and narcissistic—that can fall upon all the homosexual populations, are very recent. The conceptual terms needed to frame the synthetic effort are just emerging, and this book is especially intended as a contribution to the effort, a weaving together of all the strands of the current impulse within studies in prejudices.

# Epilogue

Within American groups oppressed by ideologies of desire or orectic prejudices, there are, currently, impulses of separatism and isolation as well as pragmatic impulses dictating concentration on immediate group goals of reform or reparation. Groups under great pressure find it difficult to get past self-defense; they resist considering the potentially divisive ethnic or race or gender diversity in their own ranks, and they are slow to build potentially collapsible coalitions with other groups. Barbara Smith, an African American lesbian activist, could complain recently that mainstream gay male and lesbian activism focuses on civil rights legislation, not revolution, while more radical "queer" activism concentrates only on "queer" issues: "racism, sexual oppression and economic exploitation do not qualify, despite the fact that the majority of 'queers' are people of color, female, or working class."[1] Nonetheless, strong currents, particularly within feminist and gay groups, do support giving attention to diversity and coalition building. Numerous publications from within the many subcultures of the gay subculture call for appreciation of the diversity in the gay community and for alliances with other minority groups.

Most oppressed groups, as they make an effort to organize and fight their oppression, stress the uniqueness of their history and their experience. They put the prejudice they suffer from at the center of their theoretical world. This tendency produces misunderstandings and iso-

541

lation. Jews have tried, for example, to understand racism on a model of antisemitism, and blacks have tried to understand antisemitism as a particular kind of racism, and both misunderstandings have contributed theoretical alienation to the other types of alienation that have marked Jewish and black relations since the 1960s. But misunderstandings also arise when oppressed groups try to make coalitions, and I think that there are theoretical reasons for this, in addition to whatever specific reasons of conflicting interests, incompatible group styles, and personality clashes that may keep potential allies apart.

Theoretical confusion also stands in the way of the one goal that all oppressed groups do have in common, no matter what social, cultural, and political differences separate them: all want and need education about prejudices to be part of each new generation's heritage. Feminists of diverse identities may have great trouble agreeing on what goals might unite them across the spectrum called "sexism-racism-classism," but all want histories and analyses of prejudices to be part of education. On the basis of what social science has produced in the way of Studies in Prejudice, however, even educators from within victim groups have either been addressing prejudice in the singular, on the assumption that all prejudices are alike, or addressing a particular prejudice without any sense of its particularity in relation to other prejudices.

Most antiprejudice teaching efforts have been shaped by the two initial queries that have launched social science questionnaires and polls—is the respondent prejudiced? how much? (phrased to ascertain degree of prejudice in an individual or to ascertain increase or decrease in a society). But the matter of querying about prejudice is no less complicated now than it was when the whole social scientific enterprise began in earnest after World War II, as can be gathered from a recent article in *The New York Review of Books* by Arthur Hertzberg, a prolific historian and commentator on Jewish affairs. In "Is Anti-Semitism Dying Out?" Hertzberg first questioned how to put his question. Should a determination that a person is prejudiced and an assessment of the degree take into account known or estimated membership in antisemitic organizations? antisemitic incidents or hate crimes? responses to polls and questionnaires about antisemitic beliefs? or, perhaps, the feelings of Jews in representative locales? Only the last assessment yields any clear result, Hertzberg noted. The majority of Jews in the United States and Europe—seven out of ten in polls—say that antisemitism is growing worse.

At the same time, the majority of non-Jews polled on the same topic say antisemitism is declining or is not very important.

The same kind of result is obtained in polls of African Americans and whites about racism. As the fortieth anniversary of the *Brown v. Board of Education* decision was marked in 1994, for example, American newspapers and journals filled with reflections on the condition of American schools, which, once desegregated, are now often resegregated. Is this resegregation process, some commentators allowed themselves to ask, the result of continued, even increased, racism? Or has racism really decreased in the country and have the schools become segregated for other reasons? Answers to these questions depend, of course, on what is being assessed, what the understanding of racism is. Most whites count the ways in which civil rights victories like *Brown v. Board of Education* have paved the way for integration, and most blacks count the broken promises and point to the deteriorating ghettos. To most whites, the existence of a sizable black middle class seems significant, to most blacks the appalling rate of black poverty overshadows the whole territory of race relations.

Taking the measure of the current prejudices is also complicated by their assuming new subforms, appropriate to new communications possibilities and new types of social interactions. The *New York Times,* for example, reported a flourishing market in Austria and Germany for video games like "KZ Manager," which invites a user to play at managing the concentration camp Treblinka.[2] The player organizes labor patrols and sells gold fillings and lamp shades to make money for buying poisonous gas and for adding gassing facilities in the camp to kill not just Jews but Turks, the major population of "Jew"-like immigrants in today's Germany. Sexism, too, fits well into new technological forms, especially ones that provide the kind of sex that is, so to speak, a narcissist's dream—virtual sex, sex without a body that might in any way disturb a narcissistic one-sex fantasy.

Those assessing the current conditions of prejudices or of a prejudice must take into account the obvious increase around the globe of nationalism and corresponding ethnocentrisms, a function of the end of the Cold War superpower stalemate and the breakup of the twentieth-century empires and imperiums. Because no clear distinctions are made between ethnocentrism and the ideologies of desire, many people assume that increasing ethnocentrism means increasing prejudice in general. But even those who recognize that antisemitism, for instance, is not the same as ethnocentrism, still blur the distinction. A recent report on Europe from the Institute for Jewish Affairs in London acknowledged that "antisemitism is by no means the primary form of bigotry apparent today. Racial prejudice and violence are experienced most acutely by blacks, Turks, Gypsies, Moslems, Asians and other ethnic minority groups and by foreign workers, immigrants, refugees, and asylum-seekers."[3] This list puts together extremely diverse phenomena, each one calling for an exploration appropriate to it, and conveys the general impression that a single phenomenon, general prejudice, is burgeoning everywhere. The report lacks any sense that some of the phenomena on the list—such as prejudice against Turks in Germany—are of the same type as antisemitism, and can, in the manner of obsessional prejudices, replace antisemitism in a given society. Antisemitism may decrease while the level of obsessional prejudice stays the same or increases. An individual may be antisemitic until the growing Turkish population in his town convinces him that the real conspiracy to take over the government is Turkish, not Jewish.

These kinds of theoretical confusions carry right over into educational decisions. Within the contemporary world Jewish community, for example, a great divide on the topic of how to combat antisemitism has arisen from a controversy over causality. Most studies of recent antisemitism indicate that Christian doctrine and Christian anti-Jewish habits of thought and action are not central to the most vocal and public antisemites, including neo-Nazis of various nationalities. (The studies cast doubt on the idea that the Christian doctrinal background has been central through the whole history of political antisemitism, that is, since the turn of the century.) Much more crucial, these studies show, are the resentments antisemites feel about their own precarious economic situations, their sense of being short-changed, threatened, by national and global recessions and depressions. But many Jews, nonetheless, view antisemitism as a Christian disease, a matter of Christian doctrine as set forth in the New Testament.[4] They make no distinction between ethnocentrism and antisemitism, and no distinction between social and political antisemitism.

The causal analyses are expected to yield instructions. On the one hand, those who charge recent antisemitism primarily to Christianity's long tradition of prejudice believe that educational campaigns addressed to Christians, particularly the young, and public discussions of Christian doctrine and practice are the keys to ameliorating antisemitism. Many leaders of Jewish organizations take this tack and point to the success of Jewish efforts to get the World Council of Churches and the Vatican to denounce antisemitism.[5] On the other hand, those who focus on social and economic turbulence and discontent believe that only relieving people of their social and economic anxieties will keep them from blaming the Jews for their troubles. These theorists point to the lack of effect Christian official admissions of responsibility for antisemitism have had on the rising tide of antisemitism in Eastern Europe and the former Soviet Union.

I definitely agree with those who focus on the social and economic conditions that promote antisemitism. Prevention of depression or fear of depression is the best prevention for prejudices that flourish in the syndrome I have called depression and disillusion. Education about antisemitism is also crucial, however—but not education directed primarily at Christian doctrine and practice. Prejudiced Christians will certainly use the Christian tradition of Jew hatred to frame their prejudices, but they will also use other cultural images and symbols, as the Nazis did in their pagan Teutonic mode. The educational and therapeutic approach has to be more encompassing and also addressed not just to antisemitism but to antisemitism as an obsessional prejudice. Analysis of the obsessional dynamic needs to become common understanding: the construction of a penetrating, infiltrating group, the attribution of blame for state controlled economic disaster, the ingredient of envy and imitation of the alleged world-conquering power, the sadistic and ultimately genocidal impulse.

More direct political activity must be undertaken when an obsessional prejudice becomes political and is directed against governments, which are held to be controlled by a Jewish or some other kind of conspiracy. For example, during the 1992 U.S. presidential campaign, Americans should have exposed Ross Perot's bid for what it was: an attack on government as a front for foreign lobbying conspiracies. And they should have related Perot's views to the specifically antisemitic attack on government at the center of the Reverend Pat Robertson's campaign, an attack he has laid out quite clearly in his books, especially *The New World Order* (1991), a harangue about international Jewish banking designed to justify the eventual takeover of America's government by the Christian Coalition. Both of these campaigns were influential in stoking paranoid distrust of government in the alienated American electorate. They were also far more dangerous for promoting the conditions in which antisemitism flourishes than anything emanating from the Nation of Islam, which receives so much attention from the press. The Nation of Islam, though antisemitic, is a separatist organization without designs to defeat the government. Rhetoric like that about the Zionist Organization Government imagined in the White Aryan Resistance camp is also, of course, antisemitic but much less influential on the conditions promoting antisemitism and the other obsessional prejudices than mass mainstream antigovernment national campaigns.

Analysis of racism as a hysterical prejudice similarly yields an educational concentration and a political action focus. If the main psychosocial goal of racists is to perpetuate a two-tier family constellation, either in the immediate family, in a local community, or in a family imagined more nationally, in order to keep a group of inferior people in their place and available as such for actual or fantasied use as nonincestuous sexual figures or nonsibling sibling rivals, then this motivational complex must be the focus of teaching about racism. Racists have as their political goal making their governments the instruments for perpetuating the "natural" family of the superior race with its inferior domestics; they tend toward state racism. So the focus of political action needs to be against any effort to institute racism legally, any Jim Crow or anti–civil rights legislation. Legislative change is the barometer. Caste perpetuation—or, more simply, perpetuation of race-specific poverty— is the main legislative arena of racists, although it may be called welfare reform or criticism of affirmative action.

Feminists have tried to educate about sexism, and to get schools to be less sexist, but their project has been enormously contested. Education about sexism hardly exists except at the most superficial behavioral level, because this prejudice is so multilayered and complexly tied to familial and more general social arrangements, and also because it is a prejudice that is narcissistically totalizing, extending from the details of behavior on out to cosmological visions. More than antisemitism and racism, sexism flows through every facet of a sexist's existence, leaving, as it were, no place to stand to see it. The prejudice is ego syntonic in the strongest meaning of the term, that is, the prejudice constitutes the ego ideal of the sexist.

In practical political terms, sexism does not have a single pattern of relation to states. It is neither antistate like the obsessional prejudices, which aim at destroying a "corrupted" government and at creating a suprastate with super defenses, nor state appropriating like the hysterical prejudices, which want to make a state into a hierarchical family. The phrase "the personal is political" registered the feminist understanding that sexism suffuses institutions of all sorts, from what Kate Millett called "the fundamental level of copulation"—the prevailing conventions of sexual behavior—through to the laws that govern even those conventions of sex behavior. Sexists do not organize to appropriate the state for state sexism; but they do use laws to assure that the narcissism that is fundamentally located in intimate spheres is not threatened by laws that support women's liberation.

As the prejudices differ, so the educational and active responses of the victim groups differ, and must differ. But efforts can be coordinated and coalitions built if the differences are compassed and accounted for. Groups that allow great diversity among the victims and that incorporate experiences of being victimized in multiple ways can be models of achieved—not presupposed—solidarity. These are the groups, as I have tried to show, of the experiential and analytical present-tense pioneers, of the intelligentsia needed for the new world of late-twentieth-century sociopolitical structures and mass population movements or reconfigurations.

# Notes

## Introduction

1. This and the following quotations are from the preface to Gordon Allport, *The Nature of Prejudice* (Reading, Mass.: Addison-Wesley, 1954; New York: Anchor, 1958).

2. To emphasize the evolution of these group names and highlight historical differences, when I am writing about American contexts prior to the 1960s, I will use the term Negroes; for the 1960s, Blacks; and for the period since, African Americans. I will use "blacks" and "whites," both with lowercase letters, in my general theoretical discussions because the usage "Blacks" and "whites" makes "whites" seem like a politically unproblematic designation.

3. See Charles Saunders, "Assessing Race Relations Research," in *The Death of White Sociology,* ed. Joyce Ladner (New York: Random House, 1973).

4. Albert Murray, *The Omni-Americans* (New York: Vintage, 1983, orig. 1970), p. 31.

5. Many gay men and lesbians reject the word "homosexual" because it was and still is part of a medical vocabulary that stigmatized them as ill. I will use the term for its historical meaning, when I am writing about how "homosexuals" came into existence at the turn of the century and how they have been constructed since. I will use "gay people" as the group name for gay men and lesbians (rather than adopting the provocative, polemical "queers"—which some activist gay people use in the way African Americans once used "Blacks," that is, to turn a derogatory term into an assertive one—as I do not think "queers" is widely enough in use to avoid misunderstanding).

6. Theodor Adorno et al., *The Authoritarian Personality* (New York: Harper, 1950), p. 105.

7. Ibid., pp. 102, 150, where the authors noted that the term "ethnocentrism" was introduced in 1906 by W. G. Sumner but went beyond Sumner's emphasis on provincialism or cultural narrowness. "Ethnocentrism is based on a pervasive and rigid in-group–out-group distinction; it involves stereotyped

549

negative imagery and hostile attitudes regarding out-groups, stereotyped positive imagery and submissive attitudes regarding in-groups, and a hierarchical,
authoritarian view of group interaction in which in-groups are rightly dominant, out-groups subordinate." This use of "ethnocentrism" came close to the
use of "xenophobia" that was common among anthropologists and sociologists
before World War II. In the late 1920s, E. S. Bogardus, working in this anthropological tradition, had developed a "social distance scale" for measuring and
comparing hostilities held by one person toward different out-groups.

8. Recently the U.S. military has been pressed to compromise on the usual
branding procedure of homophobia. The "Don't ask, don't tell" policy is only
acceptable because it implies that if a gay person tells—or touches—he or she
will be immediately evicted; in effect, the gay person does his or her own branding.

9. As an example, see Karen Sacks's interesting piece "Toward a Unified
Theory of Class, Race, and Gender," *American Ethnologist* (1989), in which the
theoretical unification actually depends on how "feminist theories and case
studies are, or can be read as sustaining the centrality of class and class struggle
as key forces for social transformation" (p. 534).

10. The *ab novo* quality common to feminism and gay liberation gives those
movements a deep affinity for another contemporary form of politics and discourse of the "household" or nonpublic sphere—the environmental movement. Until recently, the environment was generally thought to be outside the
public realm and uninfluenced by its affairs. The natural resources of mother
earth were simply there, ready to hand, to supply and sustain the public activities of people, as the household was there to perpetuate the species—a natural
process—and supply and sustain men. Nature was the opposite of culture,
which included all kinds of political formations. But it has slowly become apparent that the earth is not simply there to be used and abused. Resources are
finite and they can be used in such a way that they are ruined, transformed,
and poisonous to societies needing them. The natural, like the personal, is
political. But, like feminists, environmentalists have no customary political
grouping; they have no nation, and their concerns have no national borders;
their analyses are outside or aslant to the democracy-versus-totalitarianism conflict and to movements for national liberation. In multiparty nations, they organize "Green" parties, as feminists have tried organizing feminist parties, but
otherwise they have to invent ways to make their concerns important to those
who think in terms of national liberation and those who think in terms of
democracy versus totalitarianism.

11. Recently a relatively synthetic work on prejudice did finally appear. It is
*The Social Psychology of Prejudice* (New York: Praeger, 1992), by John Duckitt, a
South African. But his *Prejudice* essentially refers only to race prejudice. The
book does, however, include a general history of theories of prejudice, which

I have found instructive if incomplete. Because the history is constructed from within the discipline of social psychology, it neglects both sociology or social theory and the antecedents of current social psychology that are considered obsolete, like psychoanalysis. More interesting theoretically is Arthur Brittan and Mary Maynard, *Sexism, Racism, and Oppression* (Oxford: Blackwell, 1984).

12. Ernst Kris, "Notes on the Psychology of Prejudice (1946)," in *Selected Papers of Ernst Kris* (New Haven: Yale University Press, 1975), p. 469.

13. Developments as diverse as a breakthrough in the Middle East peace process involving Israel and its neighbors and the formal or legal cessation of apartheid in South Africa reflect the changing contexts I am tracing and will return to consider in more detail. Given the nature of sexism and homophobia, important changes will not be reflected in document-signing ceremonies— changes in these areas will register at the borders between public and private realms.

14. Elaine Pinderhughes, *Understanding Race, Ethnicity, and Power: The Key to Efficacy in Clinical Practice* (New York: Free Press, 1982), p. 18.

15. Cited in Eric Norden, "The Paramilitary Right," *Playboy* 16, no. 6 (1969).

16. Adolf Hitler, *Mein Kampf*, trans. Ralph Manheim (Boston: Houghton Mifflin, 1943), p. 430.

## 1. Theories of Prejudice

1. Otto Klineberg, "Prejudice: The Concept," *International Encyclopedia of Social Sciences*, vol. 12. New York: Macmillan, 1968.

2. Pierre van den Berghe, *Race and Racism* (New York: John Wiley, 1967), p. 12. I will note later the importance of van den Berghe's work for the development of comparative historical studies of racism, particularly the post-1967 essays of C. Vann Woodward and the anthology he edited, *The Comparative Approach to American History* (New York: Basic Books, 1968).

3. I discuss the "culture and personality" or "social character" tradition in Chapter 6.

4. The ethnopsychoanalyst George Devereux formulated the idea that sociological and psychological approaches should be viewed in terms of their complimentarity, although he did not apply this approach to study of prejudices. I consider Devereux's work in Chapter 6.

5. See, for example, Lester Thurow, *Poverty and Discrimination* (Washington: Brookings Institution, 1969).

6. Emory Bogardus, *Social Distance* (Los Angeles: Antioch, 1959). T. F. Pettigrew (*Social Forces* 38 [1959]: 246–253) did social distance studies in South Africa for comparative purposes and determined that three light-skinned groups—English, Afrikaaner, and Jewish—shared a "pattern of prejudice" toward dark-skinned Africans: they registered most distance from first urban

and then rural "Coloreds," and then from Indians. Among the whites, Jews registered least distance at each descending step.

7. I will discuss these views in more detail below. See Cedric Robinson, *Black Marxism: The Making of the Black Radical Tradition* (Atlantic Highlands, N.J.: Zed Books, 1983).

8. J. D. Lohman and D. C. Reitzes, "Note on Race Relations in Mass Society," *American Journal of Sociology* 58 (1952): 424.

9. See the following sections in *The Standard Edition of the Complete Psychological Words of Sigmund Freud,* 24 vols., trans. James Strachey (London: Hogarth, 1953–1974): "Types of Onset of Neurosis" (12:229–258) and Lecture 22 of the 1916–17 *Introductory Lectures* (16:339–357); in the "Wolf Man" case Freud added to his usual list of types of frustration one called "narcissistic" (17:118), which I will consider in Part 2.

10. Bruno Bettelheim and Morris Janowitz, *Social Change and Prejudice, including "The Dynamics of Prejudice"* (Glencoe, Ill.: Free Press, 1964), p. 131.

11. The first collection of criticisms was edited by Richard Christie and Marie Jahoda, *Studies in the Scope and Method of "The Authoritarian Personality"* (Glencoe, Ill.: Free Press, 1954).

## 2. What Happened to the "Prejudiced Personality"

1. Max Horkheimer and Theodor Adorno, *Dialectic of Enlightenment* (New York: Seabury Press, 1972, orig. 1944), p. 192.

2. Adorno et al., *The Authoritarian Personality,* p. 10.

3. Wilhelm Reich, *The Mass Psychology of Fascism* (New York: Farrar, Straus, and Giroux, 1970), pp. 5, 163. This book was first published in Germany in 1933 (the first English edition appeared in 1946), but it was continually revised and reissued, becoming progressively more filled with Reich's wild "bio-energetics" theories.

4. Adorno et al., *The Authoritarian Personality,* p. 228.

5. On the 1970s feminist theories of the patriarchal family as the origin of sexism, see Chapter 6.

6. Nathan Ackerman and Marie Jahoda, "The Dynamic Basis of Antisemitic Attitudes," *Psychoanalytic Quarterly* 17 (1948): 257–258.

7. Adorno et al., *The Authoritarian Personality,* p. 107. Of course, in colonial contexts, the majority is often the victim group—but "Eurocentric" theorists like those in the Adorno group do not speak the language of postcolonialism, they speak the language of superpower confrontation.

8. See Edward Shils, "Authoritarianism: 'Right' and 'Left,' " in *Studies in the Scope and Method of "The Authoritarian Personality,"* ed. Richard Christie and Marie Jahoda (Glencoe, Ill.: Free Press, 1954), pp. 24–49.

9. From Harry Truman's address in Chicago, March 17, 1945, cited in *The Radical Right,* ed. Daniel Bell (New York: Doubleday, 1964), p. 331.

10. Richard Hofstader, *The Paranoid Style in American Politics and Other Essays* (New York: Knopf, 1966).

11. Richard Ashmore and Frances DelBoca, "Psychological Approaches to Understanding Intragroup Conflict," in *Towards the Elimination of Racism,* ed. Phyllis A. Katz (New York: Pergamon Press, 1976), pp. 73–124. This survey article, which seems to be based on Collins's textbook, provides, in turn, an orientation for other surveys, like Werner Bergmann, "Approaches to Antisemitism Based on Psychodynamics and Personality Theory," in Bergmann's anthology *Error without Trial: Psychological Research on Antisemitism* (New York: Gruyter, 1988). Survey histories are handed down from book to book in social science like lecture notes from one student class to the next—except that footnotes are required.

12. John F. Dovido and Samuel L. Gaertner have edited a volume called *Prejudice, Discrimination, and Racism* (Orlando, Fla.: Academic Press, 1986), in which many of the contemporary theorists of "modern racism" are represented. This volume reports the notion of "racial ambivalence" that has been developed by Irwin Katz, Joyce Wackenhut, and R. Glen Hass, and it discusses the "modern racism scale" (as opposed to an "old-fashioned racism scale") that has been created by John B. McConahay. The editors also offer several surveys of the various 1970s surveys of work on prejudice—so that it is clear that the disciplinary habit of surveying the literature has now moved into its next phase, metasurveying.

13. Many Jewish activists now use "anti-Jewism" rather than "antisemitism" for this reason.

## 3. Sociology Surveys the American Dilemma

1. Cited in Stanley Elkins, *Slavery: A Problem in American Institutional and Intellectual Life* (Chicago: University of Chicago Press, 1959).

2. Gunnar Myrdal, *Against the Stream: Critical Essays on Economics* (New York: Vintage, 1975), p. 297, which continues: "I recall from one of the early years of the Sixties that during a visit by me to the United States a conference was called in New York of professors in the disciplines concerned and responsible foundation officials. There was unanimity in regretting that even up till that time the study of the Negro problem had been downgraded and, in fact, discouraged. This both reflected and contributed to the great complacency of the American public that marked that interregnum, and it certainly had its influence on the way the Negro problem was handled."

3. It is interesting to note that the UNESCO document clearly repudiated the idea that there are racial differences in intelligence: "Available scientific

knowledge provides no basis for believing that the groups of mankind differ in their innate capacity for intellectual and emotional development." UNESCO, *The Race Concept: Results of an Inquiry* (Paris, 1951). Nevertheless, this idea has, of course, persisted up to the most recent example, Richard Hernstein and Charles Murray's *The Bell Curve* (New York: Free Press, 1994).

4. Cited in Paul G. Lauren, *Power and Prejudice: The Politics and Diplomacy of Racial Discrimination* (Boulder, Colo.: Westview Press, 1988), p. 173 (and *passim* throughout his chap. 6).

5. Charles Silberman offered a good critical survey of this "acculturation theory" in *Crisis in Black and White* (New York: Random House, 1964), chap. 3, even though he was of the opinion that Elkins's work was "the most brilliant and probing study of slavery" (p. 75). He saw no contradiction in his assessments.

6. Frantz Fanon, *Black Skin, White Masks* (New York: Grove Press, 1967, orig. 1952), p. 115.

7. Murray, *The Omni-Americans,* p. 224. Murray is alluding to a work coauthored by Nathan Glazer, *Beyond the Melting Pot,* which I will discuss below.

8. Klineberg's remark was part of his introduction to a symposium for school teachers and social workers, *Child Study* 33, no. 2 (1955–56): 2.

9. "Degrees of embeddedness" for racism in the culture is one category used to survey theories of racism in Mark Chessler's "Contemporary Sociological Theories of Racism," in *Towards The Elimination of Racism,* ed. Phyllis A. Katz (New York: Pergamon Press, 1976).

10. This discussion is quoted from the *American Journal of Orthopsychiatry* 26 (1956): 467. The participants were referring to Kenneth Clark's report on desegregated schools in *Journal of Social Issues* 9 (1953). Also of great importance in discussions such as this one were Robin Williams and Margaret Ryan, *Schools in Transition* (Durham: University of North Carolina Press, 1954). Viola Bernard, a psychoanalyst from Columbia University, who had written one of the few papers dealing with psychoanalytic treatment of minority group members (see *Journal of the American Psychoanalytic Association* 1, no. 2 [1953]), was one of the few clinicians to raise questions about the theory that behavioral change produces attitudinal change. She did not, however, simply dismiss the theory as sophisticated but simple-minded behaviorism. Rather, she pointed out that conditioning can be used for ill as well as for good. Hitler had "demonstrated all too convincingly [that] the dictator type of authority could compel social conditions that drove many German citizens to brutal behavior against their Jewish countrymen which stimulated widespread irrational attitudes of racial inferiority." Bernard was concerned about who would change attitudes through behavior modification, and for what democratic or totalitarian purposes—not with the theory of behavior modification itself. But she at least had gotten a hold on one part of the social engineering problem.

11. See *American Journal of Orthopsychiatry* 28 (1958): 32–35.

12. The report and a history of it, plus many supporting documents, can be found in L. Rainwater and W. Yancy, *The Moynihan Report and the Politics of Controversy* (Cambridge, Mass.: MIT Press, 1967). All my citations are to this edition.

13. Kenneth Clark contributed much to this figure—much more than he intended, I think—but the first work to sketch the figure was one he read and cited, a book by two psychoanalysts, Abram Kardiner and Lionel Ovesey, *The Mark of Oppression: A Psychosocial Study of the American Negro* (New York: Norton, 1951), which is full of simplified and distorted Freudian ideas. The authors suggest a "basic personality for the Negro" and show that this Negro personality is a "caricature of the corresponding white personality," that is, Negro identity is formed *only* in reaction to white prejudices. It is interesting to observe that in *The Death of White Sociology* Clark is both castigated (by Albert Murray) and praised warmly as a role model, one of the pioneers in the brief, brilliant history of Black psychology. For a summary of Clark's career, see Robert Guthrie, *Even the Rat Was White: A Historical View of Psychology* (New York: Harper and Row, 1976). For a good summary of the psychological work of the 1950s and 1960s that created the idea that Negroes are full of self-hatred and low self-esteem, see John D. McCarthy and William L. Yancey, "Uncle Tom and Mr. Charlie: Metaphysical Pathos in the Study of Racism and Personal Disorganization," *American Journal of Sociology* 7, no. 4 (1971): 648–672.

14. On Jensen's paper, see J. S. Kagan, "Inadequate Evidence and Illogical Conclusions," *Harvard Educational Review* 39 (1969): 126–129. For the historical context and antecedent efforts to link race and intelligence, see Guthrie, *Even the Rat Was White,* and Stephen Gould, *The Mismeasure of Man* (New York: Norton, 1981), chaps. 5 and 6.

15. Very recently, a type of work has emerged that flows against particularism. It urges multidimensionality of prejudice and acknowledges that prejudices change over time within any given group. In multicultural societies like the United States, Canada, and Australia, characterized by historical layers of immigration, cultural prejudice is more salient among recent immigrants and social prejudice more pervasive among settled populations. Ethnocentrism can cover and then evolve into racism. As groups become more familiar culturally, their prejudices and the prejudices against them focus more on social factors, which are less obvious and less immediately defining than such things as differences in language, costumes, holidays, etc. See Ian McAllister and Rhonda Moore, "The Development of Ethnic Prejudice: An Analysis of Australian Immigrants," *Ethnic and Racial Studies* 14, no. 2 (April 1991): 127–151.

16. This "contact theory" has been worked out in detail by the researchers represented in two collections edited by Henri Tajfel, *Differentiation between Social Groups* (New York: Academic Press, 1978) and *Social Identity and Intergroup*

*Relations* (Cambridge: Cambridge University Press, 1982). See also Thomas Pettigrew, "The Intergroup Contact Hypothesis Reconsidered," in *Contact and Conflict in Intergroup Encounters,* ed. M. Hewstone and R. Brown (Oxford: Blackwell, 1986), pp. 169–195.

17. These statistics and those in the next paragraph are reported in Bettelheim and Janowitz, *Social Change and Prejudice,* pp. 12–13.

18. And, I will argue later, actual hypocrisy is particularly characteristic of the prejudices I call hysterical.

19. Winthrop Jordan, *White over Black: American Attitudes toward the Negro, 1550–1812* (Durham: University of North Carolina Press, 1968), p. x.

20. Joel Kovel, *White Racism: A Psychohistory* (New York: Pantheon, 1970). In summary (p. 32): "The dominative type usually has a personal tie (albeit destructive) with his black object—the extreme having been slavery, when the slave owner allowed his black woman to suckle his child; the aversive type avoids the the black person as though he were a thing . . . The dominative racist, when threatened by the black resorts to violence; the aversive racist, in the same situation, turns away and walls himself off."

21. Robert Merton, "Discrimination and the American Creed," in *Discrimination and National Welfare,* ed. R. MacIver (New York: Harper, 1949).

22. Murray, *The Omni-Americans,* p. 39.

23. Walker's article, from the *Journal of the National Medical Association* 60 (1968): 396–400, is cited by Hugh F. Butts, "White Racism: Its Origins, Institutions, and the Implications for Professional Practice in Mental Health," *International Journal of Psychiatry* 8, no. 6 (1969): 914–928, which is quoted below.

## 4. The Prejudice That Is Not One

1. See the "American Indians, Blacks, Chicanos, and Puerto Ricans" issue of *Daedalus* 110 (Spring 1981) for articles on these groups in the 1970s.

2. For a brief summary of the goals of the intercultural education movement, see Mordecai Grossman, "The Schools Fight Prejudice," *Commentary* 1 (1945–46): 34–42. One of the model schools for this progressive program was located in Springfield, Massachusetts, and its work was described in Clarence Chatto et al., *The Story of the Springfield Plan* (New York: Barnes and Noble, 1945), and J. W. Wise, *The Springfield Plan* (New York: Viking, Press, 1945). The principles of the movement are well presented in an autobiography of one of the Quaker guiding lights: Rachel Davis DuBois, *All This and Something More: Pioneering in Intercultural Education* (Bryn Mawr, Penn.: Dorrance, 1984).

3. For a review of this whole topic, see D. Jenkins et al., "Racism and Educational Evaluation" in *Race, Education, and Identity,* ed. G. Verma and C. Bagley (New York: St. Martin's, 1979).

4. Ibid., p. 27.

5. William Stone, Gerda Lerderer, and Richard Christie, eds., *Strength and Weakness: The Authoritarian Personality Today* (New York: Springer Verlag, 1992).

6. Cited from a summary article Altemeyer wrote for the *Harvard Medical School Mental Health Letter;* for a fuller account, see his *Enemies of Freedom* (San Francisco: Jossey-Bass, 1988).

7. Cornel West, "Toward a Socialist Theory of Racism," in *Prophetic Fragments* (Grand Rapids, Mich.: Eerdmans, 1988), p. 102.

8. This is, of course, a question that would never occur to—for example—a South African considering white attitudes toward Blacks or coloreds, the South African majority.

9. Allport, *The Nature of Prejudice,* pp. 31–32.

10. The misunderstanding of "matriarchy" in Moynihan's report is discussed in Carol B. Stack, *All Our Kin* (New York: Harper and Row, 1974); for a recent revisiting of the report, see the special issue of the *Nation,* July 24/31, 1993, entitled "Scapegoating the Black Family."

11. C. Bagley et al., *Personality, Self-Esteem, and Prejudice* (London: Saxon House, 1979), pp. 116, 118, 124, 133, 135.

12. The problem is much wider, as is clear in Judith Stacey and Barrie Thorne, "The Missing Feminist Revolution in Sociology," *Social Problems* 32, no. 4 (April 1985): 301–316, a thorough methodological critique of the discipline.

13. Gayle Rubin, "Woman as Nigger," in *Masculine/Feminine,* ed. Betty Roszak and Theodore Roszak (New York: Harper, 1969), pp. 230–240.

14. Simone de Beauvoir, *The Second Sex* (New York: Penguin, 1972, orig. 1947), p. xxvii.

15. Gerda Lerner, *The Creation of Patriarchy* (New York: Oxford University Press, 1986), p. 240.

16. The analogy between sexism and racism is taken even further in Shulamith Firestone's *The Dialectics of Sex* (New York: Bantam, 1970), and in this book, too, the argument is made that women's liberation will come with transcendence of biological difference—by relying on advanced reproductive technologies, by overcoming motherhood.

17. Kate Millett, *Sexual Politics* (New York: Doubleday, 1970), p. 25.

18. Hazel Carby, "White Women, Listen!" in *The Empire Strikes Back* (London: Hutchinson and the Birmingham Centre for Cultural Studies, 1982), p. 213.

19. Adrienne Rich, *On Lies, Secrets, and Silence* (New York: Norton, 1979), and see the discussion of this problem in Elizabeth Spelman, *Inessential Woman: Problems of Exclusion in Feminist Thought* (Boston: Beacon Press, 1988).

20. Beauvoir, *The Second Sex,* pp. 102 and 109.

21. Although there are matrilineal and matrifocal societies and societies in which women were the chief spiritual leaders, the historical and archaeological

record does not yet hold an instance of a society in which women ruled over men in councils or governments.

22. Marielouise Janssen-Jurriet, *Sexism: The Male Monopoly on History and Thought,* trans. Verne Moberg (New York: Farrar, Straus, and Giroux, 1982; orig. 1976), p. 325.

23. The touchstone text for feminist rejection of psychoanalytic psychopathology is Phyllis Chesler's *Women and Madness* (New York: Doubleday, 1972).

24. Millett relied heavily for this education in psychoanalysis on Viola Klein's *The Feminine Character,* first published in 1946, which was part of the Frankfurt School's postwar reassessment (and desexualization) of Freudian theory. Klein's tendentious misreadings of Freud thus got second-hand best-seller influence—most unfortunately.

25. Grete Bibring, "On the 'Passing of the Oedipus Complex' in a Matriarchal Family Setting," in *Drives, Affects, Behavior,* ed. R. M. Loewenstein (New York: International Universities Press, 1953).

26. For this argument against androgyny as an ideal, see Paula Rothenberg, "The Construction, Deconstruction, and Reconstruction of Difference," *Hypatia* 5, no. 1 (Spring 1990): 42–57, with bibliographic references to the debate over androgyny.

27. George Devereux, *From Anxiety to Method in the Behavioral Sciences* (New York: Humanities Press, 1967), pp. 178–179. Devereux did not ask himself *why* humans find a divergence from their own self-model so disturbing, so anxiety producing; I am suggesting here that it signals or represents frustration, loss of the paradise of primary narcissism, and I will pursue this line of thought in Chapters 7 and 8.

## 5. The Homophobias

1. I will return to the history of feminist theory again in Chapter 15 and offer there a more detailed interpretation of the debate among feminist theorists between those who think masculine and feminine roles are constructions that cover up the sameness of *human* sexuality and those who think men and women are essentially different.

2. Hooker's technical papers can be found in the *Journal of Projective Techniques,* 21 (1957), 22 (1958), and 23 (1959). See also her summary in "Male Homosexuals and Their 'Worlds,' " in *Sexual Inversion,* ed. Judd Marmor (New York: Basic Books, 1965).

3. This and the following quotation are from *Three Essays on the Theory of Sexuality* (*Standard Edition* 7:145, note 1, and 139, note 2), a text Freud revised several times between its 1905 publication and 1924. See also the 1920 case study of a homosexual eighteen-year-old girl who was "in no way ill," "had never been neurotic, and came to the analysis without even one hysterical symp-

tom" (*Standard Edition* 18:155). Freud assumed that *repressed* homosexual object choices would play a large role in any patient's psychoneurosis, but that those who did not repress their choices would not construct a neurosis on the site of their repression; in a formula he used recurrently, "neuroses are, so to say, the negative of perversions" (*Standard Edition* 7:165).

4. Weinberg indicated clearly that "homophobia" was a condensation of "homosexualphobia," but confusion arose later among those who thought it meant fear of "the same" (homo) and was, thus, an inappropriate term. Others have questioned whether the idea that the prejudice is a phobia is helpful at all. Many prefer "heterosexism" because it is less psychological and seems to point to more systemic prejudice; it is a word that fits the analysis of prejudice I called (in Chapter 3) autonomous norms—heterosexism is the autonomous norm that all in the society are socialized to. Still others have suggested alternative words, like "antihomosexuality" (modeled on antisemitism).

5. A 1978 survey dealing with behaviors by gay faculty members felt to be objectionable by English Department chairs showed a remarkable consensus about how horrible public hand holding is. The only item topping it on the list was appearing on campus in the dress of the opposite sex. Louie Crew, "Before Emancipation: Gay Persons as Viewed by Chairpersons of English," in *The Gay Academic,* ed. Crew (Palm Springs, Calif.: ETC Publications, 1978).

6. See Evelyn Blackwood, "Breaking the Mirror: The Construction of Lesbianism and the Anthropological Discourse on Homosexuality," in *Anthropology and Homosexual Behavior,* ed. Blackwood (New York: Haworth, 1986), which reprints an issue of the *Journal of Homosexuality*.

7. See the excellent discussion in Lillian Faderman's *Odd Girls and Twilight Lovers: A History of Lesbian Life in Twentieth Century America* (New York: Columbia University Press, 1991).

8. Richard Isay, *Being Homosexual; Gay Men and Their Development* (New York: Farrar, Straus, and Giroux, 1989), p. 78.

9. A summary of this position is offered by Laura Reiter, "Developmental Origins of Antihomosexual Prejudice in Heterosexual Men and Women," *Clinical Social Work Journal* 19, no. 2 (1991): 163–175. In addition to the work of Nancy Chodorow, Carol Gilligan, and other feminists, this strand of analysis owes a great debt to the work of psychoanalyst Robert Stoller on core gender identity, which developed a line of work launched by Ralph Greenson, "On Homosexuality and Gender Identity" (1964), in *Explorations in Psychoanalysis* (New York: International Universities Press, 1978), pp. 191–197.

10. A. P. MacDonald, Jr., and Richard G. Games, "Some Characteristics of Those Who Hold Positive and Negative Attitudes toward Homosexuals," *Journal of Homosexuality* 1, no. 1 (1974): 9–27, which offers confirmation of an earlier report by MacDonald et al. in the *Journal of Consulting and Clinical Psychology* 40 (1972): 161.

11. This quote and those following are from Robert Musil, *Young Törless,* trans. E. Wilkins and E. Kaiser (New York: Signet, 1964); see pp. 48, 72, 124–126, 85, 138.

## 6. "Social Character" in Search of a Theory

1. Talcott Parsons, "The Superego and the Theory of Social Systems," *Psychiatry* 15 (1952): 15.

2. Some anthropologists spoke of the modal personality or the tribal or (very broadly, usually much too broadly) national character, others of the basic personality or the ethnic personality, while the majority of sociologists used the term "social character." As I will discuss, despite being used interchangeably, these terms were not synonymous. Most theorists would accept as a working definition of culture the one I am going to assume in what follows: "the organized group of ideas, habits and conditioned emotional responses" shared by the members of a society (to cite Ralph Linton, *Culture and Mental Disorders* [Springfield, Ill: C. C. Thomas, 1956], p. 5).

3. I borrow these working definitions from David Riesman and his coauthors Nathan Glazer and Reuel Denny, *The Lonely Crowd: A Study of the Changing American Character* (New York: Doubleday, 1955; orig. 1950), p. 18.

4. Tzvetan Todorov's *The Conquest of America: Perceiving the Other* (New York: Harper and Row, 1984) shows how the Spanish conquistadors assessed the social character of the Indians they encountered and found thereby their military vulnerabilities.

5. The single-dominating-trait characterologies of the ancients did, of course have an assumed biological base, although it was not racial. Most Greeks after Hippocrates held that every individual is born with a preponderance in him or her of one of the four bodily humors. Modern single-trait biologically based theories have tended to stress morphology—bodies and particularly heads of different shapes (endomorphs, ectomorphs, etc.) are said to house different character types.

6. Abram Kardiner and Ralph Linton, *The Individual and His Society* (New York: Columbia University Press, 1947), p. 36.

7. Linton, *Culture and Mental Disorders,* p. 23.

8. In the characterological terms I will develop below, the Comanche warriors were successful narcissists, while the Alor, so marked by their oral and general libidinal frustration, were hysterical.

9. George Devereux, *Reality and Dream: The Psychotherapy of a Plains Indian* (New York: International Universities Press, 1951), p. 51.

10. Red Bain, "Sociopathy of Antisemitism," *Sociometry* 4 (1943): 460–464.

11. Riesman, Glazer, and Denny, *The Lonely Crowd,* pp. 1–36.

12. Parsons, "The Superego and the Theory of Social Systems," p. 15.

13. David Riesman, "Some Observations on Social Science Research," in *Individualism Reconsidered and Other Essays* (Glencoe, Ill.: Free Press, 1954), p. 477.

14. Christopher Lasch, *The Culture of Narcissism* (New York: Warner Books, 1979), p. 206.

15. For historical accuracy, however, it is important to note that Kardiner and Linton worked with the developments in psychoanalytic theory that go under the name "ego psychology" and are associated with the work in child analysis of Anna Freud and with the work in adult analysis of Heinz Hartmann, Ernst Kris, Rudolf Loewenstein, and many others. Although they did not always agree with each other on details, Kardiner and Linton rightly viewed themselves as having gone many steps beyond the crudest form of culture and personality studies, which had been based entirely on Freud's instinctual drive theory. In the 1920s, the Hungarian anthropologist Geza Roheim had, for example, argued that societies (like individuals) inevitably developed through oral, anal, and phallic-genital phases, and that individuals in their oral, anal, and phallic-genital phases recapitulated societal and species developments. Theodor Reik continued this strand of work. In 1934, Wilhelm Reich had put succinctly the central problem of this kind of ultra-Freudianism (or ultra-early-Freudianism): "A social organization cannot be studied by psychoanalytic interpretation, for society has no drives, no unconscious, no superego, no inner life. It consists of social interrelations between men possessing a psychic apparatus of a certain structure" (quoted in William C. Manson, *The Psychodynamics of Culture: Abram Kardiner and Neo-Freudian Anthropology* [New York: Greenwood Press, 1988], p. 14).

16. As I noted earlier, Pierre van den Berghe distinguished very clearly between ethnocentrism and racism, and I am here building upon his *Race and Racism* (1967). But van den Berghe focused on only one aspect of racism's ideology—the derivation of mental and cultural characteristics from bodily characteristics—and he did not distinguish between established group identities and projected ones. There is also a recent tendency among sociologists to distinguish prejudice from racism, but usually along the traditional dividing line between individuals and societies. Prejudice, then, is an attitude held by an individual and racism is an ideology of exploitation, equated with a society's culture. Prejudice is a subject for psychology, racism for sociology. For example: "An individual can be described as prejudiced or racist—or both; but a culture can only be described as racist . . . Racism is not an aggregation of individual ideas; it is rather a distinct cultural orientation sustained and expressed by the society's basic institutions" (Donald Neal, *The Origins of American Slavery and Racism* [Columbus, Ohio: Merrill, 1972], p. 159). No way to connect society's basic institutions to individuals' prejudices is suggested by this distinction.

17. I am making a dynamic distinction between ethnocentrisms and ideolo-

gies of desire, a distinction related to how these prejudices function for people in their group-sustaining or group-creating behavior. This dynamism makes impossible such a crude and static distinction as this one: prejudice arises from "assumed belief dissimilarities" so that "distinctions among the groups based on belief systems . . . are all more elemental than the distinction based on race (skin color)." Ranking prejudices, saying that one kind is the most fundamental, is, to my mind, completely simplistic. Cf. R. A. James and R. D. Ashmore, "The Structure of Intergroup Perception," *Journal of Personality and Social Psychology* 25 (1973): 438.

18. I will turn to the particular modern social and political conditions that produce and sustain orecticisms in Chapter 10. Occasionally, the distinction between ethnocentrisms and orecticisms that I am drawing is acknowledged by historians of the modern period, as it was, in part, by O. Cox in his Marxist *Caste, Class, and Race* (Garden City, N.Y.: Monthly Review Press, 1970, orig. 1948). Cox argued that ethnocentrism is a general, even universal "we feeling," an aspect of all group relations, whether these involve families, teams, communities, or nations. Dominant groups, Cox went on, also everywhere and always are intolerant. They refuse to tolerate the "we beliefs" and practices of the subordinate groups they control and persecute. But racism is a modern historical product confined to a special domain of control. It originated with and grew during the rise of capitalism, culminating in the late nineteenth century, and it functioned as the bourgeoisie's means for rationalizing and extending control over labor populations—slave labor populations and then wage labor populations. To fulfill its rationalizing function, racism had to convey much more than intolerance; it had to allege the innate inferiority of labor populations. Racism is the ideology that justifies labor exploitation. "The dominant group is intolerant of those it can define as antisocial, while it holds race prejudice against those it can define as sub-social. Persecution and capitalist exploitation are the respective behavior aspects of these two social attitudes" (p. 400). So rigidly class-based was Cox's distinction, however, that he classified antisemitism as a form of ethnocentric intolerance, by which he meant that it does not allege the innate inferiority of the Jews and does not serve the bourgeoisie's capitalism.

19. Cited in Leon Poliakov, *The Aryan Myth* (New York: Basic Books, 1974), p. 319.

20. Ibid., p. 322 (citing Wenninger's *Geschlecht und Charakter,* Vienna, 1905).

21. One of the clearest indications that it has not been antisemitism that has motivated the majority of postwar Palestinian refugees is the willingness of so many in the third generation, now, to seek peace with the Israelis.

22. Sándor Ferenczi, "The Ontogenesis of the Interest in Money," in *Contributions to Psychoanalysis,* trans. Ernest Jones (Boston: R. G. Badger, 1916), p. 277. I will return to develop this distinction between displacements and projections

later, and to indicate how the particular kind of orectic prejudice that I will designate obsessional is also rooted in and reflective of anal-phase experiences but in a different way than ethnocentrism is.

23. The idea that long-simmering ethnic conflicts suddenly burst into war with the dissolution of Yugoslavia is quite false. There was no active ethnic conflict among the groups now waring, which lived in relative harmony in Bosnia, especially in cities like Sarajevo. Ethnic parties had to be formed, each promoting fear of minority status and hatred of the state envisioned by conspiring ethnic others. The complex war was precipitated by Serbian aggression, and specifically by a calculated Nazi-like policy of extermination aimed at the Muslims, who were viewed as conspirators aiming at a Muslim state in Bosnia. That is, an expansionary ideological policy, not an ethnocentrism, precipitated the war. The preparatory economic deterioration of Yugoslavia is part of a precipitating pattern typical of obsessional prejudices, as I will indicate in Chapters 10 and 11.

24. Walter Lippmann, *Public Opinion* (New York: Free Press, 1965, orig. 1922), p. 21.

25. Hannah Arendt, *The Origins of Totalitarianism* (New York: Harcourt, Brace, 1973, orig. 1951), p. 66.

## 7. Character Types and Their Ideologies of Desire

1. Riesman, Glazer, and Denny, *The Lonely Crowd*, p. 18.

2. Otto Fenichel took up Freud's scheme and formulated a theory of sublimative and reactive character types, the latter divided into Freud's threesome—pathological behavior toward the id, the superego, and external objects. But he interpreted the reactive character types only in terms of the ego's behavior. (See *The Psychoanalytic Theory of the Neurosis* [New York: Norton, 1945], pp. 470ff.) Contemporary analysts do, of course, operate with other characterologies, but usually they offer them without any theoretical justification for why they have chosen the types and number of types they have chosen. Otto Kernberg, for example, bases a scheme on 'levels' (not stages) of instinctual development in "A Psychoanalytic Classification of Character Pathology," *Journal of the American Psychoanalytic Association* 18 (1970): 800–822. David Shapiro, whose book *Neurotic Styles* (1965) is often cited as a rich contemporary investigation of character, speaks of obsessive-compulsive style, paranoid style, hysterical style, and impulsive styles, but again offers no explanation of why these and not others are the neurotic styles. I have discussed the history and theory of characterology in a book called *Creative Characters* (New York: Routledge, 1991).

3. The chronology of the defenses Anna Freud proposed in *The Ego and the Mechanisms of Defense* (New York: International Universities Press, 1966) was contested at the time (particularly by Melanie Klein) and has been ever since.

This important area of psychoanalytic theory is little discussed in contemporary writing. See J. Sandler, ed., *The Analysis of Defense: The Ego and the Mechanisms of Defense Revisited* (New York: International Universities Press, 1983).

4. They also stressed that children may suffer developmental disorders that do not at all resemble the classical Freudian neuroses—hysteria, obsessional neurosis, narcissistic neurosis—particularly if they are severely traumatized, if they have to contend with disabilities, organic conditions, or anything that inhibits physical or more general growth. In a sense, it can be said that developmental disorders inhibit character formation and make impossible the integration of structures and functions that is character.

5. I mean "obsessional neurotics" to include those suffering from what is currently known as Obsessive Compulsive Disorder (OCD), a condition in which repetitive thoughts and behaviors are out of control, completely dominating a life. The onset is usually late adolescence and often associated with an emotional or physical trauma or an infection (for example, strep) that effects the basal ganglia, known to be abnormal in most OCD patients. It is estimated that 1–2 percent of the American population suffers from OCD, about 4 million people, some of whom are helped by serotonin altering antidepressants.

6. Defenses can, of course, be reflected in many other ways—including, as I will note further along, in theories of prejudice.

7. Nathan Ackerman, "Antisemitic Motivation in a Psychopathic Personality: A Case Study," *Psychoanalytic Review* 34 (1947): 76–101.

8. Kenneth Kenniston, "Psychological Development and Historical Change," *Journal of Interdisciplinary History* 2 (1971): 337–338.

9. Else Frenkel-Brunswik and R. Nevitt Sanford, "The Anti-Semitic Personality: A Research Report," in *Anti-Semitism: A Social Disease,* ed. Ernst Simmel (New York: International Universities Press, 1948), p. 110. This report is particularly important, because it shows what the Adorno group discovered about antisemitism before they submerged antisemitism in the larger category of ethnocentrism that is central to *The Authoritarian Personality.*

10. One study found that 37 percent of those visiting a dermatological clinic with nonspecific dermatitis were obsessive compulsives who had produced their condition by excessive hand washing; but none of these people had ever sought treatment for their obsessions. That is, many people function reasonably well even with OCD.

11. This description is from a work by Max Weber's colleague Ernst Troeltsch, *Protestantism and Progress,* trans. W. Montgomery (Boston: Beacon Press, 1958), p. 133.

12. Theodor Adorno, "Anti-Semitism and Fascist Propaganda," in *Anti-Semitism: A Social Disease,* ed. Ernst Simmel (New York: International Universities Press, 1948).

13. Freud, *Inhibitions, Symptoms, Anxieties,* in *Standard Edition* 20:99.

14. Freud, "Psychoanalytical Notes on an Autobiographical Account of a Case of Paranoia," in *Standard Edition* 12:3–84.

15. For a catalog of this stereotype's attributes, see Evelyn Torton Beck, "From 'Kike' to 'JAP,' " in *Race, Class, and Gender: An Anthology,* ed. Margaret Andersen and Patricia Hill Collins, (Belmont, Calif.: Wadsworth, 1992).

16. Their emphasis in displacing is not that of ethnocentrists, who put unacceptable desires onto others in order to preserve the harmony in their group—they get rid of intergroup hate by converting it into intragroup hate (as I noted in Chapter 6). The obsessional seeks, primarily, purity on an individual level, for which group membership then becomes a confirmation. That is, the obsessional needs to form a group with like-minded people, not defend an existing group.

17. Otto Fenichel noticed this aspect of antisemitism in his "Elements of a Psychoanalytic Theory of Anti-Semitism," in *Anti-Semitism: A Social Disease,* ed. Ernst Simmel (New York: International Universities Press, 1948), pp. 11–32.

18. Ralf Georg Reuth, *Goebbels* (New York: Harcourt, 1994), p. 26.

19. Maurice Samuel, *The Great Hatred* (New York: Knopf, 1940), pp. 42–43.

20. Cited in Robert J. Lifton and Eric Markusen, *The Genocidal Mentality: Nazi Holocaust and Nuclear Threat* (New York: Basic Books, 1990), p. 58.

21. In general, the psychic differences and fantasy differences between males and females of this character type are smaller and fewer than in the other two prejudice types, for reasons that will be explored below.

22. This and the following quotations are from Freud, "Fragment of an Analysis of a Case of Hysteria," in *Standard Edition* 7:54–55.

23. Eugene Genovese, *The Political Economy of Slavery* (New York: Pantheon, 1965), pp. 23, 28.

24. P. Chodoff and H. Lyons, "The Hysterical Personality and Hysterical Conversion," *American Journal of Psychiatry* 1, no. 4 (1958): 734–740.

25. Freud, "Some General Remarks on Hysterical Attacks," *Standard Edition* 9:234.

26. Freud's colleague Karl Abraham particularly stressed a distinction between the phallic and the fully genital stage, noting that hysteria referenced to the former; he also stressed in his clinical papers how frequently hysterics are terrified of and refuse to acknowledge the genitals of the opposite sex.

27. E. R. Zetzel, "So-Called Good Hysterics," *International Journal of Psychoanalysis* 49 (1968): 256.

28. The claim, repeated since the turn of the century, that there are more hysterical females than males is made without regard to the differences in male and female action possibilities—those who have the theater of the world to act in are not counted among the hysterics; only those who act in the theater of their own bodies are. Similarly, clinicians who note that there is not much "classic" hysteria in contemporary America are not paying attention to the

nonclassic forms hysteria currently takes—for example, in fitness crazes, diet fads, initiations into ecstatic groups, etc. There may be fewer hysterics in therapy settings but not in the population.

29. Linton, *Culture and Mental Disorders,* p. 132.

30. Freud, "On Beginning the Treatment," in *Standard Edition* 12:134.

31. Some more sociologically minded psychoanalysts believe that infants are psychically organized for relationships from birth, that there is no such thing as primary narcissism, although there is "cognitive narcissism" in the sense that an infant is incapable of drawing a cognitive line between itself and its maternal caretaker. From this point of view, embraced by most American feminists of the object relations and interpersonal varieties, Freud's primary narcissism theory, which is integral to his instinctual drive theory, is one of the main obstacles to a psychoanalysis that does not devalue human beings' capacities for relationships. See Nancy Chodorow, "Toward a Relational Individualism," in *Feminism and Psychoanalytic Theory* (New Haven: Yale University Press, 1989) for a clear account of the feminist critique. From my point of view, this feminist critique has been one of the main obstacles to feminism's understanding of sexism.

32. M. S. Mahler, "On the First Three Sub-phases of the Separation-Individuation Process," *International Journal of Psychoanalysis* 41 (1972): 338.

33. Janine Chassequet-Smirgel, *The Ego Ideal: A Psychoanalytic Essay on the Malady of the Ideal,* trans. Paul Barrows (New York: Norton, 1985; orig. 1974).

34. Heinz Kohut, in *The Analysis of Self* (New York: International Universities Press, 1971) used the terminology "grandiose self" and "idealized parental imago" for the subjective and objective dimensions of narcissism, but he did not relate the preponderance of one or the other to a social role, leader or follower.

35. Freud, "Introductory Lectures," in *Standard Edition* 16:318: "The feeling of having been defrauded by grown-up people, and put off with lies, contributes greatly to a sense of isolation and to the development of independence." (Like so many of Freud's remarks about narcissism, this one has the ring of autobiography about it.)

36. This distinction does not, to my knowledge, exist in clinical literature, but it was noted by the dissident Freudian Wilhelm Stekel in his *Patterns of Psychosexual Infantilism* (New York: Grove Press, 1959), p. 320: "The narcissistic process may lead either to physical or to mental self-love: that is, one narcissist will be infatuated with his own body (specifically, with his genital organs), another will adore his psychic personality, his intellectual abilities . . . In many instances, the two aspects merge in varied combinations. One narcissist may feel certain to approach very closely to his bodily ideal and smart under the gap separating him from the spiritual ideal; others regard themselves as physically repellent, but they are full of admiration for 'the beauty of the inner personality' which they are sure to possess." Chassequet-Smirgel (*The Ego Ideal,*

pp. 23ff.) and others did acknowledge that many narcissistic perverts must idealize their objects and their desires, often by creating for themselves an aesthetic or cultural ambience in which to enjoy their bodily pleasures. The physical/mental distinction has been made in historical terms by Freud's colleague Hanns Sachs in "The Delay of the Machine Age," *Psychoanalytic Quarterly* 2 (1933): 404–424. Sachs observed that the Greeks and the Romans exhibited bodily narcissism—so that they had no interest, for example, in developing machines that might replace physical labor—while the narcissism of the Christians was mental. Freud had argued that the ego is "first and foremost a body-ego" (*Standard Edition* 19:27) so that ego love is first and foremost body love; mental love follows with capacities for idealization and sublimation.

37. I will explore these gender differences in narcissisms in Chapter 8.

38. Devereux, *From Anxiety to Method in the Behavioral Sciences,* p. 178.

39. Otto Fenichel, *The Psychoanalytic Theory of Neurosis* (New York: Norton, 1945), pp. 243–244, see also p. 54.

40. As I noted in Chapter 2, reporting on Aboud's *Children and Prejudice,* cognitive psychologists stress that children between the ages of eight and ten are generally less prejudiced than younger children, but this empirical observation was connected only to cognitive development, not to any psychodynamic understanding of latency. I treat prejudices in adolescence in Chapter 9.

41. Robert Waelder, "Notes on Prejudice," in *Psychoanalysis: Observation, Theory, Application* (New York: International Universities Press, 1976), p. 448.

42. Cited in Elinor Langer, "The American Neo-Nazi Movement Today," *Nation* 16 (July 1990): 88.

43. These notes on Simmons and quotations are based on Arnold Rose, *The Ku Klux Klan in American Politics* (Washington, D.C: Public Affairs Press, 1962, orig. 1921).

44. D. M. Chalmers, *Hooded Americanism: The First Century of the Ku Klux Klan, 1865–1965* (Garden City, N.Y.: Doubleday, 1965), p. 33.

45. J. M. Mecklin, *The Ku Klux Klan: A Study of the American Mind* (New York: Harcourt, Brace, 1924), p. 25.

46. Ibid., citing an article by Frank Tannenbaum in *Century,* 1923, p. 873.

47. M. Newton and J. A. Newton, *The Ku Klux Klan: An Encyclopedia* (New York: Garland, 1991), p. 373.

48. Mecklin, *The American Mind,* p. 27.

49. *New York Times,* April 20, 1965, p. 24.

50. Newton and Newton, *The Ku Klux Klan,* p. 514.

51. Ibid., p. 173.

52. Helen Zia, "Women in Hate Groups," *Ms. Magazine,* March/April, 1991, p. 26.

53. Much of this antisemitic propaganda emerges, however, not from the

Klan but from Metzger's White Aryan Resistance, which has a *Race and Reason* radio show on nearly sxity cable-access channels. Current technologies offer modes of linkage to dispersed groups and weigh somewhat against the perennial Klan factionalism, while electoral successes like those David Duke managed in Louisiana provide publicity. For the Klan groups, antisemitism functions as it did in the early 1920s—it is an outreach prejudice, one that connects the Klan to people who feel manipulated by unseen forces and victimized by complex economic trends.

54. Jeff Coplon, "The Skinhead Reich," *Utne Reader,* May/June, 1989, p. 89.

## 8. Origins and Developmental Lines

1. Bruno Lasker, *Race Attitudes in Children* (New York: Henry Holt, 1929). Page citations in text refer to this edition.

2. Kenneth Clark, *Prejudice and Your Child* (Boston: Beacon Press, 1963, orig. 1955).

3. Mary Ellen Goodman, *Race Awareness in Young Children* (Reading, Mass.: Addison-Wesley, 1964, orig. 1952), p. 217.

4. Ruth Horowitz, "Racial Aspects of Self-Identification in Nursery School Children," *Journal of Psychology* 7 (1939): 91–99.

5. Goodman, *Race Awareness,* p. 44, and citation following, p. 136.

6. Phyllis Katz, "The Acquisition of Racial Attitudes in Children," in *Towards The Elimination of Racism,* ed. Kate (New York: Pergamon Press, 1976), pp. 125–154.

7. Marjorie McDonald, *Not by the Color of Their Skins: The Impact of Racial Differences on the Child's Development* (New York: International Universities Press, 1970).

8. Ibid., p. 95.

9. Freud, *Standard Edition* 14:195 (the other five passages are 7:168, 13:123 [note], 17:120, 18:117–120, 20:168). Subsequent citations in text are to the *Standard Edition.*

10. Freud's translator James Strachey was the first to point out (7:216, note 1) that the discovery of sex hormones required little modification in Freud's hypothesis that as yet unknown chemical substances underlie sexuality. There is, however, no simple or monocausal relationship between changing levels of hormones and sexual activity, sexual aim, or sexual object. This view, often equated with Freud's descriptions of *Trieb,* is not Freud's.

11. The clearest statement Freud made of his position can be found in *Standard Edition* 18:170:

> The mystery of homosexuality is . . . by no means so simple as it is commonly depicted in popular expositions—"a feminine mind, bound therefore to love a man, but unhappily attached to a masculine body; a masculine mind, irresistibly

attracted by women, but, alas! imprisoned in a feminine body." It is instead a question of three sets of characteristics, namely—

Physical sexual characteristics
(physical hermaphroditism)
Mental sexual characteristics
(masculine or feminine attitude)
Kind of object-choice

which, up to a certain point, vary independently of one another, and are met with in different individuals in manifold permutations.

12. Anna Freud, *Normality and Pathology in Childhood* (New York: International Universities Press, 1965), pp. 64–65.

13. Phyllis Katz, in her review of the literature on children's acquisition of prejudice (see note 6), claims that there has been no research on children less than three years old, but she ignores completely the psychoanalytic literature. See especially Rene Spitz, "Environment versus Race," in *Psychoanalysis and Culture: Essays in Honor of Geza Roheim,* ed. G. B. Wilbur and W. Munsterberger (New York: International Universities Press, 1951), pp. 32–41. Also Rene Spitz, *The First Year of Life* (New York: International Universities Press, 1965).

14. McDonald, *Not by the Color,* p. 113.

15. James Baldwin, "Stranger in the Village," in *Notes of a Native Son* (Boston: Beacon Press, 1984, orig. 1957), p. 162.

16. Goodman, *Race Awareness,* p. 120.

17. Lawrence Kubie, "The Ontogeny of Racial Prejudice," *Journal of Nervous and Mental Disease* 141, no. 3 (1965): 267–268.

18. McDonald, *Not by the Color,* p. 178, cites this example, and compares it to Freud's description of the Wolf Man, who was compelled as a child to breathe out whenever he passed a crippled person in the street, in order to avoid incorporating or identifying with the frighteningly damaged and pitiable person (see *Standard Edition* 17:66–67, 88–89).

19. McDonald, *Not by the Color,* p. 105.

20. Ibid., p. 136.

21. Cited in another context by John Duckitt, *The Social Psychology of Prejudice* (New York: Praeger, 1992), p. 131.

22. Allport, *The Nature of Prejudice,* p. 300.

23. See A. Davey, *Learning to Be Prejudiced: Growing up in Multi-Ethnic Britain* (London: Edward Arnold, 1983): Altemeyer's work on RWAs (discussed in Chapter 4); and, for an earlier American study showing weak correlation, Else Frenkel-Brunswik and J. Havel, "Prejudice in the Interviews of Children," *Journal of Genetic Psychology* 82 (1953): 91–136.

24. Richard Sterba, "Some Psychological Factors in Negro Race Hatred and in Anti-Negro Riots," in *Psychoanalysis and the Social Sciences,* ed. Geza Roheim, vol. 1 (New York: International Universities Press, 1947), p. 420; citations following, pp. 411–427.

25. Mardi Horowitz, ed., *Hysterical Personality Style and the Histrionic Personality Disorder* (Northvale, N.J.: J. Aronson, 1991), p. 46.

26. Citations are from "The Dynamic Basis of Antisemitic Attitudes," *Psychoanalytic Quarterly* 17 (1948): 240–260, which is a shorter, less technical version of *Anti-Semitism an Emotional Disorder* (New York: Harper, 1950).

27. Bettelheim and Janowitz, *Social Change and Prejudice,* p. 134.

28. As I noted in Chapter 7 and will note again below, obsessionals do have strong, if faulty, superegos but often do not feel guilt because they have projected it onto others; their prejudices relieve them of it.

29. Anna Freud, "Obsessional Neurosis: A Summary of Psychoanalytic Views," in *The Writings of Anna Freud,* vol. 5 (New York: International Universities Press, 1969), pp. 242–261.

30. Bela Grunberger, "The Anti-Semite and the Oedipal Conflict," *International Journal of Psychoanalysis* 45 (1964): 380. "Part objects" are the important, impressive, libidinally invested body parts of the parental figures, such as the breast and the penis, which are incorporated by children not yet mature enough to incorporate whole objects or full parental images.

31. All citations from Hitler, *Mein Kampf,* trans. Ralph Manheim (Boston: Houghton Mifflin, 1943).

32. Erik Erikson, "The Legend of Hitler's Childhood," in *Childhood and Society* (New York: Norton, 1963, orig. 1950), p. 330. Erikson uses the term "hysteria," but everything else in his description of Hitler's habits suggests obsessionality, particularly things like rigid abstinence from meat, coffee, alcohol, and sexual activity, as Erikson himself notes.

33. Grunberger, "Anti-Semite and Oedipal Conflict," p. 382.

34. Wilhelm Reich, *Character Analysis,* trans. T. Wolfe (New York: Farrar, Straus, Groux, 1970), p. 202.

35. Harold Blum, "Masochism, the Ego Ideal, and the Psychology of Women," in *Female Psychology: Contemporary Psychoanalytic Views,* ed. Blum (New York: International Universities Press, 1977), pp. 168, 170.

36. Most anatomy texts still do not accurately treat female genitalia, as Josephine Lowndes Sevely, a Harvard Medical School researcher, has shown in *Eve's Secrets: A New Theory of Female Sexuality* (New York: Random House, 1987). Sevely demonstrates the similarities of female and male sexual anatomy by reversing the usual route—that is, she shows what male anatomy has in common with female.

37. On the man who fathers himself, see Freud, "A Special Type of Object Choice Made by Men" (1910), in *Standard Edition* 11:173.

38. Peter Blos, "Prolonged Adolescence," *American Journal of Orthopsychiatry* 24 (1954): 733–742.

39. Donald Rinsley, *Developmental Pathogenesis and the Treatment of Borderline and Narcissistic Personalities* (New York: J. Aronson, 1989), p. 43.

40. In Klein's technical terms, infants go through a schizoid position, associated with weaning and characterized by frustrated and envious rage, and into a depressive position in which they make reparations to their mothers for the aggression loosed on her earlier. Mental health depends upon whether they emerge from the depressive position with its guilt and self-punishment.

41. Klein held that the infant has an ego at birth, and therefore she did not agree with Freud's notion that there is a primary narcissistic stage before ego differentiation. She thought of idealization as the child's means for denying the existence of the death instinct, not as a displacement of primary narcissism that comes about when the infant, experiencing dissatisfactions, tries to retain its satisfying state.

42. Chassequet-Smirgel, *The Ego Ideal,* p. 43.

43. Ibid., p. 35: Chassequet-Smirgel notes that if a female child denies the differences between the sexes and the generations, desires to be able to be the right sex and to be big enough to be the father with her mother, then she will entertain the fantasy that making a baby does not require a father—she alone is sufficient. She connects this with adult women's utopian fantasies in which females are able to reproduce without men, which, given current technologies, can refer to artificial insemination rather than invoking immaculate conception or some kind of Herland fantasy.

44. Elizabeth L. Mayer argues this proposition with clinical examples in " 'Everybody Must Be Just Like Me': Observations on Female Castration Anxiety," *International Journal of Psychoanalysis* 66 (1985): 331.

45. Susan Stern, *With the Weathermen* (New York: Doubleday, 1975), p. 243, cited in Lasch, *Culture of Narcissism.*

46. See Annie Reich, "Narcissistic Object Choice in Women," in *Psychoanalytic Contributions* (New York: International Universities Press, 1973), pp. 179–208, a study of women who either attach themselves to one man who supplies them with a kind of vicarious phallic power or go quickly from one "deified" phallic creature to the next in rapid succession.

47. The great contemporary literary explorer of these female fantasies is Monique Wittig, especially in *Les guérillières.*

## 9. Adolescence and the Aims of Hatreds

1. Charles Glock et al., *Adolescent Prejudice* (New York: Harper and Row, 1975), is based on an elaborate five-year University of California sociological study of antisemitism and racism in three high schools. Its central claim is that prejudice is strongest among those who are socially and educationally deprived, who lack the cognitive skills to combat stereotyping. Except for some remarks on peer group formation and peer pressure, the authors give no indication at all that adolescence is a developmental stage with particular developmental tasks; the

approach is entirely cognitive and, like all "social distance" measuring, assumes that what subjects say on questionnaires gives a full picture of their prejudices.

2. Robert Lindner, *The Fifty-Minute Hour* (New York: Bantam, 1973, orig. 1954): all quotations from chaps. 2 and 4.

3. Ernest Jones, "Some Problems of Adolescence," in *Papers on Psychoanalysis* (Boston: Beacon Press, 1961, orig. 1923).

4. Siegfried Bernfeld, "Types of Adolescence," *Psychoanalytic Quarterly* 7 (1938): 244.

5. Anna Freud, *The Ego and the Mechanisms of Defense*, pp. 137–165, cited in the following paragraphs.

6. See Chapter 4 above, citing Allport, *The Nature of Prejudice*, p. 31.

7. Moses Laufer and M. Egle Laufer, *Adolescence and Developmental Breakdown* (New Haven: Yale University Press, 1984), pp. 8–10.

8. Ibid., p. 6.

9. Victor Eisenstein, "Obsessive Hobbies," *Psychoanalytic Review* 34 (1948): 151–170.

10. Freud, "The Dissection of the Psychical Personality," in *Standard Edition* 22:67.

11. For a thorough review of the ways in which the ego ideal and the superego have been defined and differentiated, see Joseph Sandler, Alex Holder, and Dale Meers, "The Ego Ideal and the Ideal Self," *Psychoanalytic Study of the Child* 18 (1963): 139–158. My remarks are indebted to Annie Reich, *Psychoanalytic Contributions* (New York: International Universities Press, 1973), pp. 179–208, 288–311, 323–324.

12. Anna Freud, "On Adolescence," in *The Writings of Anna Freud*, vol. 5 (New York: International Universities Press, 1969), p. 149, and citations following, pp. 155–165.

13. Karl Mannheim, "The Problem of Generations," in *Essays on the Sociology of Knowledge*, ed. Paul Kecskeneti (New York: Oxford University Press, 1952).

14. Harrison Salisbury, *The Shook-Up Generation* (New York: Fawcett, 1959), p. 32.

15. The cultural circumstances that promote bisexuality as a self-designated identity in adolescents seem to me to be two: those in which trespassing of gender roles is hip or cool and those in which adolescents are encouraged to behave or remain like small children. The two circumstance may coincide, as they do in trendy milieus where sexual liberation ideals play a large role but the adults also fear having their children grow up and become sexually active (often with the rationale that they will then be exposed to danger and disease).

16. Peter Blos, "The Second Individuation Process," in *The Adolescent Passage* (New York: International Universities Press, 1979), p. 68.

17. As an example: in her memoir of her childhood and adolescence, *I Know Why the Caged Bird Sings*, Maya Angelou tells of her sixteen year old fear of being

a lesbian and how she resolved it—by collaring the first beautiful young man she met on the street and persuading him to sleep with her.

18. Blos, "The Second Individuation," p. 69; Heinz Hartmann, Ernst Kris, and Rudolf Loewenstein, *Papers on Psychoanalytic Psychology* (New York: International Universities Press, 1988), p. 52.

19. Joseph Adelson, "The Political Imagination of the Young Adolescent," in *Twelve to Sixteen: Early Adolescence,* eds. Jerome Kagan and Robert Coles (New York: Norton, 1972), pp. 106–144, cited again in following paragraphs. An interesting (but rather superficial) comparison piece focused on children is Robert Coles's *The Political Life of Children* (Boston: Atlantic Monthly Press, 1986).

20. Among the many factors producing the frequently obtained research result that many girls suffer a drop in self-esteem at about age twelve are these two: there is little cultural encouragement for girls to project their bad feelings onto others and also less support for their narcissism in peer groups than most boys find.

21. Samuel Ritvo, "Late Adolescence," *Psychoanalytic Study of the Child* 26 (1971): 254.

22. I. A. Newby, ed., *The Development of Segregationist Thought* (Homewood, Ill.: Dorsey Press, 1968), p. 7, citing James Ford Rhodes, *History of the United States* (1909).

23. Ibid., p. 68, citing Howard Odum, *Social and Mental Traits of the Negro* (1910).

24. Ibid., p. 89, citing Lambert Schuyler and Patricia Schuyler, *Close That Bedroom Door!* (1957).

25. The American historian Winthrop Jordan, introducing an issue of *Daedalus* devoted to adulthood (Spring 1976) summarized this story: "Throughout the nineteenth century the fertility rate in the United States fell quite markedly. At the same time, particularly at the end of the century, the mortality rate declined. The combined result was that grown persons no longer spent such a large portion of their lives in the parental role; the 'empty nest' syndrome is a relatively recent one." Jordan made this remark to indicate that the same social and demographic changes that brought "adolescence" in the modern sense into being brought "adulthood" into being. The word "adulthood," built upon the word "adult," which derives from the past participle of the Latin *adolescere* ("to grow up"), appeared only at the time of the Civil War. And it pointed to the period in a grown-up's life between the moment when he or she was officially ready to parent and the moment when his or her child finished adolescence and became, in turn, an adult.

26. Natalie Zemon Davis, "The Reasons of Misrule," *Past and Present* 50 (1971): 40–75.

27. Joseph Kett, *Rites of Passage: Adolescence in America, 1790 to the Present* (New York: Basic Books, 1977).

28. Margaret Mead, *Coming of Age in Samoa* (New York: Morrow Quill, 1973), preface, chap. 5, and p. 246 cited below. Mead's work was certainly influenced by her reformist agenda, but not, I think, completely distorted by it, as a contemporary critic, Derek Freedman, has charged in a debunking study of Mead's fieldwork. I am going to ignore the detailed foci of this controversy by staying with the broad lines of Mead's study.

29. This formulation comes from J. W. M. Whiting, R. Kluckholm, and A. Anthony, "The Function of Male Initiation Ceremonies at Puberty," in *Readings in Social Psychology,* ed. E. E. Macoby, T. M. Newcomb and E. L. Hartley (New York: Henry Holt, 1958), pp. 359–370. It has been contested by, for example, J. K. Brown, "Adolescent Initiation Rites among Preliterate Peoples," in *Studies in Adolescence,* ed. R. E. Grinder (New York: Macmillan, 1963), pp. 75–85.

30. The intellectual sloppiness and hyperbole characteristic of many of the student rebels was apparent in Jerry Farber's widely reprinted *The Student as Nigger* (New York: Pocket Books, 1970), which blasted what he called "the Auschwitz educational system" in America.

## 10. Shared Prejudices, Societal Styles

1. Peter Loewenberg, "The Psychohistorical Origins of the Nazi Youth Cohort," *American Historical Review* 76 (1972): 1457–1502.

2. The anthropological-sociological approach to ethnocentrism is richest and most complexly comparative in Donald Horowitz, *Ethnic Groups in Conflict* (Berkeley: University of California Press, 1985).

3. Lee Bridges and Liz Fekete, "Victims, the 'Urban Jungle' and the New Racism," *Race and Class* 27, no. 1 (1985): 46.

4. Bigots of the far right and progressive feminists can meet on the common ground of antipornography to work against unrestricted free speech—and what is most deeply shared is the fear that people will be infiltrated by the pornography and corrupted. See Chapter 15.

5. The Nation of Islam, for example, is a separatist organization that demands endogamy and requires of its members vows of pure living that are designed to protect them from all the infiltrations of the devilish white world—the drugs whites use to destroy black communities, the alcohol, the vicious ideas about black inferiority. Economically, the Muslims advocate separatism as well, and their programs are not free of antisemitic allegations. Similarly, in various visions of feminist separatism there are programs for independence from male contributions to reproduction (such as *Herland* utopias), preventing infiltration of male ideas and practices, establishing censorship (most recently, of male-produced pornography). Victims of obsessional prejudices can also respond in kind to the obsessionality that has come their way, as do many Zionists who insist for political (rather than religious) reasons on strict endogamy, who reject

conversion and establish purification rituals and constant proofs of group loyalty.

6. The Nazis, the ultimate bureaucrats, made museums of Jewish artifacts, to preserve the history of the Jews, while they set out to destroy the Jews utterly—that is, by cremation or mass burial. I see this contradiction as a way to incorporate Jewish brain power, Jewish culture, but cleanse it of any materiality, any flesh. It is like eating only the spirit of a totemic animal. On a less intense level, Americans who are Japanophobic (to borrow the title of Bill Emmott's *Japanophobia: The Myth of the Invincible Japanese* [New York: Times Books, 1993]) also study assiduously Japanese educational methods, business practices, management styles, etc.

7. All citations in what follows are from the title essay in Hofstader's *The Paranoid Style in American Politics and Other Essays* (New York: Knopf, 1966).

8. Cited in Hannah Arendt, *The Origins of Totalitarianism,* p. 418.

9. Carey McWilliams, *A Mask of Privilege,* p. 22.

10. When minorities involved in trade become the object of violent prejudice, it is because they have become identified with a hated and corrupt government or political movement. So it was with the Chinese trading community in Thailand in 1945, which was identified with the Kuomintang, and with the Chinese trading community in Indonesia in 1965, which was identified with the Communists and said to have ties with China, Indonesia's enemy. Middleman minorities like the Chinese in Southeast Asia, the Asians in East and South Africa, and the Jews in prewar Europe, are particularly vulnerable to obsessional prejudice, but so are groups that are perceived as having an imperialistic government or power behind them—as Catholic immigrants have Rome behind them. Northern Ireland is a terroristic standoff between two groups that each describe the other as manipulated from behind the scenes—the Catholics by Rome and the Southern Irish Catholics, and the Protestants by England. In the American South, Abolitionists—or the Yankees generally—were seen as conspiratorial infiltrators during Reconstruction, and some have argued that this is one reason why antisemitism was less prevalent in the South than elsewhere in the United States before World War II—the Yankees were the "other Jews" to hate. See Thomas Pettigrew, "Parallel and Distinctive Changes in Anti-Semitic and Anti-Negro Attitudes," in *Jews in the Mind of America,* ed. C. H. Stember (New York: Basic Books, 1966), pp. 391–393.

11. Americans generally were much more receptive to refugees from Communist persecution just after the war than they had been to refugees from Nazi persecution, which seems to imply an identification with the victims of Communism but a prejudice against the victims of antisemitism. Nevertheless, Americans were much less given to equating Jews and Communists than Europeans were.

12. In the logic of fantasy, anal penetration makes a man into a (passive)

woman, but it can also make a woman into a man if her fantasy is that this penetration is incorporation of a penis. The obsessional prejudices take very similar forms in men and women, as I have implied before, because they can be built up in defense against the same sexual fantasy of being anally penetrated.

13. Inner-city African Americans and immigrant people of color may hate not the Japanese but their more local or regional middleman minorities, the Koreans who own the grocery store, the Vietnamese who have bought up the Gulf shrimp boats, the Indians who run the outpatient clinic, the Arabs who are buying real estate, and so forth.

14. American anti-Communism in the early Cold War period, when fear of a postwar depression spread, was directed at (alleged) domestic Communists. After the early 1970s, when it was no longer possible to rally around the image of a domestic Communist threat, anti-Communism was directed toward the Evil Empire (as Ronald Reagan put it) of the Soviet Union itself, which then lacked the key ingredients for galvanizing obsessionality (the clannishness, separatism, cultural aloofness, etc.) because it was opening Westward. In this context, Gorbachev, a leader who behaved like a Westerner, could be welcomed as "one of us." Anti-Communism metamorphosed into a vast ethnocentrism.

15. Arendt, *The Origins of Totalitarianism,* p. 3; subsequent page citations given in text.

16. The term "nation-state" presents graphically its referent: it is a sovereign state in which the citizens are also a nation—a population bound together by common place of origin and language, by culture. Nation-states began to emerge in the late Renaissance, but the term dates to the decade after World War I, when Europeans realized just how problematic modern states containing more than one national population could be. We generally speak now not of multinational states but of multicultural ones—the emphasis has shifted from birth group to culture group.

17. In Arendt's terms, a person of the masses is selfless "in the sense that the self does not matter." He or she has been reduced by a lack of interests and connections to a kind of nothingness or numbness of being: "the source of all worries and cares which make human life troublesome and anguished is gone" (p. 312). A vacuum arises, which the leader fills, so that Hitler could announce to his followers quite correctly: "All that you are you are through me, all that I am I am through you alone." What Arendt was describing in social and existential terms could also be described as a feeling of having been robbed of one's precious inner goods, one's desires and hopes, all emotion, and having this inner emptiness then miraculously filled by the leader's power.

18. There has been an enormous amount of speculation about why dark skin, usually called "black" even when it is brown, and blackness are so commonly—so cross-culturally—considered inferior or evil. Blackness, many have noted, is

associated with dirt or feces, with the fearsome night or the night in which sexual activities are overheard or witnessed by children. (See Kenneth J. Gergen, "The Significance of Skin Color in Human Relations," *Color and Race,* ed. J. H. Franklin [Boston: Houghton Mifflin, 1968].) But it seems to me that the genitalization that so marks the hysterical prejudices indicates that black is crucially associated with genitals and pubic hair, particularly in females, where the hair is felt to hide or cloak the genitals. The "superior" lighter skin is degenitalized, or disassociated from the genitals, and purified. According to a rule of thumb Freud developed, feelings about the genitals are displaced upward, usually onto the face, particularly by those tending toward hysteria. So noses and lips and male beards are taken as indexes to the size of the genitals. But so, too, is fair (unclothed, always visible) facial skin taken as an index to the purity or nonsexuality of the genitals, so that white women can be imagined as unthreateningly sexless. The woman who is the exception that proves this rule is the (usually lower-class) "dumb blond"—she is, so to speak, a white Negro.

19. I will recount some of these analyses—by Frantz Fanon, Malcolm X, James Baldwin and others—in Chapter 14.

20. Charles Herbert Stember, *Sexual Racism: The Emotional Barrier to an Integrated Society* (New York: Elsevier, 1976), p. 45.

21. Like many American commentators on racism, Stember thinks in terms of a white majority and a black minority, which makes his analysis inapplicable in social terms to, say, South Africa or Brazil, which are also both multiracial and multicultural societies.

22. See George Devereux, "Neurotic Downward Identification," *American Imago* 22 (1965): 75–95.

23. In effect, this is the theory to which Stember subscribes in *Sexual Racism* when he assumes that all male sexuality is pursuit of defilement pleasure, as it is the theory to which Kate Millett subscribes in *Sexual Politics.* Many in our current society hold the view that male sexuality is by nature violent and conquering, that all men are testosterone driven, abusive, rapacious, etc. Under these conditions, a man can easily align part of himself with the omnipresent male brute and turn that part loose on a lower woman, a whore. It seems to me that stereotypes about always-aggressive male sexuality promote both racism and sexism.

24. If they are predisposed to identify with their mothers in such a scene—like Freud's famous Wolf Man or the case presented by Rogers, which I discussed in Chapter 8—they may anticipate or desire assault from the father, assuming a passive homosexual position. Or they may identify with both parents, bisexually.

25. Psychodynamically, it seems to me that one of the key reasons why the American approach to crime control emphasizes building prison after prison is that these are the places where lower-class and minority men are—routinely—

sexually humiliated. When prison inmates carry out the racism of the taxpayers, the taxpayers do not have to be directly involved. A similar kind of indirectness is attained when there is black on black violence in inner cities, in South African homelands, or in other types of prisons.

26. While the psychic mechanism of hysterical prejudice among women seems to be, in general, different from that among men, I noted before that the two sexes seem to develop obsessional prejudices along quite similar lines. In comparing the prejudices, one finds that the obsessional prejudices are much more closely tied—in psychoanalytic terms, one would say "fixated"— to the anal phase of development, which is less sexually differentiated, while the hysterical prejudices are genitalized. Fear of impotence or of insufficient power—whether explicitly played out in sexual terms or translated into other power domains—may be present in some women, but the more usual dynamic seems to rest on fear of loss of love.

27. Newby, *The Development of Segregationist Thought,* p. 26, citing John Morgan, "The Race Question in the United States."

28. Pierre van den Berghe, *Race and Ethnicity: Essays in Comparative Sociology* (New York: Basic Books, 1970), p. 163.

29. Some anthropologists argue that the status of outcast or pariah groups originates in their work. At any rate, such groups share designations around the world. They are always "dull, disorderly, sexually loose, rude, violently aggressive, and physically unclean." This list happens to come from a study of the Burakumin of Japan, who were once called by the name Eta, which means "full of filth," and who are still sometimes called Yottsu, meaning four and indicating that they are four-legged beasts (A. De Vos, *Japan's Outcasts* [London: Minority Rights Group, 1973]). Oral and phallic images abound in the characterizations of pariah groups. The Samal Luwaan of the Southern Philippines, whom the dominant Tausug regard as repulsive, get their name from the word *luwaan,* meaning "that which is spat out," rejected by God (after having been in God's mouth). In the Tausug's mythology, the Luwaan are said to come from the same race as the monkeys. In Sri Lanka, the Sinhalese have as their outcast group the Rodiya, whose name means "filth" and whose women are not allowed to cover their breasts (or, in more recent times, not allowed to wear jackets). See Horowitz, *Ethnic Groups in Conflict,* chap. 1. Although the Jews are often called a pariah group, it is important to note that historically they have never been fully a caste—they have never played as a group, for example, a fixed role in divisions of labor, although they have been concentrated in certain labor and work sectors. The middleman minorities fixed upon by the obsessionally prejudiced are not castes.

30. C. Vann Woodward, *The Strange Career of Jim Crow* (New York: Oxford University Press, 1974, orig. 1955), p. 25.

31. Ibid., p. 86.

32. C. Vann Woodward, *American Counterpoint: Slavery and Racism in the North-South Dialogue* (New York: Oxford University Press, 1983, orig. 1971), p. 45.

33. Newby, *The Development of Segregationist Thought*, p. 108.

34. Gerda Lerner, *The Creation of Patriarchy* (New York: Oxford University Press, 1986), p. 29; subsequent page citations given in text.

35. This formulation differentiates the approach of Lerner, who is indebted in this part of her argument to Claude Meillassoux and Peter Aaby, from Friedrich Engels, who held that it is the existence of private property that brings about the subordination of women.

## 11. Constructing Ideal Types

1. Woodward, *American Counterpoint*, p. 12.

2. Sartre, *Anti-Semite and Jew*, p. 25.

3. Arendt, *The Origins; of Totalitarianism*, p. 232; subsequent page citations appear in text.

4. But it is also important to remember that Arendt thought the quality of social antisemitism would, when political antisemitism was in a regnant phase, have an influence on the way political antisemitism was put into practice: "The deciding forces in the Jews' fateful journey to the storm center of events were without doubt political; but the reactions of society to antisemitism and the psychological reflections of the Jewish question in the individual had something to do with the specific cruelty, the organized and calculated assault upon every single individual of Jewish origin, that was already characteristic of the antisemitism of the Dreyfus Affair . . . Social factors . . . changed the course that mere political antisemitism would have taken if left to itself, and which might have resulted in anti-Jewish legislation and even mass expulsion but hardly in wholesale extermination" (p. 87).

5. Arthur M. Schlesinger, Jr., *The Politics of Upheaval* (Boston: Houghton Mifflin, 1960), p. 628.

6. Seymour Martin Lipset, "Three Decades of the Radical Right," in *The Radical Right*, ed. Daniel Bell (New York: Doubleday, 1964), p. 442, citing a 1955 essay by Peter Viereck.

7. Ibid., pp. 408; subsequent quotations on pp. 410–413, 420, 440–446.

8. Lifton and Markusen, *The Genocidal Mentality*, p. 47.

9. Ibid., p. 13.

10. The science fiction fantasies that go along with this form of obsessionality are filled with invaders from another planet, aliens, creatures in UFOs, and so forth. But, once on earth, these fantasy beings behave in the traditional manner of obsessional fantasy creations, that is, they are skilled at getting inside human bodies and taking them over—they do not bring about the end of the world, usually.

11. *New York Times,* February 6, 1994, p. 16.

12. This and the following quotes from Robert Sullivan, "An Army of the Faithful," *New York Times Magazine,* April 25, 1993.

13. On these groups and their programs, see Norman J. Cohen, ed., *The Fundamentalist Phenomenon* (Grand Rapids, Mich.: W. B. Erdmans, 1990).

14. B. E. Trainor and E. L. Chase, "Keep Gays Out," *New York Times,* March 29, 1993, p. A15.

15. In the seventeenth and eighteenth centuries, the word "race" was used by the English primarily in the sense of lineage or line of descent. Its main political usage was in controversies about the rights of kings, of nobles, and of commoners. "Race" was a word for historical claims. But the linguistic and conceptual landscape began to change in the early decades of the 1800s, when the practice of appealing to origins for explanations became zoological and when the Bible receded as the historical document of highest authority, the one proclaiming the ultimate origin of the entire human species in a single ancestor, Adam. Then scientific writers began to use the word "race" as though it were equivalent to "species," and as though humans were not a single species but a genus consisting of a plurality of species or races. Those who believed that all of Adam's heirs belong to the same species protested, but their arguments were met with a literary and scientific outpouring of new ideas.

16. Woodward, *American Counterpoint,* p. 273 (note), credited W. J. Cash, author of *The Mind of the South* (New York: Knopf, 1941) with the insight that "the lower class white's obsessive anxiety for racial hegemony trapped him into submission to upper class hegemony. More than anywhere else in the country, this class hegemony prevailed in the South."

17. Gunnar Myrdal, *The American Dilemma: The Negro Problem and Modern Democracy,* 2 vols. (New York: Random House, 1972, orig. 1944), 2:1142.

18. Philip Mason, *Prospero's Magic: Some Thoughts on Clan and Race* (Westport, Conn.: Greenwood Press, 1975, orig. 1962), p. 29.

19. Ibid., p. 32.

20. The transition from paternalism to competitiveness generally takes place more slowly in nonurban regions where plantation-like traditions stay strong than in towns and cities; in colonial settings, it is also slow in institutions, like the military, which are hierarchical (as, for example, in the Indian Army before the British departed).

21. Mason, *Prospero's Magic,* p. 31.

22. Ibid., p. 39.

23. When a whining complaint of this sort about affirmative action admissions was posted on the community bulletin board at my college, and a black student responded to it angrily, the white author wrote, "Fuck you and your family" on the black student's reply. To me that comment meant, "I feel like an or-

phan; I have passed all the tests for academic excellence and I still get no love, so you can't have any."

24. Failing to appreciate the successive layers of racism, some current sociologists, following the work of William Julius Wilson at Chicago, argue that it is not race prejudice that today perpetuates the poor economic situation of African Americans, but the effects of entrapment in the lower class or underclass. The ways in which racism and classism are the same are not explored. Moreover, this argument cannot explain why, for example, interracial sexual and marital relationships still rouse such opposition.

25. James Baldwin, *The Fire Next Time* (New York: Dell, 1988, orig. 1962), p. 35.

## 12. The Body and Soul of Narcissism

1. Gilberto Freyre, *The Masters and the Slaves* (New York: Knopf, 1946), pp. 404, 70–71, 326.

2. Ibid., p. 360.

3. Ibid., p. 428, and see pp. 430, 182, 324.

4. Gilberto Freyre, *The Mansions and the Shanties* (New York: Knopf, 1963), pp. 99–100.

5. Karen Horney, "The Flight from Womanhood," in *Psychoanalysis and Women,* ed. Jean Baker Miller (New York: Penguin, 1973), pp. 5–20.

6. For examples of the socialist critique, see Joan Smith, "Feminist Analysis of Gender: A Mystique," in *Woman's Nature: Rationalizations of Inequality,* ed. M. Lowe and R. Hubbard (New York: Pergamon Press, 1983), pp. 90–109, and Iris Young, "Is Male Gender Identity the Cause of Male Domination?" in *Throwing Like a Girl and Other Essays* (Bloomington: Indiana University Press, 1990), pp. 36–61.

7. Howard S. Levy, *Chinese Footbinding: The History of a Curious Erotic Custom* (New York: Walton Rawls, 1966), cited by Marilyn French, *The War against Women* (New York: Summit Books, 1992), p. 99.

8. In both majority and minority groups, sexism of various sorts will be aggravated in individuals who are socially marginalized, downwardly mobile, physically or socially traumatized, frustrated, and locked out of sexual competitions by virtue of their socioeconomic status or their personal characteristics (their ugliness or dysfunctionality or antisocial traits). But it is no more possible to understand anything about sexism by beginning the analysis from such aggravating conditions than it is to understand anything about racism by claiming that racism grows worse in bad economic times. For example, it could be noted that empirical research shows the majority of rapists to be men who are blocked from sexual gratification by their inabilities to function well socially. But the size of such a disaffected and dysfunctional group is not the key factor in rape rates. Such a group is inhibited in a society that is very sexist and very repressive,

a society in which women are sequestered and protected from attack. By contrast, in a society that is less sexist, in the sense of more permissive, women are more vulnerable to rapists, even though the availability of gratification by other means than force keeps the number of rapists down in such a society. It is in permissive societies, further, that women who are relatively free to move about in the public world are especially vulnerable to the kind of rape called "date rape" or "acquaintance rape," which thrives on ambiguous situations and is most difficult to prove in court, and which is not as commonly committed by the disaffected and dysfunctional. Rape rates in the United States are the highest in the developed world, and this dismal statistic seems to reflect the riptides of a society that is at once becoming more and more permissive as certain forms of sexism recede and becoming more and more repressive as other forms rigidify. There is no simple or direct relationship between specific types of sexist behavior (like rape) or the level of sexist violence and the "sexism"—which is not a single phenomenon—of a society. What usually comes from analyses of sexism that start with aggravations of it is a claim that all men are rapists, or that all sexual imagery is pornographic, or that all sexual encounters are degrading.

9. See Michael Young and Peter Wilmott, *The Symmetrical Family* (New York: Pantheon, 1972), on the "principle of stratified diffusion," which indicates that family life trends that are first visible in the upper end of the class spectrum appear later at the lower.

10. A possible exception is the Native American female *berdache* (female-female marriage). In a certain sense, one could say that the heterosexual narcissistic fantasy is a lesbian marriage in which one of the lesbians is a male, and it is not unlikely that envy is an ingredient of the homophobias currently being directed at lesbians who are "married" and raising children. See the section below on the role of envy in hysterical homophobias. Women who decide to be single parents can feel that they can give themselves (and a child)—as though they played both parts in a marriage—the mothering they desire; or at least that they will not be disappointed by a man.

11. *New York Times,* July 26, 1994.

12. In a certain sense, this could be described as a type of fetishism—males get not a female's phallus but a male's. But it is possible—clinical inquiry would be needed to test the hypothesis—that the male's phallus functions in its receptor's fantasy much as the women's phallus does; that is, it reassures him that everyone has a phallus.

13. In the contemporary world, this generalization could apply to homophobic authoritarian states on the right (Argentina) and the left (Cuba, China).

14. John Boswell, *Christianity, Homosexuality, and Social Tolerance* (Chicago: University of Chicago Press, 1980), pp. 157, 164.

15. Cited in ibid., p. 131.

16. Ibid., p. 15.

17. This is a persistent theme in Boswell's book: "No charge against a minority seems to be more damaging than the claim that they pose a threat of some sort to the children of the majority," he noted (p. 273) in discussing the charge of ritual murder of children made against Jews in the twelfth century. It seems to me, however, that this kind of charge is built on or extrapolated and derived from the anxieties prejudiced adults feel for themselves and defend against. Prejudiced people fear for their children as narcissistic extensions of themselves. I think Boswell's historical judgment was influenced by the strength when he was writing in the late 1970s of the "Save our children" dimension of American homophobia (on which see below).

18. Boswell, *Chrstianity, Homosexuality, and Social Tolerance*, pp. 32, 34.

19. Boswell himself admitted (p. 37) that his typological distinction between intolerant rural and tolerant urban cultures has to be qualified for the history of homophobia in Rome, where "gay people were actually safer under the Republic, before the state had the authority or the means to control aspects of the citizenry's personal lives" than they were under the more urbanized empire. He also admitted that the distinction had no bearing on the later transition from tolerance to hostility in the late twelfth century, which was closely tied not to any regressive deurbanization but to "the rise of corporate states and institutions with the power and desire to regulate increasingly personal aspects of human life." About the intolerance of gay people that grew up in the thirteenth century, Boswell wrote: "It does not seem . . . to have any relation to the 'urban/rural' dichotomy mentioned earlier in this study" (p. 270).

20. Those who follow Boswell's typology generally find the *berdache* to have a limited role. For example, Dennis Altman, *The Homosexualization of America: The Americanization of the Homosexual* (New York: St. Martin's, 1982), p. 48: "Traditional societies . . . are organized in such a way as to disallow the possibility of a child's choosing a way of life other than that prescribed by tradition and her elders, thus exclusive homosexuals, where they exist, take on particular roles, often religious ones (as in the case of the Amerindian *berdaches*), or become outcasts (which appears to be literally the case among some Hindus). It is only with the breakdown of the ascriptive family and the very narrowly defined social roles of traditional cultures that it becomes possible to live as a homosexual in other than this very rigid way. And only in urban societies, where social institutions can develop independently of the family and the clan can a homosexual subculture develop." The working definition of a homosexual here is the exclusive homosexual—a definition that came into play only in the nineteenth century (see below).

21. Boswell, *Christianity, Homosexuality, and Social Tolerance*, p. 207.

22. Cited in ibid., p. 211.

23. Cited by Louis Crompton, "Gay Genocide: From Leviticus to Hitler," in

*The Gay Academic,* ed. Louie Crew (Palm Springs, Calif.: ETC Publications, 1978). It is not clear, as a lesbian would have but one clitoris to lose, which second "member" (*membre* is the euphemism for penis) was condemned in this passage, unless the code is assuming the one-sex theory of the female's interior penile shaft. But it is more likely that the passage refers to a tradition of dismembering homosexuals (cutting off arms and legs) that is reflected in other codes of the period.

24. See the discussion in Chapter 10.

25. William F. Buckley, Jr., "Crucial Steps in Combating the AIDS Epidemic," *New York Times,* March 18, 1986.

26. Michel Foucault, *The History of Sexuality* (New York: Vintage, 1979), p. 43. Such a conception had existed earlier, particularly in the Renaissance, but it was neither widespread nor backed by medical and systematic (often Darwinian) theories of innateness or congenital deformation.

27. Greenberg, *The Construction of Homosexuality,* pp. 400–401.

28. Altman, *The Homosexualization of America.*

29. Phillipe Ariès, "Thoughts on the History of Homosexuality," in *Western Sexuality,* eds. Ariès and Andre Bejin, trans. Anthony Forster (New York: Blackwell, 1986, French orig. 1985), p. 63.

30. Within both the male and female gay communities there are subcommunities of people who engage in sadomasochistic practices, sometimes in organized or commercial settings; but these groups—to judge from their literature—are often quite self-conscious parodiers of sadomasochism; they play its roles and insist upon a peculiar respectfulness for the dominated person's wishes and for the line between play and not-play. The topic of sadomasochism is, however, a source of great debate, particularly among lesbians, many of whom view it as an importation of extreme sexism into lesbian life.

31. Edmund White, *States of Desire* (New York: Dutton, 1980), p. 16.

## 13. Varieties of Silencing

1. Cited in Saul Friedlander, *Memory, History, and the Extermination of the Jews of Europe* (Bloomington: University of Indiana Press, 1993), p. 34.

2. Ibid., pp. 1–21.

3. Ibid., pp. 49–51, and see Saul Friedlander, ed., *Probing the Limits of Representation: Nazism and the "Final Solution"* (Cambridge, Mass.: Harvard University Press, 1992).

4. See Chapters 7 and 9.

5. The Nazi-created "Jewish councils" (*Judenrate*) charged with certain administrative responsibilities for organizing deportations from Jewish towns and ghettos were, of course, part of the Nazi system for implicating the Jews in their own destruction. By noting the cruelty of questions raised about Jewish passivity,

I do not mean to imply that it is not crucially important to understand exactly how the Nazi antisemitic policy was effected in such a way as to render Jewish resistance nearly impossible, including by creating the *Judenrate*.

6. Primo Levi, *The Drowned and the Saved*, trans. Raymond Rosenthal (New York: Vintage, 1989), p. 39.

7. Fernando Camon, *Conversations with Primo Levi*, trans. John Shepley (Marlboro, Vt.: Marlboro Press, 1989), p. 4.

8. Levi, *The Drowned and the Saved*, pp. 117–118.

9. It is currently being republished in English by a Jewish press. At the time of the volume's original English publication, many American Jewish intellectuals, particularly on the Left, criticized it. Two of the most trenchant critiques came from Harold Rosenberg, "Does the Jew Exist? Sartre's Morality Play about Antisemitism" *Commentary* 7 (1949): 8–18, and Sidney Hook, "Reflections on the Jewish Question," *Partisan Review* 16 (1949): 463–482. Since then, it has become a classic, protected by such praise as this comment on its dust jacket: "[A] fervent and brilliant challenge to antisemitism" *(New York Times)*.

10. Otto Fenichel's essay is in *Anti-Semitism: A Social Disease*, ed. Ernst Simmel (New York: International Universities Press, 1948), and also in his own *Collected Papers of Otto Fenichel*, second series (New York: Norton, 1954), pp. 335–338.

11. On this essay of Sartre's, and the reaction to it of the African and Caribbean intelligentsia in Paris, see Chapter 14.

12. Sartre, *Anti-Semite and Jew*, p. 54; subsequent citations, pp. 65, 85, 137.

13. Ibid., p. 151.

14. Sartre (ibid., pp. 135–136) goes even further at one point and holds not just the antisemites but all non-Jews responsible for inventing the Jews: "We have created this variety of men who have no meaning except as artificial products of a capitalist (or feudal) society, whose only reason for existing is to serve as scapegoat for a still prelogical [not yet rational] community—this species that bears witness for essential humanity better than any other because it was born of secondary reactions within the body of humanity—this quintessence of man, disgraced, uprooted, destined from the start to either inauthenticity or martyrdom. In this situation there is not one of us who is not totally guilty and even criminal; the Jewish blood that the Nazis shed falls on all our heads."

15. Ibid., p. 55.

16. Levi, *The Drowned and the Saved*, p. 174.

17. Levi, *Survival in Auschwitz and The Reawakening: Two Memoirs* (New York: Summit Books, 1985), p. 148.

18. Levi, *The Drowned and the Saved*, pp. 26–27.

19. Ibid., p. 78.

20. Richard Wright, *Black Boy* (New York: NAL, 1963, orig. 1937), p. 70.

21. James Baldwin, *Notes of a Native Son* (Boston: Beacon Press, 1955), p. 55.

22. Louis Lomax, *The Negro Revolt* (New York: NAL, 1963), p. 180.
23. Ibid., p. 201.

## 14. On Resistance to Hysterical Repression

1. Eric Dingwall, *Racial Pride and Prejudice* (London: Watts, 1946), p. 227.

2. See March 20, 1994, p. E2. On April 2, 1994, the *Times* reported (p. 10) that the school board had rejected a call from its superintendent for the principal's resignation. The vote was four to two, with the only black member in the minority. Later, the principal was disciplined.

3. The anthology *Who Speaks for the Negro?* edited by the white poet Robert Penn Warren in 1965 has a representative range of opinion.

4. Myrdal, *The American Dilemma,* pp. 563 and 591. Myrdal also proposed exactly the opposite explanation: "The violence of the Southerner's reaction to equality in each of the spheres rises with the degree of its relation to the sexual and the personal, which suggests that his prejudice is based on fundamental attitudes toward sex and personality" (p. 1142, note). But Myrdal marginalized this theory in *The American Dilemma.*

5. St. Claire Drake, *Black Folk Here and There,* vol. 1 (Berkeley: University of California Press, 1987), p. 35 (in a very thorough bibliographic essay on theories of racism).

6. Cited in ibid., p. 35.

7. W. J. Cash, *The Mind of the South* (New York: Vintage, 1969, orig. 1941), p. 119.

8. Myrdal made a much-cited (but very skimpily documented) claim that Blacks have a "rank order of discrimination" that is the opposite of whites. For whites, the attitude most resistant to change upheld the ban on intermarriage or sexual intercourse involving white women, while for Blacks this issue was of least concern. As Charles Herbert Stember pointed out in *Sexual Racism* (p. 16), Myrdal may well have failed to understand that Blacks were little concerned with intermarriage, which was then hardly a possibility for a Black, while what the whites had in mind was any form of sexual interaction or cohabitation. Myrdal also presented the opinions of Southern whites generally but of Black leaders only, who at the time renounced intermarriage as a matter of policy. (W. E. B. Du Bois, for example, refused to marry a woman who was so light-skinned that she was often mistaken for white, but in later times he advocated repealing miscegenation laws.)

9. William Brink and Louis Harris, *Black and White* (New York: Simon and Schuster, 1967), p. 132.

10. John Howard Griffin, *Black Like Me* (New York: NAL, 1961), p. 85.

11. W. E. B. Du Bois, *The Soul of Black Folks* (New York: Signet, 1982, orig. 1903), p. 45: "After the Egyptian and Indian, the Greek and the Roman, the

Teuton and the Mongolian, the Negro is a sort of seventh son, born with a veil, and gifted with second sight in this American world—a world which yields him no true self-consciousness, but only lets him see himself through the revelation of the other world. It is a peculiar sensation, this double-consciousness, this sense of always looking at one's self through the eyes of others, of measuring one's soul by the tape of a world that looks with amused contempt and pity. One ever feels this twoness—an American, a Negro; two souls, two thoughts, two unreconciled strivings; two warring ideals in one dark body, whose dogged strength alone keeps it from being torn asunder."

12. Under the title "Black Orpheus" Sartre's preface was translated into English and issued as a pamphlet by his French publisher, Gallimard (no date).

13. Fanon, *Black Skin, White Masks,* p. 115.

14. Ibid., p. 133.

15. Senghor 's remarks at a conference on the future of Africa are cited in *French News* 16 (April 1962): 8, as noted by Irene Dobbs Jackson, "Negritude: A Study in Outline," in *Negritude: Essays and Studies,* ed. A. H. Berrian and R. A. Long (Hampton, Va.: Hampton Institute Press, 1967).

16. Fanon, *Black Skin, White Masks,* p. 160.

17. Ibid., p. 150.

18. Ibid., p. 155.

19. Ibid., pp. 190–191.

20. The quotations following from ibid., pp. 160, 162, 165.

21. James Baldwin, *No Name in the Street* (New York: Dell, 1972), pp. 53–54.

22. Ibid., p. 63.

23. *The Autobiography of Malcolm X,* with Alex Haley (New York: Grove Press, 1966, orig. 1965), p. 153.

24. Ibid., p. 163.

25. Ibid., p. 185.

26. Ibid., p. 168.

27. Ibid., p. 333.

28. Ibid., p. 304.

29. Ibid., p. 91.

30. Ibid., p. 95.

31. Ibid., p. 120.

32. Ibid., p. 94.

33. Ibid., p. 362.

34. Ibid., p. 349. But Malcolm was always a learner, and his second trip to Africa in 1964 taught him, he said in one of his last speeches, about the importance of education for women and the importance of women in "our struggle for freedom." See Malcolm X, *By Any Means Necessary: Speeches, Interviews, and a Letter by Malcolm X,* ed. George Breitman (New York: Pathfinder, 1970), p. 179.

35. *The Autobiography of Malcolm X,* p. 350.

36. *By Any Means Necessary,* pp. 160, 165.

37. Calvin Hernton, *Sex and Racism in America,* (New York: Grove Press, 1965), p. 120. Hernton's work, like that of so many African American writers of the postwar period, is deeply in debt to Sartre's *Anti-Semite and Jew,* and the summary cited follows on the general statement of the Sartrean scapegoat theory: "Like any paranoiac, the racist experiences himself as an authentic individual only when he projects his fears onto others and imagines they are attacking him. In Germany the 'others' were Jews. In America they are Negroes."

38. In some texts, several universalisms are tried, as, for example, the Southern Negro-improvement Christian version of Booker T. Washington and the Northern Communist Party version that the hero of Ralph Ellison's *Invisible Man* finds fraudulent on his way to his brief turn into separatist revolutionary action.

39. Baldwin, *The Fire Next Time,* pp. 130, 136.

40. Ibid., p. 130.

41. And this American renaissance is, of course, only a part of a much greater phenomenon across the entire African diaspora and throughout the postcolonial world.

42. Darlene Clark Hine, " 'In the Kingdom of Culture': Black Women and the Intersection of Race, Gender, and Class," in *Lure and Loathing: Essays on Race, Identity, and the Ambivalence of Assimilation,* ed. Gerald Early (New York: Penguin, 1993), p. 340.

43. bell hooks and Cornel West, *Breaking Bread: Insurgent Black Intellectual Life* (Boston: South End Press, 1991), p. 154.

44. Barbara Christian, *Black Feminist Criticism* (New York: Pergamon Press, 1985), p. 161, who cites Giovanni.

45. Ibid., p. 162.

46. Audre Lorde, "The Master's Tools Will Never Dismantle the Master's House," in *This Bridge Called My Back,* ed. Cherrie Moraga and Gloria Anzaldua (New York: Kitchen Table Press, 1981), p. 100.

## 15. Feeling the Contradictions of Sexism and Being the Targets of Homophobias

1. Hazel Carby gives a good summary of the clarifications black feminists have offered in "White Woman Listen! Black Feminism and the Boundaries of sisterhood," in *The Empire Strikes Back;* but her correct conclusion that "Black women have been dominated 'patriarchally' in different ways by men of different 'colours' " is historical and sociological and does not compass the psychological differences between in-group and out-groups sexisms.

2. Olive Banks, *Faces of Feminism* (Oxford: Martin Robertson, 1981), p. 102.

3. Reprinted in S. Firestone and A. Koedt, eds., *Notes from the Second Year: Women's Liberation* (New York: New York Radical Feminists, 1970), p. 112.

4. The title "cultural feminism" seems to have been bestowed in 1975 by a radical feminist collective called Redstockings (New York) and then made part of feminist historiography by Alice Echols, "The Taming of the Id: Feminist Sexual Politics, 1968–1983," in *Pleasure and Danger,* ed. Carol Vance (New York: Routledge, 1984), an essay later elaborated in Echols's *Daring to Be Bad: Radical Feminism in America, 1967–1975* (Minneapolis: University of Minnesota Press, 1989).

5. See Ann Snitow, Christine Stansell, and Sharon Thompson, eds., *Powers of Desire: The Politics of Sexuality* (New York: Monthly Review Press, 1983), p. 230.

6. Cited by Carol Lee Bacchi, *Same Difference: Feminism and Sexual Difference* (Boston: Allen and Unwin, 1990), p. 249.

7. See Ellen Willis, "Feminism, Moralism, and Pornography," in *Powers of Desire* (see note 5 above), pp. 460–467.

8. Schlafly made this remark in her nationally syndicated column.

9. Mary Daly, *Gyn/Ecology* (Boston: Beacon Press, 1978), p. 365. In "The Fourth World Manifesto," a precursor of cultural feminism from 1971 that argued for considering all women as a Fourth World, not defined by the socio-economic orders of the first three worlds, its author stated: "A woman's class is almost always determined by the man she is living with . . . Class is therefore bascially a distinction between males, while the female is defined by her sexual caste status" (cited in Echols, *Daring to Be Bad,* p. 246).

10. Mary Daly, *Beyond God the Father: Toward a Philosophy of Women's Liberation* (Boston: Beacon Press, 1973), p. 49.

11. Caroline Ramazanoglu's *Feminism and the Contradictions of Oppression* (New York: Routledge, 1989) is a good survey of the transition from 1960s and 1970s feminism to the third-wave or postfeminist concerns of the present.

12. For a thorough comparative history of the debates in America, Britain, and Australia, see Bacchi, *Same Difference,* from which this quotation comes (p. 21).

13. Theorists like Michel Foucault, who saw all kinds of discourses of power as basically alike in their effects on victims, argue that all victim groups should refuse to theorize in their oppressors' terms. He specifically rejected all constructions of "oppositional subjects"—whether "the proletariat," "woman," or even "the oppressed" in general. Thus struggles against victimizers can only be negative—they consist of dismantling the oppressor's categories and any confining oppositional categories as well. This approach is, I think, a variation on the notion that all prejudices are one: all oppressive discourses are one. I have been arguing that sexism, because it is a form of narcissism, constructs its victims differently—more purely narcissistically—than prejudices stemming from other psychosocial configurations.

14. A good example of work focused on a practical political issue but also conducted with an intricate display of postmodernist theoretical maneuvering is the account of an Indian divorce settlement trial by Zakia Pathak and Rajeswari Sunder Rajan, "Shahbano," in *Feminist Theory in Practice and Process,* ed. M. Malson, J. O'Barr, S. Westphal-Wihl, and M. Wyer (Chicago: University of Chicago Press, 1989), pp. 249–274.

15. Susan Sontag, "Notes on 'Camp,' " in *Against Interpretation* (New York: Dell, 1969), pp. 291–292.

16. Dennis Altman, *Homosexual Oppression and Liberation* (New York: Outerbrige and Dienstfrey, 1971), p. 86.

17. Ken Plummer, "Speaking Its Name: Inventing a Lesbian and Gay Studies," in *Modern Homosexualities,* ed. Plummer (New York: Routledge, 1992), p. 13.

18. Seymour Kleinberg, *Alienated Affections: Being Gay in America.* (New York: St. Martin's, 1980), p. 39.

19. Faderman, *Odd Girls and Twilight Lovers,* p. 255.

20. Monique Wittig, preface to the English translation of *The Lesbian Body,* trans. David LeVay (New York: William Morrow, 1975), p. 9.

21. Kate Adams, "Making the World Safe for the Missionary Position," in *Lesbian Texts and Contexts,* ed. Karla Jay and Joanne Glasgow (New York: New York University Press, 1990), p. 265.

22. Cited by S. A. Bogus, "The 'Queen B' Figure in Black Literature," in *Lesbian Texts and Contexts* (see preceding note), p. 280.

## Epilogue

1. Barbara Smith, "Where's the Revolution?" *Nation* (special issue entitled "A Queer Nation"), July 5, 1995, p. 13.

2. *New York Times,* May 1, 1991, p. 1.

3. Quoted in Arthur Hertzberg, "Is Anti-Semitism Dying Out?" *New York Review of Books,* June 24, 1993.

4. Leon Poliakov, chief historian and theoretician for this position, also argued in his four-volume history of modern antisemitism that nineteenth-century antisemitic race theory expressed in secular terms the Christian claim upon exclusive truth and hatred of the Jews for refusing that truth.

5. Hertzberg, "Is Anti-Semitism Dying Out?" p. 56.

# Bibliography

Abelove, Henry, et al. *The Lesbian and Gay Studies Reader.* New York: Routledge, 1993.

Aboud, Frances E. *Children and Prejudice.* New York: Blackwell, 1988.

Ackerman, Nathan. "Antisemitic Motivation in a Psychopathic Personality: A Case Study." *Psychoanalytic Review* 34 (1947): 76–101.

Ackerman, Nathan, and Marie Jahoda. *Anti-Semitism, an Emotional Disorder.* New York: Harper, 1950.

———. "The Dynamic Basis of Antisemitic Attitudes." *Psychoanalytic Quarterly* 17 (1948): 240–260.

Adelson, Joseph. "The Political Imagination of the Young Adolescent." In *Twelve to Sixteen: Early Adolescence,* ed. Jerome Kagan and Robert Coles. New York: Norton, 1972, pp. 106–144.

Adorno, Theodor. "Anti-Semitism and Fascist Propaganda." In *Anti-Semitism: A Social Disease,* ed. Ernst Simmel. New York: International Universities Press, 1948.

Adorno, T. W., et al. *The Authoritarian Personality.* New York: Harper, 1950.

Alexander, Franz. *The Psychoanalysis of the Total Personality,* trans. Bernard Glueck. New York and Washington Nervous and Mental Disease Pub. Co., 1930.

Alexander, I. E., and S. Blackman. "Castration, Circumcision, and Antisemitism." *Journal of Abnormal and Social Psychology* 55 (1957): 143–144.

Alexander, Leo. "Sociopsychologic Structure of the SS." *Archives of Neurology and Psychiatry* 59 (1948): 622–634.

Allen, D. W. *The Fear of Looking: Or Scopophilic—Exhibitionistic Conflicts.* Charlottesville: University Press of Virginia, 1974.

Allen, Jeffner, ed. *Lesbian Philosophies and Cultures.* New York: State University of New York Press, 1990.

Allport, Gordon. *Becoming: Basic Considerations for a Psychology of Personality.* New Haven: Yale University Press, 1955.

————. "The Historical Background of Modern Social Psychology." In *The Handbook of Social Psychology,* vol. 1, ed. G. Lindzay and E. Aronson. New York: Addison-Wesley, 1968.

————. *The Nature of Prejudice.* Reading, Mass.: Addison-Wesley, 1954.

————. "Some Roots of Prejudice." *Journal of Psychology* 22 (1946): 9–39.

Altemeyer, Robert. *The Enemies of Freedom.* San Francisco: Jossey-Bass, 1988.

————. "Marching in Step: A Psychological Explanation of State Terror." *Sciences* April 1988, pp. 30–38.

Altman, Dennis. *The Homosexualization of America: The Americanization of the Homosexual.* New York: St. Martin's, 1982.

————. *Homosexual Oppression and Liberation.* New York: Outerbridge and Dienstrey, 1971.

"American Indians, Blacks, Chicanos, and Puerto Ricans." *Daedalus* 110 (1981).

Angelou, Maya. *I Know Why the Caged Bird Sings.* New York: Bantam, 1977, orig. 1969.

Anzieu, Didier. *The Group and the Unconscious,* trans. Benjamin Kilborne. Boston: Routledge, 1984.

Apostle, Richard A., et al. *The Anatomy of Racial Attitudes.* Berkeley: University of California Press, 1983.

Arendt, Hannah. *The Origins of Totalitarianism.* 1951. New York: Harcourt, Brace, 1973, orig. 1951.

Ariès, Philippe, and Andre, Bejin. *Western Sexuality,* trans. Anthony Forster. New York: Blackwell, 1985.

Ashmore, Richard, and Frances DelBoca. "Psychological Approaches to Understanding Intergroup Conflict." In *Towards the Elimination of Racism,* ed. Phyllis A. Katz. New York: Pergamon Press, 1976, pp. 73–124.

Bacchi, Carol Lee. *Same Difference: Feminism and Sexual Difference.* Boston: Unwin and Allen, 1990.

Badcock, C. R. *Madness and Modernity.* Oxford: Blackwell, 1983.

Bagley, C., G. K. Verma, K. Mallick, and L. Young. *Personality, Self-Esteem, and Prejudice.* London: Saxon House, 1979.

Bain, Red. "Sociopathy of Antisemitism." *Sociometry* 4 (1943): 460–464.

Baird, Robert M., and Stuart E. Rosenbaum, eds. *Bigotry, Prejudice, and Hatred.* Buffalo: Prometheus Books, 1992.

Bak, Robert C. "The Phallic Woman: The Ubiquitous Fantasy in Perversions." *Psychoanalytic Study of the Child* 23 (1968): 15–36.

Baldwin, James. *The Fire Next Time.* New York: Dell, 1988, orig. 1962.

————. *No Name in the Street.* New York: Dell, 1972.

————. *Notes of a Native Son.* Boston: Beacon Press, 1955.

————. "Stranger in the Village." In *Notes of a Native Son.* Boston: Beacon Press, 1957.

Baluner, Bob. *Black Lives, White Lives: Three Generations of Race Relations in America.* Berkeley: University of California Press, 1989.

Barker, Martin. *The New Racism.* Frederick, Md.: Altheia, 1981.

Bar Tal, Daniel, et al. *Stereotyping and Prejudice: Changing Conceptions.* New York: Springer Verlag, 1989.

Bastide, Roger. "Color, Racism, and Christianity." In *Color and Race,* ed. J. H. Franklin, Boston: Houghton Mifflin, 1968.

———. *The Sociology of Mental Disorders,* trans. Jean McNeil. New York: McKay, 1972.

Beauvais, Cheryl. "Gender, Prejudice, and Categorization." *Sex Roles,* January 1987, pp. 89–100.

Beauvoir, Simone de. *The Second Sex.* New York: Penguin, 1972, orig. 1947.

Bell, Daniel, ed. *The Radical Right.* New York: Doubleday, 1964.

Benedict, Ruth. *Race: Science and Politics.* New York: Greenwood, 1982.

Bergman, Shlomo. "Some Methodological Errors in the Study of Antisemitism." *Jewish Social Studies,* January 1943, pp. 43–60.

Bergman, Werner, ed. *Error without Trial: Psychological Research on Anti-Semitism.* New York: Gruyter, 1988.

Berke, Joseph H. *The Tyranny of Malice.* New York: Summit Books, 1988.

Berkeley, O. A. R. "The Labor Question from a Psychoanalytical Point of View." *Psychoanalytical Review* 11 (1924): 246–253.

Berkowitz, L. "Anti-Semitism, Judgmental Processes, and the Displacement of Hostility." *Journal of Abnormal and Social Psychology* 62 (1961): 210–215.

Bernfeld, Siegfried. "Types of Adolescence." *Psychoanalytic Quarterly* 7 (1938).

Bernstein, Doris. "Female Genital Anxieties, Conflicts, and Typical Mastery Modes." *International Journal of Psychoanalysis* 71 (1990): 151–165.

Bethlehem, Douglas W. *A Social Psychology of Prejudice.* New York: St. Martin's, 1985.

Bettelheim, Bruno, and Morris Janowitz. *Social Change and Prejudice, including "The Dynamics of Prejudice."* Glencoe, Ill.: Free Press, 1964.

———. "The Victim's Image of the Anti-Semite." *Commentary* 5 (1948): 173–179.

Bibring, Grete. "On the 'Passing of the Oedipus Complex' in a Matriarchal Family Setting." In *Drives, Affects, Behavior,* ed. R. M. Lowenstein. New York: International Universities Press, 1953.

Biddiss, Michael D. "Fascism and the Race Question: A Review of Recent Historiography." *Journal of African History* 10, no. 3 (1969): 251–267.

Bierly, Margaret N. "Prejudice toward Contemporary Outgroups as a Generalized Attitude." *Journal of Applied Psychology* 15, no. 2 (1985): 189–199.

Billingsley, Andrew. "The Treatment of Negro Families in American Scholarship." In *Black Families in White America.* Englewood Cliffs, N.J.: Prentice-Hall, 1968.

Bird, Brian. "A Consideration of the Etiology of Prejudice." *Journal of the American Psychoanalytic Association* (1957): 490–513.

Blackwood, Evelyn. "Breaking the Mirror: The Construction of Lesbianism and the Anthropological Discourse on Homosexuality." In *Anthropology and Homosexual Behavior,* ed. Blackwood. New York: Haworth, 1986.

Blos, Peter. *The Adolescent Passage.* New York: International Universities Press, 1979.

———. *On Adolescence: A Psychoanalytic Interpretation.* New York: Macmillan, 1962.

———. "Prolonged Adolescence." *American Journal of Orthopsychiatry* 24 (1954): 733–742.

Blum, Harold. "Masochism, the Ego Ideal, and the Psychology of Women." In *Female Psychology: Contemporary Psychoanalytic Views,* ed. H. Blum. New York: International Universities Press, 1977.

Blumenfeld, Warren J., ed. *Homophobia: How We All Pay the Price.* Boston: Beacon Press, 1992.

Bogardus, Emory. *Social Distance.* Los Angeles: Antioch, 1959.

Boswell, John. *Christianity, Social Tolerance, and Homosexuality: Gay People in Western Europe from the Beginning of the Christian Era to the Fourteenth Century.* Chicago: University of Chicago Press, 1980.

Bovell, Gilbert Balfour. "Psychological Considerations of Color Conflicts among Negroes." *Psychoanalytic Review* 30 (1943): 447–459.

Bradbury, William C. "Evaluation of Research in Race Relations." *Inventory: Research in Racial-Cultural Relations* 5, nos. 2–3 (1953): 99–133.

Brenner, Arthur B. "Some Psychoanalytic Speculations on Anti-Semitism." *Psychoanalytic Review* 35 (1948): 20–32.

Bridges, Lee, and Liz Fekete. "Victims, the 'Urban Jungle,' and the New Racism." *Race and Class* 27, no. 1 (1985): 45–61.

Brink, William, and Louis Harris. *Black and White.* New York: Simon and Schuster, 1967.

Brittan, Arthur, and Mary Maynard. *Sexism, Racism, and Oppression.* Oxford: Blackwell, 1984.

Brody, Eugene B. "Psychosocial Aspects of Prejudice." In *American Handbook of Psychiatry,* vol. 2, rev. ed. 1975.

Brooks, Roy L. *Rethinking the American Race Problem.* Berkeley: University of California Press, 1990.

———. "Twentieth Century Black Thought: Ideology and Methodology." *Phi Betta Kappa* 53 (1973): 46–57.

Brown, J. F. "The Origin of the Anti-Semitic Attitude." In *Jews in a Gentile World,* ed. I. Graeber and S. H. Britt. New York: Macmillan, 1942, pp. 124–148.

Brown, J. K. "Adolescent Initiation Rites among Preliterate Peoples." In *Studies in Adolescence,* ed. R. E. Grinder. New York: Macmillan, 1963, pp. 75–85.

Brunner, Constantin. *Tyranny of Hate: The Roots of Antisemitism,* trans. Graham Harrison, ed. Aron M. Rappaport. Lewiston, N.Y.: Edwin Mellen, 1992.

Bulhan, Hussein Abdilahi. *Frantz Fanon and the Psychology of Oppression.* New York: Plenum, 1985.

Bulkin, Elly, et al., eds. *Yours in Struggle: Three Feminist Perspectives on Anti-Semitism and Racism.* Ithaca, N.Y.: Firebrand Books, 1988.

Burgin, Victor, James Donald, and Cora Kaplan, eds. *Formations of Fantasy.* New York: Routledge, 1989.

Butts, Hugh F. "White Racism: Its Origins, Institutions, and the Implications for the Professional Practice in Mental Health." *International Journal of Psychiatry* 8, no. 6 (1969): 914–928.

Camon, Fernando. *Conversations with Primo Levi,* trans. John Shepley. Marlboro, Vt.: Marlboro Press, 1989.

Campbell, Angus. *White Attitudes toward Black People.* Ann Arbor: University of Michigan Press, 1971.

Carby, Hazel et al., eds. *The Empire Strikes Back.* London: Hutchinson and the Birmingham Centre for Cultural Studies, 1982.

Carmichael, Stokely, and Charles Hamilton. *Black Power: The Politics of Liberation in America.* New York: Random House, 1967.

Cash, W. J. *The Mind of the South.* New York: Vintage, 1969, orig. 1941.

Chalmers, David Mark. *Hooded Americanism: The First Century of the Ku Klux Klan, 1865–1965.* Garden City, N.Y.: Doubleday, 1965.

Chandler, David P. *The Tragedy of Cambodian History.* New Haven: Yale University Press, 1991.

Chassequet-Smirgel, Janine. *The Ego Ideal: A Psychoanalytic Essay on the Malady of the Ideal,* trans. Paul Barrows. New York: Norton, 1985, orig. 1974.

Chatto, Clarence. *The Story of the Springfield Plan.* New York: Barnes and Noble, 1945.

Chesler, Mark. "Contemporary Sociological Theories of Racism." In *Towards the Elimination of Racism,* ed. Phyllis A. Katz. New York: Pergamon Press, 1976.

Chesler, Phyllis. *Women and Madness.* New York: Doubleday, 1972.

Chodoff, P., and H. Lyons. "The Hysterical Personality and Hysterical Conversion." *American Journal of Psychiatry* 4 (1958).

Chodorow, Nancy. *Feminism and Psychoanalytic Theory.* New Haven: Yale University Press, 1989.

———. *The Reproduction of Mothering.* Berkeley: University of California Press, 1978.

Christian, Barbara. *Black Feminist Criticism.* New York: Pergamon Press. 1985.

Christie, Richard. "Authoritarianism and Related Constructs." In *Measures of Personality and Social Psychological Attitudes.* New York: Academic Press, 1981.

———. *Studies in Machiavellianism.* New York: Academic Press, 1970.

Christie, Richard, and Marie Jahoda, eds. *Studies in the Scope and Method of "The Authoritarian Personality."* Glencoe, Ill.: Free Press, 1954.

Clark, Kenneth. *Dark Ghetto.* New York: Harper and Row, 1965.

———. "Desegregation: An Appraisal of the Evidence." *Journal of Social Issues* 9, no. 4 (1953).

———. *Prejudice and Your Child.* Boston: Beacon Press, 1955.

———. *The White Problem in America.* Chicago: Johnson, 1966.

Cleaver, Eldridge. *Soul on Ice.* New York: McGraw, 1968.

Cohen, Norman J., ed. *The Fundamentalist Phenomenon.* Grand Rapids, Mich.: Eerdmans, 1990.

Cohn, Norman. *The Pursuit of the Millennium.* New York: Oxford University Press, 1970.

———. *Warrant for Genocide: The Myth of the Jewish World-Conspiracy and the Protocols of the Elders of Zion.* Chicago: Scholars Press, 1983.

Coles, Robert. *The Political Life of Children.* Boston: Atlantic Monthly Press, 1986.

Collins, Barry E. *Social Psychology: Social Influence, Attitude Change, Group Processes, and Prejudice.* Reading, Mass.: Addison-Wesley, 1970.

Cook, Mercer, and Stephen E. Henderson. *The Militant Black Writer in Africa and the United States.* Madison: University of Wisconsin Press, 1969.

Coplon, Jeff. "The Skinhead Reich," *Utne Reader,* May/June, 1989.

Cox, Oliver C. *Caste, Class, and Race.* Garden City, N.Y.: Monthly Review Press, 1970, orig. 1948.

Crew, Louie, ed. *The Gay Academic.* Palm Springs, Calif.: ETC Publications, 1978.

Cruse, Harold. *The Crisis of the Negro Intellectual.* New York: Morrow, 1967.

Curtis, Michael, ed. *Antisemitism in the Contemporary World.* Boulder, Colo.: Westview Press, 1986.

Daly, Mary. *Beyond God the Father: Toward a Philosophy of Women's Liberation.* Boston: Beacon Press, 1973.

———. *Gyn Ecology.* Boston: Beacon Press, 1978.

Davey, A. *Learning to be Prejudiced: Growing up in a Multi-Ethnic Britain.* London: Edward Arnold, 1983.

Davis, Allison. *Children of Bondage: The Personality Development of Negro Youth in the Urban South.* Washington, D.C.: American Council on Education, 1940.

Davis, Angela Yvonne. *Women, Culture, and Politics.* New York: Random House, 1989.

———. *Women, Race, and Class.* New York: Random House, 1981.

Davis, Jerome. *Character Assassination.* New York: Philosophical Library, 1950.

Davis, Natalie Zemon. "The Reasons of Misrule." *Past and Present* 50 (1971): 40–75.

Degler, Carl. "Slavery and the Genesis of American Race Prejudice." *Comparative Studies in Society and History* 2 (1959): 49–66.

Devereux, George. *Basic Problems of Ethnopsychiatry*. Chicago: University of Chicago Press, 1980.

————. *Ethnopsychoanalysis: Psychoanalysis and Anthropology as Complementary Frames of Reference*. Berkeley: University of California Press, 1978.

————. *From Anxiety to Method in the Behavioral Sciences*. New York: Humanities Press, 1967.

————. "Neurotic Downward Identification." *American Imago* 22 (1965): 75–95.

————. *Reality and Dream: The Psychotherapy of a Plains Indian*. New York: International Universities Press, 1951.

————. *A Study of Abortion in Primitive Societies*. New York: International Universities Press, 1976.

Devine, Patricia G., Margo J. Monteith, and Julia R. Zuwerink. "Prejudice with and without Compunction." *Journal of Applied Social Psychology,* June 1991, pp. 817–830.

De Vos, A. *Japan's Outcasts*. London: Minority Rights Groups, 1973.

Dicks, Henry Victor. *Licensed Mass Murder: A Socio-Psychological Study of Some SS Killers*. New York: Basic Books, 1972.

————. "Psychological Factors in Prejudice." *Race* 1 (1959).

Dingwall, Eric. *Racial Pride and Prejudice*. London: Watts, 1946.

Dinnerstein, Dorothy. *The Mermaid and the Minotaur*. New York: Harper and Row, 1976.

Dollard, John. *Caste and Class in a Southern Town*. Garden City, N.Y.: Doubleday, 1949.

Dollard, John, et al. *Frustration and Aggression*. New Haven: Yale University Press, 1939.

Donald, James, ed. *Psychoanalysis and Cultural Theory: Thresholds*. London: Macmillan, 1990.

Dorsey, John M. "A Psychotherapeutic Approach to the Problems of Hostility." *Social Forces* 29 (1950): 197–206.

Dovido, John F., and Samuel L. Gaertner. *Prejudice, Discrimination, and Racism*. Orlando, Fla.: Academic Press, 1986.

Doyle, Anna-Beth, et al. "Developmental Patterns in the Flexibility of Children's Ethnic Attitudes." *Journal of Cross-Cultural Psychology* 19 (1988): 3–18.

Drake, St. Claire. *Black Folk Here and There: An Essay in History and Anthropology*. Berkeley: University of California Press, 1987.

Du Bois, Cora. *The People of Alor*. New York: Harper, 1961.

DuBois, Rachel Davis. *All This and Something More: Pioneering in Intercultural Education*. Bryn Mawr, Penn.: Dorrance, 1984.

Du Bois, W. E. B. *Darkwater, Voices from the Veil*. Millwood, N.Y.: Kraus-Thomson, 1975.

————. *The Soul of Black Folks.* New York: Signet, 1982, orig. 1903.

Duckitt, John. *The Social Psychology of Prejudice.* New York: Praeger, 1992.

Dworkin, Andrea. *Woman Hating.* New York: Dutton, 1974.

Echols, Alice. *Daring to Be Bad: Radical Feminism in America, 1967–1975.* Minneapolis: University of Minnesota Press, 1989.

Ehrlich, Howard J. *The Social Psychology of Prejudice: A Systematic Theoretical Review and Propositional Inventory of the American Social Psychological Study of Prejudice.* New York: John Wiley, 1973.

Eisenstein, Hester, and Alice Jardine, eds. *The Future of Difference.* New Brunswick, N.J.: Rutgers University Press, 1985.

Eisenstein, Victor W. "Obsessive Hobbies." *Psychoanalytic Review* 34 (1948): 151–170.

Elkins, Stanley. *Slavery: A Problem in American Institutional and Intellectual Life.* Chicago: University of Chicago Press, 1959.

Elliott, W. A. *Us and Them: A Study of Group Consciousness.* Aberdeen: Aberdeen University Press, 1986.

Ellison, Mary. "David Duke and the Race for the Governor's Mansion." *Race and Class* 33 (1991): 71–79.

Emmott, Bill. *Japanophobia: The Myth of the Invincible Japanese.* New York: Times Books, 1993.

Erikson, Erik. *Childhood and Society.* New York: Norton, 1963, orig. 1950.

Faderman, Lillian. *Odd Girls and Twilight Lovers: A History of Lesbian Life in Twentieth Century America.* New York: Columbia University Press, 1991.

Fairbairn, W. Ronald D. "Observations on the Nature of Hysterical States." *British Journal of Medical Psychology* 27 (1954): 105–125.

Fanon, Frantz. *Black Skin, White Masks.* New York: Grove Press, 1952.

————. *The Wretched of the Earth.* New York: Grove Press, 1968.

Farber, Jerry. *The Student as Nigger.* New York: Pocket Books, 1970.

Fausto-Sterling, Anne. *Myths of Gender: Biological Theories about Women.* New York: Basic Books, 1985.

Fenichel, Otto. "Elements of a Psychoanalytic Theory of Anti-Semitism." In *Anti-Semitism: A Social Disease,* ed. Ernst Simmel. New York: International Universities Press, 1948, pp. 11–32.

————. *The Psychoanalytic Theory of Neurosis.* New York: Norton, 1945.

Ferenczi, Sándor. *Contributions to Psychoanalysis,* trans. Ernest Jones. Boston: R. G. Badger, 1916.

Ficarrotto, Thomas J. "Racism, Sexism, and Erotophobia: Attitudes of Heterosexuals toward Homosexuals." *Journal of Homosexuality* 19, no. 1 (1990): 111–116.

Fine, Reuben. *Narcissism, the Self, and Society.* New York: Columbia University Press, 1986.

Firestone, Shulamith. *The Dialectics of Sex.* New York: Bantam, 1970.

Ford, C., and F. Beach. *Patterns of Sexual Behavior*. New York: Harper and Row, 1951.

Forster, Arnold, and B. Epstein. *The New Antisemitism*. New York: McGraw, 1974.

Foucault, Michel. *The History of Sexuality*. New York: Pantheon Books, 1978.

Franklin, John Hope. *Color and Race*. Boston: Houghton Mifflin, 1968.

———. *Race and History: Selected Essays, 1938–1988*. Baton Rouge: Louisiana State University Press, 1989.

Fredrickson, George M. *The Black Image in the White Mind; The Debate on Afro-American Character and Destiny*. New York: Harper and Row, 1971.

Freeman, Thomas. "Some Aspects of Pathological Narcissism." *Journal of the American Psychoanalytic Association* 12 (1964): 540–561.

French, Marilyn. *The War against Women*. New York: Summit Books, 1992.

Frenkel-Brunswik, Else. "A Study of Prejudice." *Human Relations* 1 (1948): 295–306.

Frenkel-Brunswik, Else, and J. Havel. "Prejudice in the Interviews of Children." *Journal of Genetic Psychology* 82 (1953): 91–136.

Frenkel-Brunswik, Else, and R. Nevitt Sanford. "The Anti-Semitic Personality: A Research Report." In *Anti-Semitism: A Social Disease,* ed. Ernst Simmel. New York: International Universities Press, 1948.

———. "Some Personality Factors in Anti-Semitism." *Journal of Psychology* 20 (1945): 271–291.

Freud, Anna. *The Ego and the Mechanisms of Defense*. New York: International Universities Press, 1966.

———. *Normality and Pathology in Childhood*. New York: International Universities Press, 1965.

———. "Obsessional Neurosis: A Summary of Psychoanalytic Views." In *The Writings of Anna Freud*, vol. 5. New York: International Universities Press, 1969, pp. 242–261.

———. "On Adolescence." In *The Writings of Anna Freud*, vol. 5. New York: International Universities Press, 1969.

Freud, Sigmund. *Standard Edition of the Complete Psychological Works of Sigmund Freud*, 24 vols, trans. James Strachey. London: Hogarth, 1953–1974.

Freyre, Gilberto. *The Mansions and the Shanties*. New York: Knopf, 1963.

———. *The Masters and the Slaves*. New York: Knopf, 1946.

Friedlander, Saul. *Memory, History, and the Extermination of the Jews of Europe*. Bloomington: Indiana University Press, 1993.

———. *Probing the Limits of Representation: Nazism and the 'Final Solution.'* Cambridge, Mass.: Harvard University Press, 1992.

Fromm, Erich. *Escape from Freedom*. New York: Farrar and Rinehart, 1941.

Fuss, Diana. *Essentially Speaking: Feminism, Nature, and Difference*. New York: Routledge, 1989.

Gabriel, J., and G. Ben-Tovim. "Marxism and the Concept of Racism." *Economy and Society* 7, no. 2 (1977).

Geahchan, Dominique J. "Deuil et nostalgie." *Revue Française de Psychanalyse* 32 (1968): 39–65.

Genovese, Eugene. *The Political Economy of Slavery.* New York: Pantheon, 1965.

Gergen, Kenneth J. "The Significance of Skin Color in Human Relations." In *Color and Race,* ed. J. H. Franklin. Boston: Houghton Mifflin, 1968.

Gerth, Hans. *Character and Social Structure.* New York: Harcourt, Brace, 1964.

Gilman, Sander L. *Difference and Pathology: Stereotypes of Sexuality, Race, and Madness.* Ithaca, N.Y.: Cornell University Press, 1985.

————. *Jewish Self-Hatred: Anti-Semitism and the Hidden Language of the Jews.* Baltimore: Johns Hopkins University Press, 1986.

————. *The Jew's Body.* New York: Routledge, 1991.

————. *On Blackness without Blacks: Essays on the Image of the Black in Germany.* Boston: G. K. Hall, 1982.

Ginsburg, Morris. "Anti-Semitism." *Sociological Review,* January–April 1943, pp. 1–11.

Glazer, Nathan. "The Social Scientists Dissect Prejudice." *Commentary* 1 (1949): 79–85.

Glazer, Nathan, and Daniel Patrick Moynihan. *Beyond the Melting Pot.* Cambridge, Mass.: MIT Press, 1963.

Glock, Charles, Robert Wuthnow, Jane Allyn Piliavin, and Melitta Spencer. *Adolescent Prejudice.* New York: Harper and Row, 1975.

Glock, Charles Y., and Ellen Siegelman, eds. *Prejudices, U.S.A.* New York: Praeger, 1969.

Goffman, Irving. *Stigma: Notes on the Management of Spoiled Identity.* Englewood Cliffs, N.J.: Prentice-Hall, 1963.

Goldberg, David. "The Socio-Discursive Formation of Racism." *Journal for the Study of Black Philosophy* 1, no. 2 (1985).

Goldberg, David Theo, ed. *Anatomy of Racism.* Minneapolis: University of Minnesota Press, 1990.

Goldstein, Jan. "The Wandering Jew and the Problem of Psychiatric Anti-Semitism in Fin-de-Siecle France." *Journal of Contemporary History* 20 (1985): 538–545.

Goldstein, Naomi Friedman. *The Roots of Prejudice against the Negro in the United States.* Boston: Boston University Press, 1948.

Gonsiorek, John G., and James D. Weinrich. *Homosexuality: Research Implications for Public Policy.* Newbury Park, Calif.: Sage Publications, 1991.

Goodman, Mary Ellen. *Race Awareness in Young Children.* Reading, Mass.: Addison-Wesley, 1952.

Gould, Stephen. *The Measure of Man.* New York: Norton, 1981.

Graber, I., and S. H. Britt. *Jews in a Gentile World.* New York: Macmillan, 1942.

Greenberg, David F. *The Construction of Homosexuality.* Chicago: University of Chicago Press, 1988.

Greenson, Ralph R. "On Homosexuality and Gender Identity." In *Explorations in Psychoanalysis.* New York: International Universities Press, 1978.

Griffin, John Howard. *Black Like Me.* New York: NAL, 1961.

Grossman, Mordecai. "The Schools Fight Prejudice." *Commentary* 1 (1945–46): 34–42.

Grunberger, Bela. "The Anti-Semite and the Oedipal Conflict." *International Journal of Psychoanalysis* 45 (1964): 380–385.

————. *Narcissism: Psychoanalytic Essays,* trans. Joyce S. Diamanti. New York: International Universities Press, 1979.

Guthrie, Robert V. *Even the Rat Was White: A Historical View of Psychology.* New York: Harper and Row, 1976.

Hacker, Andrew. *Two Nations Black and White, Separate, Hostile, Unequal.* New York: Ballantine, 1992.

Hall, G. Stanley. *Adolescence: Its Psychology and Its Relations to Physiology, Anthropology, Sociology, Sex, Crime, Religion, and Education.* New York: Appleton, 1904.

Halperin, David M. *One Hundred Years of Homosexuality.* New York: Routledge, 1990.

Halpern, David. "What Is Antisemitism?" *Modern Judaism* 1 (1981): 251–262.

Halsell, Grace. *Black/White Sex.* New York: Morrow, 1972.

Hamberg, David A. "New Risks of Prejudice, Ethnocentrism, and Violence." *Science,* February 7, 1986, p. 533.

Hamilton, James. "Some Dynamics of Anti-Negro Prejudice." *Psychoanalytic Review* 51 (1966–67): 5–15.

Hansen, Gary L. "Measuring Prejudice against Homosexuality (Homosexism) among College Students." *Journal of Social Psychology,* August 1982, pp. 233–236.

Haring, Douglas Gilbert. *Personal Character and Cultural Milieu; a Collection of Readings.* Syracuse: Syracuse University Press, 1956, orig. 1949.

Harris, Adrienne. "Gender as Contradiction." *Psychoanalytic Dialogues* 1, no. 2 (1991): 197–224.

Hartley, E. L. *Problems in Prejudice.* New York: King's Crown, 1946.

Hartmann, Heinz, Ernst Kris, and Rudolf Loewenstein. *Papers on Psychoanalytic Psychology.* New York: International Universities Press, 1988.

Heer, Friedrich. *Challenge of Youth,* trans. Geoffrey Skelton. Tuscaloosa: University of Alabama Press, 1974.

Helmriech, William B. *The Things They Say behind Your Back.* New Brunswick, N.J.: Transaction Books, 1982.

Henriques, Fernando. *Children of Conflict: A Study of Interracial Sex and Marriage.* New York: Dutton, 1975.

Hermann, Imre. "The Giant Mother, the Phallic Mother, Obscenity." *Psycho-analytic Review* 36 (1949).

Hernton, Calvin C. *Sex and Racism in America.* New York: Grove Press, 1965.

Herskovits, Melville Jean. *The Myth of the Negro Past.* Boston: Beacon Press, 1958.

Hertzberg, Arthur. "Is Anti-Semitism Dying Out?" *New York Review of Books,* June 24, 1993, pp. 51–57.

Hine, Darlene Clark. " 'In the Kingdom of Culture': Black Women and the Intersection of Race, Gender, and Class." In *Lure and Loathing: Essays on Race, Identity, and the Ambivalence of Assimilation,* ed. Gerald Early. New York: Penguin, 1993.

Hitler, Adolf. *Mein Kampf,* trans. Ralph Manheim. Boston: Houghton Mifflin, 1943.

Hoetink, H. *The Two Variants in Caribbean Race Relations,* trans. Eva M. Hooykaas. London: Oxford University Press, 1967.

Hofstader, Richard. *The Paranoid Style in American Politics and Other Essays.* New York: Knopf, 1966.

Holms, J. E. *Black and White Racial Identity: Theory, Research, and Practice.* New York: Greenwood, 1990.

Hook, Sidney. "Reflections on the Jewish Question." *Partisan Review* 16 (1949): 463–482.

Hooker, Evelyn. "The Adjustment of the Male Oriented Homosexual." *Journal of Projective Techniques* 21 (1957).

———. "Male Homosexuality in the Rorschach." *Journal of Projective Techniques* 22 (1958).

———. "Male Homosexuals and Their 'Worlds.' " In *Sexual Inversion,* ed. Judd Marmor. New York: Basic Books, 1965.

hooks, bell. *Black Looks: Race and Representation.* Boston: South End Press, 1992.

———. *Outlaw Culture: Resisting Representations.* New York: Routledge, 1994.

hooks, bell, and Cornell West. *Breaking Bread: Insurgent Black Intellectual Life.* Boston: South End Press, 1991.

Horkheimer, Max, and Theodor Adorno. *The Dialectic of Enlightenment.* New York: Seabury Press, 1972, orig. 1944.

Horney, Karen. "The Flight from Womanhood." In *Psychoanalysis and Women,* ed. Jean Baker Miller. New York: Penguin, 1973.

Horowitz, Donald. *Ethnic Groups in Conflict.* Berkeley: University of California Press, 1985.

Horowitz, Mardi, ed. *Hysterical Personality Style and the Histrionic Personality Disorder.* Northvale, N.J.: Aronson, 1991.

Horowitz, Ruth. "Racial Aspects of Self-Identification in Nursery School Children." *Journal of Psychology* 7 (1939): 91–99.

Huggins, Nathan, et al., eds. *Key Issues in the African American Experience.* New York: Harcourt, Brace, 1971.

Isay, Richard. *Being Homosexual: Gay Men and Their Development.* New York: Farrar, Straus, and Giroux, 1989.

Jacobson, Edith. "Development of the Wish for a Child in Boys." *Psychoanalytic Study of the Child* 6 (1951): 139–152.

Jahoda, Marie. "Race Relations: A Psycho-analytical Interpretation." In *Man, Race, and Darwin,* ed. Philip Mason. London: Oxford University Press for the Institute of Race Relations, 1960.

James, R. A., and R. D. Ashmore. "The Structure of Intergroup Perception." *Journal of Personality and Social Psychology* 25 (1973).

Janssen-Jurriet, Marielouise. *Sexism: The Male Monopoly on History and Thought,* trans. Verne Moberg. New York: Farrar, Straus, and Giroux, 1982, orig. 1976.

Jay, Karla and Joanne Glasgow, eds. *Lesbian Texts and Contexts.* New York: New York University Press, 1990.

Jenkins, D., S. Kemmis, B. MacDonald, and G. Verma. "Racism and Educational Evaluation." In *Race, Education, and Identity,* ed. G. Verma and C. Bagley. New York: St. Martin's, 1979.

Johnson, Miriam M. "Reproducing Male Dominance: Psychoanalysis and Social Structure." In *Advances in Psychoanalytic Sociology,* ed. Jerome Rabow, Gerald Platt, and Marion S. Goldman. Malabar, Fla.: Krieger, 1987.

———. *Strong Mothers, Weak Wives.* Berkeley, Calif.: University of California Press, 1988.

Johnston, James Hugo. *Race Relations in Virginia and Miscegenation in the South, 1776–1860.* Amherst: University of Massachusetts Press, 1970.

Jones, Ernest. *Papers on Psychoanalysis.* Boston: Beacon Press, 1961.

Jones, James M. *Prejudice and Racism.* New York: Random House, 1972.

Jones, Reginald Lanier, ed. *Black Psychology.* New York: Harper and Row, 1972.

Jordan, Winthrop D. "Modern Tensions and the Origins of American Slavery." *Journal of Southern History* 28 (1962): 18–30.

———. *The White Man's Burden: Historical Origins of Racism in the United States.* New York: Oxford University Press, 1974.

———. *White over Black: American Attitudes toward the Negro, 1550–1812.* Durham: University of North Carolina Press, 1968.

Josephs, Lawrence. *Character Structure and the Organization of the Self.* New York: Columbia University Press, 1992.

Kagan, J. S. "Inadequate Evidence and Illogical Conclusions." *Harvard Educational Review* 39 (1969): 126–129.

Kaplan, Louise J. *Adolescence, the Farewell to Childhood.* New York: Simon and Schuster, 1984.

Karasu, Tokroz B., and Charles Socarides, eds. *On Sexuality: Psychoanalytic Observations.* New York: International Universities Press, 1979.

Kardiner, Abram. *The Psychological Frontiers of Society*. New York: Columbia University Press, 1945.

Kardiner, Abram, and Ralph Linton. *The Individual and His Society*. New York: Columbia University Press, 1947, orig. 1939.

Kardiner, Abram, and Lionel Ovesey. *The Mark of Oppression; A Psychosocial Study of the American Negro*. New York: Norton, 1951.

Katz, Jacob. *Exclusiveness and Tolerance; Studies in Jewish-Gentile Relations in Medieval and Modern Times*. London: Oxford University Press, 1961.

———. *From Prejudice to Destruction: Anti-Semitism, 1700–1933*. Cambridge, Mass.: Harvard University Press, 1980.

———. "Zionism vs. Antisemitism." *Commentary* 67, no. 4 (1979): 46–52.

Katz, Phyllis. *Towards the Elimination of Racism*. New York: Pergamon Press, 1976, pp. 125–54.

Kecskemeti, Paul. "The Psychological Theory of Prejudice." *Commentary* 17 (1954): 359–366.

———. "Some Psychological Hypotheses on Nazi Germany." *Journal of Social Psychology* 26 (1947): 158–165 and 27 (1948): 91–107, 253–270.

Kenniston, Kenneth. "Psychological Development and Historical Change." *Journal of Interdisciplinary History* 2 (1971): 337–338.

Kernberg, Otto F. *Aggression in Personality Disorders*. New Haven: Yale University Press, 1992.

———. *Borderline Conditions and Pathological Narcissism*. New York: J. Aronson, 1975.

———. *Internal World and External Reality: Object Relations Theory Applied*. New York: J. Aronson, 1980.

———. "A Psychoanalytic Classification of Character Pathology." *Journal of the American Psychoanalytic Association* 18 (1970).

Kett, Joseph. *Rites of Passage: Adolescence in America, 1790 to the Present*. New York: Basic Books, 1977.

Kinsey, Alfred, et al. *Sexual Behavior in the Human Male*. Philadelphia: W. R. Saunders, 1953.

Kirk, Marshall, and Hunter Madsen. *After the Ball: How America Will Conquer Its Fear and Hatred of Gays in the 90s*. New York: Doubleday, 1989.

Kirkpatrick, Martha, ed. *Women's Sexual Development*. New York: Plenum, 1980.

Kittay, Eva Feder. "Rereading Freud on 'Femininity' or Why Not Womb Envy." *Women's Studies International Forum* 7, no. 5 (1984): 385–391.

Kitzinger, Celia. *The Social Construction of Lesbianism*. Newbury Park, Calif.: Sage Publications, 1987.

Kleinberg, Seymour. *Alienated Affections: Being Gay in America*. New York: St. Martin's 1980.

Klineberg, Otto. "Introduction: The Many Faces of Prejudice." *Child Study* 33, no. 2 (1955–56): 2–3.

————. "Prejudice: The Concept." In *International Encyclopedia of Social Sciences*, vol. 12. New York: Macmillan, 1968.

Kohut, Heinz. *The Analysis of the Self.* New York: International Universities Press, 1971.

————. *The Restoration of the Self.* New York: International Universities Press, 1977.

Kosofsky, Eve. *Epistemology of the Closet.* Berkeley: University of California Press, 1990.

Kovel, Joel. *White Racism: A Psychohistory.* New York: Pantheon, 1970.

Kris, Ernst. "Notes on the Psychology of Prejudice." In *Selected Papers of Ernst Kris.* New Haven: Yale University Press, 1975.

Kubie, Lawrence. "The Ontogeny of Racial Prejudice." *Journal of Nervous and Mental Disease* 141, no. 3 (1965): 267–268.

Kulka, O. D. "Critique of Judaism in European Thought: On the Historical Meaning of Modern Antisemitism." *Jerusalem Quarterly* 52 (1989): 126–144.

Kuper, Leo. *Genocide.* New Haven: Yale University Press, 1981.

Ladner, Joyce, ed. *The Death of White Sociology.* New York: Vintage Books, 1973.

Landauer, Karl. "Some Remarks on the Formation of the Anal-Erotic Character." *International Journal of Psychoanalysis* 20 (1939): 418–425.

Langer, Elinor. "The American Neo-Nazi Movement Today." *Nation* 16 (July 1990): 82–108.

Langmuir, Gavin. *Toward a Definition of Antisemitism.* Berkeley, Calif.: University of California Press, 1990.

Laqueur, Thomas. *Making Sex: Body and Gender from the Greeks to Freud.* Cambridge, Mass.: Harvard University Press, 1990.

Lasch, Christopher. *The Culture of Narcissism.* New York: Warner Books, 1979.

Lasker, Bruno. *Race Attitudes in Children.* New York: Henry Holt, 1929.

Laufer, Moses, and M. Egle Laufer. *Adolescence and Developmental Breakdown.* New Haven: Yale University Press, 1984.

Lauren, Paul G. *Power and Prejudice: The Politics and Diplomacy of Racial Discrimination.* Boulder, Colo.: Westview Press, 1988.

Lee, Gloria, and Ray Loveridge, eds. *The Manufacture of Disadvantage: Stigma and Social Closure.* Philadelphia: Open University Press, 1987.

Lehne, Gregory K. "Homophobia among Men." In *The Forty-Nine Percent Majority: The Male Sex Role,* ed. Deborah S. David and Robert Brannon. Reading, Mass.: Addison-Wesley, 1976.

Leites, Nathan Constantin. "Psychocultural Hypotheses about Political Acts." *World Politics,* 1948.

————. *Psychopolitical Analysis: Selected Writings of Nathan Leites,* ed. Elizabeth Wirth Marvick. Beverly Hills: Sage Publications, 1977.

Lendval, Paul. *Anti-Semitism without Jews: Communist Eastern Europe*. Garden City, N.Y.: Doubleday, 1971.

Lerner, Gerda. *The Creation of Patriarchy*. New York: Oxford University Press, 1986.

Lerner, Harriet E. "Early Origins of Envy and Devaluation of Women: Implications for Sex Role Stereotypes." *Bulletin of the Menninger Clinic* 38, no. 6 (1974): 538–553.

Levenkron, Steven. *Obsessive-Compulsive Disorders*. New York: Warner, 1991.

Levi, Primo. *The Drowned and the Saved*, trans. Raymond Rosenthal. New York: Vintage, 1989.

———. *Survival in Auschwitz and The Reawakening: Two Memoirs*. New York: Summit Books, 1985.

Levine, Robert Allen, and Donald Campbell. *Ethnocentrism: Theories of Conflict, Ethnic Attitudes, and Group Behavior*. New York: John Wiley, 1972.

Levy, Howard S. *Chinese Footbinding: The History of a Curious Erotic Custom*. New York: Walton Rawls, 1966.

Lewin, Bertram D. "The Body as Phallus." *Psychoanalytic Quarterly* 2 (1933): 24–47.

Lewis, Bernard. *Semites and Anti-Semites: An Inquiry into Conflict and Prejudice*. New York: Norton, 1986.

Lewis, Helen Block. *Freud and Modern Psychology*. New York: Plenum, 1981–1983.

Lifton, Robert Jay, and Eric Markusen. *The Genocidal Mentality: Nazi Holocaust and Nuclear Threat*. New York: Basic Books, 1990.

Limentani, Adam. "To the Limits of Male Heterosexuality: The Vagina-Man." *Analytic Psychotherapy and Psychopathology* 1 (1984): 115–129.

Lind, W. *Race Relations in World Perspective*. Honolulu: Hawaii University Press, 1955.

Lindner, Robert. *The Fifty-Minute Hour*. New York: Bantam, 1973, orig. 1954.

Linton, Ralph. *Culture and Mental Disorders*, ed. George Devereux. Springfield, Ill.: C. C. Thomas, 1956.

Lippman, Walter. *Public Opinion*. New York: Free Press, 1922.

Lipset, Seymour Martin, and Leo Lowenthal, eds. *Culture and Social Character: The Work of David Riesman Reviewed*. New York: Free Press, 1961.

———. "Three Decades of the Radical Right." In *The Radical Right*, ed. Daniel Bell. New York: Doubleday, 1964.

Lipstadt, Deborah E. *Beyond Belief: The American Press and the Coming of the the Holocaust*. New York: Free Press, 1986.

———. *Denying the Holocaust: The Growing Assault on Truth and Memory*. New York: Free Press, 1993.

Locke, Alain LeRoy, ed. *When Peoples Meet: A Study in Race and Culture Contacts*. New York: Committee on Workshops, Progressive Education Assoc., 1942.

Loewald, Hans W. *Sublimation: Inquiries into Theoretical Psychoanalysis.* New Haven: Yale University Press, 1988.

Loewenstein, Rudolph M. *Christians and Jews: A Psychoanalytic Study.* New York: International Universities Press, 1951.

Lohman, J. D., and D. C. Reitzes. "Note on Race Relations in Mass Society." *American Journal of Sociology* 58 (1952): 424.

Lomax, Louis E. *The Negro Revolt.* New York: NAL, 1964.

Lowenberg, Peter. "The Psychohistorical Origins of the Nazi Youth Cohort." *American Historical Review* 76 (1972): 1457–1502.

Lowenfeld, Henry. "Some Aspects of a Compulsion Neurosis in a Changing Civilization." *Psychoanalytic Quarterly* 13 (1944): 1–13.

Lowenthal, Leo. *Prophets of Deceit: A Study of the Techniques of the American Agitator.* Palo Alto, Calif.: Pacific Books, 1970, orig. 1949.

Lowie, Robert Harry. *Are We Civilized? Human Culture in Perspective.* New York: Harcourt, Brace, 1929.

——— . *Toward Understanding Germany.* Chicago: University of Chicago Press, 1954.

Lynch, Dennis Tylden. *The Wild Seventies.* New York: Appelton-Century, 1941.

MacDonald, A. P., Jr., and Richard G. Games. "Some Characteristics of Those Who Hold Positive and Negative Attitudes toward Homosexuals." *Journal of Homosexuality* 1, no. 1 (1974): 9–27.

Maddox, Albert. "Some Psychophysical Aspects of the Race Problem." *Psychoanalytic Review* 30 (1943): 325–329.

Mahler, M. S. "On the Three First Sub-phases of the Separation-Individuation Process," *International Journal of Psychoanalysis* 41 (1972).

Mahon, Eugene J. "A Note on the Nature of Prejudice." *Psychoanalytic Study of the Child* 46 (1991): 369–379.

Malcolm X. *By Any Means Necessary: Speeches, Interviews, and a Letter by Malcolm X,* ed. George Breitman. New York: Pathfinder, 1970.

Malcolm X and Alex Haley. *The Autobiography of Malcolm X.* New York: Grove Press, 1966.

Malson, M., J. O'Barr, S. Westphal-Wihl, and M. Wyer. *Feminist Theory in Practice and Process.* Chicago: University of Chicago Press, 1989.

Mannheim, Karl. "The Problem of Generations." In *Essays on the Sociology of Knowledge,* ed. Paul Kecskeneti. New York: Oxford University Press, 1952, pp. 276–320.

Manning, Marable. *How Capitalism Underdeveloped Black America.* Boston: South End Press, 1983.

Mannoni, O. *Prospero and Caliban: The Psychology of Colonialization.* London: Methuen, 1956.

Manson, William C. *The Psychodynamics of Culture: Abram Kardiner and Neo-Freudian Anthropology.* New York: Greenwood Press, 1988.

Margolies, Liz, Martha Becker, and Larla Jackson-Brewer. "Internalized Homophobia: Identifying and Treating the Oppressor Within." In *Lesbian Psychologies: Explanations and Challenges,* ed. Boston Lesbian Psychologies Collective. Urbana: University of Illinois Press, 1987.

Martin, James Gilbert. *The Tolerant Personality.* Detroit: Wayne State University Press, 1964.

Mason, Philip. *Patterns of Dominance.* London: Oxford University Press, 1970.

———. *Prospero's Magic: Some Thoughts on Clan and Race.* Westport, Conn.: Greenwood Press, 1975, orig. 1962.

———. *Race Relations.* London: Oxford University Press, 1970.

Massing, Paul. *Rehearsal for Destruction: A Study of Political Anti-Semitism in Imperial Germany.* New York: Harper, 1949.

Mayer, Elizabeth Lloyd. " 'Everybody Must Be Just Like Me': Observations on Female Castration Anxiety." *International Journal of Psychoanalysis* 66 (1985): 331–347.

McAllister, Ian, and Rhonda Moore. "The Development of Ethnic Prejudice: An Analysis of Australian Immigrants." *Ethnic and Racial Studies* 14, no. 2 (April 1991): 127–151.

McCarthy, John D., and William L. Yancy. "Uncle Tom and Mr. Charlie: Metaphysical Pathos in the Study of Racism and Personal Disorganization." *American Journal of Sociology* 7, no. 4 (1971): 648–672.

McDonald, Marjorie. *Not by the Color of Their Skins: The Impact of Racial Differences on the Child's Development.* New York: International Universities Press, 1970.

McLean, Helen V. "Psychodynamic Factors in Racial Relations." In *Race Prejudice and Discrimination,* ed. Arnold M. Rose. New York: Knopf, 1951.

McWhirter, David P., et al., eds. *Homosexuality/ Heterosexuality: Concepts of Sexual Orientation.* New York: Oxford University Press, 1990.

McWilliams, Carey. *A Mask for Privilege: Antisemitism in America.* Boston: Little, Brown, 1948.

Mead, Margaret. *And Keep Your Powder Dry: An Anthropologist Looks at America.* New York: Morrow, 1942.

———. *Coming of Age in Samoa.* New York: Morrow Quill, 1973.

Mead, Margaret, and James Baldwin. *A Rap on Race.* Philadelphia: Lippincott, 1971.

Mecklin, J. M. *The Ku Klux Klan: A Study of the American Mind.* New York: Harcourt, Brace, 1924.

Merton, Robert. "Discrimination and the American Creed." In *Discrimination and National Welfare,* ed. R. MacIver. New York: Harper, 1949.

Miller, Jean Baker. *Toward a New Psychology of Women.* Boston: Beacon Press, 1986.

Miller, Norman, and Marilyn B. Brewer, eds. *Groups in Contact: The Psychology of Desegregation.* Orlando, Fla.: Academic Press, 1984.

Millett, Kate. *Sexual Politics.* New York: Doubleday, 1970.

Milner, David. *Children and Race.* London: Penguin, 1975.

Minh-ha, Trinh T. *Women, Native, Other: Writing Postcoloniality and Feminism.* Bloomington: Indiana University Press, 1989.

Mitchell, Juliet. *Psychoanalysis and Feminism.* New York: Pantheon Books, 1974.

Mitscherlich, Alexander. *Society without the Father: A Contribution to Social Psychology,* trans. Eric Mosbacher. New York: Harcourt, 1969.

Moller, Herbert. "Sex Ratio, Misegenation, and Race Relations." In *Race: Individual and Collective Behavior,* ed. Edgar T. Thompson and Everett C. Hughes. Glencoe, Ill.: Free Press, 1958.

Money, John. *Love and Love Sickness: The Science of Sex, Gender Difference, and Pair-Bonding.* Baltimore: Johns Hopkins University Press, 1980.

Money-Kyrle R. E. "On Prejudice—a Psychoanalytical Approach." *British Journal of Medical Psychology* 33 (1960): 205–209.

Montagu, Ashley. *The Natural Superiority of Women.* New York: Collier Books, 1979.

Moraga, Cherrie, and Gloria Anzaldua, eds. *This Bridge Called My Back: Writings by Radical Women of Color.* New York: Kitchen Table Press, 1983, orig. 1981.

Morrison, Andrew P., ed. *Essential Papers on Narcissism.* New York: New York University Press, 1986.

Morrison, Toni. *Playing in the Dark.* Cambridge, Mass.: Harvard University Press, 1992.

Morse, Nancy C., and Floyd H. Allport. "The Causation of Anti-Semitism: An Investigation of Seven Hypotheses." *Journal of Psychology* 34 (1952): 197–233.

Moscovici, S. *The Age of the Crowd.* Cambridge: Cambridge University Press, 1985.

Mosse, George L. *Germans and Jews: The Right, the Left, and the Search for a 'Third Force' in Pre-Nazi Germany.* New York: Fertig, 1970.

Muensterberger, Werner. *Man and His Culture: Psychoanalytic Anthropology after "Totem and Taboo."* New York: Taplinger, 1970.

Murray, Albert. *The Omni-Americans.* New York: Vintage, 1983.

Murray, John M. "Narcissism and the Ego Ideal." *Journal of the American Psychoanalytic Association* 12 (1964): 477–511.

Musil, Robert. *Young Törless,* trans. E. Wilkins and E. Kaiser. New York: Signet, 1964.

Mussen, Paul. "Some Personality and Social Factors Related to Changes in Children's Attitudes towards Negroes." *Journal of Abnormal and Social Psychology* 45 (1950): 423–441.

Muuss, Rolf Eduard Helmut, ed. *Adolescent Behavior and Society: A Book of Readings.* New York: Random House, 1980.

Myrdal, Gunnar. *The American Dilemma: The Negro Problem and Modern Democracy,* 2 vols. New York: Random House, 1972, orig. 1944.

Nager, Norma. "Racism and White Women: Keeping Sexism Intact." *Social Policy* 15 (Summer 1984): 53–54.

Nain, Gemma Tang. "Black Women, Sexism and Racism: Black or Antiracist Feminism?" *Feminist Review* 37 (Spring 1991): 1–22.

Neal, Donald. *The Origins of American Slavery and Racism.* Columbus, Ohio: Merrill, 1972.

Needham, Rodney. *Primordial Characters.* Charlottesville: University of Virginia, 1978.

Nelson, Marie Coleman. *The Narcissistic Condition: A Fact of Our Lives and Times.* New York: Human Sciences, 1977.

Newby, I. A., ed. *The Development of Segregationist Thought.* Homewood, Ill.: Dorsey Press, 1968.

————. *Jim Crow's Defense: Anti-Negro Thought in America.* Baton Rouge: Louisiana State University Press, 1965.

Newton, M., and J. A. Newton. *The Ku Klux Klan: An Encyclopedia.* New York: Garland, 1991.

Nicholson, Linda J. *Gender and History.* New York: Columbia University Press, 1986.

Norden, Eric. "The Paramilitary Right." *Playboy* 16, no. 6 (1969).

Odum, Howard. *Social and Mental Traits of the Negro.* New York: Columbia University Press, 1910.

Ovesey, Lionel, and Ethel Person. "Gender Identity and Sexual Pathology in Men." *Journal of the American Academy of Psychoanalysis* 1, no. 1 (1973): 53–72.

Paranjpe, A. C. "Introduction—Ethnic Identities and Prejudices: Perspectives from the Third World." *Journal of Asian and African Studies* 20 (1985): 133–139.

Parin, Paul. "The Mark of Oppression: Jews and Homosexuals as Strangers." *Psychoanalytic Study of Society* 14 (1989): 15–39.

Parsons, Talcott. "Postscript to the Sociology of Modern Anti-Semitism." *Contemporary Jewry* 1 (1980): 31–38.

————. "The Sociology of Modern Anti-Semitism." In *Jews in a Gentile World,* ed. I. Graeber and S. H. Britt. New York: Macmillan, 1942.

————. "The Superego and the Theory of Social Systems." *Psychiatry* 15 (1952).

Paz, Octavio. *One Earth, Four or Five Worlds: Reflections on Contemporary History,* trans. Helen R. Lane. San Diego: Harcourt, Brace, Jovanovich, 1985.

Pearson, Gerald Hamilton Jeffrey. *Adolescence and the Conflict of Generations.* New York: Norton, 1958.

Pedersen, Stefi. "Unconscious Motives in Pro-Semitic Attitudes." *Psychoanalytic Review* 38 (1951): 361–373.

Pettigrew, Thomas. "The Intergroup Contact Hypothesis Reconsidered." In *Contact and Conflict in Intergroup Encounters,* ed. M. Hewstone and R. Brown. Oxford: Blackwell, 1986: 169–195.

———. "Parallel and Distinctive Changes in Anti-Semitic and Anti-Negro Attitudes." In *Jews in the Mind of America,* ed. C. H. Stember. New York: Basic Books, 1966, pp. 391–393.

———. *A Profile of the Negro American.* Princeton: Van Nostrad, 1964.

———. *Racially Separate or Together.* New York: McGraw Hill, 1971.

———. *Sociology of Race Relations: Reflection and Reform.* New York: Free Press, 1980.

Pharr, Suzanne. *Homophobia: A Weapon of Sexism.* Inverness, Calif.: Chardon Press, 1988.

Philipson, Ilene. "Narcissism and Mothering: The 1950s Reconsidered." *Women's Studies International Forum* 5 (1982): 29–40.

Pinderhughes, Elaine. *Understanding Race, Ethnicity, and Power: The Key to Efficacy in Clinical Practice.* New York: Free Press, 1989.

Pinson, K. S. *Essays on Antisemitism.* New York: Basic Books, 1946.

Plant, Richard. *The Pink Triangle.* New York: Henry Holt, 1966.

Plummer, Ken, ed. *Modern Homosexualities.* New York: Routledge, 1992.

Poliakov, Leon. *The Aryan Myth.* New York: Basic Books, 1974.

———. *The History of Anti-Semitism.* New York: Vanguard, 1965.

Porter, Judith D. R. *Black Child, White Child: The Development of Racial Attitudes.* Cambridge, Mass.: Harvard University Press, 1971.

Posner, Richard A. *Sex and Reason.* Cambridge, Mass.: Harvard University Press, 1994.

Poussaint, Alvin F., and Joyce Ladner. "Black Power." *Archives of General Psychiatry,* April 1968.

Prager, Dennis. *Why the Jews? The Reason for Antisemitism.* New York: Simon and Schuster, 1983.

"Prejudice." Symposium. *Public Opinion* July–August 1987.

Proshansky, H. "The Development of Intergroup Attitudes." In *Review of Child Development Research,* ed. M. L. Hoffman. New York: Russell Sage Foundation 1966.

Pulzer, Peter G. J. *The Rise of Political Anti-Semitism in Germany and Austria.* 1964. Cambridge: Harvard University Press, 1988.

Raab, Earl, and Seymour M. Lipset. *Prejudice and Society.* New York: Anti-Defamation League of B'nai B'rith, 1968.

Rabkin, R. "Conversion-Hysteria as Social Maladaption." *Psychiatry* 27 (1964): 349–363.

Rado, Sandor. "Obsessive Behavior: So-Called Obsessive Compulsive Neurosis." In *Psychoanalysis of Behavior: Collected Papers,* vol. 2 (New York: Grune and Stratton 1956–1962, pp. 53–83.

Rainwater, Lee and William Yancy. *The Moynihan Report and the Politics of Controversy.* Cambridge, Mass.: MIT Press, 1967.

Ramazanoglu, Caroline. *Feminism and the Contradictions of Oppression.* New York: Routledge, 1989.

Rank, Otto. *Beyond Psychology.* New York: Dover, 1958, orig. 1941.

Reich, Annie. *Psychoanalytic Contributions.* New York: International Universities Press, 1973.

Reich, Wilhelm. *Character Analysis,* trans. T. Wolfe. New York: Farrar, Straus and Giroux, 1970.

———. *The Mass Psychology of Fascism.* New York: Farrar, 1970.

Reiser, Martin. "On Origins of Hatred towards Negroes." *American Imago* 18 (1961): 167–182.

Reiter, Laura. "Developmental Origins of Antihomosexual Prejudice in Heterosexual Men and Women." *Clinical Social Work Journal* 19, no. 2 (1991): 163–175.

Reuth, Ralf Georg. *Goebbels.* New York: Harcourt Brace, 1994.

Rex, John. "The Concept of Race in Sociological Theory." In *Race and Racialism,* ed. Sami Zubaide. London: Tavistock, 1970.

Rich, Adrienne Cecile. *On Lies, Secrets, and Silence.* New York: Norton, 1979.

Richards, Barry. *Images of Freud: Cultural Responses to Psychoanalysis.* New York: St. Martin's, 1989.

Riesman, David. "Some Observations on Social Science Research." In *Individualism Reconsidered and Other Essays.* Glencoe, Ill.: Free Press, 1954.

Riesman, David, Nathan Glazer, and Reuel Denny. *The Lonely Crowd: A Study of the Changing American Character.* (New York: Doubleday, 1955, orig. 1950).

Rile, Arnold. *The Ku Klux Klan in American Politics.* Washington, D.C.: Public Affairs Press, 1962.

Rinsley, Donald. *Developmental Pathogenesis and the Treatment of Borderline and Narcissistic Personalities.* New York: J. Aronson, 1989.

Ritvo, Samuel. "Late Adolescence." *Psychoanalytic Study of the Child* 26 (1971): 254.

Robinson, Cedric. *Black Marxism: The Making of the Black Radical Tradition.* Atlantic Highlands, N.J.: Zed Books, 1983.

Rochlin, Gregory. *Man's Aggression: The Defense of the Self.* Boston: Gambit, 1973.

Rodgers, Terry C. "The Evolution of an Active Anti-Negro Racist." *Psychoanalytic Study of Society* 1 (1960): 237–247.

Rokeach, Milton. *The Open and Closed Mind.* New York: Basic Books, 1960.

Rosaldo, Michelle, and Louise Lamphere, eds. *Woman, Culture, and Society.* Stanford, Calif.: Stanford University Press, 1974.

Rose, Arnold Marshall. "Anti-Semitism's Root in City-Hatred." *Commentary* 6 (1948) 374–378.

———. *The Ku Klux Klan in American Politics.* Washington, D.C.: Public Affairs Press, 1962, orig. 1921.

———. *Studies in Reduction of Prejudice: A Memorandum Summarizing Research on Modification of Attitudes.* Chicago: The Council, 1947.

Rose, Arnold, and Catherine Rose. "The Psychology of Prejudice." In *America Divided*. New York: Knopf, 1948.

Rosen, George. *Madness in Society: Chapters in the Historical Sociology of Mental Illness*. New York: Harper, 1969.

Rosenberg, Harold. "Does the Jew Exist? Sartre's Morality Play about Antisemitism" *Commentary* 7 (1949): 8–18.

Rothenberg, Paula. "The Construction, Deconstruction, and Reconstruction of Difference." *Hypatia* 5, no. 1 (Spring 1990): 42–57.

———. *Racism and Sexism: An Integrated Study*. New York: St. Martin's, 1988.

Rothstein, Arnold. *The Narcissistic Pursuit of Perfection*. New York: International Universities Press, 1980.

Rubin, Gayle. "Woman as Nigger." In *Masculine/Feminine*, ed. Betty Roszak and Theodore Roszak. New York: Harper, 1969.

Rubin, Theodore Isaac. *Antisemitism: A Disease of the Mind*. New York: Continuum, 1990.

Ryan, William. *Blaming the Victim*, rev. ed. New York: Random House, 1976.

Sachs, Hanns. "The Delay of the Machine Age." *Psychoanalytic Quarterly* 2 (1933): 404–424.

Sacks, Karen. "Toward a Unified Theory of Class, Race, and Gender." *American Ethnologist*, 1989, p. 534.

Sahakian, William S. *History and Systems of Social Psychology*. Washington, D.C.: Hemisphere, 1982.

Salisbury, Harrison. *The Shook-Up Generation*. New York: Fawcett, 1959.

Samuel, Maurice. *The Great Hatred*. New York: Knopf, 1940.

Sandler, J., ed. *The Analysis of Defense: The Ego and the Mechanisms of Defense Revisited*. New York: International Universities Press, 1983.

Sandler, J., and A. Hazari. "The 'Obsessional': On the Psychological Classification of Obsessional Character Traits and Symptoms." *British Journal of Medical Psychology* 33 (1960): 113–121.

Sandler, J., Alex Holder, and Dale Meers. "The Ego Ideal and the Ideal Self." *Psychoanalytic Study of the Child* 18 (1963): 139–158.

Sandler, J., Ethel Spector Person, and Peter Fonagy, eds. *On Narcissism—An Introduction*. New Haven: Yale University Press, 1991.

Sanger, Gerhart. *The Social Psychology of Prejudice: Achieving Intercultural Understanding and Cooperation in a Democracy*. New York: Harper, 1953.

Sartre, Jean-Paul. *Anti-Semite and Jew*. New York: Schocken, 1949.

———. *Black Orpheus*, trans. S. W. Allen. Paris: Gallimard, 1963.

Saunders, Charles. "Assessing Race Relations." In *The Death of White Sociology*, ed. Joyce Ladner. New York: Random House, 1973.

Schlesinger, Arthur M., Jr. *The Politics of Upheaval*. Boston: Houghton Mifflin, 1960.

Schuyler, Lambert and Patricia Schuyler. *Close That Bedroom Door*. Winslow: Heron House, 1957.

Searle, Chris. *The Forsaken Lover: White Words and Black People.* Boston: Routledge, 1972.

See, Katherine O'Sullivan, and William J. Wilson. "Race and Ethnicity." In *Handbook of Sociology,* ed. Neil Smelser. Newbury Park, Calif.: Sage Publications, 1988.

Seeley, John R. *The Americanization of the Unconscious.* New York: International Science Press, 1967.

Seidenberg, Robert. "The Sexual Basis of Social Prejudice." *Psychoanalytic Review* 38 (1952): 94.

Settlage, Calvin F. "Cultural Values and the Superego in Late Adolescence." *Psychoanalytic Study of the Child* 18 (1972): 74–92.

Sevely, Josephine Lowndes. *Eve's Secrets: A New Theory of Female Sexuality.* New York: Random House, 1987.

Shapiro, David. *Neurotic Styles.* New York: Basic Books, 1965.

Sherwood, Rae. *The Psychodynamics of Race: Vicious and Benign Spirals.* Atlantic Highlands, N.J.: Humanities Press, 1980.

Shils, Edward. "Authoritarianism: 'Right' and 'Left.' " In *Studies in the Scope and Method of "The Authoritarian Personality,"* ed. R. Christie and M. Jahoda. Glencoe, Ill.: Free Press, 1954, pp. 24–49.

———. *The Torment of Secrecy.* Glencoe, Ill.: Free Press, 1956.

Silberman, Charles. *Crisis in Black and White.* New York: Random House, 1964.

Simpson, George, and J. Milton Yinger. *Racial and Cultural Minorities: An Analysis of Prejudice and Discrimination.* New York: Harper, 1958.

Sivanandan, A. "The New Racism." *New Statesman and Society* 4 (November 1988).

Smelser, Neil J. *Theory of Collective Behavior.* New York: Free Press, 1962.

Smith, Joan. "Feminist Analysis of Gender: A Mystique." In *Woman's Nature: Rationalizations of Inequality,* ed. M. Lowe and R. Hubbard. New York: Pergamon Press, 1983.

Snitow, Ann, Christine Stansell, and Sharon Thompson. Introduction to *The Powers of Desire: The Politics of Sexuality,* ed. Snitow, Stansell, and Thompson. New York: Monthly Review Press, 1983.

Sobo, Simon. "Narcissism as a Function of Culture." *Psychoanalytic Study of the Child* 32 (1977): 155–172.

Socarides, Charles W., and Vamik D. Volkman, eds. *The Homosexualities: Reality, Fantasy, and the Arts.* Madison, Conn.: International Universities Press, 1990.

Solomon, Joseph C. "The Fixed Idea as an Internalized Transitional Object." *American Journal of Psychotherapy* 16 (1962): 632–644.

Solomon, Marion Fried. *Narcissism and Intimacy: Love and Marriage in an Age of Confusion.* New York: Norton, 1989.

Sontag, Susan. *Against Interpretation.* New York: Dell, 1969.

Spelman, Elizabeth V. *Inessential Women: Problems of Exclusion in Feminist Thought.* Boston: Beacon Press, 1988.

Spitz, Rene. "Environment versus Race." In *Psychoanalysis and Culture: Essays in Honor of Geza Roheim,* ed. G. B. Wilbur and W. Munsterberger. New York: International Universities Press, 1951.

———. *The First Year of Life.* New York: International Universities Press, 1965.

Stacey, Judith, and Barrie Thorne. "The Missing Feminist Revolution in Sociology." *Social Problems* 32, no. 4 (April 1985): 301–316.

Stachura, Peter D. *The German Youth Movement, 1900–1945: An Interpretation and Documentary History.* New York: Macmillan, 1981.

Stack, Carol B. *All Our Kin.* New York: Harper and Row, 1974.

Stanton, Alfred H. "Comparison of Individual and Group Psychology." *American Psychoanalytic Journal,* January 1958, pp. 121–130.

Staples, Robert. *The Black Woman in America.* Chicago: Nelson-Hall, 1973.

———. *The Urban Plantation: Racism and Colonialism in the Post-Civil Rights Era.* Oakland, Calif.: Black Scholars Press, 1987.

Staub, Ervin. *The Roots of Evil: The Origins of Genocide and Other Group Violence.* Cambridge: Cambridge University Press, 1992.

Steeley, John. *The Americanization of the Unconscious.* New York: International Science, 1967.

Stekel, Wilhelm. *Patterns of Psychosexual Infantilism.* New York: Grove Press, 1959.

Stember, Charles Herbert. *Sexual Racism: The Emotional Barrier to an Integrated Society.* New York: Elsevier, 1976.

Stember, Charles Herbert, et al. *Jews in the Mind of America.* New York: Basic Books, 1966.

Sterba, Richard. "Some Psychological Factors in Negro Race Hatred and in Anti-Negro Riots." In *Psychoanalysis and the Social Sciences,* vol. 1, ed. Geza Roheim, New York: International Universities Press, 1947.

Stern, Susan. *With the Weathermen.* New York: Doubleday, 1975.

Stewart, Abigail J., and David G. Winter. "The Nature and Causes of Female Suppression." *Signs: Journal of Women in Culture and Society* 2, no. 3 (1977): 531–553.

St. Lawrence, Janet S., et al. "The Stigma of AIDS: Fear of Disease and Prejudice toward Gay Men." *Journal of Homosexuality* 19, no. 3 (1990): 85–101.

Stoller, Robert J. *Observing the Erotic Imagination.* New Haven: Yale University Press, 1985.

———. *Presentations of Gender.* New Haven: Yale University Press, 1985.

———. *Sex and Gender: On the Development of Masculinity and Femininity.* New York: Science House, 1968.

Stone, John. *Race, Ethnicity, and Social Change.* North Scituate, Mass.: Duxbury, 1977.

Stone, William, Gerda Lederer, and Richard Christie, eds. *Strength and Weakness: The Authoritarian Personality Today.* New York: Springer Verlag, 1992.

Sugar, Max, ed. *Female Adolescent Development.* New York: Brunner/Mazel, 1979.

Suleiman, Susan Rubin, ed. *The Female Body in Western Culture.* Cambridge, Mass.: Harvard University Press, 1985.

Sullivan, Robert. "An Army of the Faithful." *New York Times Magazine,* April 25, 1993.

Tajfel, Henri. *Differentiation between Social Groups.* New York: Academic Press, 1978.

———. *Human Groups and Social Categories.* Cambridge: Cambridge University Press, 1981.

———. *Social Identity and Intergroup Relations.* Cambridge: Cambridge University Press, 1982.

Tannenhill, Rae. *Sex in History.* New York: Stein and Day, 1980.

Theweleit, Klaus. *Male Fantasies,* trans. Stephen Conway. Minneapolis: University of Minnesota Press, 1987–1989.

Thibaut, John W., and Harold H. Kelley. *The Social Psychology of Groups.* New York: John Wiley, 1986.

Thomas, Alexander, and Samuel Sillen. "The Sexual Mystique." In *Racism and Psychiatry.* Seacaucus, N.J.: Citadel Press, 1974.

Thompson, Clara. "Some Effects of the Derogatory Attitude toward Female Sexuality." *Psychiatry* 13 (1950).

Thurow, Lester. *Poverty and Discrimination.* Washington, D.C.: Brookings Institution, 1969.

Tiger, Lionel. *Men in Groups.* New York: Random House, 1969.

Todorov, Tzvetan. *The Conquest of America: Perceiving the Other.* New York: Harper and Row, 1984.

Trainer, B. E., and E. L. Chase. "Keep Gays Out." *New York Times,* March 29, 1993, p. A15.

Troeltsch, Ernst. *Protestantism and Progress: A Historical Study of the Relation of Protestantism to the Real World,* trans. W. Montgomery. Boston: Beacon Press, 1958.

Tumin, Melvin Marvin. *An Inventory and Appraisal of Research on American Anti-Semitism.* New York: Freedom Press, 1961.

Turkel, Ann Ruth. "Reflections on the Development of Male Chauvanism." *American Journal of Psychoanalysis* 52, no. 3 (1992): 263–272.

UNESCO. *The Race Question in Modern Science: Race and Science.* New York: Columbia University Press, 1961.

Van den Berghe, Pierre L. *The Ethnic Phenomenon.* New York: Elsevier, 1981.

———. *Man in Society: A Biosocial View.* New York: Elsevier, 1975.

———. *Race and Ethnicity: Essays in Comparative Sociology.* New York: Basic Books, 1970.

———. *Race and Racism.* New York: John Wiley, 1967.

Van Ophuijsen, J. "On the Origin of Feelings of Persecution." *International Journal of Psychoanalysis* 1 (1920): 235–239.

Vickery, William E., and Stewart G. Cole. *Intercultural Education in American Schools.* New York: Harper, 1943.

Volkan, Vamik D. *The Need to Have Enemies and Allies.* Northvale, N.J.: J. Aronson, 1988.

Waelder, Robert. "Notes on Prejudice." In *Psychoanalysis: Observation, Theory, Application.* New York: International Universities Press, 1976.

Walker, Herbert. "Some Reflections on the Death of Dr. Martin Luther King— A Commentary on White Racism." *Journal of the National Medical Association* 60 (1968): 396–400.

Wangh, Martin. "National Socialism and the Genocide of the Jews." *International Journal of Psychoanalysis* 45 (1944): 386–395.

Warren, Robert Penn. *Who Speaks for the Negro?* New York: Vintage, 1966.

Watson, Peter, ed. *Psychology and Race.* Chicago: Aldine, 1974.

Weatherly, D. "Anti-Semitism and the Expression of Fantasy Aggression." *Journal of Abnormal and Social Psychology* 62 (1961): 891–892.

Weinberg, George H. *Society and the Healthy Homosexual.* New York: St. Martin's, 1972.

Weinstein, Fred, and Gerald M. Platt. *Psychoanalytic Sociology.* Baltimore: Johns Hopkins University Press, 1973.

Wellman, David. "The New Political Linguistics of Race." *Socialist Review* 87–88 (1986): 43–62.

———. *Portraits of White Racism.* Cambridge: Cambridge University Press, 1977.

Welsing, Frances Cress. *The Isis Papers: The Keys to the Colors.* Chicago: Third World Press, 1991.

Werner, David S. "Normal and Pathological Nostalgia." *Journal of the American Psychoanalytic Association* 25 (1977): 387–398.

West, Cornel. *Prophesy Deliverance: An Afro-American Revolutionary Christianity.* Philadelphia: Westminster, 1982.

———. "Toward a Socialist Theory of Racism." In *Prophetic Fragments.* Grand Rapids, Mich.: Eerdmans, 1988.

West, Louis Jolyon. "The Othello Syndrome." *Contemporary Psychoanalysis* 4 (1968).

———. "The Psychology of Racial Violence." *Archives of General Psychiatry* 16 (June 1967): 648.

Westie, Frank R. "Race and Ethnic Relations." In *Handbook of Modern Sociology,* ed. Robert E. L. Faris. Chicago: Rand McNally, 1964.

White, Edmund. *States of Desire.* New York: Dutton, 1980.

Whiting, J. W. M., R. Kluckholm, and A. Anthony. "The Function of Male Initiation Ceremonies at Puberty." In *Readings in Social Psychology,* ed. E. E. Macoby, T. M. Newcomb, and E. L. Hartley. New York: Henry Holt, 1958, pp. 359–370.

Whitlow, Roger. "Baldwin's Going to Meet the Man: Racial Brutality and Sexual Gratification." *American Imago* 34 (1977): 351–356.

Whyte, William. *The Organization Man.* New York: Simon and Schuster, 1956.

Wilson, E. O. *Sociobiology: The New Synthesis.* Cambridge, Mass.: Harvard University Press, 1975.

Wilson, Glenn D., ed. *The Psychology of Conservatism.* New York: Academic Press, 1976.

Wise, J. W. *The Springfield Plan.* New York: Viking, 1945.

Wistrich, Robert S. *Antisemitism: The Longest Hatred.* London, Thames Metheun, 1991.

Wood, Forrest G. *Black Scare: The Racist Response to Emancipation and Reconstruction.* Berkeley: University of California Press, 1968.

Woods, Sherwyn M. "Some Dynamics of Male Chauvinism." *Archives of General Pyschiatry,* January 1976, pp. 63–65.

Woodward, C. Vann. *American Counterpoint: Slavery and Racism in the North-South Dialogue.* New York: Oxford University Press, 1983, orig. 1971.

———. *The Comparative Approach to American History.* New York: Basic Books, 1968.

———. *The Future of the Past.* New York: Oxford University Press, 1989.

———. *The Strange Career of Jim Crow.* New York: Oxford University Press, 1974, orig. 1955.

Wright, Richard. *Black Boy.* New York: NAL, 1963, orig. 1945.

Wrong, Dennis. "The Psychology of Prejudice and the Future of Antisemitism in America." In *Jews in the Mind of America,* ed. C. H. Stember. New York: Basic Books, 1966.

Yarrow, Marion Radke. "Interpersonal Dynamics on Desegregation Process." *Journal of Social Issues* 14–1 (1958).

Young, Iris Marion. "Abjection and Oppression: Dynamics of Unconscious Racism, Sexism, and Homophobia." In *Crises in Continental Philosophy,* ed. A. B. Dallery et al. Albany: State University of New York Press, 1990.

———. "Is Male Gender Identity the Cause of Male Domination?" In *Throwing Like a Girl and Other Essays.* Bloomington: Indiana University Press, 1990.

Young, Michael, and Peter Wilmott. *The Symmetrical Family.* New York: Pantheon, 1972.

Young-Bruehl, Elisabeth. *Creative Characters.* New York: Routledge, 1991.

Zetzel, E. R. "So-Called Good Hysterics." *International Journal of Psychoanalysis* 49 (1968): 256.

Zia, Helen, "Women in Hate Groups." *Ms. Magazine,* March/April, 1991.

Zilboorg, Gregory. "Psychopathology of Social Prejudice." *Psychoanalytic Quarterly,* July 16, 1947, pp. 303–324.

Zimmermann, Moshe. *Wilhelm Marr: The Patriarch of Anti-Semitism.* New York: Oxford University Press, 1986.

# Index

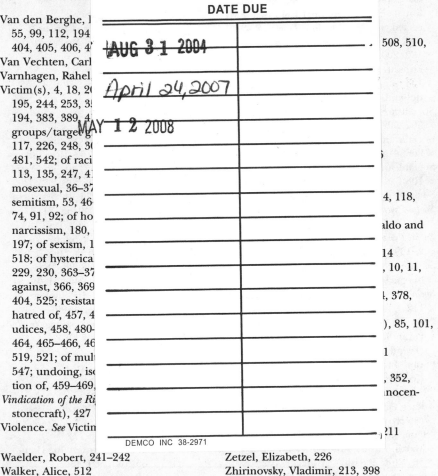